HANDBOOKS

S0-AET-825

# COASTAL MAINE

HILARY NANGLE

**PARK LOOP ROAD**

TWO-WAY

ONE-WAY

The Beehive

Great Head

Sand Beach

★ THUNDER HOLE OVERLOOK

Gorham Mountain

Otter Cliffs

Pemetic Mountain

BLACKWOODS

Otter Creek

WILDWOOD STABLES ★

Day Mountain

Seal Harbor

Penobscot Mountain

Jordan Pond

JORDAN POND HOUSE

ASTICOU AZALEA GARDEN

★ THUVA GARDEN

Parkman Mountain

Hadlock Ponds

Little Long Pond

Bear Island

Eastern Way

Sutton Island

Little Cranberry Island

Islesford

Crow Island

Green Nubble

Baker Island

*Acadia National Park*

Norumbega Mountain

SARGENT

3

198

Northeast Harbor

INFORMATION CENTER

DR

CLARK POINT RD

Greening Island

Great Cranberry Island

Western Way

ATLANTIC

OCEAN

Sound

Hall Quarry

Acadia Mountain

102

FERNALD POINT RD

SOUTHWEST HARBOR/ TREMONT CHAMBER OF COMMERCE

WENDELL GILLEY MUSEUM

Southwest Harbor

Manset

Park

SEAWALL

102A

Great Gott Island

Echo Lake

Beech Mountain

LONG POND RD

National

Long Pond

Mansell Mountain

Bernard Mountain

102

Bass Harbor

BASS HARBOR HEAD LIGHT

Hodgdon Pond

WESTERN MOUNTAIN RD

Seal Cove Pond

Acadia

SEAL COVE RD

Seal Cove

Tremont

Bernard

SWANS ISLAND FERRY TERMINAL

Pretty Marsh Harbor

Folly Island

Moose Island

West Tremont

102

*Blue Hill Bay*

2 mi

2 km

0

0

# DISCOVER
# COASTAL MAINE

From the glacier-scoured beaches of the Southern Coast to the rugged boulders Down East, Maine's coastline follows a zigzagging route that would measure about 5,500 miles if you stretched it taut. But taut it isn't – it's a wrinkled landscape whose countless bony fingers jut into the sea. Eons ago, glaciers came crushing down from the north, inch by massive inch, and squeezed Maine's coastline into these splayed fingers.

Sure, lots of states have ocean shorelines – at least a third of them. But most of them look out onto azure seas, which can be mesmerizing, lonely, scary, and – let's face it – a little boring after a while. But, thanks to its geography, Maine coast vistas are much more intimate, full of spruce-clad islands and gray granite and sometimes-forbidding headlands. Along this coast are 64 lighthouses, 90 percent of the *nation's* lobsters, and the eastern seaboard's highest

Sailboats fill Rockport's pretty harbor.

peak. Each of the peninsulas has its own character, as does each island offshore and each harbor village.

And then there are the coastal Mainers who lend this place its special character. No individuals are more rugged than the ump-teenth-generation fishermen who make their honest living from these bone-chilling waters. And even the summerfolk tend to be different here – many have come back year after year to the same place and the same neighbors and the same pursuits. Some came as kids and now return to share this remarkable place with their grandchildren.

The landscape and the pureness of the environment are big draws. Coastal Maine is easy on the senses. The air is clean and clear, and breezes often are perfumed with pine, balsam, or rugosa rose mingling with the briny scent of the sea. In many places, you can almost taste the salt in the air. Even in Portland, the state's biggest city (okay, it's tiny by most standards), you can escape into the quiet of a preserve or forest and hear the birds sing, streams gurgle, and leaves rustle.

**Cruises on the four-masted *Margaret Todd* depart from Bar Harbor.**

And then there's the food. Of course, lobster is king, and Maine's seafood is ultra fresh, but don't overlook luscious Maine wild blueberries, sweet Maine maple syrup, delicious local farmstead cheeses and yogurts, and homemade pies sold at roadside stands. Access to this bounty along with plentiful farmstands and farmers markets is one reason why talented chefs are drawn to the state.

Even if you don't dine at one of the hot restaurants with nationally known chefs, you can partake from the bounty of cheesemakers, fish smokers, artisan bakers, microbrewers, and organic farmers. But balance that with classic Maine fare: a bean-hole or chowder supper, where you can share a table with locals and, if you're lucky, hear a genuine Maine accent (here's a hint: "Ayuh" isn't so much a word as a sharp two-part intake of breath).

There's a reason why more than eight million people visit Maine every year, why longtime summerfolk finally just pick up stakes and *settle* here. Maine boldly promotes itself as "The Way Life Should Be" – spend a little time in this extraordinarily special place and you'll see why.

sunset on Corea Harbor

# Contents

The Lay of the Land . . . . . . . . . . . . . . . . . . . . . . . . . . . . . . . . . . . . . . . . . . . . 14
Planning Your Trip. . . . . . . . . . . . . . . . . . . . . . . . . . . . . . . . . . . . . . . . . . . . . 17
Explore Coastal Maine . . . . . . . . . . . . . . . . . . . . . . . . . . . . . . . . . . . . . . . . . 19
Icons of the Maine Coast . . . . . . . . . . . . . . . . . . . . . . . . . . . . . . . . . . . . . . . 19
Lighthouses, Lobster, and L. L. Bean. . . . . . . . . . . . . . . . . . . . . . . . . . . . . . 21
14-Day Best of the Real Maine. . . . . . . . . . . . . . . . . . . . . . . . . . . . . . . . . . . 22
Destination Dining Tour . . . . . . . . . . . . . . . . . . . . . . . . . . . . . . . . . . . . . . . . 24
Antiques and Junktiques: A Shopper's Tour. . . . . . . . . . . . . . . . . . . . . . . . 26
Cultural Heritage "Trails" . . . . . . . . . . . . . . . . . . . . . . . . . . . . . . . . . . . . . . 27

Southern Coast . . . . . . . . . . . . . . . . . . . . . . . . . . . . . . . . . . . . . . . . . 29
Kittery. . . . . . . . . . . . . . . . . . . . . . . . . . . . . . . . . . . . . . . . . . . . . . . . . . . . . . 32
The Berwicks . . . . . . . . . . . . . . . . . . . . . . . . . . . . . . . . . . . . . . . . . . . . . . . . 35
The Yorks . . . . . . . . . . . . . . . . . . . . . . . . . . . . . . . . . . . . . . . . . . . . . . . . . . . 37
Ogunquit and Wells . . . . . . . . . . . . . . . . . . . . . . . . . . . . . . . . . . . . . . . . . . . 48
The Kennebunks . . . . . . . . . . . . . . . . . . . . . . . . . . . . . . . . . . . . . . . . . . . . . 60
Old Orchard Beach Area. . . . . . . . . . . . . . . . . . . . . . . . . . . . . . . . . . . . . . . 76

Greater Portland . . . . . . . . . . . . . . . . . . . . . . . . . . . . . . . . . . . . . . . 82
Portland . . . . . . . . . . . . . . . . . . . . . . . . . . . . . . . . . . . . . . . . . . . . . . . . . . . . 86
Freeport . . . . . . . . . . . . . . . . . . . . . . . . . . . . . . . . . . . . . . . . . . . . . . . . . . . 116

Mid-Coast Region . . . . . . . . . . . . . . . . . . . . . . . . . . . . . . . . . . . . 125
Brunswick Area . . . . . . . . . . . . . . . . . . . . . . . . . . . . . . . . . . . . . . . . . . . . . 128
Bath Area . . . . . . . . . . . . . . . . . . . . . . . . . . . . . . . . . . . . . . . . . . . . . . . . . . 139
Wiscasset Area . . . . . . . . . . . . . . . . . . . . . . . . . . . . . . . . . . . . . . . . . . . . . 153

Boothbay Peninsula .............................................. 160
Pemaquid Region ................................................ 172

## Penobscot Bay.............................................. 191
Thomaston Area ................................................ 194
Cushing Peninsula.............................................. 196
St. George Peninsula .......................................... 198
Monhegan Island............................................... 203
Rockland Area................................................. 209
Vinalhaven and North Haven Islands............................ 219
Camden-Rockport Area.......................................... 226
Lincolnville.................................................. 240
Belfast Area.................................................. 243
Searsport Area ............................................... 250

## Blue Hill Peninsula and Deer Isle .................... 257
Bucksport Area................................................ 260
Blue Hill..................................................... 263
Brooklin/Brooksville/Sedgwick ................................ 271
Castine ...................................................... 280
Deer Isle .................................................... 286
Isle au Haut ................................................. 302

## Acadia Region............................................. 306
Ellsworth..................................................... 310
Acadia National Park on Mount Desert Island .................. 315
Bar Harbor and Vicinity ...................................... 322
Northeast and Seal Harbors ................................... 338
The Quiet Side ............................................... 344
Islands near Mount Desert..................................... 355
Schoodic Peninsula............................................ 359

## The Down East Coast ..................................... 375
Milbridge........................................................ 378
Jonesport/Beals Area ...................................... 383
Machias Bay Area .......................................... 388
Lubec and Vicinity.......................................... 396
Campobello Island.......................................... 402
Eastport and Vicinity ...................................... 406
Calais and Vicinity.......................................... 415

## Background.................................................. 421
The Land........................................................ 421
History .......................................................... 426
Government and Economy................................ 433
The People .................................................... 434
Culture .......................................................... 436

## Essentials .................................................. 444
Getting There.................................................. 444
Getting Around .............................................. 447
Tips for Travelers .......................................... 449
Health and Safety .......................................... 452
Information and Services.................................. 456

## Resources.................................................... 459
Glossary ........................................................ 459
Suggested Reading.......................................... 461
Internet Resources .......................................... 465

## Index.......................................................... 468

# MAP CONTENTS

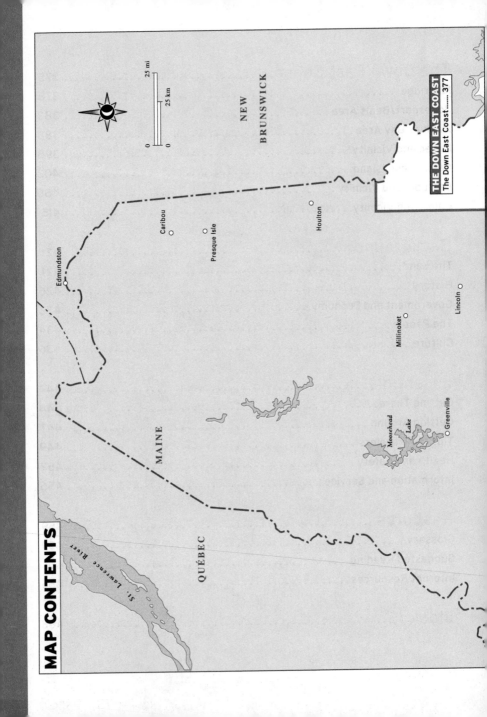

**THE DOWN EAST COAST**
The Down East Coast ...... 377

St. Lawrence River

QUÉBEC

MAINE

NEW BRUNSWICK

Edmundston

Caribou

Presque Isle

Houlton

Moosehead Lake

Greenville

Millinoket

Lincoln

0    25 mi

0    25 km

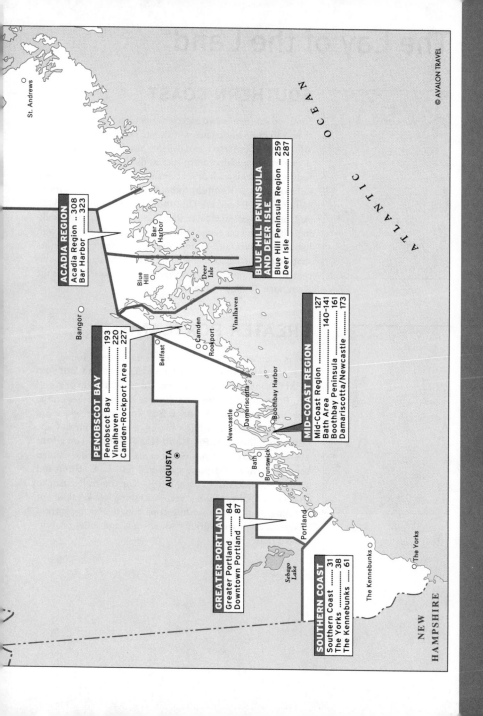

© AVALON TRAVEL

The Lay of the Land

SOUTHERN COAST

ATLANTIC OCEAN

ATLANTIC

St. Andrews

**ACADIA REGION**
Acadia Region .... 308
Bar Harbor ....... 323

Bar Harbor

Blue Hill

Deer Isle

**BLUE HILL PENINSULA AND DEER ISLE**
Blue Hill Peninsula Region ... 259
Deer Isle ....... 287

Bangor

Vinalhaven

Belfast

Camden
Rockport

**PENOBSCOT BAY**
Penobscot Bay ........... 193
Vinalhaven ............... 220
Camden-Rockport Area ..... 227

**MID-COAST REGION**
Mid-Coast Region .............. 127
Bath Area .............. 140-141
Boothbay Peninsula ......... 161
Damariscotta/Newcastle ......... 173

Newcastle

Damariscotta

Boothbay Harbor

AUGUSTA

Bath
Brunswick

Portland

Sebago
Lake

**GREATER PORTLAND**
Greater Portland ....... 84
Downtown Portland ....... 87

The Kennebunks

The Yorks

**SOUTHERN COAST**
Southern Coast ....... 31
The Yorks ......... 38
The Kennebunks ....... 61

NEW
HAMPSHIRE

# The Lay of the Land

## SOUTHERN COAST

Sand and sun are the two biggest draws to this region of Maine, thanks to miles of beaches, but they're not the only reasons to visit. Maine's Southern Coast delights history buffs, with homes dating from the 17th century, such as those at **Old York;** architecture buffs, with scads of sea captains' and shipbuilders' homes in towns such as **Kennebunkport;** art connoisseurs, with its plentiful galleries and the **Ogunquit Museum of American Art;** outdoors-oriented folks, with numerous preserves for walking, hiking, and canoeing; maritime-heritage aficionados, with lighthouses, forts, and fishing villages; shoppers with antiques shops and outlets galore; and families, with the state's best concentration of amusement parks and amusing places, such as the **Seashore Trolley Museum.**

## GREATER PORTLAND

As far as cities go, Maine's largest is not overwhelming, and most of its must-see sights, including the **Portland Museum of Art, Victoria Mansion, Portland Observatory,** and **Old Port** are within walking distance of one another on the downtown peninsula. A **Casco Bay Tour** will introduce you to the nearby islands, while a biking or driving tour to Cape Elizabeth will include **Portland Head Light.** Go on a **lobstering cruise,** and you might actually catch your dinner. Venture north to Freeport, and you'll find **L. L. Bean** and nearly 180 outlets to browse. But if what you really want to do is to go hiking, birding, deep-sea fishing, sea kayaking, or bicycling, all that's at your fingertips, too, thanks to plentiful preserves, a vibrant working waterfront, and miles of well-marked trails.

## MID-COAST REGION

Between Brunswick and Waldoboro, long granite-tipped fingers of land are dotted with small fishing villages, sea captains' homes, lobster wharves, nature preserves, antiques and artisans' shops, and occasionally beautiful stretches of sand, such as **Popham Beach**. Brunswick is home to **Bowdoin College** and the **Joshua Chamberlain Museum**, which honors the Civil War hero. Maine's shipbuilding heritage is brought to life in Bath's **Maine Maritime Museum**. Wiscasset is famed for its antiques shops, while Boothbay is the departure point for many excursion boats, including one that takes in a living-history lighthouse tour of **Burnt Island**. The adjacent Pemaquid Peninsula is tipped by **Pemaquid Point Lighthouse**. And no place along the Maine Coast has as many places for enjoying al fresco **lobster in the rough**.

## PENOBSCOT BAY

Island-studded Penobscot Bay is a sailor's dream. The rugged coastline hides protected harbors and links fishing villages with rather cosmopolitan towns. The jagged coastline is punctuated by beacons, such as **Owls Head Light** and **Rockland Breakwater Light**. Islands, including **Monhegan**, which is south of Penobscot Bay, frame the seaward background, while the **Camden Hills** are the inland backdrop. Lighthouses and lobster are two of the region's calling cards, but they're complemented by museums, such as **The Farnsworth Museum**, **Owls Head Transportation Museum**, and **Penobscot Marine Museum**. Throughout the region are antiques shops, art galleries, and artisans' studios. It's places such as **BlueJacket Shipcrafters**, where museum-quality ship models are handcrafted, that tie the seemingly diverse elements tidily together.

## BLUE HILL PENINSULA AND DEER ISLE

Water, water everywhere. That's certainly how it feels in a region edged by a mapmaker-challenging coastline (a magnet for **sea kayakers**) that makes it possible to watch the sun both rise—and set—over the Atlantic. Flavoring the region is an odd mix of genteel retirees, back-to-the-landers, summer folk, traditional boatbuilders, rugged fishermen, and talented artists, many of whom join together to perform as the **Flash in the Pans Community Steel Band**. Equally eclectic are the dozens of artists, many first drawn here by the **Haystack Mountain School of Craft.** Well off the usual path is **Castine,** a peaceful and beautifully preserved village where historical markers throughout explain its turbulent past. From Stonington, it's a short boat ride to **Isle au Haut** and a remote and rugged section of **Acadia National Park.**

# ACADIA REGION

Acadia National Park, the region's icon, is a miniature masterpiece, a gem of a natural and cultural resource. Get a taste with the **Park Loop** or the famed **carriage roads,** or go all out and hike rugged trails, kayak along undeveloped coastline, or canoe quiet ponds. Afterward, take part in a long-standing tradition, tea and popovers at the **Jordan Pond House.** Busy Bar Harbor anchors Mount Desert Island, but venture to Northeast Harbor's two fabulous gardens, **Asticou** and **Thuya,** and then loop around **Somes Sound** to the quiet side. Hop aboard an excursion boat to an offshore island or take an educational cruise narrated by a park ranger. While it's tempting to think that if you've been to Mount Desert, you've experienced Acadia, more parkland along with dozens of artists' studios and two scenic byways awaits on the quiet **Schoodic Peninsula** and environs.

# THE DOWN EAST COAST

East of Acadia the coastal geography changes, with blueberry barrens a frequent sight and huge tides ruling daily life. Traffic subsides; fast-food joints, shopping plazas, and chain motels all but disappear; and the stretch of road between towns gets longer. Artisans are plentiful. Fishing and lobstering are big business. But the biggest attraction is the wild expanse of coastline. Hiking and birding are renowned here and easy, thanks to a multitude of refuges, parks, and preserves, places such as **Maine Coastal Islands National Wildlife Refuge, Great Wass Preserve, West Quoddy Head State Park,** and **Shackford Head,** to name just a few. And offshore there's **Machias Seal Island,** a nesting ground for puffins, those clowns of the sea. Venture inland and find the Grand Lakes, ideal for fishing, boating, swimming, and lazy summer vacations.

# Planning Your Trip

If you truly want to see *everything,* you'll need three weeks to a month, minimally, especially if you're someone who would rather do than just see. If your plans don't permit getting away for that long, the best strategy is to focus on a region or two or three and immerse yourself in it.

## WHEN TO GO
### Spring
You might have to rethink your definition of spring. Melting winter snows combined with spring rains have earned March and April the well-deserved title Mud Season. Spring doesn't really begin to arrive until late April. By May, flowers are beginning to bloom and trees are beginning to leaf in most regions of the coast. While it might seem to be a beautiful time to visit, the scourge of Maine, the blackfly, is at its worst mid-May–mid-June, making outdoor activities northeast of Greater Portland pretty miserable.

Most businesses in larger coastal towns and cities remain open year-round, but smaller towns and villages don't even begin to wake up until mid-May and sometimes not even until mid-June. That said, there are always a few stretches of fine weather in May and June, and a good breeze keeps the bugs at rest. Better yet, many coastal accommodations are still on off-season or shoulder-season rates, and it's far easier to get dinner reservations.

### Summer
Summer can be idyllic, with moderate temperatures, clear air, and wispy breezes, but it can also close in with fog, rain, and chills. Prevailing winds are from the southwest. July and August are the peak season for visiting Maine and with good reason. These are the warmest months of the year and also the easiest times for families to travel. It's also when you'll have the greatest choice of recreation options. Of course, that means peak-season rates, congested roads (especially from Kittery through Wiscasset), and difficulty getting reservations at the best restaurants and accommodations, unless you've planned well ahead. If your schedule permits, consider late June or late August. Perhaps because of school's starting or ending, those weeks tend to be a bit quieter.

### Autumn
Ahhh, September. Mainers heave a collective sigh of relief after Labor Day, the first Monday of September. It is arguably the best time of the year to travel in the state. Days are warm and mostly dry, nights are cool, fog is rare, bugs are gone, and crowds are few. Foliage is turning by early October, usually reaching its peak by the middle of the month. While the prevailing wisdom sends people inland, seeing those brilliant reds, oranges, and yellows mixed with evergreens against a deep blue sea is without compare. And here's a plus: At many accommodations, rates are lower in autumn.

### Winter
The Maine Coast slumbers in winter, often blanketed in white. Snow tends not to last as long as inland, and often predicted snow is in reality ice. Choices in lodging, dining, and activities are far fewer than in other months, but the rates are at their lowest (except for special events). Instead of sunbathing on the sand, bundle up and take an invigorating walk or cross-country ski across a beach. In Camden, you can glide down alpine trails overlooking Penobscot Bay and then warm yourself with a bowl of lobster stew. On Mount Desert, when a nor'easter rumbles up the coast, you can snowshoe or ski on the carriage roads. Shop Kittery's and Freeport's outlets without crowds and take advantage of low-season sales. In areas with solid year-round populations, life goes on

full tilt, with an impressive array of cultural activities in cities such as Portland, and college towns, such as Brunswick.

## WHAT TO TAKE

The adage "If you don't like the weather, wait a minute" certainly applies to Maine. I've seen June days that begin in the 70s and finish in the 30s. Similarly, it can be 80°F and sunny a mile or so inland and damp and foggy along the coast. A coastal breeze can make it feel much cooler than the temperature indicates. Layering clothing is the best option.

Do bring a fleece jacket or pullover, a windbreaker, a lightweight sweater, and rain gear. In spring and autumn, add a wool sweater and a micro-fleece top for cool, damp days. In the peak of summer, temperatures can range from the 60s to the 80s, with usually a handful of hot, muggy days that might reach into the 90s. Bring pants and shorts—I've found pants that convert to shorts to take me through a long day of touring, from foggy morning through hot afternoon to cool evening.

Unless you're dining at the White Barn Inn or Arrows, you won't need fancy clothing. Resort casual is the dress code in most good restaurants and in downtown Portland, with nice T-shirts and shorts being acceptable almost everywhere in beach communities.

Good walking shoes are a must. If you're planning on getting afloat in a canoe or kayak, bring backup footwear. Little is worse than spending a day in wet, squishy sneakers.

A bathing suit, quick-drying shorts, a brimmed hat, and sunglasses are all useful.

Either take or plan to buy on arrival sunscreen and, in late spring and early summer especially, bug dope. You can find Lewey's Eco-Blends, a bug repellent based on a Native American herbal recipe, in many shops. Unless you're heading into deep woods, it works well and has a pleasant scent.

If you're planning on going out on a windjammer, whale watch, puffin excursion, or kayak tour, check with the outfitter on appropriate gear for the outing. Many of these boats venture well offshore, where it can be significantly colder. Extra fleece, wool sweaters, gloves, and a hat can be worth their weight in gold, even in summer. If you're prone to motion sickness, pack appropriate precautions.

In winter and spring, add warm, waterproof boots, gloves, hat, and winter-weight clothing to your list.

No matter when you come, bring a camera and plenty of film or memory cards (you can buy both here, and many photo shops in larger communities will download images onto a CD for a small fee). Don't forget prescription glasses, prescription medicines, binoculars, perhaps a journal or sketchpad, and any financial cards you plan to use, such as debit, credit, and ATM. If you're planning to venture into Canada, make sure you have appropriate identification and paperwork.

Other handy items are a small backpack for day trips or light hiking and a small or collapsible cooler for picnics or storing food. You can greatly reduce the cost of eating by buying food at grocery stores or supermarkets instead of dining out.

# Explore Coastal Maine

## ICONS OF THE MAINE COAST

It's a tough job to single out Maine's sightseeing icons. There are just so many. But, unless you have years to spend, such a big, meandering chunk of real estate needs some whittling to be made explorable. This itinerary exposes you to a good chunk of Maine while taking in most of the state's icons in 10 days. The downside: You'll be doing a fair bit of driving on Route 1, the major thoroughfare that strings these sights together. It's primarily a two-lane road, where speeds through towns are often 25 mph or below. It's not exactly ideal for a speed trip through Maine. While this itinerary is planned as 10 days, if your schedule permits, you'll be rewarded if you spend longer in any of the locations, but especially on Mount Desert.

If you're arriving by airplane, your best bet is to arrive at Portland International Jetport and depart from Bangor International, but if you can't swing that, use Portland only (but add an extra last night in Portland). Book your first two nights' lodging in Portland, nights three and four in Rockland or vicinity, nights five and six on Mount Desert Island, nights seven and eight in either the Jonesport or Cutler areas, to coincide with taking a puffin-sighting trip from either location (make reservations). Book your ninth night in the Calais area or Eastport.

### Day 1

Stretch your legs after your journey to Maine with a refreshing walk on **Ogunquit Beach,** one of Maine's prettiest and proof that there's plenty of sand along Maine's fabled rockbound coast. Afterward, head to **Kennebunkport** and indulge your passions: shopping in the boutiques and galleries that crowd Dock Square, taking a walking tour to view the historic homes, or enjoying a leisurely drive along the waterfront.

### Day 2

Begin the day with a visit to **Portland Head Light,** a Cape Elizabeth landmark and Maine's oldest lighthouse (1791), at the edge of 94-acre Fort Williams Park. Spend the afternoon in the **Portland Museum of Art,** Maine's premier art museum, smack in the heart of the state's largest city. End the day with a sunset cruise on Casco Bay.

### Day 3

Make a pilgrimage to gigunda sports retailer

and outfitter **L. L. Bean,** hub of the hub-bub in Freeport—Maine's outlet bonanza. Either spend the morning shopping or taking a Walk-on Adventure class. In the afternoon, visit the **Maine Maritime Museum** in Bath, 10 acres of indoor and outdoor exhibits celebrating the state's nautical heritage.

## Day 4

Take a day trip to **Monhegan Island** from Port Clyde. This car-free, carefree gem, about a dozen miles off the coast, is laced with hiking trails and has earned a place in art history books as the Artists' Island.

## Day 5

Drive or hike to the top of **Mt. Battie,** in Camden Hills State Park, on the northern fringe of Camden. The vistas are magnificent, with the broad sweep of Penobscot Bay for a backdrop. Then continue up the coast to Mount Desert Island and begin your explorations of **Acadia National Park.** If you've arrived on the island before noon, pick up a picnic lunch and then drive the **Park Loop,** a perfect introduction to Acadia that covers many of the highlights. Otherwise, take a whale-watching trip from Bar Harbor (reservations are wise).

## Day 6

Welcome the day by watching the sunrise from the summit of **Cadillac Mountain.** Afterward, if you haven't either driven or bicycled the Park Loop, do so. If you have, then explore the park more in depth: Go hiking, bicycling, or sea kayaking, take a carriage ride, or book an excursion boat to Islesford or a whale-watching excursion.

## Day 7

Depart Mount Desert Island and continue north on Route 1, dipping down the Gouldsboro Peninsula and looping through the **Schoodic section of Acadia National Park.** Continue to either the Jonesport or Cutler areas (wherever your lodging reservations are for that night).

## Days 8 and 9

These two days are interchangeable. Book a **puffin-sighting** trip on day eight, with day nine as a weather backup. You will need reservations. Afterward, drive to Lubec and visit **West Quoddy Head State Park.** On day nine, drive north to Calais, visiting Eastport, home of the highest tides in the country, if time permits.

## Day 10

Travel day. Return to Bangor via Route 9 (allow three hours) and then connect to I-95 if you're heading to Portland (allow three hours) or points south or west.

# LIGHTHOUSES, LOBSTER, AND L. L. BEAN

Maine's biggest draws are the three L's: lighthouses, lobster, and L.L. Bean. Maine's 64 lighthouses stretch from York's Nubble, lighted annually for the holidays, to candy-striped West Quoddy Head, in Lubec. Lobster, of course, can be found practically everywhere along the coast, but the best way to enjoy it is at a no-fuss lobster shack. Bean's ever-expanding campus in Freeport is the gigunda outdoor retailer's mothership, but it also has outlets in downtown Portland and in Ellsworth.

This six-day tour concentrates on the Southern Coast, Greater Portland, Midcoast, and Penobscot Bay regions. Book your first two nights' lodging in Portland, the second two in Damariscotta/Newcastle, and the final two in the Thomaston/Rockland area. If you're arriving by airplane, use Portland International Jetport. If you simply must stay in an accommodation that resembles a lighthouse, add an extra night or two in Phippsburg in the lighthouse building at Sebasco Harbor Resort, or tag on an extra couple of days at the end in Blue Hill at the First Light B&B.

## Day 1

Begin in York and view **The Nubble,** and then head north to **The Lighthouse Depot,** in Wells, allowing plenty of time to shop for all manner of lighthouse-related souvenirs and gifts. If time permits, veer down to East Point Sanctuary for distant views of Wood Island Light (bring binoculars).

## Day 2

Loop out to South Portland and Cape Elizabeth, beginning with visits to the **Portland Harbor Museum** and nearby **Spring Point**

**Ledge Lighthouse.** You won't find a better setting for lunch than Lobster Shack at Two Lights, overlooking **Cape Elizabeth Light.** Next, visit **Portland Head Light,** a Maine icon, and its museum. Allow time for a late-afternoon cruise with **Lucky Catch Lobster Tours;** perhaps you'll catch your dinner. If not, you can still enjoy a lobster on the waterfront.

## Day 3

Get an early start and begin at **L. L. Bean,** in Freeport. Be sure not to miss the famed outlet store. You might even take a **Walk-on Adventure** with Bean's Discovery School. In the afternoon, visit the **Maine Maritime Museum,** in Bath, and, if time permits, take a lighthouse cruise on the Kennebec River. Perhaps mosey down to Georgetown for dinner at Five Islands or stop in Wiscasset at either Red's Eats or Sprague's for a lobster roll.

## Day 4

Spend the morning in Boothbay Harbor, stepping back in time for a visit with light keeper Joseph Muise and his family on a **Burnt Island Tour.** In the afternoon, drive down to Pemaquid Point to view **Pemaquid Light,** perhaps climbing to the top. Be sure to also visit the Fisherman's Museum in the keeper's house. End the day with **lobster in the rough** in Round Pond.

### Day 5

Begin the day with a visit to **Marshall Point Light,** in Port Clyde, and then board the mail boat to **Monhegan Island.** Be sure to visit the museum in the lighthouse keeper's house. Alternatively, take a lighthouse-themed cruise or sea kayak tour out of Rockport or Rockland. Either way, be sure to visit the James Beard award–winning lobster shack **Waterman's Beach Lobster** in Spruce Head.

### Day 6

Greet the day with a sunrise walk out the breakwater to **Rockland Breakwater Light.** Before heading home, tour the **Maine Lighthouse Museum** and, if time permits, take a short jaunt out to **Owls Head Light,** in Owls Head, before returning to Portland for a late-afternoon flight home.

## 14-DAY BEST OF THE REAL MAINE

For many folks, the Down East, Acadia, and Blue Hill-Deer Isle regions represent the *real* Maine. With the notable exception of Ellsworth through Bar Harbor, life's pace really is slower here. Traffic congestion is rare; chain restaurants and accommodations are few.

Spend two weeks poking around, and you can visit Acadia National Park, browse the studios of megatalented artisans, go whale-watching or puffin-sighting, hike magnificent trails, kayak along undeveloped coastline, experience working lobstering villages, and view lighthouses. This tour circles you clockwise through the region, beginning in Calais and ending with the Blue Hill Peninsula, but you can do it in reverse.

The best air access is via Bangor International Airport. Book your first two nights' lodging in Eastport, the third in Lubec, nights four and five in or around Jonesport (Addison, Jonesboro, Columbia Falls), nights six and seven on the Gouldsboro Peninsula, nights 8–10 on Mount Desert Island, and your last three nights on the Blue Hill Peninsula (Blue Hill and Brooksville lodgings will be most central to all activities).

### Day 1

A travel day. From Bangor, drive Route 9 (The Airline) to Calais and then head south on Route 1 to Eastport (allow about three hours).

### Day 2

Begin your day early to catch sunrise; Eastport is the first U.S. city to see the sun rise each morning. It's also home to some of the largest tides on the East Coast, so check the height of the tide at the waterfront and then revisit it six hours later. In between, take a **whale-watching** cruise, tour Raye's Mustard Mill, browse downtown shops, take an easy hike out to Shackford Head, and just soak up the small-town Down East life.

## Day 3

Drive south to **Lubec** and visit **West Quoddy Head State Park,** allowing time to visit the museum at the base of the candy-striped lighthouse and to walk the trail edging the seaside cliffs. If time permits, head over the bridge to Campobello Island for a look-see at the Roosevelt estate.

## Day 4

Spend the morning on an excursion with **Tours of Lubec and Cobscook,** getting an insider's view, and then work your way down to the Jonesport area, noticing the blueberry barrens and perhaps touring some of the historical sites in Machias en route.

## Days 5 and 6

You'll need two days in the Jonesport area to maximize your odds of taking a puffin-watching trip to **Machias Seal Island.** While in the area, go hiking and bird-watching on **Great Wass Island** and/or **Petit Manan National Wildlife Refuge;** poke around Jonesport, the real deal when it comes to lobstering; and take in two unusual sights, the **Maine Central Model Railroad,** in Jonesport, and the **Ruggles House,** in Columbia Falls. For local color, don't miss a meal at Tall Barney's; sit at the Liar's Table, if you dare, and gossip with the lobstermen.

## Day 7

Begin with a drive or bicycle loop around the **Schoodic section of Acadia National Park.** Depending on your interests, spend the rest of the day hiking in the park, sea kayaking, or browsing the numerous artisans' galleries tucked in all corners of the region.

## Day 8

Head for Mount Desert Island. Begin on the outskirts, visiting **Northeast Harbor** and **Southwest Harbor,** with stops to see the As-ticou and Thuya Gardens, **Somes Sound,** and the **Wendell Gilley Museum.** Enjoy a lobster dinner at Thurston's Lobster Pound.

## Day 9

Spend the day in **Acadia National Park.** Begin by driving or bicycling the Park Loop to take in the park's highlights and then indulge your passions: hiking, sea kayaking, bicycling, a carriage tour. Be sure to stop for tea and popovers at the **Jordan Pond House.**

## Day 10

Visit the **Abbe Museum** and go **whale-watching,** and in-between poke around Bar Harbor.

## Day 11

Depart Mount Desert for the Blue Hill Peninsula. En route, visit **Birdsacre,** a peaceful preserve and bird refuge. In **Blue Hill,** begin with a tour of the **Parson Fisher House.** Afterward, visit some of the many galleries in town. Do ask locally to see if the **Flash-in-the-Pans Community Steel Band** is performing during your days on the peninsula, and make it a point to hear it.

## Day 12

Noodle over to **Castine** and pick up a brochure for a self-guided walking tour. Spend the afternoon on a guided sea-kayaking tour.

## Day 13

Explore **Deer Isle** and **Stonington,** allowing plenty of time to browse the galleries along the way or hike on one of the island's preserves. If time permits, hop a cruise to **Isle au Haut.**

## Day 14

Visit **Fort Knox** and the **Penobscot Narrows Bridge and Observatory** in the morning before heading home. If you're flying out of Bangor, you can either mosey up Route 15 or connect via Route 174 to Route 1A North.

# DESTINATION DINING TOUR

In recent years, Maine's restaurant scene has gained increasing national attention, with top awards and mentions in foodie magazines such as *Bon Appétit, Food and Wine, Gourmet,* and *Saveur.* If you want to dine your way through Maine, here's where to go to hit the biggies. You definitely want to plan well in advance for a summer visit, and even then, you might have to be flexible in your seating time.

## SOUTHERN COAST

### Arrows

A quiet country farmhouse is the understated setting for this restaurant, named by *Gourmet* as one of America's Top 50 Restaurants. Chefs Clark Frasier and Mark Gaier were nominated for a James Beard award in 2004 and have received accolades from, besides *Gourmet,* magazines such as *Bon Appétit* and even *Time.* They're renowned for their fresh flavorful cuisine, with many ingredients sourced from the restaurant's gardens. Jacket preferred for men.

### White Barn Inn

Maine's only five-diamond restaurant regularly gets kudos from publications such as *Food and Wine, Travel and Leisure,* and *Condé Nast Traveler.* The dining room is an elegantly restored barn, where chef Jonathan Cartwright's fixed-price, four-course menu, offering contemporary New England cuisine with European accents, is served by formally dressed waiters. Jackets are required for gentlemen.

### And While You're Here...

Don't miss **Provence,** a fabulous country French Ogunquit restaurant, owned by chef Pierre Gignac, that always wins top marks from local critics, and **Blue Sky,** Boston celebrity chef Lydia Shire's new restaurant in York Beach.

### Local Color

Slather on the secret sauce at **Flo's Steamed Dogs,** in Cape Neddick, and pick up taffy kisses at **The Goldenrod** in York Beach.

## GREATER PORTLAND

For any of these three, you'll feel most comfortable in resort casual wear. There's no need for jackets, although you wouldn't feel out of place, either.

### Fore Street

Ask any Maine foodie who the dean of Maine foods is, and likely the answer will be Sam Hayward. Here, Hayward has teamed with another highly regarded restaurateur, Dana Street, of Street and Company. The result won Hayward the "Best Chef in the Northeast" award from the James Beard Foundation in 2004.

### Hugo's

In 2004, *Food and Wine* named chef Rob Evans one of America's 10 Best New Chefs. You'll learn why when you step into this fine restaurant, decorated in soothing shades, where Evans prepares New American cuisine.

### Five Fifty-Five

And in 2007, *Food and Wine* gave chef Steve Corry the same endorsement. Corry's ever-changing menu takes advantage of whatever's fresh and local.

### And While You're Here...

New in 2007 and quickly gaining a following among area foodies was **Bresca,** where chef Krista Kerns prepares Italian-accented dishes in a tiny spot.

### Local Color

Watch boats come and go while chowing down all you can eat at **The Porthole**'s Friday-night fish fry, or grab an Italian sandwich, Maine's twist on a sub, at **Amato's.**

# PENOBSCOT BAY

## Primo

James Beard award–winning chef Melissa Kelly and her partner Price Kushner keep earning kudos for their farmhouse restaurant on the Rockland/Owls Head border. Resort casual is the preferred dress.

## Waterman's Beach Lobster

What's a lobster-in-the-rough spot doing on this list? Well, the folks at the James Beard House thought it deserved an award, and we think you deserve a night where you can dress down and drink in the view (if you want anything more potent to drink, be sure to bring it with you). You'll be eating lobster on a picnic table; jeans, shorts, and T-shirts are the dress code.

## And While You're Here...

Don't miss Francine, chef/owner Brian Hill's lovely little bistro in a residential section of downtown Camden.

## Local Color

Fried seafood is served with a dose of local color and a slab of pie at both Anglers Restaurant and Just Barb's.

# ACADIA REGION

## Le Domaine

It doesn't look like much from the road, but step inside. Former chef/owner Nicole Purslow created a touch of France on the coast of Maine, right down to the wine list, and her successors are keeping up the tradition. Before dinner, stroll the lovely grounds, laced with trails. When you make dining reservations, book a room for the night, too. Then all you'll have to do after wining and dining is head upstairs. Any local folks celebrating a special occasion likely will be dressed to the nines, but resort casual is fine.

## And While You're Here...

Have dinner at Burning Tree, long considered one of Mount Desert Island's best restaurants. Chef/owners Allison Martin and Elmer Beal Jr. create imaginative entrées that honor the best of what's fresh, local, and when possible, organic.

## Local Color

Gossip's served all day along with mighty-fine home cooking at Chester Pike's Galley, in Sullivan, but go early if you want to snag one of the homemade doughnuts. The locals don't order it, but it's doubtful you'll find lobster ice cream anywhere else but Ben and Bill's Chocolate Emporium, in Bar Harbor.

# ANTIQUES AND JUNKTIQUES: A SHOPPER'S TOUR

Searching for treasures? Whether you have a practiced eye or just enjoy the thrill of the hunt, you'll find these the best places for finding genuine antiques and collectibles or can't-resist treasures. This six-day tour stretches from Wells, in the Southern Coast region, to Searsport, in the Penobscot Bay region. Book your first two nights in Wells or a nearby town, your third night in Bath, fourth night in Wiscasset or one of the towns north of it, and your last two nights in Belfast or Searsport. If you're arriving by air, fly in and out of Portland.

## Days 1 and 2

**Wells and Vicinity:** Flea-market–style shops, antiquarian bookstores, huge barns, and old houses filled with genuine antiques or overflowing with "good stuff" line both sides of Route 1 in Wells and overflow into nearby towns. Don't miss **R. Jorgensen Antiques,** with 11 rooms filled with fine European and American antiques, or **Douglas N. Harding Rare Books** for antiquarian volumes and ephemera. Continue up to Kennebunk to **Antiques on Nine** for more finds.

## Day 3

**Brunswick and Bath:** Spend the first morning in Brunswick. A choice selection fills five rooms at **Day's Antiques.** For more variety, explore **Cabot Mill Antiques,** where more than 140 dealers show and sell their wares in the renovated Fort Andross mill complex next to the Androscoggin River. Then continue to Bath. The lower end of Bath's Front Street has side-by-side antiques shops, some with good-size collections of antiquarian books. While here, take a gander at the lovely historical homes lining Washington Street, and don't miss the **Maine Maritime Museum,** with its emphasis on nautical and boat-building antiquities.

## Day 4

**Woolwich and Wiscasset:** Get an early start for the best pickings at famous **Montsweag Flea Market.** Afterward, continue north on Route 1, stopping at **Avalon Antiques Market,** a large, multidealer shop along the way. Spend the afternoon in downtown Wiscasset, prowling though your choice of about two dozen antiques shops. If time permits, visit two antiques-filled treasure houses in Wiscasset, **Castle Tucker** and the **Nickels-Sortwell House,** and the **Musical Wonder House,** brimming with antique music boxes.

## Day 5

Dozens of antiques dealers have set up shops in the **Pemaquid Region.** Mosey down Route 130, where numerous barns have been converted into shops. Return to Route 1 and continue north, stopping at the many antique shops and auction houses along the way. You'll find clusters in **Nobleboro, Thomaston,** and **Lincolnville.** Do stop at **Nobleboro Antique Exchange,** a multidealer antique mall that's much, much larger than it first appears.

### Day 6

**Searsport:** Hard to believe there could be a town that rivals Wiscasset for the title Antiques Capital, but Searsport does. Sea captains' homes and big barns now house individual and group shops, such as **Pumpkin Patch,** which emphasizes Maine antiques, and the **Searsport Antique Mall,** with more than 70 dealers. You'll also find a few roadside flea markets worth poking around. Learn more about how all these treasures arrived here by visiting the **Penobscot Maritime Museum.**

### Day 7

Return to Belfast and then take Route 17 West, stopping in Liberty to visit **Liberty Tool Company,** three floors of antiques, with most of the wares being tools. Then continue west to I-95, and head south to Portland for an afternoon flight home.

# CULTURAL HERITAGE "TRAILS"

After years of fielding requests from visitors for lists of cultural-heritage sites and special-interest activities, the Maine Office of Tourism has teamed up with the state's arts and culture organizations to create a whole range of "trails" that cover maritime history, art museums, outstanding gardens, outdoor sculpture, and Wabanaki (Native American) sites. With state support, several counties and groups have produced their own regional cultural maps. Request copies of any of the first five publications at any of the state Visitor Information Centers or call 800/782-6497. The Wabanaki guide is available for a fee (see entry below).

### Maine Architecture Trail

Travelers in Maine pass through many small towns and villages, and it's not uncommon for them to stop and marvel at the wondrous architectural details. Presented in this brochure are six specific routes, three emphasizing coastal sights, each explaining the connection between the landscape, the people, and the architecture by focusing on specific sights and putting it all in historical context.

### Maine Art Museum Trail

An attractive brochure focuses on the state's seven significant art museums, containing more than 50,000 works of art—ancient to contemporary, painting and sculpture, furniture and textiles. Four of the seven are in coastal Maine. From south to north: Ogunquit Museum of Art (Ogunquit); Portland Museum of Art (Portland); Bowdoin College Museum of Art (Brunswick); and Farnsworth Art Museum (Rockland). (The museums inland are Bates College Museum of Art in Lewiston, the Colby Museum of Art in Waterville, and the University of Maine Museum of Art in Orono.) The trail website is www.maineartmuseums.org.

### Maine Archives and Museums Directory

More than 125 institutions are listed by region in this 72-page directory of museums, historical societies, historic sites, and archives. Four of the regions fall within coastal Maine. (The directory includes some of the highlights of the maritime-heritage and art-museum trails.) The website is www.mainemuseums.org.

### Maine Garden and Landscape Trail

A handy foldout map lists and locates more than 50 gardens—a huge variety from pocket parks to city parks; formal, English, and experimental gardens; even a monastery and a cemetery. Although the trail covers the entire state, two-thirds of the sites are in Coastal Maine. You'll find the finest displays in June and July, when garden tours are also on the agenda. Best of these tours are in Camden, Damariscotta, the Kennebunks, and Mount Desert Island. The "trail" map also lists several dozen garden and plant centers with wonderful display gardens where you can indulge your horticultural habit.

## Maine Maritime Heritage Trail

Any state that claims more than 5,000 miles of in-and-out coastline logically can also claim a rich maritime heritage. The Maritime Heritage Trail focuses on the sites that represent Coastal Maine's rich history—maritime museums, boatbuilding schools, lighthouses, and sea captains' mansions. Also part of the story are maritime celebrations—windjammer and lobster-boat races, lighthouse tours, and clam and lobster festivals. The special large-format, two-sided map serves as a handy reference as you travel the trail. The website www.maritimemaine.org has even more sights and information.

## Maine Outdoor Sculpture Guide

Three tours are highlighted in this handy and fun-to-read 64-page guidebook. The Seacoast Tour visits outdoor sculptures from Kittery to Machias, detailing each sculpture and explaining its history. The Sculpture Garden Tour highlights classic and whimsical coastal sculpture gardens in Ogunquit, Bath, Islesboro, and Mount Desert. The Civil War Tour explains coastal Civil War–related monuments in York and Calais. Noncoastal outdoor sculptures are also featured in the guide, which also includes walking tours of outdoor sculpture in Portland and Bangor. Call 207/287-2724 to request a copy.

## A Wabanaki Guide to Maine: A Visitor's Guide to Native American Culture in Maine

Although a bit outdated, this splendid 86-page spiral-bound booklet, published in 2001, is an excellent guide. The Wabanaki Trail is a go-at-your-own-pace route that leads you to museums, workshops, festivals, shops, significant landmarks, and even ancient canoe routes. Two trail sections are in the Acadia and Down East regions of Coastal Maine, where two of Maine's four tribes live. The guide is available for $10 (check or money order) from the Maine Indian Basketmakers Alliance (P.O. Box 3253, Old Town 04468, 207/827-0391).

# SOUTHERN COAST

Drive over the I-95 bridge from New Hampshire into Maine's Southern Coast region on a bright summer day and you'll swear the air is cleaner, the sky bluer, the trees greener, the roadside signs more upbeat: Welcome to Maine: The Way Life Should Be. (*Is* it? Or maybe the way life *used* to be?)

Most visitors come to this region for the spectacular attractions of the justly world-famous Maine coast—the inlets, islands, and especially the beaches, but it's rich in history, too.

Southernmost York County, part of the Province of Maine, was incorporated in 1636 (only 16 years after the *Mayflower* pilgrims reached Plymouth, Massachusetts) and reeks of history: ancient cemeteries, musty archives, and architecturally stunning homes and public buildings. Probably the best places to dive

into that history are in the sites of the Old York Historical Society in York Harbor.

Geological fortune smiled on this 50-mile ribbon, endowing it with a string of sandy beaches—nirvana for sun worshipers, less enchanting to swimmers, who need to steel themselves to spend much time in the ocean (especially in early summer, before the water temperature has reached a tolerable level).

Complementing those beaches are amusement parks and arcades, fishing shacks turned chic boutiques, a surprising number of good restaurants (given the region's seasonality), and some of the state's prettiest parks and preserves.

Spend some time poking around the small villages that give the region so much character. Many have been gussied up and gentrified

© TOM NANGLE

SOUTHERN COAST

# HIGHLIGHTS

**◖ Old York Historical Society:** York dates from the 1640s, and on this campus of historic buildings, you can peek into early life (page 39).

**◖ Nubble Light/Sohier Park:** You'll likely recognize this often-photographed Maine Coast icon, which is the easiest lighthouse to see in the region (page 39).

**◖ Ogunquit Museum of American Art (OMAA):** It's hard to say which is more jaw dropping, the art or the view (page 48).

**◖ Marginal Way:** Escape the hustle and bustle of Ogunquit with a stroll on this paved, shorefront path (page 48).

**◖ Wells Reserve at Laudholm Farm:** Orient yourself at the visitors center, where you can learn about the history, flora, and fauna, and then take a leisurely walk to the seashore, passing through a variety of habitats (page 49).

**◖ Seashore Trolley Museum:** Ring-ring-ring goes the bell...and zing-zing-zing go your heartstrings, especially if you're a trolley fan (page 60).

**◖ Dock Square:** Busy, busy, busy is this heart of Kennebunkport, and with good reason. Brave the crowds and explore (page 63).

**◖ St. Anthony's Monastery:** It's hard to believe this oasis of calm is just a short stroll from busy-busy-busy Dock Square (page 64).

LOOK FOR ◖ TO FIND RECOMMENDED SIGHTS, ACTIVITIES, DINING, AND LODGING.

**◖ East Point Sanctuary:** A must for birders, this coastal preserve provides dramatic views (page 77).

quite a bit but retain their seafaring or farming bones.

Some Mainers refer to the Southern Coast as northern Massachusetts. Sometimes it can seem that way, not only for the numbers of commonwealth plates in evidence but also because many former Massachusetts residents have moved here for the quality of life and commute to jobs in the Boston area. The downside is escalating real-estate prices that have forced families with deep roots off land that's been in their families for generations

and pushed those in traditional seafaring occupations inland. Still, if you nose around and get off the beaten path, you'll find that real Maine is still here.

## PLANNING YOUR TIME

The good news is that Maine's Southern Coast is a rather compact region. The bad news is that it's heavily congested, especially in summer. Still, with a minimum of four days, you should be able to take in most of the key sights, from beaches to museums, as

SOUTHERN COAST

Casco Bay

112  Gorham  25  Portland

Newfield

110

Westbrook

Peaks Island

5

22

22

Hollis Center

29

South Portland

1

Waterboro Center

CUMBERLAND

9

77  Two Lights State Park

109  11

YORK

4

112  Scarborough

35

TURNPIKE

Cape Elizabeth

Crescent Beach State Park

202

Old Orchard Beach

Scarborough Beach Park

Prouts Neck

Saco River

5

Saco

Ocean Park

Springvale

Alfred

111

Biddeford

1

Ferry Beach State Park

Sanford

4

Kennebunk River

35

MAINE

9  Biddeford Pool

**(  EAST POINT SANCTUARY**

202

99

Kennebunk

**(  DOCK SQUARE**

Goose Rocks Beach

11

109

9A

Cape Porpoise

**(  WELLS RESERVE AT LAUDHOLM FARM**

Kennebunkport

Kennebunk Beach

North Berwick

Wells

Berwick  4

95

Wells Beach

Moody

South Berwick

Ogunquit Beach

Mt Agamenticus

Ogunquit

**(  OGUNQUIT MUSEUM OF AMERICAN ART (OMAA)**

236

**(  MARGINAL WAY**

Cape Neddick

York Beach

4

103  101

York River

1A

York Village

Eliot

★ **(  OLD YORK HISTORICAL SOCIETY**

Piscataqua River

Kittery

**(  NUBBLE LIGHT/ SOHIER PARK**

Portsmouth

Kittery Point

**NEW HAMPSHIRE**

1

ATLANTIC OCEAN

Salmon Falls River

0     0.5 mi

0     0.5 km

95

© AVALON TRAVEL

long as you don't want to spend hours basking in the sun.

Route 1, the region's primary artery, is often bumper-to-bumper traffic. If you're hopscotching towns, consider using I-95, which has exits for York, Kennebunk, and Saco/Biddeford/Old Orchard Beach. Parking, too, can be a challenge and expensive, but a trolley system operates in summer and connects most towns,

making it easy to avoid the hassles and help the environment.

July and August are the busiest months. If you can avoid them, do. Spring and fall are lovely times to visit, and most attractions are open. In winter, you can walk the beaches without running into another soul, it's easy to get dinner reservations, and lodging prices plummet—the trade-off is that fewer businesses are open.

# Kittery

Besides being a natural point of entry into the state, Kittery also competes with Freeport, farther up the coast, as an outlet-shopping mecca. Kittery boasts more than 120 factory outlets lining both sides of U.S. 1. But before or after you overdose on shoes, china, tools, toys, candles, and underwear, take time to explore the back roads of Maine's oldest town—settled in 1623 and chartered in 1647. Maine is home to a lot of well-kept secrets, Kittery being one of them. Parks, a small nautical museum, historic architecture, and lobster restaurants are only a few of the attractions in Kittery and its "suburb," Kittery Point. It was also on Kittery's Badger Island where the sloop *Ranger* was launched in 1777. The shipbuilding continues at Portsmouth Naval Shipyard, on Kittery's Dennet's Island, the first government shipyard in America.

To reach Kittery's shops and services from I-95 northbound take the Exit 3 cloverleaf, designated Kittery, Coastal Route 1 North, and continue to Route 1. From I-95 southbound, take the Yorks/Berwicks exit, and then take Coastal Route 1 South. Follow signs; the twists and turns can be confusing.

## SIGHTS

Avoid the outlet sprawl and see the prettiest part of the area by driving along squiggly Route 103 from the Route 1 rotary in Kittery through Kittery Point (administratively part of Kittery) and on to Route 1A in York. You can even make a day of it, stopping at the sites mentioned here. Be very careful and watch for cyclists and pedestrians, as there are no shoulders and lots of blind corners and hills.

### Kittery Historical and Naval Museum

Maritime history buffs shouldn't miss the small but well-stocked Kittery Historical and Naval Museum (Rogers Road Ext., near the junction of Rtes. 1 and 236, Kittery, 207/439-3080, 10 A.M.–4 P.M. Tues.–Sat. June–mid-Oct., $3 adults, $1.50 kids 7–15, family max. $6). A large exhibit hall and a small back room contain ship models, fishing gear, old photos and paintings, and an astonishing collection of scrimshaw (carved whale ivory).

### Lady Pepperrell House

The 1760 Georgian Lady Pepperrell House (Pepperrell Rd., Rte. 103, shortly before the Fort McClary turnoff) is now privately owned and no longer open to the public, but it's worth admiring from afar. Nearby, across from the First Congregational Church, is the area's most-visited burying ground. Old-cemetery buffs should bring rubbing gear here for some interesting grave markers. The tomb of Levi Thaxter (husband of poet Celia Thaxter) bears an epitaph written for him by Robert Browning.

### Fort McClary Historic Site

Since the early 18th century, fortifications have stood on this 27-acre headland, protecting Portsmouth Harbor from seaborne foes. Contemporary remnants at Fort McClary (Rte. 103, Kittery Point, 207/439-2845, $2 adults, $1 kids 5–11) are several outbuildings, an 1846 blockhouse, granite walls, and earthworks—all with a view of Portsmouth Harbor. Opposite are the sprawling buildings of the Portsmouth Naval Shipyard. Bring a picnic (covered tables and a lily pond are across the street) and turn the kids loose to run and play. It's officially open May 30–October 1, but the site is accessible in off-season. The fort is 2.5 miles east of Route 1.

### Fort Foster

The only problem with Fort Foster (Pocahontas Rd., off Rte. 103, Gerrish Island, Kittery Point, 207/439-3800, 10 A.M.–8 P.M. Memorial Day–Labor Day and weekends May and Sept., $10 vehicle pass, $5 adult walk-in, $1 child walk-in) is that it's no secret, so parking can be scarce (and expensive) at this 90-acre municipal park at the entrance to Portsmouth Harbor. On a hot day, arrive early. Then you can swim, hike the nature trails, fish off the

© TOM NANGLE

Fort McClary has guarded Portsmouth Harbor since the early 18th century.

bridge is a pullout on the left. You have a couple of options for hikes: a 1.8-mile loop trail, including a spur, or a half-mile loop. Bring binoculars to spot waterfowl in the marshlands.

## Captain and Patty's Piscataqua River Tours

Take a spin around the Piscataqua River Basin with Captain and Patty's Piscataqua River Tours (Town Dock, Pepperrell Rd., Kittery Point, 207/439-8976 home or 207/451-8156 boat). The 80-minute historical tour departs seven times daily, including once in the evening for a two-hour twilight cruise for adults only. Along the way, Captain Neil Odams points out historic forts, lighthouses, and the Naval shipyard.

## ENTERTAINMENT
### Concerts in the Park

Kittery Recreation presents a free, summer concert series on Memorial Field, Old Post Road, 6:30–8 P.M. on Wednesday evenings mid-July–mid-August.

## SHOPPING

No question, you'll find bargains at Kittery's 120-plus factory outlets (www.thekitteryoutlets.com)—actually a bunch of minimalls clustered along Route 1. All the household names are here: Bass, Calvin Klein, Eddie Bauer, J Crew, Mikasa, Esprit, Lenox, Timberland, Tommy Hilfiger, GAP, Villeroy and Boch, and a hundred more (all open daily). Anchoring it all is the **Kittery Trading Post** (301 Rte. 1, 207/439-2700 or 888/587-6246, www.kitterytradingpost.com), a humongous sporting-goods and clothing emporium. Try to avoid the outlets on weekends, when you might need to take a number for the try-on rooms. Most of the minimalls have telephones; several have ATMs; all have restrooms.

## ACCOMMODATIONS

Put a little oooh and aaaah into your touring with a visit to the **Portsmouth Harbor Inn and Spa** (6 Water St., Kittery, 207/439-4040, www.innatportsmouth.com, $160–200

pier (no license needed), picnic, and investigate the tide pools. Bring your sailboard and a kite—there's almost always a breeze. From nearby **Seapoint Beach** (park in the small roadside lot and walk down to the beach; the lower lot is for residents only, no facilities) on a clear day, there's a wide-open view of the offshore Isles of Shoals, owned jointly by Maine and New Hampshire.

## RECREATION
### Brave Boat Harbor

One of the Rachel Carson National Wildlife Refuge's 10 Maine coastal segments is Brave Boat Harbor (207/646-9226), a beautifully unspoiled, 560-acre wetlands preserve in Kittery Point with a four-mile (round-trip) trail. Carry binoculars, wear rubberized boots to maneuver the squishy areas, and slather on the insect repellent. The habitat is particularly sensitive here, so be kind to the environment. Take Route 103 to Chauncey Creek Road, and continue past the Gerrish Island bridge to Cutts Island Lane. Just beyond it and across a small peak). The handsome brick inn, built in 1889, looks out over the Piscataqua River, Portsmouth, and the Portsmouth Naval Shipyard. Five attractive Victorian-style rooms (most with water views) are furnished with antiques and have air-conditioning, TV, and phones. There's an outdoor hot tub, and beach chairs are available. Breakfasts are multicourse feasts. Request a back room if you're noise sensitive, although air-conditioning camouflages traffic noise in summer. Rooms on the third floor have the best views, but these also have hand-held showers. Now for the aaaah part. The inn also has a full-service spa. The inn has lots of intriguing special packages. It's an easy walk across the bridge to Portsmouth for plentiful dining options.

Shopaholics take note: **Chicadee Bed and Breakfast** (63 Haley Rd., 207/439-0672 or 888/502-0876, www.chicadeebandb.net, $125 d) is within walking distance of Kittery's famed outlets. A full country breakfast should power you through a shopping spree. Afterward, return for a dip in the pool. Walter and Brenda Lawrence's family home is comfortably furnished with country flair. No pets—four dogs are in residence.

## FOOD
### Local Flavors
Kittery has an abundance of excellent specialty food stores that are perfect for stocking up for a picnic lunch or dinner. Most are along the section of Route 1 between the Portsmouth bridge and the traffic circle.

Three are within steps of each other. At **Beach Pea Baking Co.** (53 Rte. 1, 207/439-3555, 7:30 A.M.–6 P.M. Mon.–Sat.) you can buy fabulous breads and pastries. Sandwiches and salads are made to order 11 A.M.–3 P.M. daily. There's pleasant seating indoors and on a patio. Next door is **Golden Harvest** (7 A.M.–6:30 P.M. Mon.–Sat. and 9 A.M.–6 P.M. Sun.), where you can load up on luscious produce. Across the street is **Terracotta Pasta Co.** (52A, Rte. 1, 207/475-3025, 10 A.M.–6 P.M. Mon., 9 A.M.–6:30 P.M. Tues.–Sat., and noon–4 P.M. Sun.), where in addition

to handmade pastas you'll find salads, soups, sandwiches, prepared foods, and lots of other goodies.

Just off Route 1 is **Enoteca Italiana** (20 Walker St., 207/439-7216, 10 A.M.–7 P.M. Mon. and Wed.–Sat. and noon–4 P.M. Sun.), which carries wine, an extensive selection of cured meats, fine cheeses, and other gourmet items.

What's a meal without chocolate? At **Cacao** (64 Government St., just off the town green, 207/438-9001, noon–6 P.M. Tues.–Fri. and 10 A.M.–4 P.M. Sat.), Susan Tuveson handcrafts outrageously decadent chocolate truffles and caramels. Flavors vary from the familiar to the exotic: Some are made with chilies (habanero lime!), some with cheeses. The strawberry balsamic vinegar with black pepper truffle and the fleur de sel caramel are particularly sublime.

Old World artisan breads made from organic ingredients are available at the company store for **When Pigs Fly** (447 Rte. 1, 207/439-3114, www.sendbread.com).

In Kittery Point, **Frisbee's Supermarket** (207/439-0014, 7 A.M.–8 P.M. Mon.–Sat., 8 A.M.–8 P.M. Sun.) is an experience in itself. Established in 1828, the store has marginally modernized but still earns its label as North America's oldest family store—run by the fifth generation of Frisbees.

At the **Sunrise Grill** (182 State Rd., Rte. 1, Kittery Traffic Circle, Kittery, 207/439-5748, 6:30 A.M.–2 P.M. daily), order waffles, granola, omelettes, or Diana's Benedict or at lunch, salads, sandwiches, and burgers. In downtown Kittery, **Crooked Lane Café** (Wentworth St., 207/439-2244), in a Victorian building with a tin ceiling and both indoor and outdoor seating, is a bit more polished and serves a full menu of espresso-style coffees along with breakfast and lunch fare.

Craving Mex? Some of the recipes in Luis Valdez's **Loco Coco's Tacos** (36 Walker St., Kittery, 207/438-9322, www.locococos.com, 11 A.M.–3 P.M. and 4–8 P.M. Mon.–Fri., to 9 P.M. Sat.) have been passed down for generations, and the homemade salsas are fab. If you're feeling really decadent, go for the artery-busting California fries. There's a kids' menu, too. Nothing costs more than $9.

## Casual Dining

Dining in Kittery took a bit of an upswing with the opening of ❰ anneke jans (60 Wallingford Sq., Kittery, 207/439-0001, www.annekejans.net, 5–10 P.M. Tues.–Sat.). Charcoal walls, white-clothed tables with moss centerpieces, a wine bar, and windows that open to the street create an especially hip and stylin' atmosphere. The French/American bistro menu might include blue-corn-dusted sea scallops, herb-roasted chicken, or Angus strip sirloin, with prices ranging $14–31. The extensive wine list has more than 30 available by the glass. This is a local hot spot with a lively crowd; reservations are recommended.

## Lobster and Clams

If you came to Maine to eat lobster, **Chauncey**

**Creek Lobster Pier** (16 Chauncey Creek Rd., off Rte. 103, Kittery Point, 207/439-1030, www.chaunceycreek.com, 11 A.M.–8 P.M., to 7 P.M. after Labor Day, mid-May–Columbus Day) is the real deal. Step up to the window, place your order, take a number, and grab a table (you may need to share) overlooking tidal Chauncey Creek and the woods on the close-in opposite shore. It's a particularly picturesque—and extremely popular—place. Parking is a nightmare. BYOB and anything else that's not on the menu.

If clams are high on your must-have list, you can't do much better than **Bob's Clam Hut** (315 Rte. 1, Kittery 03904, 207/439-4233, www.bobsclamhut.com, 11 A.M.–9 P.M. Mon.–Thurs., to 9:30 P.M. Fri. and Sat., to 8:30 P.M. Sun.), next to the Kittery Trading Post. Using vegetable oil for frying, Bob's turns out everything from scallops to shrimp to calamari to, of course, clams—the tartar sauce is the secret weapon. Expect to pay market rates, but nothing is too pricey. Bob's is open all year.

# The Berwicks

Probably the best known of the area's present-day inland communities is the riverside town of South Berwick—thanks to a historical and literary tradition dating to the 17th century, and antique cemeteries to prove it. The 19th-and 20th-century novels of Sarah Orne Jewett and Gladys Hasty Carroll have lured many a contemporary visitor to explore their rural settings—an area aptly described by Carroll as "a small patch of earth continually occupied but never crowded for more than three hundred years."

Also here is the 150-acre hilltop campus of **Berwick Academy,** Maine's oldest prep school, chartered in 1791 with John Hancock's signature. The coed school's handsome gray-stone William H. Fogg Memorial Library ("The Fogg") is named for the same family connected with Harvard's Fogg Art Museum. The highlight of the library is an incredible collection

of dozens of 19th-century stained-glass windows, most designed by Victorian artist Sarah Wyman Whitman, who also designed jackets for Sarah Orne Jewett's books. Thanks to a diligent fund-raising effort, the windows were recently restored to their former glory.

## SIGHTS
### Sarah Orne Jewett House

Don't blink or you might miss the tiny sign outside the 1774 Sarah Orne Jewett House (5 Portland St., Rtes. 4 and 236, South Berwick, 207/384-2454, www.historicnewengland.org, 11 A.M.–5 P.M. Fri.–Sun. June 1–Oct. 15, $8 adults, $7 seniors, $4 ages 12 and younger) smack in the center of town. Park on the street and join one of the tours—you'll learn details of the Jewett family and its star, Sarah (1849–1909), author of *The Country of the Pointed Firs,* a New England classic. Books by and about

Author Sarah Orne Jewett made her home in South Berwick.

© TOM NANGLE

Sarah are available in the gift shop. House tours are at 11 A.M. and 1, 2, 3, and 4 P.M. The house is a Historic New England property.

## Hamilton House
Dramatically crowning a bluff overlooking the Salmon Falls River and flanked by handsome colonial revival gardens, 18th-century Hamilton House (40 Vaughan's La., South Berwick, 207/384-2454, www.historicnewengland.org, 11 A.M.–5 P.M. Wed.–Sun. June 1–Oct. 15, $8 adults, $7 seniors, $4 ages 12 and younger) evokes history and tradition. Like the Jewett House, the 35-acre site is owned by Historic New England. Knowledgeable guides relate the house's fascinating history. Tours begin only on the hour—last one at 4 P.M. In July, the **Sunday in the Garden** concert series takes place on the lawn ($8 admission, including a free pass to come back and see the house). Pray for sun; the concert is moved indoors on rainy days. From Route 236 at the southern edge of South Berwick (watch for a signpost), turn left onto Brattle Street and take the second right onto Vaughan's Lane.

## Vaughan Woods State Park
A path connects Hamilton House to adjoining Vaughan Woods State Park (28 Oldfields Rd., South Berwick, 207/384-5160, 9 A.M.–8 P.M. late May–early Sept., but accessible all year, $2 adults, $1 children 5–11, free over 65 or under 5), but it's not easy to find, and there's much more parking space at the main entrance to the 250-acre river's-edge preserve. Three miles of maintained trails wind through this under-used park, and benches are scattered here and there. There's even a bench looking out over the river and Hamilton House.

## Old Berwick Historical Society/ Counting House
Based in a onetime cotton-mill building known as the Counting House, the Old Berwick Historical Society (Liberty and Main Sts., Rte. 4, P.O. Box 296, South Berwick 03908, 207/384-0000, www.obhs.net, 1–4 P.M. Sat.–Sun. in July, Aug., and Sept.,), sees a steady stream of genealogists looking for their roots in one of Maine's oldest settlements. Books and docu-

ments are only part of the museum's collection, which includes old photos and tools, boat models and nautical instruments, plus special annual exhibits. Admission to the 19th-century Counting House is by donation.

## ENTERTAINMENT

Theatergoers head to the Berwick area for the long-running (since 1972) **Hackmatack Playhouse** (538 School St./Rte. 9, Berwick, 207/698-1807, www.hackmatack.org), midway between North Berwick and Berwick. The popular summer theater, based in a renovated barn reminiscent of a past era, has 8 P.M. performances (comedies and musical comedies) Wednesday–Saturday and a 2 P.M. matinee Thursday. The ambience is relaxed and casual but quality is high, though it's a non-Equity house. The Hackmatack season runs late June–early September. Tickets are $20; discounts for seniors and students except Saturday.

## ACCOMMODATIONS

Once the headmaster's residence for nearby Berwick Academy, the elegant, turn-of-the-20th-century **Academy Street Inn Bed and Breakfast** (15 Academy St., South Berwick, 207/384-5633) has crystal chandeliers, leaded-glass windows, working fireplaces, and high-ceilinged rooms full of antiques. Paul and Lee Fopeano's handsome home has five rooms with private baths ($84–94 d). Full breakfast

or afternoon lemonade on the 60-foot screened porch is a real treat. It's open all year.

## FOOD

A local institution since 1960, **Fogarty's** (471 Main St., South Berwick, 207/384-8361, 11 A.M.–8 P.M., to 9 P.M. Sat.) has expanded through the years from a simple takeout to a local favorite for inexpensive, family-friendly dining. Ask for a river-view table in the back room.

Newer on the scene is **Pepperland Café** (279 Main St., South Berwick, 207/384-5535, 11 A.M.–11:30 P.M. Tues.–Sat., 9 A.M.–3 P.M. Sun.), a family-friendly pub-meets-bistro serving comfort food with pizzazz. Make a meal from smaller plates and salads ($5–10) or go big with the entrées ($16–19). Everything's prepared from scratch, and more than half of the waste is recycled.

Now here's a find: a cozy French bistro serving simple yet classic fare created from farm-fresh ingredients. **Margaux: Bistro Populaire** (404 Main St., South Berwick, 207/384-8249, 5:30–9 P.M. Tues.–Sat.) is an intimate, low-key neighborhood bistro, where Linda Robinson and Christine Prunier provide a warm welcome into the simple white house, with dining on the enclosed porch, one small dining room, and at the small bar. The frequently changing menu might include escargot au Pernod, braised lamb shank, duck confit, or seared sea scallops. Mix and match from small and large plates. Entrée range is $18–25.

# The Yorks

Four villages with distinct personalities—upscale York Harbor, historic York Village, casual York Beach, and semirural Cape Neddick—make up the Town of York. First inhabited by Native Americans, who named it Agamenticus, the area was settled as early as 1624—so history is serious business here. Town high points were its founding, by Sir Ferdinando Gorges, and the arrival of well-to-do vacationers in the 19th century. In between were Indian massacres,

economic woes, and population shuffles. The town's winter population explodes in summer (pretty obvious in July and August, when you're searching for a free patch of York Beach sand or a parking place). York Beach, with its seasonal surf and souvenir shops and amusements, has long been the counterpoint to genteel York Village, but that's changing with the restoration and rebirth of downtown buildings and the arrival of tony restaurants, shops, and condos.

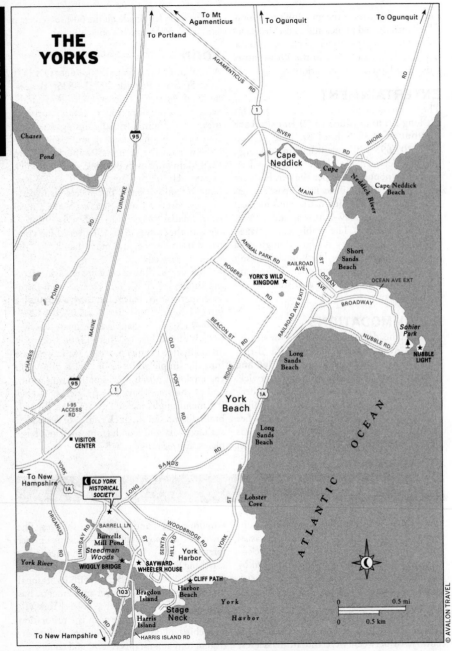

THE
YORKS

History and genealogy buffs can study the headstones in the Old Burying Ground or comb the archives of the Old York Historical Society. For lighthouse fans, there are Cape Neddick Light Station ("Nubble Light") and, six miles offshore, Boon Island. You can rent horses or mountain bikes on Mt. Agamenticus, board a deep-sea fishing boat in York Harbor, or spend an hour hiking the Cliff Path in York Harbor. For the kids, there's a zoo, a lobster-boat cruise, a taffy maker, or, of course, back to the beach.

## SIGHTS
### ◖ Old York Historical Society

Based in York Village, the Old York Historical Society (207 York St., P.O. Box 312, York 03909, 207/363-4974, www.oldyork.org, museum buildings open 10 A.M.–5 P.M. Mon.–Sat. early June–early Oct., $10 adults or $5 one building, $8 seniors or $4 one building, $5 children 4–16 or $3 one building) is the driving force behind a collection of eight colonial and postcolonial buildings (plus a research library) open throughout the summer. Start at the Jefferds' Tavern Visitor Center (5 Lindsay Rd., York), where you'll need to pick up tickets for visiting. Don't miss the Old Burying Ground, dating from 1735, across the street (rubbings are a no-no). Nearby are the Old Gaol and the School House (both fun for kids), Ramsdell House, and the Emerson-Wilcox House. About one-half mile down Lindsay Road, on the York River, are the John Hancock Warehouse and the George Marshall Store Gallery (140 Lindsay Rd., operated in the summer as a respected contemporary-art gallery); across the river is the Elizabeth Perkins House. Antiques buffs shouldn't miss the Wilcox and Perkins Houses. These two are open by guided tour; other buildings are self guided. Visit some or all of the buildings, at your own pace—no one leads you from one to another. In July and August, an architectural walking tour of York Village begins at 10 A.M. every Wednesday ($2 pp; meet at Jefferds' Tavern). At 196 York Street, across from the jail, is the well-stocked Museum Shop. Note: Some sites you can walk

to from the tavern; others you'll need a car to reach and parking may be limited.

### ◖ Nubble Light/Sohier Park

The best-known photo op in York is the distinctive 1879 lighthouse known formally as Cape Neddick Light Station and familiarly as "The Nubble." Although there's no access to the lighthouse's island, Sohier Park Welcome Center (Nubble Rd., off Rte. 1A, between Long and Short Sands Beaches, York Beach, 207/363-7608, 10 A.M.–8 P.M. daily June–mid-Sept. and weekends in May and to early Oct.) provides the perfect viewpoint (and has restrooms). Parking is limited, but the turnover is fairly good. Not a bad idea, however, to walk from the Long Sands parking area or come by bike, even though the road has inadequate shoulders. Weekdays this is also a popular spot for scuba divers.

### Sayward-Wheeler House

Owned by the Boston-based Historic New England, the 1718 Sayward-Wheeler House (9 Barrell La. Ext., York Harbor, 207/384-2454, www.historicnewengland.org, $5) occupies a prime site at the edge of York Harbor. It's open with tours on the hour 11 A.M.–4 P.M. the first and third Saturday of the month, from June through mid-October. In the house are lots of period furnishings—all in pristine condition. Take Route 1A to Lilac Lane (Rte. 103) to Barrell Lane and then to Barrell Lane Extension.

### York's Wild Kingdom

More than 250 creatures—including tigers, zebras, llamas, deer, lions, elephants, and monkeys—find a home at York's Wild Kingdom (102 Railroad Ave., off Rte. 1, York Beach, 207/363-4911 or 800/456-4911, www.yorkzoo.com). It's not what you'd call a state-of-the-art zoo, but it keeps the kids entertained. Elephant shows and other animal "events" occur three times daily in July and August—usually at noon, 2 P.M., and 4 P.M., but the schedule is posted, or you can call ahead. Between the zoo and the amusement-park rides, it's easy to spend a day here—and

# SOUTHERN COAST LIGHTHOUSE TOUR

The lure of lighthouses is understandable. Legends tell of heroic keepers, prank-playing ghosts, and death-defying storms. Lighthouse lovers will find five in southern Maine, all viewable (binoculars will help) from land. Most of these were built in the 19th century on the wrecks of earlier lights that couldn't withstand winter storms.

Begin your journey by taking Route 103, off Route 1 in Kittery, and heading north. The best place to view **Whaleback Lighthouse,** which guards the Portsmouth Harbor and the mouth of the Piscataqua River, is from Fort Foster, on Gerrish Island, which is connected to the mainland via a bridge.

Continue on Route 103 until it merges with Route 1A, and then follow this north, bearing right, at the end of Long Sands Beach, on Nubble Road. The Cape Neddick Light, better known as **The Nubble,** stands just 200 yards or so off Cape Neddick Point and is easily seen from Sohier Park.

Sohier Park is also the best place to view the **Boon Island Light,** six miles offshore. The first three lighthouses constructed on this remote pile of rock were destroyed before the current light, dating from the mid-19th century, was constructed of hand-hewn granite blocks.

Continue on 1A until it joins Route 1, and then head north. Break from viewing real lighthouses for a visit to the king of lighthouse emporia, **Lighthouse Depot,** on Route 1 in Wells.

After touring, browsing, buying, and learning everything there is to know about lighthouses, continue north on Route 1 until Route 9 East splits from it, just north of Wells. Follow Route 9 through the Kennebunks and on to the village of Cape Porpoise. The town pier, at the end of Pier Road, is the best place to view the **Goat Island Lighthouse,** which has the distinction of being the last manned lighthouse in the state. It was finally automated in 1990. There's also a great view from the Vaughn's Island Preserve, in Kennebunkport, but you'll have coordinate your visit with the tide.

Return to Route 9, and continue east until it merges with Route 208. You'll turn right, following signs for Biddeford Pool. The **Wood Island Lighthouse,** on the east end of Wood Island, marks the entrance to the Saco River. It can be seen from several points in Biddeford Pool and Hills Beach, but the best view is from the East Point Audubon Sanctuary.

there are snack bars on the grounds. Admission (covering the zoo and some of the rides) is in the neighborhood of $18 adults, $15 children 4–10, $4 age 3 and younger. Zoo-only admission is $14 adults, $9 or $1 kids. The zoo's open 10 A.M.–5 P.M., to 6 P.M. weekends and July and August, from late May to late September; amusement park hours are noon–9:30 P.M. late June through early September.

## Spooky Sightseeing

Flickering candles and a black-hooded guide get you right in the spirit of things during imaginative evening candlelight walking tours of historic York village. **Ghostly Tours** (250 York St., Rte. 1A, York, 207/363-0000, www.ghostlytours.com) specializes in ghost stories and 18th-century folklore during its 45-minute meanders through burial grounds in the oldest part of town. (Even the phone number is kinda weird.) Cost is $10 pp. To continue the theme, **Gravestone Artwear** (same address, 207/351-1434 or 800/564-4310) carries wizard capes, gravestone rubbing kits (but don't try them out in the Old Burying Ground), notecards, T-shirts, and lots of other cemetery-centered items.

## RECREATION
### Walk the Walks

Next to Harbor Beach, near the Stage Neck Inn, a sign marks the beginning of the **Cliff Path,** a walkway worth taking for its dramatic harbor views in the shadow of elegant summer cottages. On the one-hour round-trip, you'll pass the York Harbor Reading Room (an ex-

© TOM NANGLE

The Wiggly Bridge leads to Steedman Woods preserve.

clusive club). The path is on private property, traditionally open to the public courtesy of the owners, but controversy surfaces periodically about property rights, vandalism, and the condition of some sections of the walk. Note: It's called the Cliff Path for a reason. It's not a good choice for little ones.

A less strenuous route is known variously as the **Shore Path, Harbor Walk,** or **Fisherman's Walk,** running west along the harbor and river from Stage Neck Road (next to Edwards' Harborside Inn) and passing the Sayward-Wheeler House before crossing the tiny, green-painted Wiggly Bridge leading into the **Steedman Woods** preserve. Carry binoculars for good boat watching and birding in the 16-acre preserve, owned by the Old York Historical Society. A one-mile double-loop trail takes less than an hour of easy strolling.

## Mt. Agamenticus

Drive to the summit of Mt. Agamenticus ("The Big A") and you're at York County's highest

point. It's only 692 feet, but on a clear day you'll have panoramic views of ocean, lakes, woods, and sometimes the White Mountains. The preserve, comprising 7,000 acres of conservation land and 4,500 acres of water district land, is considered among the most biologically diverse wildernesses in Maine, and its landscape includes vernal pools and ponds and it's home to rare and endangered species. At the top are a billboard map of the 40-mile trail network and a curious memorial to St. Aspinquid, a 17th-century Algonquian Indian leader. Also here are riding stables, offering trail rides Memorial Day to mid-September. Mountain biking is also hugely popular on Agamenticus. Take a picnic, a kite, and binoculars. In the fall, if the wind's from the northwest, watch for migrating hawks; in winter, bring a sled for the best downhill run in southern Maine. Contact the **York Parks and Recreation Department** (207/363-1040) for info about the trail rides and other activities at the mountain park. Fortunately, in recent years, conservationists have been particularly active here, saving thousands of acres from development. The efforts continue, with a goal of 14,000 acres. From Route 1 in Cape Neddick, take Mountain Road (also called Agamenticus Rd.) 4.2 miles west to the access road.

## Golf

The **Ledges Golf Club** (1 Ledges Dr., off Rte. 91, York, 207/351-9999, www.ledgesgolf.com) is an 18-hole course with daily public tee times.

## Swimming

Sunbathing and swimming are big draws in York, with four beaches of varying sizes and accessibility. Bear in mind that traffic can be gridlocked along the beachfront (Rte. 1A) in midsummer, so it may take longer than you expect to get anywhere. **Lifeguards** are on duty 9:30 A.M.–4 P.M. mid-June–Labor Day at Short Sands Beach, Long Beach, and Harbor Beach. Bathhouses at Long Sands and Short Sands are open 9 A.M.–7 P.M. daily in midsummer. The biggest parking space (metered) is at Long Sands, but that 1.5-mile beach also draws the most customers. Scarcest parking is at Harbor Beach, near the Stage Neck Inn, and at Cape Neddick (Passaconaway) Beach, near the Ogunquit town line.

## Sea Kayaking

Kayak rentals are available for $30 a day, single, $45 double, from **Excursions: Coastal Maine Outfitting Company** (1399 Rte. 1, Cape Neddick, 207/363-0181, www.excursionsinmaine.com), owned by Mike Sullivan and Scott Leighton. Or sign up for one of their half-day tours: $55 (afternoon) or $60 (morning, with lunch). Kids 10–15 are $5 less. A four-hour basics clinic for ages 16 and older is $75; another for those comfortable with basics is also $75. Sea-kayak rental is $30/day or $45 for 24-hour period per double, $45/$60 for a single. Excursions is on Route 1 four miles north of the I-95 York exit.

**Harbor Adventures** (Harris Island Rd., York Harbor, 207/363-8466, www.harboradventures.com) offers instruction and guided sea-kayaking trips from Kittery through Kennebunkport. Prices begin around $40 for a two-hour harbor tour.

## Scuba and Surfing

**York Beach Scuba** (19 Railroad Ave., P.O. Box 850, York Beach 03910, 207/363-3330), a source for rentals, air, and trips, is conveniently situated not far from Sohier Park, a popular dive site. It also offers diving packages, including lodging and meals. For surfing information, lessons, or rentals, call **Liquid Dreams Surf Shop** (171 Long Beach Ave., York, 207/351-2545). It's open 10 A.M.–5 P.M. weekends, and it's right across from the beach.

## Fishing

Local expert on fly-fishing, spin fishing, and conventional tackle is **Eldgrege Bros. Guide Service** (1480 Rte. 1, Cape Neddick, 207/373-9269, www.eldredgeflyshop.com). Four-hour guided trips for one or two anglers begin at $250 freshwater, $300 salt water. Kayak and rod and reel rentals are available.

# ENTERTAINMENT
## Live Music

**Inn on the Blues** (7 Ocean Ave., York Beach, 207/351-3221, www.innontheblues.com) has live music (acoustic, blues, reggae) every night but Monday during the summer. If you want to be close to both the music and the beach, consider booking one of the suites upstairs ($155–390).

The **Ship's Cellar Pub** in the York Harbor Inn frequently has live entertainment, too.

Free concerts are often held at the **Ellis Park Gazebo,** usually 7–9 P.M. from early July to early September.

## FESTIVALS AND EVENTS

Each year, the Old York Historical Society invites decorators to transform a local house for the **Decorator Show House,** culminating in an open house from mid-July to mid-August.

From late July into early August, the **York Days** festivities enliven the town for 10 days with concerts, dances, walking tours, a road race, sandcastle contests, antiques and art shows, a dog show, fireworks, a parade, and public suppers.

York Village's **Annual Harvestfest** takes place 10 A.M.–4 P.M. the weekend after Columbus Day in October and combines colonial crafts and cooking demonstrations, hayrides, museum tours, entertainment for adults and kids, and an ox roast with beanhole beans. This is one of the town's most popular events; most activities are free.

The annual **Lighting of the Nubble,** in late November, includes cookies, hot chocolate, music, and an appearance by Santa Claus. The best part, though, is seeing the lighthouse glowing for the holidays.

## SHOPPING

Park in York Village and wander around the handful of small shops. **York Village Marketplace** (211 York St., Rte. 1A, York Village, 207/363-4830) is a three-level emporium based in a restored 1834 church. Lots of tasteful stuff, with an emphasis on antiques—bet you won't leave empty-handed. A model train shop occupies the entire third floor—go just to see the elaborate model set up in the shop.

Expect to wash your hands before examining any of the 400-plus, museum-quality antique quilts at Betsy Telford's **Rocky Mountain Quilts** (130 York St., York Village, 207/363-6800 or 800/762-5940, www.rockymountainquilts.com). This isn't a place for browsers.

Fans of fine craft shouldn't miss **Panache** (1949 Rte. 1, Cape Neddick, 207/646-4878). It boasts of having New England's largest selection of fine contemporary art glass, but there's so much more here. It's a visual treat. Find it just south of the Ogunquit Playhouse, on the York-Ogunquit town line.

## ACCOMMODATIONS
### York Harbor

**Bed-and-Breakfasts:** Hosts Donna and Paul Archibald have turned Fannie Chapman's 1889 summer cottage into the elegant and romantic ◖ **Chapman Cottage** (370 York St., P.O. Box 575, York Harbor 03911, 207/363-2059 or 877/363-2059, www.chapmancottagebandb.com, $155–250), a truly special retreat. Rooms are huge and plush, with air-conditioning, Wi-Fi, TV, and spacious baths; most have whirlpool baths and fireplaces (some in the bathrooms), and a few have private decks and river views. The pampering includes a welcome fruit basket, fresh flowers, bathrobes, and fine linens. The inn also has a lovely dining room and an inviting lounge with tapas menu and martini/wine bar.

Inviting Adirondack-style chairs accent the green lawn rolling down to the harbor at **Edwards' Harborside Inn** (7 Stage Neck Rd., P.O. Box 866, York Harbor 03911, 207/363-3037 or 800/273-2686, www.edwardsharborside.com, $150–220 rooms, $150–320 suites). Many of the 10 rooms can be combined into suites, and most have water views. All have TV, phone, and air-conditioning. One suite has a party-size whirlpool tub facing the harbor, another a grand piano. Watch the sunset from the inn's 210-foot pier, stroll the adjacent shorefront paths, wander over to the beach, or just settle into one of those shore-

front chairs and watch the world go by. A full lovely buffet breakfast is served in the water-view sunporch.

Bill and Bonney Alstrom, former innkeepers at Tanglewood Hall, weren't looking to downsize, but on a lark, they stumbled upon this woodland cottage, and they were smitten. After more than a year of renovations, they opened **Morning Glory Inn** (120 Seabury Rd., York, 207/363-2062, www.morninggloryinnmaine.com, $155–225 peak). A boutique B&B, catering to romantics, the Morning Glory has just three rooms, all very spacious and private, and all with doors to private patios or yards, air-conditioning, TV with DVD, fridge, Wi-Fi, and plentiful other little amenities. The living room, in the original section of the house, was a 17th-century cottage, barged over from the Isle of Shoals; the newer post-and-beam great room doubles as a dining area, where a hot breakfast buffet is served. The property is ultraquiet—listen to the birds singing in the gardens; it's truly a magical setting, far removed yet convenient to everything York offers.

**Full-Service Inns: York Harbor Inn** (Rte. 1A, P.O. Box 573, York Harbor 03911, 207/363-5119 or 800/343-3869, www.yorkharborinn.com, $99–349 d) is an accommodating in-town spot with a country-inn flavor and a wide variety of room and package-plan options throughout the year. The oldest section of the inn is a 17th-century cabin from the Isles of Shoals. Accommodations are spread out in the inn, adjacent Yorkshire building, and two elegantly restored houses, both with resident innkeepers: neighboring Harbor Hill, and 1730 Harbor Crest, about a half mile away. All have TV, phones, free Wi-Fi, and air-conditioning; some have four-poster beds, fireplaces, and whirlpools; many have water views. Rates include a generous continental breakfast.

You can't miss the **Stage Neck Inn** (100 Stage Neck Rd., P.O. Box 70, York Harbor 03911, 207/363-3850 or 800/340-9901, www.stageneck.com), occupying its own private peninsula overlooking York Harbor. Modern, resort-style facilities include two pools (one indoors), tennis courts, golf privileges, fitness center, and spectacular views from balconies and terraces. The formal Harbor Porches restaurant (no jeans; entrées $21–30) and the casual Sandpiper Bar and Grille are open to the public. Peak-season rates are $235–345 d mid-May–Labor Day (special packages and MAP are available). Open all year.

## York Beach

**Hotel and Motel:** For more than 150 years, **The Union Bluff** (8 Beach St., P.O. Box 1860, York Beach 03910, 207/363-1333 or 800/833-0721, www.unionbluff.com, $159–329 peak) has stood sentry, like a fortress, overlooking Short Sands Beach. Many of the rooms have ocean views. All have TV, air-conditioning, and phone; some have fireplace, whirlpool bath, or ocean-view deck. Furnishings are modern motel-style. Also on the premises are the Beach Street Grill dining room and a pub serving lighter fare. Best deals are the packages, which include breakfast and dinner. The hotel and pub are open year-round; the restaurant is seasonal.

**Bed-and-Breakfasts:** Everything's casual and flowers are everywhere at the brightly painted **Katahdin Inn** (11 Ocean Ave. Ext., P.O. Box 193, York Beach 03910, 207/363-1824, www.thekatahdininn.com, $65–125 d), overlooking the breakers of Short Sands Beach. Longtime owners Rae and Paul LeBlanc appropriately refer to it as a "bed and beach." It was built in 1863 and has always been a guesthouse. Nine smallish first-, second-, and third-floor rooms (eight with water views) have lots of four-poster beds and mostly shared baths. Breakfast is not included, but coffee is always available, the rooms have refrigerators, and several eateries are nearby. It's open mid-May–October.

Not oceanfront, but offering ocean views from many rooms and just a short walk from Short Sands Beach, is Barbara and Michael Sheff's **Candleshop Inn** (44 Freeman St., P.O. Box 1216, York Beach 03910, 207/363-4087 or 888/363-4087, www.candleshopinn.com, $110–170 peak). The 10 guest rooms (private and shared baths) are decorated in a country cottage style, with area rugs, painted furniture, and florals; many are set up for families. The day begins with a vegetarian breakfast and a stretch-and-relaxation class. Spa services, including massage and Reiki, are available on-site by appointment.

**Condominium Suites:** Fabulously sited on the oceanfront and overlooking the Nubble Light, the high-end **ViewPoint** (229 Nubble Rd., York Beach, 207/363-2661, www.viewpointhotel.com, $295 one bedroom–$575 three bedroom per night, $2,100–3,695 per week) comprises luxuriously appointed one-, two-, and three-bedroom suites. All have gas fireplace, fully equipped kitchen, washer/dryer, TV/VCR, phone, private patio, porch, or deck, Wi-Fi, and daily maid service. On the premises are an outdoor heated pool, grilling area, gardens, and playground.

## Cape Neddick

A convenient location is the biggest selling point for the **Country View Motel and Guesthouse** (1521 Rte. 1, Cape Neddick, 207/363-7260 or 800/258-6598, www.countryviewmotel.com, $89–220 peak), a well-cared-for property with a variety of accommodations. Motel rooms vary from standard to ones with full kitchens; those in the 18th-century guesthouse have more of a B&B flair; all have air-conditioning, phone, and TV. On the premises are a pool and a picnic area with gas grills. Rates include continental breakfast. Pets are permitted in the motel.

## Seasonal Rentals

Several companies manage week- or month-long rental properties, usually houses or condos. Weekly rentals begin and end on Saturday. Best is **Seaside Vacation Rentals** (Meadowbrook Plaza, 647 Rte. 1, P.O. Box 2000, York 03909, 207/363-1825, www.seasiderentals.com), a longtime family-operated firm with more than 500 properties in York, Ogunquit, Wells, Kennebunk, and Kittery.

# CAMPING

**Dixon's Coastal Maine Campground** (1740 Rte. 1, Cape Neddick, 207/363-3626, www

© TOM NANGLE

Cape Neddick Light Station is locally known as "The Nubble."

.dixonscampground.com, $30–36) has more than 100 well-spaced sites on 40 wooded and open acres. It can accommodate tents and small RVs. Electric and water hookups are available. Facilities include a playground and a good-size outdoor heated pool. It's also the base for Excursions Sea Kayaking.

## FOOD
### Seacoast Fine Dining Club

More than two dozen restaurants on Maine's Southern Coast participate in the Seacoast Fine Dining Club (P.O. Box 228, Newmarket, NH 03857, 603/292-5093, www.seacoastfinedining.com). Membership costs $29.95 and entitles you to buy one entrée and get a second one of equal or lesser value free. It also provides discounts on some area attractions.

### Local Flavors

Both *Gourmet* and *Saveur* know where to get dogs. Sometimes the line runs right out the door of the low-ceilinged, reddish-brown roadside shack that houses local institution **Flo's**

**Steamed Dogs** (Rte. 1, opposite the Mountain Rd. turnoff, Cape Neddick). Founder Flo Stacy died at age 92 in June 2000, but her legend and her family live on. No menu here—just steamed Schultz wieners, buns, chips, beverages, and an attitude. The secret? The spicy, sweet-sour hot-dog sauce (allegedly once sought by the H. J. Heinz corporation, but the proprietary Stacy family isn't telling or selling). The cognoscenti know to order their dogs only with mayonnaise and the special sauce—nothing heretical such as catsup or mustard. It's open all year, 11 A.M.–3 P.M., and not a minute later, Thursday–Tuesday. Flo's has added stands in Kittery, Sanford, and Wells.

See those people with their faces pressed to the glass? They're all watching the taffy makers inside **The Goldenrod** (2 Railroad Ave., York Beach, 207/363-2621), where machines spew out 180 Goldenrod Kisses a minute, 65 tons a year—and have been at it since 1896. (The shop also accepts mail orders.) The Goldenrod is an old-fashioned place, with a tearoom, gift shop, old-fashioned soda fountain (135 ice-cream flavors), and casual dining room, with equally old-fashioned prices. It's open for breakfast (8 A.M.), lunch, and dinner daily late May–Columbus Day.

Tucked behind the York County Federal Credit Union is a delicious find, **Food and Co.** (1 York St./Rte. 1, York, 207/363-0900, www.foodnco.com, 7 A.M.–7 P.M. Mon.–Sat.). The combination gourmet food store and café does everything right: breakfast, lunch, and dinners to go (order by 3 P.M. and pick up after 5 P.M.). Prices are reasonable—most breakfast and lunch items are around $7—and the flavors creative and divine.

The *best* pies and other goodies come from **Pie in the Sky Bakery** (corner of Rte. 1 and River Rd., Cape Neddick, 207/363-2656, www.pieintheskymaine.com, 9 A.M.–6 P.M. Fri.–Mon.). You can pick up a slice for $4.50 or the whole pie for $25. Possibilities are numerous: apple crumb, blueberry, bumbleberry, jumbleberry, peach raspberry, and so on; all are handcrafted and made without preservatives or trans fats.

After viewing The Nubble, head across the road to **Brown's Ice Cream** (232 Nubble Rd., York Beach, 207/363-1277), where unusual flavors complement the standards.

Stop in at the **Gateway Farmers Market** (York Chamber of Commerce Visitor Center, Rte. 1, York, 9 A.M.–noon Sat., mid-June–mid-Oct.) and stock up for a picnic. If you still need more, head next door to Stonewall Kitchen.

## Good Eats

The York Harbor Inn's **Ship's Cellar Pub** (11:30 A.M.–12:30 A.M. Mon.–Sat. and 4 P.M.–midnight Sun.) attracts even the locals. On the menu are soups, sandwiches, and salads as well as heftier entrées ($16–31), such as chicken scalopinne and pan lobster supreme. The food's good; the service is so-so. The pub doubles as a favorite local watering hole, with live music Wednesday–Sunday. Happy hour, with free munchies, is 4–6 P.M. and sometimes draws a raucous crowd.

Wood-fired pizza and finger-licking ribs are the best sellers at **Ruby's Genuine Wood Grill** (433 Rte. 1, a mile south of the I-95 exit, York, 207/363-7980, www.rubysgrill.com, 11:30 A.M.–10 P.M., to 11 P.M. Fri. and Sat.), but there's plenty more on the menu. Some of the pizzas are downright intriguing—pulled pork and barbecue sauce, for instance. Entrées vary from St. Louis ribs to fajitas to mahimahi, most priced in the low teens. Pastas, sandwiches, salads, and burgers fill out the menu. Lots of variety and flair here. In nice weather, opt for the enclosed deck, where there's often live music Saturday night.

**Wild Willy's** (765 Rte. 1, York, 207/3363-9924, www.wildwillysburgers.com, 11 A.M.–8 P.M. Mon.–Sat.) has turned burgers into an art form. More than a dozen hefty, mouthwatering burgers, all made from certified Angus beef, are available, from the classic Willy burger to the Rio Grande, with roasted green chiles from New Mexico and cheddar cheese. Don't miss the hand-cut fries. Chicken sandwiches, steak chili, and frappes are also served, as are beer and wine. Order at the counter before grabbing a seat in the dining area or out on the back deck; the servers will find you when it's ready. Cash only; burgers run about $6.

Locals swear by **Rick's All Seasons Cafe** (240 York St., York, 207/363-5584), where the food is good, and the gossip is even better. Go for breakfast or lunch—the fried clams earn raves. Have patience: Almost everything is cooked to order. It's worth the wait.

## Casual to Fine Dining

It's hard to know whether Food or Shopping is the right category for **Stonewall Kitchen** (Stonewall La., York, 207/351-2712 or 800/207-5267, www.stonewallkitchen.com), a phenomenally successful company that concocts imaginative condiments and other food products, many of which have received national awards. The headquarters building—including a handsome shop with tasting areas and a "viewing gallery" where you can watch it all happen—is next to the Yorks Chamber of Commerce building, on Route 1. Go hungry: There are an espresso bar and an excellent café on the premises, open daily for breakfast and lunch and light fare in the late afternoon. Dinner may be served during peak season; call.

Don't let the forlorn and faded exterior deter you. Serving "food that loves you back," **Frankie and Johnny's Natural Foods** (1594 Rte. 1 N, Cape Neddick, 207/363-1909, www.frankie-johnnys.com, opens 5 P.M. Wed.–Sun., $17–26) is vibrant inside. Chef/owner John Shaw's eclectic menu varies from bean-curd satay, vegan delight, and Cajun crab cakes to toasted peppercorn-seared sushi-grade tuna, blackened pork Delmonico, and smoked mozzarella ravioli. It's the best vegetarian menu in York, and the house-made pastas are excellent. Reservations are recommended for summer weekends. Be forewarned: Portions are more than generous. No credit cards ("plastic is not natural"). BYOB.

For a memorable meal, book a table at █ **Chapman Cottage** (370 York St., P.O. Box 575, York Harbor 03911, 207/363-2059 or 877/363-2059, www.chapmancottage-bandb.com). Dinner is served in two connected rooms, each with fireplace, and both are decorated in a style fitting the 1899 home. Nicely spaced tables, soft lighting, classical music, and comfortable chairs make it easy to settle in for a night of leisurely fine dining. Service is professional without being stuffy, and the menu is small but intriguing, with selections such as stuffed pork tenderloin, hazelnut ravioli, and duck ($18–27).

The glass-walled dining room at the **York Harbor Inn** (5:30–9:30 P.M. daily and 9:30 A.M.–2:30 P.M. Sun. brunch) gets high marks for creative cuisine (the head chef has been here since 1982), so reservations are essential. Entrées run $25–35. Ask about an early-bird special.

Renowned Boston chef Lydia Shire's new restaurant **Blue Sky on York Beach** (Rte. 1A, York Beach, 207/363-0050) is adding a new tone to downtown York Beach. Opened in late 2007, the second-floor restaurant in The Atlantic House is elegant yet welcoming, with gleaming wood floors, a see-through fireplace, white chairs, and big windows taking in the views. In summer, dinner also will be served on the ocean-view porch. The dining room opens nightly at 5:30 P.M. The menu ranges from pizza to lobster, with most entrées around $20; a lounge menu is less pricey. For more casual eats, try Shire's first-floor cafe, **Clara's Cupcake Café,** named after her granddaughter and serving sandwiches, soups, and baked goods.

## Lobster

Before heading for the **Cape Neddick Lobster Pound/Harborside Restaurant** (Shore Rd., Cape Neddick, 207/363-5471), check the tide calendar. The rustic shingled building dripping with lobster-pot buoys has a spectacular harbor view (especially from the deck) at high tide, a rather drab one at low tide, so plan accordingly. Entrées are $15–24. Open at noon daily. It offers entertainment beginning at 10 P.M. Friday and Saturday in summer.

## INFORMATION AND SERVICES

The Maine Tourism Association operates a Maine State Visitor Information Center (207/439-1319) in Kittery, between Route 1 and I-95, with access from either road. It's chock-full of brochures and has restrooms and a picnic area.

For York area information, head for the Shingle-style palace of the Yorks Chamber of Commerce (1 Stonewall La., off Rte. 1, York, 207/363-4422, www.gatewaytomaine.org), at I-95's York exit. Inside are restrooms. It's open daily in summer.

## GETTING AROUND

The Maine Turnpike, a toll road, is generally the fastest route, if you're trying to get between two towns. Route 1 parallels the turnpike, on the ocean side. It's mostly two lanes and is lined with shops, restaurants, motels, and other tourist-oriented sites, which means stop-and-go traffic that often slows to a crawl. If you're traveling locally, it's best to walk or use the local trolley systems, which have the bonus of saving you the agony of finding a parking spot.

The **York Trolley** (207/748-3030, www.yorktrolley.com) provides a number of options for getting around the Yorks. A York tour departs hourly 10 A.M.–2 P.M. Monday and Friday with stops at Short Sands, York Village, York Harbor, York Beach, and Nubble Lighthouse. A day pass is $8 adult, $4 kids 3–10.

The company also operates a **York Beach Shuttle** from late June to early September. The service between Long and Short Sands beaches runs every 30 minutes 9:30 A.M.–10:30 P.M. ($1.50 one-way, $3 complete loop).

The **Shoreline Shuttle** operates hourly between York's Short Sands Beach and Ogunquit's Perkins Cove from late June through Labor Day. Fare is $1 each way; a 12-ride pass is $10; 18 and younger ride free.

# Ogunquit and Wells

Ogunquit has been a holiday destination since the indigenous residents named it "beautiful place by the sea." What's the appeal? An unparalleled, unspoiled beach, several top-flight (albeit pricey) restaurants, a dozen art galleries, and a respected art museum with a view second to none. The town has been home to an art colony attracting the glitterati of the painting world starting with Charles Woodbury in the late 1880s. The summertime crowds continue, multiplying the minuscule year-round population of just under 1,400. These days, it's an especially gay-friendly community, too. Besides the beach, the most powerful magnet is Perkins Cove, a working fishing enclave that looks more like a movie set. The best way to approach the cove is via trolley-bus or on foot, along the shoreline Marginal Way from downtown Ogunquit—midsummer parking in the cove ($3 per hour) is madness.

Wells, once the parent of Ogunquit and since 1980 its immediate neighbor to the north, was settled in 1640. Nowadays, it's best known as a long, skinny, family-oriented community with about 10,300 year-round residents, seven miles of splendid beachfront, and heavy-duty commercial activity: lots of antiques and used-book shops, and a handful of factory outlets. It also claims two spectacular nature preserves worth a drive from anywhere. At the southern end of Wells, abutting Ogunquit, is **Moody,** an enclave named after 18th-century settler Samuel Moody and even rating its own post office.

If swimming isn't your top priority, plan to visit Ogunquit and Wells after Labor Day, when crowds let up, lodging rates drop dramatically, weather is still good, and you can find restaurant seats and parking spots.

## SIGHTS
### ◖ Ogunquit Museum of American Art (OMAA)

Not many museums can boast a view as stunning as the one at the Ogunquit Museum of American Art (543 Shore Rd., P.O. Box 815, Ogunquit 03907, 207/646-4909, www.ogunquitmuseum.org), nor can many communities boast such renown as a summer art colony. Overlooking Narrow Cove, 1.4 miles south of downtown Ogunquit, the museum prides itself on its distinguished permanent collection. Works of Marsden Hartley, Rockwell Kent, Walt Kuhn, Henry Strater, and Thomas Hart Benton, among others, are displayed in five galleries. Special exhibits are mounted each summer, when there is an extensive series of lectures, concerts, and other programs. OMAA has a well-stocked gift shop, wheelchair access, and landscaped grounds with sculptures, a pond, and manicured lawns. Admission is $7 adults, $5 seniors, $4 students, and free for kids under 12. It's open 10:30 A.M.–5 P.M. Mon.–Sat., 2–5 P.M. Sunday July 1 to late October; closed Labor Day and for four days in mid-August for rehanging.

### ◖ Marginal Way

No visit to Ogunquit is complete without a leisurely stroll along the Marginal Way, the mile-long foot path edging the ocean from Shore Road (by the Sparhawk Resort) to Perkins Cove. It's been a must-walk since Josiah

© TOM NANGLE

The Marginal Way was a gift to the town of Ogunquit in the 1920s.

Chase gave the right-of-way to the town in the 1920s. The best times to appreciate this shrub-lined, shorefront walkway in Ogunquit are early morning or when everyone's at the beach. En route are tide pools, intriguing rock formations, crashing surf, pocket beaches, benches (though the walking's a cinch, even partially wheelchair-accessible), and a marker listing the day's high and low tides. When the surf's up, keep a close eye on the kids—the sea has no mercy. A midpoint access is at Israel's Head (behind a sewage plant masquerading as a tiny lighthouse), but getting a parking space is pure luck. Best advice is to stroll the Marginal Way to Perkins Cove for lunch, shopping, and maybe a boat trip, and then return to downtown Ogunquit via trolley-bus.

## Perkins Cove

Turn-of-the-20th-century photos show Ogunquit's Perkins Cove lined with gray-shingled shacks used by a hardy colony of local fishermen—fellows who headed offshore to make a tough living in little boats. They'd hardly recognize it today. Though the cove remains a working lobster-fishing harbor, several old shacks have been reincarnated as boutiques and restaurants, and photographers go crazy shooting the quaint inlet spanned by a little pedestrian drawbridge. In midsummer, you'll waste precious time looking for one of the three or four dozen parking places ($3 an hour), so take advantage of the trolley-bus service. In the cove are galleries, gift shops, a range of eateries (fast food to lobster to high-end dining—see *Ogunquit* under *Food*), boat excursions, and public restrooms.

## ◖ Wells Reserve at Laudholm Farm

Known locally as Laudholm Farm (the name of the restored 19th-century visitors center), Wells National Estuarine Research Reserve (342 Laudholm Farm Rd., Wells, 207/646-1555, www.wellsreserve.org) occupies 1,690 acres of woods, beach, and coastal salt marsh on the southern boundary of the Rachel Carson National Wildlife Refuge, just one-half

© TOM NANGLE

Laudholm Farm is the site of the Wells National Estuarine Research Reserve.

mile east of Route 1. Seven miles of trails wind through the property. The best trail is the Salt Marsh Loop, with a boardwalk section leading to an overlook with panoramic views of the marsh and Little River inlet. Another winner is the Barrier Beach Walk, 1.3-mile round-trip that goes through multiple habitats all the way to beautiful Laudholm Beach. Allow 1.5 hours for either; you can combine the two. Lyme disease ticks have been found here, so tuck pant legs into socks and stick to the trails (some of which are wheelchair-accessible). The informative exhibits in the visitors center (open 10 A.M. to 4 P.M. Mon.–Sat. and noon–4 P.M. Sun. May–Oct., weekdays Oct.–Mar., closed mid-Dec.–mid-Jan.) make a valuable prelude for enjoying the reserve. An extensive program schedule, April–November, includes lectures, nature walks, and children's programs. Reservations are required for some programs. Trails are accessible 7 A.M.–dusk. From late May to mid-October, admission is charged, $2 adult, $1 ages 6–16.

## Rachel Carson National Wildlife Refuge

Ten chunks of coastal Maine real estate—now more than 4,700 acres, eventually 7,600 acres, between Kittery Point and Cape Elizabeth—make up this refuge (Rte. 9, 321 Port Rd., Wells, 207/646-9226, http://rachelcarson.fws.gov) headquartered at the northern edge of Wells, near the Kennebunkport town line. Pick up a *Carson Trail Guide* at the refuge office (parking space is very limited) and follow the mile-long walkway (wheelchair-accessible) past tidal creeks, salt pans, and salt marshes. It's a birder's paradise during migration seasons. As with the Laudholm Farm reserve, the Lyme disease tick has been found here, so tuck pant legs into socks and stick to the trail. Office hours are 8 A.M.–4:30 P.M. weekdays year-round; trail access is sunrise to sunset, year-round. Leashed pets are allowed.

## Ogunquit Arts Collaborative Gallery

Closer to downtown Ogunquit is the Ogunquit Arts Collaborative Gallery (also known as the Barn Gallery, Shore Rd. and Bourne La., P.O. Box 529, Ogunquit 03907, 207/646-8400), featuring the works of member artists—an impressive group. The OAC is the showcase for the Ogunquit Art Association, established by Charles Woodbury, who was inspired to open an art school in Perkins Cove in the late 19th century. Special programs throughout the season include concerts, workshops, gallery talks, and an art auction. The gallery is open 11 A.M.–5 P.M. Monday–Saturday and 1–5 P.M. Sunday late May–Oct. 1. Admission is free.

### Wells Auto Museum

More than 80 vintage vehicles, plus a collection of old-fashioned nickelodeons (bring nickels and dimes, they work), are jam-packed into the Wells Auto Museum (Rte. 1, Wells, 207/646-9064). From the outside, it just looks like a big warehouse, right on the highway. Admission is $5 adults, $2 children 6–12. It's open 10 A.M.–5 P.M. daily Memorial Day–Columbus Day.

### Local History Museums

Ogunquit's history is preserved in the **Ogunquit Heritage Museum** (86 Obeds La., Dorothea Jacobs Grant Common, Ogunquit, 207/646-0296, www.ogunquitheritagemuseum.org, 12:30–4:30 P.M. Tues.–Sat. June–Sept.). The museum opened in 2002 in the restored Captain James Winn House, a 1785 cape listed on the National Register. Plans call for the construction of a fishing shack and boat shop to display appropriate exhibits, including an Ogunquit dory.

Right on the historic Post Road that once linked Boston with points north stands the **Historic Meetinghouse Museum** (938 Post Rd., Rte. 1, opposite Wells Plaza, P.O. Box 801, Wells 04090, 207/646-4775, 10 A.M.–4 P.M. Tues.–Thurs., to 1 P.M. Sat. June–mid. Oct, Wed. and Thurs. only in winter), a handsome steepled structure on the site of the town's first church (1643). Preserved and maintained by the Historical Society of Wells and Ogunquit, its displays include old photos, ship models, needlecraft, and local memorabilia. On the

second floor is a genealogical library where volunteers will help you research your roots. Enter in the rear.

## RECREATION
### Beaches

One of Maine's most scenic and unspoiled sandy beachfronts, the 3.5-mile stretch of sand fringed with seagrass is a major magnet for hordes of sunbathers, spectators, swimmers, surfers, and sandcastle builders. Getting there means crossing the Ogunquit River via one of three access points. For Ogunquit's **Main Beach**—with a spanking new bathhouse and high crowd content—take Beach Street. To reach **Footbridge Beach,** marginally less crowded, either take Ocean Street and the footbridge or take Bourne Avenue to Ocean Avenue in adjacent Wells and walk back toward Ogunquit. **Moody Beach,** at Wells's southern end, technically is private property—a subject of considerable legal dispute. Lifeguards are on duty all summer at the public beaches, and there are restrooms in all three areas. The beach is free, but parking is not; parking lots charge by the hour ($4 an hour at the Main Beach) or the day ($15 per day at Main Beach, Footbridge Beach, and Moody Beach), and they fill up early on warm midsummer days. After 3 P.M., some are free. It's far more sensible to opt for the frequent trolley-buses.

Wells beaches continue where Ogunquit's leave off. **Crescent Beach,** Webhannet Drive between Eldredge and Mile Roads, is the tiniest, with tide pools, no facilities, and limited parking. **Wells Beach,** Mile Road to Atlantic Avenue, is the major (and most crowded) beach, with lifeguards, restrooms, and parking. Around the other side of Wells Harbor is **Drakes Island Beach** (take Drakes Island Road, at the blinking light), a less crowded spot with restrooms and lifeguards. Walk northeast from Drakes Island Beach and you'll eventually reach Laudholm Beach, with great birding along the way. Summer beach-parking permits are available from the town hall in Wells: it's $15 a day for nonresidents ($5 for a motorcycle, $25 for an RV); if you're staying longer, a $50 10-visit pass is a better bargain.

## Bike, Kayak, and Surfboard Rentals

At **Wheels and Waves** (579 Post Rd., Rte. 1, Wells, 207/646-5774, www.wheelsnwaves.com), mountain-bike rentals begin at $20 a day; tandems are $40. Surfboards are $25.

Put in right at the harbor and explore the estuary from **Webhannet River Kayak and Canoe Rentals** (345 Harbor Rd., Wells, 207/646-9649, www.webhannetriver.com). Rates begin at $25 for two hours.

## Boating Excursions

Depending on your interest, you can go deep-sea fishing or whale-watching or just gawking out of Perkins Cove, Ogunquit. Between April and early November, Captain Tim Tower runs half-day (departing 4 P.M.; $45 pp) and full-day (departing 7 A.M.; $70 pp) **deep-sea-fishing trips** aboard the 40-foot *Bunny Clark* (P.O. Box 837, Ogunquit 03907, 207/646-2214, www.bunnyclark.com). Reservations are necessary. Tim has a science degree, so he's a wealth of marine biology information. All gear is provided, and the crew'll fillet your catch for you; dress warmly and wear sunblock.

Perkins Cove (Barnacle Billy's Dock) is also home port for the Hubbard family's **Finestkind Cruises** (207/646-5227, www.finestkindcruises.com), offering 1.5-hour, 14-mile Nubble Lighthouse cruises (10 A.M., noon, 2 and 4 P.M. daily; $18 adults, $10 kids) and one-hour cocktail cruises (5:45 P.M. daily; two extra trips in July and Aug.; $12 adults, $7 kids; cash bar) in a sheltered powerboat. A 75-minute breakfast cruise, complete with coffee, juice, and muffin, departs at 9 A.M. daily ($15 adults, $10 kids). The family also does 50-minute lobster-boat trips, 4–6 cruises Monday–Saturday; look and listen—no helping; $12 adults, $7 kids) in a real lobster boat (no toilets). Also available are 1.75-hour sails aboard *The Cricket,* a locally built wooden sailboat. It departs three times daily and costs $27.50 pp. High season runs July 1 through Labor Day; limited schedule May, June, September, October. Reservations are advisable but usually unnecessary midweek. No credit cards.

## Golf

The 18-hole, Donald Ross–designed **Cape Neddick Country Club** (650 Shore Rd., 207/361-2011, www.capeneddickgolf.com) is a semiprivate 18-hole course with restaurant and driving range.

## Sea Kayaking

**World Within Sea Kayaking** (746 Ocean Ave., Wells, 207/646-0455, www.worldwithin.com) has both tours and rentals. Rentals are available on the tidal Ogunquit River to experienced kayakers for $15/hour single, $25/hour double. Guided tours begin with one hour of land instruction followed by two hours on the water for $70 pp. World Within also has an outlet at Wheels and Waves.

# ENTERTAINMENT
## Theater

Having showcased top-notch professional theater since the 1930s, the 750-seat **Ogunquit Playhouse** (Rte. 1, P.O. Box 915, Ogunquit 03907, 207/646-5511, www.ogunquitplayhouse.org) knows how to do it right: presenting comedies and musicals each summer, with big-name stars. The air-conditioned building is wheelchair-accessible. The box office is open daily in season, beginning in early May. Performances are at 8 P.M. Tuesday–Friday, 8:30 P.M. Saturday, matinees at 2:30 P.M. Wednesday and Thursday and 3:30 P.M. Sunday mid-June–Labor Day. Prices range $39–48. The playhouse also presents a children's series and a handful of Sunday night concerts. Parking can be a hassle; consider walking the short distance from the Bourne Lane trolley-bus stop.

## Live Music

Ogunquit has several nightspots with good reputations for food and live entertainment. Best known is **Jonathan's** (2 Bourne La., P.O. Box 1879, Ogunquit 03907, 207/646-4777 or 800/464-9934 in Maine), where national headliners often are on the schedule upstairs. Advance tickets are cheaper than at the door, and dinner guests get preference for seats. Reservations are essential at this popular spot. The well-respected downstairs restaurant has creative entrées for $18–30 and ethnic flavors at the oyster bar. Highlighting the dining room are contemporary artwork and a 600-gallon aquarium. It's open 5–9:30 P.M., to 10 P.M. Friday and Saturday.

**Ogunquit Performing Arts** (207/646-6170) presents a full slate of programs, including classical concerts, ballet, and theater.

The **Wells Summer Concert Series** runs from early July through early September at the Hope Hobbs Gazebo in Wells Harbor Park. A wide variety of music is represented, from sing-alongs to swing.

## FESTIVALS AND EVENTS

The **Fourth of July** celebration on Ogunquit Beach includes fireworks and live music. **Harbor Fest,** a concert, craft fair, parade, chicken barbecue, and children's activities, takes place the second weekend of July in Harbor Park in Wells.

In mid-August, Ogunquit Beach hosts a **Sandcastle-Building Contest** and in late August is the annual **Sidewalk Art Show and Sale.**

**Capriccio** is a performing arts festival, with daytime and evening events as well as a kite festival, held during the first week of September. Then, the second weekend that month, Wells National Estuarine Research Reserve (Laudholm Farm) hosts the **Laudholm Nature Crafts Festival,** a two-day juried crafts fair with children's activities and guided nature walks. This is an especially fine event. And the *third* weekend of September, the **Annual Ogunquit Antiques Show** benefits the Historical Society of Wells and Ogunquit. It's held at the Dunaway Center, School Street, Ogunquit.

In late October is **OgunquitFest,** a family-oriented weeklong event with pumpkin decorating, scarecrow contest, and other seasonal activities.

**Christmas by the Sea,** the second weekend of December, features caroling, tree lighting, shopping specials, Santa Claus, a chowderfest, and a beach bonfire in Ogunquit.

## SHOPPING
### Antiques and Antiquarian Books

Antiques are a Wells specialty. You'll find more than 50 shops, with a huge range of prices. The majority are on Route 1. **R. Jorgensen Antiques** (502 Post Rd., Rte. 1, R.R. 1, Box 1125, Wells 04090, 207/646-9444), is a phenomenon in itself, filling 11 showrooms in two buildings with European and American 18th- and 19th-century furniture and accessories. **MacDougall-Gionet Antiques and Associates** (2104 Post Rd., Rte. 1, Wells, 207/646-3531) has been here since the mid-1960s, and its reputation is stellar. The 65-dealer shop—in an 18th-century barn—carries American and European country and formal furniture and accessories.

If you've been scouring antiquarian bookshops for a long-wanted title, chances are you'll find it at **Douglas N. Harding Rare Books** (2152 Post Rd., Rte. 1, P.O. Box 184, Wells 04090, 207/646-8785 or 800/228-1398). Well cataloged and organized, the sprawling bookshop at any given time stocks upward of 100,000 books, prints, and maps, plus a hefty selection of Maine and New England histories. Don't count on leaving empty-handed—there are too many temptations.

### Art Galleries

There's no scarcity of the spectacular scenery that drew artists to Ogunquit in the early 20th century, but it's not the artistic magnet it once was. Yet galleries have popped up here and there. After you've been to the art museum, do your art browsing along Shore Road and in Perkins Cove.

### Lighthouse Extravaganza

Several minilighthouses stand watch over the **Lighthouse Depot** (Post Rd., Rte. 1, P.O. Box 1690, Wells 04090, 207/646-0608 or 800/758-1444, www.lighthousedepot.com), a truly amazing mecca for lighthouse aficionados. Imagine this: two floors of lighthouse books, sculptures, videos, banners, Christmas ornaments, lawn ornaments, paintings, and replicas running the gamut from pure kitsch to attractive collectibles. Its *Maine Lighthouse*

The Cliff House Resort and Spa is on the edge of Bald Head.

*Map and Guide* ($5.95) is particularly helpful for tracking down the state's sentinels. Depot owners Tim Harrison and Kathy Finnegan also publish the *Lighthouse Digest*, a monthly magazine focusing on North American lighthouses (annual subscription $28), and produce a large mail-order catalog. The shop is about 1.5 miles north of the junction of Routes 1 and 109.

## ACCOMMODATIONS
### Ogunquit

Motel-style accommodations are everywhere in Ogunquit, most along Route 1, yet finding last-minute rooms in July and August can be a challenge, so book well ahead if you'll be here then. Most properties are open only seasonally.

**Hotels and Motels:** You're almost literally within spitting distance of Perkins Cove at the 37-room **Riverside Motel** (159 Shore Rd., P.O. Box 2244, Ogunquit 03907, 207/646-2741, www.riversidemotel.com), where you can perch on your balcony and watch the action—or, for that matter, join it. Rooms with

phone, air-conditioning, refrigerators, cable TV, and fabulous views are $130–160, with continental breakfast.

**Juniper Hill Inn** (336 Main St., Rte. 1, P.O. Box 2190, Ogunquit 03907, 207/646-4501 or 800/646-4544, www.ogunquit.com) is a particularly well-run motel-style lodging on five acres close to downtown Ogunquit and the beach. Amenities include refrigerators, cable TV, coin-operated laundry, fitness center, indoor and outdoor pools, and golf privileges. Rooms have all the amenities, plus free Wi-Fi. Peak rates are $149–219. Open all year.

You can't get much closer to the water than the **Above Tide Inn** (66 Beach St., P.O. Box 2188, Ogunquit 03907, 207/646-7454, www.abovetideinn.com, $170–250), which is built on a wharf over the tidal Ogunquit River and has views to the open Atlantic. It's steps from the beach and downtown Ogunquit. Each of the nine rooms has air-conditioning, TV, and minifridge; a light breakfast is provided; no in-room phone.

**Cottage Colony:** It's nearly impossible to land a peak-season cottage at **The Dunes** (518 Main St., P.O. Box 917, Ogunquit 03907, 207/646-2612, www.dunesonthewaterfront.com), but it's worth trying. The property is under its third generation of ownership and guests practically will their weeks to their descendents. Tidy, well-equipped white housekeeping cottages and a handful of guest rooms are generously spaced on a shady, grassy lawns that roll down to the river, with the dunes just beyond. Facilities include a dock with rowboats, pool, and lawn games. It's all meticulously maintained. In peak season, one- and two-bedroom cottages require a one- or two-week minimum stay; guest rooms require three nights. Rooms begin at $105, cottages at $190 per night; weekly cottage rentals begin at $1,330.

**Eclectic Properties:** It's not easy to describe the **Sparhawk Oceanfront Resort** (41 Shore Rd., P.O. Box 936, Ogunquit 03907, 207/646-5562), a sprawling, one-of-a-kind place popular with honeymooners, sedate families, and seniors. There's lots of tradition in this thriving, six-acre complex—it's had various incarnations since the turn of the 20th century—and the Happily Filled sign regularly hangs out front. Out back is the Atlantic, with forever views, and the Marginal Way starts right here. It offers tennis courts, gardens, heated freshwater pool. No restaurant, but Ogunquit has plenty of options, and breakfast is included with your room. The 87 rooms vary in the different buildings—from motel-type rooms (best views) and suites to inn-type suites; rates run $170–300 (seven-night minimum July 4 to mid-August).

Nor is it easy to describe **The Beachmere Inn** (62 Beachmere Pl., Ogunquit, 207/646-2021 or 800/336-3983, www.beachmere inn.com, $150–390), a private, oceanfront property comprising a Victorian-style inn, an updated motel, and other buildings as well as its own beaches. All rooms have air-conditioning, TV, and phone; many rooms have kitchenettes; most have balconies, decks, or terraces; some have fireplaces. Morn-

ing coffee and muffins are provided. Reservations require three-night to one-week minimum in July and August; closed January–late March.

**Bed-and-Breakfasts:** Built in 1899 for a prominent Maine lumbering family, **C Rockmere Lodge** (40 Stearns Rd., P.O. Box 278, Ogunquit 03907, 207/646-2985, www .rockmere.com, $160–225 peak), underwent a meticulous six-month restoration in the early 1990s, thanks to preservationists Andy Antoniuk and Bob Brown, and in 2006 the duo, along with Doug Flint, gave the inn and grounds a complete rejuvenation, lightening the decor. Near the Marginal Way on a peaceful street, the handsome home has eight very comfortable Victorian guest rooms, all with CD players and cable TV (a 1,000-title library of DVDs and VCR tapes and CDs is available) and most with ocean views. Rates include a generous breakfast, with a hot entrée every other day. A wraparound veranda, a gazebo, and "The Lookout," a third-floor windowed nook with comfy chairs, make it easy to settle in and just watch the passersby on the Marginal Way. The woodwork throughout is gorgeous, and the grounds double as a public garden. Beach towels, chairs, and umbrellas are provided for guests. Closed March and April. No pets; four dogs in residence.

Floors glisten, brass gleams, and breakfast is served on the glass-walled porch at the **Hartwell House** (118 Shore Rd., P.O. Box 393, Ogunquit 03907, 207/646-7210 or 800/235-8883, www.hartwellhouseinn.com, $175–300), where the 13 rooms and three good-sized suites, all with air-conditioning, are divided between two buildings straddling Shore Road. Rooms are beautifully decorated with antiques and reproductions; try for a garden-view room in the main house. Rates include a full breakfast and afternoon tea.

**Resorts:** Founded in 1872, **The Cliff House Resort and Spa** (Shore Rd., P.O. Box 2274, Ogunquit 03907, 207/361-1000), a self-contained Victorian-era complex, sprawls over 70 acres topping the edge of Bald Head Cliff, midway between the centers of York and Ogunquit. Third-generation innkeeper Kathryn Weare keeps updating and modernizing the facilities. Among the most recent additions are a spa building with oversize rooms with king-size beds, gas fireplaces, and balconies, as well as a full-service spa, indoor pool, outdoor vanishing-edge pool, and glass-walled fitness center overlooking the Atlantic. A new central check-in building with indoor amphitheater connects the main building to the spa building. The 150 room and suite styles and prices vary widely in decor, from old-fashioned to contemporary; all have cable TV and phones, some have gas fireplaces, most have a spectacular ocean view ($265–370). Packages are the way to go here. Other facilities include a dining room, lounge, family indoor and outdoor pools, games room, and tennis courts. Eight pet-friendly rooms ($25 per night) have bowl, bed, and treats, and there's a fenced-in exercise area. Open late March–early December.

### Wells

Like Ogunquit, Wells has a long list of motel-type lodgings, mostly on Route 1, and everything fills up in late July and early August. If you're arriving then, don't count on finding last-minute space.

Once part of a giant 19th-century dairy farm, the **Beach Farm Inn** (97 Eldredge Rd., Wells, 207/646-8493, www.beachfarm inn.com) is a 2.5-acre oasis in a rather congested area 0.2 mile off Route 1. Guests can swim in the pool, relax in the library, or walk one-quarter mile down the road to the beach. If you bring your own bikes, storage is provided; rentals are available within walking distance. Eight rooms (five with private baths, two detached) are $100–135 d, including a full breakfast; two cottages go for $650 and $950 a week. Third-floor rooms have air-conditioning. Open all year.

Even closer to the beach is **( Haven by the Sea** (59 Church St., Wells Beach, 207/646-4194, www.havenbythesea.com, $169–350), a lovely and modern B&B in a former church. Innkeepers John and Susan Jarvis have

kept the original floor plan, which allows some surprises. Inside are hardwood floors, cathedral ceilings, and stained-glass windows. The confessional is now a full bar, and the altar has been converted to a dining area that opens to a marsh-view terrace—the bird-watching is superb. Guest rooms have sitting areas, and the suite has a whirlpool tub and fireplace. Guests have plenty of room to relax, including a living area with fireplace. Rates include a full breakfast and afternoon hors d'oeuvres. Also available are a three-bedroom, ocean-view cottage and an apartment.

## FOOD
### Ogunquit

**Local Flavors: The Egg and I** (501 Maine St., Rte. 1, 207/646-8777, www.eggandibreak-fast.com) earns high marks for its omelettes and waffles. You can't miss it—there's always a crowd. Open 6 a.m.–2 p.m. daily for breakfast, with lunch choices also served after 11 a.m. No credit cards.

Equally popular is **Amore Breakfast** (178 Shore Rd., 207/646-6661, www.amore breakfast.com, 7 a.m.–1 p.m. Fri.–Tues.). Choose from a baker's dozen omelettes, seven versions of eggs Benedict (including lobster and a spirited rancheros version topped with salsa and served with guacamole), as well as various French toast, waffles, and all the regulars and irregulars.

Eat in or take out from **Village Food Market** (Main St., Ogunquit Center, 207/646-2122, www.villagefoodmarket.com). A breakfast sandwich is less than $3; subs and sandwiches are available in three sizes, and there's even a children's menu.

Scrumptious baked goods, tantalizing salads, and panini sandwiches are available to go at Mary Breen's fabulous **( Bread and Roses** (28A Main St., 207/646-4227, www.breadan-drosesbakery.com), a small bakery right downtown with a few tables outside.

**Harbor Candy Shop** (26 Main St., 207/646-8078 or 800/331-5856) is packed with the most outrageous chocolate imaginable. Fudge, truffles, and turtles are all made here in the shop. Fortunately (or maybe unfortunately), it also accepts mail orders. Open all year.

**Lobster:** Creative marketing, a knockout view, and efficient service help explain why more than 1,000 pounds of lobster bite the dust every summer day at **Barnacle Billy's** (Perkins Cove, 207/646-5575 or 800/866-5575, 11 A.M.–9 P.M. daily seasonally). For ambience, stick with the original operation; Barnacle Billy's Etc., next door (formerly the Whistling Oyster), is an upmarket version of the same thing with a broader menu. Full liquor license. Try for the deck, with a front-row seat on Perkins Cove.

**Ethnic:** The closest thing to an upscale-rustic French country inn is the dining room at ◖ **Provence,** also referred to as 98 Provence (262 Shore Rd., 207/646-9898, www.98provence.com). Chef/owner Pierre Gignac produces the cuisine to match, turning out appetizers such as stewed pheasant in baked tomato and chevre gratin and superb entrées in the $26–33 range, but there are also three fixed menus (around $29–37). Duck, venison, seafood, veal, and lamb are all represented. Service is attentive and well paced. Don't miss it, and be sure to make reservations. Open for the season at 5:30 P.M. Wednesday–Monday beginning in mid-April.

Cross the street from Provence and you're in Italy—sort of. Vegetarians and pasta fanatics gravitate to **The Impastable Dream** (261 Shore Rd., 207/646-3011, www.impastabledream.com). Entrée range is $12–19; choices are predictable (ravioli, gnocchi, lasagna, Mediterranean tomato-based sauces over pasta, etc.) in this comfortable, casual spot. No reservations, so you may have to wait. It's open 5–9 P.M. daily, and a kids' menu is available until 6 P.M.

The best and most authentic Italian dining is at **Angelina's Ristorante** (655 Main St./Rte. 1, 207/646-0445), opened by popular local chef and owner David Giarusso in late 2005. Dine in the dining room or lounge or out on the deck, choosing from pastas, risottos (the house specialty), and main courses such as *rollantini di pollo*, a boneless chicken breast

stuffed with prosciutto, mozzarella, and basil and baked with a light spinach cream sauce, or a hand-cut filet mignon grilled and finished with a chianti-portobello-gorgonzola demiglace. More than 30 wines are available by the glass. Most choices run $16–24. It opens nightly at 5 P.M.

**Casual Dining: Gypsy Sweethearts** (10 Shore Rd., 207/646-7021, www.gypsysweethearts.com, 5:30–9 P.M. Tues.–Sun.) serves in four rooms on the ground floor of a restored house, and on a rooftop deck, too. It's one of the region's most reliable restaurants, and the creative menu is infused with ethnic accents and includes vegetarian choices (entrées $17–30). Seating is both inside and out. Reservations advised in midsummer.

Equally reliable, and just south of it is **Five-O** (50 Shore Rd., 207/646-6365, www.fiveoshoreroad.com, 5–10 P.M. daily), where executive chef Jonathan MacAlpine turns out classics with flair complemented by well-conceived inspirations. The menus changes frequently, but entrées such as pan-seared Atlantic salmon or Peking chicken are $25–33. Lighter fare ($9–16) is available in the lounge to 11 P.M., where martinis are a specialty. Service is excellent. In the off-season, multicourse regional dinners are held about once a month ($70). There's even valet parking.

**The View's the Thing:** There's not much between you and Spain when you get a window seat at **MC** (Oarweed La., Perkins Cove, Ogunquit, 207/646-6263, www.mcperkinscove.com), sister restaurant of the mega-high-end Arrows Restaurant. Actually, almost every table on both floors has a view, and the sophisticated decor doesn't compete with it. Service is extremely attentive, and the food is fab, creative, and in keeping with chefs Mark Gaier and Clark Frasier, ultrafresh. If you can't justify the splurge for Arrows, get a taste of their cuisine here. Reservations are essential for dinner. It's open 11:30 A.M.–2:30 P.M. for lunch (entrées $9–19) and 5:30–11 P.M. for dinner (entrées $22–34), with a bar menu served until 11 P.M. A jazz brunch is served beginning at 11 A.M. Sundays. Closed Tuesdays and January.

Equally if not more impressive are the views from the dining room at **The Cliff House** (Shore Rd., Ogunquit, 207/361-1000), open to the public for breakfast, lunch, and dinner daily. Try for the brunch buffet, 7:30 A.M.–1 P.M. Sunday. Service can be so-so. Reservations are required for dinner (no jeans, T-shirts, or sneakers); entrée range is $23–33. Before or after dining, wander the grounds. Open late March–early December.

**Destination Dining:** Restrain yourself for a couple of days and then splurge on an elegant dinner at **Arrows** (Berwick Rd., about 1.5 miles west of Rte. 1, Ogunquit, 207/361-1100, www.arrowsrestaurant.com), definitely one of Maine's finest restaurants. In a beautifully restored 18th-century farmhouse overlooking well-tended gardens (including a one-acre kitchen garden that supplies about 90 percent of the produce), co-owners/chefs Mark Gaier and Clark Frasier do everything right here, starting with the artistic presentation. Prices are stratospheric by Maine standards—with wine and all, count on paying at least $250 a couple—but well worth it. "Innovative" is too tame to describe the menu; entrées cost close to $50. Consider the six-course tasting menu ($95); serious foodies might splurge on the indulgence tasting menu, 10 courses for $135. A credit card is required for reservations—essential in midsummer and on weekends. Jackets are preferred for men; no shorts. It's open for dinner at 6 P.M. mid-April–early December: Tuesday–Sunday in July and August, Wednesday–Sunday in June and September–Columbus Day; mostly weekends other months. Off-season, ask about winemaker, regional, bistro nights, and specialty dinners and cooking classes (most $69–89 for a five-course meal).

## Wells

**Local Flavors:** Best homemade doughnuts in Wells (and beyond), hands down, are at **Congdon's Doughnuts** (Rte. 1, Wells, 207/646-4219). Also try the strata. Open 6 A.M.–3 P.M. daily for breakfast and lunch year-round, closed Tuesday.

**Bean suppers** are held 5–7 P.M. on the first Saturday of the month, May–October, at the Masonic Hall on Sanford Road, and on the second Saturday at the Wells Congregational Church, on Route 1.

**Flo's** (Rte. 1, Wells, 11 A.M.–7 P.M. daily), an offspring of the York institution, has opened a stand in Wells. The famous hot dogs are served, but so are burgers and sandwiches. Order at the window, and then grab a picnic table under the pines.

For scrumptious baked goods and made-to-order sandwiches, head to **Borealis Bread** (Rte. 1, Wells, 8:30 A.M.–5:30 P.M. Mon.–Fri., 9 A.M.–4 P.M. Sat. and Sun.), in the Aubuchon Hardware plaza adjacent to the Wells Auto Museum. There are only two tables inside, so take it to the beach.

Pick up all sorts of fresh goodies at the **Wells Farmers Market** in the Town Hall parking lot, 3–6 P.M. Wednesdays.

**Family Favorites:** No eatery in this category qualifies as heart healthy, so don't say you weren't forewarned.

Longtime favorite **Billy's Chowder House** (216 Mile Rd., just off Rte. 1, 207/646-7558, www.billyschowderhouse.com) has a prime marsh-view location—with wall-to-wall cars in the parking lot. Seafood is the specialty here, but you can get just about anything. It's open 11:30 A.M.–10 P.M. July and August, to 9 P.M. other months, mid-January–early December.

The **Maine Diner** (2265 Post Rd., Rte. 1, Wells, 207/646-4441, www.mainediner.com) has a reputation built on lobster pie and award-winning seafood chowder. Beer and wine only. It's open 7 A.M.–9:30 P.M. (8 P.M. in winter) daily for breakfast, lunch, and dinner (breakfast available anytime). Prices run from less than $10 for diner food to $20 for surf and turf.

Newest among the family favorites is **Mainiax Restaurant** (Rte. 1, Wells, 207/646-0808, www.mainiaxrestaurant.com, 11:30 A.M.–8 P.M., to 9 P.M. Fri. and Sat.) The menu is huge—everyone in the family is sure to find something, the prices are moderate, and the decor is moosey. It's casual and fun.

**Turf and Surf:** A good steak in the land of lobster? You betcha. **The Steakhouse** (1205 Post Rd., Rte. 1, 207/646-4200, www.the-steakhouse.com, 4–9:30 P.M. Tues.–Sun.) is a great big barn of place where steaks are hand cut from USDA prime and choice, corn-fed Western beef that's never been frozen. Chicken, seafood, lobster (great stew), and even a vegetarian stir-fry are also on the menu (entrées $13–26); children's menu available. Service is efficient. No reservations, so be prepared for a wait. This place is *very* popular.

Locals rave about the seafood chowder and the lobster stew at **Lord's Harborside Restaurant** (Harbor Rd., Wells Harbor, 207/646-2651, www.lordsharborside.com, noon–9 P.M. Wed.–Mon., to 8 P.M. spring and fall). They should also rave about the view, a front-row seat on the Wells working harbor. Sure, it's touristy, but with these views, who cares? The menu has a bit of everything, but the emphasis is on fish and seafood, with most prices in the teens; lobster higher. Kids' menu available.

**Fine Dining:** Chef Joshua W. Mather has brought true fine dining to Wells with **Joshua's** (1637 Rte. 1, 207/646-3355, www.joshuas.biz). Chef Joshua grew up on his family's organic farm, just six miles distant, and produce from the farm highlights the menu. In a true family operation, his parents not only still work the farm, but they also work in the restaurant, a converted 1774 home with many of its original architectural elements. Everything is made on the premises, from the fabulous bread to the hand-churned ice cream. Entrées range $19–29. The Atlantic haddock, with carmelized onion crust, chive oil, and wild mushroom risotto is a signature dish and alone worth coming for. A vegetarian pasta entrée is offered nightly. Do save room for the maple walnut pie with maple ice cream. Yes, it's gilding the lily, but you can always walk the beach afterward. Reservations are essential for the dining rooms, but the full menu is also served in the bar. It's open 5–10 P.M. Monday–Saturday.

## INFORMATION AND SERVICES

At the southern edge of Ogunquit, right next to the Ogunquit Playhouse, the Ogunquit Chamber of Commerce's Welcome Center (Rte. 1, Box 2289, Ogunquit 03907, 207/646-2939, www.ogunquit.org), provides all the usual visitor information, including restaurant menus. Ask for the *Touring and Trolley Route Map,* showing the Marginal Way, beach locations, and public restrooms. The chamber of commerce's annual visitor booklet thoughtfully carries a high-tide calendar for the summer. It also has public restrooms.

Just over the Ogunquit border in Wells (actually in Moody) is the Wells Information Center (Rte. 1 at Bourne Ave., P.O. Box 356, Wells 04090, 207/646-2451, www.wellschamber.org). A touch-pad kiosk takes over when the office is closed.

The handsome fieldstone Ogunquit Memorial Library (74 Shore Rd., Ogunquit, 207/646-9024) is the downtown's only National Historic Register building. Or visit the Wells Public Library (1434 Post Rd., Rte. 1, 207/646-8181, www.wells.lib.me.us).

## GETTING THERE

Amtrak's **Downeaster** (800/872-7245, www.thedowneaster.com), which connects Boston's North Station with Portland, Maine, stops in Wells. The Shoreline Explorer trolley connects in season.

## GETTING AROUND

The Maine Turnpike, a toll road, is generally the fastest route if you're trying to get between two towns. Route 1 parallels the turnpike, on the ocean side. It's mostly two lanes and is lined with shops, restaurants, motels, and other tourist-oriented sites, which means stop-and-go traffic that often slows to a crawl. If you're traveling locally, it's best to walk or use the local trolley systems, which have the bonus of saving you the agony of finding a parking spot.

### Trolleys

The **Shoreline Explorer** (207/324-5762,

www.shorelineexplorer.com) trolley system makes it possible to connect from York to Kennebunkport without your car. Each town's system is operated separately and has its own fees.

**Ogunquit Trolley Co.** (207/646-1411, www.ogunquittrolley.com) operates seasonal service in Ogunquit, with 39 stops (signposted) weaving through Ogunquit. Each time you board, it'll cost you $1.50 (kids 10 and younger $1), exact fare, but for the same price you can go the whole route—a great way to get your bearings—in about 40 minutes. Hours are 8:30 A.M.–8 P.M. late May–late June and Labor Day to Columbus Day, and 8 A.M.–11 P.M. late June–Labor Day.

Wells's seasonal **Shoreline Trolley System** on Route 1 runs every 20–30 minutes, 9 A.M.–11 P.M. late June–Labor Day. Fare is $1 per trip or $3 for a day pass; family day passes are also available. It operates between Wells and Kennebunk's Lower village.

Another option is the **Hotel Shuttle** (800/696-2463, www.shorelineexplorer.com), which operates between the Amtrak station in Wells and lodging properties within the Shoreline Explorer communities. Fares vary by zone and day, and reservation is required.

# The Kennebunks

The world may have first learned of Kennebunkport when George Herbert Walker Bush was president, but Walkers and Bushes have owned their summer estate here for three generations. Visitors continue to come to the Kennebunks (the collective name for Kennebunk, Kennebunkport, Cape Porpoise, and Goose Rocks Beach—combined population about 15,200) hoping to catch a glimpse of the former first family, but they also come for the terrific ambience, the B&Bs, boutiques, boats, biking, and beaches.

The Kennebunks' earliest European settlers arrived in the mid-1600s. By the mid-1700s, shipbuilding had become big business in the area. Two ancient local cemeteries—North Street and Evergreen—provide glimpses of the area's heritage. Its Historic District reveals Kennebunk's moneyed past—the homes where wealthy shipowners and shipbuilders once lived, sending their vessels to the Caribbean and around the globe. Today, unusual shrubs and a dozen varieties of rare maples still line Summer Street—the legacy of ship captains in the global trade. Another legacy is the shiplap construction in many houses—throwbacks to a time when labor was cheap and lumber plentiful. Closer to the beach, in Lower Village, stood the workshops of sailmakers, carpenters, and mastmakers whose output drove the booming trade to success.

While Kennebunkport draws most of the sightseers and summer traffic, Kennebunk feels more like a year-round community. It boasts an interesting, old-fashioned downtown and a mix of shops, restaurants, and attractions. Yes, its beaches, too, are well known, but many visitors drive right through the middle of Kennebunk without stopping to enjoy its assets.

The Kennebunks are communities with conscience—loaded with conservationists working to preserve hikeable, bikeable green space for residents and visitors. Be sure not to miss these trails, bikeways, and offshore islets. Gravestone rubbers will want to check out Evergreen Cemetery, and history buffs should pick up a copy of *Walking in the Port,* the Kennebunkport Historical Society's well-researched booklet of three self-guided historic walking tours. To appreciate the area another way, climb aboard the Intown Trolley, with regular summertime service and lots of entertaining tidbits from the driver.

## SIGHTS
### ◖ Seashore Trolley Museum
There's nothing quite like an antique electric trolley to dredge up nostalgia for bygone days. With a collection of more than 250

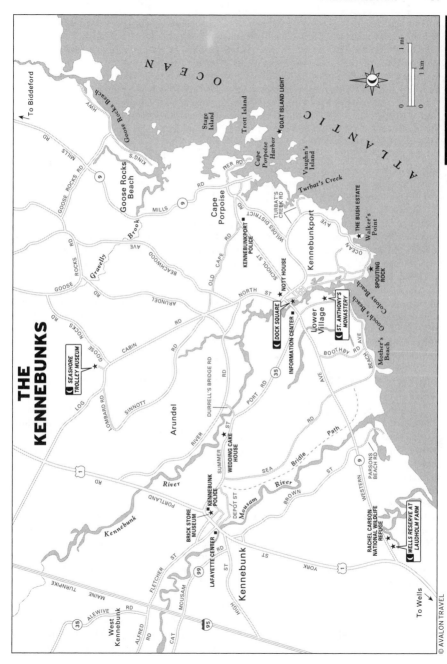

# THE KENNEBUNKS

ATLANTIC OCEAN

To Biddeford

Goose Rocks Beach

Stage Island

Trott Island

Cape Porpoise Harbor

GOAT ISLAND LIGHT

Vaughn's Island

Turbat's Creek

Cape Porpoise

KENNEBUNKPORT POLICE

WILDES DISTRICT

MOTT HOUSE

Kennebunkport

THE BUSH ESTATE

Walker's Point

SPOUTING ROCK

Colony Beach

Goodd's Beach

DOCK SQUARE

INFORMATION CENTER

Lower Village

ST. ANTHONY'S MONASTERY

SEASHORE TROLLEY MUSEUM

Arundel

WEDDING CAKE HOUSE

Mother's Beach

Bridle Path

KENNEBUNK POLICE

BRICK STORE MUSEUM

Kennebunk

RACHEL CARSON NATIONAL WILDLIFE REFUGE

WELLS RESERVE AT LAUDHOLM FARM

LAFAYETTE CENTER

West Kennebunk

MAINE TURNPIKE

To Wells

1 mi

1 km

© AVALON TRAVEL

transit vehicles (more than two dozen trolleys on display), the Seashore Trolley Museum (195 Log Cabin Rd., P.O. Box A, Kennebunkport 04046, 207/967-2800, www.trolleymuseum.org) verges on trolley-mania. Whistles blowing and bells clanging, restored streetcars do frequent trips (between 10:05 A.M. and 4:15 P.M.) on a 3.5-mile loop through the nearby woods. Ride as often as you wish, then check out the activity in the streetcar workshop, and go wild in the trolley-oriented gift shop. Bring a picnic lunch and enjoy it here. Special events are held throughout the summer, including Ice Cream and Sunset Trolley Rides at 7 P.M. every Wednesday and Thursday in July and August. Cost is $4 and includes ice cream. And here's an interesting wrinkle: Make a reservation, plunk down $50, and you can have a one-hour "Motorman" experience driving your own trolley (with help, of course). Museum tickets are $8 adults, $6 seniors, $5.50 kids 6–16, and free for kids 5 and under. The museum is 1.7 miles southeast of Route 1. It's open 10 A.M.–5 P.M. daily mid-June–Columbus Day, and weekends in May, late October, and Christmas Prelude.

## Walker's Point: The Bush Estate

There's no public access to Walker's Point, but you can join the sidewalk gawkers on Ocean Avenue overlooking George and Barbara Bush's summer compound. The 41st president and his wife lead a low-key, laid-back life when they're here, so if you don't spot them through binoculars, you may well run into them at a shop or restaurant in town. Intown Trolley's regular narrated tours go right past the house—or it's an easy, scenic family walk from Kennebunkport's Dock Square. On the way, you'll pass **St. Ann's Church,** whose stones came from the ocean floor, and the paths to **Spouting Rock** and **Blowing Cave**—two natural phenomena that create spectacular water fountains if you manage to be there midway between high and low tides.

## Wedding Cake House

The Wedding Cake House (104 Summer St.,

Kennebunk) is a private residence, so you can't go inside, but it's one of Maine's most-photographed buildings. Driving down Summer Street (Rte. 35), midway between the downtowns of Kennebunk and Kennebunkport, it's hard to miss the yellow and white Federal mansion with gobs of gingerbread and Gothic Revival spires and arches. Built in 1826 by shipbuilder George Bourne as a wedding gift for his wife, the Kennebunk landmark remained in the family until 1983.

## Cape Porpoise

When your mind's eye conjures an idyllic lobster-fishing village, it probably looks a lot like Cape Porpoise—only 2.5 miles from busy Dock Square. Follow Route 9 eastward from Kennebunkport; when Route 9 turns north, continue straight, and take Pier Road to its end. From the small parking area, you'll see lobster boats at anchor, a slew of working wharves, and 19th-century **Goat Island Light,** now automated, directly offshore. In Cape Porpoise are a handful of B&Bs, restaurants, galleries, historic Atlantic Hall, and the extra-friendly Bradbury Bros. Market.

## Local History Museums

Occupying four restored 19th-century buildings (including the 1825 William Lord store) in downtown Kennebunk, **The Brick Store Museum** (117 Main St., Kennebunk, 207/985-4802, www.brickstoremuseum.org, 10 A.M.–4:30 P.M. Tues.–Fri. and 10 A.M.–1 P.M. Sat.) has garnered a reputation for unusual exhibits: a century of wedding dresses, a two-century history of volunteer firefighting, life in southern Maine during the Civil War. Admission is by donation ($5 suggested). The museum encourages appreciation for the surrounding Kennebunk Historic District with hour-long **architectural walking tours,** mid-June to mid-October (call for current schedule). Cost is $5. If the schedule doesn't suit, the museum sells a walk-it-yourself booklet for $5.

Owned and maintained by the Kennebunkport Historical Society, **The Nott House** (8 Maine St., Kennebunkport) is a mid-19th-cen-

The Wedding Cake House was built by a local shipbuilder as a wedding gift for his wife.

tury Greek Revival mansion filled with Victorian furnishings. Be sure to visit the restored gardens. It's open 1–4 P.M. Tuesday–Friday and 10 A.M.–1 P.M. Saturday mid-June–Columbus Day. Tour tickets are $5 adults, under 18 are free. Hour-long architectural walking tours of the Kennebunkport Historic District depart from the Nott House at 11 A.M. Thursday and Saturday in July and August, and Saturday only in September. Cost is $3 pp. At the house, you can buy a guidebook for a do-it-yourself tour for $4.

The Kennebunkport Historical Society also owns and maintains a five-building **History Center** (125–135 North St., Kennebunkport, 207/967-2751, www.kporthistory.org). The Town House School, dating from the turn of the 20th century, is the society's research center. The Pasco Exhibit Center, containing the society's offices, also has permanent and rotating exhibits of local memorabilia. It's open 10 A.M.–4 P.M. Tuesday–Friday all year. Admission is $3 adults, free for children under 18. If you call ahead for an appointment, a

staff member will let you into the tiny old jail on the grounds.

### ◖ Dock Square

Even if you're not a shopper, make it a point to meander through the heart of Kennebunkport's shopping district, where one-time fishing shacks have been restored and renovated into upscale shops, boutiques, galleries, and dining spots. Some shops, especially those on upper floors, offer fine harbor views. If you're willing to poke around a bit, you'll find some unusual items that make distinctive souvenirs or gifts—pottery, vintage clothing, books, specialty foods, and, yes, T-shirts.

## PARKS AND PRESERVES

Thanks to a dedicated coterie of year-round and summer residents, the foresighted **Kennebunkport Conservation Trust (KCT),** founded in 1974, has become a nationwide model for land-trust organizations. The KCT has managed to preserve from development several hundred acres of land (including 11 small

© HILARY NANGLE

Dock Square is the center of the action in busy Kennebunkport. Shops and restaurants make it easy to spend hours here browsing.

islands off Cape Porpoise Harbor), and most of this acreage is accessible to the public, especially with a sea kayak. The trust has even assumed ownership of 7.7-acre Goat Island, with its distinctive lighthouse visible from Cape Porpoise and other coastal vantage points. Contact the KCT (P.O. Box 7028, Cape Porpoise 04014, www.thekennebunkportconservationtrust.org) for information on its holdings or to volunteer for trail maintenance.

### ◖ St. Anthony's Monastery

Long ago, 35,000 Native Americans used this part of town for a summer camp. They knew a good thing. So did a group of Lithuanian Franciscan monks who in 1947 fled war-ravaged Europe and acquired the 200-acre St. Anthony's Franciscan Monastery (Beach St., Kennebunk, mailing address P.O. Box 980, Kennebunkport 04046, 207/967-2011). From 1956 to 1969, they ran a high school here. The monks occupy the handsome Tudor great house, but the well-tended grounds (sprinkled with shrines and a

recently restored sculpture created by Vytautas Jonynas for the 1964 World's Fair) are open to the public sunrise–sunset. A short path leads from the monastery area to a peaceful gazebo overlooking the Kennebunk River. No pets or bikes. Public restrooms are available. The grounds are open 6 A.M.–8:30 P.M. in summer, closing at 6 P.M. in winter.

### Vaughn's Island Preserve

Thanks to the Kennebunkport Conservation Trust, 96-acre Vaughn's Island has been saved for posterity. You'll need to do a little planning, tidewise, since the island is about 600 feet offshore. Consult a tide calendar and aim for low tide close to the new moon or full moon (when the most water drains away). Allow yourself an hour or so before and after low tide, but no longer, or you may need a boat rescue. Wear treaded rubber boots, since the crossing is muddy and slippery with rockweed. Keep an eye on your watch and explore the ocean (east) side of the island, along the beach. It's all worth the effort, and there's a great view of Goat Island Light off to the east. From downtown Kennebunkport, take Maine Street to Wildes District Road. Continue to Shore Road (also called Turbat's Creek Rd.), go 0.6 mile, jog left 0.2 mile more, and park in the tiny lot at the end.

## Emmons Preserve

Also under the stewardship of the Kennebunkport Conservation Trust, the Emmons Preserve has two trails (blazed yellow and pink) meandering through 146 acres of woods and fields on the edge of Batson's River (also called Gravelly Brook). The yellow trail gives best access to the water. Fall colors here are brilliant, birdlife is abundant, and you can do a loop in half an hour. But why rush? This is a wonderful oasis in the heart of Kennebunkport. From Dock Square, take North Street to Beachwood Avenue (right turn) to Gravelly Brook Road (left turn). The trailhead is on the left.

## Picnic Rock

About 1.5 miles up the Kennebunk River from the ocean, Picnic Rock is the centerpiece of the **Butler Preserve,** a 14-acre enclave managed by The Nature Conservancy. Well named, the rock is a great place for a picnic and a swim, but don't count on being alone. A short trail loops through the preserve. Consider bringing a canoe or kayak (or renting one) and paddle with the tide past beautiful homes and the Cape Arundel Golf Club. From Lower Village Kennebunk, take Route 35 west and hang a right onto Old Port Road. When the road gets close to the Kennebunk River, watch for a Nature Conservancy oak-leaf sign on the right. Parking is along Old Port Road; walk down through the preserve to Picnic Rock, right on the river.

## RECREATION
### Beaches

Ah, the beaches. The Kennebunks are well endowed with sand but not with parking spaces. Between mid-June and mid-September, you'll need to buy a **parking permit** ($10 a day, $20 a week, $50 a season) from the Kennebunk

Town Hall (4 Summer St., 207/985-3675) or the Kennebunkport Police Station (101 Main St., 207/967-4243) or the chamber of commerce. (The police station is open 24 hours; other locations are not.) *You need a separate pass for each town.* Many lodgings provide free permits for their guests—be sure to ask when making room reservations. Or you can avoid the parking nightmare altogether by hopping aboard the Intown Trolley, which goes right by the major beaches.

The main beaches in **Kennebunk** (east to west, stretching about two miles) are 3,346-foot-long Gooch's (most popular), Kennebunk (locally called Middle or Rocks Beach), and Mother's (a smallish beach next to Lords Point, where there's also a playground). Lifeguards are on duty at Gooch's and Mother's Beaches July–Labor Day. Mother's Beach is the home of the Kennebunk Beach Improvement Association. Ask locally about a couple of other beach options.

**Kennebunkport's** claim to beach fame is three-mile-long Goose Rocks Beach, one of the loveliest in the area. Parking spaces are scarce and biking on Route 9 can be dicey, so if sun and sand are your primary goals, the best solution is to book a room nearby. You'll be about five miles east of all the downtown action, however. To reach the beach, take Route 9 from Dock Square east and north to Dyke Road (Clock Farm Corner). Turn right and continue to the end (King's Hwy.).

The prize for tiniest beach goes to Colony (officially Arundel) Beach, near The Colony resort complex. It's close to many Kennebunkport lodgings and an easy walk from Dock Square.

### Bicycling

A mandatory stop for anyone interested in bicycles and biking is **Cape-Able Bike Shop** (83 Arundel Rd., Town House Corners, Kennebunkport, 207/967-4382, www.capeable-bikes.com), a local institution since 1974. The shop has all kinds of rentals and accessories, repairs your wounded gear, sponsors Saturday morning group rides, and provides a free area bike map and the best insider information. (The bike map is also available at the chamber of commerce.) One-day hybrid bike rental is $22. Road- or mountain-bike rental is $27 a day. Map, helmet, and lock are included. Delivery service is available, but the shop operates a seasonal outpost in Lower Village, next to the chamber of commerce.

Cape Abel also offers tours. The 10–15 mile Comfort Beach Tour lasts about 2.5–3 hours and costs $59 adults, $29 kids 15 and younger, including a snack. A Singletrack Adventure moderate to advanced mountain bike tour covers 6–8 miles and lasts about three hours and costs $59 adults, $29 kids, and includes a snack. Tours include rental bike, helmet, carry bag, and water bottle.

## Golf

Three 18-hole golf courses make the sport a big deal in the area. **Cape Arundel Golf Club** (19 River Rd., Kennebunkport, 207/967-3494), established in 1897, and **Webhannet Golf Club** (8 Central Ave., Kennebunk, 207/967-2061), established in 1902, are semiprivate and open to nonmembers; call for tee times at least 24 hours ahead. At Cape Arundel, where George Bush plays, no jeans or sweatpants are allowed. In nearby Arundel, **Dutch Elm Golf Course** (5 Brimstone Rd., Arundel, 207/282-9850) is a public course with rentals, pro shop, and putting greens.

## Whale Watches and Lobster-Boat Cruises

Whale sightings offshore include finbacks, minkes, and humpbacks, and the local cruise boats have had remarkable success. The 80-foot **Nick's Chance** (4 Western Ave., Lower Village, Kennebunk, 207/967-5507 or 800/767-2628, www.firstchancewhalewatch.com) departs twice daily in July and August for 4.5-hour whale watches to Jeffrey's Ledge, weather permitting. Cost is $40 adults, $25 children ages 3–12, $10 up to age 3. Departure is from Performance Marine in Kennebunk Lower Village (behind Bartley's Restaurant).

Under the same ownership and departing from the same location is the 65-foot open lobster boat **Kylie's Chance,** which departs four times daily in July and August for 1.5-hour scenic lobster cruises. A lobstering demonstration is given on most trips, but never on the evening one. Cost is $18 adults, $12 ages 3–12.

## Boating Excursions

For day sailing, the 37-foot one-ton former racing yacht **Bellatrix** (95 Ocean Ave., Kennebunkport, 207/590-1125, www.sailingtrips.com) charges $50 pp for a three-hour sail. The handsome 55-foot gaff-rigged schooner **Eleanor** (Arundel Wharf, 43 Ocean Ave., Kennebunkport, 207/967-8809, www.gwi.net/schoonersails) heads out for two-hour sails, weather and tides willing, 1–3 times daily during the summer. Cost is $40 pp.

## Canoe and Kayak Rentals

Explore the Kennebunk River. **Kennebunkport Marina** (67 Ocean Ave., Kennebunkport, 207/967-3411) rents canoes and single kayaks for $25/two hours or $45 half day; double kayaks are $45/two hours or $60 half day. Hint: Check the tide before you depart, and plan your trip to paddle with it, rather than against it.

## Sportfishing

Saltwater, light tackle, and fly sportfishing are the specialties of **Lady J Sportfishing Charters** (10 Kimball La., Kennebunk, 207/985-7304, www.ladyjcharters.com) aboard the *Rebecca Lynn.* Two-hour trips for kids ($175) include hauling lobster traps. Inshore trips for stripers and bluefish are $300 four hours, $400 six hours. Eight-hour specialty trips for shark or groundfish are $600. Trips leave from the Arundel Wharf Restaurant (Ocean Ave., Kennebunkport).

## Surfing

If you want to catch a wave, stop by **Aquaholics Surf Shop** (166 Port Rd., Kennebunk, 207/967-8650, www.aquaholicsurf.com). The shop has boards, wetsuits, and related gear for both sale and rental, and it offers lessons and surf camps.

© TOM NANGLE

Boats are always coming and going in Kennebunkport's harbor.

## ENTERTAINMENT

Live entertainment is featured, mostly weekends, at Federal Jack's Brewpub and Windows on the Water, and at the Kennebunkport Inn and The Colony.

Kennebunk Parks and Recreation sponsors **Concerts in the Park,** a weekly series of free concerts 6:30–7:30 P.M. Wednesdays late June to mid-August, in Rotary Park on Water Street.

At 7 P.M. on Thursday evenings in July, the **River Tree Arts Summer Concert Series** brings music to the lawn of the South Congregational Church, Kennebunkport.

Live, professional summer theater is on tap at the **Arundel Barn Playhouse** (53 Old Post Rd., Arundel, 207/985-5552, www.arundelbarnplayhouse.com), with productions staged in a renovated 1888 barn, June–September; tickets $19–24.

### River Tree Arts (RTA)

The area's cultural spearhead is River Tree Arts (35 Western Ave., Kennebunk, 207/967-9120, www.rivertreearts.org), an incredibly energetic,

volunteer-driven organization that sponsors concerts, classes, workshops, exhibits, and educational programs throughout the year.

## FESTIVALS AND EVENTS

Concerts and kids' activities are part of the **Summer Solstice Festival** in June. Take the kids to the **Kennebearport Teddy Bear Show,** usually the second Saturday in August, but watch the reactions of all the grown-ups.

The first two weekends of December mark the festive **Christmas Prelude,** during which spectacular decorations adorn historic homes, candle-toting carolers stroll through the Kennebunks, stores have special sales, and Santa Claus shows up in a lobster boat.

## SHOPPING

Lots of small, attractive boutiques surround **Dock Square,** the hub of Kennebunkport, so gridlock often develops in midsummer. Avoid driving through here at the height of the season. Take your time and walk, bike, or ride the local trolley-bus.

## Antiques and Art

English, European, and American furniture and architectural elements and garden accessories are just a sampling of what you'll find at **Antiques on Nine** (Rte. 9, Lower Village, Kennebunk, 207/967-0626). Another good place for browsing high-end antiques as well as home accents is **Hurlburt Designs** (Rte. 9, Lower Village, Kennebunk, 207/967-4110). More than 30 artists are represented at **Wright Gallery** (Pier Rd., Cape Porpoise, 207/967-5053).

Jean Briggs represents nearly 100 artists at her topflight **Mast Cove Galleries** (Maine St. and Mast Cove La., Kennebunkport, 207/967-3453), in a handsome Greek Revival house near the Graves Memorial Library. Prices vary widely, so don't be surprised if you spot something affordable. The gallery sponsors 2.5-hour Wednesday evening jazz concerts in July and August ($10 donation includes light refreshments). Call for the schedule. **The Gallery on Chase Hill** (10 Chase Hill Rd., Kennebunkport, 207/967-0049), in the stunningly restored Captain Chase House, next to the Windows on the Water restaurant, mounts rotating exhibits and represents a wide variety of Maine and New England artists. **Compliments** (Dock Sq., 207/967-2269) has a truly unique and fun collection of contemporary fine American crafts, with an emphasis on glass and ceramic wear.

## Books, Clothing, and Gifts

The number of shops in this category in the Kennebunks is vast. You'll need to do your own exploring and discovering. Treasures are to be found all over the Kennebunks, but most are clustered around Dock Square (Kennebunkport) and in Lower Village (Kennebunk).

To appreciate the friendly, funky **Kennebunk Book Port** (10 Dock Sq., Kennebunkport, 207/967-3815 or 800/382-2710), climb to the second floor of the antique rum warehouse and read the shop slogan: "Ice cream, candy, children, bare feet, short, long, or no hair, cats, dogs, and small dragons are welcome anytime." This place has character.

Since 1968, **Port Canvas** (9 Ocean Ave.,

Kennebunkport, 207/985-9765 or 800/333-6788) has been turning out the best in durable cotton-canvas products. Need a new double-bottomed tote bag? It's here. Also here are golf-bag covers, belts, computer cases, day packs, and of course duffel bags.

Quilt fans should make time to visit **Mainely Quilts** (108 Summer St., Rte. 35, Kennebunk, 207/985-4250), behind the Waldo Emerson Inn. The shop has a nice selection of contemporary and antique quilts.

Most of the clothing shops clustered around Dock Square are rather pricey. Not so **Arbitrage** (28 Dock Sq., 207/967-9989), which combines designer consignment clothing with new fashions, vintage designer costume jewelry, shoes, and handbags.

Irresistible eye-dazzling costume jewelry, hair ornaments, handbags, lotions, cards, and other delightful finds fill every possible space at **Dannah** (123 Ocean Ave., Kennebunkport, 207/967-8640), in the Breakwater Spa building, with free customer-only parking in the rear.

## Earth-Friendly Toiletries

Lafayette Center, a handsomely restored mill building housing boutiques and eateries, is also home to the **Tom's of Maine Natural Living Store** (Storer St., just off Main St., Kennebunk, 207/985-3874), an eco-sensitive local-turned-global firm that makes soaps, toothpaste, oils, and other products. "Factory seconds" are real bargains.

# ACCOMMODATIONS

Rates listed are for peak season; most stay open through Christmas Prelude.

## Inns and Hotels

Graciously dominating its 11-acre spread at the mouth of the Kennebunk River, **The Colony Hotel** (140 Ocean Ave. at King's Hwy., P.O. Box 511, Kennebunkport 04046, 207/967-3331 or 800/552-2363, www.thecolonyhotel.com/maine), springs right out of a bygone era, and its distinctive cupola is an area landmark. It's had a long-time commitment to the environment, with recycling, waste-reduction, and educational programs. There's a special feeling here, with cozy corners for reading, lawns and gardens for strolling, a beachfront swimming pool, room service, tennis privileges at the exclusive River Club, bike rentals, massage therapy, and lawn games. Doubles begin at $190, including breakfast, but not $5 pp daily service charge. Pets are $25 per night. Higher-priced rooms have ocean views, others have garden views. The hotel dining room is open to the public for breakfast, lunch, and dinner; reservations are advisable. Brunch is a big winner, 11 A.M.–2 P.M. Sunday mid-June–Labor Day. Open mid-May–late October.

The The White Barn Inn and its siblings have cornered the ultrahigh-end, boutique inn market, with four in this category. Most renowned is the **White Barn Inn** (37 Beach Ave., Kennebunk, mailing address P.O. Box 560, Kennebunkport 04046, 207/967-2321, www.whitebarninn.com, $340–780). Also part of the empire are **The Beach House Inn** (211 Beach Ave., Kennebunk, 207/967-3850, www.beachhseinn.com, $299–525), **The Breakwater Inn, Hotel, and Spa** (127 Ocean Ave., Kennebunkport, 207/967-3118, www.thebreakwaterinn.com, $290–345), **The Yachtsman Lodge and Marina** (Ocean Ave., Kennebunkport, 207/967-2511, www.yachtsmanlodge.com, $299–314), and three restaurants. Rooms in all properties have air-conditioning, phones, satellite TV, VCR and CD players; bikes and canoes are available for guests. Rates include bountiful continental breakfasts and afternoon tea, but check out the off-season packages, especially if you wish to dine at one of the restaurants. All but the Beach House are within easy walking distance of Dock Square.

The White Barn Inn is the most exclusive, with five-diamond and Relais and Chateaux status. It's home to one of the best restaurants in the *country* (see *Food*). Many rooms have fireplaces and marble baths with separate steam showers and whirlpool tubs (you can even arrange for a butler-drawn bath). Service is impeccable, and nothing has been overlooked in terms of amenities. There's an outdoor heated European-style brimming pool, where lunch is available, weather permitting, and a full-service spa. For a truly away-from-it-all feeling, consider staying at one the inn's ultraprivate riverfront Wharf Cottages ($585–1,300—ouch!), which face Dock Square from across the river. The inn also has a Hinckley Talaria-44 available for charter.

The Beach House Inn faces Middle Beach and is a bit less formal than the White Barn, but the service is on par. The Breakwater, at the mouth of the Kennebunk River, comprises a beautifully renovated, historical inn with wrap-around porches and an adjacent, more modern, newly renovated building that houses rooms and a full-service spa. The complex also is home to Stripers Restaurant (see *Food*). Finally, there's the Yachtsman, an innovative blend of a motel and B&B, with all rooms opening onto patios facing the river and the marina where George H. W. Bush keeps his boat.

Innkeeper (and restaurateur and artist) Jack Nahil seems to have a magic touch with everything he undertakes. Now he's rehabbed the **◖ Cape Arundel Inn** (208 Ocean Ave., Kennebunkport, 207/967-2125, www.capearundelinn.com), making it (and its restaurant) a prime destination. The fabulous ocean view (all but two rooms overlook the Bush estate) doesn't hurt, either. The Cape Arundel compound comprises the Shingle-style main inn building (seven rooms, most with water view; $295–375 peak), the Rockbound motel-style building (six rooms with sea-view balconies; $315–375 peak), and the Carriage House Loft, a large suite on the upper floor of the carriage house ($295 peak); an expanded continental breakfast buffet is included. Most rooms have fireplaces; Rockbound and Carriage House have TV. Open March–January 1. The inn's restaurant, where every table has an ocean view, earns raves for its intriguingly creative cuisine; entrées are $20–34.

If nonstop beaching is your vacation goal, book one of the 22 rooms at **Tides Inn by-the-Sea** (252 Kings Hwy., Goose Rocks Beach, Kennebunkport, 207/967-3757, www.tidesinnbythesea.com), directly across the street from superb Goose Rocks Beach. Decor at the John Calvin Stevens–designed Victorian inn is funky, whimsical (faux painting, costumed dummies, a resident ghost named Emma), and altogether fun. Next door is **Tides Too**, a modern, condo-type building with one- and two-bedroom efficiencies by the week ($3,500 for four people). Inn rooms, early June–Labor Day, go for $195–325 d, including continental breakfast. Open mid-May–mid-October. The inn's first-rate Belvidere Club is open to the public Wednesday–Sunday for breakfast and creative dinners with a small but select menu (entrées $22–25).

The sprawling, riverfront **Nonantum Resort** (95 Ocean Ave., P.O. Box 2626, Kennebunkport 04046, 207/967-4050 or 800/552-5651, www.nonantumresort.com, $189–439) complex, which dates from 1884, includes a bit of everything, from simple rooms with an old-fashioned, Victorian decor to modern family suites with kitchenettes. Some rooms have views to the open ocean. Facilities include a dining room, outdoor heated pool and whirlpool, and docking facilities—two tour boats are based here. All 115 rooms have air-conditioning, Wi-Fi, and TV; some have refrigerators. Rates include a full breakfast. The dining room is also open for dinner and, in July and August, lunch. Packages, many of which include dinner, are a good choice. Do note: Weddings take place here almost every weekend. Open April–early December.

Innkeepers and chefs Brian and Shanna O'Hea (they met at the Culinary Institute of America) have created a lovely escape at **The Kennebunk Inn** (45 Main St., Kennebunk, 207/985-3351, www.thekennebunkinn.com, $125–160 peak), a rambling 1799 inn in downtown Kennebunk. No two rooms are alike, and renovation is an ongoing process. Some have air-conditioning or antique claw-foot tubs or fireplaces, all have Wi-Fi, TV, and phone. The inn has both a dining room (5–9 P.M. Wed.–Sat., entrées $19–28) and pub (5–9 P.M. daily, $7–15). Rates include a continental breakfast. A few pet-friendly rooms ($20 per stay) are available.

## Bed-and-Breakfasts

Three of Kennebunkport's lovliest inns are rumored to have been owned by brothers-in-law, all of whom were sea captains. Rivaling the White Barn Inn for service, decor, amenities, and overall luxury is the three-story **( The Captain Lord Mansion** (P.O. Box 800, Kennebunkport 04046, 207/967-3141 or 800/522-3141, www.captainlord.com, $215–450), which is one of the finest B&Bs anywhere. And no wonder. Innkeepers Rick and Bev Litchfield have been at it since 1978, and they're never content to rest on their laurels. Each year the inn improves upon seeming perfection. If you want to be pampered and stay in a meticulously decorated and historical B&B with marble bathrooms (heated floors, many with double whirlpool tubs), fireplaces, original artwork, phones, and air-conditioning in all rooms and even a few cedar closets, then look no further. Even breakfast is a special affair, with fresh-squeezed orange juice made from oranges flown in daily. Bicycles and beach towels and chairs are available. Afternoon treats are provided.

The elegant, Federal-style **The Captain Jefferds Inn** (5 Pearl St., P.O. Box 691, Kennebunkport 04046, 207/967-2311 or 800/839-6844, www.captainjefferdsinn.com, $150–360), in the historic district, provides the ambience of a real captain's house. Each of the 15 rooms and suites (11 in the main house and four more in the carriage house) have plush linens, fresh flowers, down comforters, CD players, and air-conditioning; some have fireplaces, whirlpool tubs, and other luxuries. A three-course breakfast and afternoon tea are included.

**The Captain Fairfield Inn** (8 Pleasant St., P.O. Box 3089, Kennebunkport 04046, www.captainfairfield.com, $225–340) is perhaps the most modest architecturally of the three, but it doesn't scrimp on amenities. Innkeepers Rob and Leigh Blood are slowly replacing traditional decor with a more contemporary style. All rooms have flat-screen TVs, air-conditioning, and Wi-Fi; some have gas fireplaces. The lovely grounds are a fine place to retreat for a snooze in the hammock or a game of croquet. Rates include a four-course breakfast.

Hidden in a woodsy, private residential neighborhood, the lovely **Old Fort Inn** (Old Fort Ave., P.O. Box M, Kennebunkport 04046, 207/828-3678, www.oldfortinn.com) is the kind of place that you might not want to leave, even for touring or shopping. Once part of a Colony-style grand hotel, the stable has been renovated into elegant, spacious guest rooms, many with fireplaces and/or jetted tubs, all with wetbars equipped with fridge and microwave. The main building houses a huge common room and a screened porch. On the 15-acre premises are a heated pool, tennis court, and antiques shop. Breakfast is a lavish hot-and-cold buffet. Rates are $160–375.

The inspiration for the **English Meadows Inn** (141 Port Rd., Lower Village, Kennebunk, 207/967-5766, www.englishmeadowsinn.com, $175–305 peak) came from those lovely English manor homes, elegant yet comfortable. The 1860s original Greek Revival architecture was married to the Victorian Queen Anne style later in the century. Inside, the woodwork gleams, the floors, scattered with Asian-style rugs, shine, and the antiques and country comfort pieces mix with an unusual collection of Asian and English antiques, collected by the owner when living abroad. Books fill the inn's many nooks and crannies. Rooms are split between the main house, carriage house (where children are welcome), and a pet-friendly, two-bedroom cottage, a good choice for young families. Breakfast is elaborate.

The low-key, turn-of-the-20th-century **Green Heron Inn** (126 Ocean Ave., Kennebunkport, 207/967-3315, www.greenheroninn.com) sees many repeat guests. Ten rooms and a two-story cottage have TV, phones, air-conditioning, private baths; some have fireplace, microwave, or refrigerator; and most have cove views. Prices are $145–175 d (cottage is $250). Children are welcome; some pets are accepted ($10 per night). Also included is breakfast—one of the best in town—served in the coveside breakfast room.

Neighboring the Wedding Cake House, **The**

**Waldo Emerson Inn** (108 Summer St., Rte. 35, Kennebunk, 207/985-4250, www.waldoemersoninn.com) has a charming colonial feel—as it should, since the main section was built in 1784. Poet Ralph Waldo Emerson spent many a summer in this, his great-uncle's home. Six attractive rooms, three with working fireplaces, are $135–150 peak, including full breakfast. In-room massages are available. Quilters, take note: In the barn is Mainely Quilts, a well-stocked quilt shop, open daily in summer.

You'll awake to the drone of lobster-boat engines at **The Inn at Harbor Head** (41 Pier Rd., Cape Porpoise, Kennebunkport, 207/967-5564, www.harborhead.com), an idyllic spot on Cape Porpoise Harbor, 2.5 miles from Dock Square. Hand-painted murals, monogrammed bathrobes, flower bouquets, a superb library, hammocks in the yard, Wi-Fi, and outstanding views are just a few of the many pluses here. It offers three rooms and one good-size suite, some with whirlpool tub, fireplace, or private deck. Rates are $195–325 d.

Here's a bargain: The nonprofit **Franciscan Guest House** (28 Beach Ave., P.O. Box 980, Kennebunkport 04046, 207/967-4865, www.franciscanguesthouse.com), on the grounds of the monastery, has accommodations spread among two buildings, as well as three other Tudor-style cottages. Accommodations are basic, but they do have some nice amenities, including TV, air-conditioning, saltwater pool, and beach passes. A buffet breakfast is included in the rates, and a buffet dinner often is available. There is no daily mail service, but fresh towels are provided daily. Rooms are $92–154, and one- to three-bedroom suites are $149–279. No credit cards.

## Motels and Cottages

Patricia Mason is the 12th-generation innkeeper at **( The Seaside Motor Inn and Cottages** (80 Beach Ave., Kennebunk, mailing address P.O. Box 631, Kennebunkport 04046, 207/967-4461 or 800/967-4461 www.kennebunkbeach.com, $229–249), a property that has been in her family since the mid-1600s. What a location! The 22-room motel and 10 cottages sit on 20 acres bordered by the Atlantic Ocean, the Kennebec River, and Gooch's River. It's the only truly beachfront property in the area, with a private beach for guests. Motel rooms are spacious, with TV, air-conditioning, and refrigerators. A continental breakfast is included in the rates. The one- to four-bedroom cottages are rented by the week early and late season and by the month in July and August.

With indoor and outdoor heated pools and whirlpools and a good-size fitness center, the **Rhumb Line Motor Lodge** (Ocean Ave., P.O. Box 3067, Kennebunkport 04046, 207/967-5457 or 800/337-4862, www.rhumblinemaine.com) is a magnet for families. This well-managed two-story establishment in a quiet residential area three miles from Dock Square has easy access to the trolley-bus service. Fifty-nine large rooms have private balcony or patio, phones, air-conditioning, Wi-Fi, cable TV, and small refrigerators. Free continental breakfast. From late May to mid-September, weather permitting, there are nightly poolside lobster bakes. Rates are $155–185; kids 12 and under stay free. Closed in January.

Compared with other intown properties, the **Fontenay Terrace Motel** (128 Ocean Ave., Kennebunkport, 207/967-3556, www.fontenaymotel.com, $140–175 peak) is a bargain. Second-generation innkeepers David and Paula Reid keep the place spotless. It borders a tidal inlet and has a private grassy and shaded lawn, perfect for retreating from the hubbub of busy Kennebunkport. Each of the eight rooms has air-conditioning, minifridge, microwave, Wi-Fi, cable TV, and phone; some have water views. A small beach is 300 yards away, and it's a pleasant one-mile walk to Dock Square.

The clean and simple **Cape Porpoise Motel** (12 Mills Rd., Rte. 9, P.O. Box 7218, Cape Porpoise 04014, 207/967-3370, www.capeporpoisemotel.com, $125–150 peak) is a short walk from the harbor. All rooms have TV and air-conditioning, some have kitchenettes; rates include a continental breakfast, with muffins, fruit, and other surprises. Also available by the

week or month are efficiencies with full kitchens, phones, and one or more bedrooms.

## FOOD

Hours are for peak season, when reservations are advised. Call ahead September–June.

### Local Flavors

**All Day Breakfast** (55 Western Ave., Rte. 9, Lower Village, Kennebunk, 207/967-5132) is a favorite meeting spot, offering such specialties as invent-your-own omelettes and crepes, Texas French toast, and the ADB sandwich. ADB is open 7 A.M.–1:30 P.M. weekdays in summer (to 2 P.M. weekends). Closed mid-December–mid-January.

It's hard to choose the perfect pastry from the large selection at **Port Bakery and Café** (181 Port Rd., Kennebunk, 207/967-2263, opens at 7 A.M. daily). Hot breakfasts are also available, as are soups and sandwiches and other goodies. Eat in or outside on the deck or take it all to go.

Conveniently near the Kennebunk and Kennebunkport Chamber of Commerce, **H. B. Provisions** (15 Western Ave., Lower Village, Kennebunk, 207/967-5762) has an excellent wine selection, along with plenty of picnic supplies, newspapers, and all the typical general-store inventory. It also serves breakfast and prepares hot and cold sandwiches, salads, and wraps. It's open daily all year.

The name says it all at **The Bakery and Café** (50 Main St., Kennebunk, 207/985-7888, 6 A.M.–6 P.M. daily and 5–8 P.M. Fri.), a bright and airy downtown spot. Soups, salads, sandwiches, fancy coffees, and pastries are the usuals, but it's also open Friday nights for pizza and stromboli.

Equal parts fancy food and wine store and gourmet café, **Cape Porpoise Kitchen** (Rte. 9, Cape Porpoise, 207/967-1150, 7 A.M.–7 P.M. daily) sells sandwiches, salads, prepared foods, desserts, and everything to go with.

While away an afternoon with a traditional English tea at the **English Meadows Inn** (141 Port Rd., Lower Village, Kennebunk, 207/967-5766, 2–4 P.M. Thurs.–Sat.). Choose from a cream tea ($12.95), with tea, scones, and sweets, or a Queen's tea ($19.95), which adds petite sandwiches to the tray. It's beautifully presented, served in a lovely room or perhaps the garden. Reservations required.

The **Kennebunk Farmers Market** sets up shop mid-May–mid-October in the Grove Street municipal parking lot off Route 1 (behind the Mobil station). Hours are 8 A.M.–noon Saturday. Vendors sell crafts, condiments, fresh produce (including organic), flowers, breads, biscotti; special events (tastings, etc.) are sometimes on the agenda.

### Family Favorites

The nearest thing to being afloat is sitting at a riverfront deck table at **Arundel Wharf** (43 Ocean Ave., Kennebunkport, 207/967-3444), where passing tour and lobster boats provide lunchtime entertainment. Captain's chairs and chart-topped tables complete the nautical picture. Burgers and fries are always on the menu for kids; adults might want to limit their choices to similar fare—dinner entrées are $14–30. Open at 11:30 A.M. daily for lunch and dinner mid-May–mid-December; reservations are wise for dinner.

A bit off the beaten track is **Lucas on 9** (62 Mills Rd./Rte. 9, Cape Porpoise, 207/967-0039, www.lucason9.com), a family-friendly, family-operated restaurant, and the Lane family knows food. Chef Jonathan Lane makes everything from scratch and delivers on his mother Deborah's mission of "Good American food at affordable prices." Jonathan's travels have infused his preparations with more than a bow toward his work on Southern riverboats (Louisiana spicy crab soup, bread pudding with whisky). There are at least six specials nightly in addition to plenty of other choices ($13–30). The restaurant is named for Jonathan's brother Lucas, who died in 2005. It's open 11:30 A.M.–9 P.M., closed Tuesday and mid-December–early April.

Grab a stool at the counter, slip into a booth, or wait for a table at the **Wayfarer** (Pier Rd., Cape Porpoise, 207/967-8961), a casual restaurant that serves breakfast, lunch, and dinner

to locals and in-the-know tourists (dinner entrées $10–19). It's open 7 A.M.–12:30 P.M. and 5–8 P.M. Tuesday–Saturday and 7 A.M.–noon Sunday. Good lobster stew; nightly dinner specials. Most choices are in the $10–19 range. No credit cards.

### Casual Dining

Brian and Shanna O'Hea met at the Culinary Institute of America, and they've had a fine time creating **Académe** (The Kennebunk Inn, 45 Main St., Kennebunk, 207/985-3351, www.kennebunkinn.com), which they bill as a Maine brasserie and tavern. The choices vary from panini and pizzas to cashew-crusted wild salmon, which puts it within most budgets. The lunch menu, served Monday–Friday, comprises mostly soups and salads. A full dinner menu is served Tuesday–Saturday; a limited menu on Sunday and Monday. Children's menu selections are $4.50.

Just west of the junction of Routes 9 and 35 is the casually elegant **Grissini Trattoria** (27 Western Ave., Kennebunk, 207/967-2211, 5:30–9 P.M., Fri. and Sat. to 9:30 P.M.), a sibling of the White Barn Inn. Attentive service, an inspired Tuscan menu (entrées $15–33), and a bright, open-beamed space make it an appealing spot. In nice weather, try for the sunken patio.

The views complement the food at **Hurricane Restaurant** (29 Dock Sq., Kennebunkport, 207/967-9111, www.hurricanerestaurant.com), where the dining room hangs over the river. A longtime favorite in Ogunquit, this is now the only location, but it continues to reel in the crowds, both for location and for quality and creativity. Dinner entrées begin at $19.

Eat well and feel good about it at **Bandaloop** (2 Dock Sq., Kennebunkport, 207/967-4994, www.bandaloop.biz, 5:30–9:30 P.M. daily), a hip, vibrant restaurant where chef/owner W. Scott Lee likes to push boundaries. Lee named the restaurant for author Tom Robbins's fictional tribe that knew the secret to eternal life. Lee believes the secret is fresh, local, organic, and cruelty free. Selections vary from meats and fish to vegetarian and vegan

($14–24); pair a "center of plate selection" with one of eight sauces, choose from nightly specials, or simply make a meal from the appetizers.

## Fancy to Fine Dining

Every table at the **Cape Arundel Inn** (208 Ocean Ave., Kennebunkport, 207/967-2125, www.capearundelinn.com) has a knockout view of crashing surf, and the food matches the view. White-clothed tables topped with cobalt blue glassware add to the inn's casual yet elegant feel. Local artwork covers the walls. Chef Rich Lemoine's menu emphasizes fish and seafood in classic preparations, all prepared and served with care. Prices range from high $20s to mid $30s. Open for dinner daily (closed Mon. off season).

Floor-to-ceiling windows frame the Kennebunk River breakwater, providing perfect views for those indulging at **Stripers** (at the Breakwater Inn, 127 Ocean Ave., Kennebunkport, 207/967-5333), another White Barn Inn sibling. The emphasis on fish is also accented by a saltwater tank with coral reef and exotic fish. It's no surprise that fish and seafood are the specialties, with most entrées in the $18–28 range. Dress is casual. Valet parking is available. It's open 5:30–9 P.M., to 9:30 P.M. Friday and Saturday, April–late October, also 11:30 A.M.–2 P.M. Memorial Day–Labor Day.

Fusion cuisine reigns at **On the Marsh** (46 Western Ave./Rte. 9, Lower Village, Kennebunk, 207/967-2299, www.onthemarsh.com), a restored barn overlooking marshlands leading to Kennebunk Beach. Entrée range is $21–35. The decor here is astonishing, courtesy of owner Denise Rubin, an interior designer: raspberry exterior and art and antiques on both floors of the interior. Dining choices include both an "owner's table" and a "kitchen table." Entrées might include grilled tuna with French bean salad and seared sea scallops with lobster risotto. Quiet piano music adds to the elegant but unstuffy ambience; service is attentive. Reservations are essential in midsummer. It's open for dinner 5:30–9:30 P.M. daily. Closed January.

Winner of a raft of culinary awards, **Windows on the Water** (12 Chase Hill Rd., Kennebunk 04043, 207/967-3313 or 800/773-3313, www.windowsonthewater.com, 11:30 A.M.–2:30 P.M. and 5:30–9:30 P.M., to 10:30 P.M. Fri. and Sat.) has been filling its screened porch, patio, and dining rooms since 1985. It's appropriately named, with big windows providing views over nearby shops to the busy harbor. Lunch entrées are $9–17; dinner entrées are $19–39, the high end for such dishes as lobster ravioli and Thai lobster; and the White Porch Bistro (opens for dinner at 5 P.M.) serves pub-style fare. Best deals are the five-course lunch for $15 and the three-course dinner for $33; add $10 for a bottle of wine. Reservations are advisable—essential in midsummer.

Both the view and the food are outstanding at **Pier 77** (77 Pier Rd., Cape Porpoise, 207/967-8500, 11:30 A.M.–2:30 P.M. and 5–9 P.M. daily). Chef Peter and his wife, Kate, have created an especially welcoming restaurant, where the menu varies from duck three ways to seafood mixed grill (entrées $16–30). Frequent live entertainment provides nice background and complements the views over Cape Porpoise Harbor, with lobster boats hustling to and fro. Reservations are advisable. Practically hidden downstairs is **The Ramp Bar and Grille** (11:30 A.M.–10 P.M. daily), with lighter fare and a sports-pub decor.

## Destination Dining

One of Maine's biggest splurges is **The White Barn Inn** (37 Beach Ave., Kennebunkport, 207/967-2321, www.whitebarninn.com, 6–9 P.M. Mon.–Thurs., 5:30–9:15 P.M. Fri.–Sun.), with haute cuisine, haute prices, haute-rustic barn. In summer, don't be surprised to run into members of the senior George Bush clan (probably at the back window table). Soft piano music accompanies impeccable service and chef Jonathan Carter's outstanding four-course fixed-price menu ($92 pp, excluding wine). Reservations are essential—well ahead during July and August—and you'll need a credit card (cancel 24 hours ahead or you'll have a charge). No jeans or sneakers—jackets are required. It's New England's only four-star, five-diamond, Relais Gourmand restaurant. Closed early–late January.

## Lobster and Clams

**Nunan's Lobster Hut** (9 Mills Rd., Cape Porpoise, 207/967-4362, 5 P.M.–close daily) is an institution. Sure, other places might have better views, but this casual dockside eatery with indoor and outdoor seating has been serving lobsters since 1953.

Adjacent to the bridge connecting Kennebunkport's Dock Square to Kennebunk's Lower Village is another time-tested classic, the **Clam Shack** (Rte. 9, Kennebunkport, 207/967-2560, www.theclamshack.net). The tiny take-out stand serves perhaps the state's best lobster rolls, jam-packed with meat and available with either butter or mayo, and dee-lish fried clams. It opens at 11 A.M. daily May–October for lunch and dinner.

Bush-watchers often head to **Mabel's Lobster Claw** (Ocean Ave., Kennebunkport, 207/967-2562, 11:30 A.M.–3 P.M. and 5–9 P.M. daily), hoping to spot the former president (the little place is just around the corner from Walker's Point). Try Mabel Hanson's chowder or a lobster roll and see why the restaurant's a favorite (entrées top off around $30); reservations are wise.

## INFORMATION AND SERVICES
### Information

The Kennebunk and Kennebunkport Chamber of Commerce (17 Western Ave., Rte. 9, Lower Village, P.O. Box 740, Kennebunk 04043, 207/967-0857, www.visitthekennebunks.com) produces an excellent area guide to accommodations, restaurants, area maps, bike maps, tide calendars, recreation, and beach parking permits.

Check out Louis T. Graves Memorial Public Library (18 Maine St., Kennebunkport, 207/967-2778, www.graves.lib.me.us) or Kennebunk Free Library (112 Main St., 207/985-2173, kennebunklibrary.org).

## Public Restrooms

Public toilets are at Gooch's and Mother's Beaches and at St. Anthony's Monastery, the chamber of commerce building (17 Western Ave.), and at the chamber's Dock Square Hospitality Center.

## GETTING THERE AND AROUND

Amtrak's **Downeaster** (800/872-7245, www.thedowneaster.com) connects Boston's North Station with Portland, Maine, with stops in Wells, Saco, and Old Orchard Beach (seasonal).

**Vermont Transit** (800/552-8737, www.vermonttransit.com), a division of Greyhound bus lines, stops at the Wells Regional Transportation Center daily on the Boston–Portland–Bangor route. The trolley connects with the bus in season and stops in Kennebunk's Lower Village.

From Memorial Day to mid-October, the **Intown Trolley** (207/967-3686, www.intowntrolley.com) operates a 45-minute narrated sightseeing tour throughout Kennebunk and Kennebunkport, originating in Dock Square and making regular stops at beaches and other attractions. The entire route takes about 45 minutes, with the driver providing a hefty dose of local history and gossip. Seats are park bench–style. An all-day ticket is $13 adults, $6 children 3–14. You can get on or off at any stop. The trolley operates hourly 10 A.M.–5 P.M. in July and August, to 4 P.M. in spring and fall.

The free **Shoreline Explorer Kennebunk Shuttle** (www.shorelineexplorer.com) circulates hourly between Grove Street parking lot, Stop and Shop, Landing Store, Lower Village, and the beaches 10 A.M.–10:30 P.M. late June–Labor Day. It connects with the Shoreline and Intown trolleys.

SOUTHERN COAST

# Old Orchard Beach Area

Seven continuous miles of white sand beach has been drawing vacation-oriented folks for generations to the area stretching from Camp Ellis, in Saco, to Pine Point, in Scarborough. Cottage colonies and condo complexes dominate at the extremities, but the center of activity has always been and remains Old Orchard Beach.

In its heyday, Old Orchard Beach's pier reached far out into the sea, huge resort hotels lined the sands, and wealthy Victorian folk (including Rose Fitzgerald and Joe Kennedy, who met on these sands in the days when men strolled around in dress suits and women toted parasols) came each summer to see and be seen.

Storms and fires have taken their toll through the years, and the grand resorts have been replaced by endless motels, many of which display *Nous parlons Français* signs to welcome the masses of French Canadians who arrive each summer. They're accompanied by young families, who come for the sand and surf, and T-shirted and body-pierced young pleasure seekers, who come for the nightlife. (You'd better like people if you stop here, because this town welcomes tourists—the population expands from about 8,000 in winter to about 100,000 in midsummer.)

Although some residents are pushing gentrification, and a few projects are pushing it in that direction, Old Orchard Beach remains somewhat honky-tonk, and most of its visitors would have it no other way. French fries, cotton candy, and beach-accessories shops line the downtown, and as you get closer to the pier, you pass arcades and amusement parks. There's not a kid on earth who wouldn't have fun in Old Orchard—even if some parents might find it all a bit much.

Much more sedate are the villages on the fringes. The **Ocean Park** section of Old Orchard, at the southwestern end of town, was established in 1881 as a religious summer-cottage community. It still offers interdenominational services and vacation Bible school, but it also has an active cultural association that sponsors concerts, Chautauqua-type lectures, films, and other events throughout the summer. All are open to the public.

South of that is **Camp Ellis.** Begun as a small fishing village named after early settler Thomas Ellis, Camp Ellis is crowded with longtime summer homes that are in a constant battle with the sea. A nearly mile-long granite jetty—designed to keep silt from clogging the Saco River—has taken the blame for massive beach erosion since constructed. But the jetty is a favorite spot for wetting a line (no fishing license needed) and for panoramic views off toward Wood Island Light (built in 1808) and Biddeford Pool. Camp Ellis Beach is open to the public, with lifeguards on duty in midsummer. Parking—scarce on hot days—is $10 a day.

As you head north from Old Orchard you'll pass **Pine Point,** another longtime community of vacation homes. Services are few and parking is $10 a day.

Most folks get to Old Orchard by passing through **Saco** and **Biddeford,** which have long been upstairs/downstairs sister cities, with wealthy mill owners living in Saco and their workers (and workplaces) in Biddeford. But even those personalities have always been split—congested, commercial Route 1 is part of Saco, and the exclusive enclave of Biddeford Pool is, of course, in below-stairs Biddeford. Saco still has an attractive downtown, with boutiques and stunning homes on Main Street and beyond.

Blue-collar Biddeford is working hard to change its milltown image. It's home to the magnificent Biddeford City Theater and the University of New England, and as a Main Street community, it's getting a much-needed sprucing up. New shops and restaurants are balancing the numerous thrift shops downtown, and artisans and woodworkers are filling vacant mills. Another Biddeford hallmark is its Franco American tradition—thanks to the French-speaking workers who sustained the textile and shoemaking industries in the 19th century. Never is the heritage more evident than during Biddeford's annual La Kermesse festival in late June.

## SIGHTS

Founded in 1866, the **Saco Museum** (371 Main St., Saco, 207/283-3861, www.dyerlibrarysacomuseum.org, noon–4 P.M. Tues.–Sun., to 8 P.M. Thurs., $4 adults, $3 seniors, $2 students) rotates selections from its outstanding collection, including 18th- and 19th-century paintings, furniture, and other household treasures. Lectures, workshops, and concerts are also part of the annual schedule. Admission is free after 4 P.M. Thursday.

## PARKS AND PRESERVES

Saco Bay Trails, a local land trust, has produced a very helpful trail guide that includes the Saco Heath, the East Point Sanctuary, and more than a dozen other local trails. The Cascade Falls trail, for example, is a half-mile stroll ending at a waterfall. Copies are available for $5 at a number of Biddeford and Saco locations (including the Dyer Library) or from Saco Bay Trails (P.O. Box 7505, Ocean Park 04063). Trail information is also on the organization's website: www.sacobaytrails.org.

## ◖ East Point Sanctuary

Owned by Maine Audubon, the 30-acre East Point Sanctuary is a splendid preserve at the eastern end of Biddeford Pool. Crashing surf, beach roses, bayberry bushes, and offshore Wood Island Light are all features of the two-part perimeter trail here—skirting the golf course of the exclusive Abenakee Club. Allow at least an hour; even in fog, the setting is dramatic. During spring and fall migrations, it's one of southern Maine's prime birding locales, so you'll have plenty of company if you show up then, and the usual streetside parking may be scarce. It's open sunrise–sundown all year. It's poorly signposted (perhaps deliberately?), so here are the directions: From Route 9 (Main St.) in downtown Biddeford, take Route 9/208 (Pool Rd.) southeast about five miles to the

Route 208 turnoff to Biddeford Pool. Go 0.6 mile on Route 208 (Bridge Rd.), and then left onto Mile Stretch Road. Continue to Lester B. Orcutt Boulevard, turn left, and go to the end. For further information, contact Maine Audubon (20 Gilsland Farm Rd., P.O. Box 6009, Falmouth 04105, 207/781-2330).

### The Heath

Owned by The Nature Conservancy, 870-acre **Saco Heath Preserve** is the nation's southernmost "raised coalesced bog," where peat accumulated through eons into two above-water dome shapes that eventually merged into a single natural feature. For a bit of esoterica, it's the home of the rare Hessel's hairstreak butterfly. Pick up a map at the parking area and follow the mile-long, self-guided trail through the woods and then into the heath via a boardwalk. Best time to come is early–mid-October, when the heath and woodland colors are positively brilliant and insects are on the wane. You're likely to see deer and perhaps even spot a moose. The preserve entrance is on Route 112, Buxton Road, two miles west of I-95. Open all year, sunrise–sunset, it's also popular with snowshoers and cross-country skiers in winter.

### Ferry Beach State Park

When the weather's hot, arrive early at Ferry Beach State Park (Bay View Rd., off Rte. 9, Saco, 207/283-0067, $3 adults, $1 children 5–11, free for seniors and kids under 5), a pristine beach backed by dune grass on Saco Bay. In the 117-acre park are changing rooms, restrooms, lifeguard, picnic tables, and five easy interconnected nature trails winding through woodlands, marshlands, and dunes. (Later in the day, keep the insect repellent handy.) It's open daily, late May–late September, but accessible all year. (Trail markers are removed in winter.)

## RECREATION
### Golf

Opened in 1922 as a nine-hole course, the **Biddeford-Saco Country Club** (101 Old

# AMUSEMENT PARKS AND AMUSING PLACES

If you've got kids or just love amusement parks, you'll find Maine's best in the Old Orchard area, where sand and sun just seem to complement arcades and rides perfectly.

The biggie is **Funtown/Splashtown USA** (774 Portland Rd., Rte. 1, Saco, 207/284-5139 or 800/878-2900, www.funtownsplashtownusa.com). Ride Maine's only wooden roller coaster; fly down New England's longest and tallest log flume ride; free fall 200 feet on Dragon's Descent; get wet and go wild riding speed slides, tunnel slides, raft slides, and river slides or splashing in the pool. Add a huge kiddie ride section, games, food, and other activities for a full day or family fun. Funtown opens weekends in early May, Splashtown in mid-June; everything's up and running daily late June–Labor Day, when Funtown is open 10 A.M.–9 P.M., to 10 P.M. Saturday, and Splashtown 10 A.M.–6 P.M. Rates vary by height, with Big for those 48 inches and taller, Little for those 38–48 inches tall and seniors, and free for kids less than 38 inches tall. A Funtown USA Ride Pass provides two rides on the Grand Prix Racers and unlimited use of all other rides for $25 Big, $17 Little, and a night special valid after 5 P.M. is $18 Big and $12 Little. A Splashtown unlimited slide pass is $20 Big and $17 Little. Combo passes for two rides on the Grand Prix Racers and unlimited use of all other rides, slides, and pools, is $34 Big and $25 Little. Season passes also are available.

Three miles north of Funtown/Splashtown USA, **Aquaboggan Water Park** (980 Portland Rd., Rte. 1, Saco, 207/282-3112, www.aquabogganwaterpark.com) is wet and wild, with such stomach turners as the Yankee Ripper, the Suislide, and the Stealth, with an almost-vertical drop of 45 feet – enough to accelerate to 30 mph on the descent. Wear a bathing suit that won't abandon you in the rough-and-tumble. Also, if you wear glasses, safety straps and plastic lenses are required. Besides all the water stuff, there are shuffleboard courts, minigolf, an arcade, picnic tables, and snack bars. Lots of ticket options cover varying numbers of attractions. You can pay as you go, one attraction at a time, but it adds up quickly; Mondays and Fridays are $10 for the day. It's open 10 A.M.–6 P.M. daily late June–Labor Day.

The biggest beachfront amusement park, **Palace Playland** (1 Old Orchard St., Old Orchard, 207/934-2001, www.palaceplayland.com) has more than 25 rides and attractions packed into four acres, including a giant water slide, fun house, bumper cars, Ferris wheel, roller coaster, and a 24,000-square-foot arcade with more than 200 games. For a bird's-eye view of the area, ride the 75-foot-high gondola Sunwheel. Get soaked riding the Log Flume. Rev up the action on two roller coasters, one with a five-story drop, both with high-speed twisting turns. Kiddie Land has more than a dozen rides, including a fun house and a splashing whale. An unlimited pass is $26.50 per day; a kiddie pass good for all two-ticket rides is $19.50; two-day, season, and per ride tickets ($2–4) are available. Open Memorial Day–Labor Day.

**The Old Orchard Pier,** jutting 475 feet into the ocean from downtown, is a minimall of shops, arcades, and fast-food outlets. Far longer when it was built in 1898, it's been lopped off gradually by fires and storms. The current incarnation has been here since the late 1970s.

Old-time amusements are still a big draw in Old Orchard Beach.

© HILARY NANGLE

Orchard Rd., Saco, 207/282-5883) added a back nine in 1987 (toughest hole on the par-71 course is the 11th). Tee times not usually needed. Fees are moderate.

Covering more than 300 acres is the challenging 18-hole, par-71 **Dunegrass Golf Club** (200 Wild Dunes Way, Old Orchard Beach, 207/934-4513 or 800/521-1029). Greens fees are a bit steep, but well worth a splurge. Tee times are essential. The sprawling modern clubhouse has a restaurant and pro shop.

## Sea Kayaking

**Gone with the Wind** (Yates St., Biddeford Pool, 207/283-8446, www.gwtwonline.com) offers two tours, afternoon and sunset, with prices varying with the number of people on the tour (two people are about $85 pp). Wetsuits are supplied. The most popular trip is to Beach Island. Also available are rentals ($40 half day, $60 full day). Kids and seniors get a $10 pp discount.

## Surfing

A seasonal branch of **Aquaholics Surf Shop** (www.aquaholicsurf.com) rents surfboards, bodyboards, wetsuits, and related gear from a kiosk next to the pier and Palace Playland.

## ENTERTAINMENT
### Biddeford City Theater

Designed by noted architect John Calvin Stevens in 1896, the 500-seat National Historic Register Biddeford City Theater (205 Main St., P.O. Box 993, Biddeford 04005, 207/282-0849, www.citytheater.org) has been superbly restored, and acoustics are excellent even when Eva Gray, the resident ghost, mixes it up backstage. A respected community theater group mounts a winter drama season and showcases other talent throughout the year. Check local papers or call for schedule.

## Fireworks

Fireworks are set off by the pier in Old Orchard Beach at 9:45 P.M. every Thursday late June–Labor Day.

## Live Music and Performances

You'll find plenty of it in Old Orchard Beach at places including **Pier Patio Pub, Village Inn, PICS Pizza,** and **Surf 6.** In Biddeford, there's live music at **Bebe's Burritos** (140 Main St., 207/283-4222, www.bebesburritos.com) 7–10:30 P.M. every Thursday, Friday, and Saturday.

**Free concerts** are staged by the pier at 7 P.M. every Monday and Tuesday in July and August.

Another option for family concerts and other performances is the **Old Orchard Beach Pavilion** (Union Ave. and 6th St., 207/934-2024, www.oobpavilion.org).

Ocean Park's **Temple,** a 19th-century octagon that seats 800-plus, is the venue for Sunday-night concerts (7:30 P.M., $8 adults) and many other programs throughout the summer.

## EVENTS

**La Kermesse** (meaning the fair or the festival) is Biddeford's summer highlight, when nearly 50,000 visitors pour into town on the last full weekend in June (Thurs.–Sun.) to celebrate the town's Franco American heritage. Local volunteers go all out to plan block parties, a parade, games, carnival, live entertainment, and traditional dancing—most of it centered on Biddeford's Waterhouse Field. Then there's *la cuisine franco-américaine;* you can fill up on *boudin, creton, poutine, tourtière, tarte au saumon,* and crepes (although your arteries may rebel).

Generally scheduled for the Saturday of the same weekend, the **Saco Sidewalk Arts Festival** involves more than 150 artists exhibiting their work all along Saco's Main Street. Strolling musicians, kids' activities, and food booths are all part of the well-organized, daylong event.

In July, the parishioners of St. Demetrios Greek Orthodox Church (186 Bradley St., Saco, 207/284-5651) go all out to mount the annual **Greek Heritage Festival,** a three-day extravaganza of homemade Greek food, traditional Greek music and dancing, and a craft fair. Be sure to tour the impressive $1.5 million domed church building.

Football fans might want to watch the annual **Shriner's Lobster Bowl,** an all-star high school football game to benefit Shriner's Hospitals for Children.

The beaches come to life in July. Early July brings the annual **parade and Sandcastle Contest** to Ocean Park.

One weekend in mid-August, Old Orchard Beach's **Beach Olympics** is a family festival of games, exhibitions, and music benefiting Maine's Special Olympics program.

## ACCOMMODATIONS

The area has hundreds of beds—mostly in motel-style lodgings. The chamber of commerce is the best resource for motels, cottages, and the area's more than 3,000 campsites. Only recently have a few B&Bs popped up.

**The Old Orchard Beach Inn** (6 Portland Ave., Old Orchard Beach, 207/934-5834 or 877/700-6624, fax 207/934-0782, www.oldorchardbeachinn.com, $110–185) was rescued from ruin by owner Steve Cecchetti and opened in summer 2000. Built in 1730, and most recently known as the Staples Inn, the National Historic Register building seemed destined for the wrecker's ball in 1997. Now it's been transformed, with 18 antiques-filled rooms with air-conditioning, phones, and TV. Continental breakfast is included in the rates; a two-bedroom suite is $250–400. Open all year.

Practically next door is **The Atlantic Birches Inn** (20 Portland Ave., Rte. 98, P.O. Box 334, Old Orchard Beach 04064, 207/934-5295 or 888/934-5295), with 10 guest rooms with air-conditioning in a Victorian house and separate cottage. Breakfast is hearty continental, and there's a swimming pool. The beach is an easy walk. Rates run $101–131 d. It's open all year, but call ahead off-season.

Look out to sea from the porch or deck of **Cristina's Bed and Breakfast** (36 Main Ave., Camp Ellis Beach, Saco, 207/282-7483, trahan@prexar.com, $75–135), Cristina and Paul Trahan's vintage gingerbread-trimmed cottage with three pleasant guest rooms (one with private bath), all with Victorian furnishings. Rates include continental breakfast. No credit cards.

Brand spanking new and adjacent to the pier is the **Grand Victorian** (1 East Grand Ave., Old Orchard Beach, 207/934-0759, www.grandvictorianwaterfront.com), with oceanfront condominiums available for the week. Rates begin around $2,000 for a one-bedroom sleeping five. On-site are an indoor heated pool, fitness room, sauna, and spa.

## FOOD
### Old Orchard Beach

Dining is not Old Orchard's strong point. Nicest (although service and quality are inconsistent) is **Joseph's by the Sea** (55 W. Grand Ave., Old Orchard Beach, 207/934-5044, www.josephsbythesea.com, 7–11 A.M. and 5–9 P.M. daily), a quiet, shorefront restaurant amid all the hoopla. Request a table on the screened patio. The menu—French with a dash of Maine—has entrées in the $18–30 range. Reservations advisable in midsummer.

Immerse yourself in a Victorian manor at **Landmark** (28 E. Grand Ave., Old Orchard Beach, 207/934-0156, 5–8 P.M., to 9 P.M. Fri. and Sat.). Ornate tin ceilings, shining wood floors, and paintings distinguish the dining areas, which include an enclosed porch. Entrées ($19–22) vary from Parmesan haddock to lacquered duck; a kid's menu is available. Early-bird specials are served until 6 P.M.

### Camp Ellis

Two well-seasoned family restaurants service Camp Ellis. **Wormwood's Restaurant** (16 Bay Ave., Camp Ellis Beach, Saco, 207/282-9679, 11:30 A.M.–9 P.M.), next to the stone jetty, still draws the crowds and keeps its loyal clientele happy with ample portions and $6–16 entrées. Cajun-style seafood is a specialty.

At **Huot's Seafood Restaurant** (Camp Ellis Beach, Saco, 207/282-1642, www.huotsseafoodrestaurant.com, 11 A.M.–9 P.M. Tues.–Sun.), portions are large, prices are not.

### Saco

Craving fast-ish food? The Camire family operates Maine's best home-grown option, **Rapid Ray's** (189 Main St., 207/283-4222, www.rapidrays.biz, 11 A.M.–12:30 A.M. Mon.–Thurs., to 1:30 A.M. Fri. and Sat., and noon–10 P.M. Sun.). Burgers, dogs, and fried foods are the specialty at the standing-room only joint.

For more leisurely dining, book a reservation at **Mia's** (17 Pepperell Square, Saco, 207/284-6427, www.miasatpepperellsquare.com, 11 A.M.–2 P.M. and 5:30–9:30 P.M. Tues.–Sat., 9 A.M.–2 P.M. Sun.), where chef-owner Steve Rogers prepares classic fare without fuss. Dinner entrées, such as filet mignon and seared duck breast, run $17–25.

### Biddeford/Biddeford Pool

For a town grounded in Franco American culture, Biddeford has an expanding array of ethnic choices, including a few that garner praise far beyond city limits: **Jewel of India** (26 Alfred St., 207/282-5600), the Vietnamese **Que Huong** (49 Main St., 207/571-8050), **Thai Siam** (144 Main St., 207/294-3300), and **Bebe's Burritos** (140 Main St., 207/283-4222), all serving lunch and dinner.

**Buffleheads** (122 Hills Beach Rd., 207/284-6000, www.buffleheadsrestaurant.com) is a family dining find with spectacular ocean views. Ray and Karen Wieczoreck opened the restaurant in 1994 and have built a strong local following through the years. The kids can munch on pizza, burgers, spaghetti, and other favorites while adults savor well-prepared seafood with a homestyle spin or landlubber classics. Lobster pie and a turkey dinner with all the trimmings are both perennial favorites here. Prices range $6–25. It's open 11:30 A.M.–2 P.M. and 5–8:30 P.M. daily, closed Monday off-season. Hills Beach Road branches off Route 9 at the University of New England campus.

Take your lobster or fried seafood dinner to an oceanfront picnic table on the grassy lawn behind **F. O. Goldthwaite's** (3 Lester B. Orcott Blvd., Biddeford Pool, 207/284-8872, 11 A.M.–7:30 P.M. daily), an old-fashioned general store. Salads, fried seafood, sandwiches (grilled salmon BLT!), and kid-friendly fare round out the menu ($3–15).

## INFORMATION AND SERVICES

Sources of tourist information are Biddeford-Saco Chamber of Commerce and Industry (110 Main St., Saco 04072, 207/282-1567, fax 207/282-3149, www.biddefordsacochamber. org), Old Orchard Beach Chamber of Commerce (1st St., P.O. Box 600, Old Orchard Beach 04064, 207/934-2500 or 800/365-9386, www.oldorchardbeachmaine.com), and Ocean Park Association (P.O. Box 7296, Ocean Park 04063, 207/934-9068, www.oceanpark.org).

The Dyer Library (371 Main St., Saco 04072, 207/282-3031, www.sacomuseum.org), next door to the Saco Museum, attracts scads of genealogists to its vast Maine history collection. Also check out Libby Memorial Library (Staples St., Old Orchard Beach, 207/934-4351, www.ooblibrary.org).

## GETTING THERE

Amtrak's **Downeaster** (800/872-7245, www.thedowneaster.com) connects Boston's North Station with Portland, Maine, with stops in Wells, Saco, and Old Orchard Beach (seasonal).

## GETTING AROUND
### Bus and Trolley

The **Biddeford-Saco-Old Orchard Beach Transit Committee** (207/282-5408, www.shuttlebus-zoom.com) operates three systems that make getting around simple. Between late June and Labor Day, the **Old Orchard Beach Trolley** operates on a regular schedule, connecting restaurants and campgrounds. Service begins at 10 A.M. and ends at midnight. Cost is $1 per ride; children under five ride free. **ShuttleBus Tri-Town Service** provides frequent weekday and less-frequent weekend service (except national holidays) between Biddeford, Saco, and Old Orchard Beach. One-way fare is $1.25 ages five and older, exact change required. **ShuttleBus InterCity Service** connects Biddeford, Saco, and Old Orchard with Portland, South Portland, and Scarborough. Fares vary by zones, topping at $5 for anyone over five.

# GREATER PORTLAND

Whenever national magazines have articles highlighting the 10 best places to live, Greater Portland often makes the list. The very reasons that make the area so popular with residents make it equally attractive to visitors. Small in size, but big in heart, Greater Portland entices visitors with the staples—lighthouses, lobster, and L. L. Bean—but wows them with everything else it offers. It's the state's cultural hub, with performing arts centers, numerous festivals, and varied museums; a dining destination, with nationally recognized chefs as well as an amazing assortment and variety of everyday restaurants; and despite its urban environment, it has a mind-boggling amount of recreational opportunities.

Portland's population hovers around 65,000, but when the suburbs are included, it climbs to nearly a quarter of a million souls, making it Maine's largest, by far. Take a swing through the bedroom communities of Scarborough, Cape Elizabeth, and South Portland, and you'll better understand the area's popularity: easily accessible parks, beaches, rocky ledges, and lighthouses, all minutes from downtown. Then head north, passing through suburban Falmouth and Yarmouth and into Freeport, home of mega–sports retailer L. L. Bean. If you look carefully during your travels through suburbia, you'll still see the vestiges of the region's heritage: sailboats and lobster boats, traps and buoys piled on lawns or along driveways and, tucked here and there, farms with farmstands brimming with fresh produce.

Greater Portland also marks a transitional point on Maine's coastline. The long sand

© TOM NANGLE

# HIGHLIGHTS

**The Old Port:** Plan to spend at least a couple of hours browsing the shops, dining, and enjoying the energy of this restored historic district (page 91).

**Portland Museum of Art (PMA):** This museum houses works by masters such as Winslow Homer, John Marin, Andrew Wyeth, Edward Hopper, and Marsden Hartley, as well as works by Monet, Picasso, and Renoir (page 92).

**Victoria Mansion:** This house is considered one of the most richly decorated dwellings of its period remaining in the country (page 93).

**Portland Observatory:** Climb the 103 steps to the orb deck of the only remaining maritime signal tower on the Eastern Seaboard, and you'll be rewarded with views from the White Mountains to Casco Bay's islands (page 93).

**Portland Head Light:** This lighthouse, commissioned by President George Washington, is fabulously sited on the rocky ledges of Cape Elizabeth (page 97).

**Casco Bay Tour:** Take a three-hour tour on the mailboat, which stops briefly at five islands en route (page 97).

**Lobstering Cruise:** Go out on a working lobster boat in Portland Harbor, see the sights, and perhaps return with a lobster for dinner (page 101).

**L. L. Bean:** The empire's flagship store is in Freeport, and no trip to this shopping mecca is complete without a visit (page 116).

LOOK FOR �({ TO FIND RECOMMENDED SIGHTS, ACTIVITIES, DINING, AND LODGING.

**L. L. Bean Outdoor Discovery Schools:** Don't miss the opportunity for an inexpensive introduction to a new sport (page 120).

**Atlantic Seal Cruises:** Cruise with Captain Tom Ring to Eagle Island, once home to Arctic explorer Admiral Robert Peary (page 120).

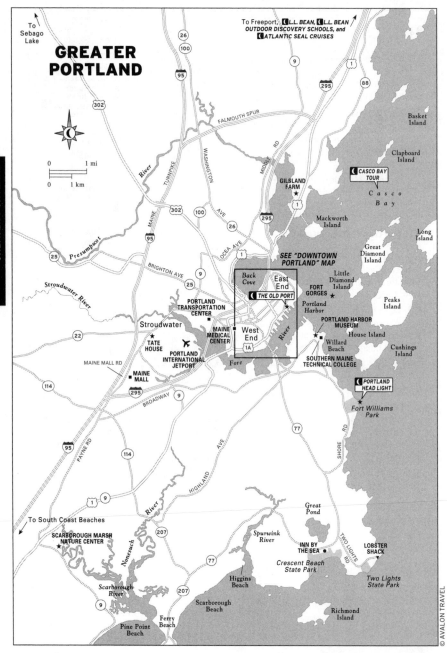

# GREATER PORTLAND

To Sebago Lake

To Freeport, **L.L. BEAN**, **L.L. BEAN** *OUTDOOR DISCOVERY SCHOOLS*, and **ATLANTIC SEAL CRUISES**

0    1 mi
0    1 km

FALMOUTH SPUR

GILSLAND FARM

**CASCO BAY TOUR**

*Casco Bay*

Basket Island

Clapboard Island

Mackworth Island

Long Island

Great Diamond Island

*Presumpscot*

*Stroudwater River*

Stroudwater

SEE "DOWNTOWN PORTLAND" MAP

Back Cove

East End

**THE OLD PORT**

West End

FORT GORGES

Little Diamond Island

Peaks Island

Portland Harbor

*Portland River*

**PORTLAND HARBOR MUSEUM**

House Island

Cushings Island

PORTLAND TRANSPORTATION CENTER

MAINE MEDICAL CENTER

TATE HOUSE

PORTLAND INTERNATIONAL JETPORT

MAINE MALL RD

**MAINE MALL**

BRIGHTON AVE

MAINE MALL RD

*Fore*

Willard Beach

**SOUTHERN MAINE TECHNICAL COLLEGE**

**PORTLAND HEAD LIGHT**

Fort Williams Park

BROADWAY

HIGHLAND AVE

SHORE RD

To South Coast Beaches

**SCARBOROUGH MARSH NATURE CENTER**

*Nonesuch River*

Great Pond

Spurwink River

**INN BY THE SEA**

**LOBSTER SHACK**

TWO LIGHTS RD

*Crescent Beach State Park*

*Two Lights State Park*

Higgins Beach

*Scarborough River*

Scarborough Beach

Pine Point Beach

Ferry Beach

Richmond Island

© AVALON TRAVEL

beaches of the Southern Coast begin to give way to a different coastline, one dotted with islands and edged with a jumble of rocks and ledges interrupted by rivers and coves.

While it might seem tempting to dismiss Portland in favor of seeking the Real Maine elsewhere along the coast, the truth is, the Real Maine is here. And while Portland alone provides plenty to keep a visitor busy, it's also an excellent base for day trips to places such as the Kennebunks, Freeport, Brunswick, and Bath, where more of that Real Maine flavor awaits.

## PLANNING YOUR TIME

July and August are the most popular times to visit, but Greater Portland is a year-round destination. Spring truly arrives by mid-May, when most summer outfitters begin operations at least on weekends. September is perhaps the loveliest month of the year weatherwise, and by mid-October, those fabled New England maples are turning crimson. No matter when you visit, pack layered clothing. Damp, foggy mornings can quickly give way to warm sunshine. Truly, there are usually only a handful of days each summer when folks wish they had an air conditioner, but for those days, you'll want to dress accordingly. A light sweater, fleece, or windbreaker is always handy when a sea breeze kicks up or after the sun sets.

To do the region justice, you'll want to spend at least three or four days here, more if your plans call for using Greater Portland as a base for day trips to more distant points. You can easily kill two days alone in downtown Portland, what with all the shops, museums, historical sites, waterfront, and neighborhoods to explore. If you're staying in town and are an avid walker, you won't need a car to get to the in-town must-see sights.

You will need a car to reach beyond the city. Allow a full day for a leisurely tour through South Portland and Cape Elizabeth and on to Prouts Neck in Scarborough.

Rabid shoppers should either stay in Freeport or allow at least a day for L. L. Bean's and the 100 or so outlets nearby. If you're traveling with a supershopper, don't despair. Freeport has parks and preserves that are light-years removed from the frenzy of its downtown, and from the fishing village of South Freeport, you can take an excursion boat to Eagle Island, home of Arctic explorer Admiral Peary. Really, you simply must get out on the water, whether from Portland's waterfront or from South Freeport. Hop a ferry to one of the islands of Casco Bay, take an evening sail, an excursion to Eagle Island, or even a paddle around the islands in a kayak.

## HISTORY

Portland's downtown, a crooked-finger peninsula projecting into Casco Bay and today defined vaguely by I-295 at its "knuckle," was named Machigonne (Great Neck) by the Wabanaki, the Native Americans who held sway when English settlers first arrived in 1632. Characteristically, the Brits renamed the region Falmouth (it included present-day Falmouth, Portland, South Portland, Westbrook, and Cape Elizabeth) and the peninsula Falmouth Neck, but it was 130 years before they secured real control of the area. Anglo-French squabbles, spurred by the governments' conflicts in Europe, drew in the Wabanaki from Massachusetts to Nova Scotia. Falmouth was only one of the battlegrounds, and it was a fairly minor one. Relative calm resumed in the 1760s, only to be broken by the stirrings of rebellion centered on Boston. When Falmouth's citizens expressed support for the incipient revolution, the punishment was a 1775 naval onslaught that wiped out 75 percent of the houses—a debacle that created a decade-long setback. In 1786, Falmouth Neck became Portland, a thriving trading community where shipping flourished until the 1807 imposition of the Embargo Act. Severing trade and effectively shutting down Portland Harbor for a year and a half, the legislation did more harm to America's fledgling colonies than to the French and British it was designed to punish.

In 1820, when Maine became a state, Portland was named its capital. The city became a crucial transportation hub with the arrival of the railroad. The Civil War was barely a blip in

Portland's history, but the year after it ended, the city suffered a devastating blow: exuberant Fourth of July festivities in 1866 sparked a conflagration that virtually leveled the city. The Great Fire spared only the Portland Observatory and a chunk of the West End. Evidence of the city's Victorian rebirth remains today in many downtown neighborhoods.

After World War II, Portland slipped into decline for several years, but that is over. The city's waterfront revival began in the 1970s and continues today, despite commercial competition from South Portland's Maine Mall; Congress Street has blossomed as an arts and retail district; public green space is increasing; and an influx of immigrants is changing the city's cultural makeup. With the new century, Portland is on a roll.

# Portland

Often compared to San Francisco (an oft-cited, unchallenged, but never verified statistic boasts it has more restaurants per capita than any city but San Francisco), Portland is small, friendly, and easily explored on foot—although at times, it may seem that no matter which direction you head, it's uphill. The heart of Portland is the peninsula jutting into Casco Bay. It's bordered by the Eastern and Western Promenades, Back Cove, and the working waterfront. Salty sea breezes cool summer days and make winter ones seen even chillier. Unlike that other city by the bay, snow frequently blankets Portland from December into March.

Portland is Maine's most ethnically diverse city, with active refugee resettlement programs and dozens of languages spoken in the schools. Although salty sailors can still be found along the waterfront, Portland is increasingly a professional community, with young, upwardly mobile residents spiffing up Victorian houses and infusing new energy and money into the city's neighborhoods.

The region's cultural hub, Portland has a striking art museum housing three centuries of art and architecture and a world-class permanent collection, performing arts centers, active historical and preservation groups, an art school and a university, a symphony orchestra, numerous galleries, coffeehouses, and enough activities to keep culture vultures busy well into the night, especially in the thriving, handsomely restored Old Port and the up-and-coming Arts District.

Portland's also a sports- and outdoor-lovers' playground, with trails for running, biking, skating, and cross-country skiing, watersports aplenty, and a beloved minor league baseball team, the Sea Dogs. When city folks desire to escape, they often hop a ferry for one of the islands of Casco Bay or head to one of the parks, preserves, or beaches in the suburbs.

Still, Portland remains a major seaport. Lobster boats, commercial fishing vessels, long-distance passenger boats, cruise ships, and local ferries dominate the working waterfront, and the briny scent of the sea—or bait—seasons the air.

## PORTLAND NEIGHBORHOODS

The best way to appreciate the character of Portland's neighborhoods is on foot. So much of Portland can (and should) be covered on foot that it would take a book to list all the possibilities, but several dedicated volunteer groups have produced guides to facilitate the process.

**Greater Portland Landmarks** (207/774-5561, www.portlandlandmarks.org) is the doyenne, founded in 1964 to preserve Portland's historic architecture and promote responsible construction. The organization has published more than a dozen books and booklets, including *Discover Historic Portland on Foot*, a packet of four well-researched walking-tour guides to architecturally historic sections of Portland's peninsula: Old Port, Western Promenade, State Street, and Congress Street. It's available for $5.95 at local bookstores, some gift shops,

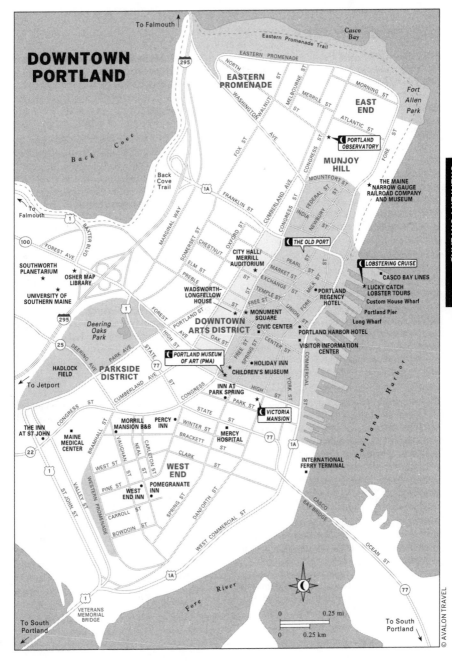

# DOWNTOWN PORTLAND

To Falmouth

Casco Bay

Eastern Promenade Trail

EASTERN PROMENADE

EASTERN PROMENADE

NORTH ST

Fort Allen Park

EAST END

MORNING ST

ATLANTIC ST

★ ☾ PORTLAND OBSERVATORY

MUNJOY HILL

MOUNTFORT ST

★ THE MAINE NARROW GAUGE RAILROAD COMPANY AND MUSEUM

Back Cove

To Falmouth

Back Cove Trail

FRANKLIN ST

MARGINAL WAY

FOX ST

WASHINGTON/WALNUT AVE

CUMBERLAND AVE

CONGRESS ST

FEDERAL ST

INDIA ST

NEWBURY ST

FORE ST

SOMERSET ST

CHESTNUT ST

OXFORD ST

☾ THE OLD PORT

ELM ST

PREBLE ST

WADSWORTH-LONGFELLOW HOUSE

CITY HALL/ MERRILL AUDITORIUM

PEARL ST

MARKET ST

EXCHANGE ST

TEMPLE ST

FREE ST

UNION ST

FORE ST

MIDDLE ST

1ST ST

☾ LOBSTERING CRUISE

■ CASCO BAY LINES

■ LUCKY CATCH LOBSTER TOURS

Custom House Wharf

PORTLAND REGENCY HOTEL

Portland Pier

Long Wharf

DOWNTOWN ARTS DISTRICT

PORTLAND ST

FOREST AVE

HIGH ST

OAK ST

MONUMENT SQUARE

CIVIC CENTER

CENTER ST

MARKET ST

PORTLAND HARBOR HOTEL

VISITOR INFORMATION CENTER

☾ PORTLAND MUSEUM OF ART (PMA)

77

FREE ST

SPRING ST

●HOLIDAY INN

CHILDREN'S MUSEUM

HIGH ST

YORK ST

COMMERCIAL ST

Portland Harbor

PARKSIDE DISTRICT

Deering Oaks Park

HADLOCK FIELD

PARK AVE

STATE ST

CUMBERLAND AVE

CONGRESS ST

INN AT PARK SPRING

PARK ST ★

STATE ST

★ ☾ VICTORIA MANSION

77

1A

To Jetport

THE INN AT ST JOHN

CONGRESS ST

MAINE MEDICAL CENTER

BRAMHALL ST

MORRILL MANSION B&B ●

PERCY INN

VAUGHAN ST

NEAL ST

CARLETON ST

WINTER ST

BRACKETT ST

CLARK ST

● MERCY HOSPITAL

International Ferry Terminal

22

WEST ST

PINE ST

● WEST END INN

POMEGRANATE INN

WEST END

SPRING ST

DANFORTH ST

WESTERN PROMENADE

ST JOHN ST

CARROLL ST

BOWDOIN ST

WEST COMMERCIAL ST

VALLEY ST

CASCO BAY BRIDGE

OCEAN ST

SOUTHWORTH PLANETARIUM ★

OSHER MAP LIBRARY ★

UNIVERSITY OF SOUTHERN MAINE ★

FOREST AVE

BAXTER BLVD

100

1A

1

295

25

1

To South Portland

VETERANS MEMORIAL BRIDGE

1

Fore River

0        0.25 mi

0        0.25 km

To South Portland

77

© AVALON TRAVEL

# CASCO BAY ISLANDS

Casco Bay is dotted with so many islands that an early explorer thought there must be at least one for every day of the year and so dubbed them the Calendar Islands. Truthfully, there aren't quite that many, even if you count all the ledges that appear at low tide. No matter, the islands are as much a part of Portland life as the Old Port.

Casco Bay Lines is the islands' lifeline, providing car and passenger service daily in summer. Perhaps the best way to see the highlights is aboard the daily mail-boat run. Indeed, on hot days, it may seem as if half the city's population is hopping a ferry to enjoy the cool breezes and calming views.

## PEAKS ISLAND

Peaks Island is a mere 20-minute ferry ride from downtown Portland, so it's no surprise that it has the largest year-round population. Historically a popular vacation spot – two lodges were built for Civil War veterans – it's now an increasingly popular suburb.

Although you can walk the island's perimeter in 3-4 hours, the best way to see it is to take a bike ($5 extra on the ferry) and pedal around clockwise. It can take less than an hour to do the five-mile island circuit, but plan on relaxing on the beach, savoring the views, and visiting the museums. Rental bikes are available on the island from Brad Burkholder at **Brad's and Wyatt's Bike Shop** (115 Island Ave., Peaks Island, 207/766-5631, about $20/day, hourly rental available, 10 A.M.-6 P.M.).

Another way to see the island is on a golf-cart tour with **Island Tours** (207/653-2549, islandtours@att.net, $15 adults, $12 seniors, $8 child), which offers a variety of 90-minute island tours as well as one-hour sunset tours ($10 adults, $8 seniors, $5 child). Admission to the Fifth Maine Regiment Museum is included in longer tours.

Civil War buffs have two museums worth a visit. The **Fifth Maine Regiment Center** (45 Seashore Ave., Peaks Island, 207/766-3330, www.fifthmainemuseum.org, 11 A.M.-4 P.M. daily July 1-Labor Day, to 5 P.M. weekends late May-July 1 and early Sept.-mid-Oct., $5 donation requested), a Queen Anne-style cottage built by Civil War veterans in 1888, now houses exhibits on the war and island history. Just a few steps away is the **Eighth Maine Regimental Memorial** (13 Eighth Maine Ave., Peaks Island, 207/766-5086, noon-3 P.M. Tues.-Sat. July 1-early Sept., $5 donation requested). Tours detail the building's fascinating history and its collection of artifacts pertaining to the Eighth Maine as well as material on the island, World War II, and more. Rustic lodging is available.

Another museum perhaps worthy of a visit just for its quirkiness is the **Umbrella Cover Museum** (207/766-4496), where owner Nancy 3. Hoffman (yes, 3) displays her collection.

Hungry? **The Cockeyed Gull** (78 Island Ave., 207/766-2880, www.cockeyedgull.com) is the best choice for either lunch or dinner.

## GREAT DIAMOND ISLAND

Great Diamond is a totally different scene. In 1891, the U.S. government began building an Army post on Great Diamond, a quick ferryboat ride from the Portland harbor front. Completed in 1907, **Fort McKinley** (named after President William McKinley) became part of Portland Harbor's five-fort defense system during World Wars I and II. When peace descended, the fort's red-brick structures were left to crumble for nearly five decades. In 1984, developers stepped in, bought the derelicts, and began restoration – albeit not without financial setbacks and opposition from environmental organizations.

Today, the 193-acre **Diamond Cove** enclave boasts barracks-turned-townhomes, single-family houses, a general store (open daily late May-Labor Day), outdoor theater, a beach bar (open mid-June-mid-September), an art gallery, no cars (only bikes and golf carts), and the **Diamond's Edge Restaurant** (207/766-5850, www.diamondsedge.com).

## GREAT CHEBEAGUE

Everyone calls Great Chebeague just "Chebeague" (shuh-BIG). Yes, there's a Little Che-

© HILARY NANGLE

The Casco Bay Lines ferry dock on Peaks Island requires precise maneuvering by the captain.

beautiful small stretch of sand lined with dune grass, not far from the Chebeague Island Inn. Also on this part of the island is **East End Point,** with a spectacular panoramic view of Halfway Rock and the bay.

Chebeague Transportation Company, from Cousins Island, Yarmouth, also services the island.

## EAGLE ISLAND

Seventeen-acre Eagle Island (207/624-6080, www.pearyeagleisland.org, 10 A.M.–5 P.M. mid-June–early Sept.) juts out of Casco Bay, rising to a rocky promontory 40 feet above the crashing surf. On the bluff's crest, Robert Edwin Peary, the first man to lead a party of fellow men to the North Pole without the use of mechanical or electrical devices, built his dream home. It's now a state historic site that's accessible via excursion boats from Portland or Freeport. The half-day trip usually includes a narrated cruise to the island and time to tour the house, filled with Peary family artifacts, and wander the nature trails. (Note: Trails are usually closed until approximately mid-July to protect nesting eider ducks).

Peary envisioned the island's rocky bluff as a ship's prow and built his house to resemble a pilot house. Wherever possible, he used indigenous materials from the island in the construction, including timber drift, fallen trees, beach rocks, and cement mixed with screened beach sand and small pebbles. From the library, Peary corresponded with world leaders, adventurers, and explorers, such as Teddy Roosevelt, the Wright Brothers, Roald Amundson, and Ernest Shackleton, and planned his expeditions. Peary reached the North Pole on April 6, 1909, and his wife, Josephine, was on Eagle when she received word via telegraph of her husband's accomplishment. After Peary's death, in 1920, the family continued to spend summers on Eagle until Josephine's death, in 1955. It was a unanimous family decision to donate the island to the state of Maine. Check the website for information on guided tours to the island led by Peary's grandson.

beague, but it's a state-owned park, and no one lives there. Chebeague is the largest of the bay's islands – 4.5 miles long, 1.5 miles wide – and the relatively level terrain makes it easy to get around. Don't plan to bring a car; it's too complicated to arrange.

You can bike the leisurely 10-mile circuit of the island in a couple of hours, but unless you're in a hurry, allow time to relax and enjoy your visit. Pick up an island map at the Portland terminal or on the ferry; all the high points are listed, including two beach access points off North Road.

If the tide is right, cross the sandspit from The Hook and explore **Little Chebeague.** Start out about two hours before low tide (preferably around new moon or full moon, when the most water drains away) and plan to be back on Chebeague no later than two hours after low tide.

Back on Great Chebeague, when you're ready for a swim, head for **Hamilton Beach,** a

# LIGHTHOUSES AND PARKS TOUR

Whether in a car or on a bike, it's easy to loop through South Portland and Cape Elizabeth on a route that takes in lighthouses, forts, beaches, and parks.

Begin just over the Casco Bay Bridge from downtown Portland (Rte. 77), take Broadway and continue to the end at **Southern Maine Community College (SMCC),** overlooking the bay. (Best time to come here is evenings and weekends, when there's ample parking.) Unless it's foggy (when the signal is deafening) or thundering (when you'll expose yourself to lightning), walk out along the 1,000-foot granite breakwater to the **Spring Point Ledge Light,** with fabulous views in every direction. Also here are picnic benches, the remains of Fort Preble, and the Portland Harbor Museum. At the southern edge of the SMCC campus is the **Spring Point Shoreline Walkway,** a scenic three-mile pathway with views off to House, Peaks, and Cushings Islands. At the end of the shoreway, you'll reach crescent-shaped **Willard Beach,** a neighborhoody sort of place with lifeguards, a changing building, a snack bar, and those same marvelous views.

From the SMCC campus, return on Broadway to the major intersection with Cottage Road and bear left. Cottage Road becomes Shore Road at the Cape Elizabeth town line. Loop into Fort Williams Park and make a pilgrimage to **Portland Head Light** before continuing on Shore Road to its intersection with Route 77. Bear left and follow to Two Lights Road and follow signs to 40-acre **Two Lights State Park.** Almost a vest-pocket park, it has picnicking and restroom facilities, but its biggest asset is the panoramic ocean view from atop a onetime gun battery. Summer admission is $4.50 adults 12-64, $1 kids 5-11.

Before or after visiting the park, take a left just before the park entrance (it's a continuation of Two Lights Road; the sign says Lighthouses). Continue to the parking lot at the end, where you'll see the signal towers for which Two Lights is named. (There's no access to either one; only one still works.) If you haven't brought a picnic for the state park, enjoy the food and the view at **The Lobster Shack.**

To eke out some beach time, return to Route 77 and continue to **Crescent Beach State Park,** a 243-acre park with changing rooms, lifeguard, restrooms, picnic tables, and a snack bar. Admission is $3.50 adults, 12-64, $1 kids 5-11. Directly offshore is Saco Bay's **Richmond Island,** a 200-acre private preserve with a checkered past dating to the 17th century.

and the Visitor Information Center (245 Commercial St., 207/772-5800).

Also available at the Visitor Information Center is a map, $1, detailing 36 significant **antislavery sites** in Portland. It also includes stories and information about the slave trade and what life was like for blacks during the slavery era. Six significant sites, each marked, are included in a 1.6-mile walking tour.

The *Portland Women's History Trail* details four loops—Congress Street, Munjoy Hill, State Street, and the West End—with about 20 stops on each loop. Among the sites: a long-gone chewing-gum factory where teenage girls worked 10-hour shifts. The trail guide is available for $8.50 in selected bookstores and at the Maine History Gallery gift shop (489 Congress St., Portland, 207/879-0427).

**Portland Trails** (1 India St., Portland, 207/775-2411, www.trails.org), a dynamic membership conservation organization incorporated in 1991, continually adds to the mileage it has mapped out for hiking and biking around Portland. The group's accomplishments include the 2.1-mile Eastern Promenade Trail, a landscaped bayfront dual pathway circling the base of Munjoy Hill and linking East End Beach to the Old Port, and a continuing trail connecting the Eastern Prom with the 3.5-mile Back Cove Trail, on the other side of I-295. Nearly two dozen trails are maintained, and the group also holds organized events—a great way to meet some locals. Contact Portland Trails for

# WINSLOW HOMER

Discovering Maine in his early 40s, Winslow Homer (1836-1910) was smitten – enough to spend the last 27 years of his life in Prouts Neck (Scarborough, south of Portland), a small fishing village gradually morphing into an exclusive summer enclave. Here, in a cluttered, rustic studio converted from a onetime stable (recently acquired by the Portland Museum of Art, which eventually plans to open it to the public on a limited basis), he produced his finest works, the seascapes that have become so familiar to us all. He painted the sea in every mood, the rocks in every light, the snow in all its bleakness, the hardy trees bent to the wind. Occasional forays to the Bahamas, the Adirondacks, and the Canadian wilderness inspired other themes, but Prouts Neck always lured him back. Homer's last work, an oil titled *Driftwood*, painted in 1909 when his health was in major decline, depicts once again the struggle of man against the roiling surf that Homer knew so intimately from his life on the coast of Maine.

a colorful foldout map of Portland's entire trail and park system—including some proposed routes—a joint effort of Portland Trails and the Greater Portland Council of Governments' Kids and Transportation Program. Better still, join Portland Trails ($35 a year) and support its ambitious efforts.

## ◖ The Old Port

Tony shops, cobblestone sidewalks, replica streetlights, and a casual, upmarket crowd (most of the time) set the scene for a district once filled with derelict buildings. The 1970s revival of the Old Port has infused funds, foot traffic, and flair into this part of town. Scores of unusual shops, ethnic restaurants, and spontaneous street-corner music make it a fun area to visit year-round. Nightlife centers on the Old Port, where a couple of dozen bars keep everyone hopping until after midnight. Police

keep a close eye on the district, but it can get a bit dicey after 11 P.M. on weekends. Caveat emptor—or maybe caveat peregrinator!

At 10:30 A.M. daily July–September, knowledgeable guides from Greater Portland Landmarks (207/774-5561, www.portland-landmarks.org) lead fascinating 90-minute **Old Port walking tours** in downtown Portland. No reservations needed. Buy tickets at the Visitor Information Center (245 Commercial St.), where the tours begin and end. Cost is $8 pp; kids under 16 with an adult are free.

## Congress Street/Downtown Arts District

Bit by bit, once-declining Congress Street is becoming revitalized, showcasing the best of the city's culture. Artists, starving and otherwise, spend much of their time here, thanks largely to encouragement from the energetic grassroots Downtown Arts District Association (DADA). Galleries, artists' studios, coffeehouses, cafés and bistros, craft shops, two libraries, the State Theatre, the Merrill Auditorium (in City Hall), the Portland Museum of Art, the Maine College of Art, and even L. L. Bean and the Portland Public Market are all part of the ongoing renaissance.

## West End

Probably the most diverse of the city's downtown neighborhoods, and one that largely escaped the Great Fire of 1866, the West End includes the historically and architecturally splendid Western Promenade, Maine Medical Center (the state's largest hospital), the city's best B&Bs, a gay-friendly community with a laissez-faire attitude, a host of cafés and restaurants, as well as a few niches harboring the homeless and forlorn.

## Munjoy Hill/East End

A once slightly down-at-the-heels neighborhood enclave with a pull-'em-up-by-the-bootstraps attitude, Portland's East End is rapidly gentrifying. Munjoy Hill is probably best known for the distinctive wooden tower that

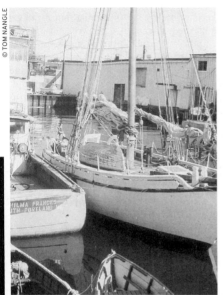

© TOM NANGLE

Portland's waterfront wharves are lined with both pleasure and working craft.

adorns its summit (see *Portland Observatory* under *Sights*).

Named for George Munjoy, a wealthy 17th-century resident, this district has a host of architectural and historic landmarks—well worth a walking tour. Fortunately, Greater Portland Landmarks (207/774-5561, www.portlandlandmarks.org) has produced a 24-page booklet, *Munjoy Hill Historic Guide* ($3), which documents more than 60 notable sites, including the National Historic Register Eastern Cemetery and, with spectacular harbor views, the Eastern Promenade and Fort Allen Park. From early June to early October, Landmarks also offers guided walking tours of the historic **Eastern Cemetery,** the oldest burial ground on the peninsula, at 10:30 A.M. on Thursdays, beginning at the Portland Observatory (138 Congress St.). Cost is $7 adult, free under 16.

## Bayside and Parkside

A Babel of languages reverberates in these districts just below Portland City Hall. Bayside experienced the arrival of refugees—Cambodian, Laotian, Vietnamese, Central European, and Afghan families—from war-torn lands during the 1980s and 1990s. Nowadays, you'll hear references to Somali Town, an area named for all the resettled refugees from that shattered country. Others have come from Sudan and Ethiopia. Portland's active Refugee Resettlement Program has assisted all. Many have found employment with Barber Foods, a fantastically conscientious firm that hires many new immigrants in its processing plant and provides opportunities for employees to learn English and obtain social services. Many newcomers have also become entrepreneurs, opening restaurants and small markets catering to their compatriots but increasingly gaining customers among local residents. Real-estate pressures are contributing to changes in these neighborhoods, too. The city is working to relocate scrap-metal yards and replace them with housing and small businesses.

## Beyond the Peninsula

At the western edge of Portland, close to the Portland Jetport, is the historic area known as **Stroudwater,** once an essential link in Maine water transport. The 20-mile-long **Cumberland and Oxford Canal,** hand-dug in 1828, ran through here as part of the timber-shipping route linking Portland Harbor, the Fore and Presumpscot Rivers, and Sebago Lake. Twenty-eight wooden locks allowed vessels to rise the 265 feet between sea level and the lake. By 1870, trains took over the route, condemning the canal to oblivion. Centerpiece of the Stroudwater area today is the historic 18th-century Tate House (see under *Beyond the Downtown Peninsula*).

## SIGHTS
### ◖ Portland Museum of Art (PMA)

Three centuries of art and architecture: That's what you'll discover at Maine's oldest (since 1882) and finest art museum, the Portland Museum of Art (7 Congress Sq., Portland, 207/775-6148, recorded info 207/773-2787 or 800/639-4067, www.portlandmuseum.org, 10 A.M.–5 P.M., to 9 P.M. Fri., closed Mon. mid-Oct.–late May, $10 adults, $8 seniors and students, $4 ages 6–17, free admission 5–9 P.M. every Friday). The museum's topflight collection of American and impressionist masters and fine and decorative arts is displayed in three architecturally stunning, connected buildings: the award-winning Charles Shipman Payson building, designed by I. M. Pei and opened in 1983, the newly restored Federal-era McLellan House, and the beaux-arts L. D. M. Sweat Memorial Galleries, designed by noted Maine architect John Calvin Stevens. The museum also has a well-stocked gift shop and a pleasant café that's open for lunch daily (11 A.M.–4 P.M.) and for dinner Friday (to 7:30 P.M.). Call for information about family activities, lectures, and other events.

### C Victoria Mansion

Jaws literally drop when their owners enter the Italianate Victoria Mansion, also called the Morse-Libby Mansion (109 Danforth St., Portland, 207/772-4841, www.victoriamansion.org, 10 A.M.–4 P.M. Mon.–Sat. and 1–5 P.M. Sun. May–Oct., special hours in Dec., $10 adults, $9 seniors, $3 6–17, holiday season $12 adults, $5 ages 6–17, $25 per family), widely considered the most magnificently ornamented dwelling of its period remaining in the country. The national Historic Landmark is rife with Victoriana—carved marble fireplaces, elaborate porcelain and paneling, a free-standing mahogany staircase, gilded glass chandeliers, a recently restored 6- by 25-foot stained-glass ceiling window, and unbelievable trompe l'oeil touches. It's even more spectacular at Christmas, with yards of roping, festooned trees, and carolers. (This is the best time to bring kids, as the house itself may not particularly intrigue them.) The mansion was built in the late 1850s by Ruggles Sylvester Morse, a Maine-born entrepreneur whose New Orleans–based fortune enabled him to hire 93 craftsmen to complete the house. The interior, designed by Gustave Herter, still boasts 90 percent of

© TOM NANGLE

GREATER PORTLAND

The Victoria Mansion is a nationally renowned gem, although you wouldn't know it from the exterior.

the original furnishings. Guided 45-minute tours begin every half hour (on the quarter hour) in season; tours are self-guided during the holidays.

### C Portland Observatory

Providing a head-swiveling view of Portland (and the White Mountains on a clear day), the octagonal red-painted Portland Observatory (138 Congress St., Portland, 207/774-5561, www.portlandlandmarks.org, 10 A.M.–5 P.M. late May–Columbus Day, last tour at 4:30 P.M., $6 adults, $4 ages 6–16) is the only remaining marine signal tower on the Eastern Seaboard. Built in 1807 at a cost of $5,000 by Captain Lemuel Moody to keep track of the port's shipping activity, the tower has 122 tons of rock ballast in its base. Admission in those days (only men were allowed to climb the 103 interior steps) was 12.5 cents. Today, admission includes the small museum at the tower's base and a guided tour to the top.

© TOM NANGLE

Climb the 103 steps to the orb deck of the Portland Observatory for 360-degree views.

## The Longfellow Connection

A few blocks down Congress Street from the PMA, you'll step back in time to the era of Portland-born poet Henry Wadsworth Longfellow, who lived in the accurately restored **Wadsworth-Longfellow House** (485 Congress St., Portland, 207/774-1822, www.mainehistory.org, 10 A.M.–4 P.M. Mon.–Sat., noon–4 P.M. Sun. May 1–Oct. 31, special holiday hours Nov. and Dec., $7 adults, $6 seniors and students, $3 ages 5–17), as a child in the early 1800s—long before the brick mansion was dwarfed by surrounding high-rises. Wadsworth and Longfellow family furnishings fill the three-story house (owned by the Maine Historical Society), and savvy guides provide insight into Portland's 19th-century life. Don't miss the urban oasis—a wonderfully peaceful garden—behind the house (same hours, free admission). Buy tickets at the adjacent Center for Maine History, which also houses the **Maine History Gallery** (489 Congress St., 207/774-1822, www.mainehistory.org, 10 A.M.–5 P.M. Mon.–Sat., noon–5 P.M. Sun., $4 adults, $3 seniors, $2 children), where you can take in the Maine Historical Society's current exhibits and find an extensive collection of Maine history books in the gift shop.

## Maine Narrow Gauge Railroad and Museum

A three-mile ride along Portland's waterfront is the highlight of a visit to the Maine Narrow Gauge Railroad Company and Museum (58 Fore St., Portland, 207/828-0814, www.mngrr.org). The museum (10 A.M.–4 P.M. daily late May–late Oct., weekends only off-season, $2 adult, $1 seniors and ages 3–12 or free with train ticket) owns more than three dozen train cars and has others on long-term loan—most from Maine's five historic narrow-gauge railroads (the last one closed in 1943). You can board a number of the cars and see others undergoing restoration. For a fee, you can ride the two-foot rails aboard a multicar train. The schedule roughly follows museum hours, with rides on the hour ($10 adults, $9 seniors, $6 ages 3–12). The track edges Casco Bay along the Eastern Promenade—a short but enjoyable excursion that's a real kid pleaser. Years ago, hundreds of steam engines were built here, but steam locomotives now operate only for special occasions. Trains also operate during school vacation weeks; call for schedule. At the eastern end of Fore Street, turn at the railroad-crossing sign on the waterside; the museum is at the back of the complex.

## Museum of African Culture

Founded in 1998, the Museum of African Culture (13 Brown St., Portland, 207/871-7188, www.museumafricanculture.org, 10:30 A.M.–4 P.M. Tues.–Sat., $5 donation) is the brainchild of Nigerian-born Oscar Mokeme (the director) and Arthur Aleshire. It's devoted to sub-Saharan African arts and culture. Among the museum's 300 or so treasures—not all on display at once—are Nigerian tribal masks and

Kids love riding the Narrow Gauge Railroad along the Eastern Prom waterfront.

Benin lost-wax bronzes. The museum also has an ambitious outreach program, educating the community about African art and culture. Ask about Friday night programs.

## Children's Museum of Maine

Here's the answer to parents' prayers—a whole museum in downtown Portland catering to kids. At the Children's Museum of Maine (P.O. Box 4041, 142 Free St., next to the Portland Museum of Art, Portland 04101, 207/828-1234, www.kitetails.com, 10 A.M.–5 P.M. Mon.–Sat., noon to 5 P.M. Sun., closed Mon. early Sept.–late May, $7, children 1 and younger free, free admission 5–8 P.M. first Fri. of each month), lots of hands-on displays encourage interaction and guarantee involvement for a couple of hours. What's here? A submarine, computer lab, TV studio, L. L. Bean's Discovery Woods, a space shuttle, a supermarket, bank (with an ATM), lobster boat, a camera obscura (one of only three in the country, $3 for that exhibit only) and more than a dozen other activities. There's even an animal hospital. Call to check on the special-events schedule.

## Portland Freedom Trail

Pick up a copy of this free map and brochure detailing a self-guided walking tour of a baker's dozen marked sights related to Portland's role in Maine's Underground Railway (www.portlandfreedomtrail.org). Among the highlights are the Abyssinian Meeting House, the third-oldest African American Meeting House still standing in the United States (undergoing restoration); First Parish Unitarian Universalist Church, where abolitionist William Lloyd Garrison spoke in 1832; Mariners' Church, location of an antislavery bookstore and print shop that printed the first Afrocentric history of the world; and Franklin Street Wharf, where stowaway slaves often arrived on vessels from Southern ports.

## Breweries

Look for the keg topping the flagpole at **Shipyard Brewery** (86 Newbury St., Portland,

207/761-0807, www.shipyard.com). Tours of the award-winning microbrewery are offered on the hour noon–4 P.M. Tours begin with a short promotional video explaining the brewing process and end with a tasting. Even if you're not a beer/ale drinker, go and enjoy the root beer that's also brewed on the premises.

Other Portland breweries offering tours are **Allagash Brewing Company** (50 Industrial Way, 207/878-5385), at 3 P.M. weekdays; **Beary's Brewing Company** (38 Evergreen Dr., 207/878-2337), at 2:30 P.M. weekdays; and **Casco Bay Brewing Company** (57 Industrial Way, 207/797-2020), by appointment.

# BEYOND THE DOWNTOWN PENINSULA

## Seeing Stars

Under a 30-foot dome with comfy theater seats and a state-of-the-art laser system, the **Southworth Planetarium** (96 Falmouth St., Science Building, lower level, University of Southern Maine, Portland, 207/780-4249, www.usm.maine.edu/~planet, 7 and 8:30 P.M. Fri. and Sat., $5–6 adults, $4–6 seniors and children) presents astronomy shows. Computer-savvy kids will head for the interactive computers in the exhibit area; the gift shop stocks astronaut ice cream and other science-type stuff. For recorded information on moon and planet positions, eclipses, and other astronomical happenings, call the **Skywatch Hotline** (207/780-4719). Take Exit 6B off I-295 and go west on Forest Avenue to Falmouth Street (left turn). The Science Building is on the left, after the parking lot.

## Osher Map Library

Also on the University of Southern Maine's campus is the Osher Map Library (207/780-4850 or 800/800-4876, ext. 4850, www.usm.maine.edu/~maps, call for schedule). The library's collection, primarily a teaching resource, documents the history of Western cartography from its inception to modern times. Themed exhibits feature highlights from the library's original maps, atlases, geographies, and globes dating from the late 15th century. Other artifacts include texts depicting explorers' narratives, accounts of early travelers, and works of cosmography, astronomy, navigation, and geography.

## Tate House

Just down the street from the Portland International Jetport, in the Stroudwater district, is the 1755 Tate House (1270 Westbrook St., 207/774-6177, www.tatehouse.org, 10 A.M.–4 P.M. Tues.–Sat. 1–4 P.M. and first Sun. of each month June 15–Oct. 15, $7 adults, $5 seniors, $2 age 6–12), a National Historic Landmark owned by the Colonial Dames of America. Built by Captain George Tate, who was prominent in shipbuilding, the house has superb period furnishings and a lovely 18th-century herb garden (more than 70 varieties) overlooking the Stroudwater River. Tours last 40 minutes. Wednesdays mid-June–mid-September are "summer garden days," when tea and goodies follow tours of the garden (for an extra charge). Other special hour-long tours focusing on the architecture and the historic Stroudwater neighborhood can be arranged by appointment. Across the street, in the Means House, is the museum's gift shop. From downtown Portland, it's 3.2 miles; take Congress Street West (Rte. 22), under I-295, and out as far as Waldo Street, just after the Fore River. Turn left onto Waldo and then turn right onto Westbrook Street. If you find yourself with spare time at the Portland Jetport, Tate House is an easy walk from the terminal. Ask for directions at the airport information desk.

## Portland Harbor Museum

The maritime history of Casco Bay and Maine is the focus of the small Portland Harbor Museum (Fort Rd., South Portland, 207/799-6337, www.PortlandHarborMuseum.org, 10 A.M.–4:30 P.M. daily late May–mid-Oct., and Fri.–Sun. spring and fall, $4 adults) on the waterfront campus of Southern Maine Community College (SMCC). To reach the museum, head over from downtown Portland (Rte. 77) and continue onto Broadway. Watch for SMCC signs. The museum now holds the title to the nearby Spring Point Ledge lighthouse, which is open for tours periodically during the summer. Call for the schedule. Also nearby are the remains of Fort Preble and the Spring Point Shoreline Walkway leading to Willard Beach.

## ◖ Portland Head Light

Just four miles from downtown Portland, Fort Williams, in Cape Elizabeth, feels a world away. This oceanfront town park, a former military base, is home to Portland Head Light (1000 Shore Rd., Fort Williams Park, Cape Elizabeth, 207/799-2661, www.portlandhead-light.com, open dawn–dusk). Commissioned by President George Washington and first lighted in 1791, it has been immortalized in poetry, photography, and philately. The surf here is awesome—perhaps too awesome. The *Annie C. Maguire* was shipwrecked below the lighthouse on Christmas Eve, 1886. There's no access to the 58-foot automated light tower, but the superbly restored keeper's house has become **The Museum at Portland Head**

© HILARY NANGLE

Portland Head Light guards the ledgy shores of Cape Elizabeth.

**Light** (10 A.M.–4 P.M. daily late May–mid-Oct. and weekends late spring and late fall, but call first to confirm, $2 adults, $1 kids 6–18). It's filled with local history and lighthouse memorabilia. The 90-acre oceanfront park offers much else to explore, including ruins of the fort and the Goddard mansion. Walk the trails, play a game of tennis, dip your toes in the surf at the rocky beach, but be careful, as there's a strong undertow here. You might even catch the Portland Symphony Orchestra, which occasionally performs here in summer. The grassy headlands are great places to watch the boat traffic going in and out of Portland Harbor. Bring a picnic lunch, and don't forget a kite. From downtown Portland, take Route 77 and then Broadway, Cottage Road, and Shore Road.

## TOURS
### ◖ Casco Bay Tour

Casco Bay Lines (Commercial and Franklin Sts., Old Port, Portland, 207/774-7871, www.cascobaylines.com), the nation's oldest continuously operating ferry system (since the 1920s), is the lifeline between Portland and six inhabited Casco Bay islands. What better way to sample the islands than to go along for the three-hour ride with mail, groceries, and island residents? The Casco Bay Lines mail boat stops—briefly—at **Long Island, Chebeague, Cliff,** and **Little** and **Great Diamond Islands.** Departures are 10 A.M. and 2:15 P.M. daily mid-June–Labor Day (plus 7:45 A.M. weekdays), 10 A.M. and 2:45 P.M. other months. Fares are $13 adults, $11.50 seniors, and $6.50 ages 5–9. The longest cruise on the Casco Bay Lines schedule is the five-hour, 45-minute narrated summertime trip (late June–Labor Day) to **Bailey Island,** with a two-hour stopover, departing from Portland at 10 A.M. daily ($18.50 adults, $16.50 seniors, $8.50 ages 5–9). Dogs (on leashes) and bicycles need separate tickets—$6 for bikes, $3.75 for animals.

### Walking Tours
The best tours of the area are offered by

**Greater Portland Landmarks** (207/774-5561, www.portlandlandmarks.org), which sponsors neighborhood walking tours as well as an annual **summer tour program,** featuring four or five walking trips and excursions to offshore islands, historic churches, revamped buildings, and gardens. Many of the destinations are private or otherwise inaccessible, so these are special opportunities. Registration is limited, and there's only one trip to each site. Tours run mid-July–mid-October, primarily on weekends.

## Land and Sea Tours

Three commercial operators offer area land-and-sea tours, but frankly, none is first rate. On each, guides often present incorrect information. Still, such tours are a good way to get the city's general layout. The best of the lot is the 1.5-hour narrated sightseeing tour of Portland in a trolley-bus, by **Mainely Tours** (3 Moulton St., Old Port, Portland, 207/774-0808, www.mainelytours.com). Cost is $16 adults, $15 seniors, $9 ages 3–12. You can combine this tour with a 90-minute Lighthouse Lover's boat tour on Casco Bay. The combined price is $27 adult, $25 senior, and $16 kids.

An alternative, especially if you're traveling with kids, is the 60–70 minute **Downeast Duck Adventures** (office at Harbor View Gifts, 177 Commercial St., 207/774-3825, www.downeastducktours.com, early June–early Oct., $22 adult, $19 senior, $17 ages 6–12, $5 age 5 and younger). Prepare to do a lot of quacking on the tour and to hear a lot of quackery regarding local history.

## PARKS, PRESERVES, AND BEACHES

Greater Portland is blessed with green space, thanks largely to the efforts of 19th-century mayor James Phinney Baxter, who foresightedly hired the famed Olmsted Brothers firm to develop an ambitious plan to ring the city with public parks and promenades. Not all the elements fell into place, but the result is what makes Portland such a livable city.

## Portland Peninsula

Probably the most visible of the city's parks, 51-acre **Deering Oaks** (Park and Forest Aves. and Deering St.) may be best known for the quaint little duck condo in the middle of the pond. Other facilities and highlights here are tennis courts, playground, horseshoes, rental paddleboats, a snack bar, the award-winning Rose Circle, a Saturday farmers market (7 A.M.–noon), and, in winter, ice skating. After dark, steer clear of the park.

At one end of the Eastern Promenade, where it meets Fore Street, **Fort Allen Park** overlooks offshore Fort Gorges (coin-operated telescopes bring it closer). A central gazebo is flanked by an assortment of military souvenirs dating as far back as the War of 1812. All along the Eastern Prom are walking paths, benches, play areas, even an ill-maintained fitness trail—all with that terrific view. Down by the water is **East End Beach,** with parking, token sand, and the area's best launching ramp for sea kayaks or powerboats.

## West of Downtown

Just beyond I-295, along Baxter Boulevard (Rte. 1) and tidal **Back Cove,** is a skinny green strip with a 3.5-mile trail for walking, jogging, or just watching the sailboards and the skyline. Along the way, you can cross Baxter Boulevard and spend time picnicking, playing tennis, or flying a kite in 48-acre **Payson Park.**

Talk about an urban oasis. The 85-acre **Fore River Sanctuary,** owned by Maine Audubon, has two miles of blue-blazed trails that wind through a salt marsh, link with the historic Cumberland and Oxford Canal towpath, and pass near **Jewell Falls,** Portland's only waterfall, protected by Portland Trails. From downtown Portland, take Congress Street West (Rte. 22), past I-295. From here there are two access routes: either turn right onto Stevens Avenue (Rte. 9), continue to Brighton Avenue (Rte. 25), turn left and go about 1.25 miles to Rowe Avenue, and then turn left and park at the end of the road; or continue past Stevens Avenue, about one-half mile to Frost Avenue, take a hard right, and then left into the Maine Orthopedic Center parking lot. Portland Trails raised the funds for the handsome, 90-foot pedestrian bridge at this entrance to the sanctuary. Open sunup to sundown daily. No pets, free admission.

Bird-watchers flock to 239-acre **Evergreen Cemetery** (Stevens Ave.) in May to see warblers, thrushes, and other migratory birds that gather in the ponds and meadows. During peak periods, it's possible to see as many as 20 warbler species in a morning, including the Cape May, bay breasted, mourning, and Tennessee. Naturalists from Maine Audubon often are on-site helping to identify birds. For more info, check the events calendar at www.Mainebirding.net.

## Scarborough

**Scarborough Beach Park** (Black Point Rd., Rte. 207, 207/883-2416, www.scarborough-beachstatepark.com, $4 adult, $2 child), a long stretch of sand, is the best beach for big waves. Between the parking area and the lovely stretch of beach, you'll pass Massacre Pond, named for a 1703 skirmish between resident Indians and resident wannabes. (Score: Indians 19, wannabes 0.) The park is open all year for swimming, surfing, beachcombing, and ice skating, but on weekends in summer, the parking lot fills early.

At 3,100 acres, **Scarborough Marsh** (Pine Point Rd., Rte. 9, 207/883-5100, www.maine-audubon.org, 9:30 A.M.–5:30 P.M. June–Labor Day, and weekends in late May and Sept.), Maine's largest salt marsh, is prime territory for birding and canoeing. Rent a canoe ($15 an hour if you're not an Audubon member or $50 per half day) at the small nature center, operated by Maine Audubon, and explore on your own. Or join one of the daily 90-minute guided tours (call for the schedule, $11 adults, $9 children, subtract $1.50 pp if you have your own canoe). Guided full-moon tours ($12 per adult, $10 per child) June–September are particularly exciting; dress warmly and bring a flashlight. Other special programs, some geared primarily for children, include wildflower walks, art classes, and dawn birding trips; all require reservations and very reasonable fees. Also here is a walking tour trail of less than one mile. Pick up a map at the center.

Overlooking the marsh is 52-acre **Scarborough River Wildlife Sanctuary** (Pine Point Rd./Rte. 9), with 1.5 miles of walking trails that loop to the Scarborough River and by two ponds.

## Falmouth (North of Portland)

Nearly a dozen of Falmouth's parks, trails, and preserves, official and unofficial, are described and mapped in the *Falmouth Trail Guide,* a handy little booklet published by the Falmouth Conservation Commission. Copies are available at Gilsland Farm, Falmouth Town Hall, and local bookstores. Two of the best options are described below.

A 65-acre wildlife sanctuary and environmental center on the banks of the Presumpscot River, **Gilsland Farm** (20 Gilsland Farm Rd., 207/781-2330, www.maineaudubon.org, dawn–dusk daily) is state headquarters for

When you need to stretch your legs, take a walk around Mackworth Island for a different view of the city skyline and Casco Bay.

Maine Audubon. More than two miles of easy, well-marked trails wind through the grounds, taking in salt marshes, rolling meadows, woodlands, and views of the estuary. Observation blinds allow inconspicuous spying during bird-migration season. In the education center (9 A.M.–5 P.M. Mon.–Sat. and 1–4 P.M. Sun.) are hands-on exhibits, a nature store, and classrooms and offices. Fees are charged for special events, but otherwise it's all free. The visitors center is one-quarter mile off Route 1.

Once the summer compound of the prominent Baxter family, Falmouth's 100-acre **Mackworth Island,** reached via a causeway, is now the site of the Governor Baxter School for the Deaf. Limited parking is just beyond the security booth on the island. On the 1.5-mile, vehicle-free perimeter path (great Portland Harbor views), you'll meet bikers, hikers, and dog walkers. Just off the trail on the north side of the island is the late Governor Percival Baxter's stone-circled pet cemetery, maintained by the state at the behest of Baxter, who donated this island as well as Baxter State Park to the people of Maine. From downtown Portland, take Route 1 across the Presumpscot River to Falmouth Foreside. Andrews Avenue (third street on the right) leads to the island. Open sunup–sundown, all year.

## RECREATION
### Bicycling
The **Bicycle Coalition of Maine** (P.O. Box 5275, Augusta 04332, 207/623-4511, www .bikemaine.org) has an excellent website that lists nearly two dozen trails in Greater Portland. You'll also find info on events, organized rides, bike shops, and more. Another good resource is **Casco Bay Bicycle Club** (www.cascobaybicycleclub.org), a recreational cycling club with rides several times weekly. Check its website for details.

For rentals (hybrids are $25 a day) and repairs visit **Cycle Mania** (59 Federal St., 207/774-2933, www.cyclemania1.com).

The best locales for island bicycling—fun for families and beginners but not especially challenging for diehards—are Peaks and Great Chebeague Islands (see sidebar *Casco Bay Islands*), but do remember to follow the rules of the road.

## Golf
You'll have no problem finding a place to tee off in Greater Portland. Some of the best courses are private, so if you have an "in," so much the better, but there are still plenty of public and semiprivate courses for every skill level. Free advice on helping you choose a course is offered by Maine's Golf Concierge (info@golfme.com).

Let's just consider Greater Portland's 18-hole courses. For all, it's a smart move to reserve tee times. **Sable Oaks Golf Club** (505 Country Club Dr., South Portland, 207/775-6257, www.sableoaks.com) is considered one of the toughest and best of Maine's public courses. Since 1998, **Nonesuch River Golf Club** (304 Gorham Rd., Rte. 114, Scarborough, 207/883-0007 or 888/256-2717, www.nonesuchgolf.com) has been drawing raves for the challenges of its par-70 championship course and praise from environmentalists for preserving wildlife habitat; full-size practice range and green, too. The City of Portland's **Riverside Municipal Golf Course** (1158 Riverside St., Portland, 207/797-3524) has an 18-hole par-72 course (Riverside North) and a nine-hole par-35 course (Riverside South). Opt for the 18-hole course.

## Sea Kayaking
With all the islands scattered through Casco Bay, Greater Portland has become a hotbed of sea-kayaking activity. The best place to start is out on Peaks Island, 15 minutes offshore via Casco Bay Lines ferry. **Maine Island Kayak Company (MIKCO)** (70 Luther St., Peaks Island, 207/766-2373 or 800/796-2373, www.maineislandkayak.com) is a successful tour operation that organizes half-day, all-day, and multiday local kayaking trips as well as national and international adventures. An introductory half-day tour in Casco Bay is $65 pp; a full day is $110, including lunch. Reservations are essential. MIKCO also does private lessons and group courses and clinics (some require previous experience). MIKCO's owner, Tom Bergh, has a flawless reputation for safety and

© HILARY NANGLE

Maine Island Kayak Company operates from a beachfront location on Peaks Island, making it easy to tour the waters of Casco Bay.

skill. Send for the extensive trip schedule. In early October (usually Columbus Day weekend), there's a daylong sale of used boats and gear—lots of real bargains.

For a quickie intro, **L. L. Bean** (180 Commercial St., 207/400-4814) offers 90-minute Portland Harbor kayak tours three times daily late June–August, and then weekends into October. Cost is $29 adults, $19 ages 10–15.

### ◖ Lobstering Cruise

Learn all kinds of lobster lore and maybe even catch your own dinner with **Lucky Catch Lobster Tours** (170 Commercial St., 207/233-2026 or 888/624-6321, www.luckycatch.com, $22 adult, $20 seniors or juniors ages 13–18, $14 ages 12 and younger). Captain Tom Martin offers five different, 80–90-minute cruises on his 37-foot lobster boat. On each (except late Saturdays and all-day Sundays, when state law prohibits it), usually 10 traps are hauled and the process and gear explained. You can even help, if you're willing. Any lobsters caught are available for purchase after the cruise for wholesale boat price (and you can have them cooked

nearby for a reasonable rate). Now wouldn't that make a nice story to tell the folks back home?

### Sailboat and Powerboat Excursions

Down on the Old Port wharves are several excursion-boat businesses. Each has carved out a niche, so choose according to your interest and your schedule. Dress warmly and wear rubber-soled shoes. Remember that all cruises are weather-dependent.

**Bay View Cruises** operates the 66-foot *Bay View Lady* (184 Commercial St., Fisherman's Wharf, Old Port, 207/761-0496, www .bayviewcruises-me.com, daily June–Sept., weekends May and June) and has five different cruises ranging from 40 minutes to two hours. On longer cruises, you can add a complete lobster bake, with notice. The main deck is enclosed and heated; the upper deck has the best views.

Cruise up to 20 miles offshore seeking whales with **Odyssey Whale Watch** (Long Wharf, 170 Commercial St., 207/775-0727, www.odysseywhalewatch.com, $40 adult, $35 ages 60-plus and 13–17, and $30 under

12). Five-hour whale watches aboard the *Odyssey* depart daily at 10 A.M. late June–early September, plus spring and fall weekends. (Don't overload on breakfast that day, and take preventive measures if you're motion-sensitive.) **Eagle Island Tours** (Long Wharf, Old Port, 207/774-6498, www.eagleislandtours.com, no credit cards) offers several excursion options, but the best is the four-hour cruise, departing at 10 A.M., to 17-acre **Eagle Island** (Tues. and Thurs.–Sun. late June–early Sept., and some weekends June and September, $26 adults, $24 seniors, $14 ages 3–12) where Arctic explorer Admiral Robert Peary built his summer home. The cruise allows time on the island to visit the house and wander the grounds. Pack a picnic, or order a box lunch 24 hours in advance.

Sail quietly across the waters of Casco Bay aboard a windjammer with **Portland Schooner Company** (Maine State Pier, 40 Commercial St., 207/766-2500, www.portlandschooner.com, late May–mid-Oct., $30 adult, $15 ages 2–12). Three or four two-hour sails are offered daily on two schooners, the 72-foot *Bagheera* and the 88-foot *Wendameen,* both historical vessels designed by John G. Alden and built in East Boothbay. Overnight windjammer trips also are available for $240 pp, including dinner and breakfast.

## Spectator Sports

A pseudofierce mascot named Slugger stirs up the crowds at baseball games played by the **Portland Sea Dogs** (Hadlock Field, 271 Park Ave., 207/879-9500 or 800/936-3647, www.portlandseadogs.com), a AA Boston Red Sox farm team. Ever since the team arrived, in 1994, loyal local fans have made tickets scarce, so it's wise to reserve well ahead (you'll pay a minimal reservation surcharge) with a major credit card. The season schedule (early Apr.–Aug.) is available after January 1. General-admission tickets are $6 adults, $3 seniors (62 and over) and kids 16 and under. Reserved seats are $7 adults, $6 all others.

For ice hockey action, the **Portland Pirates** (207/775-3458, www.portlandpirates.com,

$8–21), a farm team for the American Hockey League Anaheim Ducks, plays winter and spring home games at the 8,700-seat Cumberland County Civic Center.

The civic center is also the locale for year-round special sporting events and exhibition games, and ice shows, concerts, and college hockey games. Check the *Portland Press Herald* for schedules or call the center.

## ENTERTAINMENT AND NIGHTLIFE

The best places to find out what's playing at area theaters, cinemas, concert halls, and nightclubs are the *The Portland Phoenix* and the *Go* supplement in the Thursday edition of the *Portland Press Herald.* Both are available at bookstores and supermarkets; the *Phoenix* is free.

### Merrill Auditorium

The magnificently restored Merrill Auditorium (20 Myrtle St., box office 207/874-8200) is a 1,900-seat theater inside Portland City Hall (on Congress Street) with two balconies and one of the country's only municipally owned pipe organs, the **Kotzschmar Organ.** A summer organ classical concert series with guest artists is held at 7:30 P.M. most Tuesdays mid-June–August, $10 donation. Call for more information on the Pops series (207/883-9525).

Special events and concerts are common at Merrill, and the auditorium is also the home to a number of the city's arts organizations. The **Portland Symphony Orchestra** (207/842-0800, www.portlandsymphony.org) and **PCA Great Performances** (207/773-3150, www.pcagreatperformances.org) have extensive, well-patronized fall and winter schedules; the PSO presents three summer Independence Pops concerts as well. The **Portland Opera Repertory Theatre** (437 Congress St., 207/879-7678, www.portopera.org) performs a major opera each summer, usually in late July. In addition, there are films, lectures, and other related events throughout July. Tickets for the PSO, PCA, and PORT are available through PortTix (207/942-0800, www.porttix.com).

## St. Lawrence Arts and Community Center

Proof of what enthusiastic, determined activists can accomplish is the new St. Lawrence Arts and Community Center (76 Congress St., 207/775-5568, www.stlawrencearts. org), formerly St. Lawrence Congregational Church. Built in 1897 in Queen Anne style, the church is a distinctive landmark with more than 90 stained-glass windows. On the same street as the Portland Observatory on Munjoy Hill, the center is a vibrant venue for professional and semiprofessional theater and concerts.

## 1 Longfellow Square

The former Center for Cultural Exchange has been reborn as 1 Longfellow Square (207/761-1257, www.onelongfellowsquare.com), a venue for performances and lectures at the corner of Congress and State Streets.

## Drama

Innovative staging and controversial contemporary dramas are typical of the **Portland Stage Company** (Portland Performing Arts Center, 25A Forest Ave., 207/774-0465, www.portlandstage.com), established in 1974 and going strong ever since. Equity pros present a half dozen plays each winter season in a 290-seat performance space.

## Live Music

The Portland Conservatory of Music presents the free, weekly **Noonday Concerts** at First Parish Church (425 Congress St., 207/773-5747) at 12:15 P.M. Thursdays October–early April (excluding late November). The music varies widely, from saxophone to Scottish fiddle and dance, a string quartet to Irish baroque.

Portland Parks and Recreation sponsors **Summer in the Parks** (207/756-8275, www.ci.portland.me.us/summer.htm, July and Aug., free), a number of evening concert series, a noontime kids' series, and even movies, in downtown parks.

In summer, take the ferry to Peaks Island for sunset cocktails and often live entertainment on the deck at **Jones Landing** (at the ferry landing, Peaks Island, 207/766-4400).

## Brewpubs and Bars

Not only is **Gritty McDuff's** (396 Fore St., Old Port, 207/772-2739, 11:30 A.M.–1 A.M. daily) one of Maine's most popular breweries, its brewpub was the state's first—opened in 1988. The menu includes pub classics such as fish-and-chips and shepherd's pie, as well as burgers, salads, and sandwiches. Among the Gritty's beers and ales on tap are Sebago Light and Black Fly Stout. Gritty's also books live entertainment fairly regularly. Tours by appointment. Gritty's also has a branch in Freeport.

**Sebago Brewing Company** (164 Middle St., Old Port, 207/775-2337, 11:30 A.M.–1 A.M. daily) is newer on the scene, but prolific, with brewpubs also in Gorham and at the Maine Mall. The Portland location has seating indoors and out and a menu that varies from munchies to steak and lobster. Tours on request.

A longtime favorite pub, **$3 Dewey's** (241 Commercial St., Old Port, 207/772-3310) is so authentic that visiting Brits, Kiwis, and Aussies often head here to assuage their homesickness. Inexpensive fare, 36 brews on tap, free popcorn, and live music on Sunday, Tuesday, Wednesday, and Thursday make it a very popular spot.

Especially popular in the late afternoon and early evening is **J's Oyster** (5 Portland Pier, 207/772-4828, 11:30 A.M.–1 A.M.), a longtime fixture on the waterfront known for its raw bar and for pouring a good drink.

Of all Portland's neighborhood hangouts, **Ruski's** (212 Danforth St., 207/774-7604, 7 A.M.–12:45 A.M. Mon.–Sat., 9 A.M.–12:45 A.M. Sun.) is the most authentic—a small, usually crowded onetime speakeasy that rates just as high for breakfast as for nighttime schmoozing. Expect basic, homemade fare for well under $10, darts and big-screen TV, too. Dress down or you'll feel out of place. No credit cards.

That said, it's **Rosie's** (330 Fore St., 207/772-5656) that *Esquire* named as one of America's best bars. **Blackstones** (6 Pine St.,

207/775-2885, www.blackstones.com) claims to be Portland's oldest neighborhood gay bar.

West of I-295, **The Great Lost Bear** (540 Forest Ave., 207/772-0300, www.greatlostbear.com, 11:30 A.M.–11:30 P.M. Mon.–Sat., noon–11 P.M. Sun.) has Portland's hugest inventory of designer beers, with 54 brews on tap, representing 15 Maine microbreweries and others from New England. The bear motif and the punny menus are a bit much, but the 15 or so varieties of burgers are not bad. It's a kid pleaser.

For more upscale tippling, head for **Top of the East** (157 High St., near Congress Sq., 207/775-5411), the lounge at the top of the Eastland Park Hotel, where all of Portland's at your feet. Happy hour is 4–6 P.M. weekdays; the lounge is open until 1 A.M. Thursday–Saturday, midnight other nights. Live jazz begins at 9:30 P.M. Friday and Saturday. **Una** (505 Fore St., 207/828-0300) is a hip cocktail and wine bar serving a tapas-style menu. Another longtime favorite is **The Wine Bar** (38 Wharf St., 207/773-6667).

### Bars with Entertainment

So many possibilities are in this category, but not a lot of veterans. The Portland club scene is a volatile one, tough on investors and reporters. The best advice is to scope out the scene when you arrive; the *Portland Phoenix* has the best listings. Most clubs have cover charges. A sampling of some Portland options follows. **Asylum** (121 Center St., 207/772-8274, www.portlandasylum.com) caters to a young crowd with dance jams, CD release parties, DJ nights, and live bands. **Geno's** (13 Brown St., 207/772-7891) has been at it for years—an old reliable for rock, with an emphasis on punk rock. **Brian Boru** (57 Center St., Old Port, 207/780-1506, www.bboru.com) is an Irish pub with live Irish music and $2 pints of Guinness on Sundays. Another venue for live music is **The Big Easy** (55 Market St., 207/871-8817, www.bigeasyportland.com). **Blue** (650A Congress St., 207/774-4111, www.portcityblue.com) presents local artists and musicians in a small space and serves beer, wine, tea, and light fare; traditional Irish music is always featured on Wednesday evenings, jazz on Saturdays. Another *Esquire* recommendation is **The White Heart** (551 Congress St., 207/828-1900), a hip cocktail lounge with live music on weekends and often a DJ midweek.

### Comedy

Portland's forum for stand-up comedy is the **Comedy Connection** (6 Custom House Wharf, 207/774-5554, www.mainecomedy.com, open Thurs.–Sun. evenings), a crowded space that draws nationally known pros. Avoid the front tables unless you're inclined to be the fall guy/guinea pig, and don't bring anyone squeamish about the F-word. Bring your sense of humor, enjoy the show, and patronize the waitstaff; they have a tough job. Reservations advised on weekends.

## EVENTS

Pick up a free copy of the *Portland Area Arts and Events Calendar* at Portland shops and cafés, the Visitor Information Center, or City Hall (389 Congress St.).

June brings a host of events. The **Old Port Festival** (one of Portland's largest festivals), usually the first weekend, has entertainment, food and craft booths, and impromptu fun in Portland's Old Port. The **Greek Heritage Festival,** usually the last weekend, features Greek food, dancing, and crafts at Holy Trinity Church (133 Pleasant St., Portland).

Some of the world's top runners join upward of 500 racers in the **Beach to Beacon Race,** held in late July/early August. The 10K course goes from Crescent Beach State Park to Portland Head Light in Cape Elizabeth.

In mid-August, the **Italian Street Festival** showcases music, Italian food, and games at St. Peter's Catholic Church (72 Federal St.).

Artists from all over the country set up in 350 booths along Congress Street for the annual **Sidewalk Arts Festival,** in late August.

The **Maine Brewers' Festival,** the first weekend in November at the Portland Exposition Building, is a big event that expands every year, thanks to the explosion of Maine microbreweries. Samples galore. And from Thanksgiving weekend to Christmas Eve, **Victorian Holiday,** in downtown Portland, harks back with caroling, special sales, concerts, tree lighting, horse-drawn wagons, and Victoria Mansion tours and festivities.

## SHOPPING

The Portland peninsula—primarily Congress Street and the Old Port waterfront district—is thick with non-cookie-cutter shops and galleries. This is just a taste to spur your explorations.

### Bookstores

**Carlson-Turner Books** (241 Congress St., 207/773-4200 or 800/540-7323), based on Munjoy Hill, seems to have Portland's largest used-book inventory. Look for unusual titles and travel narratives. For good reads, contemporary fiction, and a big selection of cookbooks, visit **Cunningham Books** (199 State St., Longfellow Sq., 207/775-2246). Antique maps and atlases are the specialty at the Old Port's **Emerson Booksellers** (18 Exchange St., 207/874-2665), but it also has an excellent used-book selection.

Cookbook mavens will drool over the collection at **Rabelais Books** (86 Market St., 207/774-1044, www.rabelaisbooks.com), ideally situated in Portland's foodie neighborhood. Don and Samantha Hoyt Lindgren specialize in food and wine, carrying a delicious blend of thousands of current, rare, and out-of-print books covering culinary history, food lit, cookbooks, wine, and related topics.

For current works, **Books Etc.** (38 Exchange St., 207/774-0626) is a independent shop with a wide-ranging inventory.

### Art Galleries

Intown Portland's galleries host a **First Friday Artwalk** on the first Friday evening of each month, with exhibition openings, open houses, meet-the-artist gatherings, and other such artsy activities.

A handful of galleries specializing in contemporary art are clustered in the Arts District. These include **Aucocisco** (613 Congress St., 207/553-2222, www.aucocisco.com), **June Fitzpatrick Gallery** (112 High St., 207/879-5742, www.junefitzpatrickgallery.com), and **Institute for Contemporary Art** (Maine College of Art, 522 Congress St., 207/879-5742), with walk-in tours at 12:15 P.M. every Wednesday. In the Old Port, find **Greenhut Galleries** (146 Middle St., 207/772-2693, www.greenhutgalleries.com), another well-respected gallery showing contemporary Maine art and sculpture.

### Crafts

More than 15 Maine potters—with a wide variety of styles and items—market their wares at the **Maine Potters Market** (376 Fore St., 207/774-1633), an attractive shop in the heart of the Old Port. Established in 1980, the cooperative remains a consistently reliable outlet for some of Maine's best ceramic artisans.

Just around the corner is **Abacus** (44 Exchange St., 207/772-4880), where craft rises to a high art. Whimsy is the byword here; if you don't arrive smiling, you'll leave that way. Open all year. Abacus has branches in Kennebunkport and Freeport, and a seasonal shop in Boothbay Harbor.

### Offbeat Shopping

Trustmi, you have to see **Suitsmi** (35 Pleasant St., 207/772-8285, www.suitsmi.com), which carries wearables (including jewelry) perfect for rock concerts, funky cafés, and, if you're dying to make a statement, your class reunion. Top it all off with a hat from **Queen of Hats** (560 Congress St., 207/772-2379, www.queenofhats.com). **Shipwreck and Cargo** (207 Commercial St., Old Port, 207/775-3057, www.shipwreckandcargo.com) stocks a wide assortment of marine-related items—boat models, barometers, navy surplus stuff, and more. Even more fun and offbeat is **China Sea Marine Trading Co.** (Wharf St., 207/773-0081, www.chinaseatrading.com), where Steve Bunker and his macaw Singapore sell his wild and eclectic finds.

Woof. The company outlet **Planet Dog** (211 Marginal Way, Portland, 207/347-8606, www.planetdog.com) is a barking good time for dogs and their owners. You'll find all sorts of wonderful products, and Planet Dog, committed to "think globally and act doggedly," has established a foundation to promote and serve causes such as therapy, service, search and rescue, bomb sniffing, and police dogs.

## ACCOMMODATIONS
### Downtown Portland

Portland's peninsula doesn't have an overwhelming amount of sleeping space, but it does have good variety in all price ranges. Rates reflect peak season.

**Inns/Bed-and-Breakfasts:** Railroad tycoon John Deering built **The Inn at St. John** (939 Congress St., 207/773-6481 or 800/636-9127, www.innatstjohn.com, $85–180) in 1897. The clean, comfortable, moderately priced 37-room hostelry has the feel of a European-style hotel. It welcomes children and pets and even has bicycle storage. Cable TV, air-conditioning, free local calls, free parking, free airport pickup, and continental breakfast are provided. Most rooms have private baths (some are detached); some have fridge and microwave. The only downsides are the lack of an elevator and the lackluster neighborhood—in the evening you'll want drive or take a taxi when going out. It's about a half-hour walk to the Old Port or an $8 taxi fare.

Staying at ( **The Pomegranate Inn** (49 Neal St. at Carroll St., 207/772-1006 or 800/356-0408, www.pomegranateinn.com, $175–285) is an adventure in itself, with faux painting, classical statuary, art, antiques, and whimsical touches everywhere—you'll either love it or find it a bit much. The elegant 1884 Italianate mansion has seven guest rooms and a suite, all with private baths, air-conditioning, TV, and phones, some with fireplaces. Afternoon refreshments are served.

Take an 1830s townhouse, add contemporary amenities and a service-oriented innkeeper, and the result is the **Morrill Mansion Bed and Breakfast** (249 Vaughan St., 207/774-6900 or 888/566-7745, www.morrillmansion.com, $189–219), on the West End. Six rooms and one suite are spread out on the second and third floors (no elevator) in a carefully renovated town house. No frilly Victorian accents here—rather, the decor is understated, yet tasteful, taking advantage of hardwood floors and high ceilings. You'll find free Wi-Fi and local calls and TV/DVD in each room. A continental breakfast is included; off-street parking is free. It's near the hospital, so you might hear a siren or two. The only real negative is the lack of a comfortable living room–type area.

Former travel writer Dale Northrup put his experience to work in opening the **Percy Inn** (15 Pine St., 207/871-7638 or 888/417-3729, www.percyinn.com, $119–199), just off Longfellow Square. You can easily hole up in the guest rooms, which are furnished with phones, fax machines, CD players, TVs with VCRs, wet bars, and stocked refrigerators, and they have air-condtioning. It's best suited for independent-minded travelers who don't desire much contact with the host or other guests, as public rooms are few and the innkeeper is rarely on-site. Breakfast is a continental buffet.

Built in 1835, **The Inn at Park Spring** (135 Spring St., 207/774-1059 or 800/427-8511, www.innatparkspring.com, $149–175) is one of Portland's longest-running B&Bs. Current innkeepers Nancy and John Gonsalves are adding their own touches to make guests feel right at home. The location is just steps from most Arts District attractions. Six guest rooms are spread out on three floors (no elevator, steep stairs). All have air-conditioning and phones, some have Internet access; one has a private patio and entrance. There's a guest fridge on each floor. Rates include a full breakfast.

Built in 1877, the handsome Georgian-style **The West End Inn** (146 Pine St. at Neal St., 207/772-1377 or 800/338-1377, www.westendbb.com, $159–209) has six nicely decorated second- and third-floor guest rooms with TV, and a first-floor room with private porch. A full breakfast is served. Pack light if you're on the third floor.

**Full-Service Hotels:** You might have trouble finding the **The Portland Regency** (20 Milk St., 207/774-4200 or 800/727-3436, www.theregency.com, $199–249). That's because this lovely hotel is secreted in a renovated armory in the heart of the Old Port. Local calls are free, Wi-Fi and laptop rentals are available, and free shuttles are provided to all major Portland transportation facilities. Room configurations vary widely—some provide little natural window light or are strangely shaped. All have 27-inch TVs, minibars, and air-conditioning. A restaurant, spa, and fitness center are on-site.

Newest and most luxurious is the ◖ **Portland Harbor Hotel** (468 Fore St., 207/775-9090 or 888/798-9090, www.portlandharborhotel.com, $249–379), an upscale, boutique hotel in the Old Port built around a garden courtyard. Rooms are plush, with chic linens, duvets, down pillows on the beds, Wi-Fi and digital cable TV, and bathrooms with separate soaking tubs and showers. Bike rentals are available for $15 per day, and the hotel offers a free local car service. The restaurant is excellent. The downside is that the neighborhood can be noisy at night, so request a room facing the interior courtyard, preferably on the upper floors.

Yes, it's a chain, and yes, it's downright ugly, but the **Holiday Inn by the Bay** (88 Spring St., 207/775-2311 or 800/345-5050, www.innbythebay.com, $176–188) provides a lot of bang for the buck. It's conveniently situated between the waterfront and the Arts District; rooms on upper floors have views either over Back Cove or Portland Harbor; Wi-Fi and parking are free as is a shuttle service. It also has an indoor pool, sauna, and fitness room and on-site laundry facilities, in addition to a restaurant and lounge.

## Beyond Downtown

South of Portland are a number of inns and resorts, some right on the ocean, others within walking distance.

Just down the street from neighborhoody Higgins Beach is the informal **Higgins Beach Inn** (34 Ocean Ave., Scarborough, 207/883-6684 or 800/836-2322, www.higginsbeachinn.com, mid-May–mid-Oct., $125–165), what your mind's eye might conjure as a traditional, turn-of-the-20th-century summer hotel. It has 24 no-frills rooms, some with shared bath, a few with ocean views. The inn's **Garofalo's Restaurant** has a creative Italian slant, emphasizing seafood (entrées $18–26). In summer, the restaurant is open to the public for breakfast 7:30–10:30 A.M. and dinner 5–9 P.M.; reservations are advisable for dinner, especially on weekends.

In 2007, the **Black Point Inn Resort** (510 Black Point Rd., Prouts Neck, Scarborough, 207/883-2500 or 800/258-0003, www.blackpointinn.com, $190–289 pp, including breakfast, afternoon tea, and dinner) reopened after being dramatically downsized and upscaled. The historical shingle-style hotel sits at the tip of Prouts Neck, with views to Casco Bay from one side and down to Old Orchard from the other, and beaches out the front and back doors. Now owned by a local partnership, the inn has returned to its roots, catering to wealthy rusticators. The Point dining room is open to the public by reservation (6–9 P.M. daily, $19–38), but first, have cocktails on the porch at sunset. Staying here is splurge worthy. Guests have access to a private 18-hole golf course and tennis courts.

Seven miles south of downtown Portland, **Inn by the Sea** (40 Bowery Beach Rd., Rte. 77, Cape Elizabeth, 207/799-3134 or 800/888-4287, www.innbythesea.com, $399–789 d) is a well-managed modern complex with the stylishly casual feel of an upscale summerhouse. It underwent a major renovation and expansion (reopening June 2008) that added a full-service spa and cardio room. Guests stay in hotel rooms, spa suites, or two-bedroom garden cottages, all with spectacular water views. A boardwalk winds down through the salt marsh to the southern end of Crescent Beach State Park. Facilities include an outdoor pool and croquet lawn. By reservation, pets are honored guests here (they even have their own room-service menu). Make reservations early; the inn is incredibly popular. Priceless Audubon prints cover the walls in the appropriately named **Audubon Room** (207/767-0888), where moderate-to-expensive breakfasts, lunches, and dinners are served daily to guests—and to the public by reservation.

The **Peter A. McKernan Hospitality Center** (Southern Maine Technical College, Fort Rd., South Portland, front desk 207/741-5672, reservations 207/741-5662, www.hospitality.smccme.edu, $175) provides a different twist on the inn experience. In fact, it's the proving ground for students in the Lodging and Restaurant Management Program at Southern Maine Community College. The center, a 1902 brick building that once served as officers' quarters, has spectacular views of Casco Bay and the offshore islands. Students staff the inn, and they all aim to please. Shorefront walking/biking trails are nearby. The center keeps a low profile, yet rooms are booked far ahead. Rates include continental breakfast.

## Island Lodging

The **Inn on Peaks Island** (33 Island Ave., www.theinnonpeaksisland.com, $250–300) overlooks the ferry dock and has jaw-dropping sunset views over the Portland skyline. No island roughing it here. The spacious cottage-style guest rooms have fireplaces, sitting areas, whirlpool baths, TV and VCR, refrigerators, and rates include a continental breakfast. Lunch and dinner are also served in the inn's Shipyard Brewhaus restaurant ($10–22). Access is via Casco Bay Lines or a water taxi.

On the other end of the Peaks Island luxury scale is the extremely informal and communal **Eighth Maine Living Museum and Lodge** (13 Eighth Maine Ave., 207/766-5086 mid-May–mid-Sept., 914/237-3165 off-season, $80–100), a shorefront, rustic, living history lodge overlooking White Head Passage. Shared baths and a huge shared kitchen (in which every room is allocated a two-burner gas stove, cabinet space, dining table, and access to full kitchen facilities) allow you to rusticate in much the same manner as did the Civil War vets who built this place, in 1891, with a gift from a veteran who had won the Louisiana Lottery. It has no

housekeeping—you're responsible for stripping the linens and cleaning the room and your kitchen space before departing.

The **Chebeague Orchard Inn** (453 North Rd., Chebeague Island, 207/846-9488, $125–165) doubles as longtime residents Vickie and Neil Taliento's comfortable, antiques-filled home. Five rooms have handmade quilts (three have private baths and two share a bath); some have water views. The congenial Talientos are big supporters of the Maine Island Trail Association, so you'll get a discount if you arrive by kayak (the trail begins near Chebeague). Coffee's ready at 7 A.M.; breakfast is continental midweek, full on the weekends and served overlooking the backyard's bird feeders and apple orchard. There are bikes for guests, a fireplace in the common room, and tons of helpful advice about the island. For dinner, many guests pick up takeout and bring it back to the inn.

Another possibility might be the **Chebeague Island Inn,** a lovely and historical inn with a dining room that was expected to reopen once it's sold.

## FOOD

Downtown Portland alone has more than 100 restaurants, so it's impossible to list even all the great ones—and there are many. The city's proximity to fresh foods, from both farms and the sea, makes it popular with chefs, and its Italian roots and growing immigrant population mean a good choice of ethnic dining, too. Below is a choice selection, by neighborhood, with open days and hours provided for peak season. Call in advance September–June. You'll note that some restaurants don't list a closing time; that's because they shut the doors when the crowd thins, so call ahead if you're heading out much after 8 P.M., just to be safe. Do make reservations, whenever possible, and as far in advance as you can, especially in July and August. If you're especially into the food scene, check www.portlandfoodmap.com for a breakdown by cuisine of Portland restaurants with links to recent reviews.

If you'll be in Maine for more than a few days,

check out the **Portland Dine Around Club** (P.O. Box 15338, Portland 04112, 207/775-4711 or 877/732-2582, www.dineportland.com, $29.95). This discount card gets you two-for-the-price-of-one meals (usually dinner entrées) at more than 150 restaurants with a wide variety of menus, decor, and price ranges as well as discounts at numerous attractions, museums, performing arts venues, and even lodging, statewide. Check the website to see if the discounts are valid where and when you want them.

In addition to the many restaurant options listed here, check the *Community News* listings in each Wednesday's *Portland Press Herald*. Under "Potluck," you'll find listings of **public meals,** usually benefiting nonprofit organizations. Prices are always quite low (under $10 for adults, $2–4 for children), mealtimes quite early (5 or 6 P.M.), and the flavor quite local.

When you need a java fix, **Coffee by Design** (620 Congress St., 67 India St., and 43 Washington Ave.) is the local choice, not only for its fine brews but also for its support of local artists and community causes.

**The Portland Farmers Market** sets up on Wednesdays on Monument Square and on Saturdays in Deering Oaks Park.

## The Old Port and the Waterfront

All of these are east of the Franklin Street Arterial, between Congress and Commercial Streets.

Best known for the earliest and most filling breakfast, **Becky's Diner** (Hobson's Wharf, 390 Commercial St., Old Port, 207/773-7070, 4 A.M.–9 P.M. daily) has more than a dozen omelette choices, just for a start. It also serves lunch and dinner, all at downright cheap prices.

The color's a lot more local just down the street at **The Porthole** (20 Custom House Wharf, Commercial St., Old Port, 207/774-6652, 7 A.M.–2 A.M. Mon.–Sat.), a onetime dive that's been gussied up a bit. The all-you-can-eat Friday fish fry pulls in *real* fishermen, in-the-know locals, and fearless tourists. Eat inside or on the wharf. I like it for breakfast or the Friday $5.95 all-you-can-eat fish fry.

Pizza with a view is on tap at **Flatbread Company** (72 Commercial St., 207/772-8777, www.flatbreadcompany.com, 11:30 A.M.–10 P.M. daily), part of a small, New England chain. The all-natural pizza is baked in a primitive, wood-fired clay oven and served in a dining room with a wall of windows overlooking the ferry terminal and Portland Harbor. Half- and whole-size pizzas include choices such as nitrate-free pepperoni, vegan (dairy-free) flatbread, cheese and herb, and you-choose combos.

Healthful fast food? Stonyfield Farm CEO Gary Hirshberg proved it wasn't an oxymoron with **O'Natural's** (88 Exchange St., 207/321-2050, www.onaturals.com, 7:30 A.M.–8 P.M., to 8:30 P.M. Fri. and Sat., 10 A.M.–3 P.M. Sun.). The emphasis is on fresh, local, and organic, with choices including flatbread sandwiches, tossed salads, Asian noodles, soups, and even a kids' menu. Wheat-free, dairy-free, and veggie choices are available. It's all served in a historical bank building, where the huge safe is now a safe play area for kids.

For "gourmet goodies" don't miss **Browne Trading Market** (Merrill's Wharf, 262 Commercial St., 207/775-7560). Owner Rod Mitchell became the Caviar King of Portland by wholesaling Caspian caviar, and he's now letting the rest of us in on it. Ultimately fresh fish and shellfish fill the cases next to the caviar and cheeses. The mezzanine is wall-to-wall (literally) wine, specializing in French.

**Sweet Treats:** When you're craving carbs, want pastries for breakfast, or need to boost your energy with a sweet, follow your nose to **Standard Baking Company** (75 Commercial St., 207/773-2112), deservedly famous for its handcrafted breads and pastries. Chocoholics take note: When a craving strikes for scrumptious homemade chocolates or ice cream, head to **Fuller's** (Wharf St., 207/253-8010).

**Fish and Seafood:** Ask around, and everyone will tell you the best seafood in town is at **Street and Company** (33 Wharf St., Old Port, 207/775-0887, 5–9:30 P.M., to 10 P.M. Fri. and Sat.). Fresh, beautifully prepared fish (entrées begin about $18) is what you get, often with a Mediterranean flair. Tables are tight, and it's often noisy in the informal, brick-walled rooms.

If that's a little too limited, consider **Old Port Sea Grille and Raw Bar** (www.theold-portseagrill.com, opens 11:30 A.M. daily), a sleek, modern spot near the waterfront, with a fabulous raw bar and 500-gallon aquarium inside. Entrées run $20–33, and no surprise, seafood is the specialty.

For lobster in the rough, head to **Portland Lobster Company** (180 Commercial St., 207/775-2112, 11 A.M.–9 P.M. daily). There's a small inside seating area, but it's much more pleasant to sit out on the wharf and watch the excursion boats come and go. Expect to pay in the low $20 range for a one-pound lobster with fries and slaw. Other choices ($8–23) and a kids' menu are available.

**Ethnic Fare:** Be forewarned: Your first foray into 【 **Bresca** (111 Middle St., 207/772-1004, opens 5:30 P.M. Tues.–Sat.) won't be your last. Chef Krista Kerns delivers big flavor in this small, Italian-flavored space next to Portland's police station. She shops each morning, buying just enough for that night's meal (yes, items do sell out). You'll need a reservation to land one of the 20 seats. Service is personal, the meal is leisurely, the food divine. Do save room for dessert: Krista initially made her name as a pastry chef.

Top-notch for northern Italian is **Cinque Terre Ristorante** (36 Wharf St., 207/347-6154, www.cinqueterremaine.com, 5–9 P.M. Sun.–Thurs., to 10 P.M. Fri. and Sat.). Chef Lee Skawinski is committed to sustainable farming, and much of the seasonal and organic produce used comes from the restaurant owners' Laughing Stock Farm and other Maine farms. The restaurant is housed in a former ship's chandlery that's been transformed into a comfortable, Tuscan-accented dining area, with an open kitchen and seating either on the main floor or a second-floor balcony that rims the open space. Choose from half- or full-size portions ranging $12–28. Do begin with the antipasto plate, and don't miss the hand-made pastas or the lobster risotto. More than

100 Italian wines are on the award-winning list. Service can be iffy.

Cinque Terre's sister restaurant, **Vignola** (10 Dana St., 207/772-1330, www.vignolamaine.com, 11 A.M.–2:30 P.M. and 5 P.M.–midnight daily, opens 10 A.M. Sun. for brunch), is more casual and less pricey ($10–18) and wins points for late-night dining.

Ask locally about **Village Café,** an ever-popular family favorite for its respectable Italian food (entrées $10–23), healthful specials, and fried clams. In biz since 1936, it expected to reopen in a new Portland location in 2008.

Irish fare with a Maine accent fills the menu at **Ri-Ra** (72 Commercial St., Old Port, 207/761-4446, www.rira.com, 11:30 A.M.–10 P.M. daily). How about beef stew made with Guinness? Or grilled salmon with leeks? Entrées in the glass-walled second-floor dining room (overlooking the Casco Bay Lines ferry terminal) are $11–29. Appetizers and desserts are superb, too. The ground-floor pub, elegantly woody, with an enormous bar, is inevitably stuffed to the gills on weekends—a great spot for such traditional fare as corned beef and cabbage (pub entrées $8–16) as long as you can stand the din. No reservations, so be prepared to wait, especially on weekends.

**Eclectic Dining:** The people-watching can't be beat from the patio or deck of **Mims Brasserie** (205 Commercial St., Old Port, 207/345-7478, www.mimsportland.com, 8 A.M.–9:30 P.M. Mon.–Fri., 9 A.M.–10 P.M. Sat.–Sun.). The à la carte French-inspired menu features naturally raised meats. Dinner entrées are $12–25; side dishes are extra and designed to be mixed, matched, and shared. Create your own omelette at breakfast; Benedicts are the specialties during weekend brunch.

One of Portland's old reliables, **Walter's** (15 Exchange St., 207/871-9258, www.walters-cafe.com, 11 A.M.–2:30 P.M. and 5–9 P.M., no lunch Sun.) has been serving creative fusion fare since 1990s, and despite the longevity, it's never tiresome. The two-level dining room can be noisy. Entrées run around $16–26.

Okay, it's not exactly on the city's waterfront, but you take a Casco Bay Lines ferry from there to get to **Diamond's Edge Restaurant** (Great Diamond Island, 207/766-5850, www.diamondsedge.com, 11:30 A.M.–2:30 P.M. and 5–9 P.M. daily late May–late Sept.). You'll need to coordinate your dining with the ferry schedule, but it's worth it for the views along the way. Best bet: Go for lunch. The restaurant, in a renovated Fort McKinley Quartermaster Corps building, is elegant without being at all stuffy. In fine weather, you can dine outside.

**Destination Dining:** Plan well in advance to get a reservation at 【 **Fore Street** (288 Fore St., Old Port, 207/775-2717, www.forestreet.biz, 5:30–10 P.M. Sun.–Thurs., to 10:30 P.M. Fri. and Sat.). Chef Sam Hayward, a fixture on the Maine food scene who is well known for his creative use of Maine-sourced ingredients, won the James Beard Award for Best Chef in the Northeast in 2004 and has been featured in most of the foodie publications. Even though the copper-topped tables, open kitchen, and the industrial decor create a din in this ex-warehouse, no one seems to mind much. Game is roasted on a spit and seafood is grilled over apple wood or roasted in the wood oven. Appetizers are particularly imaginative. Entrées begin around $20. The restaurant is a joint project with Street and Company owner Dana Street.

## Arts District

These restaurants are clustered from Danforth Street (an area sometimes referred to as the Studio District) up to and around Congress Street. If you feel like just browsing and finding a spot, walk Congress Street, from around Longfellow Square down to Congress Square, for an ever-evolving variety of ethnic and mainstream choices. Be sure to ask about renowned chef Erik Desjarlais's planned new restaurant **Evangeline** (190 State St.) on Longfellow Square. Expected are both three-course a-la-carte and seven-to-fifteen-course degustation menus, bar and table seating, a well-chosen wine menu, and artwork on view.

**Local Flavors:** Even the name **Norm's Bar and Grill** (617 Congress St., 207/828-9944, 11:30 A.M.–10 P.M., opens at 4 P.M. Sun.) is reminiscent of *Cheers*. Locals would prefer this neighborhood eatery were kept secret, but the food is too good not to share. One of the reasons Norm's is so popular is that you can cobble together a meal that meets your appetite from a menu that includes selections for tapas, sandwiches, salads, entrées, and sides in addition to chalkboard specials. Norm's doesn't take reservations, so you'll probably have to relax in the equally popular bar while waiting for a table. Norm also operates the tavern across the street and a barbecue joint in the Old Port.

Ole! Healthful Mexican is served at **Mesa Verde** (618 Congress St., 774-6089, 11:30 A.M.–9 P.M. Tues.–Thurs., to 9:30 P.M. Fri. and Sat., to 8:30 P.M. Sun.), a colorful restaurant and juice bar that also is rightfully famous for its margaritas.

If your sweet tooth is calling, answer it at **geo's patisserie café** (27 Forest Ave., 207/699-2655, www.geospatisserie.com, 7 A.M.–6 P.M. Mon.–Fri., 8 A.M.–5 P.M. Sat.), a European-style scratch bakery where chef George Gilfoil creates delicious pastries and also serves lunch.

Can't make up your mind? Peruse the choices available at **Public Market House** (28 Monument Sq., 207/228-2056, http://publicmarkethouse.com, 8 A.M.–6 P.M. Mon.–Fri., 9 A.M.–6 P.M. Sat., 10 A.M.–3 P.M. Sun.), which came about after the closure of the Portland Public Market. This is far smaller, but the quality and the fun are still there. It's a growing space, with maybe a half dozen vendors selling sandwiches, baked goods, soups, and other fresh fare.

**Eclectic:** Ever-popular 【 **Local 188** (685 Congress St., 207/761-7909, www.local188.com, 11 A.M.–3 P.M. and 5:30–10:30 P.M. daily) moved from its funky digs to a larger, more comfortable space, keeping its spirit but maturing (a bit) in decor. This place serves fabulous Mediterranean-inspired food with a tapas-heavy menu. It doubles as an art gallery, with rotating exhibits. Spend lunch, Saturday or Sunday brunch (10 A.M.–3 P.M.), or an evening grazing through marinated mushrooms, vegetable salads, imaginative soups, mussel stew, even paella. Tapas selections are all under $10, heartier choices and entrées run $10–18. Free parking behind the building.

Be sure to have a reservation if you're going, pretheater, to **BiBo's Madd Apple Café** (23 Forest Ave., 207/774-9698, 11:30 A.M.–2 P.M. Wed.–Fri., 5:30–9 P.M. Wed.–Sat., 11 A.M.–2 P.M. and 4–8 P.M. Sun.)—it's right next to the Portland Performing Arts Center. On the other hand, it's popular anytime, thanks to chef Bill Boutwell (BiBo). There's no way of predicting what will be on the bistro-fusion menu, although the sweet soy-marinated salmon is so popular that it's almost always available. Dinner entrée range is $15–25.

Well off most tourists' radar screens is **Artemesia Café** (61 Pleasant St., 207/761-0135, 11 A.M.–3 P.M. Mon.–Fri., 9 A.M.–2 P.M. Sat. and Sun., and from 5 P.M. Thurs.–Sat.), but it's another one of Portland's little surprises. It's a bright spot serving a creative menu that draws upon international influences.

**Ethnic Fare:** Portland has a number of good Japanese restaurants. **Yosaku** (1 Danforth St., 207/780-0880, 11:30 A.M.–2 P.M. and 5–9:30 P.M. Mon.–Thurs., to 10:30 P.M. Fri. and Sat., to 9 P.M. Sun., and noon–3 P.M. Sat. and Sun.) is an old standby serving delicious sushi along with noodle dishes, tempuras, and other Japanese favorites.

Newer on the scene is **Miyake** (129 Spring St., 207/871-9170, noon–2 P.M. Tues.–Fri., 5–9 P.M. Mon.–Thurs., to 9:30 P.M. Fri. and Sat.), chef Masa Miyake's tiny, ultra informal neighborhood joint, which quickly established itself as a must-go; BYOB. The decor is Pepsi and plastic, but don't let that dissuade you, you can always get it to go.

**Destination Dining:** Fun, whimsical, and artsy best describes most restaurants in the Arts District, but not **Five Fifty-Five** (555 Congress St., 207/761-0555, www.fivefifty-five.com, 5–10 P.M. Mon.–Thurs., to 10:30 P.M. Fri. and Sat., 10:30 A.M.–2:30 P.M. (brunch) and 5–9:30 P.M. Sun.), where chef Steve Corry was named by *Food and Wine* as one of the top 10 best new chefs in the country. The bilevel dining area is bright and elegant. Fresh, local, and seasonal are blended in creative ways on

his ever-changing menu, which is divided into small plates, green plates, savory plates, cheese plates, and sweet plates, with prices ranging about $8–30. A five-course tasting menu is available with 24-hour notice. If you can't afford to splurge in the main restaurant, Corry serves lighter fare in the lounge.

## West End

Chef Abby Harmon's **Caiola's Restaurant** (58 Pine St., 207/772-1111, www.caiolas.com, 5:30–9:30 P.M. Tues.–Thurs., to 10 P.M. Fri. and Sat.) delivers a taste of Europe derived from local farms and gardens. It deserves its buzz as far more than a neighborhood spot. Harmon draws upon her experience at some of Maine's top restaurants, and her staff is well trained. Entrées begin around $14.

Superb, thin-crust pizzas in usual and unusual flavor combos emerge from the wood-fired oven at chef Oliver Outerbridge's **Bonobo** (Pine and Bracket Sts., 207/347-8267, 11 A.M.–11 P.M. Mon.–Sat.). After the pizza, head to the ice-cream window, serving Maple's Organics gelato.

Have breakfast or lunch or pick up prepared foods at **Aurora Provisions** (64 Pine St., 207/871-9061, www.auroraprovisions.com, 8 A.M.–6:30 P.M. Mon.–Sat.), a combination market and café with irresistible goodies, most made on the premises.

Tiny **Dogfish Cafe** (953 Congress St., 207/253-5400, 11:30 A.M.–10 P.M. Mon.–Sat.) packs 'em in for salads and sandwiches and grilled goodies, averaging around $10, with heartier dinner specials ($11–18) served evenings Wednesday–Saturday. It's just a couple of doors down from the Inn on St. John.

## Bayside

**Fine Dining:** For an elegant meal, look no farther than the **( Back Bay Grill** (65 Portland St., near the main post office, 207/772-8833, 5:30–9:30 P.M. Mon.–Thurs., to 10 P.M. Fri. and Sat.). The serene dining room is accented by a colorful mural, and arts-and-crafts wall sconces cast a soft glow on the white linen-draped tables. The menu, which highlights fresh, seasonal ingredients, ranks among the best in the city, and the wine list is long and well chosen. Service is professional. Entréees are $19–35 and worth every penny.

**Casual Dining:** In-the-know Portlanders have long favored **Bintliff's American Café** (98 Portland St., 207/774-0005, www.bintliffscafe.com, 7 A.M.–2 P.M. daily and 5–9 P.M. Wed.–Sat.) for its fabulous brunches ($7–12); the menu is humongous. It also serves a much smaller dinner menu (entrées $17–25) to equally rave reviews. It takes no reservations for brunch, so expect to wait in line on weekends (it's worth it).

## East End

These dining spots are all east of the Franklin Street Arterial, with most concentrated in the food-oriented neighborhood of India and Middle Streets. Poke around this end of the city, and you'll find quite a few ethnic hole-in-the-wall places on and around Washington Avenue. It's an ever-changing array, but if you're adventurous, give one a try.

**Local Flavors:** The most incredible fries come from ◖ **Duckfat** (43 Middle St., 207/774-8080, www.duckfat.com, 11 A.M.–8 P.M. Mon.–Thurs., to 9 P.M. Fri. and Sat., noon–6 P.M. Sun.), an ultracasual, order-at-the-counter joint owned by chef Rob Evans (of Hugo's fame), so you know it's not only good, but it has that spark, too. Fries, fried in duck fat, of course, are served in a paper cone and accompanied by your choice of sauce from six options; the truffle ketchup is heavenly. Want to really harden those arteries? Order the *poutine*, Belgian fries topped with Maine cheese curd and homemade duck gravy. In addition, Duckfat serves paninis, soups, salads, and really good milk shakes; wine and beer are available, too. Mmmmm, mmmm. For finger-lickin' barbecued ribs and chicken, fried chicken, blackened catfish, and pulled pork or beef brisket sandwiches, it's **Norm's East End Grill** (37 Middle St., 207/253-1700, 11:30 A.M.–10 P.M. Mon.–Sat., 5–9 P.M. Sun.). All barbecue items are smoked on the premises with hickory and apple wood. Of course, this being Maine, clam

and corn chowder, homemade fish cakes, and lobster stew are also available.

Mainers love their Italian sandwiches, and **Amato's** (71 India St., 207/773-1682, www.amatos.com, 6:30 A.M.–11 P.M. Mon.–Fri., opens 7 A.M. Sun.) is credited with creating this drool-worthy sub, made with ham, cheese, tomatoes, green peppers, black olives, and onions (or various other combinations), all wrapped in a doughy roll and drizzled with olive oil. Also available are calzones, salads, and other Italian-inspired foods. Amato's has outlets throughout southern Maine. This one has outdoor patio seating.

**Micucci's Grocery Store** (45 India St., 207/775-1854) has been servicing Portland's Italian community since 1949. It's a great stop for picnic fixings and a nice selection of inexpensive wines. It's also home to baker Stephen Lanzalotta's to-die-for breads and pastries, soups, little pizzas, and other healthful, delicious Mediterranean-style foods.

Huge portions at rock-bottom prices makes **Silly's** (40 Washington Ave., 207/772-0360, www.sillys.com, 11:30 A.M.–9 P.M. Tues.–Sun.) an ever-popular choice among the young and budget minded; it has a huge menu, too, with lots of international flair and milk shakes in dozens of wacko flavors. And the decor? Vintage 1950s Formica and chrome.

It's hard not to like **North Star Cafe** (225 Congress St., 207/699-2994, www.northstarmusiccafe.com, 7 A.M.–10 P.M. Mon.–Wed., to 11 P.M. Thurs.–Sat., 8 A.M.–4 P.M. Sun.), a low-key and comfy coffeehouse serving excellent soups, sandwiches, and salads, most made from locally sourced and organic ingredients. Music or readings occur almost every evening.

Just try *not* to walk out with something from **Two Fat Cats Bakery** (47 India St., 207/347-5144); the cookies! the breads! the pies!

**Casual Dining: Blue Spoon** (89 Congress St., 207/773-1119, 11 A.M.–3 P.M. and 5–9 P.M. Tues.–Sat.) was one of the first upscale eateries on Portland's gentrifying East End. Chef/owner David Iovino, who studied at the French Culinary Institute, has created a warm, welcoming, and inexpensive bistro (entrées

$9–13), where one of the best sellers is roast chicken that's pan seared and then roasted beneath a hot brick. Vegetarian and vegan selections are available.

A more recent addition to the neighborhood is **Bar Lola** (100 Congress St., 207/775-5652, 5–10 P.M. Wed.–Sat.), an intimate and cozy neighborhood bistro serving an all-tapas menu—small portions, big flavors.

Primo rustic Italian fare is the rule at **Ribollita** (41 Middle St., 207/774-2972, 5–9 P.M. Tues.–Thurs., to 10 P.M. Fri. and Sat.). You'll want reservations at this small, casual restaurant that's justly popular for delivering fabulous food at fair prices ($12–20); just be in the mood for a leisurely meal. Handmade pastas, such as white bean and Romano ravioli or pan-seared gnocchi, and choices such as radicchio-wrapped salmon with pesto and roast pepper sauce are typical.

You never know what'll be on the menu (Indonesian chicken, North African stuffed peppers, maybe Caribbean shrimp cakes?) at funky **Pepperclub** (78 Middle St., 207/772-0531, www.pepperclubrestaurant.com, 5–9 P.M. Sun.–Thurs., to 10 P.M. Fri. and Sat.), but take the risk. Vegetarian and vegan specials are always available, as are local and organic meats and seafood. If your kids are even vaguely adventuresome, they'll find food to like here—and prices to match (entrées $11–15). In the mornings, it morphs into **The Good Egg** (7–11 A.M. Mon.–Fri., 8 A.M.–1 P.M. Sat. and Sun.), serving breakfast, including gluten-free foods.

**Destination Dining:** In 2004, *Food and Wine* named Rob Evans as one of America's 10 Best New Chefs, and in 2007 he was a Beard nominee for Best Chef in the Northeast, making ◖ **Hugo's** (88 Middle St., corner of Franklin St., 207/774-8538, www.hugos.net, 5:30–9 P.M. Tues.–Thurs., to 9:30 P.M. Sat. and Sun.) a destination unto itself. Not that savvy Portlanders hadn't already been beating a path to his door for his outstanding New American cuisine. In 2008, Evans and partner Nancy Pugh planned to change the formal fixed-price, multicourse menu to an à la carte one (most entrées $15–28) and present a more casual face. Evans will still draw from the freshest Maine ingredients available. Bar seating is available; for the dining room, reservations are essential.

## The 'Burbs

Great sunset views over Portland's skyline, a casual atmosphere, and excellent fare have earned **Saltwater Grille** (231 Front St., South Portland, 207/799-5400, www.saltwatergrille.com, 11 A.M.–3 P.M. and 5–9 P.M. daily) an excellent reputation. Dine inside or on the waterfront deck. Dinner entrées run $15–25.

How about a four-course lunch, with a matchless view, on the cheap? The students in the hospitality program at Southern Maine Community College (Fort Rd., Spring Point, South Portland) need practice for their cooking and service skills, so their "labs" are two restaurants. During the academic year, the **Culinary Arts Dining Room** serves a four-course lunch Wednesday and Thursday and a buffet Friday noon–1:30 P.M., for $10.50, with reservations; call 207/741-5612.

**Pizza: Ricetta's Brick Oven Pizzeria** (29 Western Ave., Rte. 9, South Portland, between Maine Mall and Portland Jetport, 207/775-7400, and 240 Rte. 1, Falmouth, 207/781-3100, 11:30 A.M.–10 P.M., to 11 P.M. Fri. and Sat.) is regularly voted Greater Portland's best pizza palace. It's not surprising when you see the lunchtime-only pizza smorgasbord—all the pizza you can eat, plus salad and soup. Specialty pizzas are outstanding, or you can invent your own combo. Also on the menu are antipasti, calzones, giant salads, soups, pasta dishes, and high-calorie desserts.

**Lobster in the Rough:** Every Mainer has a favorite lobster eatery (besides home), but **The Lobster Shack** (222 Two Lights Rd., Cape Elizabeth, 207/799-1677, www.lobstershacktwolights.com, 11 A.M.–8 P.M. mid-Apr.–mid-Oct.) tops an awful lot of lists. Seniority helps—it's been here since the 1920s. Scenery, too—a panoramic vista in the shadow of Cape Elizabeth Light. Plus the menu—

seafood galore (and hot dogs for those who'd rather). Choose a lobster from the tank; indulge in the lobster stew; grab a table on the ledges and watch the world sail by. Opt for a sunny day; the lighthouse's foghorn can kill your conversation when the fog rolls in.

## INFORMATION AND SERVICES
### Information
The Visitor Information Center of the Convention and Visitors Bureau of Greater Portland (245 Commercial St., Portland 04101, 207/772-4994, www.visitportland.com) has tons of brochures, plenty of restaurant menus, and public restrooms. The Portland Downtown District (94 Free St., 207/772-6828, www.portland-maine.com) has a useful website.

Check out the Portland Public Library (5 Monument Sq., 207/871-1700, www.portlandlibrary.com).

For winter parking-ban information, call 207/879-0300.

### Public Restrooms
In the Old Port area, you'll find restrooms at the Convention and Visitors Bureau Visitor Information Center (245 Commercial St.), the Spring Street parking garage (45 Spring St.), the Fore Street Parking Garage (419 Fore St.), and the Casco Bay Lines ferry terminal (Commercial and Franklin Sts.).

On Congress Street, find restrooms at Portland City Hall (389 Congress St.) and the Portland Public Library (5 Monument Sq.). In Midtown, head for the Cumberland County Civic Center (1 Civic Center Sq.). In the West End, use Maine Medical Center.

## GETTING THERE AND AROUND
The best overall source for planning your transportation is the website www.transportme

.org. It lists schedules, fares, and other information for airlines, buses, ferries, and trains.

The ultraclean and comfortable Portland Transportation Center (100 Thompson Point Rd., Portland, 207/828-3939) is the base for **Concord Trailways** (800/639-3317, concordtrailways.com) and **Amtrak's Downeaster** (800/872-7245, www.thedowneaster.com). Parking is $3 per day, and the terminal has free coffee, free newspapers (while they last), and vending machines. The **Metro** (114 Valley St., P.O. Box 1097, Portland 04104, 207/774-0351, $1.25 exact change), **The Portland Explorer** (207/774-9891 or 800/377-4457, www.portlandexplorer.org, free), and the Zoom buses, with service from Biddeford/Saco, stop here and connect with **Portland International Jetport** (207/774-7301, www.portlandjetport.org), **Vermont Transit Lines** (950 Congress St., 207/772-6587 or 800/552-8737), and **Casco Bay Lines ferry service** (www.cascobaylines.com). If you show your Trailways or Amtrak ticket stub to the Metro bus driver, you'll have a free ride downtown. Taxis charge $1.40 for the first plus $0.25 for each additional one-ninth mile.

Parking garages and lots are strategically situated all over downtown Portland, particularly in the Old Port and near the civic center. Unless you're lucky, you'll probably waste a lot of time looking for on-street parking (meters start at $0.25 a half hour), so a garage or lot is the best option. If you land in a garage or lot with a Park and Shop sticker, you can collect free-parking stamps, each good for an hour, from participating shops and restaurants. You could even end up parking for free. A day of parking generally runs $8–16. The Casco Bay Lines website (www.cascobaylines.com) has a very useful parking map, listing parking lots and garages and their hourly and daily rates. It's good for comparison shopping.

# Freeport

Freeport has a special claim to historic fame—it's the place where Maine parted company from Massachusetts in 1820. The documents were signed on March 15, making Maine its own separate state.

At the height of the local mackerel-packing industry here, countless tons of the bony fish were shipped out of South Freeport, often in ships built on the shores of the Harraseeket River. Splendid relics of the shipbuilders' era still line the streets of South Freeport, and no architecture buff should miss a walk, cycle, or drive through the village. Even downtown Freeport still reflects the shipbuilder's craft, with contemporary shops tucked in and around handsome historic houses. Some have been converted to B&Bs, others are boutiques, and one even disguises the local McDonald's franchise.

Today, Freeport is best known as the mecca for the shop-till-you-drop set. The hub, of course, is sportswear giant L. L. Bean, which has been here since 1912, when founder Leon Leonwood Bean began making his trademark hunting boots (and also unselfishly handed out hot tips on where the fish were biting). More than 120 retail operations now fan out from that epicenter, and you can find almost anything in Freeport (pop. about 7,700)—except maybe a parking spot in midsummer.

When (or if) you tire of shopping, you can always find quiet refuge in the town's preserves and parks—Mast Landing Sanctuary, Wolfe's Neck Woods State Park, and Winslow Memorial Park—and plenty of local color at the Town Wharf in the still honest-to-goodness fishing village of South Freeport.

An orientation note: Don't be surprised to receive directions (particularly for South Freeport) relative to "the Big Indian"—a 40-foot-tall landmark at the junction of Route 1 and South Freeport Road. If you stop at the Maine Visitor Information Center in Yarmouth and continue on Route 1 toward Freeport, you can't miss it, just north of the Freeport Inn and the Casco Bay Inn.

## SHOPPING

Logically, this category must come first in any discussion of Freeport, since shopping's the biggest game in town. It's pretty much a given that anyone who visits Freeport intends to darken the door of at least one shop.

## ◖ L. L. Bean

If it's *only* one, it's likely to be "Bean's." The whole world beats a path to L. L. Bean (95 Main St., Rte. 1, 207/865-4761 or 800/341-4341, www.llbean.com)—or so it seems in July, August, and December. Established as a hunting/fishing supply shop, this giant sports outfitter now sells everything from kids' clothing to cookware on its ever-expanding downtown campus. In 2007, it moved the hunting and fishing store into the expanded main store, and in 2008, the outlet store—a great source for deals on equipment and clothing—moved into the former hunting and fishing building, behind the main store. It's also partnered on a new parking and retail facility, expected to open in 2009, with as many as 40 shops. It's under construction on land behind Bow and Main Streets.

By 2010, Bean's aspires to have a new outdoor adventure center in full operation on its 700-acre property on Desert Road. Possibilities include a restaurant, lodging, a golf course, and opportunities for extended stay and participation packages for sports in its Walk-On Adventures and other programs, such as kayaking, canoeing, cross-country skiing, snowshoeing, shooting, and archery. Some opportunities may open prior to 2010.

Until the 1970s, Bean's remained a rustic store with a creaky staircase and a closet-size women's department. Then a few other merchants began arriving, Bean's expanded, and a feeding frenzy followed. The Bean reputation rests on a savvy staff, high quality, an admirable environmental consciousness, and a no-questions-asked return policy. Bring the kids—for the indoor trout pond, the clean re-

# MAINE WILDLIFE PARK

If you want to see where Maine's wild things are, venture a bit inland to visit the Maine Wildlife Park (Shaker Rd./Rte. 26, Gray, 207/657-4977, 9:30 A.M.-6 P.M. daily, gate closes 4:30 P.M. mid-Apr.-Veterans' Day, $6 ages 13-60, $4.50 seniors, $4 kids 4-12). Nearly 25 native species of wildlife can be seen at this state-operated wildlife refuge, including such ever-popular species as moose, black bear, white-tailed deer, and bald eagle. The park began in 1931 as a state-run game farm. For more than 50 years, the Department of Inland Fish and Game reared pheasants here for release during bird-hunting season. At the same time, wildlife biologists and game wardens with the state's Department of Inland Fisheries and Wildlife needed a place to care for orphaned or injured animals.

In 1982, the farm's mission was changed to that of a wildlife and conservation education facility. Today the park is a temporary haven for wildlife, but those who cannot survive in the wild live here permanently.

Among the wildlife that have been in residence at the park are lynx, deer, opossum, black bear, bobcat, porcupine, raccoon, red-tailed hawk, barred and great horned owl, mountain lion, bald eagle, raven, skunk, woodchuck, and coyote. Other frequent guests include wild turkey, fisher, gray fox, kestrel, turkey vulture, wood turtle, and box turtle. Most are here for protection and healing, and while they're in residence, visitors are able to view them at close range.

In addition to the wildlife, there are numerous interactive exhibits and displays to view, nature trails to explore, a nature store, snack shack, and even picnic facilities. Special programs and exhibits are often offered on weekends mid-May–mid-September.

The park is 3.5 miles north of downtown Gray and Maine Turnpike Exit 63. From the coast, take Route 115 from Main Street in downtown Yarmouth, continuing through North Yarmouth (with stunning old houses) to Gray, and then head north on Route 26 for 3.5 miles.

strooms, and the "real deal" outlet store. The store's open-round-the-clock policy has become its signature, and if you show up at 2 A.M., you'll have much of the store to yourself, and you may even spy vacationing celebrities or the rock stars who often visit after Portland shows.

## Outlets and Specialty Stores

After Bean's, it's up to your whims and your wallet. The stores stretch for several miles up and down Main Street and along many side streets. Pick up a copy of the *Official Map and Visitor Guide* at any of the shops or restaurants, at one of the visitor kiosks, or at the Hose Tower Information Center (23 Depot St., two blocks east of L. L. Bean). All the big names are here, as are plenty of little ones. Don't overlook the small shops tucked on the side streets, such as **Earrings and Company, Wilbur's of Maine Chocolate Confections,** and **Edgecomb Potters.**

## PARKS, PRESERVES, AND OTHER ATTRACTIONS
### Mast Landing Sanctuary

More than two miles of easy, yellow-blazed trails wind through the 140-acre Mast Landing Sanctuary, an area that ages ago was the source of masts for the Royal Navy. Pick up a trail map at the parking area and start watching for birds. The best (and longest) route is the 1.6-mile Loop Trail, which passes fruit trees, hardwoods, and an old milldam. (Keep the kids off the dam.) Maine Audubon owns the sanctuary (see *Parks, Preserves, and Beaches* in the *Portland* section). The society operates a very popular nature day camp here late June–mid-August each summer; call for the schedule. The sanctuary is open sunrise–sunset, year-round, and is popular in winter with cross-country skiers. Admission is free. From downtown Freeport (Rte. 1), take Bow Street (opposite L. L. Bean) one mile east to Upper Mast Landing Road. Turn left (north) and go 500 feet to the parking area.

## Wolfe's Neck Woods State Park

Five miles of easy to moderate trails meander through 233-acre Wolfe's Neck Woods State Park (Wolfe's Neck Rd., 207/865-4465, $3 ages 11–64, $1 children 5–11), just a few minutes' cycle or drive from downtown Freeport. You'll need a trail map, available near the parking area. The easiest route (partly wheelchair-accessible) is the Shoreline Walk, about three-quarters of a mile, starting near the salt marsh and skirting Casco Bay. Sprinkled along the trails are helpful interpretive panels explaining various points of natural history—bog life, osprey nesting, glaciation, erosion, and tree decay. Guided tours are offered at 2 P.M. daily mid-July–late August, weather permitting. Leashed pets are allowed. Adjacent **Googins Island,** an osprey sanctuary, is off-limits. From downtown Freeport, follow Bow Street (across from L. L. Bean) for 2.25 miles; turn right onto Wolfe's Neck Road (also called Wolf Neck Rd.) and go another 2.25 miles.

## Wolfe's Neck Farm

The best time to visit Wolfe's Neck Farm (10 Burnett Rd., 207/865-4469, www.wolfes-neckfarm.org) is March and April for the annual **Calf Watch,** when about 60 calves and 15 lambs join the herd on the 620-acre farm. During calving season, the farm is open 9 A.M.–5 P.M. daily, and kids can see the latest newborns as well as chickens, turkeys, pigs, and other creatures. Sustainable agriculture and environmental sensitivity are the overriding philosophies at this working farm owned and operated by the nonprofit Wolfe's Neck Farm Foundation. Nature trails lace the property, and a small retail shop in the farmhouse (open 9 A.M.–4:30 P.M. weekdays) sells naturally raised beef, lamb, pork, and eggs.

## Winslow Memorial Park

Owned by the town of Freeport, Winslow Memorial Park (Staples Point, South Freeport, 207/865-4198, late May–late Sept., $1.50) is a spectacular 90-plus-acre seaside park, overlooking the islands of upper Casco Bay. Swim off the beach (changing house, restrooms, but no lifeguards), picnic on the shore, walk the three-quarters-mile nature trail and perch on the point, launch a canoe or kayak, or reserve one of the 100 inland or waterfront campsites ($22–29, no hookups, but some sites can take RVs). The boat landing and beach area are tidal, so boaters and swimmers should plan to be here two hours before and two hours after high tide; otherwise, you're dealing with mudflats. From the Big Indian on Route 1, take South Freeport Road one mile to Staples Point Road and continue to the end.

## Bradbury Mountain State Park

Six miles from the hubbub of Freeport and you're in tranquil, wooded, 590-acre Bradbury Mountain State Park (Rte. 9, Pownal, 207/688-4712, $3 adults, $1 children 5–11), with facilities for picnicking, hiking, mountain biking, and rustic camping, but no swimming. Pick up a trail map at the gate and take the easy, 0.4-mile (round-trip) Mountain Trail to the 485-foot summit, with superb views east to the ocean and southeast to Portland. In fall, it's gorgeous. Or take the Tote Road Trail, on the western side of the park, where the ghost of Samuel Bradbury occasionally brings a chill to hikers in a hemlock grove. A playground keeps the littlest tykes happy. The nonresident camping fee is $14 per site per night ($11 for residents). The park season is May 15–October 15, but there's winter access for cross-country skiing. From Route 1, cross over I-95 at Exit 20 and continue west on Pownal Road to Route 9.

## Pineland Farms

Once a home to Maine's mentally disabled citizens, 1,600-acre Pineland (15 Farm View Dr., New Gloucester, 207/688-4539, www.pinelandfarms.org) campus was closed in 1996. In 2000, the Libra Foundation bought it, and now the property comprises 19 buildings and 5,000 acres of farmland, and much of it is open for recreation. Walk or ski the trails, sight birds in the fields and woods, stroll through the garden, fish the pond or skate on it in winter, play tennis, go mountain biking or orienteering, or even take a horseback-riding lesson. It's a vast

© TOM NANGLE

GREATER PORTLAND

Glaciers contributed to the formation of the Desert of Maine.

outdoor playground, but your first stop should be the visitors center (9 A.M.–5 P.M. daily) to see a list of any events (frequent ones include guided farm tours and family experiences), pick up maps, pay any necessary fees, shop for farm-fresh products, or even grab lunch or snacks at Foley's Bakery Coffee House or the Commons Caféteria. (Some activities, such as cross-country mountain-biking trail access and horseback-riding lessons require fees.) Also on the premises are a variety of accommodations, with rates beginning at $325–400 per night. No dogs.

## Desert of Maine

Okay, so maybe it's a bit hokey, but talk about sands of time. More than 10,000 years ago, glaciers covered the region surrounding the Desert of Maine (95 Desert Rd., 207/865-6962, www.desertofmaine.com, early May–mid-Oct., $8.75 adults, $6.25 ages 13–16, $5.25 ages 6–12). When they receded, they scoured the landscape, pulverizing rocks and leaving behind a sandy residue that was covered by a thin layer of topsoil. Jump forward to 1797, when William Tuttle bought 300 acres and moved his family here, as well as his house and barn, and cleared the land. Now jump forward again to the present and tour where a once-promising farmland has become a desert wasteland. The guided, safari-style tram tours combine history, geology, and environmental science and an opportunity for children to hunt for "gems" in the sand. Decide for yourself: Is the desert a natural phenomenon? A man-made disaster? Or does the truth lie somewhere in the middle?

## Harrington House and Pettengill Farm

A block south of L. L. Bean is the Harrington House (45 Main St., Rte. 1, 207/865-3170, www.freeporthistoricalsociety.org, 10 A.M.–2:30 P.M. Tues., Thurs., and Fri. and 10 A.M.–7 P.M. Wed., free) home base of the Freeport Historical Society. You can pick up walking maps detailing Freeport's architecture for a small fee and tour the house. Exhibits pertaining to Freeport's history and occasionally ones by local artists are presented in two rooms in the restored 1830 Enoch Harrington House, a National Historic Register property.

Also listed on the register is the society's Pettengill Farm, a 19th-century saltwater farm comprising a circa 1810 saltbox-style house, woods, orchards, salt marsh, and lovely perennial gardens. The farmhouse is open only during the annual Pettengill Farm Days in the fall, but the grounds are open at all times. From Main Street, take Bow Street and go 1.5 miles. Turn right onto Pettengill road. Park at the gate, and then walk along the dirt road for about 15 minutes to the farmhouse.

## RECREATION AND SPORTS
### € L. L. Bean Outdoor Discovery Schools

Since the early 1980s, the sports outfitter's Outdoor Discovery Schools (888/552-3261, www.llbean.com) have trained thousands of outdoors enthusiasts to improve their skills in fly-fishing, archery, hiking, canoeing, sea kayaking, winter camping, cross-country skiing, orienteering, and even outdoor photography. Here's a deal that requires no planning. **Walk-On Adventures** provides 1.5–2.5-hour lessons in sports such as kayak touring, fly casting, archery, clay shooting, snowshoeing, and cross-country skiing for $15, including equipment. All of the longer fee programs, plus canoeing and camping trips, require preregistration, well in advance because of their popularity. Some are held in the mountains and on the rivers of western Maine, others are in Maryland and Virginia. Some of the lectures, seminars, and demonstrations held in Freeport are free, and a regular catalog lists the schedule. Bean's waterfront **Flying Point Paddling Center** hosts many of the kayaking, saltwater fly-fishing, and guiding programs and is home to the annual **PaddleSports Festival** in June, with free demonstrations, seminars, vendors, lessons, and more.

### € Atlantic Seal Cruises

Atlantic Seal Cruises (Town Wharf, South Free-

port, 207/865-6112 or 877/285-7325), owned and operated by Captain Tom Ring, makes two or three 2.5-hour cruises daily to 17-acre **Eagle Island,** a State Historic Site once owned by Admiral Robert Peary of North Pole fame. The trip includes a lobstering demonstration (except Sun., when lobstering is banned). Fee is $28 adult, $20 ages 5–12, $15 ages 1–4. Captain Ring also does daylong excursions once a week to **Seguin Island,** off the Phippsburg Peninsula, where you can climb the light tower and see Maine's only first-order Fresnel lens, the largest on the coast. (This trip, which costs $50 adult, $34 under 12, is not for the unsteady; you'll be offloaded from a small boat.) A Seal and Osprey Watch cruise is offered at twilight.

### Kayak and Canoe Rentals

**Ring's Marine Service** (Smelt Brook Rd., South Freeport, 207/865-6143 or 866/865-6143, www.ringsmarineservice.com) rents single kayaks for $38, tandems for $60, and canoes for $28 per day, with longer-term rentals available.

## ENTERTAINMENT

Shopping seems to be more than enough entertainment for most of Freeport's visitors, but don't miss the **L. L. Bean Summer Concert Series** (800/341-4341, ext. 37222). At 7:30 P.M. each Saturday early July–Labor Day weekend,, Bean's hosts free big-name, family-oriented events in Discovery Park, in the Bean's complex. Arrive early (these concerts are *very* popular) and bring a blanket or a folding chair. Call for more info.

## ACCOMMODATIONS

If you'd prefer to drop where you shop, Freeport has a large country inn, several motels, and more than two dozen B&Bs, so finding a pillow is seldom a problem, but it's still wise to have reservations. For camping, try Winslow Memorial Park and Wolfe's Neck Farm.

### Downtown

One of Freeport's pioneering B&Bs is on the main drag yet away from much of the traf-

© TOM NANGLE

Cruise to Eagle Island to the home Arctic explorer Admiral Peary built to resemble the prow of a ship.

fic, in a restored house where Arctic explorer Admiral Donald MacMillan once lived. The 19th-century **White Cedar Inn** (178 Main St., Freeport, 207/865-9099 or 800/853-1269, www.whitecedarinn.com, $145–200) has seven attractive guest rooms with antiques, air-conditioning, and Wi-Fi; some have gas fireplaces; one has a TV and accepts dogs ($20). The full breakfast will definitely power you through a day of shopping.

Two blocks north of L. L. Bean, the ◖ **Harraseeket Inn** (162 Main St., Freeport, 207/865-9377 or 800/342-6423, www.harraseeketinn.com, $199–305 peak) is a splendid 84-room country inn with an indoor pool, cable TV, air-conditioning, phones, and Wi-Fi; many rooms have fireplaces and hot tubs. A few rooms are decorated with Thomas Moser furnishings, otherwise decor is colonial reproduction in the two antique buildings and a modern addition. Rates include a hot-and-cold buffet breakfast and afternoon tea—a refreshing break from power shopping—with finger sandwiches and sweets. Pets are permitted in some rooms. The $25/night fee includes a dog bed, small can of food, treat, and dishes. Ask about packages, which offer excellent value. Children 12 and younger stay free. If you're traveling solo, the nightly Innkeeper's Table (reservation required by 5:30 P.M. for 6:30 P.M. seating, 207/865-1085) is a communal table hosted by an innkeeper and a great way to meet other guests. (See *Food* for information on its two excellent restaurants.)

Three blocks south of L. L. Bean, on a quiet side street shared with a couple of other B&Bs, is **The James Place Inn** (11 Holbrook St., Freeport, 207/865-4486 or 800/964-9086, www.jamesplaceinn.com, $155–185 peak). Innkeepers Robin and Tori Baron welcome guests to seven comfortable rooms, all with air-conditioning, Wi-Fi, and TV, a few with double whirlpool tubs, and one with a woodburning fireplace and private deck. If the weather's fine, enjoy breakfast on the deck. After shopping, collapse on the hammock for two.

## Beyond Downtown

Here's a throwback. Three miles north of downtown is the **Maine Idyll** (1411 Rte. 1, 207/865-4201, www.maineidyll.com, $59–103), a tidy cottage colony operated by the Marstaller family for three generations. Twenty studio to three-bedroom pine-paneled cottages are tucked under the trees. All have refrigerators, fireplaces, and TV, and most have limited cooking facilities. Wi-Fi is available near the office. A light breakfast is included. There are two children's play sets, and well-behaved pets are $4.

The family-run **Casco Bay Inn** (107 Rte. 1, Freeport, 207/865-4925 or 800/570-4970, www.cascobayinn.com, $99–119 peak) is a bit fancier than most motels. It has a pine-paneled lounge with fieldstone fireplace and guest Internet station, with Wi-Fi throughout. The spacious rooms have double sinks in the bath area, and some have a refrigerator and microwave. A continental breakfast with newspaper is included.

Ooohh, and here's a find, if you're lucky enough to snag it, given there's only one guest room. **Wolf Neck Bed and Breakfast** (93 Birch Point Rd., Freeport, 207/865-1725, www.wolfneckbb.com, $175) is Dianne Gaudet and Steve Norton's waterfront, newly built Shingle-style home with one guest suite, complete with sitting room and private deck. Longtime area residents, they're a great resource on the region. They also provide a full breakfast. Bring your own boat and launch it right here or rent a canoe or kayaks from the hosts.

Captain Tom Ring, of Atlantic Seal Cruises, also operates **Atlantic Seal B&B** (25 Main St., South Freeport, 207/865-6112 or 877/285-7325, $150–225) in his mid-19th-century Cape-style home on the harbor. The views are stupendous, and the house is chock-full of antiques and fascinating maritime collectibles; Tom's seafaring Maine roots go back for generations. Despite the heritage, rooms have modern amenities, including air-conditioning and private baths (one detached). Tom whips up a bountiful breakfast, and the location is just steps from Harraseeket Lunch and Lob-

ster. Note: Tom is a technophobe and has neither a computer or answerphone.

## Camping

**Recompence Shore Campsites** (134 Burnett Rd., Freeport, 207/865-9307, www.freeportcamping.com, $21–32) is part of Wolfe's Neck Farm. It's an eco-sensitive campground with 175 wooded tent sites (a few hookups are available), many on the farm's three-mile-long Casco Bay shorefront. For anyone seeking peace, quiet, and low-tech camping in a spectacular setting, this is it. Amenities include a laundry and Wi-Fi. Ice, firewood, ice cream, and snacks are available at the camp store. Quiet, leashed, attended pets are welcome. Quiet time begins at 10 P.M. Swimming depends on the tides; check the tide calendar in a local newspaper. Take Bow Street (across from L. L. Bean) to Wolfe's Neck Road, turn right, and go 1.6 miles to Burnett Road, a left turn.

## FOOD

Freeport has an ever-increasing number of places to eat, but nowhere enough to satisfy hungry crowds at peak dining hours on busy days. Go early or late for lunch, and make reservations for dinner.

## Local Flavors

South of downtown, **Royal River Natural Foods** (443 Rte. 1, Freeport, 207/865-0046, www.rrnf.com) has a small selection of prepared foods, including soups, salads, and sandwiches, and a seating area.

Craving a proper British tea? **Jacqueline's Tea Room** (201 Main St., Freeport, 207/865-2123, www.jacquelinestearoom.com, 10:30 A.M.–3 P.M.) serves a four-course tea by reservation for $20 pp in an elegant setting. Seatings for the two-hour indulgence are between 11 A.M. and 1 P.M. Tuesday–Friday and every other weekend.

At the Big Indian **Old World Gourmet Deli and Wine Shop** (117 Rte. 1, Freeport, 207/865-4477), the offerings are just as advertised, with sandwiches, soups, salads, and prepared foods. There are a few tables inside, but it's mostly a to-go place.

## Casual Dining

The Harraseeket Inn's woodsy-themed **Broad Arrow Tavern** (162 Main St., 207/865-9377 or 800/342-6423, 11:30 A.M.– 10 P.M., to 11 P.M. Fri. and Sat.), just two blocks north of L. L. Bean but seemingly a world away, is a perfect place to escape shopping crowds and madness. The food is terrific, with everything made from organic and naturally raised foods; prices run $10–23. Can't decide? Opt for the extensive, all-you-can-eat lunch buffet ($17) that highlights a bit of everything.

Good wine and fine martinis are what reels them into **Conundrum** (117 Rte. 1, Freeport, 207/865-0303, 4:30–10 P.M. Tues.–Sat.), near Freeport's Big Indian, but the food is worth noting, too. Dozens of wines by the glass, more than 20 martinis, and 20 champagnes will keep most oenophiles happy. The food, varying from pâtés and cheese platters to cheeseburgers and maple-barbecued chicken, helps keep them sober.

## Ethnic Fare

Dine indoors or out on the tree-shaded patio at **Azure Italian Café** (123 Main St., 207/865-123, www.azurecafe.com, 11 A.M.–8 P.M., to 9 P.M. Fri. and Sat.). Go light, mixing selections from antipasto, *insalate,* and *zuppa* choices or savor the heartier entrées ($13–30), such as lasagna *formaggio,* Maine seafood risotto, or lemon-and-thyme roast chicken. The service is pleasant and the indoor dining areas are accented by well-chosen contemporary Maine artwork. Live jazz is a highlight some evenings.

Down the side street across from Azure is **Mediterranean Grill** (10 School St., Freeport, 207/865-1688, www.mediterraneangrill.biz, 11 A.M.–10 P.M. daily). Because it's off Main Street, the Cigri family's excellent Turkish-Mediterranean restaurant rarely gets the crowds. House specialties such as moussaka, lamb chops, and *tiropetes* augment a full range of kebab and vegetarian choices. Or simply

make a meal of the appetizers—the platters are meals in themselves. Sandwiches and wraps are available at lunch. Entrées go for $16–25. Dine inside or on the streetside deck.

Two surprisingly good, easy-on-the-budget Asian restaurants share a building on the south end of town. **China Rose** (23 Main St., 207/865-6886, 11 A.M.–9:30 P.M., to 10 P.M. Fri. and Sat.) serves Szechuan, Mandarin, and Hunan specialties in a pleasant first-floor dining area. Upstairs is **Miyako** (207/865-6888, same hours), with an extensive sushi bar menu and it also serves other Japanese specialties, including tempura, teriyaki, *nabemono,* and noodle dishes. Luncheon specials are available at both.

Good food and attentive service has made **Thai Garden** (491 Rte. 1, Freeport, 207/865-6005, 11 A.M.–9 P.M. daily) an ever popular choice for Thai.

## Fine Dining

Priciest and worth every penny is the Harraseeket Inn's cloth-and-candles **Maine Dining Room** (207/865-1085, 6–9 P.M., to 9:30 P.M. Fri. and Sat.). The service is excellent, and chef Theda Lyden's commitment to natural and organic foods is impressive. Tableside preparations (for 2–7), such as Caesar salad, chateaubriand, and flaming desserts, add an understated note of theater. Dinner entrées are $24–38. Brunch (11:45 A.M.–2 P.M. Sun., $24.95) is a seemingly endless buffet, with whole poached salmon and Belgian waffles among the highlights.

## Lobster

In South Freeport, order lobster in the rough at **Harraseeket Lunch and Lobster Company** (36 Main St., Town Wharf, South Freeport, 207/865-4888, 11 A.M.–8:45 P.M. daily summer hours, closes at 7:45 P.M. spring and fall). Grab a waterfront picnic table, place your order, and go at it. (There's also inside dining.) Be prepared for a wait in midsummer. Fried clams are particularly good here, and they're prepared either breaded or battered. Order both and decide for yourself which is better. Another

GREATER PORTLAND

option: If you're camping nearby, call ahead and order boiled lobsters to go. BYOB; no credit cards.

## INFORMATION AND SERVICES

Freeport Merchants Association (Hose Tower, 23 Depot St., Freeport 04032, 207/865-1212 or 800/865-1994, www.freeportusa.com) produces an invaluable foldout map/guide showing locations of all the shops, plus sites of lodgings, restaurants, visitor kiosks, pay phones, restrooms, and car and bike parking. If you're serious about "doing" Freeport, send for one of these guides before you arrive so you can plan your attack and hit the ground running.

Just south of Freeport is the Maine Visitor Information Center (Rte. 1, at I-95 Exit 17, Yarmouth, 207/846-0833), part of the statewide tourism-information network. Staffers are particularly attuned to Freeport and Yarmouth, but the center has brochures and maps for the entire state. Also here are restrooms, phones, picnic tables, vending machines, and a dog-walking area.

# MID-COAST REGION

In contrast to the Southern Coast's gorgeous sandy beaches, the Mid-Coast Region features a deeply indented shoreline with snug harbors and long, gnarled fingers of land. Even though these fingers are inconvenient for driving and bicycling, this is where you'll find picturebook Maine in a panorama format. Drive to the tips of the peninsulas and come upon lighthouses, fishing villages, country inns, and lobster wharves. The Mid-Coast, as defined in this chapter, stretches from Brunswick through Waldoboro.

Visitors come for Brunswick's Bowdoin College, Bath's marine museum, Wiscasset's historic homes, the jumbled shops of Boothbay Harbor, Pemaquid Point's lighthouse, and, of course, lobster. The Bath-Brunswick area is one of the least touristy areas of the coast. Not that visitors don't come, but this area has a strong and

varied economic base other than tourism, which means that no matter when you visit, you'll find shops, restaurants, and lodgings open and activities scheduled. Bowdoin College, Bath Iron Works, and the Brunswick Naval Air Station (slated for closure by 2011) also contribute to a population more ethnically diverse than in most of Maine and draw an active retiree population. Still, as you drive down the peninsulas that reach seaward from Bath and Brunswick, the vibrancy gives way to traditional fishing villages pressed by the hard realities of maintaining such lifestyles in a modern world and hanging on to waterfront properties in the face of rapidly rising real-estate prices.

Wiscasset still clings to the nickname of prettiest village in Maine, but for many travelers heading through it on Route 1, Wiscasset

© TOM NANGLE

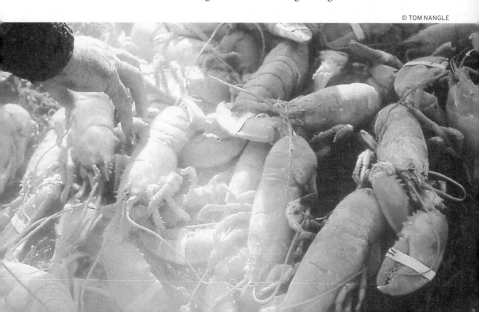

# HIGHLIGHTS

◖ **Bowdoin College:** This beautiful, shady campus is home to the Bowdoin College Museum of Art, the Peary-MacMillan Arctic Museum, and the Maine State Music Theater (page 128).

◖ **Maine Maritime Museum:** It's easy to while away a half day touring the exhibits in the main and outer buildings and just enjoying the riverfront setting (page 140).

◖ **Popham Beach:** Often winning accolades as Maine's prettiest or best beach, Popham is a long stretch of sand, anchored by a fort at one end and seabird colonies at the other (page 143).

◖ **Burnt Island Tour:** Step back in history and visit with a lighthouse keeper's family circa 1952 on a living-history tour (page 160).

◖ **Coastal Maine Botanical Gardens:** This seaside garden comprises more than 125 acres of well-planned exhibits, trails, and art (page 163).

◖ **Pemaquid Point Lighthouse:** It's hard to say which is Maine's prettiest lighthouse, but Pemaquid's is right up there. It's also depicted on the Maine state quarter (page 174).

◖ **Colonial Pemaquid/Fort William Henry:** A beautiful setting overlooking John's Bay, a partially reconstructed fort, and remnants from archaeological digs researching one of the first English settlements in America make this well worth a visit (page 175).

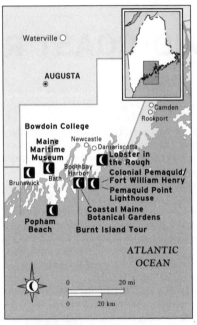

LOOK FOR ◖ TO FIND RECOMMENDED SIGHTS, ACTIVITIES, DINING, AND LODGING.

◖ **Lobster in the Rough:** Lobster wharves abound in Maine, but the Pemaquid Peninsula has a concentration of scenic spots for lobster lovers (page 189).

is nothing but an expletive deleted–producing headache. Traffic often backs up for miles, inching forward through the bottleneck village. Although many are just glad to get through it, those who take time to explore Wiscasset are rewarded with multitudes of antiques shops and lovely architecture.

The tempo changes northeast of Wiscasset. Traffic eases and there's less roadside development. Detour down the Boothbay and Pemaquid Peninsulas, and you'll be rewarded

with the Maine of postcards. These two peninsulas appear unchallenged as home to more lobster-in-the-rough spots than elsewhere on the coast, and Maine's creative economy is blossoming here, as evidenced by the artists' and artisans' studios that pepper these peninsulas.

## PLANNING YOUR TIME

Route 1 is the primary artery connecting all the points in the Mid-Coast Region, and Wiscasset, a major bottleneck, is smack-dab in the

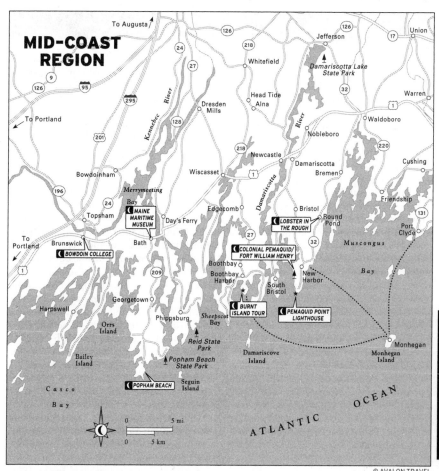

MID-COAST
REGION

© AVALON TRAVEL

middle. For this reason, it's best to split your lodging and explorations into two parts: south of Wiscasset and north of Wiscasset. Even then, driving down the long fingers of land requires patience. The towns south of Wiscasset are less touristy than those on the Boothbay or Pemaquid Peninsulas, with Orr's and Bailey's Islands and the Phippsburg Peninsula being the best places to sprout roots for old-time summer flavor.

To cover the region, you'll need 4–5 days. Antiques mavens should concentrate their efforts in Bath, Wiscasset, and Damariscotta. Allow at least two days to appreciate the fine museums in Brunswick and Bath, and another day to tour Wiscasset's historical house museums and nearby fort. If you're an avid or even aspiring kayaker, you'll want time to puzzle through the nooks and crannies of the coastline in a boat, and if you value parks and preserves, this region offers plenty worth your time. For either, the Boothbay and Pemaquid Peninsulas are good bases.

# Brunswick Area

Brunswick (pop. 20,520), straddling Route 1, relies partly on modern defense dollars—but it was incorporated in 1738 and is steeped in history. The town is home to both prestigious Bowdoin College and the sprawling Brunswick Naval Air Station—an unusual and sometimes conflicting juxtaposition that makes this a college town with a difference. You'll find lots of classic homes and churches, several respected museums, and year-round cultural attractions.

Brunswick and Topsham face each other across roiling waterfalls on the Androscoggin River. The falls, which Native Americans knew by the tongue-twisting name of Ahmelahcogneturcook ("place abundant with fish, birds, and other animals"), were a source of hydropower for 18th-century sawmills and 19th- and 20th-century textile mills. Franco Americans arrived in droves to beef up the textile industry in the late 19th century (but lost their jobs eventually in the Depression). Those once derelict mills now house shops, restaurants, and offices.

Brunswick is also the gateway to the stunning Harpswells, a peninsula/archipelago complex linked by causeways, several bridges, and a unique granite cribstone bridge. Scenic back roads on Harpswell Neck inspire detours to the fishing hamlets of Cundy's Harbor, Orr's Island, and Bailey Island, and once you're here, it's easy to want to linger.

## SIGHTS
### ◖ Bowdoin College
Bowdoin College (Brunswick, 207/725-3000, www.bowdoin.edu) got its start here nearly 150 years before the Naval Air Station landed on the nearby Brunswick Plains. Founded in 1794 as a boys' college with a handful of students, Bowdoin (coed since 1969) now has 1,550 students. The college has turned out such noted graduates as authors Nathaniel Hawthorne and Henry Wadsworth Longfellow, sex pioneer Alfred Kinsey, U.S. President Franklin Pierce, Arctic explorers Robert Peary and Donald MacMillan, U.S. Senators George Mitchell

and William Cohen, and a dozen Maine governors. Massachusetts Hall, oldest building on the 110-acre campus, dates from 1802. The stately Bowdoin pines, on the northeast boundary, are even older. The striking **David Saul Smith Union,** occupying 40,000 square feet in a former athletic building on the east side of the campus, has a café, pub, lounge, and bookstore open to the public. Call for information on admissions and campus tours (207/725-3100) and on campus concerts, lectures, and performances open to the public (207/725-3375).

Photos and artifacts bring Arctic expeditions to life at the small but fascinating **Peary-MacMillan Arctic Museum** (Hubbard Hall, 207/725-3416, http://academic.bowdoin.edu/arcticmuseum, 10 A.M.–5 P.M. Tues.–Sat., 2–5 P.M. Sun., free). Among the specimens are animal mounts, a skin kayak, fur clothing, snow goggles, and Inuit carvings—most collected by Arctic pioneers Robert E. Peary and Donald B. MacMillan, both Bowdoin grads. Permanent exhibits highlight the natural and cultural diversity of the Arctic. The small gift shop specializes in Inuit books and artifacts. Donations are welcomed.

An astonishing array of Greek and Roman artifacts is only one of the high points at the **Bowdoin College Museum of Art** (Walker Art Building, 207/725-3275, www.bowdoin.edu/art-museum, 10 A.M.–5 P.M. Tues.–Sat., 2–5 P.M. Sun., free). Designed in the 1890s by Charles McKim of the famed McKim, Mead, and White firm, it's a stunning neoclassical edifice with an interior rotunda and stone lions flanking the entry. In 2007, the museum was expanded and modernized for the 21st century, adding a striking bronze-and-glass entry pavilion to preserve the facade while also achieving accessibility. The college's prized Assyrian reliefs, previously in the magnificent Rotunda, were moved to a glass-walled addition facing Brunswick's Park Row. The renovated museum is far more user friendly and a fitting setting for the impres-

# JOSHUA L. CHAMBERLAIN, CIVIL WAR HERO

When the American Civil War began in 1861, Joshua Chamberlain was a 33-year-old logic instructor at Bowdoin College in Brunswick; when it ended, in 1865, Chamberlain earned the Congressional Medal of Honor for his "Daring heroism and great tenacity in holding his position on the Little Round Top." He was designated by Ulysses S. Grant to formally accept the official surrender of Confederate General John Gordon (both men represented the infantry). He later became governor of Maine (1867-1871) and president of Bowdoin College, but Chamberlain's greatest renown, ironically, came more than a century later – when 1990s PBS filmmakers focused on the Civil War and highlighted his strategic military role.

Joshua Lawrence Chamberlain was born in 1828 in Brewer, Maine, the son and grandson of soldiers. After graduating from Bowdoin in 1852, he studied for the ministry at Bangor Theological Seminary and then returned to his alma mater as an instructor.

With the nation in turmoil in the early 1860s, Chamberlain signed on to help, receiving a commission as a lieutenant colonel in the Twentieth Maine Volunteers in 1862. After surviving 24 encounters and six battle wounds and having been promoted to general (brigadier, then major), Chamberlain was elected Republican governor of Maine in 1866 – by the largest margin in the state's history – only to suffer through four one-year terms of partisan politics. In 1871, Chamberlain became presi-

dent of Bowdoin College, where he remained until 1883. He then dove into speechmaking and writing, his best-known work being *The Passing of the Armies*, a memoir of the Civil War's final campaigns. From 1900 to 1914, Chamberlain was surveyor of the Port of Portland, a presidential appointment that ended only when complications from a wartime abdominal wound finally did him in. He died at the grand old age of 86.

Brunswick's Joshua L. Chamberlain Museum, in his onetime home at 226 Maine Street, commemorates this illustrious Mainer, and thousands of Civil War buffs annually stream through the door in search of Chamberlain "stuff." To make it easier, the Pejepscot Historical Society has produced a helpful map titled *Joshua Chamberlain's Brunswick*, highlighting town and college ties to the man – his dorm rooms, his presidential office, his portraits, even his church pew (number 64 at First Parish Church). Chamberlain's gravesite, marked by a reddish granite stone, is in Brunswick's Pine Grove Cemetery, just east of the Bowdoin campus.

Biennially, the museum celebrates **Chamberlain Days** with a symposium that concentrates on his roles in the war and in Maine. Typically, events include lectures by authors and scholars; field trips to places of interest connected with Chamberlain's life; tours of his home, concentrating on the most recent restoration work; musical or dramatic performances; and group discussions.

sive permanent collection of 19th- and 20th-century American art and its other works.

## Pejepscot Historical Society Museums

Side by side in an unusual, cupola-topped duplex facing Brunswick's Mall (village green) are two museums operated by the Pejepscot Historical Society (159 and 160 Park Row, Brunswick, 207/729-6606), the **Pejepscot Museum** (159 Park Row, 10 A.M.–5 P.M. Tues.–Fri., free) and the **Skolfield-Whittier House** (161 Park Row,

tours on the hour to 3 P.M. Thurs.–Sat. late May–late Oct., $5 adult, $2.50 child). Focusing on local history, the museum has a collection of more than 50,000 artifacts and mounts an always interesting special exhibit each year. The 17-room Skolfield-Whittier House, on the right-hand side of the building, looks as though the owners just stepped out for the afternoon. Unoccupied 1925–1982, the onetime sea captain's house has elegant Victorian furnishings and lots of exotic artifacts collected on global seafaring stints.

**MID-COAST REGION**

Also operated by the Pejepscot Historical Society, the **Joshua L. Chamberlain Museum** (226 Maine St., Brunswick, 207/729-6606, tours on the hour 10 A.M.–3 P.M. Tues.–Sat., $5 adult, $2.50 child), across from First Parish Church, commemorates the Union Army hero of the Civil War's Battle of Gettysburg, who's now gaining long-overdue respect. The partly restored house where Chamberlain lived in the late 19th century (and Henry Wadsworth Longfellow lived 30 years earlier) is a peculiar architectural hodgepodge with six rooms of exhibits of Chamberlain memorabilia, much of it Civil War–related. A gift shop stocks lots of Civil War publications, especially ones covering the Twentieth Maine Volunteers. A combination ticket for both historical houses is $8 adults, $4 kids.

## Uncle Tom's Church

Across the street from the Chamberlain museum is the historic 1846 **First Parish Church** (9 Cleaveland St. at Bath Rd., Brunswick, 207/729-7331), a Gothic Revival (or carpenter Gothic) board-and-batten structure crowning the rise at the head of Maine Street. Scores of celebrity preachers have ascended this pulpit, and Harriet Beecher Stowe was inspired to write *Uncle Tom's Cabin* while listening to her husband deliver an antislavery sermon here. If you're a fan of organ music, arrive here before noon any Tuesday early July–early August (or call ahead for details), when guest organists present 40-minute lunchtime concerts (12:10–12:50 P.M.) on the 1883 Hutchings-Plaisted tracker organ. Admission is free, but a $5 donation is requested. At other times, the church is open by appointment.

## Brunswick's Noted Women

With more than 20 points of interest, the **Brunswick Women's History Trail** covers such national notables as authors Harriet Beecher Stowe and Kate Douglas Wiggin and lesser-known lights, including naturalist Kate Furbish, pioneering Maine pediatrician Dr. Alice Whittier, and the Franco American women who slaved away in the textile mills at

the turn of the 20th century. Buy the walking-tour booklet at the Pejepscot Museum gift shop ($2). Then set out to follow the fascinating story. The museum offers guided tours lasting about one hour once a month in June, July, and August (donation requested).

## Brunswick Literary Art Walk

Cast your eyes downward while walking along Maine Street. Four bronze plaques recognize Brunswick's most famous writers: Henry Wadsworth Longfellow, Nathaniel Hawthorne, Harriet Beecher Stowe, and Robert P. T. Coffin. Each plaque bears a quote from the author commemorated. The privately funded endeavor plans to produce a brochure with additional information on the writers along with a map. Look for it at stores, lodgings, and info bureaus.

## Go, Fish!

If you're in town between mid-May and late June, plan to visit Central Maine Power's **Brunswick Hydro** generating station, straddling the falls on the Androscoggin River, Lower Maine Street, next to Fort Andross, Brunswick-Topsham town line (207/729-7644 or 207/623-3521, ext. 2116, weekdays, or 800/872-9937). A glass-walled viewing room lets you play voyeur during the annual ritual of anadromous fish heading upstream to spawn. Amazingly undaunted by the obstacles, such species as alewives (herring), salmon, and smallmouth bass make their way from salt water to fresh via a 40-foot-high, 570-foot-long man-made fish ladder. The viewing room, which maxes out at about 20 people, is open 1–5 P.M. Wednesday–Sunday during the brief spring spawning season.

# RECREATION
## Excursion Train

Ride in restored, vintage railcars on the scenic **Maine Eastern Railroad** (207/596-6725 or 800/637-2457, www.maineeasternrailroad.com), operating between Rockland and Brunswick, with stops in Wiscasset and Bath. The train operates late May–early November, with special holiday trains in December. Adult fares are $40 round-trip, $25 one-way; ages 5–15 pay $25/$15; seniors are $35/$25; family rate is $100/$75 covering two adults and two kids. Packages with lodging, meals, and theater are available.

## Hiking and Biking

A good choice for family biking or a good walk in the Brunswick area is the 2.5-mile **Androscoggin River Bicycle Path** running between downtown Brunswick and Cooks Corner, meandering along the scenic Androscoggin River and paralleling Route 1. (Unfortunately, the traffic noise often makes the route less than tranquil.) The landscaped asphalt path is also popular with joggers, strollers, and in-line skaters. To reach the path from the lower end of Maine Street in downtown Brunswick, take Mason Street and then the next left onto Water Street. Continue about two blocks to the parking area (often very crowded) next to the boat-launching site. The path has no loop, so you'll need to return the way you came.

In the village of Bailey Island, there's a mini-walk to the **Giant Stairs,** a waterfront stone stairway of mammoth proportions. To get there, take Route 24 from Cooks Corner toward Bailey Island and Land's End, keeping an eye out for Washington Avenue, on the left about 1.5 miles after the cribstone bridge. (Or drive to Land's End, park the car with the rest of the crowds, survey the panorama, and walk 0.8 mile back along Route 24 to Washington Avenue from there.) Turn onto Washington Avenue, go 0.1 mile, and park at the Episcopal Church (corner of Ocean St.). Walk along Ocean Street to the shorefront path. Watch for a tiny sign just before Spindrift Lane. Don't let small kids get close to the slippery rocks on the surf-tossed shoreline. (The same advice, by the way, holds for Land's End, where the rocks can be treacherous.)

Thank the **Brunswick-Topsham Land Trust** (108 Maine St., Brunswick, 207/729-7694, www.btlt.org), founded in 1985, for access to two nature preserves (one on Harpswell Neck, one in Topsham). At 11-acre **Captain Alfred Skolfield Nature Preserve,** one of the two blue-blazed nature-trail loops skirts a salt marsh, where you're apt to see egrets, herons, and osprey in summer. Adjacent to the preserve is an ancient Indian portage site that linked Middle Bay and Harpswell Coves when Native Americans spent their vacations here. (No dopes, they!) Take Route 123 (Harpswell Rd.) south from Brunswick about three miles; when you reach the Middle Bay Road intersection (on the right), continue on Route 123 for 1.1 miles. Watch for a small sign, and a small parking area, on your right.

In Topsham, the 163-acre **Bradley Pond Farm Preserve** has two well-laid-out nature loops (a total of 2.5 miles) that let you sample marshes, woodlands, fields, and the pond—all astonishingly close to civilization. Farm owners Florence and Fred Call have generously agreed to share their special turf, so heed the rules and stay on the trails. From Maine Street in Brunswick, cross the river to Topsham's Main Street. At the junction of Routes 196 and 201, take 201 four miles to Bradley Pond Road (on the left). Turn in and park (or leave your bike) in the designated parking areas on the left.

The 103-acre **Cox Pinnacle,** owned by the town of Brunswick, comprises wooded hills, rocky ledges, and wetlands laced with about 1.5 miles of old logging and farming roads. The trails lead to Cox Pinnacle, the highest point of land in Brunswick (350 feet). Take the Durham Road, then turn right at the blinking light onto Hacker Road, and drive 0.3 mile to the parking lot on the left.

Also owned by the town of Brunswick is the **Town Commons** (www.brunswickme.org/commons), granted by vote of the Pejepscot proprietors on May 8, 1719. The one-mile Pitch Pine Barren Loop starts and finishes at the picnic area, by the main entrance on Route 123. The trail passes through swamplands and by a peat heath.

**Center Street Bicycles** (11 Center St., just off Maine St., Brunswick, 207/729-5309) does repairs and sells bikes and a good range of accessories. Prices vary with models, but figure about $35 for a one-day rental. The knowledgeable staff also act as a clearinghouse for route information. (For instance, they strongly urge every customer to avoid biking the Harpswells, especially Route 123; the scenic rewards are outstanding, but the risks are many on the shoulderless roads.)

## Swimming

**Thomas Point Beach** (29 Meadow Rd., Brunswick, 207/725-6009 or 877/872-4321, www.thomaspointbeach.com) is actually 85 acres of privately owned parkland with facilities for swimming (lifeguard on duty, bathhouses), fishing, field sports, picnicking (500 tables), and camping (75 tent and RV sites at $20; no water or sewer hookups, but electricity and dump station available). No pets, skateboards, or motorcycles are allowed. The sandy beach is tidal, so the swimming "window" is about two hours before high tide until two hours afterward; otherwise, you're wallowing in mudflats. (The same rule holds for kayakers or canoeists.) Toddlers head for the big playground; teenagers gravitate to the arcade and the ice-cream parlor. The park is also the site of several annual events, including the Maine Highland Games and the Bluegrass Festival. Parking is ample. At Cooks Corner, where Bath Road meets Route 24 South, go 1.5 miles on Route 24, then turn left, and follow signs for less than two miles to the park. It's open 9 A.M.–sunset mid-May–September. Admission to the park is $3.50 adults, $2 kids 3–12.

For freshwater swimming, head to town-owned **Coffin Pond** (River Rd., Brunswick, 207/725-6656), a man-made swimming hole with a sandy beach, lifeguards, water slide, picnic tables, playground, changing rooms, and snack bar. Kids' swimming lessons (ages 5–14) are held in August. It's a popular spot, so expect plenty of company. It's open 10 A.M.– 7 P.M. mid-June–early September. Nonresident admission is $3.50 adult, $2 age 12 and younger. Heading west on Route 1 (Pleasant St.), turn right onto River Road and go about a half mile to the parking area (on the right).

Another terrific but nonsecret spot for freshwater swimming is **White's Beach** (White's Beach and Campground, Durham Rd., Bruns-

wick, 207/729-0415, www.whitesbeachand-campground.com). The sandy-bottomed pond maxes out at nine feet, so it's particularly good for small kids. In mid-July, the campground hosts a popular family bluegrass festival. Park facilities include a snack bar, playground, hot showers, and campsites. Admission is $3.75 adults, $2.75 kids 12 and younger and seniors. Campsites (45) are $20–30. It's open mid-May–mid-October. From Route 1 just south of the I-95 exit into Brunswick, take Durham Road 2.2 miles northwest.

## Golf

Established in 1901 primarily for Bowdoin College students, the **Brunswick Golf Club** (River Rd., Brunswick, 207/725-8224) is now an especially popular 18-hole public course, so you'll need to call for a starting time. Another possibility is the nine-hole **Brunswick Naval Air Station Golf Club** (Bath Rd., Brunswick, 207/921-2155). You'll have access to the pro shop, snack bar, and driving range. Call for tee times.

## Boating Excursions

Departing at noon from the Cook's Lobster House wharf (Cook's Landing) in Bailey Island (off Rte. 24), a large, sturdy **Casco Bay Lines ferry** does a 1.75-hour nature-watch circuit of nearby islands, including Eagle Island, the one-time home of Admiral Robert Peary (there are no stopovers on these circuits; for excursions to Eagle Island, see *Sailboat and Powerboat Excursions* under *Recreation* in the *Greater Portland* chapter). Reservations aren't needed. Cost is $12 adults, $10 seniors, $5.50 kids 5–9. To confirm the schedule when weather is iffy, call Casco Bay Lines (207/774-7871), or Cook's Landing (207/833-6641).

For a more intimate excursion in a smaller boat, Captain Les McNelly, owner of **Sea Escape Charters** (Box 7, Bailey Island 04003, 207/833-5531, www.seaescapecottages.com), operates two-hour on-demand sightseeing cruises throughout the summer (weather permitting) for $65 pp (two people) or $35 pp (four people). Or he'll take you out to Eagle

Island for $140 a couple (lower rate if there are more passengers). He also offers fishing trips: $200 for four hours, including bait and tackle ($95 each additional person); no fishing license required; bring your own lunch. Call to schedule a trip. Trips operate out of Sea Escape Cottages, one- and two-bedroom well-equipped cottages, with full kitchens and oceanside decks that rent for $140–160 per night or $850–1,020 per week, including linens and one change of towels.

Occasionally, the grandson of Admiral Robert E. Peary, the first explorer to reach the North Pole, leads an **Eagle Island Adventure Tour** (Friends of Peary's Eagle Island, P.O. Box 70, Bailey Island 04003, 207/833-2310, www.pearyeagleisland.org, $38). Details and departure locations are subject to change—some years Harpswell, other years Portland. Space is limited and reservations are required. Check the website for details.

### Sea Kayaking

**H2Outfitters** (P.O. Box 72, Orr's Island 04066, 207/833-5257 or 800/205-2925, www.h2outfitters.com) has been a thriving operation since 1978. Based in a wooden building on the Orr's Island side of the famed cribstone bridge, this experienced company organizes multiday trips, including island camping, for $395 pp and up; all gear is included.

Newer on the scene is **Seaspray Kayaking** (207/443-3646 or 888/349-7772, www.seaspraykayaking.com), with bases on the New Meadows River, in Brunswick, as well as at Sebasco, in Phippsburg, and Bay Point, in Georgetown. The New Meadows base is particularly good for those nervous about trying the sport, as it isn't open ocean and there are no waves. Rentals and tours are available. Rentals are $10–20 for the first hour, $5–10 for additional hours, $25–50 per day. Equipment options include solo and tandem kayaks, recreational kayaks, surf kayaks, and canoes. Tours, led by Registered Maine Guides, vary from sunset paddles to three-day expeditions and include moonlight paddles, island-to-island tours, and inn-to-inn tours. Rates begin at

$50 adult, $25 child for shorter tours. A striper fishing kayak tour, including tackle and instruction, is $75. Reserve early for the popular Moonlight Paddles ($40).

If you're an experienced sea kayaker, consider exploring Harpswell Sound from the boat launch on the west side of the cribstone bridge; kayaks can also put in at Mackerel Cove, near Cook's Lobster House. There's also a boat launch with plentiful parking at Sawyer Park on the New Meadows River, on Route 1, just before you cross the river heading north.

## ENTERTAINMENT

The region's extremely active arts organization, **Five Rivers Arts Alliance** (108 Main St., Brunswick, 207/798-6964, www.fiveriversartsalliance.org), maintains a calendar of area concerts, gallery openings, art shows, lectures, exhibits, and other arts-related events and also sponsors a few key events. Listings also appear on www.midcoastmaine.com/events.

There's no lack of classical music in Brunswick each summer, but for lighter fare, the **Maine State Music Theatre** (Pickard Theater, Bowdoin College, mailing/box office 22 Elm St., Brunswick 04011, 207/725-8769, www.msmt.org), has been a summer tradition since 1959. The renovated, state-of-the-art, air-conditioned theater brings real pros to its stage for four musicals (mid-June–late Aug.). Loyal subscribers book the same seats year after year, and performances tend to sell out, so call ahead for the schedule and reservations. (Nonsubscription tickets go on sale in early May.) Performances are at 8 P.M. Tuesday–Saturday; matinees are staged at 2 P.M. on an alternating schedule—each week has matinees on different days. (No children under four are admitted, but special family shows are performed during the season.) Ticket range is $30–49.

The **Bowdoin International Music Festival** (box office 12 Cleveland St., mailing address 6300 College Station, Brunswick 04011, 207/725-3895, www.summermusic.org) is a showcase for an international array of musical talent of all kinds late June–early August. The six-week festival, part of an international music school, presents a variety of concert opportunities—enough so that there's music almost every night of the week. Venues vary and tickets range free–$30. Call or check the website for the current schedule.

The First Paris Church sponsors a **Summer Organ Concert Series** (207/729-7331) at the church between noon and 1 P.M. on Tuesdays in July and August, suggested donation $5.

**Second Friday Art Walks** (207/725-4366) take place in downtown Brunswick 5–7:30 P.M. May–November. Gallery openings, wine tastings, light refreshments, and other activities are usually part of the mix.

**Music on the Mall** presents family band concerts at 7 P.M. Wednesdays (Thursdays if it rains) in July and August on the Brunswick Mall (the lovely park in the center of town).

## FESTIVALS AND EVENTS

The first full week of August, the **Topsham Fair** is a weeklong agricultural festival with exhibits, demonstrations, live music, ox pulls, contests, harness racing, and fireworks at the Topsham Fairgrounds.

The third Saturday of August, the **Maine Highland Games,** sponsored by the St. Andrew's Society of Maine, mark the annual wearing of the plaids—but you needn't be Scottish to join in the games or watch the Highland dancing or browse the arts and crafts booths. (Only a Scot, however, can appreciate that unique concoction called haggis.) If you're seeking your clan roots, this is the place; lots of genealogical networking goes on here. It all happens at Thomas Point Beach in Brunswick.

Also at Thomas Point Beach, September's **Annual Bluegrass Festival** is a four-day event with nonstop bluegrass, including big-name artists. Kickoff is Thursday noon.

The **Family Arts Festival** (207/798-6964), in September, has hands-on workshops, music, dance, and storytelling for all ages under tents on the Mall.

## SHOPPING

Downtown Brunswick invites leisurely browsing, with most of the shops concentrated on Maine Street. Do take special care when crossing the four-lane wide street, and do so only at marked crosswalks.

A handful of small shops are part of the **Tontine Mall** (149 Maine St., Brunswick); the mall entrance is right in the middle of downtown.

## Art, Craft, and Antiques Galleries

The **Bayview Gallery** (58 Maine St., Brunswick, 800/244-3007), mounts half a dozen superb shows annually, specializing in contemporary New England artists.

Facing the Mall, **Day's Antiques** (153 Park Row, Brunswick, 207/725-6959) occupies five rooms and the basement of the handsome historic building known as the Pumpkin House. Quality is high at David Day's shop; prices are fair.

More than 140 dealers show and sell their wares at **Cabot Mill Antiques** (14 Maine St., 207/725-2855), in the renovated Fort Andross mill complex next to the Androscoggin River.

Part gallery, part resource center, **Maine Fiberarts** (13 Maine St., Topsham, 207/721-0678, www.mainefiberarts.org) is a must-stop for anyone interested in fiber-related artwork: knitting, quilting, spinning, basketry. If you're really interested in finding artists and resources statewide, buy a copy of its resource book.

Nearly two dozen local artists exhibit their works in varied media at **Sebascodegan Artists Gallery** (Rte. 24, Great Island, Harpswell, 207/833-6260).

## Bookstores

With an eclectic new-book inventory that includes lots of esoterica, **Gulf of Maine Books** (134 Maine St., Brunswick, 207/729-5083) has held the competition at bay since the early 1980s. The fiction selection is particularly good, as are the religion, health, and poetry sections. Poet/publisher/renaissance man Gary Lawless oversees everything.

**Bookland** (Cooks Corner Shopping Center, Bath Rd.d and Rte. 24 S, Brunswick, 207/725-2313), a thriving independent emporium, is also home to the very popular Hardcover Cafe.

## ACCOMMODATIONS
### Hotels, Motels, and Inns

Combining a Federal-style manse with a new hotel wing, **The Captain Daniel Stone Inn** (10 Water St., Brunswick, 207/725-9898 or 877/573-5151, www.captaindanielstone-inn.com) has 34 guest rooms and suites furnished with antiques and reproductions and a country-inn feel, despite a location edging busy Route 1. It offers private baths, air-conditioning, phones, and cable TV. The inn is walking distance to downtown Brunswick, and it's close to the bike path (bikes are available to guests). A few rooms are pet friendly ($25 per night). In summer, rooms are $135–290, suites are $220–255, including expanded continental breakfast; rates are lower other months, and special packages are available. The inn's casually elegant restaurant, **Augustine's,** is open daily for lunch 11:30 a.m.–3 p.m. and dinner 5–10 p.m., serving both in a fine dining room and more casual tavern. Breakfast is available to guests.

A dozen miles down Route 24 from Cooks Corner is the turnoff for Jo Atlass's **Little Island Motel** (44 Little Island Rd., Orr's Island, 207/833-2392, www.littleislandmotel.com, $125–135 d peak), a nine-unit complex on its own spit of land with deck views you won't believe. Basic rooms have cable TV and small fridge. Rates include buffet breakfast and use of bikes, boats, and a little beach. No credit cards. Open mid-May–mid-October.

Continue another mile down Route 24, cross the cribstone bridge, and you'll come to Chip Black's **Bailey Island Motel** (Rte. 24, P.O. Box 4, Bailey Island 04003, 207/833-2886, www.baileyislandmotel.com, $95–215), a congenial, clean, no-frills waterfront spot with 11 rooms and wowser views. Kids under 10 are free; 10 and older are $15. Continental breakfast is included, and rooms have cable TV. A dock is available for boat launching. Open mid-May–late October.

Looking rather like an old-fashioned tearjerker film set, the family-run **Driftwood Inn** (81 Washington Ave., Bailey Island, 207/833-5461, www.thedriftwoodinnmaine.com) has 25 very basic, pine-paneled rooms in four buildings (some with private toilet and sink; all with shared showers), six housekeeping cottages, a saltwater pool, a stunning view, a dining room (open to the public), and a determinedly rustic ambience. No frills, period, but it has ocean-front porches, games, and an old-fashioned simplicity that you rarely find anymore, and you'll sleep at night listening to the waves crash on the rocky shore. It's all on three oceanfront acres near the Giant Stairs. The dining room, open to the public by reservation, serves a set, home-cooked meal nightly (usually with a fish-of-the-day alternative), late June–Labor Day for $16–19. Breakfast is $6.50. Rooms are $85–120 d; all meals are extra, but rates including breakfast and dinner are available ($450 pp/week). Cottages rent by the week in season, $645–680; off-season $115–125 per night. Dogs are allowed in the cottages. No credit cards. Open mid-May–October.

### Bed-and-Breakfasts

Right downtown, facing the tree-shaded Mall, is the **Brunswick Inn on Park Row** (165 Park Row, Brunswick, 207/729-4914 or 800/299-4914, www.brunswickbnb.com, $125–190 d), a handsome, 30-room Greek Revival mansion built in 1849 and decorated with contemporary flair. Original works by Maine artists are displayed throughout the inn, including in the Cygnet Lounge Wine Bar. Fifteen elegant guest rooms are split between the main house and the newly renovated Carriage House (with two fully accessible rooms); all have Wi-Fi and phones, and Carriage House suites have TV. Breakfast is a treat. Open all year.

Within walking distance of downtown Brunswick, but across the bridge spanning the Androscoggin River, is the **Black Lantern B&B** (57 Elm St., Topsham, 207/725-4165 or 888/306-4165, www.blacklanternbandb.com, $95), Tom and Judy Connelie's lovely 1860s riverfront home. All rooms are decorated with an emphasis on comfort, and two have water views. Judy's quilts will warm you on a cool night.

On the outskirts of town, in a rural location smack-dab on Middle Bay, is ◖ **Middle Bay**

**Farm Bed and Breakfast** (287 Pennellville Rd., Brunswick, 207/373-1375, www.middlebayfarm.com, $150–170), lovingly and beautifully restored by Phyllis Truesdell, who bought the property after it sat all but abandoned for a decade. Once the site of the Pennell Brothers Shipyard, the farmhouse and sail loft now house guests seeking an away-from-it-all, yet convenient, location. Four water-view guest rooms in the 1834 farmhouse are decorated with antiques and have TV/VCR. Also in the main house is a living room with fireplace and grand piano. Two suites in the sail loft each have a living room with kitchenette and two tiny bedrooms and share an open porch. All guests receive a full breakfast in the water-view dining room. Canoes and bicycles are available to guests. Bring a sea kayak to launch from the dock. Open all year.

At the 1761 **Harpswell Inn** (108 Lookout Point Rd., South Harpswell, 207/833-5509 or 800/843-5509, www.harpswellinn.com), innkeepers Anne and Richard Moseley operate a comfortable, welcoming, antiques-filled oasis on 2.5 secluded, water-view acres. It's tough to break away from the glass-walled great room, but Middle Bay sunsets from the porch can do it. And just down the hill is Allen's Seafood, where you can watch lobstermen unload their catches in a gorgeous cove. In fall, the foliage on two little islets in the cove turns brilliant red. The B&B has nine lovely rooms (most with private baths; $110–159 d), three suites ($235–249 d), and four cottages ($950–1,400 per week). Prices are slightly higher for one-night stays. From Bath Road, in Brunswick, take Route 123 eight miles to Lookout Point Road (on the right). Open all year.

After many years as an extremely popular dining destination 13 miles south of Cooks Corner, **The Log Cabin** (Rte. 24, P.O. Box 41, Bailey Island 04003, 207/833-5546, www.logcabin-maine.com) in 1996 added lodging to its repertoire, and now it serves meals only to guests. Nine nicely decorated rooms have phones, TV/VCR, private decks facing the bay, and, weather permitting, splendid sunset views to the White Mountains. Four rooms

have kitchen facilities; some have gas fireplaces or whirlpool tubs. There's also an outdoor heated pool. Rates are $169–329 d in midsummer, lower early and late in the season. Full breakfast is included; dinner ($16–31) is available only to guests 6–6:30 P.M. Open April–October.

## Seasonal Rentals

For weekly or monthly rentals in Great, Orr's, and Bailey Islands, try **Your Island Connection** (P.O. Box 300, Bailey Island 04003, 207/833-7779, www.mainerentals.com) or **Harpswell Property Management** (P.O. Box 6, Bailey Island 04003, 207/833-7795, www.baileyisland.com). The Bath-Brunswick Chamber of Commerce also keeps a list of seasonal cottage rentals.

## FOOD

Brunswick has an abundance of inexpensive cafés, delis, coffeehouses, and ethnic restaurants lining its main and side streets as well as seasonal vendors operating cart stands on the mall. At most, you order at the counter and then select your table.

### Local Flavors

**Wild O.A.T.S. Bakery and Café** (149 Maine St., Tontine Mall, Brunswick, 207/725-6287, www.wildoatsbakery.com, 7:30 A.M.–5 P.M. Mon.–Sat., 8 A.M.–3 P.M. Sun.) turns out terrific made-from-scratch breads and pastries, especially the breakfast kind, in its cafeteria-style place. (Just so you know, the name stands for Original and Tasty Stuff.) It has inside and outside tables, moderate prices, good-for-you salads, and great sandwiches (try the Club Med or the curried chicken melt).

For food on the run—no-frills hot dogs straight from the cart—head for Brunswick's Mall, the village green where **Danny's on the Mall** (no telephone) has been cooking dirt-cheap tube steaks since the early 1980s.

**Fat Boy Drive-In** (Bath Rd., Old Rte. 1, Brunswick, 207/729-9431) is a genuine throwback—a landmark since 1955, boasting carhops, window trays, and a menu guaranteed to clog your arteries. Fries and frappes are specialties. If you insist, there are five booths indoors. No credit cards. It's open 11 A.M.–8:30 P.M. daily—get this—the third Tuesday in March to the second Sunday in October. The second Saturday in August, about 700 people show up, many in 1950s getups, for the annual sock hop. Only pre-1970 cars can park in the lot that night (if you have one, stop in ahead of time for a pass).

Afterward, stop by **Hattie's Ice Cream** (185 Park Row, Brunswick, 207/725-6139, www.hattiesicecream.com, noon–11 P.M. daily) for a scoop (or two, or three) of Maine-made organic ice cream, sorbet, or gelato in drool-worthy flavors that define creative (cardamon-ginger-infused gelato). Or how about a sundae atop a Simply Divine brownie?

Or choose from up to 32 flavors of gelato and *sorbetto* at **The Gelato Fiasco** (74 Maine St., Brunswick, 207/607-4002).

Arguments rage endlessly about who makes the best chowder in Maine, but **The Dolphin Chowder House** (Dolphin Marina, 515 Basin Point Rd., South Harpswell, 207/833-6000, 11 A.M.–8 P.M. daily May 1–Nov. 1), heads lots of lists for its fish chowder, accompanied by a blueberry muffin. Equally famed is its lobster stew. Plus you can't beat the scenic 13-mile drive south from Brunswick and the spectacular water views, through two walls of windows at the tip of Harpswell Neck.

One of Maine's best farmers markets is the **Brunswick Farmers Market,** which sets up, rain or shine, on the Mall (village green) 8 A.M.–2 P.M. Tuesday and Friday May–November (Friday is the bigger day). The market moves to Crystal Spring Farm, Pleasant Hill Road, between 8:30 A.M. and 12:30 P.M. on Saturday. You'll find produce, cheeses, crafts, condiments, live lobsters, and serendipitous surprises—depending on the season.

## Casual Dining

"Tis a gift to be local..." is the motto at Jessica Gorton's **Sweet Leaves Teahouse** (22 Pleasant St., Brunswick, 207/725-1376, 11:30 A.M.–9 P.M. Tues.–Sat.), a casual restaurant next to

the post office just south of Maine Street that serves lunch, dinner, and afternoon tea. Chef Josh DeGroot has brought his immense talent here, shaping a menu that changes daily and honors local farmers, anglers, foragers, and fromage folks (that's cheesemakers). Just about everything is made on the premises except the bread, which comes from Standard Baking in Portland. Ice creams and sorbets are made in house, and don't miss DeGroot's signature chocolate goat cheese. After 5 P.M., "dinnerly plates" such as crab cakes, potato gnocchi, or hangar steak are served. Tuesdays feature an open mic 6:30–9 P.M.

At the upper end of the downtown drag is **Scarlet Begonias** (212B Maine St., Brunswick, 207/721-0403, 11 A.M.–8 P.M. Sun.–Wed., to 8:30 P.M. Thurs., to 9:30 P.M. Fri. and Sat., opens at noon Sat.), an especially cheerful place with a Mediterranean-influenced, bistro-type pizza-and-pasta menu. Order at the counter and look for a table. How could anyone resist a $10 pasta puttanesca dubbed Scarlet Harlot? You can't go wrong here; everything's a winner. No credit cards. BYOB.

An enticing selection of small plates, soups, salads, and sandwiches is served at the tiny **111 Maine Street** (111 Maine St., Brunswick, 207/729-9111, www.111maine.com, 11 A.M.–4 P.M. Tues.–Fri., to 9 P.M. Fri., 10 A.M.–2 P.M. Sat.–Sun.). Everything's ultrafresh and seasonally driven—the market veggie plate is delish in summer. Inside are a handful of tables and a window bar with stools; in summer, there usually are a few tables outside, too.

Just off Maine Street, **Renaissance Bistro and European Wine Bar** (25 Mill St., Brunswick, 207/721-0412, www.renaissance-bistro.com) is a find for European-influenced fare created from locally sourced ingredients and served in a casual, storefront bistro setting. Dinner choices ($18–26) vary from wild mushroom ravioli to rack of lamb to duck; brunch is especially decadent. It's open for dinner beginning at 5 P.M. Tuesday–Saturday, and brunch beginning at 9 A.M. Saturday–Sunday.

Eclectic doesn't begin to describe **Frontier Cafe** (Mill 3, Fort Andross, 14 Maine St. at Rte. 1 overpass, Brunswick, 207/725-5222, www.explorefrontier.com, 9 A.M.–9 P.M. Mon.–Thurs., 11 A.M.–11 P.M. Sat.), a combination café, gallery, and cinema inspired by founder Michael Gilroy's world travels. The menu of soups, sandwiches, and salads changes weekly but usually includes wonderful market plates emphasizing the cuisine of a country or region—Maine, France, the Middle East, Italy. Desserts are homemade, and there's a kids' menu, too. Wine and beer are served. Films are screened ($7 adult), and there are frequent events, such as the monthly Knit and Fiddle, concerts, and other entertainment.

Just over the bridge from Brunswick, in the renovated Bowdoin Mill complex overlooking the Androscoggin River, is the **Sea Dog Brewery** (1 Main St., Topsham, 207/725-0162, www.seadogbrewing.com, 11:30 A.M.–1 A.M. daily), with seating inside and on a deck overhanging the river. The menu ranges from burgers and sandwiches to full plate entrées ($11–18). It offers frequent acoustic entertainment, including karaoke on Thursdays. There are also games for kids and a games room with video arcade and pool tables. A jazz brunch is served until 1 P.M. Sundays.

### Ethnic Fare

Generous portions, moderate prices, efficient service, and narrow aisles are the story at **The Great Impasta** (42 Maine St., Brunswick, 207/729-5858, www.thegreatimpasta.com, 11 A.M.–9 P.M. Mon.–Thurs., to 10 P.M. Fri.–Sat.), a cheerful, informal eatery where the garlic meets you at the door. No reservations, so expect to wait, although you can call ahead and add your name to the waiting list. Dinner entrées are $10–17. It has a small but varied wine list and a "bambino menu" for the kids.

Hip, funky, and full of personality are words often used to describe **El Camino** (15 Cushing St., Brunswick, 207/725-8228, 5–9 P.M. Wed.–Sat., to 10 P.M. Fri.–Sat.), which uses fresh, local, and often organic ingredients to create innovative Cal-Mex fare. Prices top out around $15.

Chef Richard Gnauck has been serving authentic German fare in the area for more than 20 years, and recently he's been joined by sons Erik and Wilhelm at his **Richard's Restaurant** (115 Maine St., Brunswick, 11 A.M.–2 P.M. and 5–9 P.M. Mon.–Sat., to 9:30 P.M. Fri. and Sat.). German favorites such as Wiener schnitzel and sauerbraten share the menu with American-style fare; heart-smart and petite portions are available; $12–20.

### Lobster and Seafood

In late 2006, the Holbrook Community Foundation took ownership of Holbrook's Wharf, site of **Holbrook's Wharf and Grille** (984 Cundy's Harbor Rd., 207/729-0848, 11:30 A.M.–sunset daily), along with Holbrook's General Store and the Trufant mansion, preserving this slice of Maine-fishing-village life for future generations. The wharf lobster shack, under leased operation by the Morse family, is the real thing for authentic lobster in the rough, and the view's superb. Order at the window and then choose a picnic table on the wharf, some under cover. Seafood baskets, hot dogs, and burgers are also available. BYOB.

You want fresh? Fish doesn't get any fresher than that served at **Allen's Seafood** (119 Lookout Point Rd., Harpswell, 207/833-2828, 11 A.M.–7 P.M. daily), a seasonal take-out shack overlooking Middle Bay. Chowders, fried fish, lobster, and similar fare are prepared fresh from the bounty of the daily catch. Order and then grab a picnic table. Moorings and a dock are available if you arrive by boat.

## INFORMATION AND SERVICES

The Southern Midcoast Chamber of Commerce (2 Main St., Topsham, 877/725-8797, www.midcoastmaine.com) publishes *Guide to Southern Midcoast Maine*.

For information on Harpswell, visit Harpswell Business Association (www.harpswellmaine.org).

Check the website of Curtis Memorial Library (23 Pleasant St., Brunswick, 207/725-5242, www.curtislibrary.com) for excellent local resources and guides.

# Bath Area

One of the smallest in area of Maine's cities, Bath—with a population of about 9,920 in only nine square miles—has many similarities to Brunswick. It sits astride Route 1 and a river, relies on modern military funding, yet has centuries of historical and architectural tradition, enough distinction that the National Trust for Historic Preservation named it as one of a Dozen Distinctive Destinations in 2005. The defense part is impossible to ignore, since giant cranes dominate the riverfront cityscape at the huge Bath Iron Works complex, source of state-of-the-art warships—your tax dollars at work. Less evident (but not far away) is the link to the past: Just south of Bath, in Popham on the Phippsburg Peninsula, is the poorly marked site where a trouble-plagued English settlement, a sister colony to Jamestown, predated the Plymouth Colony by 13 years. (Of course, Champlain arrived before that, and Norse-

men allegedly left calling cards even earlier.) In 1607 and 1608, settlers in the Popham Colony managed to build a 30-ton pinnace, *Virginia of Sagadahoc,* designed for transatlantic trade, but they lost heart during a bitter winter and abandoned the site. (A replica is under construction at the Maine Maritime Museum. For details, visit www.mainesfirstship.org.)

Bath is the jumping-off point for two peninsulas to the south—Phippsburg (of Popham Colony fame) and Georgetown. Both are dramatically scenic, with glacier-carved farms and fishing villages. Drive (bicycling is best left to experienced pedalers) a dozen miles down any of these fingers and you're in different worlds, ones where artists and photographers, hikers and historians go crazy with all the possibilities.

Across the soaring Sagadahoc Bridge from Bath is Woolwich, from which you can continue northeastward along the coast or detour northward on Route 128 to the hamlet of Day's Ferry. Named after 18th-century resident Joseph Day, who shuttled back and forth in a gondola-type boat across the Kennebec here, the picturesque village has a cluster of 18th- and 19th-century homes and churches—all part of the Day's Ferry Historic District. And the village's Old Stage Road saw many a stagecoach in its day; passengers would ferry from Bath and pick up the stage here to travel onward.

## SIGHTS
### Bath Iron Works

Only during one of its relatively infrequent launchings is Bath Iron Works (BIW) open to the public, and then it's a mob scene, with hordes of politicos, townsfolk, and military pooh-bahs in their scrambled eggs and brass. But the launchings are exciting occasions, with flags flying everywhere. BIW, under the umbrella of giant defense contractor General Dynamics, employs more than 8,500 in its Bath and smaller Brunswick sites. When BIW talks, everyone listens. And when BIW's

© TOM NANGLE

Front and center in downtown Bath is City Hall.

MID-COAST REGION

afternoon shift changes, everyone from Brunswick to Wiscasset feels the gridlock. Avoid approaching Bath between 3:25 and 4 P.M. on a weekday; be forewarned and plan your schedule around the witching hour. Despite the construction of the brand-new Sagadahoc Bridge, which has definitely eased the situation, traffic still backs up at shift-change time.

## ◖ Maine Maritime Museum

Spread over 20 acres on the Kennebec River is the state's premier marine museum, the Maine Maritime Museum (243 Washington St., Bath, 207/443-1316, www.mainemaritimemuseum. org, 9:30 A.M.–5 P.M. daily, $10 adult, $7 ages 7–17, $9 over 65). On the grounds are relics of the 19th-century Percy and Small Shipyard (1897–1920) and a hands-on lobstering exhibit, but the first thing you see is the architecturally dramatic Maritime History Building, locale for permanent and temporary displays of marine art and artifacts and a shop stocked with nautical books and gifts. Bring a picnic and let the toddlers loose in the children's play area. Then join one of the three daily, hour-long guided shipyard tours or the special themed tours offered at 2 P.M. weekdays (all tours late May–mid-Oct.). Shipyard demonstrations are held on a rotating schedule, and brown-bag lectures are often given. In summer, weather permitting, the museum sponsors a variety of special river cruises; call for information. Percy and Small Shipyard is open all year as long as the weather holds.

## Bath History Preserved

Sagadahoc Preservation (Box 322, Bath 04530, www.sagadahocpreservation.org), founded in 1971 to rescue the city's architectural heritage, has produced **Architectural Tours: Self-Guided Walking and Driving Tours of the City of Bath,** a terrific foldout brochure (with maps) to guide you—via car, ankle express, or bicycle—around Bath. Pick up a copy at a local business. It also offers an annual house tour, usually in June; check the website for details. Another free map and guide, **The Historic Architecture of Downtown Bath, Maine,** is

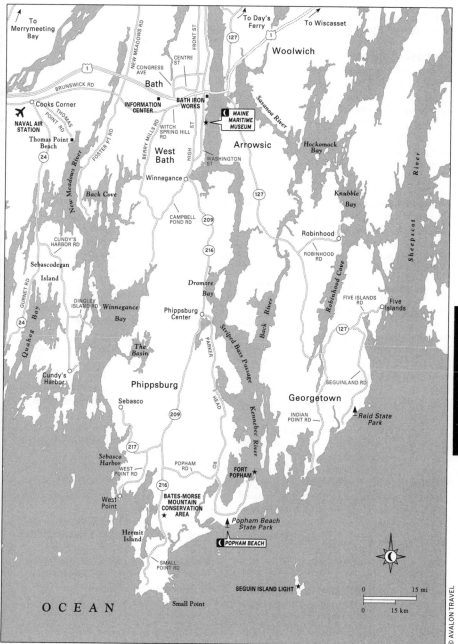

sponsored by Main Street Bath (4 Centre St., Bath, 207/442-7291, www.mainstbath.com).

## Phippsburg Peninsula

Thanks to an impressive map/brochure produced by the Phippsburg Historical Society and the Phippsburg Business Association, you can spend a whole day—or, better still, several days—exploring the peninsula that drops from Bath. Along the way are campgrounds, B&Bs, an updated traditional resort, restaurants, a unique state park, hiking trails, secluded coves, spectacular scenery, and tons of history.

About two miles south of Bath is a causeway known as **Winnegance,** a Wabanaki name usually translated as "short carry" or "little portage." Native Americans crossed here from the Kennebec to the New Meadows River. Early settlers erected nearly a dozen tide-powered mills to serve the shipbuilding industry, but they're long gone. Just before the causeway, on the Bath-Phippsburg boundary, is the **Winnegance General Store** (36 High St., Bath, 207/443-9805), a local favorite for the miscellanea that general stores offer, including inexpensive sandwiches. About 1.5 miles farther is a left turn onto Fiddler's Reach Road, leading to the **Morse Cove Public Launching Facility,** one of the state's most scenic boat-launch sites. If you have a kayak, plan to go downriver on the ebb tide and return on the flow (otherwise, you'll be battling the strong Kennebec River current). There's plenty of paved parking here, plus a restroom.

Back on Route 209, it's another 1.3 miles to the **Dromore Burying Ground** (on the right), with great old headstones; the earliest is dated 1743. The next mile opens up with terrific easterly views of Dromore Bay. Right in the line of sight is 117-acre Lee Island (which the owners sold to the state in 1995). From May through mid-July, the island is off-limits to protect nesting eagles and waterfowl.

Next you're in **Phippsburg Center,** alive with shipbuilding from colonial days to the early 20th century. Hang a left onto Parker Head Road (but avoid this detour if you're on a bicycle; it's too narrow and winding). After the Phippsburg Historical Museum (in an 1859 schoolhouse) and the Alfred Totman Library, turn left onto Church Lane to see the **Phippsburg Congregational Church,** built in 1802. Out front is a "Constitution Tree," a huge English linden planted in 1774.

Parker Head Road continues southward and meets Route 209, which takes you to **Popham Beach State Park.** Continue to the end of Route 209 for **Fort Popham Historic Site,** where parking is woefully inadequate in summer (and costs an exorbitant $7 at nearby Percy's Store). The fort is accessible Memorial Day–September. Youngsters love this place—they can fish from the rocks, climb to the third level of the 1865 stone fortress, picnic on the seven-acre grounds, and create sand castles on the tiny beach next to the fort. Resist the urge to swim, though; the current is dangerous, and there's no lifeguard. Across the river is Bay Point, a lobstering village at the tip of the Georgetown Peninsula. **Percy's Store** (207/389-2010), by the way, with a handful of tables, is the best place down here for pizza, picnic fare, and fishing tackle.

Across the cove from the fort is Fort Baldwin Road, a one-lane-wide, winding road leading to the shorefront site of the 1607 Popham Colony. Climb the path up Sabino Hill to World War I–era **Fort Baldwin,** the best vantage point for panoramic photos.

Backtrack about four miles on Route 209, turn left onto Route 216, and head toward **Small Point.** Go about 0.9 mile to Morse Mountain Road, on the left, which leads to the parking area and trailhead for **Bates-Morse Mountain Preserve.** Farther south are Head Beach and Hermit Island.

Returning northward on Route 216, you'll hook up with Route 209 and then see a left turn (Rte. 217) to Sebasco Harbor Resort (see *Accommodations*). Take the time to go beyond the resort area. When the paved road goes left (to the Water's Edge Restaurant), turn right at a tiny cemetery and continue northward on the Old Meadowbrook Road, which meanders for about four miles along the west side of the peninsula. About midway along is **the**

**Basin,** regarded by sailors as one of the Maine coast's best "hurricane holes" (refuges in high winds). As you skirt the Basin and come to a fork, bear right to return to Route 209; turn left and return northward to Bath.

## Woolwich Historical Society Museum

Next to a Route 1 flashing caution light, 2.5 miles north of Bath, the two-story Woolwich Historical Society Museum (Rte. 1 at Nequasset Rd., P.O. Box 98, Woolwich 04579, 207/443-4833, 10:30 A.M.–2:30 P.M. Tues.– Sat. July and Aug., $3 adults, $1 children over six), admirably well organized, has rooms full of early 19th- to early 20th-century quilts, clothing, tools, and tradesmen's wares. The oldest part of the building dates from the early 19th century.

# PARKS, BEACHES, AND PRESERVES

## Bath's In-Town Parks

An old-fashioned gazebo, just right for hanging out with a book (bring a cushion), is the centerpiece of **Library Park,** the manicured space fronting the Patten Free Library, Summer and Washington Streets.

**Waterfront Park,** bordering the Kennebec on Commercial Street, has covered picnic tables, restrooms, and Friday-night concerts in summer.

At the end of High Street, at the tip of land where Whiskeag Creek meets the Kennebec River, is the **Thorn Head Preserve** (www.lkrlt. org/thornehead.html), maintained by the Lower Kennebec Regional Land Trust. Allow a half hour for the easy walk to the headland and its stone "picnic" table with views toward Merrymeeting Bay. Allow longer if you wish to explore any of the side trails.

## Hamilton Sanctuary

Owned by Maine Audubon, Hamilton Sanctuary (Foster Point Rd., West Bath, no phone) is a peaceful site for walking and nature study on the New Meadows River, with 1.5 miles of trails winding through meadows and forests and along the Back Cove shoreline. From Route 1 between Bath and Brunswick, take the New Meadows Road exit. Head south on New Meadows. When it becomes Foster Point Road, go four miles to the sanctuary entrance. Open sunrise–sunset all year; free admission. For more information, contact Maine Audubon (20 Gilsland Farm Rd., Falmouth, 207/781-2330).

## Popham Beach

On hot July and August weekends, the parking lot at Popham Beach State Park (Rte. 209, Phippsburg, 207/389-1335), 14 miles south of Bath, fills up by 10 A.M., so plan to arrive early at this huge crescent of sand backed by sea grass, beach roses, and dunes. Facilities include changing rooms, outside showers, restrooms, and seasonal lifeguards. Admission is $4 adults, $1 kids 5–11, free under 5 or over 65. It's officially open April 15–October 30, but the beach is accessible all year (no winter contact number).

## Fort Popham Historic Site

A mile down the road, at the end of Route 209, is the seven-acre Fort Popham Historic Site, where kids of all ages can explore the waterfront tower and bunkers of a 19th-century granite fort. No swimming here—the current is dangerous—but there's fun fishing from the rocks (no license needed), plus picnic tables and restrooms.

## Bates-Morse Mountain Conservation Area

Consider visiting the lovely, 600-acre Bates-Morse Mountain Conservation Area (Rtes. 209 and 216, Small Point, Phippsburg Peninsula, www.bates.edu/Morse-Mountain.xml) *only* if you are willing to be extraconscientious about the rules for this private preserve. A relatively easy four-mile round-trip hike takes you through marshland (you'll need insect repellent) and to the top of 210-foot Morse Mountain, with panoramic views, and then down to privately owned Seawall Beach. On a clear day, you can see New Hampshire's Mt. Washington from the summit. No dogs or vehicles;

MID-COAST REGION

no recreational facilities; stay on the preserve road and the beach path at all times (side roads are private). Least terns and piping plovers—both endangered species—nest in the dunes, so avoid this area, especially mid-May–mid-August. Birding hint: Morse Mountain is a great locale for spotting hawks during their annual September migration southward. Pick up a map (and the rules) from the box in the parking area, Morse Mountain Road, off Route 216 (just under a mile south of the Rte. 209 intersection). No admission fee; open sunrise–sunset.

### Head Beach

Just off Route 216, about two miles south of the Route 209 turnoff to Popham Beach, is Head Beach, a sandy crescent that's open until 10 p.m. A day-use fee ($5) is payable at the small gatehouse; there's a restroom on the path to the beach and a store within walking distance.

### Phippsburg Hiking Trails

The town of Phippsburg and the Phippsburg Land Trust (207/443-6309, www.phippsburglandtrust.org) have prepared a handy free brochure with map that describes nine preserves with trails. Three—Center Pond, Spirit Pond, and Ridgewell Preserve—have detailed maps and field guides available at trailhead boxes. The Land Trust also hosts guided walks mid-June–mid-September.

### Reid State Park

Reid State Park, on the Georgetown Peninsula (Seguinland Rd., Georgetown, 207/371-2303), is no secret, so plan to arrive early on summer weekends, when parking is woefully inadequate. Highlights of the 765-acre park are 1.5 miles of splendid beach (in three distinct sections), marshlands, sand dunes, and tide pools. Kids love the tide pools, treasure troves left by the receding tide. Facilities include changing rooms (with showers), picnic tables, restrooms, and snack bars. Test the water before racing in; even in midsummer, it's breathtakingly cold. In winter, bring cross-country skis and glide along the shore-

line. The park—14 miles south of Route 1 (Woolwich) and two miles off Route 127—is open daily all year. Admission is $4.50 adults, $1 kids 5–11, free for ages 5 and under and 65 and older.

Just half a mile beyond the Reid State Park entrance is **Charles Pond,** where the setting is unsurpassed for freshwater swimming in the long, skinny pond. You'll wish this were a secret, too, but it isn't. No facilities.

### Josephine Newman Sanctuary

A must-see for any nature lover, the 119-acre Josephine Newman Sanctuary (Rte. 127, Georgetown, no phone) has 2.5 miles of blazed loop trails winding through 110 wooded acres and along Robinhood Cove's tidal shoreline. Josephine Oliver Newman (1878–1968), a respected naturalist, bequeathed her family's splendid property to Maine Audubon, which maintains it today. The 0.6-mile self-guiding trail is moderately difficult, but the rewards are 20 informative markers highlighting special features: glacial erratics, reversing falls, mosses, and marshes. The easiest route is the 0.75-mile Horseshoe Trail, which you can extend for another mile or so by linking into the Rocky End Trail. The sanctuary is open sunrise–sunset daily all year,; free admission. No pets or bikes. The best way to appreciate it is to buy *Forests, Fields, and Estuaries,* a 60-page sanctuary guide ($3.50), with lots of natural-history information useful for other preserves. Contact Maine Audubon (20 Gilsland Farm Rd., Falmouth, 207/781-2330), or stop in at the society's environmental center in Falmouth. To reach the Newman sanctuary, take Route 127 from Route 1 in Woolwich (the road to Reid State Park) for 9.1 miles. Turn right at the sanctuary sign and continue up the narrow, rutted, dirt road (pray no one's coming the other way) to the small parking lot. A map of the trail system is posted at the marsh's edge and available in the box.

### Montsweag Preserve

Owned and managed by the Chewonki Foundation, 45-acre Montsweag Preserve (Montsweag Rd., Woolwich, no phone) is a peaceful estuarine microcosm on the shore of tidal Montsweag Brook. A 1.5-mile, blue-blazed loop trail meanders through fields and woods, tidal frontage, and salt marsh. Wear long pants and waterproof shoes or boots. It's open sunrise–sunset all year. From Bath, take Route 1 northwest about 6.5 miles to Montsweag Road (not well marked). Turn right and go 1.3 miles to the preserve on the left (also not well marked). Park alongside the road and do the trail clockwise.

## Robert P. Tristram Coffin Wildflower Sanctuary

The New England Wildflower Society owns this lovely 177-acre preserve bordering Merrymeeting Bay, with more than 100 species of wildflowers. Well-marked trails lace the sanctuary. To find it, take Route 127 north for 2.2 miles, then Route 128 for 4.5 miles, and look for a small parking area on the left.

# RECREATION
## Golf

The 18-hole **Bath Country Club** (Whiskeag Rd., Bath, 207/442-8411) has moderate greens fees, a pro shop, and a restaurant serving lunch and dinner. Starting times are needed on weekends.

The **Sebasco Harbor Resort** has a nine-hole course (expanding to 18 holes) open to nonguests on a space-available basis; call the resort's pro shop (207/389-9060) to inquire. Each hole has two sets of tees. Watch out for the infamous second hole, which gives new meaning to the term water hole, and be sure to say, "Morning, Sarah," on the sixth tee. If you look nearby, you'll find a gravestone inscribed "Sarah Wallace—1862." A local rhyme goes:

Show respect to Sarah
You golfers passing by;
She's the only person on this course,
Who can't improve her lie.

The course, called Shore Acres, is open early May–late October.

## Bicycling

Bath-area headquarters for anything to do with bikes is **Bath Cycle and Ski** (Rte. 1, Woolwich, 207/442-7002 or 800/245-3626, www.bikeman.com). Rentals are $80/week, route maps are available, and the shop sponsors weekly rides on Tuesday nights and Saturday and Sunday mornings.

## Excursion Boats

The 50-foot **Yankee** operates out of Small Point's Hermit Island Campground Monday–Saturday throughout the summer. You can go on nature cruises, enjoy the sunset, or visit Eagle Island; the schedule is different each day and rates vary widely by trip. Call for information and reservations (207/389-1788).

The M/V **Ruth,** a 38-foot excursion boat, runs cruises out of Sebasco Harbor Resort late June–Labor Day. You don't need to be a Sebasco guest to take the trips, but reservations are essential. The schedule changes weekly, but possible options are a nature cruise, Cundy's Harbor lunch cruise, lobstering demos, sunset cruise, and Pirate Island at lengths varying from one to two hours. Price for nonguests is $17 adults, $9 kids 3–12. Resort guests pay $13 adult, $6 child. Call the Sebasco Harbor Resort (207/389-1161) for the schedule, which is available a week in advance. Also sailing from Sebasco Harbor Resort is **Sail Magic** (207/650-3293, www.sailmagic.com), a Tartan 41 ocean racer built in 1974.

**Long Reach Cruises** (207/442-0092 or 888/538-6785, www.longreachcruises.com) offers a variety of one- to three-plus-hour cruises, departing from the Maine Maritime Museum. Options include narrated history, lighthouses, seal-watching, eagle-watching, and sunset cruises. Prices range $20–40 adult, $10–20 child, including museum admission.

The **Maine Maritime Museum** (see *Sights*) runs excursion boats to Seguin Island in summer, weather permitting, allowing you about three hours to explore the island, where you can climb the hill to the lighthouse and then climb the 53-foot light tower for a fabulous view from the deck. Afterward, visit the three-room

Seguin Museum, loaded with lighthouse memorabilia. The nonprofit Friends of Seguin maintains the island's buildings and subsidizes the summertime caretakers, in residence Memorial Day–mid-September. The Coast Guard maintains the automated light, which has an 18-mile range. There's no dock, so you'll be offloaded by dinghy—not an experience recommended for the unsteady.

### Canoeing and Kayaking

Close to civilization, yet amazingly undeveloped, 392-acre **Nequasset Lake** is a great place to canoe. You'll see a few anglers, a handful of houses, and near-wilderness along the shoreline. Personal watercraft and motors over 10 hp are banned. Take Route 1 from Bath across the bridge to Woolwich. Continue to the flashing caution light at Nequasset Road; turn *right* and go 0.1 mile. Turn left, and left again, into the parking area for the Nequasset Stream Waterfront Park, a popular swimming hole. Launch your canoe and head upstream, under Route 1, to the lake.

Paddle the relatively calm and safe waters of Winnegance Creek with a rental boat from **Up the Creak Kayak and Canoe Rentals** (Rte. 209, Phippsburg, 207/443-4845, www.rentkayaks.com). Canoe and kayak rentals are $10 pp for three hours.

**Seaspray Kayaking** (888/349-7774) operates from bases at the Sebasco Harbor Resort, in Sebasco Estates; Hermit Island Campground, on Small Point; and Bay Point Kayaking Center, in Georgetown. Hourly rentals begin at $10–20 the first hour plus $5–10 for each additional hour, up to $20–50 daily, with longer-term rates and delivery available. A variety of guided tours also are offered, with half-day options for $50 adult, $25 child, and specialty paddles, such as sunset or moonlight, for $40 pp.

### Fishing Charters

For guided fishing trips for stripers, bluefish, pike trout, and smallmouth bass, contact **Kennebec Tidewater Charters** (207/737-4695, www.kennebectidewater.com). Captain Robin Thayer, a Master Maine Guide, offers freshwater and saltwater cruises, beginning at $300 for four hours. Tackle is provided and instruction is available. Catch-and-release is encouraged.

## ENTERTAINMENT AND EVENTS

Bath's most diversified entertainment setting is the **Center for the Arts at the Chocolate Church** (804 Washington St., Bath, 207/442-8455, www.chocolatechurch.com), a chocolate-brown board-and-batten structure built in 1846 as the Central Congregational Church. Year-round activities at the arts center include music and dance concerts, dramas, exhibits, and children's programs.

At 7 P.M. every Tuesday and Friday mid-June–August, the **Gazebo Concert Series** brings live entertainment to Bath's Library Park.

Five Rivers Arts Alliances holds **3rd Friday Art Walks** (various locations, Bath, 207/798-6964, 5–8 P.M.) June–October.

The Gothic Revival-style Winter Street Church, built in 1843, is now owned by Sagadahoc Preservation.

Throughout the summer, the **Maine Maritime Museum** (207/443-1316) schedules special events, often hinging on visits by tall ships and other vessels. Some of the visiting boats are open to the public for an extra fee. Call the museum to check.

From November through April, 60 dealers show their wares at the monthly **Bath Antiques Shows** (207/443-8983, www.bathantiques-shows.com, $4) at the Bath Middle School.

## SHOPPING

Front and Center Streets are lined with fun, independent shops, including a number of antiques shops clustered on lower Front Street.

Bath's home to yet another good independent bookstore successfully bucking the megastore trend. The **Bath Book Shop** (96 Front St., Bath, 207/443-9338) has friendly, hometown service and a discerning taste in books.

Right in the shadow of the Route 1 overpass is an incredible resource for knitters and weavers. **Halcyon Yarn** (12 School St., Bath, 207/442-7909 or 800/341-0282, www.halcyonyarn.com), a huge warehouse of a place, carries domestic and imported yarns, looms, spinning wheels, how-to videos, kits, and pattern books.

About nine miles down Route 127, you'll come to **Georgetown Pottery** (Rte. 127, Georgetown, 207/371-2801), a top-quality ceramics studio/shop.

Anyone who appreciates fine woodworking tools *has* to visit the Shelter Institute's **Woodbutcher Tools** (873 Rte. 1, Woolwich, 207/442-7938) retail shop and bookstore, five miles north of Bath.

### Flea Market

One of Maine's biggest and most enduring flea markets is right on Route 1 north of Bath, often creating near-accidents as rubbernecking motorists slam to a halt. **Montsweag Flea Market** (Rte. 1 at Mountain Rd., Woolwich, 207/443-2809) is a genuine treasure trove about seven miles northeast of Bath's Sagadahoc bridge. It's open weekends in May, September, and October and on Wednesday, Friday,

Saturday, and Sunday June–August. Sales begin at 6:30 A.M.

### Farmers Market

In Waterfront Park on Commercial Street, the **Bath Farmers Market** operates 8:30 A.M.– 12:30 P.M. every Thursday and Saturday May 1–October, featuring crafts, plants, condiments, baked goods, and cheeses in addition to seasonal produce.

## ACCOMMODATIONS
### Bath

Most of Bath's in-town B&Bs and inns are in historic residences built by shipping magnates and their families, giving you a chance to appreciate the quality of craftsmanship they demanded in their ships and their homes alike.

The flamboyant pink and plum Italianate **Galen Moses House** (1009 Washington St., Bath, 207/442-8771 or 888/442-8771, www.galenmoses.com, $119–199) is a standout in the city's Historic District. Original architectural features—soaring ceilings, friezes, chandeliers, elaborate woodwork, stained-glass windows—and period antiques make it equally appealing inside, as do hosts Jim Haught and Larry Kieft. All rooms have air-conditioning and Wi-Fi. It has plenty of common rooms to relax, including one with TV and VCR. A fancy full breakfast and afternoon refreshments are included. Pets are allowed in one room for $15 per night.

Innkeeper Elizabeth Knowlton blends elegance and comfort at the **Inn at Bath** (969 Washington St., Bath, 207/443-4294 or 800/423-0964, www.innatbath.com, $165–185). Her culinary skills, honed as chef and co-owner of a Montana fly-fishing lodge, have garnered national attention. Guest rooms in the 1810 Greek Revival–style inn are decorated with antiques and each has air-conditioning, TV/VCR, Wi-Fi, and phone. Two have wood-burning fireplaces, and two have two-person whirlpool tubs. Kids over four and dogs are welcome. One room is ADA compliant.

Just a few miles from downtown Bath, yet feeling a world away, is the **Fairhaven Inn**

**MID-COAST REGION**

The faux lighthouse is one of the most popular lodges at Sebasco Harbor Resort.

© TOM NANGLE

(118 North Bath Rd., Bath, 207/443-4391 or 888/443-4391, www.mainecoast.com/fairhaveninn, $90–145). Antiques and country pieces furnish Dawn and Andrew Omo's truly rambling 1790 colonial, built on 16 country acres with views over the Kennebec River. It has eight rooms, all with Wi-Fi and air-conditioning; some share baths. The Omos grew up in Bath, so they know the area well. Open year-round.

### Phippsburg Peninsula

The trouble with staying at the ◖ **Sebasco Harbor Resort** (Rte. 217, Sebasco Estates, 207/389-1161 or 800/225-3819, www.sebasco.com), a self-contained resort on 575 waterfront acres, is that between the beautiful setting and the bountiful offerings, you might not set foot off the premises during your entire vacation. Situated at the mouth of the saltwater New Meadows River, 12 miles south of Bath, Sebasco has attracted families who return year after year—since 1930, when it

opened. Many guests stay for a week. Sebasco changed hands in 1997, and owner Bob Smith has successfully brought the resort up to 21st-century standards, but he has kept the emphasis on families, and you'll have to look far and wide to find a better family resort. Scattered around the well-tended property are the main lodge and a variety of cottages (from 1–6 bedrooms; the two-bedroom units with shared living room are a great choice for families), a main lodge, a four-story cupola-topped lighthouse building edging the harbor, and two new suites buildings, Harbor Village and the waterfront Fairwinds Spa, with more contemporary amenities. All have private baths, phones, cable TV; many have water views, some have refrigerators or kitchenettes. Pets are allowed in a handful of cottages for $25. Most intriguing is The Lighthouse ($260–370 in July and Aug.); it's worth the splurge. Otherwise, in July and August, room rates range $199–399; suites are $349–479; cottage rates are $399–1,775; $15 per extra person; kids 10 and under are free. MAP rate, including breakfast and dinner, is an additional $48 pp (10 and younger no charge when dining with an adult and off the kids' menu), and special packages (and lower rates) are available spring and fall. The resort's **Pilot House** restaurant (7:30–9:30 A.M. and 6–9 P.M.), with a dramatic sunset water view, is also open to the public; dinner entrée range is $17–32. Below it, the patio at the casual Ledges Pub (11:30 A.M.–2 P.M. and 5–9 P.M., $8–23) is a late-day magnet, with indoor and outdoor seating. Weekly summer events include a Sunday evening reception and grand buffet, lobster bakes, family barbecues, bingo, live entertainment, and the free Camp Merrit children's program. Recreational facilities include two all-weather tennis courts, nine-hole championship golf course and a three-hole regulation course for beginners and families, the state's largest outdoor saltwater pool, boat tours aboard the *Ruth,* sailing trips, sea kayak excursions, mountain-bike tours, candlepin bowling, horseshoes, a playground, a well-equipped fitness center, and as much or as little organized activity as you want. In 2007, the resort opened an oceanfront spa. (See *Excursion Boats* under *Recreation* for info on cruises in the M/V *Ruth*.) Sebasco Harbor Resort is open early May–late October.

Right on the beach between Popham Beach State Park and Fort Popham is the **Popham Beach Bed and Breakfast** (4 Ocean View La., Popham Beach, Phippsburg, 207/389-2409, www.pophambeachbandb.com, $175–215 d), a unique hostelry in a restored 1883 Coast Guard station. Innkeeper Peggy Johannessen takes guests to the rooftop lookout tower and shares the building's history as a maritime lifesaving center. Inside are three rooms and a suite, two with gas fireplaces. A two-course breakfast is served in the dining room each morning, and guests can hang out in the large oceanfront living room. Open all year.

Magnificent gardens surround **Edgewater Farm Bed and Breakfast** (71 Small Point Rd./Rte. 216, Sebasco Estates, 207/389-1322 or 877/389-1322, www.edgewaterfarmbedandbreakfast.com, $130–140 d), Carol and Bill Emerson's comfy, unfussy 19th-century farmhouse, just south of the turnoff to Popham Beach and close to the access for Morse Mountain. Families usually choose the carriage house, where kids can play in the huge recreation room. A brunch-size breakfast served in the many-windowed solarium benefits from lots of organic produce grown on the four-acre grounds. (The Emersons always plant extra to donate to the Bath food pantry each summer.) And then there's the four-foot-deep indoor lap pool, a hot tub outside on the deck, and the Benedictine labyrinth Bill created in a wooded grove. English, Spanish, a bit of French, and German are all spoken. Pets are possible.

**Rock Gardens Inn** (Rte. 218, Sebasco Estates, Phippsburg, 207/389-1339, www.rockgardensinn.com) hosts numerous artists' workshops, and no wonder. It sits on its own peninsula, and the pretty grounds are landscaped with wild and cultivated flowers. Guests stay in one of three inn rooms ($130–150 d, $175–190 s) or 10 cottages and have use of an outdoor heated pool and sea kayaks. Cottage rates begin at $140 d pp and include breakfast and dinner—and the weekly lobster cookout. After the minimum rate is reached per cottage, kids pay $50–110, depending upon age. Sebasco Harbor Resort is just steps away, and guests have access to its facilities, too. Ask about all-inclusive art retreats.

Joe and Debbie Braun have done a masterful job restoring **The 1774 Inn at Phippsburg** (44 Parker Head Rd., Phippsburg Center, 207/389-1774, www.1774inn.com, $125–185), a four-square Georgian Colonial National Historic Register property with an ell and barn. Many Colonial details have been preserved, including shutters with peepholes and strong bars to defend against attack, paneled wainscoting, ceiling moldings, fluted columns, and wide pine floors. Most of the eight rooms (all but two with private bath) have views of the Kennebec River. Rooms are furnished with antiques or tasteful reproductions. Also on the premises is the Riverside Guest House, a four-bedroom, two-bath cottage available for $1,800 per week.

## Georgetown Peninsula

It'll be hard to tear yourself away from the scenery and sanctuary at **The Mooring Bed and Breakfast** (132 Seguinland Rd., Georgetown, 207/371-2790 or 866/828-7348, www.themooringb-b.com, $150–200), the original home of Walter Reid, who donated Reid State Park to the state. His great-granddaughter and her family have beautifully restored the house, situated on lovely, oceanfront grounds with island-studded views. Each room has a water view and air-conditioning. There's plenty of room to spread out, including the appropriately named Spanish room. A full breakfast is served.

## Campgrounds

Plan to book a site in January if you want a waterfront campsite in midsummer at the Phippsburg Peninsula's **Hermit Island Campground** (6 Hermit Island Rd., Phippsburg, 207/443-2101, www.hermitisland.com, winter mailing address 42 Front St., Bath 04530, same phone). With 275 campsites (no vehicles larger than pickup campers; no hookups) spread over a 255-acre causeway-linked island, this is oceanfront camping at its best. The well-managed operation has a store, snack bar, seasonal post office, boat rentals, boat excursions, trails, and seven private beaches. The hub of activity (and registration) is the Kelp Shed, next to the campsite entrance. No washing machines, but dryers are available. Rules are strictly enforced (no visitors allowed in the camping area). Open and wooded sites run $34–56 (two adults and two kids) mid-June–Labor Day, $32 a site early and late in the season. Reservations for a week's stay or longer and Memorial and Labor Day Weekends can be made by mail beginning in early January and by phone in early February (call for exact date). Reservations for stays of less than one week accepted as of March 1. It's open mid-May–Columbus Day, but full operation is really June–Labor Day. The campground is at the tip of the Phippsburg Peninsula. No pets, no credit cards.

## FOOD
### Local Flavors
For breakfast, lunch, or sweets, drop into the **Starlight Café** (15 Lambard St., 207/443-3005, 7 A.M.–2 P.M. Mon.–Fri.), a too-cute and too-tiny daylight-basement space across a side street from the Customs House. It's bright and cheerful, and the food is fab.

Here's a wonderful, multifaceted find. Susan Verrier's **North Creek Farm** (24 Sebasco Rd., Phippsburg, 207/389-1341, 9 A.M.–6:30 P.M. daily, lunch served 11:30 A.M.–3:30 P.M.) is an 1850s saltwater farm with fabulous organic gardens, including ornamental display gardens and lots of rugosa roses (a specialty—Susan's written two books). Visitors can meander down by a waterfall, creek, and salt marsh. Inside the barn is a small store stocked with garden and gourmet goodies and a small café, where Susan makes delicious soups and sandwiches to order ($5–7). There are tables indoors, but there also are chairs and tables scattered in the gardens. Pick up one of the illustrated catalogs—a fun read and you're almost guaranteed to find something you want.

On the Georgetown Peninsula, **Five Islands Farm** (13375 Rte. 127, Five Islands, 297/371-9383, www.fiveislandsfarm.com) is a fine stop for picnic fixings, with an excellent assortment of Maine cheeses, along with breads, meats, chips, salsa, and even wine.

Oh my! Patty Mains retired early from Bath Iron Works to pursue her passion, chocolate. Her handcrafted chocolates are made from the best ingredients and from traditional recipes—try the needhams, made with mashed potatoes. While chocolates are the centerpiece at **MainSweets** (Rte. 127, Georgetown, 207/371-2806), she also sells home-baked breads, cookies, brownies, fudge, and other sweet treats.

Bath's best pizza comes from **The Cabin** (552 Washington St., Bath, 207/443-6224, 10 A.M.–10 P.M., to 11 P.M. Thurs.–Sat.)—a local landmark since 1973. The white garlic sauce is outstanding, and the cheese steak is about the best outside of Philly. A large three-topping pizza is $15. Order food to go or eat in at this decidedly casual place across from Bath Iron Works.

### Barbecue
Finger-licking, Memphis-style barbecue along with other Southern specialties are served in big quantities at **Beale Street Barbeque and Grill** (215 Water St., Bath, 207/442-9514, 11 A.M.–9 P.M. daily, to 10 P.M. in July and Aug.). Everything's made on the premises. Find it next to the municipal parking lot.

### Casual Dining
Kate and Andy Winglass operate **Mae's Café and Bakery** (160 Centre St., at High St., Bath, 207/442-8577, www.maescafeandbakery.com), a longtime local favorite bakery and café, with seating indoors and on a front deck. It's *the* place to go for brunch (reservations essential on weekends). Breakfast and lunch are served 8 A.M.–3 P.M. daily; dinner, served to 8 P.M. Thursday–Saturday, is in the $14–20 range. Sunday brunch is served until 2 P.M. The appealing menu has creative touches—the tarragon chicken salad croissant available for lunch is a winner. Rotating art shows enliven the open and airy dining rooms.

The Mediterranean theme at **Maryellenz**

Cafe (15 Vine St., Bath, 207/442-0960, 11:30 A.M.–9:30 P.M. Tues.–Sat.) allows for some whiffs of Maine (crab cakes, for instance, and fresh fish); there's a good selection of creative pasta dishes. Or mix-and-match a meal from the tapas and meze selections. Entrée range is $10–25. The brightly colored dining rooms double as an art gallery.

The cool and contemporary Danish decor matches the food at ◖ Solo Bistro (128 Front St., Bath, 207/443-3373, www.solobistro.com, opens at 5 P.M. Mon.–Sat.), a sophisticated storefront restaurant downtown, where the choices might range from a bistro burger to pan-seared wild salmon ($12–28). A nightly three-course fixed-price menu is usually around $23. The wine bar features jazz on Friday nights.

## The View's the Thing

Even if you're not staying at **Sebasco Harbor Resort** (Rte. 217, Sebasco Estates, 207/389-1161 or 800/225-3819, www.sebasco.com), you can dine in either of its two waterfront restaurants, both with gasp-producing sunset views. Binoculars hang by windows in the **Pilot House** (5:30–9 P.M. Mon.–Sat.), the more formal of the two, so diners can get a better view of the boats or birds happening by. Dinner entrée range is $17–27. Below it is the casual Ledges Pub (11:30 A.M.–2 P.M. and 5–10 P.M. daily), with indoor and outdoor seating and a menu varying from kid-friendly burgers and fried foods to salmon salad ($6–18).

Gaze at seals playing in the Kennebec River, Fort Popham, and out to open ocean from **Spinney's Restaurant** (Rte. 209, Popham Beach, 207/389-2052, 8 A.M.–8:30 P.M. daily). Food varies in quality from year to year (best advice: Keep it simple; entrées run $10–30, but sandwiches and hot dogs are less than $5), but you can't beat the view. Keep it budget friendly by coming for breakfast. Open mid-May–late October.

## Lobster in the Rough

**Phippsburg Peninsula:** The rustic, buoy-draped **Lobster House** (395 Small Point

Rd./Rte. 216, Small Point, 207/389-1596 or 207/389-2178, 5–9 P.M. Tues., noon–9 P.M. Wed.–Sun. late May–early Sept.) overlooks a scenic tidal cove; the view is best when the tide's in. No surprise that lobster and seafood are featured, but sandwiches, soups, salads, and a few grilled items make the menu wallet-friendly for anyone.

**Georgetown Peninsula:** Just over a mile beyond the turnoff to Reid State Park, you'll reach the end of Route 127 at Five Islands. Here you'll find ◖ **Five Islands Lobster Company** (1447 Five Islands Rd., Five Islands, Georgetown, 207/371-2990, www.fiveislandslobster.com), known for its slogan: "Eat on the dock with the fishermen, but best avoid the table by the bait-shack door." Here you can pig out on lobster rolls, better-than-usual onion rings, crab cakes, and if you must, burgers and hot dogs 11:30 A.M.–8 P.M. daily mid-May–mid-October. It even takes credit cards, a rarity among lobster wharves. Dress down, BYOB, and enjoy the end-of-the-road ambience of this idyllic spot.

## Destination Dining

The building alone is worth a visit to chef Michael Gagne's **Robinhood Free Meetinghouse** (210 Robinhood Rd., HC 33, Box 1469A, Georgetown 04548, 207/371-2188, www.robinhood-meetinghouse.com, 5:30–9 P.M. daily in season), a multistar restaurant in a beautifully restored 1855 building on the Georgetown Peninsula. Most tables are on the main floor; overflow diners go to the second floor, where many of the pews remain. The enormous (more than two dozen entrées, a dozen appetizers) high-quality menu makes it even more enticing. Creativity is the menu byword for Gagne. If you're a chocoholic, save room for Gagne's swoon-worthy signature dessert: Obsession in Three Chocolates with chocolate sauce. Entrées are in the $22–28 range, and portions are large. This isn't a setting for children, but the kitchen can come up with chicken fingers or fettuccine if necessary. Reservations are essential. It's open 5:30–8 P.M. Thursday–Saturday mid-October–mid-May. In winter,

© HILARY NANGLE

It's worth the journey down the peninsula to reach Five Islands Lobster Company, for both the views and the food.

ask about special "theme" nights. Gagne sells his famed 72-layer hand-cut cream cheese biscuits frozen, so take a half dozen or so home to enjoy with your leftovers. The restaurant is on the left, about a mile east of Route 127.

## INFORMATION AND SERVICES
### Information

The Southern Midcoast Chamber of Commerce (2 Main St., Topsham, 877/725-8797, www.midcoastmaine.com) publishes *Guide to Southern Midcoast Maine*. A visitor information center is located in Bath's renovated train station (restrooms available), adjacent to the Bath Iron Works main yard. It's open year-round with brochure racks, and staffed by volunteers from May into October. Request copies of the *City of Bath Downtown Map and Guide* and the *Bath-Brunswick Region Map and Guide*.

Main Street Bath (4 Centre St., Bath, 207/442-7291, www.visitbath.com) produces a guide and has an informative website.

Check out Patten Free Library (33 Summer St., Bath, 207/443-5141, www.patten. lib.me.us).

### Public Restrooms

Public restrooms are at Bath City Hall (55 Front St.), Patten Free Library (33 Summer St.), Sagadahoc County Courthouse (752 High St.), and (summer only) Waterfront Park (Commercial St.).

## GETTING AROUND

The Bath Trolley (443-9741, www.bathtrolley.org) circulates through the area, with each one-way trip costing $1. For a schedule, visit City Hall.

# Wiscasset Area

Billing itself "The Prettiest Village in Maine," Wiscasset (pop. 1,200) works hard to live up to its slogan, with quaint street signs, well-maintained homes, and an air of attentive elegance. Behind the scenes, however, it's actually a rather workaday community—not overrun with deep-pocketed retirees. The interesting mix includes artists, antiques dealers, state government workers, worm diggers, and blue-collar types. And it seems to work.

Wiscasset ("meeting place of three rivers"), incorporated as part of Pownalborough in 1760, has had its current name since 1802. In the late 18th century, it became the shire town of Lincoln County and the largest seaport north of Boston. Countless tall-masted ships sailed the 12 miles up the Sheepscot River to tie up here, and shipyards flourished, turning out vessels for domestic and foreign trade. The 1807 Embargo Act and the War of 1812 delivered a one-two punch that shut down trade and temporarily squelched the town's aspirations, but Wiscasset yards soon were back at it, producing vessels for the pre–Civil War clipper-ship era—only to face a more lasting decline with the arrival of the railroads and the onset of the Industrial Revolution.

Just east of Wiscasset, across the Donald Davey Bridge, is Davis Island and Edgecomb, a tiny town that primarily serves as a funnel to the Boothbay Peninsula.

The Davey Bridge, built in 1983, is the most recent span over the Sheepscot. The earliest, finished in 1847, was a toll bridge that charged a horse and wagon $0.15 to cross, pedestrians $0.03 each, and pigs $0.01 apiece. Before that, ferries carried passengers, animals, and vehicles between Wiscasset and Edgecomb's Davis Island (then named Folly Island).

Wiscasset is notorious for midsummer gridlock. Especially on weekends, traffic backs up on Route 1 for miles in both directions—to the frustration of drivers, passengers, and Wiscasset merchants. The state Department of Transportation has tested traffic medians, stoplights, and other devices, but nothing seems to solve the problem. A bypass has been under discussion for years, but not-in-my-backyard opposition to every route has halted progress. (When you stop in town, try to park pointed in the direction you're going; it's impossible to make turns across oncoming traffic.)

## SIGHTS

In 1973, a large chunk of downtown Wiscasset was added to the National Register of Historic Places, and a walking tour is the best way to appreciate the Federal, Classical Revival, and even pre-Revolutionary homes and commercial buildings in the Historic District. Below are a few of the prime examples. If you do nothing else, be sure to swing by the homes on High Street.

### Castle Tucker

Once known as the Lee-Tucker House, Castle Tucker (Lee and High Sts., Wiscasset, 207/882-7169, www.historicnewengland.org, tours on the hour, 11 A.M.–4 P.M. Wed.–Sun. June–Oct. 15, $5) is a must-see. Built in 1807 by Judge Silas Lee, and bought by sea captain Richard Tucker in 1858, the imposing mansion has Victorian wallpaper and furnishings, Palladian windows, an amazing elliptical staircase, and a dramatic view over the Sheepscot River. In early 1997, Jane Tucker, Richard's granddaughter, magnanimously deeded the house to Historic New England.

### Nickels-Sortwell House

Also owned by Historic New England, the three-story Nickels-Sortwell House (121 Main St., Wiscasset, 207/882-6218, www.historicnewengland.org, tours on the hour 11 A.M.–4 P.M. Fri.–Sun. June–Oct. 15, $5) looms over Route 1, yet it's so close to the road many motorists miss it. Don't. Sea captain William Nickels commissioned the mansion in 1807 but died soon after its completion. For 70 or so years, it was the Belle Haven Hotel, before Alvin and

# RURAL RAMBLINGS

Surrounding Wiscasset are the lovely rural inland communities of Dresden, Sheepscot, and Alna, definitely worth a detour.

Begin in Dresden at the 1761 **Pownalborough Court House** (River Rd./Rte. 128, Dresden, 10 A.M.-4 P.M. Tues.-Sat., noon-4 P.M. Sun. July and Aug., weekends only June and Sept., $4 adults, $2 children 7-17), a pre-Revolutionary riverfront courthouse listed in the National Register of Historic Places. President John Adams once handled a trial here – in a mid-18th-century frontier community (named Pownalborough) established by French and German settlers. During the 30-minute tour of the three-story courthouse, guides delight in pointing out the restored beams, paneling, and fireplaces, as well as the on-site tavern that catered to judges, lawyers, and travelers. Walk a few hundred feet south, and you'll find a cemetery with Revolution-era graves. Along the river is a nature trail developed by local Eagle Scouts. For more information, call or write **Lincoln County Historical Association** (Federal St., P.O. Box 61, Wiscasset 04578, 207/882-6817, www.lincolncountyhistory.org). From Route 1 in Wiscasset, take Route 27 about nine miles north to the junction with Route 128. Turn left (south) and go 2.5 miles to the courthouse sign. The courthouse is also an easy drive from Bath.

Return to Wiscasset, and follow Route 218 north for about eight miles to Head Tide Village, an eminently picturesque hamlet at the farthest reach of Sheepscot River tides. From the late 18th century to the early 20th, Head Tide (now part of the town of Alna) was a thriving mill town, a source of hydropower for the textile and lumber industries. All that's long gone, but hints of that era come from the handful of well-maintained 18th- and 19th-century homes in the village center.

Up the hill, the stunning 1838 **Head Tide**

**Church,** another fine example of local prosperity, is usually open 2-4 P.M. Saturday in July and August. Volunteer tour guides point out the original pulpit, a trompe l'oeil window, a kerosene chandelier, and walls lined with historic Alna photographs.

Head Tide's most famous citizen was the poet **Edwin Arlington Robinson,** born here in 1869. His family home, at the bend in Route 194 and marked by a plaque, is not open to the public. Perhaps his Maine roots inspired these lines from his poem "New England":

> Here where the wind is always north-
> north-east
> And children learn to walk on frozen
> toes.

Just upriver from the bend in the road is a favorite swimming hole, a millpond where you can join the locals on a hot summer day. Not much else goes on here, and there are no restaurants or lodgings, so Head Tide can't be termed a destination, but it's a village frozen in time – and an unbeatable opportunity for history buffs and shutterbugs.

Also historic, but a bit more lively and fun for kids is the **Wiscasset, Waterville, and Farmington Railway** (97 Cross Rd., off Rte. 218, Sheepscot, 207/882-4193, www.wwfry.org, 9 A.M.-5 P.M. Sat. year-round and Sun. late May-mid-Oct.), a museum commemorating a two-foot gauge common carrier railroad that operated in the early part of the 20th century, from Wiscasset in the south, to Albion and Winslow in the north. On the grounds are a museum in the old station (free admission) and train rides along the mainline track running north from Cross Road, on the original roadbed ($6 adult, $4 kids 4-12). Trains depart Sheepscot hourly 10 A.M.-4 P.M. on weekends. From Route 1 in Wiscasset, take Route 218 north 4.7 miles to a four-way intersection and go left on the Cross Road to the museum.

Frances Sortwell's meticulous Colonial Revival restoration in the early 20th century.

## Lincoln County Jail and Museum

Wiscasset's Old Jail, completed in 1811, was the first prison in the District of Maine (then part of Massachusetts). Amazingly, it remained a jail—mostly for short-termers—until 1953. Two years after that, the Lincoln County Historical Association took over, so each summer you can check out the 40-inch-thick granite walls, floors, and ceilings; the 12 tiny cells; and historic graffiti penned by the prisoners. Attached to the prison is the 1837 jailer's house, now the Lincoln County Museum, containing antique tools, the original kitchen, and various temporary exhibits. The complex is open 10 A.M.–4 P.M. Tuesday–Saturday and noon–4 P.M. Sunday in July and August, and weekends only June and September. Admission is $4 adults, $2 ages 7–17. A Victorian gazebo, overlooking the Sheepscot River, is a great spot for a picnic. From Route 1 (Main St.) in downtown Wiscasset, take Federal Street (Rte. 218) 1.2 miles. For more information, contact Lincoln County Historical Association (Federal St., P.O. Box 61, Wiscasset 04578, 207/882-6817, www.lincolncountyhistory.org).

## Musical Wonder House

The treasures in the Musical Wonder House (18 High St., P.O. Box 604, Wiscasset 04578, 207/882-7163, www.musicalwonderhouse.com), an 1852 sea captain's mansion, are indeed astonishing, and eccentric Austrian-born museum founder Danilo Konvalinka delights in sharing them—for a price. The best way to appreciate the collection of hundreds of 19th-century European music boxes, player pianos, and musical rarities is to take a guided tour (available 10 A.M.–5 P.M. Mon.–Sat. and noon–5 P.M. Sun. late May–Oct.), reduced schedule spring and fall), including two dozen player-piano and music-box demonstrations. A 35-minute tour is $10; 75-minute tour is $20; a three-hour tour, by appointment only, is $40. A web-order sideline, offering music-boxes and music box and player-piano cassettes and CDs, continues year-round.

## Fort Edgecomb

Built in 1808 to protect the Sheepscot River port of Wiscasset, the Fort Edgecomb State Historic Site (Eddy Rd., Edgecomb, 207/882-7777, $2 adults, $1 kids 5–11) occupies a splendid, three-acre riverfront spread ideal for picnicking and fishing (no swimming). Many summer weekends, the Revolutionary encampments on the grounds of the octagonal blockhouse make history come alive with re-enactments, period dress, craft demonstrations, and garrison drills. The fort officially is open 9 A.M.–5 P.M. daily late May–early September. It's off Route 1; take Eddy Road just north of Wiscasset Bridge and go one-half mile to Fort Road.

## RECREATION

### Canoeing and Kayaking

Explore the ponds and waterways in the region with a rental canoe or kayak from **Wiscasset Trading Post** (754 Rte. 1, Wiscasset, 207/882-9645, www.wiscassettradingpost.com). Rates begin at $30 for a 24-hour rental. Delivery service is available. If you paddle any rivers or streams, check tide charts first and plan your outing to paddle with the current, rather than working against it. You might put in at the public landing in Wiscasset and paddle up the Sheepscot River into a bay rich with avian and aquatic life.

## FESTIVALS AND EVENTS

Wiscasset's daylong **Annual Strawberry Festival and Country Fair** (St. Philip's Episcopal Church, Hodge St., 207/882-7184) celebrates with tons of strawberries, plus crafts and an auction on the last Saturday in June. The church also is the site of **Monday-night fish-chowder suppers,** mid-July–mid-August. Reservations are advised (207/882-7184) for these very popular 5:30 P.M. suppers.

In early July, the daylong **Morris Farm Fair** takes place at the nonprofit community Morris

Farm on Route 27, and includes animal exhibits, farm tours, crafts, games, and food.

A summer highlight at Watershed Center for the Ceramic Arts is its annual **Salad Days,** a fund-raising event held on a July Saturday. For a $25 donation, you choose a handmade pottery plate, fill it from a piled-high buffet of fruit and veggie salads, and be part of an old-fashioned picnic social—and you even get to keep the plate! Afterward, there's plenty of time to explore the center's 32 acres. Call ahead to confirm the date (207/882-6075).

## SHOPPING
### Antiques and Art

It's certainly fitting that a town filled end-to-end with antique homes should have more than two dozen solo and group antiques shops.

Right downtown, **Blythe House Antiques** (161 Main St., Wiscasset, 207/882-1280) has multiple dealers exhibiting in room settings. Fine European antiques directly imported are the specialty at **Daybreak Manor** (106 Rte. 1, Wiscas-

© TOM NANGLE

Antiques and specialty shops line Wiscasset's streets.

set, 207/882-9786). Both fine art and antiques are sold at **French and Vandyke** (8 Federal St., Wiscasset, 207/882-8302).

European and American 19th- and 20th-century painters are the broad focus at **Wiscasset Bay Gallery** (67 Main St./Rte. 1, P.O. Box 309, Wiscasset 04578, 207/882-7682 or 888/622-9445) which schedules high-quality rotating shows throughout the season.

In the handsome open spaces of an early-19th-century brick schoolhouse, the **Maine Art Gallery** (Warren St., P.O. Box 315, Wiscasset 04578, 207/882-7511) was founded in 1954 as a nonprofit corporation to showcase contemporary Maine artists.

Two miles south of town is **Avalon Antiques Market** (563 Rte. 1, Wiscasset, 207/882-4239, www.avalonantiques market.com), a huge red barn of a place filled with more than 100 dealers showing on three floors.

### Gifts, Crafts, and Miscellanea

The oldest commercial building in town is **Wiscasset Hardware** (Water St., Wiscasset, 207/882-6622), built in 1797 as a ship chandlery on the east side of Water Street. Since 1949, the Stetson family has run this hardware-plus business. (The "plus" part is a general store with antiques, souvenirs, and Maine products.) Request a free town map and check out the great view from the river-view deck, where you can buy sandwiches, hot dogs, ice cream, and coffee.

Folk art fans must visit Lois and David Kwantz's **Butterstamp Workshop** (55 Middle St., Wiscasset, 207/882-7825), which creates and sells designs copied from antique molds. Sometimes you can watch the workshop operation, which produces butter and cookie molds, beeswax ornaments, even magnets.

**Rock, Paper, Scissors** (78 Main St., Wiscasset, 207/882-9930) is a stylish paper store with a terrific selection and interesting array of products.

### Discount Shopping

Carving out a unique niche is **Big Al's Super Values** (Rte. 1, Wiscasset, 207/882-6423), a catchall emporium specializing in odd lots, closeouts, funky souvenirs, and half-priced birthday cards. Bargains galore, plus free coffee, restroom, and a gift shop. Some tourism brochures are also available here. It's three miles south of Wiscasset, across from the Sea Basket Restaurant.

## ACCOMMODATIONS
### Bed-and-Breakfasts

Wiscasset isn't loaded with B&Bs, but the choices are intriguing. As always, off-season rates are less expensive.

Named after a famous Maine clipper ship, Paul and Melanie Harris's **Snow Squall Inn** (5 Bradford Rd. at Rte. 1, P.O. Box 730, Wiscasset 04578, 207/882-6892 or 800/775-7245, www.snowsquallinn.com, $100–170 d) is a renovated mid-19th-century house with four lovely rooms and three suites, all with phone, air-conditioning, and Wi-Fi, and two with fireplace. Relax in two public rooms, both with TV and fireplace, on the porch or gazebo, and enjoy the landscaped grounds. Ask Melanie, a licensed massage therapist and a vinyasa yoga instructor, about scheduling a massage or taking a class. The suites, in the adjacent carriage house, each sleep four and are ideal for families. It's open all year, but only by reservation November–April.

Then there's a major getaway—**The Squire Tarbox Inn** (1181 Main Rd., Rte. 144, Westport Island, 207/882-7693 or 800/818-0626, www.squiretarboxinn.com, $135–195), an elegantly casual B&B/inn. Accomplished Swiss chef/owner Mario De Pietro and his wife, Roni, have continued the inn's reputation for dining excellence. Eleven lovely rooms, some with fireplaces, are divided between the late-18th-century main house and the early-19th-century carriage house; those in the main house are more formal. Rates include breakfast, and the dining room is open to the public by reservation for dinner (see *Food*). Also on the property are walking paths, a rowboat, mountain bikes, a working pottery, and a working farm, with organic vegetable gardens, chickens, and goats. Open April–December. From downtown Wiscasset, head southwest four miles on Route 1 to Route 144. Turn left and go about 8.5 scenic miles to the inn.

## Motels

Fairly close to Route 1 but buffered a bit by century-old hemlocks, the **Wiscasset Motor Lodge** (Rte. 1, R.R. 3, Box 911, Wiscasset 04578, 207/882-7137 or 800/732-8168, www.wiscassetmotorlodge.com, $62–108) is a comfortable, well-maintained motel. Rooms have phone, TV, and air-conditioning, and a light breakfast is included in summer. Ask for a room in the back building if you're sensitive to noise.

## Resort

Stretching along the Sheepscot riverfront on Davis Island, **◖ Sheepscot Harbour Village and Resort** (306 Eddy Rd., Edgecomb, 800/437-5503, www.midcoastresort.com) comprises beautifully renovated shingle-style buildings, including an inn, lodge, and cottages all adjacent to Bintliff's Ocean Grille restaurant. You can walk to Fort Edgecomb, across the bridge into Wiscasset, meander down the back roads to Boothbay Harbor, or simply stay put and enjoy the on-site amenities, including what must be one of the longest docks ever built, bicycles, canoes, kayaks, and planned walking paths, shops, and spa. In July and August, rates range $119–209 d with pets welcome for $15/night. Packages including breakfast and dinner are available. Owner and overall good guy Roger Bintliff is a strong supporter of military families; his Project Operation Recognition provides a free weeklong vacation each week to families of Maine National Guard soldiers.

## FOOD

Across Federal Street from the Nickels-Sortwell House in downtown Wiscasset is the lovely **Sunken Garden,** an almost-unnoticed pocket park created around the cellar hole of a long-gone inn. It's a fine place for a picnic.

### Local Flavors

Let's start with the obvious, **Red's Eats** (Main and Water Sts., Wiscasset, 207/882-6128, 11 A.M.–11 P.M. Mon.–Sat. and noon–6 P.M. Sun. early May–mid-Oct.). This simple takeout stand has garnered national attention through the decades for its lobster rolls stuffed

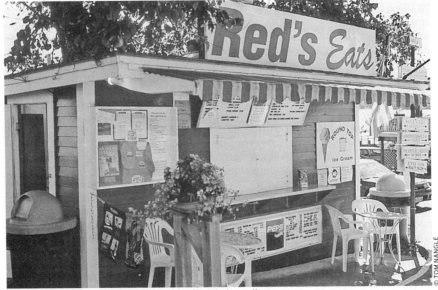

© TOM NANGLE

Red's Eats has earned national fame for its lobster rolls.

with the meat from a whole lobster. It's easy to spot because of the line. Expect to wait. And wait. And wait, perhaps for an hour or more. Is it worth it? I don't think so, but others rave about the cold lobster rolls, the fried fish, the hot dogs, and the wraps. If you're planning on one of Red's lobster rolls, ask someone who's just bought one the price before you get in line and make sure you have enough cash (no credit cards). The few tables on the sidewalk and behind the building, overlooking the river, are seldom empty (except in bad weather), but it's only a quick walk across Main to picnic tables (and a public restroom) on the Town Wharf, where **Sprague Lobster** (22 Main St., Wiscasset, 207/882-2306) has set up a competing stand. Many locals prefer Sprague's. Lines are rare and the lobster rolls also contain the meat from an entire crustacean.

Back up the street, across from the post office, is **Treat's** (80 Main St., Wiscasset, 207/882-6192, www.treatsofmaine.com, 10 A.M.–6 P.M. Mon.–Sat., noon–5 P.M. Sun.), a superb source of gourmet picnic fixings: sand-wiches, soups, wine, cheese, condiments, and artisanal breads. You won't leave here empty-handed, even if you aren't hungry.

## Family Friendly

Two miles southwest of downtown Wiscasset, **The Sea Basket Restaurant** (Rte. 1, Wiscasset, 207/882-6581, www.seabasket.com, 11 A.M.–8 P.M. Tues.–Sat.) has been serving hearty bowls of lobster stew and good-size baskets of emi-nently fresh seafood since 1981. There's always a crowd—locals eat here, too—so expect to wait. The fried fish is almost healthful, thanks to convection-style frying using trans fat–free oil. Closed January into February, with reduced hours and days in the off-season.

In a high-visibility location across Route 1 from Red's Eats, **Sarah's Cafe** (Main and Water Sts., Rte. 1, Wiscasset, 207/882-7504, www.sarahscafe.com, 11 A.M.–9 P.M., opens 7:30 A.M. Sat. and Sun.), is the home of huge "whaleboat" and "dory" sandwiches, homemade soups (self-serve), pizza, vegetarian specials, and an ice-cream fountain. Lobster meat shows up in salads, burritos, quesadillas, wraps, croissants, and more. The deck has front-row seats on the Sheepscot River. It has a beer and wine license and air-conditioning. Be forewarned that service sometimes is very sluggish, but crayons keep kids busy. It closes at 8 P.M. off-season.

Housed in a big red barn, about midway between Bath and Wiscasset, **Montsweag Roadhouse** (942 Rte. 1, Woolwich, 207/443-6563, www.montsweagroadhouse.com, 11 A.M.–9 P.M., to 10 P.M. Fri. and Sat.) gets two thumbs up for reasonably priced foods, from burgers and pizzas to steak and fried fish, and friendly service. The upstairs games room—pool and foosball tables and dart boards—keeps kids busy while the grown-ups chat. This is an especially casual place, with a strong local following. The bar remains open to 1 A.M., with live music both upstairs and down on weekends.

## Casual Dining

Overlooking the Kennebec, and just two blocks off Route 1, is **Le Garage** (15 Water St., Wiscasset, 207/882-5409, www.legaragerestaurant.com, 11:30 A.M.–2:30 P.M. and 5–8:30 P.M. daily), an enduringly popular spot serving traditional fare with flair. Request a porch/deck table, and dine by candlelight. Lamb is a specialty, as is finnan haddie (entrée range is $10–25); light suppers are thrifty choices. Reservations are wise on weekends. It's closed January, and Mondays off-season.

Across the river, with fine views of Wiscasset, is **Bintliff's Ocean Grill** (318 Eddy Rd., corner of Rte. 1, Edgecomb, 207/882-9401, 8 A.M.–3 P.M. and 5–10 P.M. daily). Owner Roger Bintliff is renowned for his extensive and creative breakfast and brunch menus, with more choices for omelettes and eggs Benedict than you could imagine, never mind pancakes, French toast, and other egg dishes. Add sandwiches, salads, and soups, and a large dinner menu ($16–32), too. No one should complain about not finding something. In summer, there's nightly live music. Bintliff is well respected in the community for supporting local needs. On Thursday nights, he makes a contribution to a local charity for every purchase. In

late 2007, he unveiled plans for a culinary arts campus, which includes being home for *The Fretz Kitchen* TV cooking show. Bintliff planned to offer cooking classes, tastings, wine dinners, and other culinary events in conjunction with his adjacent Sheepscot Harbour Resort.

Well off the beaten path, on an island connected to the mainland by bridge, is **The Squire Tarbox Inn** (1181 Main Rd., Rte. 144, Westport Island, 207/882-7693 or 800/818-0626, www.squiretarboxinn.com), where Swiss chef Mario De Pietro serves memorable meals. Entrées, such as rack of lamb, Swiss-style veal, and a fish of the day run $25–29, and are served either on the porch or in an intimate dining room. It serves dinner nightly late May–late October, and Thursday–Saturday in April, May, November, and December, when Thursday nights are Swiss night, with appropriate cuisine served. Ask about cooking classes.

On the edge of town, **Mark Antony Italian Cuisine** (65 Gardiner Rd., Wiscasset, 207/882-9888, www.markantonysitaliancuisine.com, 5–8 P.M. Wed.–Sun., to 9 P.M. Fri. and Sat.) is a cozy spot that delivers more than its humble exterior promises. Chef/co-owner Mark Buscanera draws on his North End Boston roots to prepare classic Italian fare ($10–25), and he might even serenade your table.

## INFORMATION AND SERVICES
## Information

Since there's no official information center, the best place to find the annual WRBA booklet is the display rack at Big Al's Super Values, three miles southwest of downtown. Once you get into town, stop at Wiscasset Hardware for a free walking map of the downtown area.

Check out Wiscasset Public Library (21 High St., Wiscasset, 207/882-7161, www.wiscasset.lib.me.us).

## Public Restrooms

The Town Wharf, Water Street, and the Lincoln County Court House, on Route 1 next to the sharp curve as you come down the hill from the south, have public restrooms.

# Boothbay Peninsula

East of Wiscasset, en route to Damariscotta, only a flurry of signs along Route 1 in Edgecomb (pop. around 1,000) hints at what's down the peninsula bisected by Route 27. Drive southward down the Boothbay Peninsula between Memorial Day and Labor Day and you'll find yourself in one of Maine's longest-running summer playgrounds.

The four peninsula towns of Boothbay (pop. 2,675), Boothbay Harbor (pop. 2,165), East Boothbay (pop. 540), and, connected by a bridge, Southport Island (pop. 590) have sightseeing and whale-watching excursions, a first-rate small aquarium, an antique-railway museum, wall-to-wall shops, scads of restaurants and beds, and quiet preserves for escaping the inevitable midsummer crowds.

When Route 27 arrives at the water, having passed through Boothbay Center, you're at the hub, Boothbay Harbor ("the Harbor"), scene of most of the action. The harbor itself is a boat fan's dream, loaded with working craft and pleasure yachts. Ashore, you'll face one-way streets, traffic congestion, and pedestrians everywhere (avoid July and August, if you despise crowds). Parking areas are noted on the Boothbay Harbor Region Chamber of Commerce's walking map; just be prepared to shell out about $3–5 for the day. Better yet, stay in an intown accommodation and walk. Even in peak season, though, there are plentiful places to escape the hoards.

Try to save time for quieter spots: East Boothbay, Ocean Point, Southport Island, the Coastal Botanical Gardens, or even just over the 1,000-foot-long footbridge stretching across one corner of the harbor. Cross the bridge and walk down Atlantic Avenue to the Fishermen's Memorial, a bronze fishing dory commemorating the loss of hardy souls who've earned a rugged living here by their wits and the sea. Across the street is Our Lady Queen of Peace Catholic Church, with shipwright-quality woodwork and its own fishing icon—a lobster trap next to the altar.

In the 1870s, when many scenic coastal areas experienced an influx of steamboat-borne rusticators from the Boston area and beyond, the Boothbay region entered its tourism phase—an era that shows no indication of coming to a close.

## SIGHTS
### Boothbay Railway Ridge
Boothbay Railway Village (Rte. 27, Boothbay, 207/633-4727, www.railwayvillage.org, 9:30 A.M.–5 P.M. daily early June–mid-Oct., $8 adults, $4 ages 3–16) feels like a life-size train set. More than two dozen old and new buildings have been assembled here since the museum was founded, in 1964, and a restored narrow-gauge steam train makes a 1.5-mile, 20-minute circuit throughout the day. Among the structures are a toy shop, a one-room schoolhouse, a chapel, a barbershop, a 19th-century town hall, two railroad stations, and a firehouse. You'll also find more than four dozen antique cars and trucks. The gift shop stocks train-oriented items. During the summer, special events include an antique auto meet, Children's Day, and a fall foliage festival. The village is open daily; train rides also operate on Memorial Day weekend, early June weekends, and the last weekend in October (a ghostly Halloween ride). The village is 3.5 miles north of downtown Boothbay Harbor, 7.5 miles south of Route 1.

### 🄲 Burnt Island Tour
Visit with a lighthouse keeper's family, climb the tower into the lantern room, and explore an island during a living- and natural-history program presented by the Maine Department of Marine Resources on Burnt Island (207/633-9580, www.maine.gov/dmr/education.htm, $22 adult, $12 kids under 12). The tour is offered twice daily in July and August. Travel via excursion boat from 21st-century Boothbay Harbor to Burnt Island, circa 1950, where actors portray the family of lighthouse keeper Joseph

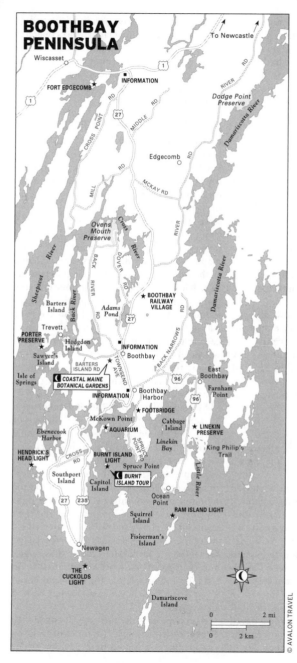

BOOTHBAY PENINSULA

Wiscasset

To Newcastle

FORT EDGECOMB ★

INFORMATION

Dodge Point
Preserve

Edgecomb

MCKAY RD

Ovens
Mouth
Preserve

★ BOOTHBAY
RAILWAY
VILLAGE

Barters
Island

Adams
Pond

Trevett

PORTER
PRESERVE

Hodgdon
Island

Sawyer's
Island

BARTERS
ISLAND RD

INFORMATION
Boothbay

Isle of
Springs

C COASTAL MAINE
BOTANICAL GARDENS

INFORMATION

Boothbay
Harbor

★ FOOTBRIDGE

East
Boothbay

Farnham
Point

McKown Point

★ AQUARIUM

Cabbage
Island

★ LINEKIN
PRESERVE

Ebenecook
Harbor

Linekin
Bay

King Philip's
Trail

HENDRICK'S
HEAD LIGHT

BURNT ISLAND
LIGHT

Spruce Point

Southport
Island

Capitol
Island

C BURNT
ISLAND TOUR

Ocean
Point

RAM ISLAND LIGHT

Squirrel
Island

Fisherman's
Island

Newagen

THE
CUCKOLDS
LIGHT

Damariscove
Island

0          2 mi

0          2 km

© AVALON TRAVEL

MID-COAST REGION

Muise, who lived here 1936–1951. During the three-hour program, you'll spend time with the light keeper, his wife, and each of his children learning about their lifestyles and views on island life. Historical documents, photographs, and lenses, from 1821 to the present, are displayed in the 45-foot covered walkway between the house and tower. You may climb the spiral stairway up to the lantern room and see how the lighthouse actually functions. On an easy hike, a naturalist explains the island's flora, fauna, and geology and recounts legends, including one about a sea serpent. During free time, you may hike other trails, listen to a program on present-day lobstering and Maine fisheries, go beach-combing, fish for mackerel off the dock, or just relax and enjoy it all.

## Marine Resources Aquarium

A 20-foot touch tank, with slimy but pettable specimens, is a major kid magnet at the Marine Resources Aquarium (McKown Point Rd., West Boothbay Harbor, 207/633-9559, www.maine.gov/dmr/education.htm, 10 A.M.–5 P.M. daily late May–early Sept., 10 A.M.–5 P.M. Wed.–Sun. in Sept., $5 adults, $3 seniors and kids 5–18), operated by the state Department of Marine Resources. Exhibits in the hexagonal aquarium include rare lobsters (oversize, albino, and blue) and other Gulf of Maine creatures, and new residents arrive periodically. Self-guiding leaflets are available. Consider bringing a picnic—it's a great setting. At the height of summer, parking is limited, and it's a longish walk from downtown around the west side of the harbor, so plan to take the free local trolley-bus, departing on the half hour from the Meadow Mall (many locals still call it the Small Mall, its former name) or from one of the downtown trolley-bus stops.

### Southport Island

A historic 1810 Cape-style building, carefully restored, is the 11-room home of the **Hendricks Hill Museum** (Rte, 27, West Southport, 207/633-4831, www.hendrickshill.org, 11 A.M.–3 P.M. Tues., Thurs., and Sat. July and Aug., donation appreciated), a community attic filled with all kinds of workaday tools and utensils and fascinating maritime memorabilia. The museum is about two miles south of the Southport Island bridge, on the right, in the center of West Southport.

Continuing down Route 27 toward Cape Newagen, stop at the **Southport Memorial Library** (207/633-2741). Here's a rare, surprising treat: a huge collection of beautifully mounted butterflies once owned by Dr. and Mrs. Stanley Marr. The library is open all year, 9–4 and 7–9 P.M. Tuesday and Thursday, plus 1–4 P.M. Saturday.

### Squirrel Island

A pioneering summer colony chartered in 1871, 130-acre Squirrel Island, at the mouth of the harbor, remains an exclusive yet low-key enclave with about 100 sizable Victorian cottages, no cars or bikes, no private phones, and a wonderfully relaxed pace. The squirrel motif is everywhere, though you won't see many examples of the real thing. Still controlled by the members-only Squirrel Island Village Corporation (message center 207/633-4715), the island is officially part of the town of Southport. The island has no interest in tourism, and there are no public facilities, but visitors are permitted on the island's paved perimeter path; allow at least an hour for the circuit, taking in open ocean, a sandy beach,

rugged cliffs, and dense woods. It's a window on another era. Balmy Days Cruises operates the seasonal Squirrel Island ferry (207/633-2284, www.balmydayscruises.com, $12 adult, $6 under 12), departing from Pier 8 on Commercial Street and landing on the northwest corner of the island.

## PARKS AND PRESERVES
### Boothbay Region Land Trust

Courtesy of the very active Boothbay Region Land Trust (1 Oak St., P.O. Box 183, Boothbay Harbor 04538, 207/633-4818, www.bbrlt.org), an ever-increasing amount of acreage on the peninsula and nearby islands has been preserved for wildlife, residents, and visitors, with about 25 miles of trails available. Individual preserve maps, as well as a general brochure/map with driving directions, are available at the information centers or at the trust office. Kiosks at the trailheads hold preserve maps. There are no trash receptacles, so carry a litterbag and help the BRLT and everyone who follows you. To do even more, make a cash donation to the BRLT (any amount is welcome). The trust also offers a free series of summertime guided walks and paddles in the various preserves as well as talks. Here's just a sampling of the possibilities.

Most popular is the **Porter Preserve,** a 19-acre property bordering the Sheepscot River. Follow the moderately easy 0.86-mile loop trail and be rewarded with spectacular views, especially at sunset. You might even spy some seals lolling in the ledges at low tide. To get there, take Route 27 south to the monument in Boothbay Center. Bear right on Cory Lane and go 0.3 mile, bearing right again on Barters Island Road. Follow it 12.2 miles (perhaps stopping at the Barters Island General Store for lobster rolls or subs to go), and then go left on Kimballtown Road. Go 0.5 mile and turn left at the fork onto Porter Point Road. Park in the small lot just beyond the cemetery.

Also popular is the 146-acre **Ovens Mouth Preserve** with almost five miles of trails on two peninsulas linked by a 93-foot bridge (wear insect repellent). The 1.6-mile trail on the east peninsula is much easier than the 3.7 miles of trails on the west peninsula. To get there, from the monument in Boothbay Center, travel 1.7 miles north and then go left on Adams Pond Road. Bear right at the fork and then continue 2.2 miles. To get to the east peninsula, bear right at the junction onto the Dover Road Extension. Proceed to the end of the tarred road to the parking lot on the left. To get to the west peninsula, bear left at the junction and continue 0.15 miles to the parking area on the right.

In East Boothbay, on the way to Ocean Point, is the 94.6-acre **Linekin Preserve,** stretching from Route 96 to the Damariscotta River. The 2.3-mile, white-blazed River Loop (best done clockwise) takes in an old sawmill site, a beaver dam, and great riverfront views. You'll meet a couple of moderately steep sections on the eastern side, near the river, but otherwise it's relatively easy. To get there, take Route 96 3.8 miles and look for the parking area and trail head on the left.

## ( Coastal Maine Botanical Gardens

Masterful and magical, yet still in their youth, are these shorefront gardens (Barters Island Rd., Boothbay, office Old Firehouse, Rte. 27, Boothbay, 207/633-4333, www.mainegardens. org, 9 A.M.–5 P.M. daily year-round, to 6 P.M. Sat. and Sun., to 8 P.M. Wed. in July and Aug., $10 adults, $8 ages 65-plus, $5 ages 5–17, $25 family of four). The nonprofit project, designed to preserve more than 125 acres of woodlands with a trail network and landscaped pocket "theme" gardens, has grown to encompass 248 acres, with formal gardens, paths, herb and kitchen gardens, woods walks, a fairy village, and nearly a mile of waterfront. Artwork is placed throughout. Plans include a five-senses and a children's garden. The visitors center has a café (10 A.M.–3 P.M. May 1–Oct. 15), library, and gift shop. Pick up a map and explore on your own, or ask whether a volunteer docent is available to provide a free tour. Allow at least two hours, although you could easily spend a

full day here. A full slate of activities is offered, with more planned. Entrance to the preserve is on Barters Island Road, about 1.3 miles west of Boothbay Center.

## Damariscove Island

Summering Wabanakis knew it as Aquahega, but Damerill's Cove was the first European name attributed to the secure, fjordlike harbor at the southern tip of 210-acre Damariscove Island in 1614, when Captain John Smith of the Jamestown Colony explored the neighborhood. By 1622, Damerill's Cove fishermen were sharing their considerable codfish catch with starving Plimoth Plantation colonists desperate for food. Fishing and farming sustained resident Damariscovers during their up-and-down history, and archaeologists have found rich deposits for tracing the story of this early island settlement about seven miles south of Boothbay Harbor.

Rumors persist that the ghost of Captain Richard Pattishall, decapitated and tossed overboard by Indians in 1689, still roams the island, accompanied by the specter of his dog. The fog that often overhangs the low-slung, bleak, almost-treeless island makes it easy to fall for the many ghost stories about Pattishall and other onetime residents. In summer, the island is awash with wildflowers, bayberries, raspberries, blackberries, and rugosa roses.

Since 1966, most of 1.7-mile-long Damariscove has been owned by The Nature Conservancy. Day-use visitors are welcome on the island anytime, but the northern section (called Wood End) is off-limits March 15–August 15 to protect the state's largest nesting colony of eiders—nearly 700 nests. Damariscove Island became a National Historic Landmark in 1978. Dogs are not allowed.

Access to the island is most convenient if you have your own boat. Enter the narrow cove at the southern end of the island and disembark at The Nature Conservancy dock on the west side of the harbor. Summertime caretakers live in the small cabin above the dock, where a trail map is available. Stay on the trail (watch out for poison ivy) or on the shore and away from any abandoned structures; the former Coast Guard station is privately owned.

For information about Damariscove Island, contact **The Boothbay Region Land Trust** (1 Oak St., 2nd Floor, P.O. Box 183, Boothbay Harbor 04538, 207/633-44818, www.bbrlt.org).

## RECREATION
### Bicycling

When you're ready to take your bike on the road, head for one of the chamber of commerce information centers and pick up a copy of the bike route for the 31-mile Barters Island/Southport loop (also a fine driving itinerary). Pack a picnic. Allow a full day to bike it, including stops and detours. The terrain is mostly easy and relatively level, but many stretches are narrow and winding, with poor shoulders, so it's *essential* to follow biking rules and exercise caution.

An alternate loop route, about 15 miles long, follows only the Southport Island section, from downtown Boothbay Harbor. If you're biking with kids, opt for this itinerary—but make sure they know the rules of the road, too. Again, take a picnic, or plan to stop at the Southport General Store (Rte. 27, 207/633-6666), about two miles south of the bridge. Also check out the nearby historic cemetery, the Hendricks Hill Museum, and the Hendricks Head Light (go west on Beach Road from the general store; the light is privately owned, so don't trespass).

When crossing the swing bridge that spans Townsend Gut, between West Boothbay Harbor and Southport Island, be especially cautious. The surface can be a bear trap for bike tires.

Another good biking (and driving) route begins at the junction of Routes 27 and 96, going through East Boothbay, then on down to Ocean Point, where the Shore Road loop skirts the rocky shoreline. (Ocean Point is about six miles from the Route 27/96 crossroads.) About halfway down Linekin Neck toward Ocean Point, hang a left onto King Philip's Trail, then left onto the loop road, clockwise, through the hamlet of Little River, returning to Route 96. As on the Southport Island

route, the roads are narrow and winding along Linekin Neck, and traffic can be heavy at the height of summer. Early morning is a great time to bike here; park your car in the Hannaford supermarket lot, the Meadow Mall, or the YMCA, back on Route 27 at the entrance to Boothbay Harbor.

### Excursion Boats

Two major fleet operators provide practically every type of sea adventure imaginable. Boothbay Harbor's veteran excursion fleet is **Cap'n Fish's Cruises** (Pier 1, Wharf St., Boothbay Harbor, 207/633-3244, 207/633-2626, or 800/636-3244, www.capnfishmotel.com/boattrips.htm). In addition to whale-watching trips (see below), Cap'n Fish's 150-passenger boats do nine varied, mostly two- to three-hour cruises. There is bound to be a length and itinerary (seal-watching, lobster-trap hauling, lighthouses, Damariscove, puffin cruises, and more) that piques your interest. Pick up a schedule at one of the information centers and call for reservations.

The harbor's other big fleet is **Balmy Days Cruises** (Pier 8, Commercial St., Boothbay Harbor, 207/633-2284 or 800/298-2284, www.balmydayscruises.com), operating three vessels on a variety of excursions. The *Novelty* does about seven daily one-hour harbor tours daily late June–Labor Day; cost is $12 adults, $6 under 12. (The boat stops at Squirrel Island for dropoffs and pickups.) Reservations usually are unnecessary. The 31-foot Friendship sloop *Bay Lady* does five 90-minute sailing trips daily in summer. Cost is $20 pp. Reservations are wise for the *Bay Lady* as well as for the fleet's most popular cruise, a daylong trip to Monhegan Island on the *Balmy Days II,* departing at 9:30 A.M. and returning at 4:15 P.M. daily early June–September, plus weekends in late May and early October. The three-hour round-trip allows about 3.5 hours ashore on idyllic Monhegan Island. Cost is $32 adults, $18 ages 3–11. You're headed 12 miles offshore on the Monhegan trip, so be sure to dress warmly, wear sturdy walking/hiking shoes, and take a camera and binoculars.

## Sailing

A trip aboard *Schooner Eastwind,* a 65-foot traditional wooden schooner built in 2004, with **Appledore Cruises** (20 Commercial St. Boothbay Harbor, 207/633-6598, www.fishermanswharfinn.com) is more than a day sail, it's an adventure. Herb and Doris Smith not only built this schooner, they've sailed around the world in their previous boats through the years, providing fodder for many tales. They take passengers on 2.5-hour cruises to the outer islands and Seal Rocks, up to four times daily, for $22. The boat departs from Fisherman's Wharf.

## Whale- and Puffin-Watching Cruises

Variations in Gulf of Maine whale-migration patterns have added whale-watching to the list of Boothbay Harbor boating options as the massive mammals travel northeastward within reasonable boating distance. **Cap'n Fish's** (Pier 1, Wharf St., Boothbay Harbor, 207/633-3244, 207/633-2626, or 800/636-3244, www.mainewhales.com) is the best choice. Three- to four-hour trips depart daily mid-June–mid-October. Cost is $35 adults, $22 kids 6–12, with a raincheck if the whales don't show up. Reservations are advisable, especially early and late in the season and on summer weekends. No matter what the weather on shore, dress warmly and carry more clothing than you think you'll need. Motion-sensitive children and adults need to plan for appropriate medication.

Cap'n Fish's also runs 2.5-hour puffin-sighting tours to Easter Egg Rock, circling the island once or twice for the best views. Cruises are offered once weekly in June, then three times weekly through late August, for $24 adult, $12 kids.

## Sea Kayaking

From Memorial Day weekend through September, **Tidal Transit** (18 Granary Way, Chowder House Building, Boothbay Harbor, 207/633-7140), near the footbridge, will get you afloat with two- to three-hour guided lighthouse, wildlife, or sunset tours for $35–

Kayaking is one way to get a closer look at the boats in Boothbay Harbor.

© TOM NANGLE

40. No experience is necessary. Reservations are required. For do-it-yourselfers, Tidal Transit rents single kayaks for $15 an hour or $50 a day, tandems for $25 an hour, $75 a day; other time options are available.

On the other side of the harbor, **East Boothbay Kayak Co.** (Ocean Point Marina, Rte. 96, East Boothbay, 207/633-7411 or 866/633-7411, www.eastboothbaykayaks.com) provides rentals and gives guided tours. Rentals range from $12 single to $20 tandem per hour; $50–75 per day. Delivery is available in the Boothbay region for $20, including pickup. Two- to four-hour guided tours are $40–60. The shop is next to the post office.

## ENTERTAINMENT

The renovated 1894 **Opera House** (86 Townsend Ave., Boothbay Harbor, 207/633-6855, www.boothbayoperahouse.org) is now the site of concerts, lectures, dramas, and special events. An upstairs bar, in the former Knights of Pythias Hall, is open to adults before performances and for intermission, and often for special events.

The **Lincoln Arts Festival** (207/633-3913, www.lincolnartsrestival.org) presents half a dozen or more concerts—classical, pops, choral, and jazz—and other arts-related events at various locations on the Boothbay Peninsula late March–early October.

Early July through August is a great time for music in Boothbay Harbor. Free **band concerts** at 8 P.M. Thursdays are performed on the Memorial Library lawn. Bring a blanket or folding chair.

## EVENTS

The **Fishermen's Festival** is a locally colorful early-season celebration, held the third weekend of April, beginning with a Friday Miss Shrimp Princess pageant. Saturday brings a lobster-crate race and afternoon contests such as trap hauling, scallop- and clam-shucking, fish-filleting, and net mending (plus a real steal—a lobster-eating contest you can enter for $5). Saturday night, church suppers feature fish and shellfish, and Sunday, a chowder luncheon precedes the blessing of the fleet to ensure a successful summer season.

June is the month for **Windjammer Days,** two days of festivities centering on traditional windjammer schooners. Highlights are the Windjammer Parade, harborfront concerts, plenty of food, and a fireworks extravaganza.

Huge sailboats arrive in the harbor in early September for the **Shipyard Cup** (www.shipyardcup.com), with racing on two days. Hop aboard an excursion boat for a close-up view or drive out to Ocean Point.

Columbus Day weekend marks the **Fall Foliage Festival,** featuring craft and food booths, a petting zoo, live entertainment, train rides, and more at Boothbay Railway Village.

## SHOPPING

Artisans' galleries pepper the peninsula. Galleries, boutiques, T-shirt, and novelty shops crowd Boothbay Harbor, providing plenty of browsing for all budgets and tastes. Here's just a sampling.

## Art and Craft Galleries

**Gleason Fine Art** (31 Townsend Ave., Boothbay Harbor, 207/633-6849) is one of Maine's top retail venues for 19th- through 21st-century painting and sculpture. Also downtown is the **Gold/Smith Gallery** (41 Commercial St., Boothbay Harbor, 207/633-6252), featuring intriguing gold jewelry and contemporary paintings.

The area's veteran craft shop is **Abacus** (12 McKown St., Boothbay Harbor, 207/633-2166 or 800/206-2166 outside Maine). It's great stuff—functional items, wearable art, and charming doodads—high-end American crafts from several hundred artisans.

It's hard not to stop at the wonderful **Edgecomb Potters Gallery** (Rte. 27, Edgecomb, 207/882-9493), filled with amazingly beautiful pottery as well as high-end crafts.

Juried works from 25 Maine artists are shown in **Boothbay Harbor Artisans** (11 Granary Way, Boothbay Harbor, 207/633-1152).

The working metalsmiths at **A Silver Lining** (17 Townsend Ave., Boothbay Harbor, 207/633-4103) create beautiful original jewelry in gold, sterling, brass, copper, and titanium.

A visit to the **Villiard Gallery** (57 Campbell St., Boothbay Harbor, 207/633-3507, www.villardstudios.com) is a must for fans of fine art crafts. Kim and Philippe Villiard split their lives between Boothbay Harbor and Southern France, where they live in an abandoned village in the midst of a national park. Philippe is a talented sculptor, Kim an equally talented painter. They collaborate on woodcuts and handmade books, and the results are in collections and museums. Call in advance if you want a demonstration of the process. They have works in all price ranges, from poster prints to the actual woodblocks themselves.

Take home a stoneware puffin, sandpiper, or seal from the **Anderson Studio** (Anderson Rd., East Boothbay, 207/633-4397 or 800/640-4397, www.andersonstudio.com).

Three miles south of Route 1 is the **Iron and Silk Forge and Gallery** (Rte. 27, Edgecomb, 207/882-4055), the 400-square-foot retail shop for Elizabeth Derecktor's hand-painted silk scarves and clothing and Peter Brown's high-end handwrought weathervanes, chandeliers, and fireplace tools.

## Books, Music, and Gifts

You're bound to find something at the two-story **Sherman's Book and Stationery (and Music) Store** (5 Commercial St., Boothbay Harbor, 207/633-7262 or 800/371-8128). It offers cards and cassettes, games and gifts, books and more books, kitchenware and kitsch.

## Antiques

Antique store or museum, you decide. The **Palabra Shop** (53 Commercial St., Boothbay Harbor, 207/633-4225) has 10 chock-full rooms of antiques and collectibles. It's also home to the world's largest collection of Moses bottles.

## ACCOMMODATIONS

Boothbay Harbor's longevity as a holiday destination means beds galore—more than anyone cares to count. Even so, late June–mid-August, you'll meet a blur of No Vacancy signs. If that's when you decide to show up here, make reservations. Here's a hint: If you want to concentrate your time in downtown Boothbay Harbor, shopping or taking boating excursions, stay in town and avoid the parking hassles.

Although the town practically rolls up the sidewalks in the winter, a few businesses do stay open year-round. Lodgings that usually do so are noted; others are seasonal (usually mid-May–mid-October). You'll often find great rates before July and after August.

## Classic Inns

To get away from it all, book in at the **Newagen Seaside Inn** (Rte. 27, Southport, 207/633-5242 or 800/654-5242 outside Maine, www.newagenseasideinn.com, $165–285), a full-service, unstuffy inn with casual fine dining and views that go on forever. Recently renovated rooms are split between the Main Inn, the Little Inn, where rooms have private decks, TV, and kitchenettes, and three cottages ($1,670 per week, with breakfast). Plus there are a long rocky

shore, a nature trail, spa, tennis courts, heated oceanfront saltwater pool and hot tub, guest rowboats, game room, candlepin bowling, and porches just for relaxing. Rates include a generous buffet breakfast. The dining room is open to the public by reservation for dinner 5:30–9 P.M. daily; entrées run $18–28. There's also a pub serving lighter fare beginning at 4:30 P.M. It's open mid-May–September. The inn is six miles south of downtown Boothbay Harbor.

Families like the easygoing style of the **Lawnmere Inn** (Rte. 27, Southport Island, P.O. Box 505, West Boothbay Harbor 04575, 207/633-2544 or 800/633-7645, www.lawnmereinn.com, $115–189), only two miles from downtown Boothbay Harbor. Built in 1898 on Southport Island, overlooking Townsend Gut, the somewhat dated rooms are split between a traditional inn and two adjacent, motel-style wings. The grounds are lovely, but road noise can be a problem in some rooms. Guests have use of bicycles and kayaks. Rates include a full breakfast buffet. Pets are allowed in some rooms for $20 per night.

Over in East Boothbay, the oceanfront **Ocean Point Inn** (Shore Rd., P.O. Box 409, East Boothbay 04544, 207/633-4200 or 800/552-5554, www.oceanpointinn.com, $129–219) wows guests with spectacular sunset views and an easygoing ambience that keeps guests returning generation after generation. The sprawling complex includes numerous lodging buildings: an inn, lodge, motel, apartments, cottages, and others. All rooms have minifridge, phone, cable TV, and air-conditioning, and some have kitchenettes. Also on the premises are a well-respected dining room, a pier, an outdoor heated pool, and Adirondack-style chairs set just-so on the water's edge. The best deals are the packages.

For those who require luxury touches, the **Spruce Point Inn and Spa** (Atlantic Ave., P.O. Box 237, Boothbay Harbor 04538, 207/633-4152 or 800/553-0289, www.sprucepointinn.com) is the answer. Accommodations are traditional inn rooms and cottages and condos, all with private decks, minifridges, and TV; some have fireplaces, kitchenettes, and whirlpool tubs. Decor and prices vary widely. The inn holds big weddings on many weekends, so try for midweek. Rates begin around $315 d. Amenities at the 15-acre resort include a full-service spa and fitness center, freshwater and saltwater pools, tennis courts, rocky shorefront, and a shuttle bus to downtown (about 1.5 miles, although it seems farther). A children's program is available 9:30 A.M.–2:30 P.M. for $35 per day, including lunch and snack. Also available is an evening program for ages 4–12 6–9 P.M. Thursday–Sunday for $25. Dining choices range from poolside to pub-style to fine dining, with prices to match each setting. The inn is open late May–mid-October.

## Bed-and-Breakfasts

Topping an intown hill with sigh-producing views over the inner and outer harbors and yet just a two-minute walk to shops and restaurants is ◖ **Topside Inn** (60 McKown St., Boothbay Harbor, 207/633-5404 or 877/486-7466, www.topsideinn.com, $120–185 d), a solid, 19th-century sea captain's home with two motel-style annexes. Innkeepers Brian Lamb and Ed McDermott have completely renovated the three-building complex with an emphasis on comfort. Rooms in the three-story main inn are mostly spacious (a small one under the eves is tight but inviting); most have nice views; some have humongous bathrooms. Good books are everywhere, and the rockers on the wraparound porch and Adirondack chairs on the lawn are perfect places to read or relax. The annexes have motelish-type rooms done in B&B style; all have decks and most have at least glimpses of the ocean. All rooms have phone and TV, and there's Wi-Fi access in the main inn. Rates in all buildings include breakfast: a self-serve cold buffet with a hot entrée that's served to the table. Hot beverages are available all day; and some afternoons, home-baked cookies appear magically in the living room.

Next door is **The Welch House** (56 McKown St., Boothbay Harbor, 207/633-3431 or 800/279-7313, www.welchhouseinn.com, $135–205), with stunning 180-degree views from the third-floor deck (and not-shabby ones from the lower deck). This 14-room B&B (all private baths, but some are down the hall) is an elegant getaway in a 19th-century shipbuilder's home. All of the rooms have air-conditioning, cable TV/VCR, Wi-Fi, and phone; many have water views; some have fireplaces or whirlpool tubs. Breakfast in the solarium is a treat. It's open year-round with lower rates off-season.

In town and on the water, the **Blue Heron Inn** (65 Townsend Ave., Boothbay Harbor, 207/633-7020 or 866/216-2300, www.blueheronseasideinn.com, $185–240 peak) opened in 2003 and quickly made a name for itself. The Victorian vintage belies the clean, bright interior. Large rooms are accented with antiques and collectibles from Phil and Laura Chapman's years overseas. Each room has a waterfront deck, air-conditioning, fridge, microwave, TV, LCD-HDTV, microwave, Wi-Fi, and phone; some also have a fireplace and whirlpool tub. A dock with kayaks and a paddleboat is available. A full breakfast is elegantly served on Wedgwood china. It's open year-round.

On the east side of the harbor, up a side street but within walking distance of in-town shops and restaurants, is Mary Huntington's **Pond House** (7 Bay St., Boothbay Harbor, 207/633-5842, www.pondhousemaine.com, $80–1155). The 1920s barn-red home is just one block off the harbor, surrounded by beautiful gardens and edging a pond. The five rooms, some with shared or detached baths, have beautiful oak woodwork and are decorated with a mix of antiques and country pieces, including quilts topping most beds. Rotating artwork covers the walls, and studio space is available to visiting artists. Wi-Fi is available throughout the inn. Mary's breakfasts are legendary.

Escape the hustle and bustle of Boothbay Harbor at the ◖ **Five Gables Inn B&B** (107 Murray Hill Rd., P.O. Box 335, East Boothbay 04544, 207/633-4551 or 800/451-5048, www.fivegablesinn.com, $150–225), which began life as a no-frills summer hotel in the late 19th century. It's gone steadily upmarket since then, and well-traveled innkeepers De and Mike Kennedy, owners since 1995, have added their unique touches, including wonderful murals throughout and window seats in the gable rooms. Fifteen of the light and airy 16 rooms have Linekin Bay views and some have fireplaces. The living room is congenial, the gardens are gorgeous, and the porch goes on forever. Rates include Mike's gourmet buffet breakfast. Book well ahead at this popular spot. The inn, on a side road off Route 96 in the traditional boatbuilding hamlet of East Boothbay, is 3.5 miles from downtown Boothbay Harbor. Arriving by boat? One mooring is available for guests.

Marti Booth and Larry Brown give guests a warm welcome to their **Linekin Bay Bed and Breakfast** (531 Ocean Point Rd., 207/633-9900 or 800/596-7420, www.linekinbaybb.com, $135–185 peak). No wonder, considering all the work they did to transform the 1878 home overlooking the bay into an inn. Begin the day with full breakfast on the deck, perhaps watching lobstermen pull their traps. Afternoon refreshments also are served. Guest rooms are spacious and beautifully decorated; all have fireplaces, air-conditioning, phone, TV/VCR, Wi-Fi, and bay views. It's open year-round.

## Motels

A great location just 100 feet from the footbridge, a good dining room, a fun lounge, an indoor pool, and harbor views combine to make the **Rocktide Inn** (35 Atlantic Ave., Boothbay Harbor, 207/633-4455 or 800/762-8433, www.rocktideinn.com, $105–195) a popular spot. Rooms are spread out among four buildings, with rates varying according to the view. All have air-conditioning, cable TV, Wi-Fi, and phone, and a full buffet breakfast is included. Even if you don't stay here, pop over for a drink in the tastefully decorated tiki bar–style lounge (open 4–11 P.M. daily) or on the expansive decks overhanging the harbor. The dining room, open to the public for dinner (5:30–9 P.M. daily) has both casual and formal areas; men must wear jackets in the latter.

Since 1955, the Lewis family has owned and operated the **Mid-Town Motel** (96 McKown St., Boothbay Harbor, 207/633-2751, www.

midtownmaine.com, $55–85), a spotless, no-frills, vintage motel that's within steps of everything. It's a classic: clean, convenient, and cheap, and the owners couldn't be nicer folks.

Here's another find for the budget bound. Spread out along 0.75-mile of 30 oceanfront acres, the **Ship Ahoy Motel** (Rte. 238, Southport, Box 235, Boothbay Harbor 04538, 207/633-5222, www.shipahoy-motel.com, $49–79 d) has simple motel-style rooms, done in vintage 1960s decor, spread out in four buildings. All have TV and air-conditioning and most have private decks and spectacular views. Take a dip in the swimming pool, tie your small boat to the dock or fish from it, and munch on so-so breakfast pastries in the coffee shop. Do note: Walls are thin, so noise can be an issue.

## Campgrounds

With 150 well-maintained wooded and open sites on 45 acres, **Shore Hills Campground** (Rte. 27, P.O. Box 448, Boothbay 04537, 207/633-4782, www.shorehills.com, $27–40) is a popular destination where reservations are essential in midsummer. Be sure to request a wooded site away from the biggest RVs. Leashed pets are allowed. Facilities include a laundry and free use of canoes. On the tidal Cross River, 7.5 miles south of Route 1 and close to the Boothbay Railway Village, Shore Hills is open mid-April–mid-October.

Much smaller and right on the ocean is the **Gray Homestead Oceanfront Camping** (21 Homestead Rd., Southport, 207/633-4612, www.graysoceancamping.com, $32–34), a family-run campground with 40 RV and tenting sites, as well as cottages and apartments. A stone beach, pier, laundry facilities, kayak rentals, and lobsters, live or cooked, are available. There's even a small sand beach. Rates cover two adults and two kids.

## Seasonal Rentals

For a long-term rental, start with the **Cottage Connection of Maine** (P.O. Box 662, Boothbay Harbor 04538, 207/633-6545 or 800/823-9501, www.cottageconnection.com). The annual tourism booklet published by the Boothbay Harbor Region Chamber of Commerce includes cottage-rental listings.

# FOOD
## Local Flavors

Right in the center of all the action, **Village Market** (24 Commercial St., Boothbay Harbor, 207/633-0944) makes sandwiches and pizzas to order. Absolutely no atmosphere, but it's cheap and convenient.

It's worth the drive over to Trevett to indulge in a lobster roll from the **Barters Island General Store** (207/633-1140), just before the bridge connecting Hodgdon and Barters Islands.

"Free beer tomorrow" proclaims the sign in front of **Bets Famous Fish Fry** (Village Common, Rte. 27, Boothbay), a take-out trailer that's renowned for its ultrafresh haddock fish-and-chips. Picnic tables are available.

Far more upscale in offerings is the seasonal **Oak Street Provisions** (43 Oak St., Boothbay Harbor, 207/633-3622, 8 A.M.–7 P.M. daily), with a wide array of prepared foods as well as picnic fixings, sandwiches, and breakfast goodies.

On the east side, the **East Boothbay General Store** (255 Ocean Point Rd., Rte. 96, East Boothbay, 207/633-4503) has been serving locals since 1893. These days, it sells wine and specialty foods in addition to pizzas, sandwiches, and baked goods.

Lots of variety is the key at the seasonal **Boothbay Area Farmers Market** (Town Commons, Boothbay, 9 A.M.–noon Thurs.), with goat cheese, chicken, meats, preserves, breads, and of course fresh produce.

Here's a sleeper: **Bakers Way** (90 Townsend Ave., Boothbay Harbor, 207/633-1119), known locally as The Doughnut Shop. This hole-in-the-wall restaurant turns out the unusual combo of excellent baked goods and Vietnamese food. Go for breakfast: The breakfast sandwiches are good and the sticky buns are renowned, not only for size but taste. Then return for lunch or dinner, when a good variety of Vietnamese dishes are available, most

for less than $10. While the inside dining area is purely functional, there's also seating in a pleasant garden in the backyard. Everything is also available to go.

The Boothbay region even has a Scottish tearoom. *Tea: A Magazine* gives a thumbs-up to **MacNab's Tea Room** (5 Lu Yu Tea La. off Back River Rd., Boothbay, 207/633-7222 or 800/884-7222, 10 A.M.–5 P.M. Tues.–Sat.), near the center of Boothbay (not the harbor). Tartans and terriers are the dominant motifs in this informal, folksy place, where Frances Browne serves lunch, high tea, afternoon tea, and royal tea, all by reservation only.

Ask any local where to go for a reliably good and reasonably priced breakfast or lunch, and you'll be directed to the **Blue Moon Café** (54 Commercial St., Boothbay Harbor, 207/633-2349, www.bluemoonboothbayharbor.com, 7:30 A.M.–2 P.M. daily). Order at the counter and then grab one of the handful of tables inside or on the harbor-view deck or in the overflow garden seating behind the restaurant. Homemade soups and salads, great sandwiches, and sinful pastries ($4–10). If you're headed out for a picnic, the café will fix you up with a box lunch.

Another locals' favorite serving breakfast, lunch, and dinner is the unassuming **Ebb Tide Restaurant** (43 Commercial St., Boothbay Harbor, 207/633-5692, 6:30 A.M.–9 P.M. daily). Booths line the tiny pine-paneled dining area, where some mighty good homestyle cooking is served. The chowders are renowned, and breakfast is served all day. Friday night is the haddock fry and Monday night is the scallop fry, both about $12 with free seconds. Look for the red-and-white awning.

## Casual Dining

Fresh fish expertly prepared has earned **93 Townsend** (93 Townsend Ave., Boothbay Harbor, 207/633-0777, www.93townsend.com, 11:30 A.M.–9:30 P.M. Mon.–Thurs., to 10:30 P.M. Fri. and Sat.) a strong local following. The menu also has steak, pasta, and kids' choices, but stick to fish and creative seafood renditions, including an award-winning lobster risotto and a decadent truffled mac and cheese; most choices are $15–25. No view, but the dining room is pleasant, and the martini options cover two pages.

Real Italian fare prepared by a real Italian chef is on the menu at **Ports of Italy** (47 Commercial St., Boothbay Harbor, 207/633-1011, 5–9:30 P.M. Mon–Thurs., to 10 P.M. Fri. and Sat., to 9 P.M. Sun.), an upper level restaurant with deck seating. This isn't a red-sauce place; expect well-prepared and innovative fare, with especially good seafood. Most choices are in the $20 range.

For spectacular sunset views and reliably good food, take a spin out to the **Ocean Point Inn** (Shore Rd., East Boothbay, 207/633-4200 or 800/552-5554, www.oceanpointinn.com, 6–8:30 P.M. daily). Every table in the two-tiered, pine-paneled dining room has a view. Most entrées are in the $20–28 range; a children's menu is available.

One of the most reliable dining experiences in town is at **The Thistle Inn** (55 Oak St., Boothbay Harbor, 207/633-3541, 5–9 P.M., to 10 P.M. Fri. and Sat.). Everything, from the salad dressings to the desserts, is prepared onsite. It would be easy to make a meal from the appetizers alone—crab cakes, brandied lobster, tempura banana salad, but then you wouldn't have room for the main event, perhaps lobster paella or port tenderloin ($18–30). On a cold night, ask for a table by one of the fireplaces; on a warm night, ask for one on the porch.

## Lobster in the Rough

Boothbay Harbor and East Boothbay seem to have more eat-on-the-dock lobster shacks per square inch than almost anywhere else on the coast. If you're a lobster fanatic, you've reached nirvana, heaven, ground zero, whatever. On the Southport Island side of the harbor, overlooking Townsend Gut next to the swing bridge, **Robinson's Wharf** (Rte. 27, Southport Island, 207/633-3830, www.robinsonswharf.net, opens at 11:30 A.M. daily) is a sprawling place with tons of indoor and outdoor seating. Lobster dinners, lobster stew, fried seafood, steamed clams, mussels—it's all here. Plus burgers, dogs, fries, pasta salad, even

BLTs and grilled cheese sandwiches. Save room for homemade pie.

Around the other side of the harbor, facing the Damariscotta River in East Boothbay, is the **Lobsterman's Wharf** (Rte. 96, East Boothbay, 207/633-3443, opens at 11:30 A.M. daily). Everything from ties to T-shirts adorns the clientele, usually a mix of locals and flatlanders. The lobsters are great; so are the baby-back ribs and the crab melt. It has nearly 200 seats inside and out. From the junction of Routes 27 and 96 in Boothbay Harbor, take Route 96 three miles to the wharf, on the left.

And then there's **The Lobster Dock** (49 Atlantic Ave., Boothbay Harbor, 207/635-7120, www.thelobsterdock.com, 11:30 A.M.–8:30 P.M.), where lobsters are delivered twice daily; now that's fresh. While there are a few choices for landlubbers—even PBJ for kids, lobster and fish are the prime attraction. It's right on the harbor, so the views are superb.

**Cabbage Island Clambakes** (Pier 6, Fisherman's Wharf, Boothbay Harbor, 207/633-7200, www.cabbageislandclambakes.com) deserves a category all its own. Touristy, sure, but it's a delicious adventure. You board the 126-passenger excursion boat *Argo* at Pier 6 in Boothbay Harbor; cruise for about an hour past islands, boats, and lighthouses; and disembark at 5.5-acre Cabbage Island. Watch the clambake in progress, if you like, explore the island, or play volleyball. When the feast is ready, pick up your platter, find a picnic table, and dig in. A cash bar is available in the lodge, as are restrooms. When the weather's iffy, the lodge and covered patio have seats for 100. For $50, you'll get two lobsters (or half a chicken), chowder, clams, corn, potatoes, dessert, beverage, and the boat ride. No credit cards. Clambake season is late June–early September. The 3.5-hour trips depart at 12:30 P.M. Monday–Friday, at 12:30 and 5 P.M. Saturday, 11:30 A.M. and 1:30 P.M. Sunday.

## INFORMATION AND SERVICES
### Information

The Boothbay Harbor Region Chamber of Commerce maintains one seasonal and one year-round information center. The seasonal center (May–mid-Oct.) is on Route 1, at the Route 27 junction. Down Route 27, 10.8 miles from Route 1, is the chamber's main office, next to Hannaford. It's open 8 A.M.–5 P.M. Monday–Friday all year. There's an information kiosk outside if the office is closed.

About eight miles south of Route 1, between the two centers above, is the Boothbay Chamber of Commerce Information Center (Rte. 27, Boothbay Center, 207/633-4743, daily mid-June–early Oct., weekends only the rest of the year).

All three centers stock brochures for the entire peninsula; wherever you stop, be sure to request the handy annual Boothbay Harbor walking map, the Boothbay Region Land Trust hiking brochure, and the tourism booklet covering the whole peninsula.

Check out Boothbay Harbor Memorial Library (4 Oak St., Boothbay Harbor, 207/633-3112, www.bmpl.lib.me.us). Thursday evenings in July and August, there are band concerts on the lawn.

## Public Restrooms

At the municipal parking lot on Commercial Street (next to Pier 1), and at the municipal lot at the end of Granary Way, are public restrooms. Saint Andrews Hospital, the town offices, the library, and the Marine Resources Aquarium also have restrooms.

## GETTING AROUND

The Rocktide Inn operates free trolley-buses on continuous scheduled routes during the summer.

# Pemaquid Region

At the head of the Pemaquid Peninsula, the two riverfront towns of Damariscotta and her Siamese twin, Newcastle, anchor the western end of the Pemaquid Peninsula; Waldoboro anchors the eastern end. Along the peninsula are New Harbor (probably Maine's most photographed fishing village), Pemaquid Point (site of one of Maine's most photographed lighthouses), and historic ports reputedly used by Captain John Smith, Captain Kidd, and assorted less-notorious types. Here, too, are a restored fortress, Native American historic sites, antiques and craft shops galore, boat excursions to offshore Monhegan, and one of the best pocket-size sand beaches in Mid-Coast Maine.

On Christmas Day 1614, famed explorer Captain John Smith anchored on Rutherford Island, at the tip of the peninsula, and promptly named the spot Christmas Cove. And thus it remains today. Christmas Cove is one of three villages belonging to the town of South Bristol, the southwestern finger of the Pemaquid Peninsula. South Bristol and Bristol (covering eight villages on the bottom half of the peninsula) were named after the British city.

As early as 1625, settler John Brown received title to some of this territory from the Wabanaki sachem (chief) Samoset, an agreeable fellow who learned snippets of English from British codfishermen. Damariscotta (dam-uh-riss-COT-ta), in fact, is Wabanaki for "plenty of alewives [herring]." The settlement here was named Walpole but was incorporated, in 1847, under its current name.

Newcastle, incorporated in 1763, earned fame and fortune from shipbuilding and brickmaking—which explains the extraordinary number of brick homes and office buildings throughout the town. In the 19th century, Newcastle's shipyards sent clippers, Downeasters, and full-rigged ships down the ways and around the world.

On the other, northeastern end of the peninsula is Waldoboro. Route 1 cuts a commercial swath through Waldoboro without revealing the attractive downtown—or the lovely Friendship Peninsula, south of the highway. Duck into Waldoboro and then follow Route 220 south 10 miles to Friendship for an off-the-beaten-track drive.

Waldoboro's heritage is something of an anomaly in Maine. It's predominantly German, thanks to 18th-century Teutons who swallowed the blandishments of General Samuel Waldo, holder of a million-acre "patent" stretching as far as the Penobscot River. In the cemetery at the Old German Church, on Route 32, is a 19th-century marker whose inscription sums up the town's early history:

> This town was settled in 1748, by Germans who emigrated to this place with the promise and expectation of finding a populous city, instead of which they found nothing but a wilderness; for the first few years they suffered to a great extent by Indian wars and starvation. By perseverance and self-denial, they succeeded in clearing lands and erecting mills. At this time [1855] a large proportion of the inhabitants are descendants of the first settlers.

(Sure makes you wonder why Waldo's name stuck to the town.)

After the mill era, the settlers went into shipbuilding in a big way, establishing six shipyards and producing more than 300 wooden vessels, including the first five-masted schooner, the 265-foot *Governor Ames,* launched in 1888. Although the *Ames*'s ill-supported masts collapsed on her maiden voyage, repairs allowed her to serve as a coal hauler for more than 20 years, and many more five-masters followed in her wake. It's hard to believe today, but Waldoboro once was America's sixth-busiest port. At the Town Landing, alongside the Medomak River, a marker describes the town's shipyards and shipbuilding heritage.

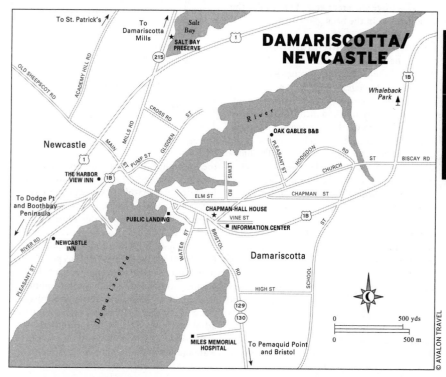

MID-COAST REGION

© AVALON TRAVEL

## SIGHTS

Pick up *A Walking Tour of the Early Dwellings of Damariscotta, Maine* at the chamber of commerce office. The book by the Damariscotta Historical Society (207/563-8441) covers sites in the Main Street Historic District and details their histories. Most are privately owned and not open for tours.

### Chapman-Hall House

Damariscotta's oldest surviving building is the Cape-style Chapman-Hall House (270 Main St., 1–5 P.M. Tues.–Sun. July and Aug., $2), built in 1754 by Nathaniel Chapman, whose family tree includes the legendary John Chapman, a.k.a. Johnny Appleseed. Highlights are a 1754 kitchen and displays of local shipbuilding memorabilia. The National Historic Register house was meticulously restored by the Chapman-Hall House Preservation Society in the styles of three different eras. Don't miss the antique roses in the back garden.

### ( Pemaquid Point Lighthouse

One of the icons of the Maine Coast, Pemaquid Point's lighthouse has been captured for posterity by many photographers and even is depicted on the Maine state quarter. The lighthouse, adjacent keeper's house, and picnic grounds are a town park. Also on the premises is an art gallery. Admission to the grounds, payable at the gatehouse, is $2 for age 12 and older. The lighthouse grounds are accessible all year, even after the museum closes for the season, when admission is free. The point is 15 miles south of Route 1, via winding, two-lane Route 130.

Lighthouses are irresistible, and the setting here makes it even more so. Commissioned in 1827, Pemaquid Point Light (www.lighthousefoundation.org) stands sentinel over some of Maine's nastiest shoreline—rocks and surf that can reduce any wooden boat to kindling. Now automated, the light tower is licensed to the American Lighthouse Foundation and is managed by the Friends of Pemaquid Point Lighthouse. Volunteers *aim* to open the tower 9 A.M.–5 P.M. daily mid-May–mid-October, weather permitting. There is no charge for

## RETURN OF THE ALEWIVES

If you're in the Damariscotta area in May and early June, don't miss a chance to go to Damariscotta Mills to see the annual Alewife Run. More than 250,000 alewives *(Alosa pseudoharengus,* a kind of herring) make their way during this time from Great Salt Bay to their spawning grounds in freshwater Damariscotta Lake, 42 feet higher. Waiting eagerly at the top are ospreys, gulls, cormorants, and sometimes eagles, ready to feast on the weary fish. Connecting the bay and the lake is a man-made stone-and-masonry "fish ladder," a zigzagging channel where you can watch the foot-long fish wriggle their way onward and upward. The ladder was built in 1807 and restored in the early 1990s. A walkway runs alongside the route, and informative display panels explain the event. It's a fascinating historical ecology lesson. To reach the fishway, take Route 215 for 1.5 miles west of Route 1. When you reach a small bridge, cross it and take a sharp left down a slight incline to a small parking area. Walk behind the barn to follow the path to the fish ladder. Try to go on a sunny day – the fish are more active and their silvery sides glisten as they go.

the tower, but donations are appreciated. Still can't get enough? Newcastle Square Vacation Rentals (207/563-6500, www.mainecoastcottages.com) manages a one-bedroom apartment available for weekly rental ($950) in the Keeper's House. Proceeds benefit preservation.

The adjacent **Fisherman's Museum** (207/677-2494), in the former light keeper's house, points up the pleasures and perils of the lobstering industry and also has some lighthouse memorabilia. The museum is open 9 A.M.–5 P.M. daily mid-May–mid-October. Museum admission is free (donations appreciated).

While here, you should also visit the **Pemaquid Art Gallery** (207/677-2752, 9 A.M.–5 P.M. Mon.–Sat., opens 1 P.M. Sun., mid-

May–mid-Oct.). It's operated by the Pemaquid Group of Artists, which has displayed its juried members' works since 1928.

Bring a picnic and lounge on the rocks below the light tower, but don't plan to snooze. You'll be busy protecting your food from the dive-bombing gulls and your kids from the treacherous surf.

## Colonial Pemaquid/ Fort William Henry

At the Colonial Pemaquid State Historic Site (end of Huddle Rd., 207/677-2423, www.friendsofcolonialpemaquid.org, 10 A.M.– 7 P.M. daily late May–early Sept., $2 ages 12– 65), visitors can gain a basic understanding of what life was like in an English frontier settlement. The 19-acre complex, listed on the National Historic Register, comprises a museum/visitors center, Fort William Henry, the Fort House, the remnants of a village, an 18th-century cemetery, picnic area, a pier and boat ramp, and restrooms, all spread out on a grassy point sloping to John's Bay and bordered by McCaffrey's Brook, the Pemaquid River, and Pemaquid Harbor. Bring a picnic, bring a kite, bring a kayak, let the kids run, but do take time to visit the historic sites (a kids' activity book is available for $1). Demonstrations, tours, lectures, and reenactments are part of the site's summer schedule. Sadly, a monstrous McMansion, perhaps appropriate in another setting but built with no respect for the locale, now dominates the view across the river, lessening the historic feel of the experience.

Three national flags fly over the ramparts of Fort William Henry, a reconstruction of a fort dating from 1692, the second of three that stood here between 1677 and the late 18th century. The forts were built to defend the English settlement of Pemaquid, settled between 1625 and 1628, from the French. From the rebuilt western tower, you'll have fantastic views of John's Bay and John's Island, named for none other than Captain John Smith; inside are artifacts retrieved from archaeological excavations of the 17th-century trading outpost.

The square, white Fort House, which dates to the late 1700s, houses a research library and archaeology lab as well as a gift shop.

Exhibits at the museum/visitors center focus on regional history, from early Native American life through the Colonial period. Selections from the more than 100,000 artifacts uncovered during archeological digs here are displayed along with a diorama of Pemaquid Village.

Take time to wander the village, 14 cellar holes of 17th- and 18th-century dwellings, a forge, trading post, jail, and other early buildings, all marked with interpretive signs. Also visit the burying ground. Note that no rubbings are permitted as they could damage the fragile old stones.

## Historic Houses of Worship

One of the oldest houses of worship in Maine that still holds services, **The Old Walpole Meeting House** (Rte. 129, Bristol Rd., Walpole, 207/563-5554), built in 1772, remains remarkably unchanged, with original hand-shaved shingles and handmade nails and hinges. The balcony—where black servants once were relegated—is paneled with boards more than two feet wide. A nondenominational service is held 3 P.M. each Sunday in August, but better still is the annual candlelight concert, a dramatic occasion in this building with no electricity and splendid acoustics. It's at 7 P.M. on a Sunday in September (usually the second Sunday, but call ahead to confirm the date). It's always a sellout, but the acoustics are so good that attendees outside can hear every note. The meetinghouse is 3.5 miles south of Damariscotta and a quarter mile south of where Routes 129 and 130 fork.

The **Harrington Meeting House** (Old Harrington Rd., off Rte. 130, 2–4:30 P.M. Mon., Wed., and Fri. July and Aug., donations welcomed), begun in 1772 and completed in 1775, now serves as Bristol's local-history museum—town-owned and run by the Pemaquid Historical Association. Behind it is an old cemetery that's fascinating to explore—if you're a fan of that sort of thing.

A remnant of Waldoboro's German connection is the **Old German Church** (Rte. 32,

© TOM NANGLE

Waldoboro's Old German Church was moved across the Medomak River in 1794.

Waldoboro, 207/832-5369 or 207/832-7742, 1–3 P.M. July and Aug.) and its cemetery. The Lutheran church, built in 1772 on the opposite side of the Medomak River, was moved across the ice in the winter of 1794. Inside are box pews and a huge hanging pulpit. One of the three oldest churches in Maine, it lost its flock in the mid-19th century, when new generations no longer spoke German.

Built in 1808, **St. Patrick's Catholic Church** (Academy Hill Rd., Damariscotta Mills, Newcastle, 207/563-3240, 9 A.M.–sundown daily), a solid brick structure with 1.5-foot-thick walls and a Paul Revere bell, is New England's oldest surviving Catholic church. Academy Hill Road starts at Newcastle Square, downtown Newcastle; the church is 2.25 miles from there, and one mile beyond Lincoln Academy. The DaPonte String Quartet often performs here.

**St. Andrew's Episcopal Church** (Glidden St., Newcastle, 207/563-3533), built in 1883, is nothing short of exquisite, with carved-oak beams, stenciled ceiling, and, for the cognoscenti, a spectacular Hutchings organ.

## Darling Marine Research Center

Not far beyond the Old Walpole Meeting House is the turnoff to the Ira C. Darling Center for Marine Research, Teaching, and Service (193 Clark's Cove Rd., off Rte. 129, Walpole, 207/563-3146, http://server.dmc.maine.edu), part of the University of Maine system. Generally known as the Darling Center, it's the hands-on laboratory for the university's marine-biology students. The Gulf of Maine Foundation sponsors a weekly lecture series mid-July–late August. Held in the waterfront conference center, the programs (at 7:30 P.M. Thursday) focus on maritime history, ecology, and marine biology. Suggested donation is $5; call ahead for schedule details (ext. 252). Also on the premises are six miles of trails through fields, woodlands, and along the river and cove. Pick up a free map at the kiosk next to the administrative building. From downtown Damariscotta, take Route 130 two miles to Route 129. Continue five miles on Route 129 to Clark's Cove Road; turn right and go about one mile to the campus.

© TOM NANGLE

Ice cutting is an annual event at the Thompson Ice House in South Bristol.

## The Thompson Ice House

On a Sunday morning in February (weather and ice permitting), several hundred helpers and on-lookers gather at Thompson Pond, next to the Thompson Ice House (Rte. 129, South Bristol, 207/644-8551), for the annual ice harvest. Festivity prevails as a crew of robust fellows marks out a grid and saws out 12-inch-thick ice cakes, which are pushed up a ramp to the ice-storage house. More than 60 tons of ice are harvested each year. Sawdust-insulated 10-inch-thick walls keep the ice from melting in this National Historic Register building first used in 1826. In 1990, the house became part of a working museum (1–4 P.M. Wed., Fri., Sat. in July and Aug., donation), with ice tools and a window view of the stored ice cakes. The grounds are accessible free all year, including a photographic display board depicting a 1964 harvest. The site is on Route 129, 12 miles south of Damariscotta. Roadside parking is allowed.

## The Gut

At the foot of a hill on Route 129 is the tiny community of **South Bristol,** the heart of the town that stretches along the western edge of the Pemaquid Peninsula. In the village center is a green-painted swing bridge (swinging sideways) spanning a narrow waterway quaintly named The Gut. Separating the mainland from Rutherford Island, The Gut is a busy thoroughfare for local lobster-boat traffic, so the bridge opens and closes often, very often. No one is in much of a hurry in this sleepy hamlet, so the frequent stoppages never seem to bother anyone, and the scenery is worth it all. So be patient.

## Waldoborough Historical Society Museum

The Waldoborough Historical Society Museum (1164 Main St., Waldoboro, 207/832-4713, 1–4:30 P.M. July–Labor Day, free) is a three-building roadside complex just 0.1 mile south of Route 1, at the eastern end of town. On the grounds are the one-room 1857 **Boggs Schoolhouse,** the 1819 **Town Pound** (to detain stray livestock), and two buildings filled with antique tools, toys, and utensils, plus period costumes, antique fire engines, and artifacts from the shipbuilding era.

## Maine Antique Toy and Art Museum

Indulge your inner child at the Maine Antique Toy and Art Museum (Rte. 1, Waldoboro, 207/832-7398, 10 A.M.–4 P.M. Thurs.–Mon. late May–mid-Oct., noon–4 P.M. Sat. and Sun. to Christmas, $4). The museum houses an extensive collection of antique toys and original comic art. See how Mickey Mouse first appeared. Browse a collection of Lone Ranger memorabilia. You'll find all the old favorites, from Popeye to Felix the Cat, Betty Boop to Snow White, Pogo to Yoda. Note: This museum is geared to nostalgic adults, not kids.

## PARKS AND PRESERVES

Residents of the Pemaquid Peninsula region are incredibly fortunate to have several foresighted local conservation organizations, each with its own niche and mission: Damariscotta River Association, Pemaquid Watershed Association, Damariscotta Lake Watershed Association, and Medomak Valley Land Trust. In addition, The Nature Conservancy, Maine Audubon, and National Audubon all have holdings on the peninsula, a natural-resource bonanza. For good descriptions of trails throughout Lincoln county, buy a copy of Paula Roberts's *On the Trail in Lincoln County* ($15.75), which describes and provides directions to more than 60 area walking trails. It's available at Salt Bay Farm, which benefits from its sale.

## Salt Bay Farm

Headquarters of the **Damariscotta River Association (DRA)** (P.O. Box 333, 109-110 Belvedere Rd., Damariscotta 04543, 207/563-1393, www.draclt.org, 9 A.M.–4 P.M. weekdays), founded in 1973, is the Salt Bay Farm Heritage Center, a late-18th-century farmhouse on a farm site. Here you can pick up maps, brochures, and other information on properties protected and managed by the DRA. It owns 40 conservation easements on 1,350 acres and owns 31 properties, preserving 700 acres, and it acts as a steward, managing another eight properties. Among these are the Dodge Point Preserve, Menigawum (Stratton Island) Preserve, and the Salt Bay Preserve. More than two miles of trails cover Salt Bay Farm's fields, salt marsh, and shore frontage and are open to the public sunrise–sunset daily year-round,. No camping or fires. DRA also has a healthy calendar of events, including birding tours, natural-history trips, concerts, and Trail Tamers, an opportunity to work on the trail system. To reach the farm from downtown Newcastle, take Mills Road (Rte. 215) to Route 1. Turn right (north) and go 1.4 miles to the blinking light (Belvedere Rd.). Turn left and go 0.4 mile.

## Salt Bay Preserve Heritage Trail

Across Great Salt Bay from the DRA Salt Bay Farm is the trailhead for the Salt Bay Preserve Heritage Trail, a relatively easy three-mile loop around Newcastle's Glidden Point that touches on a variety of habitat and also includes remnants of oyster-shell heaps ("middens") going back about 2,500 years. This part of the trail is protected by the feds; do *not* disturb or remove anything. Better still, carry a litterbag and help maintain the path.

This is a super family hike, and leashed dogs are allowed. Along the trail, watch for eagles, osprey, herons, river otters, Indian pipes, several stands of rare white oaks, and open views of Great Salt Bay. Best time to come is close to low tide, as some parts of the trail require slight detours at high tide—especially during the new or full moon. In any case, rubberized shoes or boots are a good idea. To reach the preserve from Newcastle Square, take Mills Road (Rte. 215) about two miles to the offices of the *Lincoln County News* (just after the post office). The newspaper allows parking in the northern end of its lot, but stay to the right, as far away from the buildings as possible, and be sure not to block any vehicles or access ways. Walk across Route 215 to the trailhead and pick up a brochure/map.

© TOM NANGLE

The Salt Bay Preserve Heritage Trail loops around Newcastle's Glidden Point.

## Whaleback Park

After a decade of push-me, pull-you struggling, the Damariscotta River Association, in conjunction with Maine's Bureau of Parks and Lands, finally acquired all the requisite permits in 2001 to create Whaleback Park, an eight-acre public preserve designed to highlight what remains of the "Glidden Midden," ancient oyster-shell heaps across the river from the park viewpoint. (The midden is also visible, but not as easily, from the Salt Bay Preserve Heritage Trail.) Informational signs explain the history of the midden, allegedly the largest such manmade artifact north of Florida. The "minimountain" of castoffs was even more vast until the 1880s, when a factory harvested much of it for lime. The trailhead and parking is on Business Route 1 opposite and between the Great Salt Bay School and the CLC YMCA. For information about the park, contact the DRA (207/563-1393).

## Dodge Point Preserve

In 1989, the state of Maine acquired the 506-acre Dodge Point Preserve—one of the stars in its crown—as part of a $35 million bond issue. The Damariscotta River Association, which initiated its protection, helps manage and maintain the property. To sample what the Dodge Point Preserve has to offer, pick up a map at the entrance and follow the Old Farm Road loop trail, and then hook into the Shore Trail (Discovery Trail), heading clockwise, with several dozen highlighted sites. Consider stopping for a riverside picnic and swim at Sand Beach before continuing back to the parking lot. Hunting is permitted in the preserve, so November isn't the best time for hiking here (unless you hike on Sunday, when hunting is banned). Winter brings out ice-skaters and cross-country skiers. The Dodge Point parking area is on River Road, 2.6 miles southwest of Route 1 and 3.5 miles southwest of downtown Newcastle. It's open for day use only, closing at sunset, all year. Admission is free. For more information, contact the DRA.

## Tracy Shore Preserve

Walk through a woodland wonderland that

extends to ledgy shorefront along Jones Cove, in South Bristol. Old cellars, moss-covered trails, lichen-covered rocks, a vernal pool, old pasture grounds, and spectacular views highlight this little-known gem, owned by The Nature Conservancy. It has cliffs and lots of slippery rocks, so be extra watchful of children. You can connect to another preserve, the Library Preserve, on a link crossing busy Route 129. The trailhead and parking is at the intersection of Route 129 and the S Road, 8.7 miles south of the split from Route 130.

## Rachel Carson Salt Pond/ La Verna Preserve

If you've never spent time studying the variety of sealife in a tidal pool, the Rachel Carson Salt Pond is a great place to start. Named after the famed author of *Silent Spring* and *The Edge of the Sea*, who summered in this part of Maine, the salt pond was a favorite haunt of hers. The whole point of visiting a tide pool is to see what the tide leaves behind, so check the tide calendar (in local newspapers, or ask at your lodging) and head out a few hours after high tide. Wear rubber boots and beware of slippery rocks and rockweed. Among the many creatures you'll see in this quarter-acre pond are mussels, green crabs, periwinkles, and starfish. Owned by The Nature Conservancy, the salt pond is on Route 32 in the village of Chamberlain, about a mile north of New Harbor. Parking is limited. Across the road is a trail into a 78-acre inland section of the preserve, most of it wooded. Brochures are available in the registration box.

About two miles farther north on Route 32 (or four miles south of Round Pond) is the 119-acre La Verna Preserve, also owned by The Nature Conservancy. Behind the 3,600-foot-long Muscongus Bay shorefront (spectacular views from the cliffs) are woodlands, marshlands (wear insect repellent and rubberized shoes or boots), and old cellar holes. Park on Route 32 and walk into the preserve on half-mile-long Tibbitts Road, an unpaved private road that begins opposite the red North Country barn. (Keep right when Tibbitts Road forks.) A trail leads through woodlands to the shore,

with intriguing geological formations and spectacular views.

For additional information about both preserves, which are accessible sunrise–sunset year-round, contact The Nature Conservancy, Maine Chapter (14 Maine St., Fort Andross, Brunswick, 207/729-5181).

## Todd Wildlife Sanctuary

The mainland section of a 345-acre Audubon Society property, the Todd Wildlife Sanctuary (11 Audubon Rd., Bremen) includes a visitors center and gift shop (207/529-5148, open 10 A.M.–4 P.M. daily June–Aug.), and the **Hockomock Nature Trail**, winding through the woods and down to the shore (open year-round). Pick up a trail guide at the center and follow the informative signs. Allow about an hour. Don't forget a picnic so you can have lunch on the beach. Just offshore is 333-acre **Hog Island**, site of the summertime **Audubon Ecology Camp** for youth and adults. If you have your own boat, you can walk the island's beautiful perimeter trail (no camping). Allow about three hours for the hike. Just check in beforehand at the office near the dock at the north end of the island.

# RECREATION
## Golf

The nine-hole **Wawenock Country Club** (Rte. 129, Walpole, 207/563-3938), established in the 1920s, is a challenging and very popular public course about midway down the Pemaquid Peninsula from Damariscotta. The par-3 eighth hole features a treacherous bunker named Big Bertha. Starting times are needed on summer weekends.

## Bicycling

As with so many other parts of Maine, bike lanes on the Pemaquid Peninsula are poor to nonexistent, so exercise the utmost caution. Roads are narrow, winding, and poorly shouldered.

## Swimming

Best bet (but also most crowded) on the peninsula for saltwater swimming is town-owned

**Pemaquid Beach Park,** a lovely, tree-lined sandy crescent. No lifeguard, but there are showers (cold water) and bathrooms, and the snack bar serves decent food. No alcohol is allowed on the beach. Admission is $2 for anyone over 12. At 7 P.M., the gates close (restrooms close at 5 P.M.). The beach is just off Snowball Hill Road, west of Route 130.

A much smaller beach is the pocket-size sandy area in **Christmas Cove,** on Rutherford Island. Take Route 129 around the cove and turn to the right, and then right again down the hill.

One of the area's most popular freshwater swimming holes is **Biscay Pond,** a long, skinny body of water in the peninsula's center. From Business Route 1 at the northern edge of Damariscotta, take Biscay Road (turn at McDonald's) three miles to the pond (on the right, heading east). On hot days, this area sees plenty of cars; pull off the road as far as possible.

Farther down the peninsula, on Route 130 in **Bristol Mills,** is another roadside swimming hole, between the dam and the bridge.

## Boat Excursions

At 9 A.M. each day between mid-May and early October, the 60-foot powerboat *Hardy III* departs for **Monhegan,** a Brigadoon-like island a dozen miles offshore, where passengers can spend the day hiking the woods, picnicking on the rocks, birding, and inhaling the salt air. At 3:15 P.M., everyone reboards, arriving in New Harbor just over an hour later. Dress warmly and wear rubber-soled shoes. Cost is $29 adults, $17 kids under 12. Reservations are required, and they're held until 20 minutes before departure, but plan to arrive 30 minutes ahead of time (or 45 minutes if you have luggage). Trips operate rain or shine, but heavy seas can affect the schedule. Go light on breakfast beforehand, but there are restrooms aboard. From early June through late September, there's also a second Monhegan trip—used primarily for overnighters—departing New Harbor at 2 P.M. daily. Early and late season, Monhegan trips operate only Wednesday, Saturday, Sunday, and holidays. The *Hardy III* also operates daily 1.5-hour **puffin-watching tours** (5:30 P.M. mid-May–late Aug., $21 adults, $13 kids); one-hour **seal-watching tours** (noon daily mid-June–early Sept. and Sept. weekends, $11 adults, $9 kids); and one-hour evening **lighthouse cruises** (mid-June–early Sept., $12 adults, $8 kids). **Hardy Boat Cruises** (Rte. 32, New Harbor, 207/677-2026 or 800/278-3346, www.hardyboat.com) is 19 miles south of Route 1, based at Shaw's Fish and Lobster Wharf. Parking is $2/day, at the baseball field near Shaw's.

Cruise Muscongus Bay aboard the Friendship sloop *Sarah Mead* with **Sail Muscongus** (207/380-5460, www.sailmuscongus.com) on its morning, island, or sunset cruises. Most last about three hours, with rates ranging $30–50 pp; kids under 12 are half price. Bring water and snacks. Muscongus Road is off Route 32, north of Round Pond. Parking is $5/day.

## Sea Kayaking and Canoeing

**Pemaquid Paddlers,** a local group, welcomes visitors to its weekly paddles, usually held beginning at 9 A.M. on Saturdays and lasting for about two hours. Check local papers for the schedule.

**Midcoast Kayak** (45 Main St., Damariscotta, 207/563-5732, www.midcoast-kayak.com) has rentals and offers guided tours and lessons on Muscongus Bay and the Damariscotta River. Three-hour to full-day tours range $39–99, and include introductory, adventurer, sunset, night, and explorer tours. If you would rather do it yourself, sea recreational kayaks rent for $39/day, $29/half day, $22/two hours; sea kayaks (rescue experience required) rent for $49/day, $39/half day; and tandem sea kayaks rent for $65/full day, $49/half day, $39/two hours. Instruction also is available.

Operating from a base near Colonial Pemaquid is **Maine Kayak** (113 Huddle Rd., New Harbor, 866/624-6351, www.mainekayak.com). Guided options include sunset paddle, wildlife paddle, puffin paddle, paddle-and-sail, half- and full-day trips, and a variety of overnights. Rates begin at $40 for the shorter trips. Rentals begin at $25 single, $35 tandem for two hours, with free delivery in the New Harbor area.

**Cane and Canvas** (Bristol Mills, 207/563-1280) rents canoes and kayaks for use on the Pemaquid River. Paddle upstream from its launch site to Biscay, Pemaquid, and Duck-puddle Ponds or south to a recently restored, early 19th-century stone-arch bridge that was built without mortar. There's lots of wildlife to be seen in the area. Canoes rent for $30 half day, $45 full day; kayak rentals are $20–30 half day, $30–45 full day. Multiple day rates are available. Part of the fee supports the Pemaquid Watershed Association.

If you have your own canoe, or just want to paddle the three-mile length of **Biscay Pond,** you can park at the beach area and put in there (see *Swimming*). Another good launching site is a state ramp off Route 1 in **Nobleboro,** at the head of eight-mile-long **Lake Pemaquid.**

Two preserves are accessible if you have your own boat. Owned by the Damariscotta River Association, 30-acre **Menigawum Preserve (Stratton Island)** is also known locally as Hodgdon's Island. It's at the entrance to Seal Cove on the west side of the South Bristol peninsula. The closest public boat launch is at The Gut, about four miles downriver—a trip better done *with* (in the same direction as) the tide. The best place to land is Boat House Beach, in the northeast corner—also a great spot for shelling. Pick up a map in the small box at the north end of the island and follow the perimeter trail clockwise. At the northern end, you'll see osprey nests; at the southern tip are Native American shell middens—discards from hundreds of years of marathon summer lunches. (Needless to say, do *not* disturb or remove anything.) You can picnic in the pasture, but camping and fires are not allowed. Stay clear of the abandoned homesite on the island's west side. The preserve is accessible sunrise–sunset.

Named for a 19th-century local woman dubbed "The Witch of Wall Street" for her financial wizardry, **Witch Island Preserve** is owned by Maine Audubon. The wooded, 19-acre island has two beaches, a perimeter trail, and the ruins of the "witch's" house. A quarter of a mile offshore, it's accessible by canoe or kayak from the South Bristol town landing,

just to the right after the swing bridge over The Gut. Put in, paddle under the swing bridge, and go north to the island.

## ENTERTAINMENT

Two struggling arts centers provide year-round concerts, plays, workshops, classes, and exhibits. **River Arts** (Business Rte. 1, P.O. Box 1316, Damariscotta 04543, 207/563-1507, www.riverartsme.org), previously Round Top Center for the Arts, is on 15 riverside acres, with performances held in the Darrows Barn. The neoclassic **Waldo Theatre** (916 Main St., P.O. Box 587, Waldoboro 04572, 207/832-6060, www.waldotheatre.org) was built as a cinema in 1936. Restored in the mid-1980s, it now operates as a nonprofit organization, presenting first-rate concerts, plays, films, lectures, and other year-round community events.

**Lincoln County Community Theater** (Theater St., Damariscotta, 207/563-3424, www.lcct.org) owns and operates the historic Lincoln Theater, dating from 1867. It also presents musicals and dramas, concerts, films, and more.

## FESTIVALS AND EVENTS

July brings the annual **House and Garden Tour,** a peek into some lovely private homes and gardens, and the **St. Andrew's Lawn Party and Auction,** a fun event that always draws a crowd.

The second weekend in August, **Olde Bristol Days** features a craft show, a parade, road and boat races, live entertainment, and fireworks. At Fort William Henry, in Pemaquid, it's a summer highlight on the peninsula.

In August, hundreds of diehard shoppers turn out for the annual three-day **Miles Memorial Hospital League Rummage Sale,** held under tents on Business Route 1 (close to the junction with Rte. 1) in Damariscotta.

And in October, during the **Round Pond Round About,** local galleries hold open houses and demonstrations.

## SHOPPING

Downtown Damariscotta is the region's hub, and it has a nice selection of independent shops, galleries, and boutiques. Downtown parking in summer is a major headache; the municipal lot, behind the storefronts, has a three-hour limit, and it's almost always full. You'll usually find spots on some of the side streets.

## Antiques and Antiquarian Books

Antiques shops are numerous along the Bristol Road (Rte. 130), where many barns have been turned into shops selling everything from fine antiques to old stuff. Serous antiques aficionados will find plenty to browse and buy along this stretch of road.

The multidealer **Nobleboro Antique Exchange** (104 Atlantic Hwy., Rte. 1, Nobleboro, 207/563-6800) is housed in a light blue building that goes on and on, with more than 100 display areas on three levels. The selection is diverse, from period antiques to 20th-century collectibles.

Based in a screen-fronted antique carriage house just south of Round Pond Village, **Jean Gillespie Books** (1172 Rte. 32, Round Pond, 207/529-5555) has separate rooms and alcoves, all very user friendly. Specialties are cookbooks, nautical and Maine titles, and illustrated children's books; the "Royalty" category fills six shelves.

## Art Galleries

Worth a visit for the building alone, the **Stable Gallery** (26 Water St., Damariscotta, 207/563-1991), just off Main Street, was built in the 19th-century clipper-ship era and still has original black-walnut stalls—providing a great foil for the work of dozens of Maine craftspeople. Lining the walls are paintings and prints from the gallery's large "stable" of artists.

In his **River Gallery** (Main St., Damariscotta, 207/563-6330), dealer Geoff Robinson specializes in 19th- and early-20th-century European and American fine art—a connoisseur's inventory.

Showing a high profile ever since it opened in the renovated antique fire station, **The Firehouse Gallery** (1 Bristol Rd., Damariscotta, 207/563-7299) has a tasteful, well-displayed selection of paintings, sculpture, prints,

and jewelry. The gallery mounts half a dozen shows during its season (May–Oct.).

Betcha can't leave without buying something from **Pemaquid Craft Co-op** (Rte. 130, New Harbor, 207/277-2077), with 15 rooms filled with quality works by 50 Maine artisans. There's lots of stuff to see here: iron art, woodwork, needlework, quilts, bears, candles, jewelry, and much, much more.

Contemporary art is the focus at **Gallery 170** (170 Main St., Damariscotta, 207/563-5098), housed in a lovely 1803 downtown building and displaying works by artists both local and afar in rotating shows.

If you are especially interested in arts and crafts, make Round Pond part of your itinerary. The small village is home to about a dozen galleries and studios, many within walking distance of one another.

A delightful little off-the-beaten-path find is **Tidemark Gallery** (902 Main St., Waldoboro, 207/832-5109), showing fine arts and crafts from local artists.

Head south from Waldoboro down the Friendship Peninsula to find **Old Point Comfort** (28 Pitcher Rd./Rte. 220 S, Waldoboro, 207/832-8188), the gallery and showroom where weaver Sara Hotchkiss displays her tapestry-woven carpets.

## Specialty and Eclectic Shops

The Pemaquid Peninsula is fertile ground for crafts and gifts, and many of the shop locations provide opportunities for exploring off the beaten path.

The inventory at the **Maine Coast Book Shop and Café** (158 Main St., 207/563-3207) always seems to anticipate customers' wishes, so you're unlikely to walk out empty-handed. You'll find a superb children's section, large magazine selection, helpful staff, and always something tempting in the café.

Just off Main Street (turn at Reny's) is **Weatherbird** (72 Courtyard St., Damariscotta, 207/563-8993), a terrifically eclectic shop with an inventory that defies description. Housewares, wines, toys, cards, gourmet specialties, and intriguing women's clothing are all part of the mix. Above it is **Tin Fish Etc.** (207/563-8204). Dana Moses's shop features brilliantly hand-painted tin *objets* made from recycled roofing metal. She also accepts commissions.

All sorts of finds fill the **Walpole Barn** (Rte. 129, Walpole, 207/563-7050, www.walpolebarn.com), Warren and Deb Storch's retirement fun. Browse home and garden products, whimsies, gourmet foods, even wines. Baked goods, tea, and other fare are sometimes available.

Down the peninsula, there's no question that the **Granite Hall Store** (9 Backshore Rd., off Rte. 32, Round Pond, 207/529-5864), is unique. Eric and Sarah Herndon's eclectic inventory is tough to describe but always fascinating. The first floor of this mid-19th-century emporium carries pottery, CDs, paper dolls, fudge, baskets, even catnip mice and cookie cutters. The "penny" candy, ice cream, and the old-fashioned peanut-roasting machine capture the kids. Upstairs, their parents usually succumb to books, antiques, and stunning handwoven Scottish and Irish woolens. Adding to the flavor are old ship models, hardwood floors, and a ship's bell that tolls the time. The shop is in "downtown" Round Pond, 11 miles south of Route 1.

Bells reminiscent of lighthouses, buoys, and even wilderness sounds are crafted by **North Country Wind Bells** (544 Rte. 32, Chamberlain, 207/677-2224).

A well-chosen selection of silver jewelry fills **Purple Cactus** (107 Huddle Rd., New Harbor, 207/677-2262), Elizabeth Gamage's seasonal shop on the road to Colonial Pemaquid.

Puzzle fans come from all over the country to shop at **I'm Puzzled** (246 Lower Cross Rd., Nobleboro, 207/563-5719), on the inland side of Route 1, stocked with nearly 2,000 jigsaw puzzles.

### Reny's

Whatever you do, don't leave downtown Damariscotta without visiting Reny's (207/563-5757 or 207/563-3011), with stores on each side of Main Street; one sells clothing, the other ev-erything else. This is Reny's hometown, so the selection is huge in both. If you can recognize the edges of cut-out labels, you'll find clothes from major retailers at very discounted prices. Stock up on housewares, munchies, puzzles, shoes, and whatever else floats your boat; the prices can't be beat.

## ACCOMMODATIONS
### Inns

Along a scenic side road and overlooking the Damariscotta River is **The Newcastle Inn** (River Rd., Newcastle, 207/563-5685 or 800/832-8669, www.newcastleinn.com, $175–255), an 1860s sea captain's home. Ideal for a romantic getaway, the lovely hostelry (main inn and carriage house) has 15 elegant guest rooms and suites (all with air-conditioning, some with fireplaces and whirlpool tubs), riverfront gardens, and an upscale country-inn ambience. Special packages are available off-season. Rates include a full breakfast. The inn's restaurant, **Lupines,** is open to the public by reservation. Guests gather for hors d'oeuvres at 6 P.M. Tuesday–Saturday and then move to the dining room for the four-course, fixed-price meal ($46).

Within easy walking distance of Pemaquid Light and 16 miles south of Route 1, **The Bradley Inn** (3063 Bristol Rd./Rte. 130, New Harbor, 207/677-2105 or 800/942-5560, www.bradleyinn.com, $165–325) is a beautifully restored, late-19th-century three-story building with rooms and a suite (with full kitchen and fireplace) in the inn and carriage house, a separate cottage, a spa, and lovely gardens—a great location for a quiet weekend getaway. The inn's restaurant, overlooking the gardens and open to the public, has an ambitious and pricey menu (entrées $25–32). Don't miss the granite bar in the adjoining pub. Room rates include full breakfast and afternoon tea.

Almost on top of Pemaquid Light is the rambling **Hotel Pemaquid** (3098 Bristol Rd., Rte. 130, New Harbor, 207/677-2312, www.hotelpemaquid.com, $85–155). Seventeen miles south of Route 1 but just 450 feet from the lighthouse (you can't see it from the inn, but you sure can hear the foghorn!), the hotel has been welcoming guests since 1900; it's fun to peruse the old guest registers. Hang out in the large, comfortable parlor or the wraparound veranda. The owners have gently renovated the property, updating and improving everything without losing the Victorian charm of an old seaside hotel. The inn building has rooms with private and shared baths and suites. Other buildings have motel-style units with private bath. Apartments in the annex rent for $140–200. A beautiful second-floor suite in the carriage house, with full kitchen and deck, is $200–240 per night or $1,200–1,500 per week. For the Victorian flavor of the place, request an inn room or suite. No restaurant, but The Bradley Inn and The Sea Gull Shop are nearby. No credit cards. It's open mid-May–mid-October.

Up the eastern side of the peninsula, in the middle of New Harbor, **The Gosnold Arms** (146 Rte. 32, New Harbor, 207/677-3727, off-season 561/575-9549, www.gosnold.com, $105–290) has been here since 1925 and remains deliberately old-fashioned, with pine-paneled rooms and a country-cottage common room. Customers return year after year. The family-owned operation includes the inn building and eight other buildings (with 14 units), so there's variety in layout, location, and decor. Many of the rooms include water views, but the loudspeaker at the lobster wharf across the street (Shaw's) can preclude an afternoon nap in front rooms. Rates include breakfast. It's open mid-May–mid-October.

## Bed-and-Breakfasts

A lovely water-view living room with piano and harp sets the tone for **The Harbor View Inn** (Business Rte. 1, P.O. Box 791, Newcastle 04553, 207/563-2900, www.theharborview.com, $145–210 d). Another selling point is the huge deck overlooking the twin towns and the river. Joe McEntee's family antiques fill the three beautifully decorated first- and second-floor suites. All rooms have phones, Wi-Fi, TV, comfortable chairs; two have fire-

places. Breakfast is a four-course extravaganza in the formal dining room with a printed menu, thanks to one of Joe's former careers as an executive chef (he was also a publishing executive). It's open all year.

Martha Scudder provides a warm welcome for her guests at **Oak Gables Bed and Breakfast** (Pleasant St., P.O. Box 276, Damariscotta 04543, 207/563-1476 or 800/335-7748, www.oakgablesbb.com, $95). At the end of a pretty lane, this 13-acre hilltop estate overlooks the Damariscotta River. Despite a rather imposing setting, everything's homey, informal, and hospitable. Four second-floor rooms, which can be joined in pairs, share a bath; a guest wing ($875 d) has a full kitchen, private bath, and separate entrance. The heated swimming pool is a huge plus, as is the boathouse deck, on the river. Guests can harvest blackberries from scads of bushes. Also on the grounds are a three-bedroom cottage ($1,200/week), a river-view studio apartment ($875/week), and a one-bedroom apartment ($980/week), usually booked up well ahead. It's open all year.

Wake up with a dip, after a restful sleep at the ◖ **Mill Pond Inn** (50 Main St., Rte. 215, Damariscotta Mills, Nobleboro, 207/563-8014, www.millpondinn.com, $130). The 1780 Colonial was restored and converted into an inn in 1986 by delightful owners Bobby and Sherry Whear. After a full breakfast, snooze in a hammock, watch for eagles and great blue herons, pedal a bicycle into nearby Damariscotta, or canoe the pond, which connects to 14-mile-long Damariscotta Lake. Bobby, a Registered Maine Guide, offers fishing trips and scenic tours of the lake in his restored, antique Lyman lapstrake (clinker-built) boat. Use of bicycles and canoe is free to guests. The inn is just a five-minute drive from downtown Damariscotta, but a world away. No credit cards.

The mansard-roofed **Inn at Round Pond** (1442 Rte. 32, Round Pond, 207/529-2004, www.theinnatroundpond.com, $150–190) commands a sea captain's view of the harbor as it presides over the pretty village of Round Pond. It's an easy walk to a waterfront restaurant, two dueling lobster pounds, an old-timey country store, and a handful of galleries and shops. Bay Sail boat rentals is next door. Each of three good-size rooms has harbor views and sitting areas. A full breakfast is included. It's open all year.

You can walk to Christmas Cove from **Sunset Bed and Breakfast** (16 Sunset Loop, P.O. Box 91, South Bristol 04568, 207/644-8849, www.sunsetbnb.com). Kay and Dick Miller have two small rooms, one with full bed, the other with twins, sharing one bath in their modest Cape-style house with to-die-for views. Various rates are available, from one room with private bath ($120) to a family of four ($160). Rates include a hearty continental breakfast. Bring a kayak and launch it here. It's open May–October.

About three miles south of town is **Blue Skye Farm** (1708 Friendship Rd., Waldoboro, 207/832-0300, www.blueskye-farm.com), Jan and Peter Davidson's B&B in a gorgeous 18th-century farmhouse, set amid 100 acres, with trails, gardens, and lawns. Original wall stencils by Moses Eaton decorate the entry. Breakfast is provided, and guests have full use of the country kitchen, so you can prepare other meals. Other common roams include the dining room, screened-in sun room, and a sitting room, with fireplace, that's stocked with games. Five rooms, three with private baths, are meticulously decorated. Rates range $105–145.

Just up the hill from the Waldo Theatre, hospitable Libby Hopkins has been running the **Broad Bay Inn and Gallery** (1014 Main St., P.O. Box 607, Waldoboro 04572, 207/832-6668 or 800/736-6769, www.broad-bayinn.com, $75–110) since 1984, and she's an energetic breakfast chef (she attended Le Cordon Bleu cooking school in Paris). Four antiques-filled rooms share three baths. Rates include afternoon tea or sherry. Guests can play the piano, browse through the huge art-book collection, or watch old films. The barn gallery—stocked with watercolors and some crafts—is open in July and August, when Libby also organizes art workshops run by professional teachers. It's open May–mid-October.

## Motels and Cottage Colonies

You'll have to plan well in advance to snag one of the rustic **Ye Olde Forte Cabins** (18 Old Fort Rd., Pemaquid Beach, 207/677-2261, www.yeoldefortecabins.com, $80–126 per day, $410–595 per week). These simple cabins have edged a grassy lawn dropping to John's Bay since 1922. Each has at least a toilet and sink, but a shower house and a well-equipped cookhouse are part of the colony. Although guests are expected to clean up after themselves when using the kitchen, manager Julie Powell keeps the place spotless. No frills, unless you count the private small beach. It's a great place to bring a kayak. The cabins are less than 25 yards from Colonial Pemaquid and Fort William Henry. No credit cards.

Tony and Sally Capodilupo have restored four 19th- and 20th-century houses on a 22-acre hilltop, just steps from the village and overlooking the harbor, adding 21st-century amenities while retaining the original village appeal. **The Moorings** (P.O. Box 37, New Harbor 04554, 207/677-2409 summer, 617/731-4264 winter, www.themooringsnew-harbor.com) comprises seven well-equipped weekly rental apartments, all with gas fireplace, TV/DVD, and heat, along with an indoor pool, tennis court, hot tub, laundry, cookout area, and billiards room. All sleep two and are restricted to adults. In-season rates begin at $1,200/week.

Just down the road, Dan Thompson is the third-generation innkeeper at **The Thompson House and Cottages** (95 South Side Rd., New Harbor, 207/677-2317, www.thompson-cottages.net, $400–1,650/week), a low-key, old-timey complex of mostly waterfront rooms, apartments, and cottages split among two minipeninsulas. Most have fireplaces. Row-boats are available, and there's a library with games, books, and puzzles.

Now here's a bargain. Up a long winding driveway behind Moody's Diner is **Moody's Motel** (Rte. 1, Waldoboro, 207/832-5362, www.moodysdiner.com, $44–52), in biz since 1927, and likely little has changed in the meantime. Nothing fancy here, but it's clean and well run. The motel and tourist cabins all have screened porches and TV, and a few have kitchenettes. It's open mid-May–mid-October.

## Campgrounds
The area's best-run campground is 150-acre **Lake Pemaquid Camping** (off Biscay Rd., P.O. Box 967, Damariscotta 04543, 207/563-5202, www.lakepemaquid.com, $30–44), with 280 tent and RV sites, many right on the seven-mile-long lake. It's a lively operation, with tennis, pool and lake swimming, fishing (licenses available), playground, game room, store (lobsters available), snack room, laundry, sauna, whirlpool tub, and canoe, kayak, and boat rentals. There's also plenty of entertainment, including train and hay rides, dances, movies, and performances. Rustic cabins and cottages, with full baths, are $525–1,000 per week. The campground is open Memorial Day weekend–Columbus Day.

A favorite with kayakers is **Sherwood Forest Camping** (Pemaquid Trail, P.O. Box 189, New Harbor 04554, 800/274-1593, www.sherwoodforestcampsite.com, $29–35). Facilities include a playground, sundeck, and pool, but the campground is just 800 feet from Pemaquid Beach.

## FOOD
### Local Flavors
**Damariscotta:** For breakfast, look no farther than **The Breakfast Place and Bakery** (Business Rte. 1, Main St., Damariscotta, 207/563-5434, 7 A.M.–1 P.M. daily), a small place that turns out big breakfasts. Homemade breads, muffins, and biscuits, eggs, omelettes, pancakes, waffles, and more are all reasonably priced, most $4–6. A few specials, such as crabcakes and eggs or shimp creole omelette are closer to $8.

For baked goods, sandwiches, soups, and gourmet goodies to go, head to **Weatherbird** (1168 Elm St., Damariscotta, 207/563-8993, 8 A.M.–5:30 P.M. Mon.–Sat.). Eat at one of the handful of tables out front or take it to the waterfront.

Just off Main Street, in the alley below

Sheepscot River Pottery, is **Paco's Tacos** (207/563-535, 11 A.M.–8 P.M. Mon.–Sat., to 9 P.M. Fri.), a hole in the wall where you order at the counter and then grab one of the few tables or take your meal to the waterfront. It serves Tex-Mex-style tacos, burritos, chimichangas, and fajitas, with most choices less than $7. Enchiladas are the specialty on Fridays.

In a barn-style building at the northern edge of Damariscotta is the area's best homemade ice cream—about four dozen flavors, including some unusual ones you'd never dream up. **Round Top Ice Cream** (Business Rte. 1, Damariscotta, 207/563-5307) has been in business since 1924.

For pizza, subs, and pasta, the choice is **Romeo's Pizza** (Business Rte. 1, Damariscotta, 207/563-1563, 11 A.M.–9 P.M. daily). The gourmet pizzas are superb (try the Aegean). Dinners and pasta dishes, served with garlic bread and small tossed salad, are a steal at less than $10.

**Rising Tide Natural Foods Market** (Business Rte. 1, Damariscotta, 207/563-5556) has been a thriving co-op organization since 1978, and it keeps on growing. Bulk items are available, plus books, cosmetics, and all kinds of preservative-free organic food. A self-service deli section has soups, sandwiches, salads, and entrées; you may be lucky enough to snag one of the handful of tables in the dining area. At the northern end of town, the market is open 8 A.M.–7 P.M. Monday–Saturday all year.

The **Damariscotta Area Farmers Market** sets up 9 A.M.–noon on Friday mid-May–October at Salt Bay Heritage Center, on Belvedere Road, just off Route 1, Damariscotta. Condiments, baked goods, cheeses, local shellfish, and crafts are always available from about two dozen vendors, and you never know what else will turn up at this major market. A smaller market operates in the same location 9 A.M.–noon Monday late June–August.

**Down the Peninsula:** Great coffee and good home-style breakfasts and lunches are served at the retro **Bristol Diner** (1267 Bristol Rd., Bristol, 207/563-8000, 6 A.M.–2 P.M. Tues.–Sat., 7 A.M.–1 P.M. Sun.), which promises—and delivers—"Good grub, bub."

Homemade ice cream, delicious baked goods, prepared dishes, and sandwiches to go are just a few of the reasons to stop by the seasonal **Island Grocery** (12 West Side Rd., 207/644-8552, www.islandgrocery.net). It also has breads, cheese, and all kinds of gourmet goodies—stock up for a picnic. To find it, take the first right after the swinging bridge.

Just around the corner from Colonial Pemaquid, **The Cupboard Cafe** (137 Huddle Rd., New Harbor, 207/677-3911, 8 A.M.–7 P.M. Tues.–Fri., to 3 P.M. Sat., to noon Sun.) is a homey cottage serving fresh-baked goods, breakfasts, and a nice choice of fresh salads, burgers, sandwiches, and specials.

**Waldoboro:** At the corner of Routes 1 and 220, opposite Moody's Diner, is the warehousey building that turns out superb **Borealis Breads** (1860 Atlantic Hwy., Rte. 1, Waldoboro, 207/832-0655). Using sourdough starters (and no oils, sweeteners, eggs, or dairy products), owner Jim Amaral and his crew produce baguettes, olive bread, lemon fig bread, rosemary focaccia, and about a dozen other inventive flavors (each day has its specialties). A refrigerated case holds a small selection of picnic fixings (sandwich spreads, juices). Great soups and salads, and excellent sandwiches are available to go. It's open 8:30 A.M.–5:30 P.M. Monday–Friday, 9 A.M.–4:30 P.M. Saturday and Sunday.

The **Waldoboro 5&10** (Friendship St., Waldoboro, 207/832-4624, 8 A.M.–5 P.M. Mon.–Sat.) is one of those old-fashioned, little-of-everything variety stores that disappeared ages ago. Inside are antiques, penny candy, and a deli serving excellent sandwiches and Round Top ice cream. It's a one-man operation, so service can be slow at peak times.

Pick up sandwiches, salads, and gourmet picnic fixings at **McKeen and Charles** (1587 Rte. 1, Waldoboro, 832-2221, 10 A.M.–6 P.M. Mon.–Sat., www.mckeanandcharles.com), and while you're there, ask about any scheduled wine tastings. The store also sells about 300 different beers.

Each fall, around mid-September, a tiny, cryptic display ad appears in local newspapers: "Kraut's Ready." Savvy readers recognize this as the announcement of the latest batch of ❨ **Morse's sauerkraut**—an annual ritual since 1918. The homemade kraut is available in stores and by mail order, but it's more fun (and cheaper) to visit the shop, the **Kraut House** (3856 Washington Rd., Rte. 220, Waldoboro, 207/832-5569 or 800/486-1605, www.morses-sauerkraut.com, 9 A.M.–6 P.M. Thurs.–Tues.), which also has a small café (8 A.M.–4 P.M.) serving traditional German fare. Sandwiches, such as a classic Reuben, liverwurst, or Black Forest ham are $6; homemade pierogies are $5, a sausage plate is $7, and stuffed cabbage rolls are $8. Big serve-yourself jars of Morse's pickles are on the tables. The red-painted farm store also carries Aunt Lydia's Beet Relish, baked beans, mustard, maple syrup, and other Maine foods as well as a mind-boggling selection of hard-to-find and unusual northern European specialties. It's eight miles north of Route 1.

Truck drivers, tourists, locals, and notables have been flocking to **Moody's Diner** (Rtes. 1 and 220, Waldoboro, 207/832-7785, www.moodysdiner.com, 4:30 A.M.–11 P.M. Mon.–Fri., 5 A.M.–11 P.M. Sat., 6 A.M.–11 P.M. Sun.) since the early 1930s, when the Moody family established this classic diner on a Waldoboro hilltop. The antique neon sign has long been a Route 1 beacon, especially on a foggy night, and the crowds continue, with new generations of Moodys and considerable expansion of the premises. It's gone beyond diner-dom. Expect hearty, no-frills fare and such calorific desserts as peanut-butter or walnut pie. After eating, you can buy the cookbook.

An even more humble alternative to Moody's is **Deb's Diner** (1495 Rte. 1, Waldoboro, 207/832-6144. 6 A.M.–2:30 P.M. Mon.–Sat., 7–11 A.M. Sun.), a tiny spot where the portions are big and the prices are very low. You can easily get out of here for less than $5.

## Casual Dining

A reliable standby in downtown Damariscotta, next to the Damariscotta Bank and Trust, the **Salt Bay Café** (Main St., Damariscotta, 207/563-1666, 7:30 A.M.–9:30 P.M.

Mon.–Sat., 8 A.M.–9 P.M. Sun.) has a loyal following—thanks to its imaginative, reasonably priced cuisine and cheerful, plant-filled setting. Vegetarians have their own menu, with two dozen–plus choices. Dinner entrées are $11–19; hearty lunch sandwiches run $6–8. It has a liquor license too.

An open kitchen and carefully prepared foods with an emphasis on ultrafresh seafood make **Damariscotta River Grill** (155 Main St., Damariscotta, 207/563-2992, 11 A.M.–8 P.M., to 9 P.M. Fri.–Sat., 9 A.M.–2:30 P.M. Sun.) a reliable favorite, with most entrées $14–24. The artichoke fondue is worth fighting over. Choose a table in the back with a river view, if available.

Pair fresh fish with a choice of sides and toppings, such as blue cheese merlot sauce or mango pepper relish, at **74 Maine Bistro** (74 Main St., Damariscotta, 207/563-7444, www.74maine.com, 5–9 P.M. Tues.–Sat., $16–26), just off Main Street. Other possibilities include steaks, ribs, and pastas.

One of the best meal deals in the area is Rick and Jean Kerrigan's **Anchor Inn** (Harbor Rd., Round Pond, 207/529-5584, 11 A.M.–9:30 P.M. daily mid-May–mid-Oct.), tucked away on the picturesque harbor in Round Pond, on the eastern side of the peninsula. Informal and rustic, with a menu that'll surprise you (entrées $14–25), the place always attracts a crowd. Reservations are advisable on summer weekends. After Labor Day, the schedule can be a bit erratic; call to confirm. It's a sister property to the Damariscotta River Grill.

The view's even better at **Coveside Restaurant** (105 Coveside Rd., Christmas Cove, South Bristol, 207/644-8282, www.coveside restaurant.com, 11 A.M.–9 P.M. daily, $10–28), based at a marina on Rutherford Island, just off the end of the South Bristol peninsula. It's open for lunch and dinner as well as light meals. Grab a seat on the deck and watch a steady stream of boaters and summer vacationers during the cruising season.

New owners at **The Samoset** (Rte. 130, New Harbor, 207/677-2788) have given the family standby a long-overdue freshening and livened up the menu of standards with a bit o' Southern flavor, including Cajun seasonings and a gumbo. They plan to keep it open year-round.

Location, location. Right next to Pemaquid Light is **The Sea Gull Shop** (3119 Bristol Rd., Pemaquid Point, 207/677-2374, 7:30 A.M.–7:30 P.M. daily mid-May–mid-Oct.), an oceanfront place with touristy prices, but decent food—pancakes and muffins, for instance, overflowing with blueberries.

## 🦞 Lobster in the Rough

The Pemaquid Peninsula must have more eat-on-the-dock places per capita than anyplace in Maine. Some are basic, no-frills operations, others are big-time commercial concerns. Each has a loyal following.

The biggest and best-known lobster wharf is **Shaw's Fish and Lobster Wharf** (Rte. 32, New Harbor, 207/677-2200 or 800/772-2209, 11 A.M.–9 P.M. daily), where you place your order, take a number, and wait for it to come booming back at you over the loudspeaker. (You can also order steak here. And margaritas. And oysters at the wharf raw bar.) Fried seafood dinners run $8–17. It's open mid-May–mid-October, closing one hour earlier midweek off-season.

Facing each other across the dock in the hamlet of Round Pond are the 🦞 **Round Pond Lobster Co-Op** (207/529-5725) and **Muscongus Bay Lobster** (207/529-5528). Both are good, and competition keeps prices low. Muscongus has enlarged in recent years, so it has a larger menu and covered seating, but tiny Round Pond Lobster keeps it simple and oh-so-fresh. Both usually open around 10 A.M. daily for lunch and dinner and close around sunset.

Other seasonal lobster wharves salting the peninsula are the **New Harbor Co-Op** (Rte. 32, New Harbor, 207/677-2791), **Pemaquid Fishermen's Co-Op** (Pemaquid Harbor Rd., Pemaquid Harbor, 207/677-2801), **South Bristol Fishermen's Co-op** (South Bristol, 207/644-8224), and **Broad Cove Marine Services** (off Rte. 32, Medomak, 207/529-5186), a low-key sleeper with a wowser view.

MID-COAST REGION

## INFORMATION AND SERVICES

The Damariscotta Region Chamber of Commerce (P.O. Box 13, Damariscotta 04543, 207/563-8340, www.damariscottaregion.com) publishes a free annual information booklet about the area. Its office, just off Main Street, is open 9 A.M.–5 P.M. weekdays. The Pemaquid Area Association (Chamberlain, no telephone) produces a very useful annotated map covering the lower half of the Pemaquid Peninsula. Both publications are available by mail and at the information bureaus. Also ask for a copy of *The Upper River Region Field Guide,* a foldout map/brochure produced by the Damariscotta River Association and containing excellent information about the area's preserves and natural history.

Skidompha Library (Main St., Damariscotta, 207/563-5513, www.skidompha.org) also operates a used-book shop. (Incidentally, if you're puzzled by the name, it comes from the names of the members of a local literary society who founded the library at the turn of the 20th century.) Or check out Waldoboro Public Library (Main St., Waldoboro, 207/832-4484, www.waldoborolibrary.org).

# PENOBSCOT BAY

Although considered part of the Mid-Coast, the region edging Penobscot Bay has a different feel and view. Coastal mountains in Camden and Lincolnville and an abundance of islands frame the view. These island-studded waters are renowned by sailors, so it's no surprise that Maine's famed windjammer fleet is based here.

From Thomaston through Searsport, no two towns are alike except that all are changing, as traditional industries give way to arts- and tourism-related businesses. Thomaston's Museum in the Streets, Rockland's art galleries, Camden's picturesque mountainside harbor, Lincolnville's pocket beach, Belfast's inviting downtown, Searsport's sea captains' homes, and Prospect's Fort Knox all invite exploration, as do offshore islands. From Port Clyde, take the ferry to Monhegan, an offshore idyll

known as the Artists' Island. From Rockland and Lincolnville Beach, car and passenger ferries head to Vinalhaven, North Haven, Matinicus, and Islesboro. All are occupied year-round by hardy souls and joined in summer by less-hardy ones. Except for Matinicus, they're great day-trip destinations. If what appeals to you about a ferry trip is traveling on the water, you can get a taste of the great age of sail by booking a three- or six-day cruise on one of the classic windjammer schooners berthed in Rockland, Rockport, and Camden (see the sidebar *Windjamming*). Or simply book a day sail or sea-kayak excursion.

## PLANNING YOUR TIME

To hit just the highlights, you'll need at least four days. If you want to relax a bit and enjoy

© TOM NANGLE

# HIGHLIGHTS

**Monhegan Museum:** View an impressive collection of masters at this museum adjacent to the lighthouse, then visit contemporary studios and find their inspiration by hiking island trails (page 205).

**The Farnsworth Art Museum and the Wyeth Center:** Three generations of Wyeths are represented in this recently expanded museum, which also boasts an excellent collection of works by Maine and American masters (page 209).

**Owls Head Transportation Museum:** View a fabulous collection of vintage airplanes, automobiles, and even bicycles, many of which are flown, driven, or ridden during weekend special events (page 211).

**Rockland Breakwater:** Take a walk on this nearly mile-long breakwater to the lighthouse at the end (open on weekends). It's an especially fine place to watch the windjammers sail in or out of Rockland Harbor (page 212).

**Owls Head Light State Park:** The views of Penobscot Bay are spectacular, and it's a great place for a picnic lunch (page 212).

**Camden Hills State Park:** If you have time, hike the moderate trail to the summit for a gull's-eye view over Camden Harbor and Penobscot Bay. If not, take the easy route and drive (page 229).

**Penobscot Marine Museum:** Learn what life was *really* like during the Great Age of Sail in a town renowned for the number and quality of its sea captains (page 251).

**BlueJacket Shipcrafters:** Even if you have no inclination whatsoever toward building a model ship, stop by and view some of the museum-quality models built at the oldest model company in the country (page 251).

LOOK FOR **(** TO FIND RECOMMENDED SIGHTS, ACTIVITIES, DINING, AND LODGING.

**Fort Knox:** A good restoration, frequent events, and secret passages to explore make this late-19th-century fort one of Maine's best (page 252).

**Penobscot Narrows Bridge and Observatory:** On a clear day, the views from the 420-foot-high tower, one of only three in the world, extend from Mt. Katahdin to Cadillac Mountain (page 253).

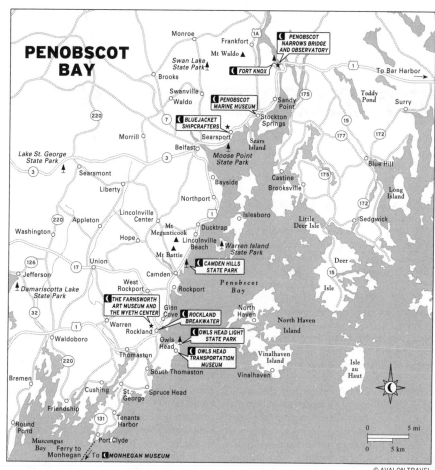

# PENOBSCOT BAY

Monroe
Frankfort
Mt Waldo ▲
**( PENOBSCOT NARROWS BRIDGE AND OBSERVATORY**
**( FORT KNOX**
Swan Lake State Park ▲
Brooks
To Bar Harbor
Swanville
Waldo
**( PENOBSCOT MARINE MUSEUM**
Sandy Point
Toddy Pond
Surry
Morrill
**( BLUEJACKET SHIPCRAFTERS** ★
Stockton Springs
Belfast
Searsport
Sears Island
Lake St. George State Park ▲
Searsmont
Moose Point State Park ▲
Blue Hill
Liberty
Bayside
Castine
Brooksville
Long Island
Northport
Appleton
Lincolnville Center
Islesboro
Little Deer Isle
Sedgwick
Washington
Hope
Mt Megunticook ▲
Ducktrap
Lincolnville Beach
Warren Island State Park ▲
Deer Isle
Mt Battie ▲
**( CAMDEN HILLS STATE PARK**
Penobscot Bay
Jefferson
Union
West Rockport
Camden
Rockport
**( THE FARNSWORTH ART MUSEUM AND THE WYETH CENTER**
Damariscotta Lake State Park ▲
Warren
Glen Cove
**( ROCKLAND BREAKWATER**
North Haven
North Haven Island
Waldoboro
Rockland
**( OWLS HEAD LIGHT STATE PARK**
Owls Head
**( OWLS HEAD TRANSPORTATION MUSEUM**
Thomaston
Vinalhaven Island
Isle au Haut
Bremen
South Thomaston
Vinalhaven
Cushing
St. George
Spruce Head
Friendship
Round Pond
Tenants Harbor
Muscongus Bay
Port Clyde
Ferry to Monhegan
To **( MONHEGAN MUSEUM**

0    5 mi
0    5 km

the area, plan on 4–5 days. Make it a full week, if you plan on overnighting on any of the offshore islands. In general, lodging is less expensive in Rockland, Belfast, and Searsport than it is in Camden. In any case, head for Monhegan or Vinalhaven on a good day and save the museums for inclement ones.

Two-lane Route 1 is the region's central artery, with veins running down the peninsula limbs. Yes, traffic backs up, especially in Camden (and in Thomaston on the Fourth of July, when it's closed for a parade), but it rarely stops moving. If your destination is Rockland, take I-95 to Augusta and then Route 17 East; if it's Belfast or north, take I-95 to Augusta and then Route 3 East. Route 90 is a nifty bypass around Thomaston and Rockland, connecting Route 1 from Warren to Rockport. For moseyers, the **Georges River Scenic Byway** is a 50-mile rural, inland route, mostly along Route 131, between Port Clyde and Liberty. It parallels the coast, but it meanders through farmlands and tiny villages, and by lakes and rivers, with antiques shops and farm stands along the way. It's simply gorgeous in autumn.

In July and August, try to avoid arriving in this region without a reservation. Helpful chamber of commerce staffers in prime locations often can work last-minute miracles, but special events and festivals can fill up all the beds for miles around.

# Thomaston Area

Thomaston is a little gem of a town, and getting more so each year thanks to the razing of the old Maine State Prison. It's also the gateway to two lovely fingers of land bordering the St. George River and jutting into the Gulf of Maine—the Cushing and St. George Peninsulas.

In 1605, British adventurer Captain George Waymouth sailed up the river now named after him (it was originally called the Georges River). A way station for Plymouth traders as early as 1630, Thomaston was incorporated in 1777 and officially named after General John Thomas, a Revolutionary War hero.

Industry began with the production of lime, which was used for plaster. A growing demand for plaster, and the frequency with which the wooden boats were destroyed by fire while carrying loads of extremely flammable lime, spurred the growth of shipbuilding and all its related infrastructure. Thomaston's slogan became "the town that went to sea."

Seeing the sleepy harborfront today, it's hard to visualize the booming era when dozens of tall-masted wooden ships slid down the ways. But the town's architecture is a testament and tribute to the prosperous past—all those splendid homes on Main and Knox Streets were funded by wealthy shipowners and shipmasters who well understood how to occupy the idle hands of off-duty carpenters.

If you're in the area in December, you're in for a treat: Thomaston's holiday decorations are stunning. All over town, but especially in the Historic District, huge wreaths, tiny white lights, and (usually) a blanket of snow create a scene lifted right out of a Currier and Ives print.

## SIGHTS AND RECREATION
### Montpelier

As you head out of Thomaston on Route 1, toward Rockland, you'll come face to face with an imposing colonial hilltop mansion at the junction with Route 131 South. (Behind it, unfortunately, is the rather ugly outline of a huge cement plant.) Dedicated to the memory of General Henry Knox, President George Washington's secretary of war, Montpelier (Rtes. 1 and 131, P.O. Box 326, Thomaston 04861, 207/354-8062, www.generalknoxmuseum.org) is a 1930s replica of Knox's original Thomaston home. The mansion today contains Knox family furnishings and other period antiques—all described with great enthusiasm during the hour-long tours, beginning on the hour and half hour. A gift shop run by the Friends of Montpelier carries books and other relevant items. Concerts, lectures, and special events occur here periodically throughout the summer; General Knox's birthday is celebrated with considerable fanfare in July. It offers tours on the half hour 10 A.M.–3 P.M. Tuesday–Saturday July and August, on the hour June, September, and October. Admission is $6 adults, $5 seniors, $3 kids 5–13, or $15 per family.

### Museum in the Streets

Montpelier is the starting point for a walking, cycling, or, if you must, driving tour (about three miles) of nearly 70 sites in Thomaston's National Historic District. Pick up a copy of the tour brochure at one of the local businesses. Included are lots of stories behind the facades of the handsome 19th-century homes that line Main and Knox Streets; the architecture here is nothing short of spectacular. Much of this history is also recounted in The Museum in the Streets, a walking tour taking in 25 informative plaques illustrated with old photos throughout town.

## EVENTS

Thomaston's **Fourth of July,** an old-fashioned hometown celebration reminiscent of a Norman Rockwell painting, draws huge crowds. A spiffy parade—with bands, veterans, kids, and pets—starts off the morning (11 A.M.), followed by races, craft and food booths, and lots more. If you need to get *through* Thomaston on the Fourth of July, do it well before the parade or well after noon; the marchers go right down Main Street (Rte. 1), and gridlock forces a detour.

## SHOPPING

Thomaston has a block-long shopping street (on Rte. 1), with ample free parking out back behind the stores.

If you arrive at Marti Reed's **Personal Book Shop** (78 Main St., Thomaston, 207/354-8058) at the right time, you're likely to run into local writers' groups that gather frequently to swap tips and gossip. That's just the kind of place this is—an independent bookstore with a warm, nurturing feel. Not to mention a dog in residence. Lots of unusual titles, too—you won't leave empty-handed. Just give Marti an idea of the type of books you enjoy, and she's bound to steer you toward winners. It's all part of her personal service. She also has a 100 percent success record, to date, for finding out-of-print books.

The **Maine State Prison Showroom Outlet** (Main St./Rte. 1, corner of Wadsworth St., Thomaston, 207/354-3131) markets the handiwork of inmate craftsmen. Some of the souvenirs verge on kitsch; the bargains are wooden bar stools, toys (including dollhouses), and chopping boards. You'll need to carry your purchases with you; prison-made goods cannot be shipped.

High-end 17th- and 18th-century American furniture and accessories are the stock-in-trade of **David C. Morey American Antiques** (161 Main St., 207/354-6033).

At the southern end of Thomaston, in a renovated chicken barn, is **Thomaston Place Auction Gallery** (51 Atlantic Hwy./Rte. 1,

Thomaston, 207/354-8141 or 888/834-5538, www.thomastonauction.com), the home of Kaja Veilleux, a longtime dealer, appraiser, and auctioneer. Auctions occur frequently throughout the summer (also in winter), with previews beforehand.

## CAMPING

The best campground is on the Thomaston/Cushing town line at **Saltwater Farm Campground** (Wadsworth St./Cushing Rd., Cushing, mailing address P.O. Box 165, Thomaston 04861, 207/354-6735, www.midcoast.com/~sfc), a 35-acre Good Sam park 1.5 miles south of Route 1. Thirty-seven open and wooded tent and RV sites ($30–39) overlook the St. George River. Cabins go for $60 a day. Facilities include a bathhouse, pool, hot tub, laundry facilities, store, and a play area. The river is tidal, so swimming is best near high tide; otherwise, you're dealing with mudflats. It's open mid-May–mid-October.

## FOOD

Often overlooked by visitors (but certainly not by locals) is casual **Thomaston Café and Bakery** (154 Main St./Rte. 1, Thomaston, 207/354-8589, 7 A.M.–2 P.M. Mon.–Sat., 8:30 A.M.–1:30 P.M. Sun., and Fri. and Sat. 5:30–8 P.M.). German-born chef Herb Peters and his wife, Eleanor, produce superb pastries, breads, and desserts (eat here or take out). Everything's homemade, there are children's options, the café uses only organic poultry. Try the incredible wild mushroom hash. Beer and wine only. Dinner entrées are $16–22, reservations essential.

## INFORMATION AND SERVICES

The Rockland-Thomaston Area Chamber of Commerce (Gateway Center, P.O. Box 508, Rockland 04841, 207/596-0376 or 800/562-2529, www.therealmaine.com) is open 9 A.M.–5 P.M. Monday–Friday and 10 A.M.–2 P.M. Saturday.

The Thomaston Public Library (42 Main St., Thomaston, 207/354-2453) occupies part of the Greek Revival Thomaston Academy.

**PENOBSCOT BAY**

# Cushing Peninsula

Cushing's recorded history goes back at least as far as 1605, when someone named "Abr [maybe Abraham] King"—presumably a member of explorer George Waymouth's crew—inscribed his name here on a ledge (now private property). Since 1789, settlers' saltwater farms have sustained many generations, and the active Cushing Historical Society keeps the memories and memorabilia from fading away. But the outside world knows little of this. Cushing is better known as "Wyeth country," the terrain depicted by the famous artistic dynasty of N. C., Andrew, and Jamie Wyeth (and assorted talented other relatives).

Even though several Wyeths still spend time here, you're not likely to meet any members of the family (unless you hang out near Fales's Store for days on end). However, if you're an Andrew Wyeth fan, visiting Cushing will give you the feeling of walking through his paintings. The flavor of his Maine work is here—rolling fields, wildflower meadows, rocky tidal coves, broad vistas, character-filled farmhouses, and some well-hidden summer enclaves. The only retail businesses are a general store, a few farmstands, and a seasonal take-out—plus a campground on the Cushing/Thomaston town line.

## SIGHTS

Cushing's town boundary begins 1.3 miles south of Route 1 (take Wadsworth St. at the Maine State Prison Showroom Outlet). Two miles farther, you'll pass giant wooden sculptures in the yard of the late artist **Bernard Langlais,** who died in 1977.

Six miles from Route 1 is the **A. S. Fales and Son Store** (locally, just "Fales's Store"), Cushing's heart and soul—source of fuel, film, gossip, and groceries. Built in 1889, the store has been in the Fales family ever since. Just be-

The Olson House inspired many of Andrew Wyeth's works.

PENOBSCOT BAY

© TOM NANGLE

# BEANHOLE BEANS

"To be happy in New England," wrote one Joseph P. MacCarthy at the turn of the 20th century, "you must select the Puritans for your ancestors...[and] eat beans on Saturday night." There is no better way to confirm the latter requirement than to attend a "beanhole" bean supper – a real-live legacy of colonial times, with dinner baked in a hole in the ground.

Generally scheduled, appropriately, for a Saturday night (check local newspapers), a beanhole bean supper demands plenty of preparation from its hosts – and a secret ingredient or two. (Don't even think about trying to pry the recipe out of the cooks.) The supper always includes hot dogs, cole slaw, relishes, home-baked breads, and homemade desserts, but the beans are the star attraction. (Typically, the suppers are also alcohol-free.) Not only are they feasts; they're also bargains, never setting you back more than about $8.

The beans at the Broad Cove Church's annual mid-July beanhole bean supper, served family-style at long picnic tables, are legendary – attracting nearly 200 eager diners. Minus the secrets, here's what happens:

Early Friday morning: Church volunteers load 10 pounds of dry pea and soldier (yellow-eye) beans into each of four large kettles and add water to cover. The beans are left to soak and soften for 6-7 hours. Two or three volunteers uncover the churchyard's four rock-lined beanholes (each about three feet deep), fill the holes with hardwood kindling, ignite the wood,

and keep the fires burning until late afternoon, when the wood is reduced to red-hot coals.

Early Friday afternoon: The veteran chefs parboil the beans and stir in the seasonings. Typical additions are brown sugar, molasses, mustard, salt, pepper, and salt pork (much of the secret is in the exact proportions). When the beans are precooked to the cooks' satisfaction, the kettle lids are secured with wire and the pots are lugged outdoors.

Friday midafternoon: With the beans ready to go underground, some of the hot coals are quickly shoveled out of the pits. The kettles are lowered into the pits and the coals replaced around the sides of the kettles and atop their lids. The pits are covered with heavy sheet metal and topped with a thick layer of sand and a tarpaulin. The round-the-clock baking begins, and no one peeks before it's finished.

Saturday midafternoon: Even the veterans start getting nervous just before the pits are uncovered. Was the seasoning right? Did too much water cook away? Did the beans dry out? Not to worry, though – failures just don't happen here.

Saturday night: When a pot is excavated for the first of three seatings (about 5 P.M.), the line is already long. The chefs check their handiwork and the supper begins. No one seems to mind waiting for the second and third seatings – while others eat, a sing-along gets under way in the church, keeping everyone entertained.

---

yond the store, take the left fork, continuing down the peninsula toward the Broad Cove Church and the Olson House.

## Broad Cove Church

Andrew Wyeth aficionados will recognize the Broad Cove Church as one of his subjects—alongside Cushing Road en route to the Olson House. Most days, it's open, so step inside and admire the classic New England architecture. The church is also well known as the site of one of the region's best beanhole bean suppers, held on a Saturday mid-July and attract-

ing several hundred appreciative diners. (See the sidebar *Beanhole Beans*.) Bear left at the fork after Fales's Store; the church is 0.4 mile farther, on the right.

## The Olson House

Many an art lover makes the pilgrimage to the Olson House (11 A.M.–4 P.M. daily late May–mid-Oct., $4), a famous icon near the end of Hathorn Point Road. The early-19th-century farmhouse appears in Andrew Wyeth's 1948 painting *Christina's World* (which hangs in New York's Museum of Modern

Art), his best-known image of the disabled Christina Olson, who died in 1968. In 1991, two philanthropists donated the Olson House to the Farnsworth Art Museum in Rockland (an $11 combination ticket includes Farnsworth admission), which has retained the house's sparse, lonely, and almost mystical ambience. The clapboards outside remain unpainted, the interior walls bear only a few Wyeth prints (hung close to the settings they depict), and it is easy to sense Wyeth's inspiration for chronicling this place. From Route 1 in Thomaston, at the Maine State Prison Showroom Outlet, turn onto Wadsworth Street and go six miles to Fales's Store. Take the left fork after the store, go 1.5 miles, and turn left onto Hathorn Point Road. Go another 1.9 miles to the house.

# St. George Peninsula

Even though the Cushing and St. George Peninsulas face each other across the St. George River, they differ dramatically. Cushing is far more rural, seemingly less approachable—with little access to the surrounding waters; St. George has a whole string of things to do and see, and places to sleep and eat—plus shore access in various spots along the peninsula.

The St. George Peninsula is actually better known by some of the villages scattered along its length: Tenants Harbor, Port Clyde, Wiley's Corner, Spruce Head—plus the smaller neighborhoods of Martinsville, Smalleytown, Glenmere, Long Cove, Hart's Neck, and Clark Island. Each has a distinct personality, determined partly by the different ethnic groups—primarily Brits, Swedes, and Finns—who arrived to work the granite quarries in the 19th century. Wander through the Seaview Cemetery in Tenants Harbor and you'll see the story: row after row of gravestones with names from across the sea.

A more famous former visitor was 19th-century novelist Sarah Orne Jewett, who holed up in an old schoolhouse in Martinsville, paid a weekly rental of $0.50, and wrote *The Country of the Pointed Firs,* a tale about "Dunnet's Landing" (Tenants Harbor).

Today the picturesque peninsula has saltwater farms, tidy hamlets, a striking lighthouse, spruce-edged tidal coves, an active yachting harbor, and, at the tip, a tiny fishing village (Port Clyde), which serves as the springboard to offshore Monhegan Island.

Port Clyde, in fact, may be the best-known community here. (Fortunately, it's no longer called by its unappealing 18th-century name—Herring Gut.) George Waymouth explored Port Clyde's nearby islands in 1605, but you'd never suspect its long tradition. It's a sleepy place, with a general store, an inn, a couple of galleries, and expensive parking.

## SIGHTS
### Marshall Point
### Lighthouse Museum
Not many settings can compare with the spectacular locale of the Marshall Point Lighthouse Museum (Marshall Point Rd., P.O. Box 247, Port Clyde 04855, 207/372-6450, www.marshallpoint.org, 1–5 P.M. Sun.–Fri., 10 A.M.–5 P.M. Sat. late May–mid-Oct., free), a distinctive 1857 lighthouse and park overlooking Port Clyde, the harbor islands, and the passing lobster-boat fleet. Bring a picnic and let the kids run on the lawn (but keep them well back from the shoreline). The tiny museum, in the 1895 keeper's house, displays local memorabilia. The grounds are accessible year-round. Take Route 131 to Port Clyde and watch for signs to the museum.

### Marine Education
Visitors are welcome to tour the facilities of **Herring Gut Learning Center** (59 Factory Rd., Port Clyde, 207/372-8677, www.herringgut.org, 8 A.M.–4 P.M. Sun.–Fri., $5 donation), a nonprofit marine education facility, with oyster

In the keeper's house at Marshall Point Light, at the tip of the St. George Peninsula, is a small museum.

and finfish hatcheries, touch tanks, exhibits, aquaponic greenhouse, and library. The center also hosts an evening lecture series in summer on topics such as sea urchins, climate change, and lobster. Enroll kids ages 5–13 in the one-day, field-based day camps ($35). Programs are organized by age groups and typically include crafts, activities, and specimen identification, collection, and examination.

## RECREATION
### Swimming and Beachcombing
**Drift Inn Beach,** on Drift Inn Beach Road (also called Candy's Cove Rd.), isn't a big deal as beaches go, but it's the best public one on the peninsula, so it gets busy on hot days. The name comes from the Drift Inn, an early-20th-century summer hotel. Drift Inn Beach Road parallels Route 131, and the parking lot is accessible from both roads. Heading south on the peninsula, about 3.5 miles after the junction with Route 73, turn left at Drift Inn Beach Road. The sign frequently disappears; watch

for an imposing square granite house and a red farm on your left. Go 0.2 mile from the turn.

### Sea Kayaking
The St. George Peninsula is especially popular for sea kayaking, with plenty of islands to add interest and shelter. **Port Clyde Kayaks** (440 Glenmere Rd., Port Clyde, 207/372-8128, www.portclydekayaks.com) offers 2.5-hour ($55) and four-hour ($69) guided tours around the tip of the peninsula, taking in Marshall Point lighthouse and the islands. Other options include full moon, starlight, kayak fishing, and, for experienced paddlers only, a puffin tour. Ask about multiday camping or B&B tours.

If you've had experience, you can launch on the ramp just before the causeway that links the mainland with Spruce Head Island, in Spruce Head (Island Rd., off Rte. 73). Parking is limited. A great paddle goes clockwise around Spruce Head Island and nearby White-head (there's a lighthouse on its southeastern

© TOM NANGLE

shore) and Norton Islands. Duck in for lunch at Waterman's Beach Lobster. Around new moon and full moon, plan your schedule to avoid low tide near the Spruce Head causeway, or you may become mired in mudflats.

## Boat Tours

The best boating experience on this peninsula is a passenger-ferry trip from Port Clyde to offshore **Monhegan Island**—for a day, overnight, or longer. (See *Monhegan Island* for more information on the island.) Perhaps because the private ferry company has a monopoly on this harbor, the trip isn't cheap, and parking adds to the cost, but it's a "must" excursion, so try to factor it into the budget. Port Clyde is the nearest mainland harbor to Monhegan; this service operates all year. **Monhegan-Thomaston Boat Line** (P.O. Box 238, Port Clyde 04855, 207/372-8848, www.monheganboat.com) uses two boats, the *Laura B.,* 70 minutes each way, and the newer *Elizabeth Ann,* 50 minutes. Round-trip tickets are $30 adults, $16 kids 2–12. (Leave your bicycle in Port Clyde; you won't need it on the island.) Reservations are essential in summer, especially for the 10:30 A.M. boat; a $5 pp fee holds the reservation until 75 minutes before departure, so you have to get to the dock early. No deposit is needed for other boats, but show up 30 minutes before departure. Parking in Port Clyde is $4 a day. If a summer day trip is all you can manage, aim for the first or second boat and return on the last one; don't go just for the boat ride.

During the summer, the Monhegan–Thomaston Boat Line also offers 2.5-hour sightseeing cruises, on a varied schedule, including a **Puffin/Nature Cruise and Lighthouse Cruise,** and mid-August–mid-September, a **Fall Fins and Feathers Cruise.** Each costs $24 adult, $10 child.

## SHOPPING
### Art

The St. George Peninsula has been attracting artists for decades, and galleries pepper the peninsula. Some have been here for years, oth-

ers started yesterday; most are worth a stop, so keep an eye out for their signs. In early August, a number of renowned artists usually coordinate on an open-studio weekend.

**The Drawing Room Gallery** (863 River Rd., St. George, 207/372-6242) mounts several theme-based group shows each summer. Philip and Barbara Anderson's gallery is just north of the junction with Route 73, about five miles south of Route 1.

Overlooking the reversing falls in downtown South Thomaston, **The Old Post Office Gallery** (Spruce Head Rd., Rte. 73, South Thomaston, 207/594-9396, www.artofthesea.com) has 11 rooms filled with marine art and antiques: ship models, prints, paintings, sculpture, scrimshaw, and jewelry.

Since 1972, Tony Oliveri has been the inspiration and the artisan behind **Keag River Pottery** (Westbrook St., South Thomaston, 207/594-7915), a small shop attached to his home just 0.1 mile off Route 73 (or 2.2 miles east of Rte. 131). He produces brilliantly glazed functional wares, such as bowls, dishes, and lamps, and readily accepts commissions.

Newer on the scene is George Pearlman's **St. George Pottery** (1012 River Rd., St. George, 207/372-6464, www.stgeorgepottery.com). His work pushes the boundaries of traditional forms.

## Used Books

Drive up to the small parking area at **Lobster Lane Book Shop** (Island Rd., Spruce Head, 207/594-7520), and you'll see license plates from everywhere. The tiny shop, in a crammed but well-organized shed that's been here since the 1960s, has 50,000 or so treasures for usedbook fans. For a few dollars, you can stock up on a summer's worth of reading. The shop is just under a mile east of Route 73, with eye-catching vistas in several directions (except, of course, when Spruce Head's infamous fog sets in).

## General Store

Despite periodic ownership changes, **Port Clyde General Store** (Rte. 131, Port Clyde, 207/372-6543) remains a character-ful destination, a two-century-old country store with a few yuppie touches. Stock up on groceries, pick up a newspaper, order a pizza, or buy a sweatshirt (you may need it on the Monhegan boat). It's open 6 A.M.–9 P.M. daily in summer, shorter hours the rest of the year. Out back is the Dip Net Restaurant, a great place to eat on the dock (see *Food*).

## ACCOMMODATIONS
### Inns

The dreamy island-dotted, oceanfront setting complements **The East Wind Inn** (Mechanic St., P.O. Box 149, Tenants Harbor 04860, 207/372-6366 or 800/241-8439, www.east-windinn.com, $109–201 peak), the perfect rendition of an old-fashioned country inn—some parts of it more old-fashioned than others. Built in 1860 and originally used as a sail loft, it has a huge veranda, a cozy parlor, harbor-view rooms, and a quiet dining room with a creditable New England menu. Rooms are divided between the main inn, some with shared bath, and the spiffed-up 19th-century Meeting House, a former sea captain's home, which also has one apartment. All rates include a full breakfast. The water-view dining room is open to the public daily for breakfast (7:30–9:30 A.M., to 10 A.M. in July and Aug.) and dinner (5:30–8:30 P.M., to 9:30 P.M. in July and Aug.). Dinner entrées are $17–26. Reservations are wise. Lunch is available in summer at a dockside take-out. Children are welcome; pets are $15 per visit. The inn is open all year; the dining room is open April–November.

### Bed-and-Breakfasts

The oceanfront **Blue Lupin** (372 Waterman's Beach Rd., South Thomaston, 207/594-2673, www.bluelupinbandb.com, $88–155) has an out-of-this-world view in an off-the-beaten-track locale. Bring a sea kayak and launch it from the beach. Or bring a bicycle to explore the area. Or simply settle in with a book or a movie. Next door is Waterman's Beach Lobster (see *Food*). It's open all year, but call ahead off-season.

In the center of South Thomaston village but overlooking the reversing falls on the tidal Wessaweskeag River, the 1830 **Weskeag at the Water** (14 Elm St., Rte. 73, P.O. Box 213, South Thomaston 04858, 207/596-6676 or 800/596-5576, www.midcoast.com/~weskeag, $120–155) has nine rooms, of which four have private baths; one has a whirlpool tub. This place is especially relaxing; congenial innkeepers Gray and Lynne Smith provide guests with games, puzzles, books, a huge video library, a great deck, and a lawn stretching to the river. Bring your sea kayak and bicycles. It's 1.5 miles from the Owls Head Transportation Museum (the Smiths love vintage cars) and a few more miles from the restaurants of downtown Rockland. It's open all year.

Smack-dab in the middle of Port Clyde, the **Seaside Inn** (5 Cold Storage Rd., P.O. Box 215, Port Clyde 04855, 207/372-0700 or 800/279-5041, www.seasideportclyde.com, $109–149) is an unfussy 1850s sea captain's home with both private and shared baths. A first-floor library has books, puzzles, TV, and a fireplace. Rates include a full breakfast. On the premises is a gallery showing the works of more than a dozen artists.

Every room has a view of Owl's Head Harbor at the **Trinity on the Ocean Bed and Breakfast** (20 Ocean Ave., Owl's Head, mailing address P.O. Box 215, Rockland 04841, 207/596-0071, www.trinityontheocean.com, $180–220 peak), an oceanfront B&B that's within walking distance of Primo restaurant. Hosts Steve and Donna Belyea are Rockland natives, so they know the area well, and they like to share their finds. Donna made the quilts topping the beds in the three guest rooms, each named after a Maine windjammer. A full breakfast is served either inside or on the oceanview deck.

### Camping

The third generation now operates **Lobster Buoy Campsites** (280 Waterman's Beach Rd., South Thomaston, 207/596-7546, www.lobsterbuoycampsites.com, $20–27), an oceanfront campground, with 40 sites, 28 with water and electric, all with fire ring and picnic table. You can launch a canoe or kayak from the small, sand beach. Rates cover two adults, two kids under 12, and one vehicle; one dog is allowed per site. Most sites are open, but a few tenting sites are in the trees. Every evening in July and August, homemade pies are sold in the Day Room.

## FOOD

All these restaurants are seasonal.

### Picnic Fare

Don't be surprised to see the handful of tables occupied at the **Keag Store** (Rte. 73, Village Center, South Thomaston, 207/596-6810, 6 A.M.–9 P.M. Mon.–Sat. and 7 A.M.–8 P.M. Sun.), one of the most popular lunch stops in the area. (Keag, by the way, is pronounced GIG—short for "Wessaweskeag.") Roast-turkey sandwiches with stuffing ($4.50) are a big draw, as is the pizza, which verges on the greasy but compensates with its flavor—no designer toppings, just good pizza. Order it all to go and head across the street to the public wharf, where you can hang out and observe all the comings and goings.

Another good spot for picnic fare is the **Port Clyde General Store** (Rte. 131, Port Clyde, 207/372-6543).

### Casual Dining

The decidedly old-fashioned **Craignair Inn Restaurant** (Clark Island Rd., off Rte. 71, Spruce Head, 207/594-7644, www.craig-nair.com), built in 1928 to house granite workers, serves dinner in its waterview dining room daily except Sunday, entrées $16–24. Seafood is the specialty. Also in the Main Inn and Vestry Annex are rooms, some with shared baths, $80–154 with breakfast.

Seafood is everything at **The Harpoon** (Drift Inn and Marshall Point Rds., Port Clyde, 207/372-6304, www.the-harpoon .com, 5–9 P.M., to 10 P.M. Fri. and Sat.) and it's about as fresh as it gets. Steaks are also on the menu, along with Cajun dishes ($17–23). Lobster's available, but save that for an outdoor deck (see *Lobster in the Rough*). Rebuilt from the ashes of an early 1990s fire, the informal restaurant is just over a low hill from the center of Port Clyde.

### Lobster in the Rough

These open-air lobster wharves are the best places in the area to get down and dirty and manhandle a steamed or boiled lobster.

Out back behind the Port Clyde General Store, and overlooking the Port Clyde lobster-boat fleet, is the **Dip Net** (Rte. 131, Port Clyde, 207/372-6307, www.dipnetrestaurant.com, open 11 A.M.–10 P.M. daily mid-May–mid-Sept.) with indoor and outdoor seating. It's all quite casual. The menu emphasizes seafood, with a raw bar, light fare ($4.50–9) and more substantial choices ($9–20) available. It's a great place for a shore dinner: lobster, clams, mussels, corn, and bread, at market price.

Poking right into Wheeler's Bay, **Miller's Lobster Company** (Eagle Quarry Rd., off Rte. 73, Spruce Head, 207/594-7406, www.millerslobster.com, 11 A.M.–7 P.M. daily) is the quintessential lobster pound, a well-run operation that draws crowds all summer long. Lobster rolls, steamed clams, crabmeat rolls, homemade pies—the works. Even hot dogs if you need them. Several picnic tables are under cover for chilly or rainy weather. BYOB.

A broad view of islands in the Mussel Ridge Channel is the bonanza at ◖ **Waterman's Beach Lobster** (343 Waterman's Beach Rd., South Thomaston, 207/596-7819, 11 A.M.–7 P.M. Thurs.–Sun.). This tiny operation has a big reputation: It's won a James Beard Award. It turns out well-stuffed lobster and crabmeat rolls and superb pies. Step up to the window and place your order. Service can be slow, but why rush with a view like this? Choose a good day; there's no real shelter from bad weather. BYOB; no credit cards. Next door to the Blue Lupin B&B, the wharf is on a side road off Route 73 between Spruce Head Village and South Thomaston; watch for signs on Route 73.

# Monhegan Island

Eleven or so miles from the mainland lies a unique island community with gritty lobstermen, close-knit families, a can-do spirit, a longstanding summertime artists' colony, no cars, astonishingly beautiful scenery, and some of the best birding on the Eastern Seaboard. Until the 1980s, the island had only radiophones and generator power; with the arrival of electricity and real phones, the pace has quickened a bit—but not much. Welcome to Monhegan Island.

But first a cautionary note: Monhegan has remained idyllic largely because generations of residents, part-timers, and visitors have been ultrasensitive to its fragility. When you buy your ferry ticket, you'll receive a copy of the regulations, all very reasonable, and the captain of your ferry will repeat them. *Heed them or don't go.*

Many of the regulations have been developed by The Monhegan Associates, an island land trust founded in the 1960s by Theodore Edison, son of the inventor. Firmly committed to preservation of the island in as natural a state as possible, the group maintains and marks the trails, sponsors natural-history talks, and insists that no construction be allowed beyond the village limits.

The origin of the name Monhegan remains up in the air; it's either a Maliseet or Micmac name meaning "out-to-sea island" or an adaptation of the name of a French explorer's daughter. In any case, Monhegan caught the attention of Europeans after English explorer John Smith stopped by in 1614, but the island had already been noticed by earlier adventurers, including John Cabot, Giovanni da Verrazzano, and George Waymouth. Legend even has it that Monhegan fishermen sent dried fish to Plimoth Plantation during the Pilgrims' first winter on Cape Cod. Captain Smith returned home and carried on about Monhegan, snagging the attention of intrepid souls who established a fishing/trading outpost here in 1625. Monhegan has been settled continuously since 1674, with fishing as the economic base.

In the 1880s, lured by the spectacular setting and artist Robert Henri's enthusiastic reports, gangs of artists began arriving, lugging their easels here and there to capture the surf, the light, the tidy cottages, the magnificent headlands, fishing boats, even the islanders' craggy features. American, German, French, and British artists have long (and continue to) come here; well-known signatures associated with Monhegan include Rockwell Kent, George Bellows, Edward Hopper, James Fitzgerald, Andrew Winter, Alice Kent Stoddard, Reuben Tam, William Kienbusch, and Jamie Wyeth.

Officially called Monhegan Plantation, the island has about 75 year-rounders. Several hundred others summer here. A handful of students attend the tiny school through eighth grade; high-schoolers have to pack up and move "inshore" to the mainland during the school year.

At the schoolhouse, the biggest social event of the year is the Christmas party, when everyone brings casseroles, salads, and desserts to complement a big beef roast. Kids perform their Christmas play, Santa shows up with presents, and dozens of adults look on approvingly. The islanders turn out en masse for almost every special event at the school, and the adults treat the island kids almost like common property, feeling free to praise or chastise them any time it seems appropriate—a phenomenon unique to isolated island communities.

For years, Monhegan's lobster-fishing season—a legislatively sanctioned period—perversely began on December 1 (locally known as Trap Day), but in 2007, that was moved forward to October 1, making it possible for visitors to view the action. An air of nervous anticipation surrounds the dozen or so lobstermen after midnight the day before as they prepare to steam out to set their traps on the ocean floor. Of course, with the lack of competition from mainland fishermen that time of year,

## TEN RULES FOR MONHEGAN VISITORS

1. Smoking is banned everywhere except in the village.
2. Rock climbing is not allowed on the wild headlands on the back side of the island.
3. Preserve the island's wild state – do not remove flowers or lichens.
4. Bicycles and strollers are not allowed on island trails.
5. Camping and campfires are forbidden islandwide.
6. Swim only at Swim Beach, just south of the ferry landing – if your innards can stand the shock. Wait for the incoming tide, when the water is warmest (and this warmth is relative). It's wise not to swim alone.
7. Dogs must be leashed; carry a pooper-scooper to remove their waste.
8. Be respectful of private property; stay on the trails. (As the island visitors guide puts it, "Monhegan is a village, not a theme park.")
9. If you're staying overnight, bring a flashlight; the village paths are very dark.
10. Carry the island trail map when you go exploring; you'll need it.

A strong suggestion: Carry a trash bag, use it, and take it off the island when you leave.

and a supply of lobsters fattening up since the previous June, there's a ready market for their catch. But success still depends on a smooth "setting." Meetings are held daily during the month beforehand to make sure everyone will be ready to "set" together. The season ends on June 25.

March brings the annual town meeting, an important community event that draws every able-bodied soul and then some.

Almost within spitting distance of Monhegan's dock (but you'll still need a boat) is whale-shaped **Manana Island,** once the home of an ex-New Yorker named Ray Phillips. Known as the Hermit of Manana, Phillips lived a solitary sheepherding existence on this barren island for more than half a century until his death in 1975. His story had spread so far afield that even *The New York Times* ran a front-page obituary when he died. (Photos and clippings are displayed in the Monhegan Museum.) In summer, youngsters with skiffs often hang around the harbor, particularly Fish Beach and Swim Beach, and you can usually talk one of them into taking you over, for a fee. (Don't try to talk them down too much or they may not return to pick you up.) Some curious inscriptions on Manana (marked with a yellow X near the boat landing) have led archaeologists to claim that Vikings even made it here, but cooler heads attribute the markings to Mother Nature.

### When to Go

If a day trip is all your schedule will allow, visit Monhegan between Memorial Day weekend and mid-October, when ferries from Port Clyde, New Harbor, and Boothbay Harbor operate daily, allowing 5–9 hours on the island—time enough to do an extensive trail loop, visit the museum and handful of shops, and picnic on the rocks. Other months, there's only one ferry a day from Port Clyde (only three a week Nov.–April), so you'll need to spend the night—not a hardship, but definitely requiring planning.

Almost any time of year, but especially in spring, fog can blanket the island, curtailing photography and swimming (although usually not the ferries). A spectacular sunny day can't be beat, but the fog lends an air of mystery you won't forget, so don't be deterred. Rain, of course, is another matter; some island trails can be perilous even in a misty drizzle.

### Other Points to Consider

Monhegan has no bank, but there are a couple of ATMs. Credit cards are not accepted everywhere. Personal checks, travelers checks, or cash will do. The few public telephones in the village require phone credit cards.

The only public restroom unconnected to a restaurant or lodging is on Horn Hill, at the southern end of the village (near the Monhegan House), and it will cost you $1 to use it. Outrageous, perhaps, but the restroom was installed to protect the woods and trails and deter daytrippers from bothering innkeepers. Unfortunately, the fee inspires some people to spurn these facilities and head for the woods. Please spend the dollar and preserve the island.

White-tailed deer used to overrun the island, leading to a relatively high incidence of Lyme disease (transmitted by deer ticks), but elimination of the herd (don't ask how) in recent years seems to have alleviated the situation. Nonetheless, birders and hikers should err on the side of caution and wear long pants rather than shorts, and tuck pant legs into socks.

## SIGHTS AND RECREATION

Monhegan is a getaway destination, a relaxing place for self-starters, so don't anticipate organized entertainment beyond the occasional lecture or narrated nature tour. Bring sturdy shoes (maybe even an extra pair in case trails are wet), a windbreaker, binoculars, a camera, and perhaps a sketchpad or a journal. If you're staying overnight, bring a flashlight for negotiating the unlighted island walkways, even in the village. For rainy days, bring a book. (If you forget, there's an amazingly good library.) In winter, bring ice skates for use on the Ice Pond.

### ◖ Monhegan Museum

The National Historic Register **Monhegan Lighthouse**—activated in July 1824 and automated in 1959—stands at the island's highest point, Lighthouse Hill, an exposed summit that's also home to the **Monhegan Historical and Cultural Museum** (207/596-7003, www.monheganmuseum.org, 11:30 A.M.– 3:30 P.M. daily July and Aug., 12:30–2:30 P.M. daily June and Sept.) in the former keeper's house and adjacent buildings. Overseen by the Monhegan Historical and Cultural Museum Association, the museum contains an antique kitchen, lobstering exhibits, and a fine collection of paintings by noted and not-so-noted artists. Two outbuildings have tools and gear

© TOM NANGLE

PENOBSCOT BAY

Monhegan's lighthouse is now a museum filled with island artifacts and art.

connected with fishing and ice-cutting, traditional island industries. The assistant lightkeeper's house, recently restored top to bottom as a handsome art gallery, provides a climate-controlled environment for the museum's impressive art collection. A volunteer usually is on hand to answer questions. Admission is technically free, but donations are encouraged.

## Artists' Studios

Nearly 20 artists' studios are open to the public during the summer (usually July and Aug.), but not all at once. At least five are open most days—most in the afternoon (Mon. has the fewest choices). Sometimes it's tight timewise for day-trippers who also want to hike the trails, but most of the studios are relatively close to the ferry landing. An annually updated map/schedule details locations, days, and times. It's posted on bulletin boards in the village and is available at lodgings and shops.

Two group galleries worth a visit are **Winter Works,** a craft co-op, and **Lupine Gallery** (207/594-8131), with works by Monhegan artists and artists' supplies.

## Hiking/Walking

Just over a half mile wide and 1.7 miles long, barely a square mile in area, Monhegan has 18 numbered hiking trails, most easy to moderate, covering about 17 miles. All are described in the *Monhegan Associates Trail Map* (www.monheganassociates.org), available at mainland ferry offices and island shops and lodgings or on the website. (The map is not to scale, so the hikes can take longer than you think.)

The footing is uneven everywhere, so Monhegan can present major obstacles to those with disabilities, even on the well-worn but unpaved village roads. Maintain an especially healthy respect for the ocean here, and don't venture too close; through the years, rogue waves on the island's backside have claimed victims young and old.

A relatively easy **day-tripper loop,** with a couple of moderate sections along the backside of the island, takes in several of Monhegan's finest features starting at the southern end of the village, opposite the church. To appreciate it, allow at least two hours. From the Main Road, go up Horn Hill, following signs for the **Burnthead Trail** (no. 4). Cross the island to the **Cliff Trail** (no. 1). Turn north on the Cliff Trail, following the dramatic headlands on the island's backside. There are lots of great picnic rocks in this area. Continue to Squeaker Cove, where the surf is the wildest, but be cautious. Then watch for signs to the **Cathedral Woods Trail** (no. 11), carpeted with pine needles and leading back to the village.

When you get back to Main Road, detour up the **Whitehead Trail** (no. 7) to the museum. If you're spending the night and feeling energetic, consider circumnavigating the island via the **Cliff Trail** (nos. 1 and 1-A). Allow at least 5–6 hours for this route; don't rush it.

## Birding

One of the East Coast's best birding sites during spring and fall migrations, Monhegan is a migrant trap for exhausted creatures winging their way north or south. Avid birders come here to add rare and unusual species to their life lists, and some devotees return year after year. No birder should arrive, however, without a copy of the superb *Birder's Guide to Maine* (see *Suggested Reading* under *Resources*).

Predicting exact bird-migration dates can be dicey, since wind and weather aberrations can skew the schedule. Generally, the best times are mid- to late May and most of September, into early October. If you plan to spend a night (or more) on the island during migration seasons, don't try to wing it—reserve a room well in advance.

## Around-the-Island Tour

On most days, the Balmy Days excursion boat makes a half-hour circuit around the island 2–2:30 P.M. for a nominal fee. Ask at the ferry dock.

## ACCOMMODATIONS

The island has a variety of lodgings from rustic to comfortable; none qualify in the multistar category. Pickup trucks of dubious vintage meet all the ferries and transport luggage to the lodgings. For cottage renters, Monhegan Trucking charges a small fee for each piece of luggage.

Best lodging is the 🄒 **Island Inn** (P.O. Box 128, Monhegan 04852, 207/596-0371, www.islandinnmonhegan.com), an imposing three-story mid-19th-century building with an expansive veranda and lawns overlooking the ferry landing. The 32 harbor- and meadow-view rooms and suites (most with private baths) are $145–340 d, high season, including full breakfast, plus a $5 pp charge for a one-night stay. Cash, checks, or travelers checks are preferred. It's open late May–early October.

In the heart of the village, **Monhegan House** (P.O. Box 345, Monhegan 04852, 207/594-7983 or 800/599-7983, www.monheganhouse.com, $77–81 s, $129–185 d peak), built in 1870, is a large four-story building with 33 rooms. All have shared baths, not always on the same floor as your room. Don't miss the loose-leaf notebook in the lobby. Labeled *A Monhegan Novel*, it's the ultimate in shaggy-dog sagas, created by a long string of guests since 1992. Rates include breakfast. There's a $5 pp surcharge for one-night stays. Children are welcome. It's open late May–Columbus Day.

A more modernized hostelry, **Shining Sails** (P.O. Box 346, Monhegan 04852, 207/596-0041, www.shiningsails.com) lacks the quaintness of the other inns, but it's very comfortable, convenient to the dock, stays open all year, and has private baths. Breakfast (included only in season) is continental. Seven first- and second-floor rooms and efficiencies (some with water views) go for $115–180 May–mid-October; rates are lower for multiple nights and off-season stays. "Well-supervised" children are welcome. An additional four apartments are in a separate building and over a restaurant ($160–190). Shining Sails also manages more than two dozen weekly-rental cottages and apartments, with rates beginning around $750/week in season.

The funkiest lodging, and not for everyone, is **The Trailing Yew** (P.O. Box 98, Monhegan 04852, 207/596-0440 or 800/592-2520, www.trailingyew.com, $90 pp). Spread among five rustic buildings south of the village on the road to Lobster Cove are 35 rooms, most with shared baths (averaging five rooms per bath and not always in the same building) and lighted with kerosene (about 12 have electricity). Rates include breakfast and dinner; kids are $25 and up, depending on age. The old-fashioned, low-key 50-seat dining room is open to the public for dinner at 5:45 P.M., served family-style by reservation, and for breakfast at 7:45 A.M. Bring a sleeping bag in spring or fall; rooms are unheated. No credit cards. It's open late May–early October.

## Seasonal Rentals

More than two dozen weekly-rental cottages and apartments—categorized as very rustic, fair, very good, and excellent—are managed by **Shining Sails Real Estate** (P.O. Box 346, Monhegan 04852, 207/596-0041, www.shiningsails.com). About half have electricity; the others have gas lights and appliances. Some sleep up to six people; kids, pets, and smoking may be limited. Peak-season (July and August) weekly rates range $750–2,500, lower off-season. Credit cards are accepted. A few are available by the night, space permitting, especially off-season. To rent one of the better seasonal places, you may need to make a two-week commitment.

## FOOD

Most visitors don't arrive on Monhegan expecting gourmet cuisine. Everything is quite casual, and food is hearty and ample. None of the eateries have liquor licenses, so buy beer or wine at the North End Market or the Barnacle Café, or bring it from the mainland. All of the restaurants and food sources are in or close to the village.

Prepared foods, varying from pastries to sandwiches to pizza, are available from **Barnacle Café** (207/596-0371), under the same ownership as the nearby Island Inn, **The Novelty,** behind and operated by The Monhegan House, and **North End Market** (207/594-5546). There's seating at **The Scruffy Dog** (207/594-0949). A new choice is **Hot Fat,** a cart that, as the name suggests, fries up the fish of the day. Look for it, and try a fish taco.

## Casual Dining

The restaurant at the **Island Inn,** open to the public for breakfast, lunch (11:15 A.M.–1:30 P.M.), and dinner (opens at 6 P.M.), has developed an excellent dinner menu with creative entrées that range $15–27; the only negative is a $3 corkage fee for the wine and $1 for the beer that *you* have to supply.

Islanders and visitors flock to the **Monhegan House Café,** overlooking the village, for breakfast, lunch, and dinner (entrées $13–20). The café will pack a picnic if you want to hit the trails. Order the lobster stew—it's justifiably famous.

## Lobster in the Rough

You can't get much rougher for lobster in the rough than **Shermie's Fish House** (on Fish Beach, 11:30 A.M.–2:30 P.M. and 4–6:30 P.M. daily). Lobster and crabmeat rolls, locally smoked fish, and homemade stews and chowders are on the menu as well as fresh lobster. Take it to the picnic table on the beach and enjoy.

## INFORMATION AND SERVICES
### Information

Several free brochures and flyers, revised annually, will answer most questions about planning a day trip or overnight visit to Monhegan. At the ferry ticket office in Port Clyde, pick up the 12-page *Visitor's Guide to Monhegan Island* and the *Monhegan Associates Trail Map*. Both are also available at island shops, galleries, and lodgings, and at the New Harbor and Boothbay Harbor ferry offices. To obtain copies beforehand, contact Monhegan–Thomaston Boat Line (P.O. Box 238, Port Clyde 04855, 207/372-8848, fax 207/372-8547, www.monheganboat.com)

around mid-April. Also request a copy of the ferry schedule. For fastest service, send a self-addressed stamped envelope. The Rockland-Thomaston Area Chamber of Commerce also has some information about lodgings and other facilities on Monhegan. Monhegan info is also available online at www.monhegan.com and www.monhegan.info.

Monhegan's pleasant little library, the Jackie and Edward Library, was named after two children who drowned in the surf in the 1920s. The fiction collection is especially extensive, and it's open to everyone. At the head of Wharf Hill, it's usually open 1–4 P.M. Tuesday, Thursday, and Saturday, plus two or three evenings a week; check when you arrive.

Also check the Rope Shed, the community bulletin board next to the meadow, right in the village. Monhegan's version of a bush telegraph, it's where everyone posts flyers and notices about nature walks, lectures, excursions, and other special events. You'll also see the current *Monhegan Artists Studio Locations* map.

## GETTING THERE AND AROUND

Ferries travel to Monhegan from Port Clyde year-round (see *Boat Tours* under *Recreation* in the *St. George Peninsula* section for details on cost and schedule). Seasonal service to the island is provided from New Harbor by Hardy Boat Cruises and from Boothbay Harbor by Balmy Days Cruises.

Part of the daily routine for many islanders and summer folk is a stroll to the harbor when the ferry comes in, so don't be surprised to see a good-size welcoming party when you arrive. You're the live entertainment.

Monhegan's only vehicles are a handful of pickup trucks owned by local lobstermen and li'l ol' trucks used by Monhegan Trucking. If you're staying a night or longer and your luggage is too heavy to carry, they'll be waiting when you arrive at the island wharf.

# Rockland Area

A "Share the Pride" campaign—kicked off in the 1980s to boost sagging civic self-esteem and the local economy—was the first step in the transformation of Rockland. Once a run-down county seat best known for the aroma of its fish-packing plants, the city has undergone a sea change—most of it for the better. The expansion of the Farnsworth Museum of American Art and the addition of its Wyeth Center was a catalyst. Benches and plants line Main Street (Rte. 1), stores offer appealing wares, coffeehouses and more than a dozen art galleries attract a diverse clientele, and Rockland Harbor is home to more windjammer cruise schooners than neighboring Camden (which had long claimed the title "Windjammer Capital"). If you haven't been to Rockland in the last decade, prepare to be astonished.

Foresighted entrepreneurs had seen the potential of the bayside location in the late 1700s and established a tiny settlement here called "Shore Village" (or "the Shore"). Today's commercial-fishing fleet is one of the few reminders of Rockland's past, when multimasted schooners lined the wharves, some to load volatile cargoes of lime destined to become building material for cities all along the Eastern Seaboard, others to head northeast—toward the storm-racked Grand Banks and the lucrative cod fishery there. Such hazardous pursuits meant an early demise for many a local seafarer, but Rockland's 5,000 or so residents were enjoying their prosperity in the late 1840s. The settlement was home to more than two dozen shipyards and dozens of lime kilns, was enjoying a construction boom, and boasted a newspaper and regular steamship service. By 1854, Rockland had become a city.

Today, Rockland remains a commercial hub—with Knox County's only shopping plazas (not quite malls, but Wal-Mart and other big-box stores have arrived), a fishing fleet that heads far offshore, and ferries that connect nearby islands. Rockland also claims the title of "Lobster Capital of the World"—thanks to Knox County's shipment nationally and internationally of 10 million pounds of lobster each year. (The weathervane atop the police and fire department building is a giant copper lobster.)

With just more than 8,000 souls, Rockland is more year-round community than tourist town. But visitors pour in during two big summer festivals—the North Atlantic Blues Festival in mid-July and the Maine Lobster Festival in early August. Highlight of the Lobster Festival is King Neptune's coronation of the Maine Sea Goddess—carefully selected from a bevy of local young women—who then sails off with him to his watery domain.

## SIGHTS
### ◖ The Farnsworth Art Museum and the Wyeth Center

Anchoring downtown Rockland is the nationally respected Farnsworth Art Museum (16 Museum St., Rockland, 207/596-6457, www.farnsworthmuseum.org), established in 1948 through a trust fund set up by Rocklander Lucy Farnsworth. With an ample checkbook, the first curator, Robert Bellows, toured the country, accumulating a splendid collection of 19th- and 20th-century Maine-related American art—the basis for the permanent *Maine in America* exhibition.

The 6,000-piece collection today includes work by Fitz Hugh Lane, Gilbert Stuart, Eastman Johnson, Childe Hassam, John Marin, Maurice Prendergast, Rockwell Kent, George Bellows, and Marsden Hartley. Best known are the paintings by three generations of the Wyeth family (local summer residents) and sculpture by Louise Nevelson, who grew up in Rockland. Sculpture, jewelry, and paintings by Nevelson form the core of the third-floor Nevelson-Berliawsky Gallery for 20th-Century Art. (The only larger Nevelson collection is in New York's Whitney Museum of American Art.) The new Wyeth Center, across Union Street in a former church, contains the work

# WINDJAMMING

In 1936, Camden became the home of the "cruise schooner" (sometimes called "dude schooner") trade when Captain Frank Swift restored a creaky wooden vessel and offered sailing vacations to paying passengers. He kept at it for 25 years, gradually adding other boats to the fleet — and the rest, as they say, is history. Windjammers have become big business on the Maine coast, with Camden and Rockland sparring for the title of Windjammer Capital. Rockland wrested it from Camden in the mid-1990s and so far, has held onto it.

Named for their ability to "jam" into the wind when they carried freight up and down the New England coast, windjammers trigger images of the Great Age of Sail. Most are rigged as schooners, with two or three soaring wooden masts; their lengths range from 64 to 132 feet. Nine are National Historic Landmarks; four were built for the trade.

These windjammers head out for 3-6 days, late May–mid-October, tucking into coves and harbors around Penobscot Bay and its islands. The mostly engineless craft set their itineraries by the wind, propelled by stiff breezes to Buck's Harbor, North Haven, and Deer Isle. Everything's totally informal, geared for relaxing.

You're aboard for the experience, not for luxury, so expect basic accommodations with few frills, although newer vessels were built with passenger trade in mind and tend to be a bit more comfy. Down below, cabins typically are small and basic, with paper-thin walls — sort of a campground afloat (earplugs are often available for light sleepers). It may not sound romantic, but be aware that the captains keep track of postcruise marriages. Most boats have shared showers and toilets. If you're Type-A, given to pacing, don't inflict yourself on the cruising crowd; if you're flexible, ready for whatever, go ahead and sign on. You can help with the sails, eat, curl up with a book, inhale salt air, shoot photos, eat, sunbathe, bird-watch, eat, chat up fellow passengers, sleep, eat, or just settle back and enjoy spectacular sailing you'll never forget.

When you book a cruise, you'll receive all the details and directions, but for a typical six-day trip, you arrive at the boat by 7 P.M. for the captain's call to meet your fellow passengers. You sleep aboard at the dock that night and then depart midmorning Monday and spend five nights and days cruising Penobscot Bay, following the wind, the weather, and the whims of the captain. (Many of the windjammers have no engines, only a motorized yawlboat used as a pusher and a water taxi.) You might anchor in a deserted cove and explore the shore, or you might pull into a harbor and hike, shop, and bar-hop. Then it's back to the boat for chow — windjammer cooks are legendary for creating three hearty, all-you-can-eat meals daily, including at least one lobster feast! When the cruise ends, most passengers find it hard to leave.

On the summer cruising schedule, several weeks coincide with special windjammer events, so you'll need to book a berth far in advance for these: mid-June (Boothbay Harbor's Windjammer Days), July Fourth week (Great Schooner Race), Labor Day weekend (Camden's Windjammer Weekend), and the second week in September (WoodenBoat Sail-In).

Most windjammers offering three- to six-day sails out of Camden, Rockland, and Rockport are members of the **Maine Windjammer Association** (P.O. Box 1144, Blue Hill 04614, 800/807-9463, www.sailmainecoast.com), a one-stop resource for vessel and schedule information.

of Andrew, N. C., and Jamie Wyeth. In the summer of 2000, the Farnsworth opened its 6,000-square-foot Jamien Morehouse Wing, an elegant venue for rotating exhibits.

In the Farnsworth's library—a grand, high-ceilinged oasis akin to an English gentleman's reading room—browsers and researchers can explore an extensive collection of art books and magazines. The museum's hyperactive education department annually sponsors hundreds of lectures, concerts, art classes for adults and children, poetry readings, and field trips. Most are open to nonmembers; some require an extra fee. A glitzy gift shop stocks posters, prints, notecards, imported gift items, and art games for children.

Next door to the museum is the mid-19th-century Greek Revival **Farnsworth Homestead,** with original high-Victorian furnishings. Looking as though William Farnsworth's family just took off for the day, the house has been preserved rather than restored.

The Farnsworth also owns the **Olson House,** 14 miles away in nearby Cushing, where the whole landscape looks like a Wyeth diorama. (See details in the *Cushing Peninsula* section.) Pick up a map at the museum to help you find the house—it's definitely worth the side trip.

The Farnsworth ($10 adults, $8 seniors and students 18 and older, free for kids under 18 and Rockland residents) is open year-round, including summer holidays. Farnsworth hours are 10 A.M.–5 P.M. daily (to 8 P.M. Wed.) in summer, 10 A.M.–5 P.M. Tuesday–Sunday in winter. Call the museum for its current definition of summer and winter. The Homestead (10 A.M.–5 P.M. daily) and the Olson House (11 A.M.–4 P.M. daily) are open late May–mid-October.

## ◖ Owls Head Transportation Museum

Don't miss this place, even if you're not an old-vehicle buff. A generous endowment has made the Owls Head Transportation Museum (Rte. 73, Owls Head, 207/594-4418, www.ohtm.org, 10 A.M.–4 P.M. daily Nov.–March, $8 adults, $7 seniors, $5 ages 5–17, $20

family, special events are extra), a premier facility for celebrating wings and wheels; it draws more than 75,000 visitors a year. Scads of eager volunteers help restore the vehicles and keep them running. On weekends May–October, the museum sponsors air shows (often including aerobatic displays) and car and truck meets for hundreds of enthusiasts. The season highlight is the annual rally and aerobatic show (early Aug.), when more than 300 vehicles gather for two days of festivities. Want your own vintage vehicle? Attend the antique, classic, and special-interest auto auction (third Sunday in Aug.). The gift shop carries transportation-related items. If the kids get bored (unlikely), there's a play area outside, with picnic tables. In winter, groomed cross-country-skiing trails wind through the museum's 60-acre site. (Ask for a map at the information desk.)

## Maine Discovery Center

The headliner at the Maine Discovery Center (1 Park Dr., Rockland) is the **Maine Lighthouse Museum** (207/594-3301, www.mainelighthousemuseum.com, 9 A.M.–5 P.M. Mon.–Fri. and 10 A.M.–4 P.M. Sat. and Sun. late May–mid-Oct., closed Sun.–Wed. in winter, $5, under 12 free), home to the nation's largest collection of Fresnel lenses, along with a boatload-plus of lighthouse, Coast Guard, and maritime-related artifacts. On view are foghorns, ships' bells, nautical books and photographs, marine instruments, ship models, scrimshaw, and so much more.

Also exhibiting at the center are the Farnsworth Art Museum, Maine Lobster Festival, Penobscot Marine Museum, Owls Head Transportation Museum, Rockland Historical Society, Island Institute, and Knox Museum.

## Project Puffin Visitor Center

If you can't manage a trip to see the puffins, Audubon's Project Puffin Visitor Center (311 Main St., Rockland, 207/596-5566 or 877/478-3346, www.projectpuffin.org, 10 A.M.–5 P.M. daily, to 7:30 P.M. Wed., June 1–Oct. 31; call for off-season hours) will bring them to you. Live videos of nesting puffins are

**PENOBSCOT BAY**

just one of the highlights of the center, which also includes interactive exhibits, a gallery, and films, all highlighting successful efforts to restore and protect these clowns of the sea.

## ◖ Rockland Breakwater

Protecting the harbor from wind-driven waves, the 4,346-foot-long Rockland Breakwater took 18 years to build, with 697,000 tons of locally quarried granite. In the late 19th century, it was piled up, chunk by chunk, from a base 175 feet wide on the harbor floor (60 feet below the surface) to the 43-foot-wide cap. The Breakwater Light—now automated—was built in 1902 and added to the National Historic Register in 1981. The city of Rockland owns the keeper's house, but it's maintained by the Friends of the Rockland Breakwater Lighthouse (www.rocklandlighthouse.com). Member volunteers usually open the lighthouse to the public 9 A.M.–5 P.M. Saturday and Sunday late May–mid-October and for special events. The breakwater provides unique vantage points for photographers, and a place to picnic or catch sea breezes or fish on a hot day, but it is extremely dangerous during storms. Anyone on the breakwater risks being washed into the sea or struck by lightning (ask the local hospital staff: it *has* happened!). Do not take chances when the weather is iffy.

To reach the breakwater, take Route 1 North to Waldo Avenue and turn right. Take the next right onto Samoset Road and drive to the end, to **Marie Reed Memorial Park** (tiny beach, benches, limited parking). Or go to the Samoset Resort and take the path to the breakwater from there.

## Main Street Historic District

Rocklanders are justly proud of their Main Street Historic District, lined with 19th- and early-20th-century Greek and Colonial Revival structures, as well as examples of mansard and Italianate architecture. Most now house retail shops on the ground floor; upper floors have offices, artists' studios, and apartments. The district starts at the corner of Winter and Main Streets and runs north to the alley just after Kelsey's Appliances. The chamber of commerce has a map and details.

## Flightseeing

Get a gull's-eye view of Coastal Maine riding in an R-44 Raven chopper with **Scenic Helicopters of Maine** (207/596-7006 or 866/596-7006, www.scenic-helicopters.com). Rates begin at $50 pp, minimum two people, for an introductory flight above Rockland and Thomaston covering 5–8 miles. Flights depart from a heliport on Route 1 at the Thomaston/Rockland line.

For something a bit quieter, soar and swoop on a glider ride with **Spirit Soaring** (207/319-9514, www.spiritsoaring.org). Rates begin at $100 for a half-hour ride over coastal Penobscot Bay. It operates from Knox County Regional Airport in Owls Head, just south of Rockland.

## Excursion Train

Ride in restored, vintage railcars on the scenic **Maine Eastern Railroad** (207/596-6725 or 800/637-2457, www.maineeasternrailroad.com), operating between Rockland and Brunswick, with stops in Wiscasset and Bath. The train operates late May–early November, with special holiday trains in December. Adult fares are $40 round-trip, $25 one-way; ages 5–15 pay $15; seniors are $35/$25; family rate is $100/$75 covering two adults and two kids. Packages with lodging, meals, and theater are available.

## PARKS AND RECREATION
## ◖ Owls Head Light State Park

On Route 73, about 1.5 miles past the junction of Routes 1 and 73, you'll reach North Shore Road in the town of Owls Head. Turn left, toward Owls Head Light State Park. Standing 3.6 miles from this turn, Owls Head Light occupies a dramatic promontory with panoramic views over Rockland Harbor and Penobscot Bay. Don't miss it. The keeper's house and the light tower are off-limits, but the park surrounding the tower has easy walking paths, picnic tables, and a pebbly beach where you can sunbathe or check out Rockland Harbor's boating traffic. (If it's foggy or rainy, don't climb the steps toward the light tower: The view evaporates in the fog, the access ramp can be slippery, and the foghorn is dangerously deafening.) Follow signs to reach the park. From North Shore Road, turn left onto Main Street, then left onto Lighthouse Road, and continue along Owls Head Harbor to the parking area. This is also a particularly pleasant bike route—about 10 miles round-trip from downtown Rockland—although, once again, the roadside shoulders are poor along the Owls Head stretch.

## Harbor Park

If you're looking for a park with more commotion than quiet green space, spend some time at Harbor Park. Boats, cars, and delivery vehicles come and go, and you can corner a picnic table or a bench or a patch of grass and watch all the action. During the holidays, a lobster trap Christmas tree presides over the park. Public restrooms (open late May–mid-October) are available. The park is just off Main Street.

## Swimming

Lucia Beach is the local name for **Birch Point Beach State Park,** one of the best-kept secrets in the area. In Owls Head, just south of Rockland—and not far from Owls Head Light—the spruce-lined sand crescent (free; outhouses but no other facilities) has rocks, shells, tide pools, and very chilly water. There's ample room for a moderate-size crowd, although parking and turnaround space can get a bit tight on the access road. From downtown Rockland, take Route 73 one mile to North Shore Drive (on your left). Take the next right, Ash Point Drive, and continue past Knox County Regional Airport to Dublin Road. Turn right, go 0.8 mile, then turn left onto Ballyhac Road (opposite the airport landing lights). Go another 0.8 mile, fork left, and continue 0.4 mile to the parking area.

If frigid ocean water doesn't appeal, head for freshwater **Chickawaukee Lake,** on Route 17, two miles inland from downtown Rockland. Don't expect to be alone, though; on hot days, **Johnson Memorial Park**'s pocket-size sand patch is a major attraction. A lifeguard holds forth; there are restrooms, picnic tables, a snack bar, and a boat-launch ramp. (In winter, iceboats, snowmobiles, and ice-fishing shacks take over the lake.) A signposted bicycle path runs alongside the busy highway, making the park an easy pedal from town.

## Golf

The **Rockland Golf Club** (606 Old County Rd., Rockland, 207/594-9322, www.rocklandgolf.com, Apr.–Oct.), an 18-hole course 0.2 mile northeast of Route 17, ranks high on many a Maine golfer's list. In July and August, you'll need to reserve a starting time a day or so in advance if you plan to tee off anytime after 7 A.M. The modern clubhouse—rebuilt after a disastrous fire in the late 1980s—has a full bar and serves breakfast and lunch at reasonable prices. Parking is plentiful.

For an 18-hole course in an unsurpassed waterfront setting (but steep rental and greens fees), check out the links at the **Samoset Resort** (220 Warrenton St., Rockport, 207/594-2511 or 800/341-1650, www.samoset.com), technically in Rockport but most often reached via Rockland.

## Sea Kayaking

Veteran Maine Guide and naturalist Mark DiGirolamo is the sparkplug behind **Breakwater Kayak** (Rockland Public Landing, Rockland, 207/596-6895 or 877/559-8800, www.breakwaterkayak.com), which has a full range of tours, even multiday ones. A two-hour Rockland Harbor tour (usually offered three times a day at the height of summer) is $35, and the all-day Owls Head Lighthouse tour is $95, including lunch. Reservations are advisable. This outfit is particularly eco-sensitive—Mark has a degree in environmental science, definitely worth supporting. Maine Audubon often taps Mark to lead natural-history field trips. Dress warmly for these tours and be sure to bring a filled water bottle.

## Boating Excursions

Marine biologist Captain Bob Pratt is the skipper of *A Morning in Maine* (207/594-1844 or 207/691-7245 seasonal boat phone,

PENOBSCOT BAY

www.amorninginmaine.com), a classic 55-foot ketch designed by noted naval architect R. D. (Pete) Culler and built by Concordia Yachts. From June through October, *Morning* departs from the middle pier at the Rockland Public Landing three times daily for two-hour sails ($30), with plenty of knowledgeable commentary from Captain Pratt. A 6 P.M. sunset sail is available in July and August. Inquire about boat-and-breakfast overnights, which run $500 per couple and include a sail, lobster dinner, and continental breakfast.

Watch Captain Steve Hale set and haul lobster traps on a cruise aboard the *Captain Jack* (Rockland Harbor, 207/594-1048, www.captainjacklobstertours.com) during a 1.25-hour cruise aboard a 30-foot working lobster boat. Cruises depart five times daily, Monday–Saturday May–September; $25 adult, $15 kids under 12. Note: There are no toilets aboard. On Saturday and Sunday, Captain Jack offers a two-hour dinner cruise that includes a lobster feed with fixings for $50 pp. Reservation required; minimum two people for a trip.

## Maine State Ferry Service

Car and passenger ferries service the islands of Vinalhaven, North Haven, and Matinicus. The Vinalhaven and North Haven routes make fantastic day trips (especially with a bike), or you can spend the night; the Matinicus ferry is much less predictable.

## Bicycling

Rentals, sales, repair, and twice-weekly group rides are provided by **Bikesenjava** (481 Main St., Rockland 207/596-1004, www.haybikesenjava.com).

## ENTERTAINMENT AND EVENTS

Stop by the **Lincoln Street Center for Arts and Education** (24 Lincoln St., Rockland, 207/594-6490, www.lincolnstreetcenter.org), a community arts center with exhibitions, performances, and classes, to see what's on the schedule.

The historic **Strand Theater** (339 Main St.,

207/594-7266, www.rocklandstrand.com), opened in 1923, underwent an extensive restoration in 2005. Films as well as live entertainment are scheduled. It's also the venue for many **Bay Chamber Concerts** (207/236-2823 or 888/707-2770, www.baychamberconcerts.org) events.

If you're a film buff, you might want to see what the **Saltwater Film Society** (www.saltwaterfilmsociety.org) has on its schedule.

The Farnsworth Museum and nearly two dozen galleries stay open until 8 P.M. every Wednesday June–mid-September for **Arts in Rockland** events, with art openings coordinated once each month.

In mid-July, the **North Atlantic Blues Festival** means a weekend of festivities featuring big names in blues. Thousands of fans jam Harbor Park for the nonstop music.

August's **Maine Lobster Festival** is a five-day lobster extravaganza, with live entertainment, the Maine Sea Goddess pageant, a lobster-crate race, craft booths, boat rides, a parade, lobster dinners, and megacrowds (the hotels are full for miles in either direction). Tons of lobsters bite the dust during the weekend—despite annual protests by the People for the Ethical Treatment of Animals. (The protests, however, seem only to increase the crowds.)

## SHOPPING

Piggybacking on the fame of the Farnsworth Museum, or at least working symbiotically, art galleries line Rockland's main and many side streets. Ask around and look around. During the summer, many of them coordinate monthly openings (usually a Wednesday evening) so you can meander and munch (and sip) from one gallery to another.

Across from the Farnsworth's side entrance, the **Caldbeck Gallery** (12 Elm St., Rockland, 207/594-5935, www.caldbeck.com) has gained a top-notch reputation as a "must-see" (and "must-be-seen") space. Featuring the work of contemporary Maine artists, the gallery mounts more than half a dozen solo and group shows each year, May–September.

**Eric Hopkins Gallery** (21 Winter St., Rockland, 207/594-1996, www.erichopkins.com) shows the North Haven artist's colorful, aerial-view paintings.

**Archipelago** (Main St., Rockland, 207/596-0701), on the ground floor of the Island Institute (a nonprofit steward of Maine's 4,617 offshore islands), is an attractive retail outlet for talented craftspeople from 14 year-round islands.

Other eminently browsable downtown Rockland galleries are **Harbor Square Gallery** (374 Main St., 207/594-8700 or 877/594-8700), **Lucky Dog Gallery** (485 Main St., 207/596-0120), **Landing Gallery** (8 Elm St., 888/394-2787), and **Nan Mulford Gallery** (313 Main St., 207/594-8481). All are within steps of each other.

## Books, Crafts, Gifts, and Clothing

Downtown Rockland has plenty of interesting shops. Here's just a selection:

An independent bookstore with inventories of best-sellers, cookbooks, kids' books, remainders, magazines, and CDs, **The Reading Corner** (408 Main St., Rockland, 207/596-6651) occupies two full rooms in downtown Rockland.

**The Grasshopper Shop** (400 Main St., Rockland, 207/596-6156) is an eclectic emporium filled with jewelry, clothing, shoes, accessories, cards, toys, and unusual gifts, all tastefully displayed beneath a handsome antique tin ceiling.

**Archipelago** (Main St., Rockland, 207/596-0701), on the ground floor of the Island Institute (a nonprofit steward of Maine's 4,617 offshore islands), is an attractive retail outlet for talented craftspeople from 14 year-round islands. The shop also carries island-related books.

## ACCOMMODATIONS

If you're planning an overnight stay in the Rockland area the first weekend in August—during the Maine Lobster Festival—*be sure* to make reservations well in advance. Festival attendance runs close to 100,000, No Vacancy signs extend from Waldoboro to Belfast, and there just aren't enough beds or campsites to go around.

## Samoset Resort

The 221-acre waterfront Samoset Resort (220 Warrenton St., Rockport, 207/594-2511 or 800/341-1650, www.samoset.com) straddles the boundary between Rockland and Rockport, the next town to the north. Most guests get to it via Rockland, from the south. Built on the ashes of a classic, 19th-century summer hotel, the Samoset is a top-of-the-line modern resort with knockout ocean views from most of its 178 rooms and suites, all refurbished in 2007, plus 72 separate town houses. Peak-season (early July–Labor Day) doubles go for $265–350, suites are $299–549. Room amenities include flat-screen TV, air-conditioning, and Wi-Fi. Conferences go on here throughout the year, but it's also a great family place, particularly off-season—with special package rates, indoor and outdoor swimming pools, fitness center, lighted tennis courts, cross-country skiing, children's day camp ($50, including lunch, ages 5–12), golf simulator, and a fabulous 18-hole waterfront golf course. On-site are a fine-dining restaurant and a casual lounge, serving light fare and with entertainment in summer.

## Motel

Directly opposite the ferry terminal for boats going to the islands of Vinalhaven, North Haven, and Matinicus, the 81-room **Navigator Motor Inn** (520 Main St., Rockland, 207/594-2131 or 800/545-8026, www.navigatorinn.com, $95–155) is a five-story shingled place with TV, air-conditioning, phones, refrigerators, and laundry facilities. Rooms are basic motel-style, but upper-floor ones have plenty of space and great views of the harbor (be prepared for traffic noise from the parking lot and street). Pets are allowed in some rooms. The bright, modern Portsider Grill and Pub serves lunch and dinner year-round, and breakfast during summer, but you're just steps from Rockland's Main Street restaurants.

## Bed-and-Breakfasts

These B&Bs are in Rockland's historic district, within easy walking distance of downtown attractions and restaurants, and are members of the **Historic Inns of Rockland Maine** (www.historicinnsofrockland.com), which co-ordinates such great off-season events as Pies on Parade and the Chocolate March.

Most elegant is ( **The Berry Manor Inn** (81 Talbot Ave., P.O. Box 1117, Rockland 04841, 207/596-7696 or 800/774-5692, www.berrymanorinn.com, $155–255), on a quiet side street a few blocks from downtown. Cheryl Michaelsen and Michael LaPosta have totally restored the manse built in 1898 by wealthy Rocklander Charles Berry as a wedding gift for his wife (thoughtful fellow). High ceilings and wonderful Victorian architectural touches are everywhere, especially in the enormous front hall and two parlors. Eight second- and third-floor Victorian-decor rooms and four ultraluxurious suites in the adjacent Carriage House have private baths, gas fireplaces, air-conditioning, hair dryers, dataports, journals, and more; many have whirlpools. In-room TV upon request. A guest pantry is stocked with free soda and juices and sweets, not that you'll be hungry after the extravagant breakfasts.

Opened in 1996, the **Captain Lindsey House Inn** (5 Lindsey St., P.O. Box 864, Rockland 04841, 207/596-7950 or 800/523-2145, www.lindseyhouse.com, $156–211) is more like a boutique hotel than a B&B. The Barnes family gutted the 1835 brick structure and restored it dramatically, adding such modernities as phones, air-conditioning, Wi-Fi, and TV. The decor is strikingly handsome, not at all fussy or frilly. Don't miss the 1926 safe in the front hall or the hidden-from-the-street garden patio—not to mention the antiques from everywhere that fill the nine comfortable rooms. It's smack downtown, and a few rooms have glimpses of the water. Rates include an extensive hot-and-cold breakfast buffet and afternoon refreshments.

Filled with reproduction furnishings and unusual touches, **The Limerock Inn** (96 Limerock St., Rockland, 207/594-2257 or 800/546-3762, $130–225, www.limerockinn.com) is a lovely painted lady. The 1890s Queen Anne mansion, with wraparound porch and turret, is listed on the National Historic Register and faces a quiet street in Rockland's historic district. Each of the eight rooms has its own distinctive flavor—such as the Turret Room with a wedding canopy bed and the Island Cottage Room with a private deck overlooking the back gardens. Some have whirlpool tubs, one a fireplace; there's Wi-Fi throughout. Breakfast is a treat.

Is it too cold for an ocean swim? Book a room at the **Lakeshore Inn** (184 Lakeview Dr., Rte. 17, Rockland, 207/594-4209 or 866/540-8800, www.lakeshorebb.com, $80 s, $100–200 d peak) and swim in Lake Chickawaukie. Although the inn dates from 1767, innkeepers Susan and Jim Rodiger have chosen to keep it light and comfy rather than fill it with antiques. The result is casual yet spiffy, the kind of place where you can put your feet up without feeling guilty. Each room has air-conditioning, phone, and other amenities. Two rooms share a rooftop deck with lake views. All guests share use of an outdoor enclosed whirlpool tub. A full breakfast is provided. Spa weekends are offered in the off-season.

## FOOD
### Wineries

Head inland on Route 17 and then noodle off on the the back roads to discover not one but two wineries. At **Sweetgrass Farm Winery and Distillery** (347 Carroll Rd., Union, 207/785-3024, www.sweetgrasswinery.com, 11 A.M.–5 P.M. daily late May–late Dec.), owner Keith Bodine uses Maine-grown fruits to produce both wines and spirits, and he is eager to show interested folks how he does it. He's worked at wineries from California to China, and early reviews of his newest venture are positive. Bring a picnic to enjoy while hiking the winery's trails. Carroll Road is between Shepard Hill Road and North Union Road, both north off Route 17 west of Route 131.

Nearby is **Savage Oakes** (174 Barrett Hill Rd., Union, 207/785-5261, www.savageoakes.com, 11 A.M.–5 P.M. Fri.–Sun. May–Oct.), where Elmer and Holly Savage and their sons have added winemaking to their second-generation Belted Galloway cattle farm. They grow nine varieties of grapes, both red and white, and produce more than a half dozen wines. Barrett Hill Road is off Route 17 directly opposite Route 131 South.

## Local Flavors

A winner for creative breakfasts and lunches is **The Brown Bag** (606 Main St., Rockland, 207/596-6372 or 800/287-6372, bakery 207/596-6392, 6:30 A.M.–4 P.M. Mon.–Sat.). It's *the* place for breakfast, especially weekends, with fantastic baked goods and a full blackboard of other options. Lunches include a half-dozen veggie choices and imaginative salads. Order at the counter; no table service. The Brown Bag is at the junction of Routes 1 and 17.

Holding down the other end of Main Street is a relative newcomer, the **Brass Compass Café** (305 Main St., Rockland, 207/596-5960, www.brasscompasscafe.com, 5 A.M.–2 P.M. daily). A great choice for Maine fare, its portions are big, the prices are small, and most of the ingredients are locally sourced. Sit indoors or on the patio. If you're really hungry, try the Titanic omelette, made with "everything but the galley sink."

Hot diggity dog! Backed up against an outside wall of The Brown Bag is a long-standing Rockland lunch landmark—**Wasses Hot Dogs** (2 N. Main St., Rockland, 207/594-7472, 10:30–6 P.M. Mon.–Sat., 11 A.M.–4 P.M. Sun.), source of great chili dogs and creative ice cream (in waffle cones). This onetime lunch wagon is now a permanent modular building—only for takeout, though. It's open all year. Branch "wagons" carry on the tradition in Camden, Belfast, Thomaston, and the south end of Rockland.

Lots of Rockland-watchers credit Maine's first bookstore/café, **Rock City Books and Coffee** (328 Main St., Rockland, 207/594-4123, www.rockcitycoffee.com, 7 A.M.–6 P.M. Mon.–Fri., 8 A.M.–6 P.M. Sat.) with sparking the designer-food renaissance in town. The menu has expanded greatly since the original coffee, tea, and treats to include frozen drinks, soups, salads, sandwiches, and wraps (including

rockin' breakfast wraps, served until 11 A.M.), and plenty of vegetarian choices. Order at the counter and then peruse the shelves of more than 10,000 carefully selected new and "gently used" books while you wait. Frequently there is weekend entertainment.

Scratch-made bread, pastries, and grab-and-go sandwiches have made **Atlantic Baking Co.** (351 Main St., Rockland, 207/596-0505, www.atlanticbakingco.com, 7 A.M.–6 P.M. daily) a popular spot for a quick, informal lunch. There are plenty of tables to enjoy your treats.

If you're craving a decent breakfast (or lunch or snack) and are up for a little foray "down the peninsula," head for the **Owls Head General Store** (2 S. Shore Dr., Owls Head, 207/596-6038), where the atmosphere is friendly and definitely contagious. If you get lost, the helpful staff will steer you the right way, and they will even take your photograph in front of the store. Despite all the competition from lobster-in-the-rough places, the lobster roll here is among the best around.

The **Rockland Farmers Market** gets under way 9 A.M.–1 P.M. each Thursday June–September at Harbor Park, on Rockland's Public Landing. Wares from more than a dozen vendors include produce, crafts, syrup, poultry, mushrooms, baked goods, and cheeses. Every week, there's a special event—music, dancers, lectures, special giveaways, and occasionally a llama or goat for the kids to pet.

## Ethnic Fare

When you're *really* famished, the place to go (maybe) is **Conte's Fish Market and Restaurant** (Harbor Park, off Main St., Rockland, 207/596-5579), where portions are humongous and prices are not ($10–20). John Conte moved here from New York in 1995, bringing his family's century-old restaurant tradition. Specialties are pasta and seafood—Italian all the way, loaded with garlic. Beer and wine only. The decor is wildly funky—fishnets, marine relics, old books, even stacks of canned plum tomatoes—all with a terrific view of Rockland Harbor. Menus are handwritten on paper-towel rolls and in-your-face at the door (order before you sit down), table coverings are yesterday's newspapers, and Edith Piaf *chansons* or operatic arias sometimes play in the background. Eccentric, unpredictable, and definitely not for everyone. Bring your sense of humor and don't be put off by the exterior or the attitude; there's life behind the doors. No credit cards. It's open at 4 P.M. daily for dinner, all year (usually, but maybe not).

**Amalfi** (421 Main St., Rockland, 207/596-0012, 5–9 P.M. Tues.–Sat.) is a Mediterranean oasis. Originally downtown, in early 2008 it moved to a more spacious waterfront location in the old MBNA complex. Given the move, it's wise to call to verify hours. Most entrées are in the $16–22 range. An excellent wine list and hard-to-resist desserts round out the choices.

Sushi fans rave about Keiko Suzuki Steinberger's **Suzuki's Sushi Bar** (419 Main St., Rockland, 207/596-7447, 11 A.M.–2:30 P.M. and 5:30–8:30 P.M. Tues.–Sat.). The food matches the decor, simple yet sophisticated. Sashimi, nigiri, *maki,* and *temaki* choices range $6–10; hot entrées are $9–18. Both hot and cold sake are served, or try a saketume, made with gin or vodka, sake, and ume plum.

Southwest fare dominates the menu at **The Park Street Grille** (279 Main St. at Park St., Rte. 1, Rockland, 207/594-4944, 11:30 A.M.–2 P.M. Mon.–Sat. and 5–9 P.M. Mon.–Sun., to 10 P.M. Fri. and Sat). Steaks and seafood are also specialties at this casual, bright spot at the southern end of the main drag. The margaritas are huge and the nacho platter could make a whole meal. Entrée range is $5–14.

A small dining area decorated in avocado and gold is the appropriate setting for the Cal-Mex food dished out at **Sunfire Mexican Grill** (488 Main St., Rockland, 207/594-6196, 11 A.M.–3 P.M. Tues.–Sat. and 5–8 P.M. Thurs.–Sat.). You'll find all the usuals, from tacos ($2.95) to chipotle shrimp tostada ($11.75). Everything is prepared fresh on-site.

## Casual Dining

**Café Miranda** (15 Oak St., Rockland, 207/594-2034, www.cafemiranda.com, 5:30–9 P.M. daily, 8:30 A.M.–1:30 P.M. Sun. brunch, and

in summer, 11:30 A.M.–2 P.M. daily) is summed up in one of its slogans, "We do not serve the food of cowards." This popular, casual place is terrific—and moderately priced—with a huge (make that overwhelming) and eminently adventurous (most choices work) menu. Lots of pastas, smoked items, veggies, olive oil, greens, and way-out combinations. Entrées are $15–26, but many of the appetizers ($6.50–12) are enough for a meal. Fresh-from-the-brick-oven focaccia comes with everything. If you sit at the counter, you can watch chef Kerry Altiero's creations emerging from the oven. Beer and wine only. Reservations are essential throughout the summer and on weekends off-season.

At the end of a day exploring Rockland, relax at **In Good Company** (415 Main St., 207/593-9110, opens 4:30 P.M. Tues.–Sun.), a casual wine bar with a creative, tapas-style selection of small and large plates.

## Destination Dining

Arriving in Rockland trailing a James Beard award–winning reputation, chef Melissa Kelly opened **◀ Primo** (Rte. 73, Rockland, 207/596-0770, www.primorestaurant.com, 5:30–10 P.M. daily in summer) in the spring of 2000 and hasn't had time to breathe. Since then, she's gone on to open two other restaurants and in 2007 expanded this one in an air-conditioned Victorian home. Fresh local ingredients (many from the restaurant's gardens) are a high priority, and unusual fish specials appear every day. Appetizers are especially imaginative; entrée range is $16–30. Kelly's partner Price Kushner produces an impressive range of breads and desserts. Reservations are essential, usually at least a week ahead on midsummer weekends—and you still may have to wait when you get there. That said, Primo slipped a notch during the renovations, so ask locally about its current reputation before making a special trip. Closed January–May.

# INFORMATION AND SERVICES

## Information

Check out the Rockland-Thomaston Area Chamber of Commerce (Gateway Center,

P.O. Box 508, Rockland 04841, 207/596-0376 or 800/562-2529, www.therealmaine.com, 9 A.M.–5 P.M. Mon.–Fri. and 10 A.M.–2 P.M.) Sat.) or Rockland Public Library (80 Union St., Rockland, 207/594-0310, www.rock-landlibrary.org).

## Public Restrooms

You'll find public restrooms at the Gateway Center; the Knox County Court House, Union and Masonic Streets; the Rockland Recreation Center, across from the courthouse, next to the playground, Union and Limerock Streets; the Rockland Public Library; and the Maine State Ferry Service terminal.

## GETTING AROUND

All Aboard Trolley Co. (21 Limerock St., 207/594-9300 or 866/594-9300, www.aatrol-ley.com) offers 45-minute sightseeing tours of downtown Rockland ($8). It departs from Park Drive, next to the Maine Lighthouse Museum.

# Vinalhaven and North Haven Islands

Vinalhaven and neighboring North Haven have been known as the Fox Islands ever since 1603, when English explorer Martin Pring sailed these waters and allegedly spotted gray foxes in his search for sustenance. Nowadays, you'll find reference to that name only on nautical charts, identifying the passage between the two islands as the Fox Islands Thorofare—and there's nary a fox in sight.

Each island has its own distinct personality. To generalize, Vinalhaven is the largest and busiest, while North Haven is sedate and exclusive.

## VINALHAVEN

Five miles wide, 7.5 miles long, and covering 10,000 acres, Vinalhaven is 13 miles off the coast of Rockland—a 75-minute ferry trip. The shoreline has so many zigs and zags that no place on the island is more than a mile from water.

The island is famed for its granite. Vinalhaven granite first headed for Boston around 1826, and within a few decades, quarrymen arrived from as far away as Britain and Finland to wrestle out and shape the incredibly resistant stone. Schooners, barges, and "stone sloops" left Carver's Harbor carrying mighty cargoes of granite destined for government and commercial buildings in Boston, New York, and Washington, D.C. In the 1880s, nearly 4,000 people lived on Vinalhaven, North Haven, and Hurricane Island. After World War I, demand declined, granite gave way to concrete and steel, and the industry petered out and died. But Vinalhaven has left its mark—ornate columns, paving blocks, and curbstones in communities as far west as Kansas City.

With a full-time population of about 1,300 souls, Vinalhaven is a serious working community, not primarily a playground. Nearly 600 island residents depend on the lobster and fishing industry. Shopkeepers cater to locals as well as visitors, and increasing numbers of artists and artisans work away in their studios. For day-trippers, there's plenty to do—shopping, picnicking, hiking, biking, swimming—but an overnight stay provides a chance to sense the unique rhythm of life on a year-round island.

### Sights

One Main Street landmark that's hard to miss is the three-story, cupola-topped **Odd Fellows Hall,** a Victorian behemoth with assorted gewgaws in the streetfront display windows. Artist Robert Indiana, who first arrived as a visitor in 1969, owns the structure, built in 1885 for the IOOF Star of Hope Lodge. It's not open to the public.

At the top of the hill just beyond Main Street (corner of School and E. Main Sts.) is a greenish-blue replica **galamander,** a massive reminder of Vinalhaven's late-19th-century granite-quarrying era. Galamanders, hitched to oxen or horses, carried the stone from island

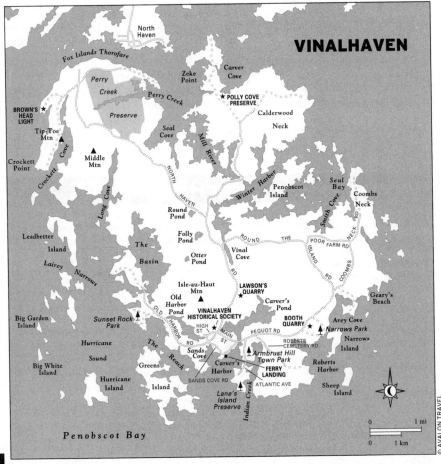

## VINALHAVEN

Penobscot Bay

© AVALON TRAVEL

quarries to the finishing shops. (By the way, the origin of the name remains unexplained.) Next to the galamander is a colorful wooden bandstand, site of very popular evening band concerts held sporadically during the summer.

The unusually energetic **Vinalhaven Historical Society** (207/863-4410, 11 A.M.–3 P.M. daily July and Aug. or by appt., free), operates a museum in the onetime town hall on High Street, just east of Carver's Cemetery. The building itself has a tale, having been floated across the bay from Rockland, where it served as a Universalist church. The muse-

um's documents and artifacts on the granite industry are particularly intriguing, and special summer exhibits add to the interest. Donations are welcomed. At the museum, request a copy of *A Self-Guided Walking Tour of the Town of Vinalhaven and Its Granite-Quarrying History,* a handy little brochure that details 17 in-town locations related to the late-19th and early-20th-century industry.

Built in 1832 and now owned by the town of Vinalhaven, **Brown's Head Light** guards the southern entrance to the Fox Islands Thorofare. To reach the grounds (no access

It's just over an hour's ferry trip to Vinalhaven Island from Rockland.

to the light itself; the keeper's house is a private residence for the town manager), take the North Haven Road about six miles, at which point you'll see a left-side view of the Camden Hills. Continue to the second road on the left, Crockett River Road. Turn and take the second road on the right, continuing past the Brown's Head Cemetery to the hill overlooking the lighthouse.

## Parks and Preserves

Vinalhaven is loaded with wonderful hikes and walks, some deliberately unpublicized. Since the mid-1980s, the foresighted **Vinalhaven Land Trust** (207/863-2543) has expanded the opportunities. When you reach the island, pick up maps at the land trust's office at **Skoog Memorial Park** (Sands Cove Road, west of the ferry terminal) or inquire at the town office or the Paper Store. The trust also offers a seasonal series of educational walks and talks.

Some hiking options are the **Perry Creek Preserve** (terrific loop trail), **Middle Mountain Park, Tip-Toe Mountain, Polly Cove Preserve,** **Isle au Haut Mountain, Arey's Neck Woods, Huber Preserve,** and **Sunset Rock Park.**

The Maine chapter of **The Nature Conservancy** (207/729-5181) owns or manages several islands and island clusters near Vinalhaven. **Big Garden** (formerly owned by Charles and Anne Morrow Lindbergh) and **Big White Islands** are easily accessible and great for shoreline picnics if you have your own boat. Other Conservancy holdings in this area are fragile environments, mostly nesting islands off-limits mid-March–mid-August. Contact The Conservancy for specifics.

No, you're not on the moors of Devon, but you could be fooled in the 45-acre **Lane's Island Preserve,** one of The Nature Conservancy's most-used island preserves. Masses of low-lying ferns, rugosa roses, and berry bushes cover the granite outcrops of this sanctuary—and a foggy day makes it even more moorlike and mystical, a Brontë novel setting. The best (albeit busiest) time to come is early August, when you can compete with the birds for blackberries, raspberries, and blueberries. Easy

© TOM NANGLE

trails wind past old stone walls, an aged cemetery, and along the surf-pounded shore. The preserve is a 20-minute walk (or five-minute bike ride) from Vinalhaven's ferry landing. Set off to the right on Main Street, through the village. Turn right onto Water Street and then right on Atlantic Avenue. Continue across the causeway on Lane's Island Road and left over a salt marsh to the preserve. The large white house on the harbor side of Lane's Island is privately owned.

Next to the ferry landing in Carver's Harbor is **Grimes Park,** a wooded, vest-pocket retreat with a splendid view of the harbor. Owned by the American Legion, the 2.5-acre park is perfect for picnics or for hanging out (especially in good weather) between boats.

Just behind the Island Community Medical Center, close to downtown, is 30-acre **Armbrust Hill Town Park,** once the site of granite-quarrying operations. Still pockmarked with quarry pits, the park has beautifully landscaped walking paths and native flowers, shrubs, and trees—much of it thanks to late island resident Betty Roberts, who made this a lifelong endeavor. From the back of the medical center, follow the trail to the summit for a southerly view of Matinicus and other offshore islands. If you're with children, be especially careful about straying onto side paths, which go perilously close to old quarry holes. Before the walk, lower the children's energy level at the large playground off to the left of the trail.

## Recreation

**Swimming:** Abandoned quarries are all over the island, and most are on private property, but two town-owned ones are easy to reach from the ferry landing. **Lawson's Quarry,** on the North Haven Road, is about a mile from downtown; **Booth Quarry** is on Pequot Road, 1.5 miles from downtown. Both are signposted. You'll see plenty sunbathers on the rocks and swimmers on a hot day, but there are no lifeguards, so swimming is at your own risk. There are no restrooms or changing rooms. *Note:* Pets and soap are not allowed in

the water; camping, fires, and alcohol are not allowed in the quarry areas.

Down the side road beyond Booth Quarry is **Narrows Park,** a town-owned space looking out toward Narrows Island, Isle au Haut, and, on a clear day, Mount Desert Island.

For saltwater swimming, continue along Pequot Road about 1.5 miles beyond Booth Quarry. At the crossroads, you'll see a whimsical bit of local folk art—the Coke lady sculpture. Turn right (east) and go a half mile to **Geary's Beach** (also called **State Beach**), where you can picnic and scour the shoreline for shells and sea glass.

**Bicycling:** Even though Vinalhaven's 40 or so miles of public roads are narrow, winding, and poorly shouldered, they're relatively level, so a bicycle is a fine way to tour the island. Bring your own, preferably a hybrid or mountain bike, or rent one at the **Tidewater Motel** (207/863-4618), on Main Street ($10 a day or $5 a half day). A wide selection of rental bikes is available on the mainland in Rockport at **Maine Sport Outfitters** (Rte. 1, Rockport, 207/236-8797 or 888/236-8796), but you have to pay extra to bring one on the ferry.

A 10-mile, 2.5-hour bicycle route begins on Main Street and goes clockwise out the North Haven Road (rough pavement), past Lawson's Quarry, to Round the Island Road (some sections are dirt), then Poor Farm Road to Geary's Beach and back to Main Street via Pequot Road and School Street. Carry a picnic and enjoy it on Lane's Island; stop for a swim in one of the quarries; or detour down to Brown's Head Light. If you're here for the day, keep track of the time so you don't miss the ferry.

**Sea Kayaking:** By reservation, kayak tours and instruction are available through **SeaEscape Kayak** (15 Harbor View Dr., Vinalhaven, 207/863-9343, www.seaescapekayak.com). An Island Picnic Tour, $85, includes a gourmet picnic lunch on an island. If you're not that gung-ho, try the two-hour Harbor Tour, $45, which is a good introduction to sea kayaking.

## Entertainment

No one visits Vinalhaven for nightlife, but concerts (Fox Island series and others), films, and lectures (most organized by the Vinalhaven Land Trust or the Vinalhaven Historical Society) are frequent. Check *The Wind* to see what's on the docket during your visit.

The Saturday morning flea markets are an island must, as much for the browsing and buying as for the gossip.

## Shopping

Vinalhaven's shops change regularly, but here are a few that have withstood the test of time. **The Paper Store** (Vinal's News Stand; Main St., 207/863-4826) carries newspapers, gifts, film, maps, and odds and ends. **Port O' Call** (Main St., 207/863-2525) is much more than a hardware store. Poke around to see what you'll find. **New Era Gallery** (Main St., 207/863-9351, www.neweragallery.com) has a well-chosen selection of art in varied media representing primarily island artisans. Don't miss the sculpture garden. A few doors away is **Second Hand Prose,** run by the Friends of the Vinalhaven Public Library and carrying a nice selection of used books.

## Accommodations

Don't even consider arriving in summer without reservations if you're planning on staying overnight. If you're going for the day, pay attention to the ferry schedule and allow enough time to get back to the boat. Islanders may be able to find you a bed in a pinch, but don't count on it. The island has no campsites. Rates listed are for peak season.

Your feet practically touch the water when you spend the night at the ◖ **Tidewater Motel and Gathering Space** (12 Main St., Carver's Harbor, P.O. Box 546, Vinalhaven 04863, 207/863-4618, www.tidewatermotel.com, $125–256), a well-maintained motel in two buildings cantilevered over the harbor. Owned by Phil and Elaine Crossman (she operates the New Era Gallery down the street), the 19-room motel was built by Phil's parents in 1970. It's the perfect place to sit on the deck and watch the lobster boats do their thing. Be aware, though, that commercial fishermen are early risers, and lobster-boat engines can rev up as early as 4:30 on a summer morning—all part of the pace of Vinalhaven. Phil is practically a one-man chamber of commerce. He can recommend hikes and other activities and, since he maintains the island's calendar of events, he always knows what's happening and when. A continental breakfast and use of bicycles are included in the rates. Kids 10 and under are free; seven units are efficiencies. It's open all year. Also on the premises is **Island Spirits,** a small gourmet-foods store stocked with wines, beers, cheeses, breads, and other goodies, even picnic baskets to pack it all in. About once a month, the motel hosts a wine tasting in the second-floor Gathering Space, overlooking the harbor. If you want to get a better sense of island life, pick up a copy of Phil's book *Away Happens,* a collection of humorous essays about island living. You can see a sample from it on the motel's website.

Also convenient to downtown is **The Libby House** (Water St., Vinalhaven, 207/863-4696, $75–150, open summer only), with five rooms, three sharing one bath.

## Food

Hours listed are for peak season. Expect reduced hours and fewer days of operation at other times.

**Baked bean suppers** are regularly held at a couple of island locations. Check *The Wind.*

Opposite the municipal parking lot is the **Harbor Gawker** (Main St., 207/863-9365, 10:30 A.M.–8 P.M. daily, to 9 P.M. July and Aug.), a local landmark since 1975, but now with a nice indoor dining area. On the menu are burgers, lobster rolls, sandwich baskets, fried seafood, terrific fish chowder (by the cup, pint, or quart), and soft ice cream. Dine in or take out.

The island's best dinner spot is the harborside room at **The Haven** (Main St., 207/863-4969, Tues.–Sat.), with a great view and a creative menu that changes nightly in summer. It has two reserved seatings—6 and

8:15 P.M. in the Harborside room. The restaurant's streetside room (6:30–9 P.M.) is more casual and less creative (it's called "pub style"), but the walls are lined with artwork on a rotating basis; no reservations, so you may need to wait, especially on summer weekends. The restaurant is a one-woman show, and Torry Pratt doubles as a local caterer and the girls' basketball coach, so hours can be sporadic.

About two miles out of town and overlooking the tidal Mill River is **What's Left Restaurant and High Tide Pub** (North Haven Rd., 207/863-4444, www.whatsleft-onvinalhaven.com, 11 A.M.–2 P.M. and 5:30–9 P.M. Tues.–Sun.). If you don't have a car, call for a ride. The menu varies from soup to steak, $7–22, and there's a full bar.

In the morning, **Island Coffee House** (Main St., 207/863-4311, 4 A.M.–noon Mon.–Sat., 5–11 A.M. Sun.) serves scrumptious baked goods. It morphs into **The Pizza Pit** 4–7 P.M. on Wednesday, Thursday, and Friday, serving pizza, wings, pastas, quesadillas, and similar fare.

If you want alcohol to pair with your meal, **The Sand Bar** (Main St., 207/863-4500, 11 A.M.–10 P.M. daily, to 9 P.M. off-season) has a full bar as well as a good menu of pub-style favorites, soups, salads, and pizza. It often has live music.

The island's best breakfast place is **Surfside** (Harbor Wharf, 207/863-2767). Eat inside or out on the wharf.

## Information and Services

For information on Vinalhaven, write the Vinalhaven Chamber of Commerce (P.O. Box 703, Vinalhaven 04863, www.vinalhaven. org). The chamber produces a helpful little flyer/map showing locations in the Carver's Harbor area. Also helpful for planning a trip to Vinalhaven is a guidebook published by Phil Crossman at the Tidewater Motel (207/863-4618, $3.50). On the island, pick up a copy of Vinalhaven's weekly newsletter, *The Wind* (P.O. Box 194, Vinalhaven 04863, 207/863-2158), named after the island's original newspaper, first published in 1884. It's loaded with island flavor: news items, public-supper announcements, editorials, and ads. A year's subscription is $25; single copies are available at most downtown locales.

Check out the Vinalhaven Public Library (E. Main and Chestnut Sts., 207/863-4401).

Public restrooms are at the ferry landing and the town office (weekdays only).

### Getting Around

I can't emphasize this enough: Don't bring a car unless it is absolutely necessary. If you're coming over for a day trip, you can get to parks and quarries, shops, restaurants, and the historical society museum on foot. If you want to explore farther, a bicycle is an excellent option, or you can rent a car from the Tidewater Motel (207/863-4618), or Phil will meet you at the ferry landing. Call well ahead to reserve.

## NORTH HAVEN

Eight miles long by three miles wide, North Haven is 12 miles off the coast of Rockland—an hour by ferry. The island boasts sedate summer homes, open fields where hundreds of sheep once grazed, about 350 year-round residents, a yacht club called the Casino, and a village gift shop that's been here since 1954.

Originally called North Island, North Haven had much the same settlement history as Vinalhaven, but, being smaller (about 5,280 acres) and more fertile, it has developed—or not developed—differently. In 1846, North Haven was incorporated and severed politically from Vinalhaven, and by the late 1800s, the Boston summer crowd began buying traditional island homes, building tastefully unpretentious new ones, and settling in for a whole season of sailing and socializing. Several generations later, "summer folk" now come for weeks rather than months, often rotating the schedules among slews of siblings. Informality remains the key, though—now more than ever.

The island has two distinct hamlets—North Haven Village, on the Fox Islands Thorofare, where the state ferry arrives, and Pulpit Harbor, particularly popular with the yachting set.

North Haven doesn't offer a lot for the day

visitor, and islanders tend not to welcome them with open arms.

## North Haven Village

Fanning out from the ferry landing is a delightful cluster of substantial, year-round clapboard homes—a marked contrast to the weathered-shingle cottages typical of so many island communities. It won't take long to stroll Main Street.

Anchoring the cluster of shops "downtown" is the **North Haven Gift Shop** (Main St., 207/867-4444), a rabbit warren of rooms that June Hopkins has been running since 1954. You'll have no problem spending money here—everything's tastefully selected, from the pottery to the notecards to the books, jewelry, and gourmet condiments. One room is a gallery with work by Maine artists.

Next door (connected via an elevated corridor) is the **Eric Hopkins Gallery** (Main St., 207/867-2229), owned by June Hopkins's son, a megatalented painter who's gained repute far beyond Maine. If you can't spring for an original (figure on several thousand dollars), his distinctive work—luminous bird's-eye views of island, sea, and forest—now appears also on notecards, postcards, T-shirts, and one-of-a-kind sweaters.

The four-story, early-20th-century **Calderwood Hall** (Main St., 207/867-2265) is artist Herb Parsons's eclectic gift shop/art gallery, with many works by island artists and artisans.

The new **Waterman's Community Center** (Main St., 207/867-2029, www.watermans.org), opened in a renovated market, provides a place for island residents and visitors to gather for entertainment, events, and even coffee and gossip. Check the schedule on its website to see what's planned.

## Bicycling

North Haven has about 25 miles of paved roads, but, just as on most other islands, they are narrow, winding, and nearly shoulderless. Starting near the ferry landing in North Haven Village, take South Shore Road east-ward, perhaps stopping en route for a picnic at town-owned Mullin's Head Park (also spelled Mullen Head) on the southeast corner of the island. Then follow the road around, counterclockwise, to North Shore Road and Pulpit Harbor. Be conscientious and obey the rules of the road and do carry out any trash (yours, or whatever you find along the way).

## Accommodations

Guest beds and food are scarce on North Haven; other than the summer folk, most visitors are day-trippers.

Within walking distance of the ferry is **Nebo Lodge** (11 Mullins La., P.O. Box 358, North Haven 04853, 207/867-2007, www.nebolodge.com, $125–225 peak), which operated as an inn during the first half of the 20th century. A group of island residents bought it in 2005, refurbished it, and it's once again welcoming guests. Nine rooms (four year-round), some with shared baths, are decorated with island art and many have rugs by Angela Adams. There's Wi-Fi throughout. Rates include a full breakfast and use of inn bikes.

Two miles from the ferry landing is **Our Place Inn and Cottages** (R.R. 1, Box 704, North Haven, 207/867-4998, www.ourplaceinn.com), Marnelle and Gordon Bubar's 19th-century farmhouse, with five rooms (three with private bath) and three simple, one-bedroom cottages, with kitchenette. Although weekly rentals are preferred, they'll take shorter reservations when space is available.

## Food

Food choices are also slim. Picnic fixings are available at Brown's Market. For a sit-down lunch (or breakfast or dinner), head for the **Coal Wharf Restaurant** (Main St., 207/867-4739), next to Brown's Boatshop. A rustic seasonal eatery that can serve 60 at a time, it's open 6 A.M.–9 P.M. Tuesday–Sunday in July and August, weekends in June, September, and early October. Reservations are wise.

Other possibilities are **Sip Ahoy at H. J. Blake's** (29 Main St., 207/867-2060, 11 A.M.–11 P.M. daily), across from the ferry terminal, serving sandwiches, chowders, and seafood, and **Waterman's Coffee Shop** (Waterman Center, 207/867-2100, 6:30 A.M.–4:30 P.M. Mon.–Sat., 10 A.M.–4 P.M. Sun.), for coffee and sweets and local news. On Saturday mornings, there's a farmers market on the ball field.

### Information

The best source of information about North Haven is the North Haven Town Office (Upper Main St., North Haven, 207/867-4433, www.northhavenmaine.org).

## GETTING THERE

**The Maine State Ferry Service** (207/596-2202, www.exploremaine.com) operates six round-trips daily between Rockland and Vinalhaven (75-minute crossing) in summer and three round-trips between Rockland and North Haven (70-minute crossing). Round-trip tickets are $14.50 adults, $6.25 kids. Both ferries take cars ($41.50 round-trip, plus $14 reservation fee), but a bicycle ($13.75 round-trip per adult bike, $7 per child's bike) will do fine unless you have the time or inclination to see every corner of the island. Getting car space on the ferry during midsummer can be a frustrating—and complicated—experience, so *avoid taking a car to the island*. If you leave a car at the Rockland lot, space available, it's $7 per day or $35 per week. If you're not spending the night on the island, watch the clock so you don't miss the last boat back to Rockland.

No official ferry service travels between Vinalhaven and North Haven, even though the two islands are almost within spitting distance. Fortunately, the J. O. Brown and Sons boat shop on North Haven provides shuttles most days from 7 A.M. on. Call the boat shop (207/867-4621) to arrange a pickup on the Vinalhaven side. (A handy outdoor pay phone is at the north end of Vinalhaven—at the end of the North Haven Road.) Don't let anyone convince you to return to Rockland for the ferry to North Haven.

**Penobscot Island Air** (207/596-7500, www.penobscotislandair.net) flies twice daily to Vinalhaven and North Haven, weather permitting, from Knox County Regional Airport in Owls Head, just south of Rockland. Seat availability is dependent on mail volume.

# Camden-Rockport Area

Driven apart by a local squabble in 1891, Camden and Rockport have been separate towns for more than a century, but they're inextricably linked. They share school and sewer systems and an often-hyphenated partnership. On Union Street, just off Route 1, a white wooden arch reads Camden on one side and Rockport on the other. These days, this area is one of the Mid-Coast's—even Maine's—prime destinations.

Camden, the better known of the two, has a year-round population of about 5,300, but that triples during the summer; Rockport, with a much lower profile, doubles in summer from about 3,500 year-round. While Rockport's harbor is relatively peaceful—with yachts, lobster boats, and a single windjammer schooner—Camden Harbor is a summer-long madhouse, jammed with dinghies, kayaks, windjammers, megayachts, minor yachts, and a handful of fishing craft.

Much of Camden's appeal is its drop-dead-gorgeous setting—a deeply indented harbor with parks, a waterfall, and a dramatic backdrop of low mountains. It is views of Camden that typify Maine nationwide, even worldwide, on calendars and postcards, in photo books, you name it.

## SIGHTS
### Self-Guided Historical Tour

The Camden-Rockport Historical Society, supported by the Whitehall Inn, has produced a handy little flyer, *A Walking Tour and Bicycle or Car Tour*, detailing more than 50 significant historic sites (mostly private residences)

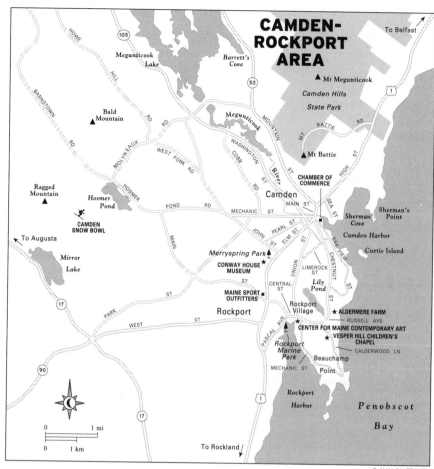

CAMDEN-ROCKPORT AREA

To Belfast

105

Megunticook Lake

Barrett's Cove

52

▲ Mt Megunticook

Camden Hills State Park

1

HOWE

HILL

BARNSTOWN RD

▲ Bald Mountain

Megunticook River

RD

RD

MOLYNEAUX

WEST FORK RD

WASHINGTON ST

COBB RD

MT BATTIE RD

BATTIE

▲ Mt Battie

HIGH ST

CHAMBER OF COMMERCE

Camden

MAIN ST

SEA ST

Sherman's Point

Ragged Mountain ▲

Hosmer Pond

HOSMER

POND        RD

MECHANIC        ST

Sherman Cove

Camden Harbor

Curtis Island

CAMDEN SNOW BOWL

To Augusta

Mirror Lake

MAIN        ST

JOHN ST

PEARL ST

ELM ST

UNION ST

BAY VIEW

Merryspring Park ★

CONWAY HOUSE MUSEUM

CENTRAL ST

LIMEROCK ST

CHESTNUT ST

Lily Pond

17

PARK

WEST        ST

ST

MAINE SPORT OUTFITTERS

Rockport

Rockport Village

★ ALDERMERE FARM

RUSSELL  AVE

90

PASCAL AVE

CENTER FOR MAINE CONTEMPORARY ART
★  VESPER HILL CHILDREN'S CHAPEL

CALDERWOOD LN

17

Rockport Marine Park

MECHANIC ST

Beauchamp Point

Rockport Harbor

Penobscot Bay

0        1 mi

0        1 km

1

To Rockland

© AVALON TRAVEL

in downtown Camden, Camden's High Street and Chestnut Street Historic Districts, and downtown Rockport. To cover it all, you'll want a car or bike; to cover segments and really appreciate the architecture, don your walking shoes. Pick up a copy of the flyer at the chamber of commerce.

## Old Conway Homestead and Cramer Museum

Just inside the Camden town line from Rockport, the Old Conway Homestead and Cramer Museum (Conway Rd., Camden, 207/236-2257, 10 A.M.–4 P.M. Mon.–Thurs. July–Aug., $5 adults, $2 kids) is a five-building complex owned and run by the Camden-Rockport Historical Society. The 18th-century Cape-style Conway House, on the National Register of Historic Places, contains fascinating construction details and period furnishings; in the barn are carriages and farm tools. Two other buildings—a blacksmith shop and a 19th-century sap house used for making maple syrup—have been moved to the grounds and restored. In the contemporary Mary Meeker Cramer Museum (named for the prime benefactor) are displays from the historical society's collection of ship models, old documents, and period clothing. For local color, don't miss the Victorian outhouse. The museum and sap house are also open for maple-syrup demonstrations on Maine Maple Sunday (fourth Sunday in March).

## Vesper Hill

Built and donated to the community by a local benefactor, the rustic, open-air **Vesper Hill Children's Chapel** is dedicated to the world's children. Overlooking Penobscot Bay and surrounded by gardens and lawns, the nondenominational chapel is an almost mystical oasis in a busy tourist region. Except during weddings or memorial services, there's seldom a crowd, and if you're lucky, you might have the place to yourself. From Central Street in downtown Rockport, take Russell Avenue east to Calderwood Lane (fourth street on right). On Calderwood, take the second right (Chapel St.) after the (private) golf course. If the sign is down, look for a boulder with Vesper Hill carved in it. From downtown Camden, take Chestnut Street to just past Aldermere Farm; turn left at Calderwood Lane and take the second right after the golf course.

**Aldermere Farm** (20 Russell Ave., Rockport, 207/236-2739, www.aldermere.org), by the way, is the home of America's original herd of Belted Galloway cattle—Anguslike beef cattle with a wide white midriff. First imported from Scotland in 1953, the breed now shows up in pastures all over the United States. The animals' startling "Oreo-cookie" hide pattern never fails to halt passersby—especially in spring and early summer, when the calves join their mothers in the pastures. Maine Coast Heritage Trust, a state conservation organization based in Brunswick, owns the 135-acre farm. Call for information on tours or other events.

## Center for Maine Contemporary Art

Once a local firehouse, this attractive building has been totally rehabbed to provide display space for the work of Maine's best contemporary artists. The nonprofit Center for Maine Contemporary Art (62 Russell Ave., Rockport, 207/236-2875, www.artsmaine.org, 10 A.M.–5 P.M. Tues.–Sat., 1–5 P.M. Sun., $5), mounts as many as a dozen shows each summer, along with special lectures, a wildly popular art auction (early Aug.), an annual juried art exhibition featuring more than 100 selections, and an annual juried craft show (mid-Oct.) spotlighting several dozen artisans. An exceptional gift shop carries high-end crafts.

## Camden Area History Center

If you want to know more about Edna St. Vincent Millay or Camden's role in Peyton Place or delve into the area's heritage, the Camden Area History Center (4 Union St., Camden, 207/236-2778, www.camdenhistorycenter.org, 9 A.M.–1 P.M. Tues. and Sat., 1–4 P.M. Thurs.) is the place to go. Opened in 2005, the center has exhibits, archives, research facilities, and plenty more to keep history hounds happy.

## PARKS AND PRESERVES

For more than a century, the Camden-Rockport area has benefited from the providence of conscientious year-round and summertime conservationists. Thanks to their benevolence, countless acres of fragile habitat, woodlands, and scenic viewpoints have been preserved. Nowadays, the most active organization is the **Coastal Mountains Land Trust (CMLT)** (101 Mt. Battie St., Camden, 207/236-7091, www.coastalmountains.org), founded in 1986. It has protected nearly 6,000 acres. Maps and information about trails open to the public are available from CMLT. Check the website for guided hikes and other events.

A Rockland-based group, **The Georges River Land Trust** (207/594-5166, www.grlt.org), whose territory covers the Georges (St. George) River watershed, is the steward for The Georges Highland Path, a low-impact hiking trail that reaches Rockport and Camden from the back side of the surrounding hills. (See *Hiking* under *Recreation*.)

## ◖ Camden Hills State Park

A five-minute drive and a small fee gets you to the top of **Mt. Battie,** centerpiece of 5,650-acre Camden Hills State Park (Belfast Rd., Rte. 1, 207/236-3109, $3 adults, $1 kids 5–11) and the best place to understand why Camden is "where the mountains meet the sea." The summit panorama is, well, breathtaking, and reputedly the inspiration for Edna St. Vincent Millay's poem "Renascence" (a bronze plaque marks the spot); information boards identify the offshore islands. Climb the summit's stone tower for an even better view. The 20 miles of hiking trails (some for every ability) include two popular routes up Mt. Battie—an easy, hour-long hike from the base parking lot (Nature Trail) and a more strenuous 45-minute one from the top of Mt. Battie Street in Camden (Mt. Battie Trail). Or drive up the paved Mt. Battie Auto Road. The park has plenty of space for picnics. In winter, ice climbers use a rock wall near the Maiden's Cliff Trail, reached via Route 52 (Mountain St.). The park entrance is two miles north of downtown Camden. Request a free trail map. The park is open mid-May–mid-October. Hiking trails are accessible all year, weather permitting.

## Merryspring Park

Straddling the Camden-Rockport boundary, 66-acre Merryspring Park (Conway Rd., Camden, 207/236-2239, www.merryspring.org) is a magnet for nature lovers. More than a dozen well-marked trails wind through woodlands, berry thickets, and wildflowers; near the preserve's parking area are lily, rose, and herb gardens. Admission is free, but donations are welcomed. Special programs (fee charged) include lectures, demonstrations, and a summer Ecology Camp for youngsters. Most programs are held in the park's modern Ross Center, named for Merryspring founders Mary Ellen and Ervin Ross. The entrance is on Conway Road, 0.3 mile off Route 1, at the southern end of Camden. Trails are open dawn to dusk daily; the visitors center is open 9 A.M.–2 P.M. Tuesday–Friday.

## Intown Parks

Just behind the Camden Public Library is the **Camden Amphitheatre** (also called the Bok Amphitheatre, after a local benefactor), a sylvan spot resembling a set for *A Midsummer Night's Dream* (which, yes, has been performed here). Concerts, weddings, and all kinds of other events take place in the park. Across Atlantic Avenue, sloping to the harbor, is **Camden Harbor Park,** with benches, a couple of monuments, and some of the best waterfront views in town. The noted landscape firm of Frederick Law Olmsted designed the park in 1931 and is listed on the National Register of Historic Places. Both the park and amphitheatre were restored to their original splendor in 2004.

Rockport's in-town parks include **Marine Park,** off Pascal Avenue, at the head of the harbor; **Walker Park,** on Sea Street, west side of the harbor; **Mary-Lea Park,** overlooking the harbor next to the Rockport Opera House; and **Cramer Park,** alongside the Goose River just west of Pascal Avenue. At Marine Park are the remnants of 19th-century lime kilns, an antique steam engine, picnic tables, a boat-launching ramp, and a polished granite sculpture of André, a harbor seal adopted by a local family in the early 1960s. André had been honorary harbormaster, ringbearer at weddings, and the subject of several books and a film—and even did the honors at the unveiling of his statue—before he was fatally wounded in a mating skirmish in 1986, at the age of 25.

## Curtis Island

Marking the entrance to Camden Harbor is town-owned Curtis Island, with a 26-foot automated light tower (and adjoining keeper's house) facing into the bay. Once known as Negro Island, it's a sight (and site) made for photo ops; the views are stunning in every direction. A kayak or dinghy will get you out to the island, where you can picnic (take water; there are no facilities), wander around, gather berries, or just watch the passing fleet. Land on the Camden (west) end of the island, allowing for the tide change when you beach your boat. Respect the privacy of the keeper's house in summer; it's occupied by volunteer caretakers.

## G. W. Hodson Park

Another good picnic spot is a tiny little town park just outside of Camden, overlooking the Megunticook River outlet from Megunticook Lake. G. W. Hodson Park is a serene, pine-needled space with a riverfront picnic table. From downtown Camden, take Route 105 (Washington St.) 2.6 miles to Molyneaux Road. Turn right and go a half mile to the park, on the right. Or take Route 52 (Mountain St.) 1.8 miles to Beaucaire Road; turn left and go 0.6 mile to the park.

## Fernald's Neck

Three miles of Megunticook Lake shoreline, groves of conifers, and a large swamp ("the Great Bog") are features of 315-acre Fernald's Neck Preserve, on the Camden-Lincolnville line (and the Knox–Waldo County line). Shoreline and mountain views are stupendous, even more so during fall-foliage season. The easiest trail is the Blue and White Loop, at the northern end of the preserve; the longer Orange Loop begins at the same point, goes past the Great Bog, and loops around the southern end of the preserve. Yellow Trails connect the loops. While on the Blue and White Loop, take the Green offshoot for a great view of the lake and hills. Some sections can be wet; wear boots or rubberized shoes, and use insect repellent. From Route 1 in Camden, take Route 52 (Mountain St.) about 4.5 miles to Fernald's Neck Road, about 0.2 mile beyond the Youngtown Inn. Turn left and then bear left at the next fork. Go past the gray farmhouse at the road's end, continue into the hayfield, and park near the woods. Head into the woods (look for signs bearing The Nature Conservancy oak leaf) and pick up a map/brochure at the trailhead register. A map is also available at the chamber of commerce office.

## Maine Institute for the Healing Arts Herb Garden

Visitors are welcome to visit Deb Soule's one-acre medicinal herb garden (219 Mill St., Rockport, 207/594-0694, www.gomiha.org, 9 A.M.–5 P.M. Mon. –Thurs. May–Oct., free) that is part of a herbal and healing-arts teaching center. Pick up a garden map and guide at the kiosk and then stroll the paths. More than 120 species of medicinal herbs are planted, and everything is labeled. It's both a teaching garden (closed to the public during workshops) and a working garden, as herbs are harvested for various preparations made by Avena Botanicals. During the same hours, the herbal apothecary is open for purchases. Better yet, check on the multitude of courses offered by the institute, which vary from women's health to cooking, healing to feng shui. It's a real gold mine for those who are open to such ideas. Mill Street is just shy of one mile south of the intersection of Routes 17 and 90 in West Rockport. Turn left on Mill Street and continue for almost one mile. Avena is on the right down a long dirt driveway.

# RECREATION
## Recreation Centers

More than an alpine ski area, the **Camden Snow Bowl** (207/236-3438, www.camden-snowbowl.com) is a four-season recreation area with tennis courts, public swimming in Hosmer Pond, and hiking trails as well as alpine trails for day and night skiing and riding and the only toboggan chute in Maine.

## Bicycling and Sea Kayaking

Local entrepreneurs Stuart and Marianne Smith have made **Maine Sport Outfitters** (Rte. 1, Rockport, 207/236-8797 or 888/236-8796, www.mainesport.com) a major destination for anyone interested in outdoor recreation. The knowledgeable staff can lend a hand and steer you in almost any direction, for almost any summer or winter sport. Nothing seems to stump them. The store sells and rents canoes, kayaks, bikes, skis, and tents, plus all the relevant clothing and accessories. A bicycle rents for $20 per day, calm-water canoes and kayaks are $25–30 per day. Sea kayaks are $40 per day single, $50 per day tandem.

**Maine Sport Outdoor School** (800/722-

© TOM NANGLE

Some trails at tiny Camden Snow Bowl have views to Penobscot Bay.

0826, a division of Maine Sport) has a full schedule of canoeing, kayaking, and camping trips. A two-hour guided Camden Harbor tour departs at least three times daily in summer and costs $35 adult, $30 ages 10–15. A four-hour, guided harbor-to-harbor tour (Rockport to Camden) is offered once each day for $75 adult, $60 child, including a picnic lunch. Multiday instructional programs and tours are available. The store is a half mile north of the junction of Routes 1 and 90.

If you have your own canoe, kayak, rowboat, or whatever, there are a number of boat-launching sites, both saltwater (Eaton Point, at the end of Sea Street, in Camden; and, even better, Marine Park, in Rockport) and freshwater (Megunticook Lake, west and east sides; Bog Bridge, on Route 105, about 3.5 miles from downtown Camden; and Barrett's Cove, on Route 52, also about 3.5 miles from Camden).

## Hiking

There's enough hiking in **Camden Hills State Park** to fill any vacation, but many other options exist. For instance, there's **Bald Mountain,** northwest of downtown Camden, for magnificent views of Penobscot Bay. From Route 1 at the southern end of town (between Subway and Exxon), take John Street for 0.8 mile. Turn left and go 0.2 mile to a fork. Continue on the left fork (Hosmer Pond Rd.) for two miles. Bear left onto Barnestown Road (passing the Camden Snow Bowl) and go 1.4 miles to the trailhead on the right, signposted Georges Highland Path Barnestown Access. Maps are available in the box; the parking lot holds half a dozen cars. The blue-blazed trail is relatively easy, requiring just over an hour round-trip; the summit views are spectacular, especially in fall. Carry a picnic and enjoy it at the top. Avoid this in late May and early June, however, when the blackflies take command. Depending on the season, you may encounter squishy areas, although trail stewards have installed some well-placed boardwalks.

**The Georges Highland Path** eventually will wind through the Georges (St. George) River watershed from the source in Liberty to the outlet in Port Clyde. Spearheaded by members of the Georges River Land Trust (207/594-5166, www.grlt.org), the blue-blazed trail now has access points on the outskirts of Camden and West Rockport. Contact the Rockland-based land trust for an up-to-date map, or pick it up from a trailhead box. The easiest access point is on Route 17 about 10 miles from downtown Rockland. Just past Mirror Lake (on your right) is a well-sign-posted parking area. The Ragged Mountain direction (north) is more strenuous than the Spruce Mountain/Mt. Pleasant section (south; across Rte. 17). The latter is a great three-hour round-trip. Views are spectacular in either direction; Ragged Mountain gets you closer to the ocean panorama.

## Swimming

The Camden area is blessed with several locales for freshwater swimming—a real boon, since Penobscot Bay can be mighty chilly, even at summer's peak. **Shirttail Point,** with limited parking, is a small sandy area on the Megunti-cook River. It's shallow enough for young kids and has picnic tables and a play area. From Route 1 in Camden, take Route 105 (Washington St.) 1.4 miles; watch for a small sign on the right. **Barrett's Cove,** on Megunticook Lake, has more parking spaces, usually more swimmers, and restrooms, picnic tables, and grills, as well as a play area. Diagonally opposite the Camden Public Library, take Route 52 (Mountain St.) about three miles; watch for the sign on the left. To cope with the parking crunch on hot summer days, bike to the beaches. You'll be ready for a swim after the uphill stretches, and it's all downhill on the way back.

Camden and Rockport both have saltwater swimming but no major sandy beaches. In Camden, it's **Laite Beach Park,** on Bay View Street about 1.5 miles from downtown Camden. Right on Camden Harbor, the park has great views, a strip of sand, picnic tables, a playground, and children's musical events 1–3 P.M. every Wednesday in July and August. Check the local papers or contact Camden Parks and Recreation (207/236-3438) for the sched-ule. Rockport has **Walker Park,** tucked away on the west side of the harbor. From Pascal Avenue, take Elm Street, which becomes Sea Street. Walker Park is on the left, with picnic tables, a play area, and a small, pebbly beach.

Indoor-pool options are the **Penobscot Bay YMCA** and the **Samoset Resort,** on the Rock-port-Rockland boundary (see *Accommodations* in the *Rockland Area* section).

## Golf

On a back road straddling the Camden-Rock-port line, the nine-hole **Goose River Golf Club** (50 Park St., Rockport, 207/236-8488) competes with the best for outstanding scenery. Starting times are needed on weekends and holidays. It has a snack bar, cart and club rentals, and moderate greens fees.

## Day Sails and Excursions

Most day sails and excursion boats operate late May–October, with fewer trips in the spring and fall than in July and August. You can't compare a two-hour day sail to a weeklong cruise on a Maine windjammer (see sidebar *Windjamming*), but at least you get a hint of what could be—and it's a far better choice for most kids, who aren't allowed on most wind-jammer cruises. Several excursion boats operate out of Camden in summer. Most weekdays, you can just show up at the dock and find a space, but on weekends, you'd better call for a reservation. Several are based at Bay View Landing, formerly known as Sharp's Wharf.

The classic wooden schooner *Olad* (207/236-2323, www.maineschooners.com, $29 adults, $17 for kids under 12) does several two-hour sails daily from Camden's Public Landing, weather permitting, late May–mid-October. Captain Aaron Lincoln is a Rock-land native, so he's got the local scoop on the all the sights.

Another historic Camden day sailer is the 57-foot, 18-passenger schooner *Surprise* (207/236-4687, www.camdenmainesail-ing.com, $30) built in 1918 and skippered by congenial educator Jack Moore and his wife, Barbara. Between May and October, they do daily two-hour sails, departing from Camden's Public Landing. Minimum age is 12.

The 49-passenger **Appledore** (207/236-8353, www.appledore2.com), built in 1978 for round-the-world cruising, sails from Bay View Landing beginning around 10 A.M. 3–4 times daily June–October. Most cruises last two hours and cost $30. Cocktails, wine, and soft drinks are available.

Over in Rockport, the schooner **Heron** (207/236-8605 or 800/599-8605, www.woodenboatco.com) is a 65-foot, John Alden–designed wooden yacht launched in 2003. Sailing options include a lobster-roll lunch sail ($50), lighthouse sail ($38), and sunset sails with hors d'oeuvres ($50).

For a short cruise—but a great way to see Camden and Rockport and their lighthouses and shorelines—head down to the Camden Public Landing and buy a ticket for the 30-passenger converted lobster boat **Betselma** (207/236-4446, www.betselma.com). Reservations usually aren't needed. Retired schooner captain Les Bex knows these waters, the wildlife, and the history. He does about eight hour-long trips daily, beginning at 10:30 A.M. June–September, for $10 adults, $5 children under 12. The last trip is at 7:30 P.M. He also does two two-hour trips—one in the morning, one in the afternoon—for $20 adults, $10 children under 12. A three-hour combo ($30 adults, $15 kids) also is available. Pets are welcome.

If the kids are bombarding you with FAQs about lobsters, here's the solution. Take a two-hour trip aboard Captain Alan Philbrick's **Lively Lady Too** (207/236-6672, $25 adults, $5 under 15), berthed at Camden's Bay View Landing. He hauls in a trap, takes out a lobster, explains all its parts, and generally provides all the answers. As a former biology teacher, he's a whiz at natural history, so there's also information about seabirds, seals, and lots more. Trips depart Monday–Saturday.

## ENTERTAINMENT

At 8 P.M. Thursday and Friday in July and August, and once a month the rest of the year, **Bay Chamber Concerts** (207/236-2823 or 888/707-2770, www.baychamberconcerts.org) draw sell-out audiences to the beautifully restored (and air-conditioned) Rockport Opera House and Rockland's Strand Theatre. Founded in the 1960s as a classical series, the summer concerts feature a resident quartet, prominent guest artists, and outstanding programs. It has expanded to include world music, jazz, and dance. The first week in August ("Next Generation Week") is devoted to classes and concerts for and by talented teenagers. Seats are reserved for summer concerts ($25–33 adults, $8 25 and younger); open seating is the rule in winter, when tickets are less expensive and programs vary from classical to pops to jazz. (Season tickets and flex passes are available.)

The beautifully renovated **Camden Opera House** (29 Elm St., Camden, 207/236-7963, box office 207/236-4884, www.camdenoperahouse.com) is the site of many performances by renowned performers.

## FESTIVALS AND EVENTS

One weekend in February is given over to the **Camden Conference,** an annual three-day foreign-affairs conference with nationally and internationally known speakers. The first weekend in February marks the **National Toboggan Championships,** two days of races and fun at the nation's only wooden toboggan chute at the Camden Snow Bowl.

The third Thursday of July is **House and Garden Day,** when you can take a self-guided tour (10 A.M.–4:30 P.M.) of significant homes and gardens in Camden and Rockport. Proceeds benefit the Camden Garden Club. And the **HarborArts,** on the third weekend in July, draws dozens of artists and craftspeople displaying and selling their wares at the Camden Amphitheatre, Harbor Park.

Labor Day weekend is also known as **Windjammer Weekend** here, with cruises, windjammer open houses, fireworks, and all kinds of live entertainment in and around Camden Harbor. Twenty top artisans open their studios for the annual **Country Roads Artists and Artisans Tour** in September.

**PENOBSCOT BAY**

Dozens of artists and craftspeople display and sell their wares at the **Fall Festival and Arts and Crafts Show,** the first weekend in October at the Camden Amphitheatre, Harbor Park.

**Christmas by the Sea** is a family-oriented early-December weekend featuring open houses, special sales, concerts, and a visit from Santa Claus.

## SHOPPING
### New and Old Books

**The Owl and Turtle Bookshop** (32 Washington St., Camden, 207/236-4769 or 800/876-4769), one of Maine's best new-books stores, with thousands of books and a wonderful children's room, moved to spacious new digs in the Knox Mill Center in 2004. Replacing it in its old location is **Sherman's** (8 Bay View St., Camden, 207/236-2223), another excellent bookstore with shops up and down the coast.

For antiquarian books, **ABCD Books** (23 Bay View St., Camden, 207/236-3903 or 888/236-3903) maintains an excellent stock of rare books and first editions (prices are a bit steep). If you simply want a good read, **Stone Soup Books** (33 Main St., Camden, no phone), a tiny second-floor shop across from the Lord Camden Inn, is Camden's best source for contemporary used fiction.

### Gifts and Crafts

You'll need to wander the streets to take in all the gift and craft shops, particularly in Camden. Some are obvious; others are tucked away on side streets and back alleys. Explore.

A downtown Camden landmark since 1940, **The Smiling Cow** (41 Main St., Camden, 207/236-3351 or 800/646-6169) is as good a place as any to pick up Maine souvenirs—a few slightly kitschy, but most reasonably tasteful. Before or after shopping here, head for the rear balcony for coffee and a knockout view of the harbor and the Megunticook River waterfall.

Follow West Street (Rte. 90) from Route 1 for almost three miles and you'll come to **Danica Candleworks** (Rte. 90, West Rockport, 207/236-3060), producers of the loveliest candle colors you've ever seen. Owner Erik

Laustsen learned the hand-dipping trade from his Danish relatives, and Danica now ships its work all over the country. The Scandinavian-style shop also carries other gift items.

Continue west to find **Messler Gallery** (Center for Furniture Craftsmanship, 25 Mill St., Rockport, 207/594-5611), where rotating shows always focus on woodworking.

### Clothing and Sporting Gear

Established in 1976, **The Admiral's Buttons** (36 Bay View St., Camden, 207/236-2617) stocks a carefully selected line of classic, high-end men's and women's clothing and accessories (bow ties, foul-weather gear, cuff links, Tilley hats, great sweaters), plus Maine-created Shard pottery and Thomas Moser furniture.

Sturdy, well-designed, homemade (by knitting machine) wool and cotton sweaters are the specialty at **Unique One** (2 Bay View St., Camden, 207/236-8717). Or you can pick out yarn and make your own.

### Discount Shopping

How could anyone resist a thrift shop with the name **Heavenly Threads** (57 Elm St., Rte. 1, Camden, 207/236-3203)? Established by Camden's community-oriented First Congregational Church (next door to the shop), Heavenly Threads carries high-quality pre-owned clothing, books, and jewelry. It's staffed by volunteers, with proceeds going to such local ecumenical causes as Meals on Wheels.

## ACCOMMODATIONS

The Camden-Rockport area (including Lincolnville) is loaded with lodgings—from basic motels to cottage complexes to elegant inns and B&Bs. Many of Camden's most attractive accommodations (especially B&Bs) are on Route 1 (variously disguised as Elm St., Main St., and High St.), heavily trafficked in summer. If you're extrasensitive to nighttime noises, request a room facing away from the street.

The chamber of commerce is very helpful with lodging information and also maintains a lengthy list of seasonal rentals. A private firm, **Camden Accommodations** (43 Elm St.,

The Camden Maine Stay is one of many inns within walking distance of downtown.

Rte. 1, Camden, 207/236-6090 or 800/344-4830, www.camdenac.com), arranges reservations at all kinds of lodgings in Camden and surrounding communities—for a week or all summer. In July and August, it's best to reserve far in advance. The toughest time to find a last-minute bed is the first weekend in August, when the Maine Lobster Festival is under way in next-door Rockland.

## Camden

A baker's dozen of Camden's finest B&Bs have banded together in the **Camden Bed and Breakfast Association** (P.O. Box 553, Camden 04843, www.camdeninns.com), with an attractive brochure and website. Some of them are described below. Rates reflect peak season.

One of Maine's most unusual (and priciest) B&Bs, **Norumbega** (61 High St., Rte. 1, Camden, 207/236-4646 or 877/363-4646, $300–475, www.norumbegainn.com) is an 1886 turreted stone castle overlooking Camden's outer harbor. Provided your wallet can stand the crunch, splurge for a night (or two) here—if only to feel like temporary royalty. Twelve rooms and suites, most named after European castles, are strikingly decorated, filled with antiques, and have all the expected amenities. Rates include a full breakfast.

The 1874 **Camden Harbour Inn** (83 Bayview St., Camden, 207/236-4200 or 800/236-4200, www.camdenharbourinn.com, $265–500) underwent a masterful renovation and restoration by new Dutch owners, reopening in 2007 as a boutique bed-and-breakfast complete with 21st-century amenities. It retains the bones of a 19th-century summer hotel, but the decor is contemporary European, with lots of crushed velvet and purples, reds, and silvers (you'll either love it or hate it). Guest rooms, some with fireplaces, patios, decks, or balconies, have at least a glimpse of Camden's harbor or Penobscot Bay; some have spectacular views. All are furnished with period pieces and have air-conditioning, Wi-Fi, flat-screen TV, refrigerator, and king-size beds. Also on the premises is Natalie's restaurant (see *Food*).

Opened for guests in 1901, the **Whitehall**

**Inn** (52 High St., Rte. 1, P.O. Box 558, Camden 04843, 207/236-3391 or 800/789-6565, www.whitehall-inn.com, $149–199) retains its century-old genteel air, right down to the telephone switchboard. Lovely gardens, rockers on the veranda, a tennis court, and attentive service all add to the appeal of this historic country inn. Ask to see the Millay Room, commemorating famed poet Edna St. Vincent Millay, who graduated from Camden High School and first recited her poem "Renascence" to Whitehall guests in 1912. Spread out between the main inn and the annex are 40 comfortable, unpretentious rooms, all with high-speed Internet access and imported linens; a few share baths. The dining room, Vincent's, is open to the public for breakfast (7–10 A.M. Mon.–Sat., to noon Sun.) and dinner (6–9 P.M. Wed.–Mon.). Also on the premises is Gossip, a bar serving pub fare. It's open mid-May–late October.

Innkeepers Bob and Juanita Topper, the hospitable hosts at **Camden Maine Stay** (22 High St., Rte. 1, Camden, 207/236-9636, www.mainestay.com, $135–250), do everything right, from the elegant decor to the delicious breakfasts to the welcoming window candles. The stunning residence, built in 1802, faces busy Route 1 and is just a bit uphill from downtown, but inside and out back, behind the carriage house and barn, you'll feel worlds away.

The **◖ Hartstone Inn** (41 Elm St., Camden, 207/236-4259 or 800/788-4823, www.hartstoneinn.com, $125–265) is Michael and Mary Jo Salmon's imposing mansard-roofed Victorian close to the heart of downtown. Although some rooms face the street (and these are insulated with triple-pane windows), most do not, and all have air-conditioning. Once inside, you're away from it all. Even more removed are rooms in two other buildings under the Hartstone's umbrella. Suites in the Manor House, tucked behind the main inn, have contemporary decor. Rooms and suites in The Hideaway, in a residential neighborhood about a block away, have country French flair. All are elegant (Wi-Fi, air-conditioning); some have fireplaces and whirlpools. Be *sure* to make reservations for dinner. And then, there's

the incredible breakfast. If you get hooked, the Salmons organize culinary classes during the winter, and you can even arrange for a one-on-one cooking experience with Michael.

The eye-grabbing **Captain Swift Inn** (72 Elm St., Camden, 207/236-8113 or 800/251-0865, www.swiftinn.com, $119–245) is named after Frank Swift, who launched Penobscot Bay's windjammer trade. All have air-conditioning and Wi-Fi, and two have gas fireplaces. Children under 10 are free.

In the heart of downtown Camden, **The Lord Camden Inn** (24 Main St., Rte. 1, Camden, 207/236-4325 or 800/336-4325, www.lordcamdeninn.com, $179–289 peak) is a hotel alternative in a historic, four-story downtown building (with elevator). Decor is reproduction Colonial with exposed brick walls and scads of old framed photos in rooms and hallways. (The brick moderates the noise level.) All 31 rooms and suites have phones, air-conditioning, TV, and Wi-Fi; a full breakfast buffet is provided. In-room spa services are available. Top-floor rooms have harbor-view balconies. Pooches are pampered in pet-friendly rooms for $20 per night, including bed, biscuits, bowls, and local dog info.

A fine choice for families is **The Lodge at Camden Hills** (Rte. 1, P.O. Box 794, Camden 04843, 207/236-8478 or 800/832-7058, www.thelodgeatcamdenhills.com, $125–225), with 20 modern suites and cottages in an especially attractive modern enclave a mile uphill from downtown Camden. Facilities include air-conditioning, phones, TV, some kitchens, some fireplaces, and some whirlpool tubs.

A hybrid of an inn, B&B, motel, and cottage three miles north of town, **The High Tide Inn on the Ocean** (Rte. 1, Camden, 207/236-3724 or 800/788-7068, www.hightideinn.com, $95–220) has enough variety for every budget—all in an outstanding, seven-acre oceanfront setting with a private pebbly beach. The two-story, eight-unit "Oceanfront" motel unit is closest to the water and farthest from Route 1. Rates include continental breakfast on the water-view porch. Pets can be accommodated in some rooms.

Step back in time at family-owned **Beloin's on the Maine Coast** (245 Belfast Rd./Rte. 1, Camden, 207/236-3262, www.beloins.com, $80–175 d). Don't judge this place from the roadside motel; down the road is another motel and cottages with spectacular oceanfront settings. Agnes Beloin keeps everything tidy, but it's all a bit old-fashioned and rustic (think 1950s). But heck, with this location, who cares! All guests have access to a private sand beach. A two-bedroom shorefront cottage is $240 d. Extra guests in rooms are $5 per night; pets are $10 per stay.

It's a short stroll into Merryspring Gardens from the **Cedar Crest Motel** (115 Elm St., Rte. 1, Camden, 207/236-4839, www.cedarcrestmotel.com, $124–139), a nicely maintained property on 3.5 wooded and landscaped acres on the southern edge of downtown. Each of the 37 rooms has air-conditioning, Wi-Fi, phone, and TV. Some have minifridges. On the premises are a guest computer, outdoor heated pool, playground, laundry, and restaurant serving all meals.

## Rockport

One of the area's spiffiest motels also has terrific Penobscot Bay views. In the Glen Cove section of Rockport (three miles south of downtown Rockport, three miles north of downtown Rockland, next door to Penobscot Bay Medical Center), the **Glen Cove Motel** (Rte. 1, P.O. Box 35, Glen Cove 04846, 207/594-4062 or 800/453-6268, www.glencovemotel.com, $129–209) sits on a 17-acre bluff with a lovely trail leading to the rocky shore. Many of the 34 units boast water views; all have air-conditioning, phones, cable TV, and refrigerators. The pool is heated. Request a room set back from Route 1.

The family-owned and operated all-suites **Country Inn** (8 Country Inn Way, Rte. 1, Rockport, 207/236-2725 or 888/707-3945, www.countryinnmaine.com, $175–210 d) is an especially good choice for families, thanks to an indoor pool, play areas, guest laundry, and fitness room. Some units have fireplaces, whirlpool tubs, and microwaves; all have air-

conditioning, phone, fridge, Wi-Fi, and TV. A continental breakfast buffet, afternoon snacks, and evening chocolate-chip cookies are included. Kids 6–16 are $5 per night; those older are $10. On-site massage is available.

## Seasonal Rentals

The chamber of commerce maintains a lengthy list of seasonal rentals. Also handling private rentals is **Camden Accommodations** (43 Elm St., Rte. 1, Camden, 207/236-6090 or 800/344-4830, www.camdenac.com).

## Camping

**Camden Hills State Park** (Belfast Rd., Rte. 1, 207/236-3109, $3 adults, $1 kids 5–11, $20 nonresident, $15 resident) has a 112-site camping area (no hookups) and is wheelchair-accessible. Pets are allowed, showers are free, and the sites are large.

**Megunticook Campground by the Sea** (Rte. 1, P.O. Box 375, Rockport 04856, 207/594-2428 or 800/884-2428, www.campgroundbythesea.com, $35–45) is the area's best-run commercial campground, a 17-acre facility with 87 wooded sites. Also on the premises are 10 camping cabins ($72). Amenities include a playground, snack bar, heated pool, laundry, and kayak rentals. Weekly lobster bakes (about $20) are held at the oceanfront picnic area. Noise rules are strictly enforced; pets are allowed. The only drawback is that the coin-op showers shut off too frequently. It's open mid-May–mid-October. The campground is three miles south of Camden, five miles north of Rockland.

## FOOD

As always, make reservations.

## Local Flavors

**Rockport:** The best source for health foods, homeopathic remedies, and fresh, seasonal produce is **Fresh Off the Farm** (Rte. 1, Rockport, 207/236-3260, 8 A.M.–7 P.M. Mon.–Sat. and 9 A.M.–5:30 P.M. Sun.), an inconspicuous red-painted roadside place that looks like an overgrown farmstand (it is). Watch for one of those permanent/temporary signs highlighting latest arrivals (Native Blueberries, Native Corn, etc.). The shop is 1.3 miles south of the junction of Routes 1 and 90.

At the southern entrance to Rockport, a sprawling red building is the home of **The State of Maine Cheese Company** (461 Commercial St., Rte. 1, Rockport, 207/236-8895 or 800/762-8895), makers of a dozen varieties of cows'-milk hard cheeses, all named after Maine locations (Aroostook Jack, Allagash Caraway, St. Croix Black Pepper, and so on). Under the cheese company's umbrella (and roof) is the Maine-Made Products Center, covering 9,500 square feet. Among the items are blueberry chutneys, maple syrup, designer breads, great jams—a one-stop-shopping (and tasting) site.

At the junction of Routes 1 and 90, a colorfully painted barn is the home of **The Market Basket** (Rte. 1, Rockport, 207/236-4371, 7 A.M.–6:30 P.M. Mon.–Fri. and 8 A.M.–6:30 P.M. Sat.), the best takeout source for creative sandwiches, homemade soups, cheeses, exotic condiments, pastries, wine (large selection), beer, and entrées-to-go. The market will also do boat provisioning. In winter, the Market Basket sponsors weeklong cooking classes. It's also open Sundays in peak season.

**Camden:** The **Camden Farmers Market,** one of the best in the state, holds forth in a parking lot at Colcord and Limerock Streets, across from Tibbetts Industries. Temporary signs are posted on Route 1 on market days—4:30–6 P.M. Wednesday mid-June–mid-September; 9 A.M.–noon Saturday mid-May–October. The market goes on, rain or shine. There's a winter market at Merry Spring November–May.

The **Camden Bagel Cafe** (Brewster Mill, 26 Mechanic St., Camden, 207/236-2661, 6:30 A.M.–2 P.M. Mon.–Sat., 7:30 A.M.–2 P.M. Sun.) has a hugely loyal clientele, drawn by *real* coffee, fresh bagels, fast service, daily newspapers, and a casual air. No credit cards.

Good coffee is a draw at the **Camden Deli** (37 Main St., Camden, 207/236-8343, 6 A.M.–10 P.M. daily), in the heart of downtown, but its biggest asset is the windowed seating overlooking the Megunticook River waterfall. The view doesn't get much better than this (go upstairs for the best angle). Made-to-order sandwiches and wraps, homemade soups, veggie burgers, and subs all add to the mix. Beer and wine only for takeout.

Since the early 1970s, **Scott's Place** (85 Elm St., Rte. 1, Camden, 207/236-8751, 10 A.M.–7 P.M. Mon.–Fri., to 4 P.M. Sat.), a roadside lunch stand near Reny's at the Camden Marketplace, has been dishing up inexpensive ($2–8) burgers and dogs, nowadays adding veggie burgers and salads. Call ahead and it'll be ready.

Peek behind the old-fashioned facade at **Boynton-McKay Food Company** (30 Main St., Camden, 207/236-2465, 7 A.M.–6 P.M. Tues.–Sat. and 8 A.M.–4 P.M. Sun., kitchen closes 3 P.M.), and you'll see an old-fashioned soda fountain, early-20th-century tables, antique pharmacy accessories, and a thoroughly modern café menu. Restored and rehabbed in 1997, Boynton-McKay had been *the* local drugstore for more than a century. The new incarnation features bagels, creative salads, homemade soups, superb wrap sandwiches, an espresso bar, and the whole works from the soda fountain. It's open for breakfast and lunch.

Facing downtown Camden's five-way intersection, **French and Brawn** (1 Elm St., Camden, 207/236-3361, 6 A.M.–8 P.M. Mon.–Sat. and 8 A.M.–8 P.M. Sun.) is an independent market that earns the description *super*. Ready-made sandwiches, soups, and other goodies complement the oven-ready takeout meals, high-cal frozen desserts, esoteric meats, and a staff with a can-do attitude.

Light breakfasts, lunches, pastries, and the area's best coffee are served at **Zoot** (31 Elm St., 207/236-9858, 8:30 A.M.–6 P.M. daily), an ultracasual espresso bar with limited but fresh and flavorful fare.

## Family Favorites

Surprise! The best pizza in town comes from the **Elm Street Grille** (Cedar Crest Motel, 115 Elm St./Rte. 1, Camden, 207/236-4839, www.cedarcrestmotel.com), serving great breakfasts, lunch, and dinner Tuesday–Sunday. It's all very reasonably priced and served in a comfortable dining room, with a handful of seats on a deck. On Friday nights, there's live jazz.

In the heart of Camden, **Cappy's** (1 Main St., Camden, 207/236-2254, www.cappyschowder.com, 11 A.M.–midnight daily) is small, a bit cramped, reliably good (it's been here for more than 25 years), and very popular with locals and out-of-towners alike. In summer, request a table in the second-floor Crow's Nest, where you'll be less squished; microbrew tastings are held here 5–7 P.M. daily in season. It's a burger-and-sandwich menu with some heartier seafood choices ($8–19); clam chowder is a specialty. During summer, Cappy's operates a bakery with takeout pastries, sandwiches, and other goodies underneath, facing on the alley that runs down to the public parking lot.

Scrumptious baked goods, as well as sandwiches, salads, and prepared foods, are available at **Three Dogs Café/Sweet Sensations Pastry Shop** (309 Commercial St./Rte. 1, Rockport, 207/230-0955). Order at the counter and then dine in or take out. In winter, a fireplace keeps everything cozy.

## Casual Dining

Chef/owner Brian Hill has created one of the region's hottest restaurants with █ **Francine Bistro** (55 Chestnut St., Camden, 207/230-0083, www.francinebistro.com, 5:30–10 P.M. daily). The well-chosen menu (entrées $24–30) is short and focused on whatever's fresh and usually locally available that day. In addition to the dining room, there's also seating at the bar and, when the weather cooperates, on the front porch.

Here's a sleeper: **Ephemere** (51 Bay View St., Camden, 207/236-4451, 5:30–9 P.M. Mon.–Sat.) is best known as a wine bar, but it also serves dinners that stretch the imagination, but that work. I mean, really, who would have paired lobster with gingerbread? The wine bar opens at 4:30 P.M. serving a light-fare menu.

Down on the harbor is the informal, art-filled **Atlantica** (1 Bay View Landing, Camden, 207/236-6011 or 888/507-8514, www.atlanticarestaurant.com, 5–9 P.M. daily), two floors of culinary creativity with an emphasis on seafood, entrées $25–36. Consider an onion-crusted halibut BLT or pan-seared day-boat scallops. In summer, try for a table on the deck hanging over the water.

**The Waterfront Restaurant** (Bay View St., Camden, 207/236-3747, 11:30 A.M.–2:30 P.M. and 5–9:30 P.M. daily) has the biggest waterside dining deck in town, but you'll need to arrive early to snag one of the tables. Lunches are the most fun, overlooking lots of harbor action; at high tide, you're eye to eye with the boats. Most entrées run $16–25.

Food as art is the idea behind the **Gallery Café** (297 Commercial St., Rte. 1, Rockport, 207/230-0061, www.prismglassgallery.com, 11 A.M.–3 P.M. and 5–9 P.M. Wed.–Sat., 10 A.M.–3 P.M. and 4–8 P.M. Sun.), a restaurant that's part of **Prismglass**, a fine-art glass gallery and working studio representing more than 50 glass artists. The menu changes seasonally, with dinner entrées, many with Italian leanings, ranging $16–30; brunch is $8–18. It's on Route 1 across from Hoboken Gardens.

Opening in 2007 to rave reviews was **Natalie's at the Camden Harbour Inn** (83 Bayview St., Camden, 207/236-4200), serving a French-accented menu nightly. The dining room is supposed to be reminiscent of the Left Bank in Paris, but instead of looking out at the Seine, you're gazing over Camden Harbor. Entrées begin in the mid-$20s.

## Fine Dining

Reservations are a must for chef Michael Salmon's five-course fixed-price extravaganzas at the **Hartstone Inn** (41 Elm St., Camden, 207/236-4259 or 800/788-4823, www.hartstoneinn.com, $45) Michael, named Caribbean chef of the year when they lived in Aruba, has cooked at the Beard House by invitation. Even Julia Child dined here. The menu changes weekly to use the freshest ingredients.

## INFORMATION AND SERVICES
## Information

The Camden-Rockport-Lincolnville Chamber of Commerce (P.O. Box 919, Camden

04843, 207/236-4404 or 800/223-5459, www.visitcamden.com) is at the Public Landing. Request a copy of its map of area streets and businesses and the official chamber guide.

Check out Camden Public Library (Main St., Rte. 1, Camden, 207/236-3440, www.camden.lib.me.us) or Rockport Public Library (1 Limerock St., Rockport, 207/236-3642, www.rockport.lib.me.us).

## Public Restrooms

Public restrooms are available at Camden's Public Landing, near the chamber of commerce, and at the Camden Public Library. In Rockport, there are restrooms at Marine Park.

# Lincolnville

Since the early 1990s, the town of Lincolnville, in Waldo County just north of Camden, has outpaced all the surrounding communities in population growth. An influx of new residents has pushed the census to the 2,000 mark. Two distinct enclaves make up the town—oceanfront Lincolnville Beach ("the Beach") and, about five miles inland, Lincolnville Center ("the Center"). Lincolnville is laid-back and mostly rural; the major activity center is a short strip of shops and restaurants at the Beach, and few visitors realize there's anything else.

About a mile north of Lincolnville Beach is a part of town with the quaint name of Ducktrap. Near the mouth of the Ducktrap River, where shoreline trees screen the water, ducks used to gather as ducks do. During moulting season, when the ducks shed their feathers and were unable to fly, foraging Native Americans would sneak up on them and capture them for dinner. Or so the story goes.

Directly offshore from Lincolnville Beach, almost within spitting distance, is the island of Islesboro, a fine day-trip destination from Lincolnville and the Camden-Rockport areas. The car ferry departs from the southern end of Lincolnville Beach.

## SIGHTS
### Islesboro

Lying three miles offshore from Lincolnville Beach, via 20-minute car ferry, is 12-mile-long Islesboro, a year-round community with a population of about 600—beefed up annually by a sedate summer colony. Car ferries are frequent enough to make Islesboro an ideal day-trip destination—and that's the choice of most visitors, partly because both dining and lodging are pretty scarce. The only camping is on nearby Warren Island State Park—and you have to have your own boat to get there. If you're not spending the night, keep an eye on the time so you don't miss the last ferry (4:30 P.M.) back to the mainland.

The best way to get an island overview is to do an end-to-end auto tour. You won't see all the huge "cottages" tucked down long driveways, and you won't absorb island life and its rhythms (that requires a longer stay), but you'll scratch the surface of what Islesboro is about. Drive off the ferry, which docks about a third of the way down the island, and go one mile to a stop sign. Turn right and go 1.2 miles to another stop sign. Turn right, onto Main Road, and go 4.3 miles south to the Town Beach at the bottom of the island. Then backtrack on Main Road, past the turnoff to the ferry dock, heading "up island" (as it's known locally) and covering 12 miles to northernmost Pripet and Turtle Head. En route, you'll pass exclusive summer estates, workaday homes, spectacular seaside vistas, and a smattering of shops. On the up-island circuit, watch for a tiny marker on the west side of the road (0.8 mile north of the Islesboro Historical Society building). It commemorates the 1780 total eclipse witnessed here—the first recorded in North America. At the time, British loyalists still held Islesboro, but they temporarily suspended hostilities, allowing Harvard astronomers to lug their instruments to the island and document the eclipse.

Allow time before the return ferry to visit the **Sailors' Memorial Museum,** a town-owned museum filled with seafaring memorabilia and allegedly home to a benevolent ghost or two. It's in the keeper's house adjacent to **Grindle Point Light** (207/734-2253, http://lighthouse.cc/grindle), built in 1850, rebuilt in 1875, and now automated.

With the closure of the Dark Harbor House, overnight accommodations are limited. Two possibilities are **The Village B&B and Café** (119 Derby Rd., Dark Harbor, Islesboro, 207/734-9772, $125 with breakfast), which also serves dinner some nights, and **Aunt Laura's B&B** (812 Main Rd., Islesboro, 207/734-8286 or 800/684-2405, www.auntlauras.com, $125 with breakfast, $75 without), which also rents bicycles and kayaks.

The car ferry *Margaret Chase Smith* departs Lincolnville Beach almost every hour on the hour, 8 or 9 A.M. to 5 P.M., and Islesboro on the half hour, 7:30 A.M.–4:30 P.M. Round-trip fares are $22.25 for car, $7.50 adults, $2.75 kids, $6.25 adult bicycles, and $3.50 kids' bikes. Reservations are $5 extra. A slightly reduced schedule prevails late October–early May. The 20-minute trip crosses a stunning three-mile stretch of Penobscot Bay, with views of islands and the Camden Hills. In summer, avoid the biggest bottlenecks: Friday afternoon (to Islesboro), Sunday afternoon and Monday holiday afternoons (from Islesboro). The *Smith* remains on Islesboro overnight, so don't miss the last run to Lincolnville Beach. For more information contact **Maine State Ferry Service** (P.O. Box 214, Lincolnville 04849, 207/789-5611, Islesboro 207/734-6935, www.exploremaine.org).

# RECREATION
## Sea Kayaking and Canoeing
**Ducktrap Kayak** (2175 Rte. 1, Lincolnville Beach, 207/236-8608) runs guided coastal tours, with rates beginning at $30 pp. Rentals are also available for $20–30, depending upon type and size, and delivery can be arranged. If you decide you need your own kayak, Ducktrap will even sell you one.

The best places to canoe are Norton Pond and Megunticook Lake, and you can even paddle all the way from the head of Norton Pond to the foot of Megunticook Lake. The only tricky part is navigating the drainage culvert between the pond and the lake.

## Swimming
Penobscot Bay flirts with Route 1 at **Lincolnville Beach,** a sandy stretch of shorefront in the congested hamlet of Lincolnville Beach. This is about as close as the road gets to the ocean. On a hot day, the sand is wall-to-wall people; during one of the coast's legendary northeasters, it's quite a wild place. There's **freshwater swimming** at several area ponds (most people would call them lakes). On Route 52 in Lincolnville Center is Breezemere Park, a small town-owned swimming/picnic area on **Norton Pond.** The Lincolnville Band, one of the oldest town bands in the country, often plays in the park's Bicentennial Bandstand, built to commemorate the town's 200th birthday. Other swimming ponds are **Coleman Pond, Pitcher Pond,** and **Knight's Pond.**

## Hiking
The boundaries of both Camden Hills State Park and Fernald's Neck extend into Lincolnville, where the major state-park hike follows the **Ski Shelter Trail** to the **Bald Rock Trail.** From Route 1 in Lincolnville Beach, take Route 173 west about 2.5 miles to the marked parking area just beyond the junction of Youngtown Road. The 1,200-foot summit—with great views of Penobscot Bay (weather permitting)—is about two miles one-way, easy to moderate hiking. The route links with the rest of the state-park trail network, but unless you've arranged for a shuttle, it's best to do Bald Rock as a round-trip hike.

# SHOPPING
Art, craft, and souvenir shops are clustered along the Route 1 strip at Lincolnville Beach;

just north of town are a couple of unusual shops and galleries worth a visit.

Handsome, dark wood buildings 0.2 mile north of the Beach are home to **Windsor Chairmakers** (Rte. 1, Lincolnville, 207/789-5188 or 800/789-5188). You can observe the operation, browse the display area, or order some of the well-made chairs, cabinets, and tables.

Professional boatbuilder Walt Simmons has branched out into decoys and wildlife carvings, and they're just as outstanding as his boats. Walt and his wife, Karen, run **Duck Trap Decoys** (Duck Trap Rd., Lincolnville, 207/789-5363), a gallery/shop that also features the work of nearly five dozen other woodcarvers.

It's a lot easier to get soft, wonderful hand-woven and hand-dyed **Swans Island Blankets** (231 Rte. 1, Northport, 297/338-9691) since the company moved its sales operation off the island near Mount Desert to the mainland, just 2.7 miles north of Lincolnville Beach. Such quality comes at a sky-high price.

The **Center General Store** (Rte. 52, Lincolnville Center, 207/763-3666) is more than just a market—it's an experience. At this old-fashioned, early-20th-century place, you can pick up baked goods, ice-cream cones, animal feed, liquor, fuel, lottery tickets, bait, and a fishing license. Stock up for a picnic or eat it here and watch the comings and goings.

## ACCOMMODATIONS
### Bed-and-Breakfasts

About four miles north of Camden and a mile south of Lincolnville, **The Victorian by the Sea** (Seaview Dr., Lincolnville Beach, mailing address P.O. Box 1385, Camden 04843, 207/236-3785 or 800/382-9817, www.victorianbythesea.com, $169–239) overlooks the bay at the end of a winding lane from Route 1. It's a dreamy Victorian with numerous fireplaces, clawfoot tubs, and a dining room in the turret, where a four-course breakfast is served.

Private, secluded, and surrounded by 22 acres of gardens, the oceanfront, Shingle-style **Inn at the Ocean's Edge** (Rte. 1, Lincolnville Beach, mailing address P.O. Box 704, Camden 04843,

207/236-0945, www.innatoceansedge.com, $245–405) is splurge-worthy. In 2004, Tim and Joan Porta, owners of the exclusive Migis Lodge, on Sebago Lake, bought it to complement their inland resort. Every room has a king-size bed, fireplace, and whirlpool tub for two, as well as TV, air-conditioning, Wi-Fi, and superb ocean views. The grounds are lovely, with a disappearing-edge pool, and chairs placed just so to take in the views. There's an excellent restaurant on the premises (see *Food*). Rates include breakfast.

Even more private and secluded is **The Inn at Sunrise Point** (Rte. 1, FR 9, Lincolnville, mailing address P.O. Box 1344, Camden 04843, 207/236-7716 or 800/435-6278, www.sunrisepoint.com, $235–545), an elegant retreat, with all the whistles and bells you'd expect at these rates. The three handsome rooms in the main lodge, four separate cottages, a loft, and two suites are all named after Maine authors or artists. Breakfast in the conservatory is divine.

### Motel

The family-run 🦀 **Mount Battie Motel** (2298 Atlantic Hwy, Rte. 1, Lincolnville, 207/236-3870 or 800/224-3870, www.mountbattie.com, $89–120) has 22 charming motel-style rooms with air-conditioning, TV, phone, fridge, and continental breakfast, including home-baked treats; Wi-Fi is available in the lobby.

**Snow Hill Lodge** (Rte. 1, HC 60, Box 550, Lincolnville Beach, 207/236-3452 or 800/476-4775, www.midcoast.com/~theview, $80–99) is an unpretentious, well-maintained motel with a splendid view of Penobscot Bay. Hospitable hosts Sitki and Marie Kocak have 30 rooms with TV and phones. Breakfast is available at the on-site café at an additional charge.

## FOOD
### Local Flavors

More local than tourist-oriented, the **Whale's Tooth Pub and Restaurant** (2431 Atlantic Hwy./Rte. 1, 207/789-5200, www.whalestooth-pub.com) is a fine choice for pub fare—try the fish-and-chips—in a cozy pub-style atmosphere. It serves lunch and dinner ($14–25) Wednesday–Sunday. In winter, snuggle by the fireplace.

French flair without the attitude is why **Chez Michel** (Rte. 1, Lincolnville Beach, 207/789-5600) is a perennial favorite, even for families. Try for one of the window tables with water views. Entrées begin around $10; it serves lunch and dinner Tuesday–Sunday.

### Fine Dining

For a romantic, classic French experience, head a bit inland to **Youngtown Inn and Restaurant** (581 Youngtown Rd., Lincolnville, 207/763-4290 or 800/291-8438, www.youngtowninn.com, 6–9 P.M. Tues.–Sun.), where chef/owner Manuel Mercier draws on his Parisian heritage and European training; entrées are $22–28.

The food matches the view at **The Edge** (Inn at the Ocean's Edge, Rte. 1, Lincolnville Beach, 207/236-4430, www.innatoceansedge.com), where you can dine inside or on the deck, overlooking Penobscot Bay. The menu features familiar foods with creative touches and an emphasis on fresh and local; most entrées are in the $30–36 range. Service is attentive, and details are noticed. Sunday night is pizza night, with fancy pies.

### Lobster in the Rough

Lincolnville's best-known landmark is **The Lobster Pound Restaurant** (Rte. 1, Lincolnville Beach, 207/789-5550, www.lobsterpoundmaine.com, 11:30 A.M.–8 P.M. daily, to 9 P.M. in July and Aug.). About 300 people—some days, it looks like more than that—can pile into the restaurant and enclosed patio, so be sure to make reservations on summer weekends. Despite the crowds, food and service are reliably good. Lobster, of course, is king, but the huge menu includes other seafood, poultry, and steaks. Entrées are $12–35.

## INFORMATION AND SERVICES

For planning, contact Camden-Rockport-Lincolnville Chamber of Commerce (P.O. Box 919, Camden 04843, 207/236-4404 or 800/223-5459, www.visitcamden.com). Also handy is a directory published by the Lincolnville Business Group (P.O. Box 202, Lincolnville 04849, www.lincolnville.org).

# Belfast Area

With a population of about 6,400, Belfast is relatively small as cities go, but changes have been occurring at lightning speed—courtesy of gigantic credit-card company MBNA (the nation's largest in affinity cards), which established a major presence here in 1996, and later was bought out by Bank of America. Even before MBNA/BA arrived, Belfast was becoming one of those off-the-beaten-track destinations popular with tuned-in travelers. Chalk that up to its status as a magnet for leftover back-to-the-landers and enough artistic types to earn the city a nod for cultural cool. Belfast has a curling club, meditation centers, an increasing number of art galleries and boutiques, dance and theater companies, the oldest shoe store in America, and half a dozen different 12-step self-help groups. The city even has a poet laureate!

This eclectic city is a work in progress, a study in Maine-style diversity. It's also a gold mine of Federal, Greek Revival, Italianate, and Victorian architecture. Take the time to stroll the well-planned backstreets, explore the shops, and hang out at the newly gussied-up waterfront.

Separating Belfast from East Belfast, the Passagassawakeag River (Puh-sag-gus-uh-WAH-keg) fortunately is known more familiarly as "the Passy." The Indian name has been translated as both "place of many ghosts" and the rather different "place

PENOBSCOT BAY

# OFF THE BEATEN PATH IN LIBERTY

Seventeen miles west of Belfast, off Route 3, is Liberty, a tiny town with a funky tool store, quirky museum, a bargain T-shirt shop, and a great state park. Everything is seasonal, running mid-May or so through mid-October or so. Call before visiting if you want to be sure everything's open.

It's a store! It's a museum! It's amazing! More than 10,000 "useful" tools – plus used books and prints and other tidbits – fill the three-story **Liberty Tool Company** (Main St., Liberty, 207/589-4771). Drawn by nostalgia and a compulsion for handmade adzes and chisels, thousands of vintage-tool buffs arrive at this eclectic emporium each year; few leave empty-handed. Nor do the thousands of everyday home hobbiests looking to pick up a hammer or find a missing wrench to fill out a set. Nor do the antiques-seekers, who browse the trash and treasures on the upper floors. The collection is beyond amazing, especially in its organization. Owner Skip Brack brings back vanloads of finds almost every week, and after sorting and cleaning, many make it into this store.

The best-of-the-best make it into Brack's **Davistown Museum** (Main St., 207/589-4900, www.davistownmuseum.org), on the third floor of the building housing Liberty Graphics, across the street. The museum houses not only a history of Maine and New England hand tools, but also local, regional, Native American. and environmental artifacts and information and an amazing collection of contemporary art, highlighted by works by artists such as Louise Nevelson (who used to buy tools across the street), Melitta Westerlund, and Phil Barter.

Downstairs is **Liberty Graphics Outlet Store** (1 Main St., 207/589-4035), selling the eco-sensitive company's overstocks, seconds, and discontinued-design T-shirts. Outstanding silkscreened designs are done with water-based inks, and many of the shirts are organic cotton; prices begin at $5.

Just down Main Street is the old **Liberty Post Office,** a unique octagonal structure that looks like an oversize box. It was built in 1867 as a harnessmaker's shop and later used as the town's post office.

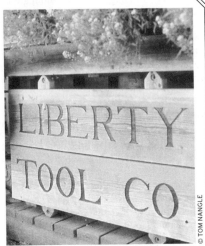

© TOM NANGLE

**You'll find practically every tool possible, and then some, at Liberty Tool Company.**

Two miles west of downtown, **Lake St. George State Park** (Rte. 3, 207/589-4255, $3 adults, $1 children 5-11) is a refreshing find. This 360-acre park has wooded picnic sites with grills along the lake, a beach, rental boats, playground, volleyball and basketball courts, and five miles of hiking trails. Also available are campsites, $20 for nonresidents. Afterward, head to **John's Ice Cream** (Rte. 3, 589-3700) for amazing flavors handcrafted (homemade is too pedestrian to describe it) on the premises.

If you're up for more inland exploring, weave your way along the **Georges River Scenic Byway,** a 50-mile auto route along the St. George River (a.k.a. Georges River) from its inland headwaters to the sea in Port Clyde. The official start is at the junction of Routes 3 and 220 in Liberty, but you can follow the trail in either direction, or pick it up anywhere along the way. Road signs are posted, but it's far better to obtain a map/brochure at a chamber of commerce or other information locale. Or contact the architects of the route, **The Georges River Land Trust** (328 Main St., Rockland, 207/594-5166, www.grlt.org).

for spearing sturgeon by torchlight." You choose. No matter, you can cross it via a pedestrian bridge.

Many travelers make Belfast a day stop on their way between Camden and Bar Harbor. Truly, Belfast is worth more time than that. Spend a full day or two here, and it's likely you'll be charmed like many of the other urban refugees into resettling here.

## SIGHTS
### Historic Walking Tour

No question, the best way to appreciate Belfast's fantastic architecture is to tour by ankle express. At the Belfast Area Chamber of Commerce, pick up the well-researched *Belfast Historic Walking Tour* map/brochure. Among more than 40 highlights on the mile-long, self-guided route are the 1818 Federal-style **First Church,** handsome residences on **High** and **Church Streets,** and the 1840 **James P. White House** (corner of Church St. and Northport Ave., now an elegant B&B), New England's finest Greek Revival residence. Amazing for a community of this size, the city actually has three distinct National Historic Districts: Belfast Commercial Historic District (47 downtown buildings), Church Street Historic District (residential), and Primrose Hill Historic District (also residential). Another walking tour is presented by the Belfast Historical Society's **Museum in the Streets,** comprising two large panels and 30 smaller ones highlighting historic buildings and people. Signs are in English and French.

### Bayside

Continuing the focus on architecture, just south of Belfast, in Northport, is the Victorian enclave of Bayside, a neighborhoody sort of place with small, well-kept, gingerbreaded cottages cheek-by-jowl on pint-size lots. Formerly known as the Northport Wesleyan Grove Campground, the village took shape in the mid-1800s as a summer retreat for Methodists. In the 1930s, the retreat was disbanded and the main meeting hall was razed, creating the waterfront park at the heart of the village. Today, many of the colorfully painted homes are rented by the week, month, or summer season, and their tenants are more likely to indulge in athletic rather than religious pursuits. The camaraderie remains, though, and a stroll (or cycle or drive) through Bayside is like a visit to another era. Bayside is four miles south of Belfast, just east of Route 1.

### Temple Heights

Continue south on Shore Road from Bayside to **Temple Heights Spiritualist Camp** (Shore Rd., Northport, mailing address P.O. Box 311, Lincolnville 04849 207/338-3029, www.templeheightscamp.org), yet another religious enclave—this one still going. Founded in 1882, Temple Heights has become a shadow of its former self, reduced primarily to the funky, 12-room Nikawa Lodge on Shore Road ($35 d, $25 s, shared bath, some with ocean view), but the summer program continues, thanks to prominent mediums from all over the country. Even a temporary setback in 1996—when the camp president was suspended for allegedly putting a hex on Northport's town clerk—failed to derail the operation. Camp programs, late June–Labor Day, are open to the public; a schedule is published each spring. Spiritualist church services and group healing sessions are free; Saturday-morning workshops are $20. Better yet, sign up for a 1.5-hour or longer **group message circle,** when you'll sit with a medium and a dozen or so others and receive insights—often uncannily on target—from departed relatives or friends. Message circles occur at 7:30 P.M. Wednesday and Saturday (arrive a half-hour early). Suggested donation is $15 pp and reservations are necessary. Private readings can be arranged for a donation of $30.

## PARKS AND RECREATION

One of the state's best municipal parks is just on the outskirts of downtown. Established in 1904, **Belfast City Park** (87 Northport Ave., 207/338-1661, free) has lighted tennis courts, an outdoor pool, a pebbly beach, plenty of picnic tables, an unusually creative playground, lots of green space for the kids, and fantastic views of Islesboro, Blue Hill, and Penobscot Bay. For more action, right in the heart of Belfast, head for **Heritage Park,** at the bottom of Main Street, with front-row seats on waterfront happenings. Bring a picnic, grab a table, and watch the yachts, tugs, and lobster boats.

## Golf

Just south of Belfast is the nine-hole **Northport Golf Club** (581 Bluff Rd., Northport, Belfast, 207/338-2270), established in 1916. Operating out of a classic shingled clubhouse, the club is open mid-April–October. Snacks and carts are available; starting times usually aren't necessary.

## Excursion Boats

Sail aboard the Friendship sloop *Amity* (evenings 207/469-0849, daytime 207/323-1443, www.friendshipsloopamity.com), based at the Belfast Public Landing for 90-minute morning ($20) or 2.5-hour afternoon ($30) sails; age 15 and younger are half price. The classic Friendship sloop, built in 1901 in Friendship, was originally used for lobstering. These days, it's been beautifully restored and carries up to six passengers. Home-baked cookies, hot coffee, and tea are served on all cruises. Captain Stephen O'Connell, a former journalist, explains the boat's history and its role in lobstering and regales passengers, when asked, with tales of his experiences living in exotic locations around the world.

Take a day trip to Castine aboard the *Good Return,* operated by Belfast Bay Cruises (207/322-5530, www.belfastbaycruises.com; ticket office 17 Main St., Belfast), departing from Thompson Wharf (between Belfast Maskers theater and the pedestrian bridge). Captain Melissa Terry, a fifth-generation descendent of a whaling captain from New Bedford, Massachusetts, is a Maine Maritime Academy graduate who enjoys sharing her love of the sea. The 4.5-hour Castine Lunch Cruise ($28 adults, $15 kids 5–15) provides time for exploring Castine and lunch (on your own). Other options include a 1.5-hour educational lobstering cruise, during which traps are hauled ($22 adults, $12 kids), one-hour harbor cruises ($11 adults, $6 kids), two-hour full-moon ice-cream cruise ($25 adult, $13 kids), and a two-hour Penobscot Bay cruise ($22 adult, $12 kids).

If you don't have your own kayak, **Water Walker** (152 Lincolnville Ave., Belfast, 207/338-6424, www.kayak-tour-maine.com) has a full range of options. Owner Ray Wirth, a Registered Maine Guide and ACA-certified open-water instructor, will arrange customized trips from a few hours to multiple days, as well as provide instruction. Rates begin at $60 for one/$70 for two for 2–3 hours.

## Winter Sports

The Scottish national sport of curling has dozens of enthusiastic supporters at Maine's only curling rink, the **Belfast Curling Club** (Belmont Ave., Rte. 3, Belfast, 207/338-9851, www.belfastcurlingclub.org), an institution here since the late 1950s. Leagues play regularly on weeknights, and the club holds tournaments *(bonspiels)* and open houses several times during the season, which runs early November–early April.

# ENTERTAINMENT

It's relatively easy to find nightlife in Belfast—not only are there theaters and a cinema, but there usually are a couple of bars open at least until midnight, and sometimes later. Some spots also feature live music, particularly on weekends.

If you don't feel like searching out a newspaper to check the entertainment listings, just go to the **Belfast Co-op Store** (123 High St., 207/338-2532) and study the bulletin board. You'll find notices for more activities than you could ever squeeze into your schedule.

Just south of Belfast, the funky **Blue Goose Dance Hall** (Rte. 1, Northport, 207/338-3003)

© HILARY NANGLE

A pedestrian bridge across the river is a favorite fishing spot.

is the site for folk concerts, contra dances, auctions, and other events. Check local papers or the Belfast Co-op Store bulletin board.

About a dozen galleries participate in Belfast Arts' **Friday Gallery Walk,** held every Friday night in July and August, and every first Friday September–December.

An old-fashioned downtown cinema—recently restored to its art deco splendor—shows first-run films for moderate ticket prices. The **Colonial Theatre** (163 High St., Belfast, 207/338-1930) has three screens, each with 1–2 showings a night and matinees Saturday, Sunday, and sometimes Wednesday. It's open all year.

Check local papers for the schedule of the **Belfast Maskers** (43 Front St., Belfast, 207/338-9668, www.belfastmaskerstheater.com), a community theater group that never fails to win raves for its interpretations of contemporary and classical dramas. In winter, wear an extra pair of socks; the floor is drafty.

Also worth checking out is the **Northport Music Theater** (851 Rte. 1, Northport, 207/338-8383, www.NorthportMusicTheater.com,

$20–25), a 136-seat theater presenting shows mid-June–late August.

## EVENTS

Belfast is a hive of activity, but lots of the surrounding Waldo County communities also put on some ambitious fairs, festivals, and public suppers. Check the newspapers for schedules.

The Belfast Garden Club sponsors **Open Garden Days** once a week mid-May–mid-September at the homes of club members and friends. Gardens are open 10 A.M.–3 P.M., rain or shine; a $3 pp donation is requested to benefit local beautification projects. Check local newspapers or ask at the chamber of commerce for the schedule.

In early July, soon after the Fourth of July, the **Arts in the Park** festival gets under way at Heritage Park, on the Belfast waterfront. It's a weekend event, two days of music, juried arts and crafts, children's activities, and lots of food booths. The **Belfast Bay Festival,** usually the third week of July, has music, carnival rides, fireworks, food, and more.

## SHOPPING

It's easy and fun to shop in downtown Belfast, a town that has so far managed to keep the big boxes away, providing fertile ground for entrepreneurs. Downtown shops reflect the city's population, with galleries and boutiques, thrift and used-goods stores, and eclectic shops.

### Books

Belfast's independent bookstore is a friendly place with good intentions but not a huge inventory. The quaintly named **Fertile Mind Bookshop** (105 Main St., Belfast, 207/338-2498) has a particularly good children's section and also carries magazines.

### Specialty Shops

Even if shoes aren't on your shopping list, stop in at "the oldest shoe store in America." Founded in the 1830s(!), **Colburn Shoe Store** (81 Main St., Belfast, 207/338-1934 or 877/338-1934) may be old, but it isn't old-fashioned—all the latest brands and styles are here.

PENOBSCOT BAY

© HILARY NANGLE

America's oldest shoe store is in downtown Belfast.

**Brambles** (70 Main St., Belfast, 207/338-3448) is a gardener's delight, with fun, whimsical, and practical garden-themed merchandise.

Perhaps it's not surprising in a city named Belfast, but **Shamrock, Thistle and Rose** (39 Main St., Belfast, 207/338-1864) is a find for lovers of Irish goods—clothing, jewelry, original art, and even music are found here.

Just over the Belfast Bridge is **Cherished Home** (31 Searsport Ave./Rte. 1, Belfast, 207/338-4111), where Genie Francis (a.k.a. Laura of the famed Luke and Laura *General Hospital* soap-opera couple) sells a nice selection of home-oriented merchandise.

About two miles east of Belfast's bridge, on the right, is the small roadside shop of **Mainely Pottery** (181 Searsport Ave., Rte. 1, Belfast, 207/338-1108). Since 1988, Jeannette Faunce and Jamie Oates have been marketing the work of more than two dozen Maine potters, each with different techniques, glazes, and styles. It's the perfect place to select from a wide range of reasonably priced work. Peek into the adjacent

studio and you'll find Jamie, who specializes in lamps (under the name of Pequog Pottery) and is happy to answer questions. Don't miss Jeannette's lovely garden out back.

## The Green Store

Calling itself a "general store for the 21st century," The Green Store (71 Main St., Belfast, 207/338-4045) carries a huge selection of environmentally friendly products. Whether you're thinking of going off the grid, need a composting toilet, want natural fiber clothing, or other natural-living products, this is the place. A very knowledgeable staff can answer nearly any question on environmentally sustainable lifestyles.

## ACCOMMODATIONS
### Bed-and-Breakfasts

On a quiet side street, **The Jeweled Turret** (40 Pearl St., Belfast, 207/338-2304 or 800/696-2304, www.jeweledturret.com, $105–159) is one of Belfast's pioneer B&Bs. Carl and Cathy Heffentrager understand the business and go out of their way to make guests comfortable. The 1898 Victorian inn is loaded with handsome woodwork and Victorian antiques— plus an astonishing stone fireplace. Carl can even fix your bike, if necessary, and he's up on all the local byways.

**The White House** (1 Church St., Belfast, 207/338-1901 or 888/290-1901, www.mainebb.com, $115–175), the handsomest manse in Belfast, is the star of the Church Street Historic District. Built in the mid-19th century, the Greek Revival building is elegant inside and out—parlors, library, and guest rooms are accented with plaster ceiling medallions; it features marble fireplaces and a magnificent stairway. A giant copper beech tree dominates the parklike grounds and gardens. Hosts Terry Prescott and Robert Hansen will lend you a tandem bike, pack you a picnic lunch, make dinner reservations—more than the comforts of home.

On the inland side of Route 1 is **Londonderry Inn** (133 Belmont Ave., Rte. 3, Belfast, 207/338-2763 or 977/529-9566, www.londonderry-inn.com, $95–140), a big farmhouse with rambling rooms, screened porch, and a huge country kitchen that innkeeper Marsha Oakes has restored into a welcoming B&B. All rooms have TV/VCR, phone, air-conditioning, and minifridge. Rates include a full farmer's breakfast and evening beverages and dessert.

## Motels and Suites

The 61 rooms at the oceanfront **Belfast Harbor Inn** (91 Searsport Ave., Belfast, 207/338-2740 or 800/545-8576, www.belfastharborinn.com, $79–149 d) have TV, air-conditioning, Wi-Fi, and phones, and there's an outdoor heated pool, a real plus for families, as is the laundry. Foxy's Steakhouse is next door. Pets are allowed in some rooms for $10 per night. Rates include a continental breakfast buffet. If you can swing it, request an ocean-view room.

Here's a nice spot with an artsy touch. **Phoenix Row** (157 High St., Belfast, 207/338-0476, www.phoenixrow.com) is a restored 1924 three-story brick building downtown, with galleries on the lower floors and four one- and two-bedroom guest suites, each with kitchen, above. All have air-conditioning and TV; a few have decks with harbor views. Rates are $115–189/night or $650–1,000/week.

## Campground

Every one of the 44 mostly open sites at the **Moorings Oceanfront RV Resort** (191 Searsport Ave., Rte. 1, Belfast, 207/338-6860, www.mooringscamp.com) has an ocean view and hookups. Views are fabulous, and the rocky beach has a pocket of sand; swimming is only for the hardy. The downsides: Many sites feel crowded, and there's often a wait for showers. Sites in midsummer are $40–48 (two adults plus three kids under 17). Coffee is available every morning, and special events are often held, including lobster shore dinners, barbecues, and deep-fried turkey fests. Facilities include laundry, play area, kayak launch, game room, Wi-Fi, and on-site restaurant.

## Seasonal Rentals

Most of the Belfast area's seasonal rentals are in Northport, specifically the charming Victorian enclave of Bayside (see *Sights*). For info,

contact **Bayside Cottage Rentals** (539 Bluff Rd., Northport, 207/338-5355, www.baysidecottagerentals.com).

# FOOD
## Local Flavors

Wraps are fast food at **Bay Wrap** (102 Main St., Belfast, 207/338-9757, www.baywrap.com, 11 A.M.–7 P.M. Mon.–Fri., to 4 P.M. Sat.). There's no limit to what the staff can stuff into various flavors of tortillas. Go for the adventure. Wraps are in the $6 range. Eat here or get them to go.

The **Belfast Co-op Store** (123 High St., Belfast, 207/338-2532, www.belfast.coop, 7:30 A.M.–8 P.M. daily) is an experience in itself. You'll have a good impression of Belfast after one glance at the clientele and the bulletin board. Open to members and nonmembers alike (with lower prices for members), the co-op store has local organic produce, fresh and frozen pesto, baked goods, teas and coffees, bulk grains and nuts, a great deli, meat and fish, dozens of cheeses, camping foods, wine and beer, and a deli-café serving lunches daily and weekend brunches.

The **Belfast Farmers Market** (Washington St. parking lot, downtown Belfast, 9 A.M.–1 P.M. Fri.) provides the perfect opportunity for stocking up for a picnic. In addition to plentiful veggies, you'll find honey, sweets, eggs, chicken pies, goat cheeses, breads, berries and apples in season, jams, medicinal and culinary herbs, jams, salsa, dillybeans, Asian vegetables, ready-to-eat Korean specialties, and even sushi.

## Ethnic Fare

Don't be put off by the lackluster exterior of **Seng Thai** (160 Searsport Ave., Rte. 1, Belfast, 207/338-0010, 11 A.M.–9 P.M. Tues.–Sun.), a small, low building across from the Comfort Inn. Inside, the ambience is pleasant, the service is good, everything's available for takeout if you prefer, and best of all, it's really good Thai food (entrées $8–14).

## Casual Dining

A longtime standby for creative (including vegetarian) world cuisine, **Darby's Restaurant**

**and Pub** (155 High St., Belfast, 207/338-2339, 11:30 A.M.–3:30 P.M. and 5–9 P.M. daily) served tofu before tofu was cool. This place has been providing food and drink since just after the Civil War; the tin ceilings and antique bar are reminders of that. Entrées $11–20.

Fresh food prepared in creative ways has earned ◖ **Chase's Daily** (96 Main St., Belfast, 207/338-0555, 7 A.M.–5 P.M. Tues.–Sat., to 8 P.M. Fri, 8 A.M.–2 P.M. Sun.) a devoted local following. The emphasis is on vegetarian fare, with most of the vegetables coming from the Chase family farm in nearby Freedom. Most choices are in the $4–7 range; dinner entrées $15–18. The restaurant doubles as an art gallery, farmers market, and bakery. It's not the place for a quiet dinner, as the space is large and tends to be loud.

Industrial chic, casual, and laid-back best describe ◖ **Three Tides** (2 Pinchy La., on Marshall Wharf, Belfast, 207/338-1707, www.3tides.com, 4 P.M.–1 A.M. Tues.–Sat. and Sun. in summer). Grab a booth inside, a seat at the bar, or a table on the deck overlooking the working harbor, and then choose from the tapas-style menu ($3.50–12). You might even play a game of bocce while waiting. Beers and ales are brewed on the premises. Also part of the operation is **LB**, a lobster pound, so lobster is almost always on the menu.

It doesn't look like much from the outside, but **Papa J's and the Lobster Bar** (193 Searsport Ave., Belfast, 207/338-6464, www.3tides.com, 4–9 P.M. Tues.–Sat., to 10 P.M. Fri. and Sat.) is warm and welcoming inside, with nice water views, a casual style, and—most important—well-prepared food ($11–24) complemented by a surprisingly good wine list. Order the lobster and feta pizza; you won't be disappointed.

## Lobster in the Rough

**Young's Lobster Pound** (2 Fairview St., Belfast, 207/338-1160, 8 A.M.–8 P.M. daily May–Nov.) is a classic eat-on-the-dock lobster place overlooking the bay. Dress down, relax, and pile into the crustaceans. BYOB. No credit cards. From downtown, cross the bridge to East Belfast and turn right at Jed's Restaurant. Continue to the end of the street.

## INFORMATION AND SERVICES
### Information

The Belfast Area Chamber of Commerce (17 Main St., P.O. Box 58, Belfast 04915, 207/338-5900, www.belfastmaine.org) has plenty of info about the region.

Check out Belfast Free Library (106 High St., Belfast, 207/338-3884, www.belfast.lib.me.us).

### Public Restrooms

Facilities are at the waterfront Public Landing, in the railroad station, at the Waldo County Court House, and at the Waldo County General Hospital.

# Searsport Area

Five miles northeast of downtown Belfast, you're in the heart of Searsport, a name synonymous with the sea, thanks to an enduring oceangoing tradition that's appropriately commemorated here in the state's oldest maritime museum. The seafaring heyday occurred in the mid-19th century, but settlers from the Massachusetts Colony had already made inroads here 200 years earlier. By the 1750s, Fort Pownall, in nearby Stockton Springs, was a strategic site during the French and Indian War (the American phase of Europe's Seven Years' War).

Shipbuilding was under way by 1791, reaching a crescendo between 1845 and 1866, with six year-round shipyards and nearly a dozen more seasonal ones. By 1885, 10 percent of all full-rigged American-flag ships on the high seas were under the command of Searsport and Stockton Springs captains—many bearing the name of Pendleton, Nichols, or Carver. Many of these were involved in the perilous China

© HILARY NANGLE

An inland lighthouse marks BlueJacket Shipcrafters, which builds museum-quality boat models.

2,600, the Searsport area's major draws are the Penobscot Marine Museum, the still-handsome brick Historic District, several B&Bs, a couple of special state parks, and wall-to-wall antiques shops and flea markets.

The Maine Historic Preservation Commission considers the buildings in Searsport's Main Street Historic District the best examples of their type outside of Portland—a frozen-in-time, mid-19th-century cluster of brick and granite structures. The ground floors of most of the buildings are shops or restaurants; make time to stop in and admire their interiors.

## SIGHTS
### Penobscot Marine Museum

Exquisite marine paintings, ship models, and unusual China-trade *objets* are just a few of the 10,000 treasures at the Penobscot Marine Museum (5 Church St., at Rte. 1, Searsport, 207/548-2529, www.penobscotmarinemuseum.org, 10 A.M.–5 P.M. Mon.–Sat., noon–5 P.M. Sun., $8 adults, $3 kids 7–15, or $18 per family), Maine's oldest maritime museum—founded in 1936. Allow several hours to explore the 13 old and new buildings just east of downtown. For a start, you'll see one of the nation's largest collections of paintings by marine artists James and Thomas Buttersworth. And the 1830s Fowler-True-Ross House is filled with exotic artifacts from foreign lands. Check out the exhibits, have a picnic, and then visit the particularly well-stocked museum store on Main Street (Rte. 1). Pick up tickets at the Museum Admissions Building (restrooms are here, as well as in the museum store and the library), first building on your left on Church Street. Call or check the website for the schedule of lectures, concerts, and temporary exhibits. This isn't a very sophisticated museum, but it is a treasure. It's open late May–mid-October.

### BlueJacket Shipcrafters

Complementing the collections at the museum are the classic and contemporary models built by BlueJacket Shipcrafters (160 E. Main St., Rte. 1, Searsport, 800/448-5567), which boasts

trade, rounding notorious Cape Horn with great regularity.

All this global contact shaped Searsport's culture, adding a veneer of cosmopolitan sophistication. Imposing mansions of seafaring families were filled with fabulous Oriental treasures, many of which eventually made their way to the Penobscot Marine Museum. Brick-lined Main Street is more evidence of the mid-19th-century wealth, and local churches reaped the benefits of residents' generosity. The Second Congregational Church, known as the Safe Harbor Church and patronized by captains and shipbuilders (most ordinary seamen attended the Methodist church), boasts recently restored Tiffany-style windows and a Christopher Wren steeple.

Another inkling of this area's oceangoing superiority comes from visits to local burial grounds: Check out the headstones at Gordon, Bowditch, and Sandy Point cemeteries. Many have fascinating tales to tell.

Today, with a population of just under

Maine's largest selection of ship models and nautical gifts. Even if you're not a hobbiest, stop in to see the incredibly detailed models on display. Shipcrafters is renowned for building one-of-a-kind museum-quality custom models—it's the official modelmaker for the U.S. Navy—but don't despair, there are kits here for all abilities (and budgets). It's easy to find: Just look for the inland lighthouse on Route 1.

## PARKS AND RECREATION
### Moose Point State Park
Here's a smallish park with a biggish view—183 acres wedged between Route 1 and a dramatic Penobscot Bay panorama. Moose Point State Park (Rte. 1, Searsport, 207/548-2882, $2 adults, $1 kids 5–11) is 1.5 miles south of downtown Searsport. Bring a picnic, let the kids hang out and play (there's no swimming, but good tide pooling at low tide), or walk through the woods or along the meadow trail. Moose-crossing signs are posted on the highway, but don't count on seeing one. It's open late May–October 1, but since it's alongside the highway, the park is accessible, weather permitting, all year.

### Mosman Park
Southeast of busy Route 1, the four-acre, town-owned Mosman Park has picnic tables, a traditional playground, lots of grassy space, a pocket-size pebbly beach, seasonal toilets, and fabulous views of the bay. Turn off Route 1 at Water Street and continue to the end.

### Sears Island
After almost two decades of heavy-duty squabbling over a proposed cargo port on Searsport's 940-acre Sears Island, the state bought the island for $4 million in November 1997. Discussions are ongoing about the establishment of visitor facilities, but for now, the only improvement on this lovely, causeway-linked island is a road. It's a fine place for biking, picnicking, walking, fishing, and cross-country skiing. From downtown Searsport, continue northeast on Route 1 two miles to Sears Island Road (on your right). Turn and go 1.2 miles to the beginning of the island, where you can pull off and park before a gate (cars aren't allowed on the island). An easy 1.5-mile walk will take you to the other side of the island, overlooking Mack Point (site of a rather unattractive cargo port) and hills off to the left. Bring a picnic and binoculars—and a swimsuit if you're hardy enough to brave the water.

### Fort Point State Park
Continuing northeast on Route 1 from Sears Island will get you to the turnoff for Fort Point State Park (Fort Point Rd., Stockton Springs, 207/567-3356, $2 adults, $1 kids 5–11) on Cape Jellison's eastern tip. Within the 154-acre park are the earthworks of 18th-century **Fort Pownall** (a British fortress built in the French and Indian War), **Fort Point Light** (a square, 26-foot, 19th-century tower guarding the mouth of the Penobscot River) and adjacent bell tower, shoreline trails, and a 200-foot pier where you can fish or bird- or boat-watch. (Birders can spot waterfowl—especially ruddy ducks, but also eagles and osprey.) Bring picnic fixings, but stay clear of the keeper's house—it's private. At the Route 1 fork for Stockton Springs, bear right onto Main Street and continue to Mill Road, in the village center. Turn right and then left onto East Cape Road, then another left onto Fort Point Road, which leads to the parking area. Officially, the park is open late May–Labor Day, but it's accessible all year, weather permitting.

### ◖ Fort Knox
Looming over Bucksport Harbor, the *other* Fort Knox (Rte. 174, Prospect, 207/469-7719, http://fortknox.maineguide.com, 9 A.M.–sunset May 1–Nov. 1, $3 adults, $1 kids 5–11) is a 125-acre state historic site, just off Route 1. Named for Major General Henry Knox, George Washington's first secretary of war, the sprawling granite fort was begun in 1844. Built to protect the upper Penobscot River from attack, it was never finished and never saw battle. Still, it was, as guide Kathy Williamson said: "very well thought out and planned, and that may have been its best defense." Begin your visit at the Visitor and Education Cen-

ter, operated by the Friends of Fort Knox, a nonprofit group that has partnered with the state to preserve and interpret the fort. Guided tours are available Memorial Day–Labor Day, and well worth it, as guides point out some of the fort's distinguishing features, including two complete Rodman canons. In 2004, restoration of the Fort Knox Officers' Quarters was completed. Wear rubberized shoes and bring a flashlight to explore the underground passages; you can set the kids loose. The fort hosts Civil War reenactments several times a summer (check with the chamber of commerce). The Halloween Fright at the Fort is a ghoulish event for the brave. The grounds are accessible all year. Bring a picnic; views over the river to Bucksport are fabulous.

### ◖ Penobscot Narrows Bridge and Observatory

Do not miss the Penobscot Narrows Bridge and Observatory (9 A.M.–5 P.M. late May–Nov. 1, $5 adults, $3 ages 5–11, includes fort admission), accessible via Fort Knox. The observatory tops the 420-foot-high west tower of the new bridge spanning the Penobscot River. It's one of only three such structures in the world and the only one in the States. You'll zip up in an elevator, and when the doors open, you're facing a wall of glass (yes, it's a bit of a shocker, downright terrifying for anyone with a serious fear of heights). Ascend two more flights (elevator available), and you're in the glass-walled observatory; the views on a clear day extend from Mt. Katahdin to Mount Desert Island. Even when it's hazy, it's still a neat experience.

### Bicycling

**Birgfeld's Bicycle Shop** (184 E. Main St., Rte. 1, Searsport, 207/548-2916 or 800/206-2916), in business since the 1970s, is a mandatory stop for any cyclist, novice or pro. Local information on about 15 biking loops, supplies, maps, weekly group rides, sales (also skateboards and scooters), and excellent repair services are all part of the Birgfeld's mix.

An especially good ride in this area is the **Cape Jellison** loop in Stockton Springs, even

© HILARY NANGLE

An observatory caps one tower of the new Penobscot Narrows Bridge.

though it means biking from Birgfeld's about four miles along congested Route 1 (be extremely cautious). If you have your own bike or a car to transport the rental, park at Stockton Springs Elementary School and do the loop from there. Including a detour to Fort Point, the ride totals less than 10 miles from downtown Stockton Springs.

### SHOPPING

The word "shopping" in Searsport usually applies to antiques—from 25-cent flea-market collectibles to well-used tools to high-end china, furniture, and glassware. The town has more than a dozen separate businesses—and some of *those* are group shops with multiple dealers. Searsport vies with Wiscasset as Maine's "Antiques Capital."

More than two dozen dealers supply the juried inventory for Bob and Phyllis Sommer's **Pumpkin Patch** (15 W. Main St., Rte. 1, Searsport, 207/548-6047)—with a heavy emphasis on Maine antiques. Specialties include quilts

PENOBSCOT BAY

(at least 80 are always on hand), silver, paint-decorated furniture, Victoriana, and nautical and Native American items.

More than 70 dealers sell their antiques and collectibles at **Searsport Antique Mall** (149 E. Main St., Rte. 1, Searsport, 207/548-2640), making it another worthwhile stop for those seeking oldies but goodies.

Close to the highway in a farm stand–style building about a mile east of downtown Searsport, the **Waldo County Craft Co-op** (1778 E. Main St., Rte. 1, Searsport, 207/548-6686) features the work of about 30 Mainers: quilts, jams, bears, dolls, jewelry, baskets, pottery, floor cloths, and lots else.

Are you a hooker? Thirteen rooms full of hooked rugs, and supplies, fill **Searsport Rug Hooking** (396 E. Main St.,/Rte. 1, Searsport, 207/548-6100, www.searsportrughooking.com), in the midst of antiques shops and flea markets at the eastern end of town. The mother-daughter team of Christine Sherman and Julie Mattison, along with a talented staff, not only sell rugs, patterns, wool, and all the other supplies and necessities of the craft, they also design the patterns, dye the wools, teach, and, demonstrate.

Teddy bear fans must stop at **Cranberry Hollow** (157 W. Main St., Rte. 1, Searsport, 207/548-2647), a shop filled with stuffed bears, quilts, and other country folk items. You can also order a custom bear.

A local fixture in Stockton Springs since 1960, **Victorian House Books/Book Barn** (E. Main St., Stockton Springs, 207/567-3351) is jam-packed with used and antiquarian books.

## ACCOMMODATIONS
### Bed-and-Breakfasts

The impressive **Carriage House Inn** (120 E. Main St., Searsport, 207/548-2167 or 800/578-2167, www.carriagehouseinmaine.com, $95–125), a National Historic Register sea captain's home, has been most recently restored by Marcia Mackwardt. Built in 1874 by Captain John McGilbery, it later became home to impressionist painter Waldo Pierce,

whose friend Ernest Hemingway visited the inn often. The architectural detailing and 12-foot ceilings add elegance to this grand property. Each of the three guest rooms, as well as the public rooms, is decorated with Victorian-era antiques and family heirlooms. A multicourse breakfast and afternoon snacks are included.

Waving pennants mark the entrance to **1794 Watchtide** (190 W. Main St., Rte. 1, Searsport, 207/548-6575 or 800/698-6575, www.watchtide.com, $135–190), in a sprawling late-18th-century sea captain's home formerly known as The College Club Inn. Each of the three rooms and two suites has a historic-name connection; the Eleanor Roosevelt Suite acknowledges visits by former first ladies in decades past. Amenities are endless, from air-conditioning and white-noise clock radios (the inn is on a busy highway) to hot and cold drinks to unusual snacks. Two rooms have whirlpool tubs. Rooms in the back have the nicest views and are most quiet. Breakfasts are fabulous. Collapse on the 60-foot sun porch, overlooking the bay, and you may never want to leave.

Deb Bush and Cathy Keating are the über-enthusiastic hosts—and gardeners—at the **Wildflower Inn** (2 Black Rd. S/Rte. 1, Searsport, 207/548-2112 or 888/546-2112, www.wildflowerinnme.com, $85–140), an easy walk to downtown shops and the museum. Once home to a sailmaker and a sea captain, the extended Cape now has four guestrooms (Wi-Fi, air-conditioning, white-noise clocks, TV) along with plenty of shared living space, including double parlors. The decor is light, a mix of antiques and contemporary pieces. A full breakfast is served at 8:30 A.M., and there's a cookie jar should you get hungry later in the day.

### Motel

The **Yardarm** (172 E. Main St., Rte. 1, P.O. Box 246, Searsport 04974, www.searsport-maine.com, $80–120 peak), a small motel set back from the road, is next door to BlueJacket Shipcrafters. Each of the 18 pine-paneled units has TV, air-conditioning, and phone; suites (per-

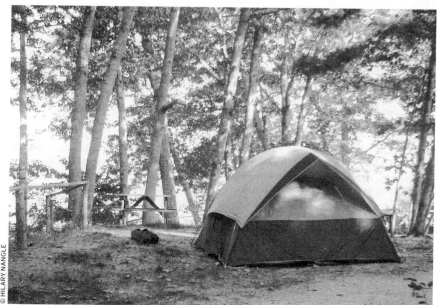
Many tenting sites at Searsport Shores have fine ocean views.

fect for families) have a dinette, microwave, and small fridge. A continental breakfast is served in a cheery breakfast room in the adjacent farmhouse. It's open May–late October.

## Campground

How can you beat 1,100 feet of tidal oceanfront and unobstructed views of Islesboro, Castine, and Penobscot Bay? **Searsport Shores Camping Resort** (216 W. Main St., Rte. 1, Searsport, 207/548-6059, www.campocean.com) gets high marks for its fabulous setting. About 120 good-size sites (including walk-in, oceanfront tenting sites) go for $36–53 a day. Facilities include a private beach, small store, free showers, laundry, play areas, recreation hall, nature trails, and volleyball court. Request a site away from organized-activity areas. Bring a sea kayak and launch it here. Leashed pets are allowed. In early September, the campground hosts Fiber Arts College, a weekend of classes, demonstrations, and camaraderie for spinners, hookers, weavers, and the like.

## FOOD

The **Anglers Restaurant** (215 E. Main St., Rte. 1, Searsport, 207/548-2405, 11 A.M.– 8 P.M. daily) is probably the least assuming and one of the most popular restaurants around. Expect hearty New England cooking, hefty portions, local color, no frills, and a bill that won't dent your wallet. Big favorites are the chowders and stews and lobster rolls. Dinner entrées are $9–14, although lobsters are higher. The "minnow menu" for smaller appetites runs $6–13. Desserts are a specialty: The gingerbread with whipped cream is divine; kids love the "bucket o' worms." If it's not too busy, and you've ordered a lobster, ask owner Buddy Hall if he'll demonstrate hypnotizing it. It's adjacent to The Bait's Motel, 1.5 miles northeast of downtown Searsport.

Good home cooking with an emphasis on fried food has made **Just Barb's** (Main St./Rte. 1, Stockton Springs, 207/567-3886) a dandy place for an unfussy meal at a low

**PENOBSCOT BAY**

price. Fried clams and scallop stew are both winners; finish up with a slab of pie or shortcake. It's open for breakfast, lunch, and dinner daily—the $6.99 all-you-can-eat fish-and-chips platter is always available, and the Friday night prime rib special always draws a crowd.

The accent is Italian at **Abbracci** (225 W. Main St., Searsport, 207/548-2010, 11:30 A.M.–8 P.M., to 5 P.M. Sun.), a combination bakery, trattoria, and espresso bar south of downtown Searsport. Choose from sandwiches, salads, soups, and specialty pizzas at lunch, and a handful of traditional entrées ($12–18), such as eggplant parm and spaghetti and meatballs at dinner.

## INFORMATION AND SERVICES

The Belfast Area Chamber of Commerce (P.O. Box 58, Belfast 04915, 207/338-5900, www.belfastmaine.org) and Waldo County Marketing Association (P.O. Box 139, Searsport 04974, 800/870-9934, www.waldocountymaine.com) have information about the Belfast area. The chamber operates a seasonal visitors information center (15 Main St.).

Searsport's small, self-serve info center is open on an unpredictable schedule. It's in a shedlike building on Route 1 (at Norris St.), across from the Pumpkin Patch antiques shop.

Check out Carver Memorial Library (Mortland Rd. at Union St., Searsport, 207/548-2303, www.carver.lib.me.us).

# BLUE HILL PENINSULA AND DEER ISLE

The Blue Hill Peninsula, once dubbed "The Fertile Crescent," is unique. Few other Maine locales harbor such a high concentration of artisans, musicians, and on-their-feet retirees juxtaposed with top-flight wooden-boat builders, lobstermen, and umpteenth-generation Mainers. Perhaps surprisingly, the mix seems to work.

Anchored by the towns of Bucksport to the east and Ellsworth to the west, the peninsula comprises several enclaves with markedly distinctive personalities. Blue Hill, Castine, Orland, Brooklin, Brooksville, and Sedgwick are stitched together by a network of narrow, winding country roads. Thanks to the mapmaker-challenging coastline and a handful of freshwater ponds and rivers, there's a view of water around nearly every bend.

You can watch the sun set from atop Blue Hill Mountain; tour the home of the fascinating Jonathan Fisher; stroll through the village of Castine (charming verging on precious), whose streets are lined with dowager-like homes; visit *WoodenBoat* magazine's world headquarters in tiny Brooklin; and browse topnotch studios and galleries throughout the peninsula. Venture a bit inland of Route 1, and you find lovely lakes for paddling and swimming and another hill to hike.

After weaving your way down the Blue Hill Peninsula and crossing the soaring pray-as-you-go bridge to Little Deer Isle, you've entered the realm of island living. Sure, bridges and causeways connect the points, but the farther down you drive, the more removed from civilization you'll feel. The pace slows,

© TOM NANGLE

# HIGHLIGHTS

◖ **The Parson Fisher House:** More than just another historic house, the Parson Fisher House is a remarkable testimony to one man's ingenuity (page 264).

◖ **Blue Hill Mountain:** It's a relatively easy hike for fabulous 360-degree views from the summit of this local landmark (page 266).

◖ **The Good Life Center:** Remember the back-to-the-land movement of the 1960s? Refresh that memory and learn how to live a sustainable life as did founders Helen and Scott Nearing (page 272).

◖ **Holbrook Island Sanctuary State Park:** Varied hiking trails and great birding are the rewards for finding this off-the-beaten-path preserve (page 274).

◖ **Flash in the Pans Community Steel Band Concerts:** Close your eyes, and you might think you're on a Caribbean island rather than in Maine when you hear this phenomenal steel-pan band (page 276).

◖ **Castine Historic Tour:** A turbulent history detailed on signs throughout town make Castine an irresistible place to tour on foot or bike (page 280).

◖ **Sea Kayaking:** Hook up with "Kayak Karen" in Castine for a tour (page 282).

◖ **Haystack Mountain School of Crafts:** Arrange your schedule to visit the architect-designed campus of this renowned oceanfront school (page 289).

◖ **Art and Craft Galleries:** The Haystack

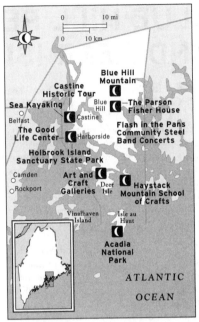

LOOK FOR ◖ TO FIND RECOMMENDED SIGHTS, ACTIVITIES, DINING, AND LODGING.

crafts school has inspired dozens of world-class artisans to set up shop on Deer Isle (page 295).

◖ **Acadia National Park:** Tipping sparsely populated **Isle au Haut** is a remote section of the national park, perfect for a day trip or longer (page 302).

the population dwindles. Fishing and lobstering are the mainstays, and lobster boats rest near many homes and trap fences edge properties. If your ultimate destination is the section of Acadia National Park on Isle au Haut, the drive down Deer Isle serves to help disconnect you from the mainland. To reach the park's acreage on Isle au Haut, after wending your way through Little Deer Isle and Deer Isle, you'll board the Isle au Haut ferryboat for the trip down Merchant Row to the island.

## PLANNING YOUR TIME

To truly enjoy this region, you'll want to spend at least three or four days here, perhaps splitting your lodging between two or three locations. The region is designed for leisurely exploring; you won't be able to zip from one location to another. Traveling along the

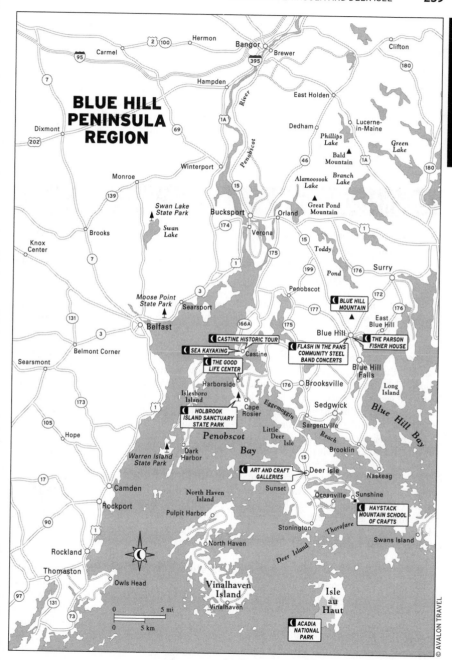

BLUE HILL PENINSULA REGION

winding roads, discovering galleries and country stores, and lodging at traditional inns are all part of the experience.

Arts fans will want to concentrate their efforts in Blue Hill, Deer Isle, and Stonington. Outdoor-oriented folks should consider Deer Isle, Stonington, or Castine as a base for sea kayaking or exploring the area preserves. For architecture and history buffs, Castine is a must. Better yet, just settle into a cottage at one of the traditional lodges for a week, enjoying breakfast and dinner at the main inn and using your days to explore all that the region has to offer.

No visit to this region is complete without at least a cruise by if not a visit to Isle au Haut, an offshore island that's home to a remote section of Acadia National Park. Allow at least a few hours for a ride on the mail boat, but if you can afford the time, spend a full day hiking the park's trails. Don't forget to pack food and water.

# Bucksport Area

The new Penobscot Narrows Bridge provides an elegant entry to the Bucksport area, a long-time rough-and-ready river port and papermaking town that's slowly gentrifying. Bucksport is no upstart. Native Americans first gravitated to these Penobscot River shores in summers, finding here a rich source of salmon for food and grasses for basketmaking. In 1764, it was officially settled by Colonel Jonathan Buck, a Massachusetts Bay Colony surveyor who modestly named it Buckstown and organized a booming shipping business here. His remains are interred in a local cemetery, where his tombstone bears the distinct outline of a woman's leg; this is allegedly the result of a curse by a witch Buck ordered executed, but in fact it's probably a flaw in the granite. Most townsfolk prefer not to discuss the matter, but the myth refuses to die—and it has immortalized a man whose name might otherwise have been consigned to musty history books. (The monument is across Route 1 from the Hannaford supermarket, on the corner of Hinks Street.)

Just south of Bucksport, at the bend in the Penobscot River, Verona Island is best known as the mile-long link between Prospect and Bucksport. Just before you cross the bridge from Verona to Bucksport, hang a left and then a quick right to a small municipal park with a boat launch and broad views of Bucksport Harbor (and the paper mill). In the Buck Memorial Library is a scale model of Admiral Robert Peary's Arctic exploration vessel, the *Roosevelt,* built on this site.

Bucksport really isn't considered part of the Blue Hill peninsula, but there are some sights here worth a look-see, a nice riverfront walkway, and area accommodations that are reasonably priced. Route 1 east of Bucksport leads to Orland, with an idyllic setting on the banks of the Narramissic River. It's also the site of a unique service organization called H.O.M.E. (Homeworkers Organized for More Employment). East Orland (officially part of Orland) claims the Craig Brook National Fish Hatchery and Great Pond Mountain (you can't miss it, jutting from the landscape on the left as you drive east on Route 1).

## SIGHTS
### Old-Time Flicks
Phoenixlike, the 1916 **Alamo Theatre** (85 Main St., Bucksport, 207/469-0924 or 800/639-1636, event line 207/469-6910, www.alamotheatre.org) has been retrofitted for a new life—focusing on films about New England produced and/or revived by unique **Northeast Historic Film (NHF),** which is headquartered here. Stop in, survey the restoration, visit the displays (donation requested), and browse the Alamo Theatre Store for antique postcards, T-shirts, toys, and reasonably priced videos on ice harvesting, lumberjacks, maple sugaring, and other traditional New England topics. One-

half mile west of Route 1, it's open 9 A.M.–4 P.M. weekdays all year. The Alamo has also become an active cinema, screening classic and current films regularly in the 120-seat theater, usually weekends. Each summer there's also a silent film festival.

### H.O.M.E.

Adjacent to the flashing light on Route 1 in Orland, H.O.M.E. is tough to categorize. Linked with the international Emmaus Movement founded by a French priest, H.O.M.E. (Homeworkers Organized for More Employment) was started in 1970 by Lucy Poulin, still the guiding force, and two nuns at a nearby convent. The quasireligious organization shelters refugees and the homeless, operates a soup kitchen and a car-repair service, runs a day-care center, and teaches work skills in a variety of hands-on cooperative programs. Seventy percent of its income comes from sales of crafts, produce, and services. At the Route 1 store (corner of Upper Falls Rd.; open 9 A.M.–4:30 P.M. daily), you can buy handmade quilts, organic produce, maple syrup, and jams—and support a worthwhile effort. You can also tour the crafts workshops on the property. To volunteer time in the workshops, store, or learning center, write P.O. Box 10, Orland 04472, or call 207/469-7961.

## PARKS AND RECREATION

For a day of hiking, picnicking, swimming, canoeing, and a bit of natural history, pack a lunch and head for 135-acre **Craig Brook National Fish Hatchery** (306 Hatchery Rd., East Orland, 207/469-2803), on Alamoosook Lake. Turn off Route 1 six miles east of Bucksport and continue 1.4 miles north to the parking area just above the visitors center (open 8:30 A.M.–3:30 P.M. weekdays and most weekends in summer; no charge; maps and restroom), with interactive displays on Atlantic salmon (don't miss the downstairs viewing area). The grounds are accessible all year, 6 A.M.–sunset daily. Established in 1871, the U.S. Fish and Wildlife Service hatchery raises sea-run Atlantic salmon for stocking seven Maine rivers, and each river has a different strain, so they're kept separate. The birch-lined shorefront has picnic tables, a boat-launching ramp, Atlantic salmon display pool, additional parking, and a spectacular cross-lake view. Watch for eagles, osprey, and loons. Also on the premises is the small Atlantic Salmon Museum, operated by the Friends of Craig Brook, with salmon and fly-fishing artifacts and memorabilia. Hiking options include nature trails through old-growth woods between Alamoosook and Craig Ponds and an easy-to-moderate two-hour (round-trip) hike up Great Pond Mountain.

Stroll the one-mile **Bucksport Waterfront Walkway,** from the Bucksport/Verona Bridge to Webber Docks. Along the way are historical markers, picnic tables, a gazebo, a restroom, and expansive views of the harbor and Fort Knox.

### Canoeing

If you've brought a canoe, **Silver Lake,** just two miles north of downtown Bucksport, is beautiful place for a paddle. There's no development along its shores, and the birding is excellent. No swimming ($500 fine); this is Bucksport's reservoir. To get to the public launch, take Route 15 north off Route 1 after crossing the Verona-Bucksport Bridge. Go 0.5 mile and turn right on McDonald Road, which becomes Silver Lake Road, and follow it 2.1 miles to the launch site.

### Hiking

The biggest rewards for the 1.8-mile easy–moderate hike up 1,038-foot **Great Pond Mountain** are 360-degree views and lots of space for panoramic picnics. On a clear day, Baxter State Park's Katahdin is visible from the peak's north side. In fall, watch for migrating hawks. Access to the mountain is via gated private property beginning about a mile north of Craig Brook National Fish Hatchery on Hatchery Road, East Orland. Roadside parking is available near the trailhead, but during fall-foliage season, you may need to park at the hatchery. Pick up a brochure from the box at the trailhead, stay on the trail, and respect the surrounding private property. The **Great Pond Mountain Conservation Trust** (P.O. Box 266, Orland 04472, 207/469-6772) acts as conscientious local steward for Great Pond Mountain and surrounding wild lands. It also hosts hikes and other activities.

## Golf

**Bucksport Golf Club** (Duck Cove Rd., Rte. 46, 1.5 miles north of Rte. 1, 207/469-7612, mid-Apr.–Sept.), running 3,397 yards, prides itself on having Maine's longest nine-hole course. Greens fees are moderate; facilities include pro shop, snack bar, driving range, and carts.

## River Cruise

See Fort Knox and the bridges from the water, on a narrated trip aboard *Lil' Toot* with **Bucksport Harbor Tours** (207/469-7498, www.littletoottours.com). Ninety-minute tours depart from the Bucksport Town Dock, five times Wednesday–Saturday late June–early September, four times Friday and Saturday through mid-October. Buy tickets, $15–20 adult, $8–10 children 16 and under, at **Dock Side Variety** (96 Main St., Bucksport).

## ACCOMMODATIONS
### Bed-and-Breakfasts

The most attractive B&B in this area is the 1820 **The Orland House** (10 Narramissic Dr., Orland, 207/469-1144, www.orlandhousebb.com, $85–105). Alvion and Cynthia Kimball's elegant, yet comfortable, Greek Revival home overlooks the Narramissic River. It's been beautifully restored with plenty of creature comforts.

Location, location, location. If only the six simple rooms at the **Alamoosook Lakeside Inn** (off Rte. 1, P.O. Box 16, Orland 04472, 207/469-6393 or 866/459-6393, www.alamoosooklakesideinn.com, $125 d) actually overlooked the lake, then it would be the perfect, rustic lakeside lodge. The property is gorgeous, the location well-suited for exploring the area, but the rooms are so-so, with tiny bathrooms. All have windows and doors opening onto a long sunporch overlooking the lake. A full breakfast is served. Alamoosook is great for wildlife-watching and

fishing, especially for bass, trout, salmon, and pickerel, and guests have access to canoes and kayaks. Paddle across the lake to the fish hatchery for a hike up Great Pond Mountain.

## Motels

In downtown Bucksport, the award for best view goes to the **Fort Knox Inn** (64 Main St., P.O. Box 826, Bucksport 04416, 207/469-3113 or 800/528-1234, $99–159), a four-story Best Western motel nudged right up to the harbor's edge. Forty modern rooms have phones, air-conditioning, and cable TV. Be sure to request a water view, or you'll be facing a parking lot.

## Campgrounds

The rivers, lakes, and ponds in the area between Bucksport and Ellsworth make it especially appealing for camping, and sites tend to be cheaper than in the Bar Harbor area. During July and August, especially weekends, reservations are wise.

Six miles east of Bucksport, across from Craig Pond Road, is Back Ridge Road, leading to **Balsam Cove Campground** (P.O. Box C, East Orland 04431, 207/469-7771 or 800/469-7771, www.balsamcove.com, $25–32). From Route 1, take Back Ridge Road 1.5 miles to the left turn for the campground, on the shores of 10-mile-long Toddy Pond. Facilities on the 50 acres include 60 wooded tent and RV sites, a one-room rental cabin ($60), on-site rental trailers ($75), dump station, store, laundry, free showers, boat rentals, and freshwater swimming. It's open late May–late September; dogs are $2/day.

The same season holds for 10-acre **Whispering Pines Campground** (Rte. 1, East Orland, 207/469-3443, www.whisperingpinesmaine.com, $26), also on Toddy Pond but with access directly from Route 1. Facilities include 50 tent and RV sites (request one close to the pond), canoes and rowboats, freshwater swimming, playground, free showers, and rec hall. Whispering Pines is 6.5 miles east of Bucksport.

## FOOD

**MacLeod's** (Main St., Bucksport, 207/469-3963, opens at 4:30 P.M. daily) is Bucksport's most popular restaurant. Slip into a booth, and choose from a varied menu. Children are welcome, it has a liquor license, and it's air-conditioned. Dinner entrées are $9–16. Reservations are wise for Saturday dinner.

On Verona Island, just before you cross the bridge to Bucksport (if you're heading north), is **Kravings Bakery and Restaurant** (42 Rte. 1, Verona, 207/469-9900, 11 A.M.–close Tues.–Sat.), a bakeshop/café with seating indoors and on an outdoor patio. The interior is pleasant, homey, and accented with knickknacks. It's also air-conditioned. Outside, you're subject to the roar of traffic on Route 1. The dinner menu varies nightly ($9–12). Fajitas and nachos are big hits during lunch, but the sandwiches are excellent, too.

In what passes as downtown Orland (hint: Don't blink), **Orland Market and Pizza** (91 Castine Rd./Rte. 175, Orland, 207/469-9999, 7 A.M.–9 P.M. daily) is a delight. Established in 1860, the old-fashioned country store has a little of this and a bit of that along with breakfast sandwiches, hot and cold sandwiches, grilled foods, salad, and all kinds of pizza. Call or drop by to find out the day's homemade specials, perhaps lasagna or spaghetti and meatballs.

Pick up produce, Maine-made goods, and other finds at the **Bucksport Riverfront Market** (waterfront, behind Town Hall, 9 A.M.–3 P.M. Sat.).

## INFORMATION AND SERVICES
### Information
The Bucksport Bay Area Chamber of Commerce (52 Main St., P.O. Box 1880, Bucksport 04416, 207/469-6818, www.bucksportbaychamber.com) is right next to the municipal office in downtown Bucksport. Office hours are 9 A.M.–5 P.M. weekdays, but the side door is always open for access to brochures, newspapers, and other publications, plus bulletin-board notices. Information is also available at the Gateway Mobil Station, at the traffic light on the corner of Route 1, between the bridge and the Hannaford supermarket.

### Public Restrooms
In Bucksport, public restrooms next to the town dock (behind the Bucksport Historical Society) are open spring, summer, and fall. Restrooms are open year-round in the Gateway Mobil gas station (at the Rte. 1 traffic light next to the Bucksport bridge) and in the Bucksport Municipal Office (weekdays) on Main Street.

# Blue Hill

Twelve miles south of Route 1 is the hub of the peninsula, Blue Hill (pop. 2,390), exuding charm from its handsome old homes to its waterfront setting to the shops, restaurants, and galleries that boost its appeal.

Eons back, Native American summer folk gave the name Awanadjo ("small, hazy mountain") to the minimountain that looms over the town and draws the eye for miles around. The first permanent settlers arrived after the French and Indian War, in the late 18th century, and established mills and shipyards. More than 100 ships were built here between Blue Hill's incorporation, in 1789, and 1882—bringing prosperity to the entire peninsula.

Critical to the town's early expansion was its first clergyman, Jonathan Fisher, a remarkable fellow who's been likened to Leonardo da Vinci. In 1803, Fisher founded Blue Hill Academy (predecessor of today's George Stevens Academy), then built his home (now a museum), and eventually left an immense legacy of inventions, paintings, engravings, and poetry.

Throughout the 19th century and into the 20th, Blue Hill's granite industry boomed, reaching its peak in the 1880s. Scratch the Brooklyn Bridge and the New York Stock Exchange and you'll find granite from Blue Hill's quarries. Around 1879, the discovery of gold and silver brought a flurry of interest, but little

The town of Blue Hill edges pretty Blue Hill Bay.

came of it. Copper was also found here, but quantities of it, too, were limited.

At the height of industrial prosperity, tourism took hold, attracting steamboat-borne summer boarders. Many succumbed to the scenery, bought land, and built waterfront summer homes. Thank these summer folk and their offspring for the fact that music has long been a big deal in Blue Hill. The Kneisel Hall Chamber Music School, established in the late 19th century, continues to rank high among the nation's summer music colonies. New York City's Blue Hill Troupe, devoted to Gilbert and Sullivan operettas, was named for the longtime summer home of the troupe's founders.

## SIGHTS
### ◖ The Parson Fisher House
Named for a brilliant renaissance man who arrived in Blue Hill in 1794, the Parson Fisher House (Rte. 15/176, 44 Mines Rd., Blue Hill, 207/374-2459, www.jonathanfisherhouse.org, 1–4 P.M. Thurs.–Sat. early July–mid-Oct.,

$5) immerses visitors in period furnishings and Jonathan Fisher lore. And Fisher's feats are breathtaking: He was a Harvard-educated preacher who also managed to be an accomplished painter, poet, mathematician, naturalist, linguist, inventor, cabinetmaker, farmer, architect, and printmaker. In his spare time, he fathered nine children. Fisher also pitched in to help build the yellow house on Tenney Hill, which served as the Congregational Church parsonage. Now it contains intriguing items created by Fisher, memorabilia that volunteer tour guides delight in explaining, including a camera obscura. Don't miss it.

### Historic Houses
A few of Blue Hill's elegant houses have been converted to museums, inns, restaurants, even some offices and shops, so you can see them from the inside out. To appreciate the private residences, you'll want to walk, bike, or drive around town. Check with the Holt House about village walking tours.

In downtown Blue Hill, a few steps off Main Street, stands the **Holt House** (3 Water St., Blue Hill, 207/326-8250, 1–4 P.M. Tues. and Fri. and 11 A.M.–2 P.M. Sat. July–mid-Sept., $3 adults, free for children 12 and under), home of the Blue Hill Historical Society. Built in 1815 by Jeremiah Holt, the Federal-style building contains restored stenciling, period decor, and masses of memorabilia contributed by local residents. In the carriage house are even more goodies, including old tools, a sleigh, carriages, and so forth.

Walk or drive up Union Street (Rte. 177), past George Stevens Academy, and wander **The Old Cemetery,** established in 1794. If gnarled trees and ancient headstones intrigue you, there aren't many good-size Maine cemeteries older than this one.

### Bagaduce Music Lending Library
At the foot of Greene's Hill in Blue Hill is one of Maine's more unusual institutions, a library where you can borrow by mail or in person from a collection of 200 titles grouped in six categories (3 Music Library La., Rte.

# GALLERY HOPPING IN BLUE HILL

Perhaps it's Blue Hill's location near the renowned Haystack Mountain School of Crafts. Perhaps it's the way the light plays off the rolling countryside and onto the twisting coastline. Perhaps it's the inspirational landscape. Whatever the reason, numerous artists and artisans call Blue Hill home, and top-notch galleries are abundant.

Judith Leighton knows contemporary art, and her **Leighton Gallery** (24 Parker Point Rd., 207/374-5001, www.leightongallery.com) is a real treat. The airy two-story-plus-basement space, in a converted barn on the Parker Point Road, is filled with a great selection. Be sure to visit the equally spectacular and extremely peaceful backyard sculpture garden. The **Liros Gallery** (14 Parker Point Rd., 207/374-5370 or 800/287-5370, www.lirosgallery.com) has been dealing in Russian icons since the mid-1960s. Prices are high, but the icons are fascinating. The gallery also carries Currier and Ives prints, antique maps, and 19th-century British and American paintings. From here, it's a short walk to **Blue Hill Bay Gallery** (Main St., 207/374-5773, www.bluehillbaygallery.com), which represents contemporary artists in various media.

Don't miss **Jud Hartmann** (Main St. at Rte. 15, 207/359-2544, www.judhartmanngallery.com). The spacious, well-lighted in-town gallery carries Hartmann's limited-edition bronze sculptures of the Woodland Tribes of the Northeast. Hartmann often can be seen working on his next model in the gallery – a real treat. He's a wealth of information about his subjects, and he loves sharing the fascinating – even mesmerizing – stories he's uncovered during his meticulous research.

Also on Main Street are three other fun, artsy gallery/shops. **Handworks Gallery** (Main St., 207/374-5613) sells a range of fun, funky,

utilitarian and fine art crafts by more than 50 Maine artists and craftspeople, including jewelry, furniture, rugs, wall hangings, and clothing. Browse **North Country Textiles** (Main St., 207/374-2715, www.northcountrytextiles.com) for fine handwoven throws, rugs, clothing, and table linens as well as other fine crafts.

Pottery is abundant in Blue Hill. **Rowantrees Pottery** (Rte. 177, 207/374-5535) and **Rackliffe Pottery** (Rte. 172, 207/374-2297 or 888/631-3321, www.rackliffepottery.com) both have well-established reputations. Rowantrees Pottery's kiln was first fired in 1934. The handmade pottery is made from local marine clay accented by rich glazes derived from local sources. Rackliffe, noted for its vivid blue wares, also makes its own glazes and has been producing lead-free pottery since 1969.

About two miles from downtown is a another don't-miss. **Mark Bell Pottery** (Rte. 15, Blue Hill, 207/374-5881), in a tiny building signaled only by a small roadside sign, is the home of exquisite, award-winning porcelain by the eponymous potter. It's easy to understand why his wares were displayed at the Smithsonian Institution's Craft Fair as well as other juried shows across the country. The delicacy of each vase, bowl, or whatever is astonishing, and the glazes are gorgeous. Twice each summer he has kiln openings, must-go events for collectors and any fans. Call for details.

Functional porcelain pottery is Melody Lewis-Kane's specialty at **Clay Forms** (Rte. 15, 207/359-2321, www.clayformspottery.com), four miles south of Blue Hill. The pitcher plant and hummingbird pieces are especially graceful.

Also worth a look-see is **Rachel Raye** (13 Schoolhouse La., East Blue Hill, 207/374-5944), a master at depicting animals and capturing their personalities.

172, P.O. Box 829, Blue Hill 04614, 207/374-5454, www.bagaducemusic.org, 10 A.M.–3 P.M. Mon.–Fri. or by appointment). Somehow this seems so appropriate for a community that's a magnet for music lovers. Annual membership is $10 ($5 for students); lending fees range $1–4 per piece, and you can keep titles for up to two months.

## Scenic Routes

**Parker Point Road** (turn off Rte. 15 at the Blue Hill Library) takes you from Blue Hill to Blue Hill Falls the back way, with vistas en route toward Acadia National Park. For other great views, drive the length of **Newbury Neck,** in nearby Surry, or head west on Route 15/176 toward Sedgwick, Brooksville, and beyond.

## PARKS AND RECREATION
### C Blue Hill Mountain

Mountain seems a fancy label for a 943-footer, yet Blue Hill Mountain stands alone, visible from Camden and even beyond. On a clear day, head for the summit and take in the wrap-around view encompassing Penobscot Bay, the hills of Mount Desert, and the Camden Hills. Climb the fire tower and you'll see even more. In mid-June, the lupines along the way are breathtaking; in fall, the colors are spectacular—with reddened blueberry barrens added to the variegated foliage. Go early in the day; it's a popular easy-to-moderate hike. A short loop on the lower slopes takes only half an hour. Take Route 15 (Pleasant St.) to Mountain Road. Turn right and go 0.8 mile to the trailhead (on the left) and the small parking area (on the right). You can also walk (uphill) the mile from the village. The trail can be squishy, especially in the wooded sections, so you'll want rubberized or waterproof shoes or boots.

## Blue Hill Heritage Trust

This fine organization (101 Union St., P.O. Box 222, Blue Hill 04614, 207/374-5118, www.bhht.org, 8 A.M.–5 P.M. weekdays) works hard at preserving the region's landscape. It also presents a Walks n Talks series, with offerings such as kayaking by preservation land along Eggemoggin Reach, a full-moon hike up Blue Hill Mountain, and walks through other trust properties, such as 700-acre Kingdom Woods Conservation Preserve and Cooper Farm at Caterpillar Hill. Many include talks by knowledgeable folks on complementary topics. Check the website, call, or stop by to see what's up when you're in town.

## Blue Hill Town Park

At the end of Water Street is a small park with a terrific view. It has a small pebble beach, picnic tables, portable toilet, and a creative playground. It's a fine place for a picnic.

## MERI Center for Marine Studies

A great way to raise kids' environmental consciousness is to enroll them in summer activities sponsored by the MERI Center for Marine Studies (55 Main St., Blue Hill, 207/374-2135, www.meriresearch.org). MERI (Marine Environmental Research Institute), a nonprofit marine-ecology organization, schedules day-long island boat trips, "eco-cruises," and island walks, plus a variety of naturalist-led morning and afternoon programs, each geared to different age groups or groupings ($20–50); cruises are limited to 12 passengers. The expanding MERI Center has a touch tank, a marine lending library, and exhibit space. At 10 A.M. on Fridays it hosts a story hour for preschoolers that concludes with a craft program. During fall, winter, and spring, MERI offers lectures and screens marine-related films. It's free, but a $3 donation is appreciated. MERI is open Monday–Saturday all year.

## Boating

A favorite spot for *experienced* kayakers and canoeists is **Blue Hill Falls,** which churns with white water when the tide turns. Check for times of high and low tide. Roadside parking is illegal, but the law is too often ignored. The Route 175 bridge is narrow, and cars often stop suddenly as they come over the hill, so be particularly cautious here.

Unless you own a boat or know a member of the Kollegewidgwok Yacht Club in East Blue

Hill (207/374-5581), there's no sailing out of Blue Hill. If you're trailing a boat, use the public boat launch down on the harbor. Kollegewidgwok, incidentally, is a Penobscot Indian word meaning "blue hill on shining green water."

## Outfitters

Anna and Barry Snow's **Rocky Coast Outfitters** (Grindleville Rd., P.O. Box 351, Blue Hill 04614, 207/374-8866, rockycoastoutfitters@verizon.net) delivers rental canoes, kayaks, and bicycles, along with the necessary helmets, paddles, and life vests, to your lodging. Delivery is free. Rates vary with equipment and rental period. Another source for rental canoes and kayaks is **The Activity Shop** (61 Ellsworth Rd., Blue Hill, 207/374-3500, www.theactivityshop.com).

## SHOPPING

Boutiques, antiques, galleries, and even two downtown bookstores make shopping a pleasure in Blue Hill, especially if you're looking for the unusual. (See the sidebar *Gallery Hopping in Blue Hill.*)

## Antiques

Historical and cottage goods are the specialty at **Salt Air Primitives** (5 Main St., Blue Hill, 207/374-8886). **Blue Hill Antiques** (8 Water St., Blue Hill, 207/374-2199 or 207/326-4973) specializes in 18th- and 19th-century French and American furniture—it attracts a high-end clientele. The same patrons seek out neighboring Brad Emerson's **Emerson Antiques** (33 Water St., Blue Hill, 207/374-5140), concentrating on early Americana, such as hooked rugs and ship models.

## Books

Blue Hill's literate population manages to support two full-service, year-round, independent bookstores. The selection is excellent at **Blue Hill Books** (2 Pleasant St., Rte. 15, Blue Hill, 207/374-5632, www.bluehillbooks.com), thanks to knowledgeable owners Nick Sichterman and Mariah Hughs. The store organizes an "authors series" during the summer.

Around the corner, ever-helpful Bonnie Myers provides free advice on the region with a money-back guarantee at **North Light Books** (Main St., Blue Hill, 207/374-5422). It's a delight to browse, the children's book selection is terrific, and out back is Blue Hill Hearth, with all sorts of treats.

## Eclectic

The Himalayas meet Blue Hill at Jeff Kaley's **Asian World Imports** (102 Pleasant St./Rte. 15, Blue Hill, 207/374-2284, www.asianworldimports.com). A Nepal Peace Corps veteran, Kaley seeks out eco-sensitive suppliers using fair-trade practices, bringing back custom-made Nepalese, Tibetan, Indian, and Thai clothing, jewelry, and artifacts, as well as organic Himalayan tea. The shop is loaded with treasures. Jeff also leads small-group cultural tours and treks in Nepal and Tibet; contact him for details.

In downtown Blue Hill is Peter Stremlau's **New Cargoes** (49 Main St., Blue Hill, 207/374-3733), following somewhat in the Pier One/Crate and Barrel tradition. Furniture, linens, notecards, candles, and on and on. The shop name is apt—new things arrive regularly.

## Wine

**Blue Hill Wine Shop** (138 Main St., Blue Hill, 207/374-2161), tucked into a converted horse barn, carries more than 1,000 wines, plus teas, coffees, and blended tobaccos and unusual pipes for diehard, upscale smokers. Monthly wine tastings (2–5 P.M. last Saturday of the month) are always an adventure.

## ENTERTAINMENT

Variety and serendipity are the keys here. Check local calendar listings and tune in to radio station WERU (89.9 and 102.9 FM, www.weru.org), the peninsula's own community radio; there might be announcements of concerts by local resident pianist Paul Sullivan or the Bagaduce Chorale, or maybe a contra dance or a tropical treat from Carl Chase's Atlantic Clarion Steel Band or Flash-in-the-Pans Community Band. The George Stevens Academy also has a weekly lecture series.

## Music

Since 1922, chamber-music students have been spending summers perfecting their skills and demonstrating their prowess at the **Kneisel Hall Chamber Music School** (Pleasant St., Rte. 15, Blue Hill, 207/374-2811, www.kneisel.org). Faculty concerts run Friday evenings and Sunday afternoons late June–late August. The concert schedule is published in the spring, and reserved-seating tickets ($30 inside, $20 on the veranda outside, nonrefundable) can be ordered by phone. There is also unreserved tent seating ($10) for the Friday evening and Sunday afternoon concerts. Other opportunities to hear the students and faculty exist, including young artist concerts, children's concerts, open rehearsals, and more. Check the website or program for details. Kneisel Hall is about a half mile from the center of town.

Chamber music continues in winter thanks to the volunteer **Blue Hill Concert Association** (P.O. Box 140, Blue Hill 04614). Five concerts are performed between January and March at the Congregational Church, a handsome, traditional New England spired edifice on Main Street.

## EVENTS

The first weekend in August, the **Academy Antiques Show** draws a huge crowd to the George Stevens Academy on Union Street in Blue Hill. Admission is $7, and lunch and tea are available.

WERU's annual Full Circle Fair is usually held in mid-August at the Blue Hill Fairgrounds (Rte. 172, north of downtown Blue Hill). Expect world music, good food, crafts, and socially and environmentally progressive talks.

On Labor Day weekend, the **Blue Hill Fair** (Blue Hill Fairgrounds, Rte. 172, Blue Hill, 207/374-9976) is one of the state's best agricultural fairs. Besides the food booths (good-for-you fare competes with fried dough), a carnival, fireworks, sheepdog trials, and live musical entertainment, you can check out the blue-ribbon winners for finest quilt, beefiest bull, or largest squash.

## ACCOMMODATIONS
### Inns and Bed-and-Breakfasts

On a quiet side street close to town, **❰ The Blue Hill Inn** (Union St., Rte. 177, P.O. Box 403, Blue Hill 04614, 207/374-2844 or 800/826-7415, www.bluehillinn.com, $158–195, mid-May–late Oct.) has been welcoming guests since 1840. If you're trying to imagine a classic country inn, this would be it. It came into new hands midsummer 2007, but new owner Sarah Pebworth planned few changes—still it's wise to inquire about particulars. Stay here if you enjoy antiques, warm hospitality, and classic New England inns; don't stay if you're on a tight budget or have small children. Ten rooms and a suite, all with air-conditioning, boast real chandeliers, four-posters, down comforters, fancy linens, and braided and Oriental rugs; three have wood-burning fireplaces. The third-floor garret suite is ideal for families with well-behaved children; a first-floor room is wheelchair-accessible. Rear rooms overlook the extensive cutting garden, with chairs and a hammock. The library, dominated by a Persian chandelier, has masses of local information. Refreshments are available all day; superb hors d'oeuvres are served 6–7 P.M. in two elegant parlors or the garden. Off-season, an adjacent suite in the elegant Cape House—the ground floor of a tiny dwelling—is $165. Twice each year, usually May and October, the inn puts on gala wine-dinner weekends; the multi-course gourmet dinners are outstanding. The innkeeper will arrange for Kneisel Hall tickets, kayak rentals, cruises, massages, and more.

What's old is new at **Barncastle** (125 South St., P.O. Box 1510, Blue Hill 04614, 207/374-2330, www.barncastlehotel.com, $125–175), a late-19th-century Shingle-style cottage that's listed on the National Register. It opens to a two-story foyer with a split stairway and balcony. Rooms and suites open off the balcony, and all are spacious, minimally decorated, and have contemporary accents, including flat-screen TVs, Wi-Fi, fridge, and microwave. Rates include a continental breakfast. Downstairs is a tavern, serving pizza, salads, and sandwiches.

The Blue Hill Inn is a classic country inn.

Two miles north of town, at Marcia and Jim Schatz's **Blue Hill Farm Country Inn** (Rte. 15, P.O. Box 437, Blue Hill 04614, 207/374-5126, www.bluehillfarminn.com, $90–110 d peak), a huge refurbished barn serves as the gathering spot for guests. If the weather is lousy, you can plop down in front of the oversize woodstove and start in on cribbage or other games. Antique sleigh-runner banisters lead to the barn's seven second-floor rooms—all with private baths, skylights, hooked rugs, and quilts. A wing of the farmhouse has seven more rooms with shared baths and more quilts. Breakfast is generous continental. During the summer, visiting jazz or classical musicians sometimes entertain in the barn, but it all eases off early. On the inn's 48 acres are well-cleared nature trails, an 18th-century cellar hole, and a duck pond. It's open year-round.

Okay, it's not a *real* lighthouse, but the waterfront **First Light B&B** (821 E. Blue Hill Rd., Blue Hill 04614, 207/374-5879, www.firstlightbandb.com, $110–200) is close enough to fool many folks. Huge windows frame views that, on a clear day, extend for five miles. Innkeeper Beverly Bartlett, a retired nursing professor, has three lighthouse-themed rooms. If you're a lighthouse buff, reserve the Lighthouse Suite, in the tower. Two other rooms share a bath or can be connected as a suite. Guests may climb the tower, built by an eccentric previous owner, for 360-degree views; it's the perfect place for seal-watching or birding. A comfortably cluttered common room, with fireplace, plentiful books, and a grand piano, faces McHeard's Cove. Breakfast is served either in the dining room or on the patio. It's open year-round.

## Seasonal Rentals

Weekly rentals (or longer) can pay off if you have a large family or are planning a group vacation. The Blue Hill Peninsula has lots of rental cottages, camps, and houses, but the trick is to plan well ahead. This is a popular area in summer, and many renters sign up for the following year before they leave town. For information, contact Sandy Douvarjo of

**Peninsula Property Rentals** (Main St., P.O. Box 611, Blue Hill 04614, 207/374-2428, www.peninsulapropertyrentals.com).

# FOOD
## Local Flavors
Picnic fare is available at **Merrill and Hinckley** (Union St., Blue Hill, 207/374-2821, 7 A.M.– 9 P.M. Mon.–Sat., 8 A.M.–9 P.M. Sun.), a quirky, family-owned grocery/general store dating from the mid-19th century.

The **Blue Hill Co-Op and Café** (Greene's Hill, Rte. 172, Blue Hill, 207/374-2165, café 207/374-8999, 8 A.M.–7 P.M. Mon.–Fri., to 6 P.M. Sat., 10 A.M.–5 P.M. Sun.) sells organic and hydroponic produce and grains, cheeses, organic coffee, and more. Breads are terrific here. Sandwiches, salads, and soups—many with ethnic flavors—are available in the café. The staff will pack it all up for a picnic, too.

Tucked behind First Light Books is **Blue Hill Hearth** (58 Main St., Blue Hill, 207/610-9090, 8 A.M.–7 P.M. Mon.–Fri., 10 A.M.–7 P.M. Sat., 10 A.M.–4 P.M. Sun.), operated by the former owner of Pain de Famille. The breads are outstanding, but you can pick up ready-made sandwiches and other goods. It's wise to call ahead for the Friday Night Pizza Plus, when two sizes of pizza are offered with about two dozen possible toppings.

Just south of town is **Barncastle** (125 South St., Blue Hill, 207/374-2300, www.barncastle-hotel.com), serving wood-fired pizzas as well as sandwiches and salads in a lovely shingle-style cottage. Everything is less than $10.

Local gardeners, farmers, and craftspeople peddle their wares at the **Blue Hill Farmers Market** (9–11:30 A.M. Sat.) It's a particularly enduring market, well worth a visit. Demonstrations by area chefs and artists are often on the agenda. The major effort is late June–September at the Blue Hill Fairgrounds (Rte. 172, just north of downtown).

## Lobster and Fried Fish
For lobster, fried fish, and the area's best lobster roll, head to **The Fish Net** (Main St., Blue Hill, 207/374-5240, 11 A.M.–8 P.M. Mon.–Thurs., to

9 P.M. Fri. and Sat.). Dine outdoors on picnic tables or inside. Nothing's pricey.

## Family-Friendly Casual Restaurants
First choice for families or anyone looking for a casual but very good meal is **The Blue Moose** (50 Main St., Blue Hill, 207/374-3274, www.thebluemooserestaurant.com, 10:30 A.M.– 3 P.M. and 5–9 P.M. Mon.–Thurs., 10 A.M.– 9:30 P.M. Fri., 7:30 A.M.–9 P.M. Sat.–Sun.), which has a wide-ranging menu and welcomes kids. Most choices are in the $8–12 range. Kids'/small appetite menu ranges $3–5.

Very popular with local folks is **Marlintini's Grill** (The Mines Rd., Blue Hill, 207/374-2500, 11:30 A.M.–9 P.M. daily, bar stays open until 1 A.M.). Inside, half is a sports bar, the other half a restaurant. You can sit in either, but the bar side can get raucous. Best bet: the screened-in porch. Expect burgers, salads, sandwiches, fried foods, and a kids' menu. The portions are big; the service is good; the food is reliable.

## Casual to Fine Dining
Here's a doubleheader: **C Arborvine and The Vinery** (Main St., Blue Hill, www.arborvine. com). For a light dinner, head to The Vinery (207/374-2441, 5:30–9 P.M. Wed.–Sun.), a piano and wine bar–style bistro in a beautifully renovated barn, where there's often evening entertainment, too. Entrées are $7–14. If you're up for something a bit more elegant, make reservations at Arborvine (207/374-2119, 5:30– 9 P.M. Tues.–Sun. summer, Fri.–Sun. winter), a conscientiously renovated two-century-old Cape-style house with four dining areas, each with a different feel and understated decor. Most entrées are in the $25–30 range; there's always at least one for vegetarians. The wine list is small but select. Chef/owner John Hikade and his wife, Beth, operate both.

Anneliese Riggall brought new life to the historical old forge building that hangs over the river downtown, reopening it as **C The Wescott Forge** (66 Main St., Blue Hill, 207/374-9909, www.thewescottforge.com, 11:30 A.M.–2 P.M. Wed.–Sat. and 5:30–10 P.M.

Mon.–Sat.). It's fabulous. The menu changes weekly but might include entrées such as seaweed-seared yellowfin tuna and Moroccan chickpea stew. Most run $16–25. The upstairs is a casual lounge, the downstairs has an easy elegance, all highlighted by beautiful forged accent pieces (check out the stairway railing). Request a table on the porch, and you'll be serenaded by the water rushing underneath as you dine.

## INFORMATION AND SERVICES
### Information
The Blue Hill Peninsula Chamber of Commerce (28 Water St., P.O. Box 520, Blue Hill 04614, 207/374-2281, www.bluehillpeninsula.org) is stocked with brochures, menus, and other information on Blue Hill and the surrounding area. You can also find information (although some is outdated) on www.bluehillme.com. One interesting feature on this site is a section on wildlife sightings.

At the Blue Hill Public Library (5 Parker Point Rd., 207/374-5515, www.bluehill.lib.me.us), ask to see the suit of armor, which *may* have belonged to Magellan. The library also sponsors a summer lecture series.

### Public Restrooms
In season, there are portable toilets behind the chamber of commerce building and in the town park. Public buildings that have restrooms are the Blue Hill Town Hall (Main St.), Blue Hill Public Library (Main St.), and Blue Hill Memorial Hospital (Water St.).

# Brooklin/Brooksville/Sedgwick

Nestled near the bottom of the Blue Hill Peninsula and surrounded by Castine, Blue Hill, and Deer Isle, this often-missed area offers superb hiking, kayaking, and sailing, plus historic homes and unique shops, studios, lodgings, and personalities.

The best-known town is Brooklin (pop. 841), thanks to two magazines: *The New Yorker* and *WoodenBoat*. Wordsmiths extraordinaire E. B. and Katharine White "dropped out" to Brooklin in the 1930s and forever afterward dispatched their splendid material for *The New Yorker* from here. (The Whites' former home, a handsome Colonial not open to the public, is on Route 175 in North Brooklin, 6.5 miles from the Blue Hill Falls bridge.) In 1977, *WoodenBoat* magazine moved its headquarters to Brooklin, where its 60-acre shoreside estate attracts builders and dreamers from all over the globe. Nearby Brooksville (pop. 911) drew the late Helen and Scott Nearing, whose *Living the Good Life* made them role models for back-to-the-landers. Their compound now verges on "must-see" status. Buck's Harbor, a section of Brooksville, is the setting for *One Morning in Maine*, one of Robert McCloskey's beloved children's books. Oldest of the three towns is Sedgwick (pop. 1,175, incorporated in 1789), which once included all of Brooklin and part of Brooksville. Now wedged *between* Brooklin and Brooksville, it includes the hamlet of Sargentville, the Caterpillar Hill scenic overlook, and a well-preserved complex of historic buildings. The influx of pilgrims continues in this area—many of them artists bent on capturing the spirit that has proved so enticing to creative types.

## SIGHTS
### WoodenBoat Publications
On Naskeag Point Road, 1.2 miles from downtown Brooklin (Rte. 175), a small sign marks the turn to the world headquarters of the *WoodenBoat* empire (Naskeag Point Rd., P.O. Box 78, Brooklin 04616, 207/359-4651, www.woodenboat.com). Buy magazines, books, clothing, and all manner of nautical merchandise at the handsome new store (www.woodenboatstore.com), stroll the grounds, or sign up for one of the dozens of one- and two-week spring, summer, and fall courses in seamanship, navigation, boatbuilding, sailmaking,

© TOM NANGLE

The famed sailing waters of Eggemoggin Reach separate Brooksville on the Blue Hill Peninsula from Little Deer Isle.

marine carving, and more. Special courses are geared to kids, women, pros, and all-thumbs neophytes; the camaraderie is legendary, and so is the cuisine. School visiting hours are 8 A.M.–5 P.M. Monday–Saturday June–October.

## Historical Sights

Now used as the museum/headquarters of the Sedgwick-Brooklin Historical Society, the 1795 **Reverend Daniel Merrill House** (Rte. 172, P.O. Box 171, Sedgwick 04676, 207/359-8086, 2–4 P.M. Sun. in July and Aug., or by appointment, donations welcomed) was the parsonage for Sedgwick's first permanent minister. Inside the house are period furnishings, old photos, toys, and tools; a few steps away are a restored 1874 schoolhouse, an 1821 cattle pound (for corralling wandering bovines), and a hearse barn. Pick up a brochure during open hours and guide yourself around the buildings and grounds. The **Sedgwick Historic District,** crowning Town House Hill, comprises the Merrill House and its outbuildings, plus the imposing 1794 Town House and the 23-acre Rural Cemetery (the oldest headstone dates from 1798) across Route 172.

## ◖ The Good Life Center

Forest Farm, home of the late Helen and Scott Nearing, is now the site of The Good Life Center (372 Harborside Rd., Box 11, Harborside, 207/326-8211, www.goodlife.org). Advocates of simple living and authors of 10 books on the subject, the Nearings created a trust to perpetuate their farm and philosophy. Resident stewards lead tours 1–5 P.M. Thursday–Tuesday in July and August (Thurs.–Mon. the rest of the year, but call ahead), $5 donation suggested. Copies of Nearing books are available for sale. From mid-June to mid-September, Monday night meetings (7 P.M.) at the farm feature free programs by gardeners, philosophers, musicians, and other guest speakers. Occasional work parties, workshops, and conferences are also on the center's schedule. The farm is on Harborside Road, just before it

# E. B. WHITE: SOME WRITER

Every child since the mid-1940s has heard of E. B. White – author of the memorable *Stuart Little*, *Charlotte's Web*, and *Trumpet of the Swan* – and every college kid for decades has been reminded to consult his *Elements of Style*, but how many realize that White and his wife, Katharine, were living not in the Big City but in the hamlet of North Brooklin, Maine? It was Brooklin that inspired Charlotte and Wilbur and Stuart, and it was Brooklin where the Whites lived very full, creative lives.

Abandoning their desks at *The New Yorker* in 1938, Elwyn Brooks White and Katharine S. White bought an idyllic saltwater farm on the Blue Hill Peninsula and moved here with their young son Joel, who became a noted architect and yachtbuilder in Brooklin before his untimely death in 1997. Andy (as E. B. had been dubbed since his college days at Cornell) produced 20 books, countless essays and letters to editors, and hundreds (maybe thousands?) of "newsbreaks" – those wry clipping-and-commentary items sprinkled through each issue of *The New Yorker*. Katharine continued wielding her pencil as the magazine's standout children's-book editor, donating many of her review copies to Brooklin's Friend Memorial Library, one of her favorite "causes." (The library also has two original Garth Williams drawings from *Stuart Little*, courtesy of E. B., and a lovely garden dedicated to the Whites.) Katharine's book, *Onward and Upward in the Garden*, a collection of her *New Yorker* gardening pieces, was published in 1979, two years after her death.

Later in life, E. B. sagely addressed the young readers of his three award-winning children's books:

> Are my stories true, you ask? No, they are imaginary tales, containing fantastic characters and events. In real life, a family doesn't have a child who looks like a mouse; in real life, a spider doesn't spin words in her web. In real life, a swan doesn't blow a trumpet. But real life is only one kind of life – there is also the life of the imagination. And although my stories are imaginary, I like to think that there is some truth in them, too – truth about the way people and animals feel and think and act.

E. B. White died on October 1, 1985, at the age of 86. He and Katharine and Joel left large footprints on this earth, but perhaps nowhere more so than in Brooklin.

turns to dirt. From Route 176 in Brooksville, take Cape Rosier Road, go eight miles, passing Holbrook Islands Sanctuary. At the Grange Hall, turn right and follow the road 1.9 miles to the end. Turn left onto Harborside Road and continue 1.8 miles to Forest Farm, across from Orrs Cove.

## Four Season Farm

Almost next door to the Nearings' place is Four Seasons Farm (609 Weir Cove Rd., Harborside, 207/326-4455, www.fourseasonfarm.com, 1–5 P.M. Mon.–Sat.), the lush organic farm owned and operated by internationally renowned gardeners Eliot Coleman and Barbara Damrosch. Both have written numerous books and articles and starred in TV gardening shows. Coleman is a driving force behind the use of the word "authentic" to mean "beyond organic," demonstrating a commitment to food that is local, fresh, ripe, clean, safe, and nourishing. He's also successfully pioneered a "winter harvest," developing environmentally sound and economically viable systems for extending fresh vegetable production from October through May in cold-weather climates. After 26 years, Coleman and Damrosch reopened their farm to the public in 2005. It's a treat for the eyes as well as the tastebuds—you've never seen such gorgeous produce. To find the farm, continue past The Good Life Center and look for a sign on the left.

## Scenic Routes

No one seems to know how **Caterpillar Hill** got its name, but its reputation comes from a panoramic vista of water, hills, and blueberry barrens—with a couple of convenient picnic tables where you can stop for lunch, photos, or a ringside view of sunset and fall foliage. From the 350-foot elevation, the views take in Walker Pond, Eggemoggin Reach, Deer Isle, Swan's Island, and even the Camden Hills; interpretive signage puts it all in context. The signposted rest area is on Route 175/15, between Brooksville and Sargentville, next to a small, but excellent, gallery; watch out for the blind curve when you pull off the road. Between Sargentville and Sedgwick, Route 175 offers nonstop views of Eggemoggin Reach, with shore access to the Benjamin River just before you reach Sedgwick village.

Two other scenic routes are **Naskeag Point,** in Brooklin, and **Cape Rosier,** westernmost arm of the town of Brooksville. Naskeag Point Road begins off Route 175 in "downtown" Brooklin, heads down the peninsula for 3.7 miles past the entrance to *WoodenBoat* Publications; past Amen Farm (207/359-8982, call for hours), home of the late author Roy Barrette, where the gardens and 10-acre arboretum are open for viewing by appointment; to a small shingle beach (limited parking) on Eggemoggin Reach, where you'll find picnic tables, a boat launch, a seasonal toilet, and a marker commemorating the 1778 Battle of Naskeag, when British sailors came ashore from the sloop *Gage,* burned several buildings, and were run off by a ragtag band of local settlers. Cape Rosier's roads are poorly marked, perhaps deliberately, so keep your DeLorme atlas handy. The Cape Rosier loop takes in Holbrook Island Sanctuary, Goose Falls, the hamlet of Harborside, and plenty of water and island views.

## PARKS, PRESERVES, AND RECREATION
### ◖ Holbrook Island Sanctuary State Park

In the early 1970s, foresighted benefactor Anita Harris donated to the state 1,230 acres in Brooksville that would become the Holbrook Island Sanctuary (207/326-4012, www.state.me.us/doc/parks, free). From Route 176, between West Brooksville and South Brooksville, head west on Cape Rosier Road, following brown-and-white signs for the sanctuary. Trail maps and bird checklists are available in boxes at trailheads or at park headquarters. The easy Backshore Trail (about 30 minutes) starts here, or go back a mile and climb the steepish trail to **Backwoods Mountain** for the best vistas. Other trails include one around a beaver flowage. Other attractions include shorefront picnic tables and grills, four old cemeteries, and super birding during spring and fall migrations. Leashed pets are allowed, but no bikes on the trails and no camping. Officially open May 15–October 15, but the access road and parking areas are plowed for cross-country skiers.

Or you can take a picnic to the **Bagaduce Ferry Landing,** in West Brooksville off Route 176, where there are picnic tables and cross-river vistas toward Castine.

A small, relatively little-known beach is Brooklin's **Pooduck Beach.** From the Brooklin General Store (Rte. 175), take Naskeag Point Road about half a mile, watching for the Pooduck Road sign on the right. Drive to the end. You can also launch a sea kayak into Eggemoggin Reach here.

## Bicycling

Bicycling in this area is hazardous. Roads here are particularly narrow and winding, with poor shoulders. If you're determined to pedal, consider either the Naskeag scenic route or around Cape Rosier, where traffic is light.

## Canoeing

**Native Trails** (Miller Rd., P.O. Box 240, Waldoboro 04572, 207/832-5255), headed by Mike Krepner, is working to re-create the ancient Minnewokun Canoe Trail, a 25-mile circuit of the southeast corner of the Blue Hill Peninsula—including the Bagaduce River and Eggemoggin Reach—used by Native Americans to tap the fisheries of the Bagaduce Estuary. The name allegedly means "many-angled route," and that it is. The 15-mile section between Castine and Walker Pond is already a popular (mostly flat-water) paddling route. Contact Native Trails for a map and an update on the project's status.

## Sailing

Captain LeCain Smith sails *Perelandra* (Buck's Harbor, 207/326-4279), a 44-foot ketch, in the waters of Penobscot Bay. Rates begin at $40 pp for a two-hour trip and increase to $60 pp for a four-hour sail. The boat holds a maximum of six passengers.

Sail on a Maine windjammer with Captain Bill Brown on the **Summertime** (207/326-8485 or 800/562-8290, www.schoonersummertime. com), which sails from various locations on the peninsula, including Brooksville, Sedgwick, and Stonington in spring and fall. Six-hour sails are $40 per adult, $20 per child younger than 12; three-hour sails are $18 and $9. The schooner takes a maximum of 20 guests.

Ensign-class Antares and Pegasus day sailboats are available for rental at **Buck's Harbor Marine** (on the dock, South Brooksville, 207/326-8839, www.bucksharbor.com). The full-keel boats rent for $130 per day. Buck's Harbor also charters bareboat sail and power yachts to qualified skippers.

## SHOPPING

Most of these businesses are small, owner-operated shops, which means they're often catch as catch can. If you want to be sure, call ahead.

## Antiques

When you need a slate sink, a clawfoot tub, brass fixtures, or a Palladian window, **Architectural Antiquities** (52 Indian Point La., Harborside, 207/326-4938, www.archantiquities.com), on Cape Rosier, is just the ticket—a restorer's delight. Prices are reasonable for what you get, and it'll ship your purchases. Open all year by appointment; ask for directions when you call. Antiques dating from the Federal period through the turn of the 20th century are the specialties at **Sedgwick Antiques** (775 N. Sedgwick Rd./Rte. 172, Sedgwick, 207/359-

8834). Early furniture, handmade furniture, and a full range of country accessories and antiques can be found at **Thomas Hinchcliffe Antiques** (26 Cradle Knolls La., off Rte. 176, W. Sedgwick, 207/326-9411). Painted country furniture, decoys, and unusual nautical items are specialties at Peg and Olney Grindall's **Old Cove Antiques** (106 Caterpillar Rd./Rte. 15, Sargentville 04673, 207/359-2031 or 207/359-8585), a weathered-gray shop, across from the Eggemoggin Country Store.

## Artists' and Artisans' Galleries

Small studio-galleries pepper Route 175 (Reach Rd.) in Sedgwick and Brooklin; most are marked only by small signs, so watch carefully. First up is **Eggemoggin Textile Studio** (off Rte. 175/Reach Rd., Sedgwick, 207/359-5083, www.chrisleithstudio.com), where the incredibly gifted Christine Leith weaves scarves, wraps, hangings, and pillows with hand-dyed silk and wool; the colors are magnificent. You might catch her at work on the big loom in her studio shop, a real treat.

Continue along the road to find **Reach Road Gallery** (Reach Rd., Sedgwick, 207/359-8803), where Holly Meade sells her detailed woodblock prints as well as prints from the children's books she's illustrated.

Only a few doors down is **Mermaid Woolens** (Reach Rd., Sedgwick, 207/359-2747), source of Elizabeth Coakley's wildly colorful hand knits—vests, socks, and sweaters. They're pricey but worth every nickel. She also does seascape paintings. Clever woman.

Continue over to Brooklin, where Virginia G. Sarsfield's handcrafts paper products, including custom lampshades, calligraphy papers, books, and lamps at **Handmade Papers** (Rte. 175 at Center Harbor Rd., Brooklin, 207/359-8345, www.handmadepapersonline. com).

Just a bit farther is **Naskeag Gallery** (Rte. 175, Brooklin, 207/359-4619), a small shop that makes browsing an art form, especially if you appreciate meandering about antiques and art. The eclectic selection might include antique sweetgrass baskets and 19th-century furnishings and accent pieces mixed with works by local artists and artisans. Fun. Talented glass artist **Sihaya Hopkins** also has a shop here, as do a few other talented artisans.

In Brooksville, more treasures await on Route 176. You'll need to watch carefully for the sign marking the long drive to **Paul Heroux and Scott Goldberg Pottery** (2032 Coastal Rd./ Rte. 176, Brooksville, 207/326-9062). The small gallery is a treat for pottery fans.

Continue southwest on Route 176 and watch closely for signs for **Bagaduce Forge** (140 Ferry Rd., Brooksville, 207/326-9676); this isn't easy to find. Joseph Meltreder is both blacksmith and farrier, and his small forge, with big views, is the real thing. He turns out whimsical pieces. Especially fun are the nail people—you'll know them when you see them.

### Wine and Gifts

Three varieties of English-style hard cider are specialties at **The Sow's Ear Winery** (Rte. 176 at Herrick Rd., Brooksville, 207/326-4649), a minuscule operation in a funky, gray-shingled building. Winemaker Tom Hoey also produces sulfite-free blueberry, chokecherry, and rhubarb wines; he'll let you sample it all. Ask to see his cellar, where everything happens. No credit cards.

Nautical books, T-shirts, gifts, food (including homemade bread and key lime pie), and boat gear line the walls and shelves of the shop at **Buck's Harbor Marine** (on the dock, South Brooksville, 207/326-8839, www.bucksharbor.com).

## ENTERTAINMENT AND EVENTS

### ◖ Flash in the Pans Community Steel Band Concerts

If you're a fan of steel-band music, check to see where and when Carl Chase's Flash in the Pans Community Steel Band (207/374-2172, www.peninsulapan.org) is performing. It usually performs somewhere on the peninsula on Monday nights (7:30–9 P.M.) mid-June–early September. The musicians aren't professionals, but you'd never know it. Local papers carry the summer schedule for the nearly three-dozen-member band, which performs in various area locales and deserves its devoted following. Admission is usually a small donation to benefit a local cause. It's worth every penny to join the fun.

### The Flye Point Music and Arts Festival

A relatively new event is getting excellent reviews. The Flye Point Music and Arts Festival at the Lookout (Flye Point Rd., off Rte. 175, North Brooklin, 207/359-2188, www.acadia.net/lookout) began in 2004. Held in late June, it features musicians such as Don McLean, Richie Havens, and Jonathan Edwards; check the website for details.

### Eggemoggin Reach Regatta

Wooden boats are big attractions hereabouts, so when a huge fleet sails in for this regatta (usually the first Saturday in August, but the schedule can change), crowds gather. Don't miss the parade of wooden boats. Best locale for watching the regatta itself is on or near the bridge to Deer Isle, or near the Eggemoggin Landing grounds on Little Deer Isle. Contact *WoodenBoat* (207/359-4651) for details.

## ACCOMMODATIONS
### Cottage Colonies

The two operations in this category feel much like informal family compounds—where you quickly become an adoptee. These are extremely popular spots, where successive generations of hosts have catered to successive generations of visitors, and reservations are usually essential for July and August. Many guests book for the following year before they leave. We're not talking fancy; cottages are old-shoe rustic, of varying sizes and decor. Most of the cottages have cooking facilities, although both colonies include breakfast and dinner in July and August. Both also have hiking trails, playgrounds, rowboats, and East Penobscot Bay on the doorstep.

Jim and Sally Littlefield are the enthusiastic fourth-generation hosts at ◖ **Oakland House Seaside Resort** (435 Herrick Rd., Brooks-

© TOM NANGLE

The Homestead at Oakland House dates from 1767, and the property has remained in the same family since it was awarded as a king's grant.

ville, 207/359-8521 or 800/359-7352, www.oaklandhouse.com), a sprawling 50-acre complex of 15 wooded and waterfront cottages, as well as Shore Oaks Seaside Inn. Much of this land, now threaded with hiking trails, was part of the original king's grant to Jim's ancestors, way back in 1765. The Homestead, where meals are served, dates from 1767. Jim is the eighth generation on the property; his daughter, Sally, is ninth, and she and her husband, Sean McGuigan, are fifth-generation hosts-in-training. Weekly rates for two people sharing a two-person cottage vary by date, but begin around $475 and top off about $1,255, plus service charge, including full breakfast and five-course dinner; lower rates for children. Thursday is lobster-picnic night on the beach. Biggest bargains are early May–mid-June and September–October, when meals and housekeeping aren't included. Rowboats are free for guests' use in season, and the staff organizes other boat excursions on request. Also ask about artist workshops—what a per-

fect location! And wait till you see the gorgeous gardens—enough to warrant a full-time gardener. Two cottages (Lone Pine and Boathouse) are winterized and available all year; the other cottages are closed in winter. Call to ask about last-minute specials and short-term getaway packages.

The fourth generation manages the **Hiram Blake Camp** (220 Weir Cove Rd., Harborside, 207/326-4951, www.hiramblake.com, Memorial Day–late Sept.), but with a difference: The second and third generations still pitch in and help with gardening, lobstering, maintenance, and kibitzing. Thirteen cottages and a duplex line the shore of this 100-acre complex. Don't bother bringing reading matter: The dining room has ingenious ceiling niches lined with countless books. There's a one-week minimum (beginning Sat. or Sun.) July and August, when cottages go for $600–2,700 a week (including breakfast, dinner, and linens). Off-season rates (no meals or linens, but cottages have cooking facilities) are $600–850 a week. The best chances for getting a reservation are in June and September. No credit cards.

## Bed-and-Breakfasts

A few steps up from the half-mile-long shorefront at the Oakland House Seaside Resort's cottage colony is ◖ **Shore Oaks Seaside Inn** (435 Herrick Rd., Brooksville, 207/359-8521 or 800/359-7352, www.oaklandhouse.com/inn.html), a handsome green-trimmed stone mansion carefully restored to its arts-and-crafts heritage. No in-room phones, no TV, no noise; just peaceful bliss. Hang out for too long in the common rooms or the veranda rockers and you might never leave; this place is magical and restorative. Ten first-, second-, and third-floor rooms (seven with private baths) top out at $105–265 d, $80–140 s, plus service charge, including breakfast; for an additional $25 pp, include a five-course dinner. Shoulder-season rates (May and late Oct.) are less expensive but still include breakfast.

In 2005, Joe Moore turned an 1874 mansard-roofed Victorian in what passes as downtown Brooklin into the **Dragonflye Inn** (Naskeag Point Rd., P.O. Box 220, Brooklin 04616, 207/359-808, www.dragonflye-inn.com, $135). It's a casual put-your-feet-up kind of place, with a special invitation issued to *WoodenBoat* school students, gallery fans (lots of work by local artisans), and kayakers. Moore's goal is sustainability: Towels and linens are made from organic cotton; soaps and shampoos are local and all natural; cleaning products are all natural, biodegradable, and earth friendly. Plans call for the roof to be replaced with faux slate comprising recycled auto tires, recycled bottle insulation, and power generated on-site from the sun or the wind. Breakfast is light continental. Wi-Fi available. Bicycles are available for guests. Kayak trips can be arranged, including local shuttles. An all-inclusive, three-hour guided sea-kayaking trip off Naskeag Point is available for $75 per person.

Best known for its restaurant and pub, **The Brooklin Inn** (Rte. 175, Brooklin, 207/359-2777, www.brooklininn.com, $105–125 with breakfast; add $10 for a one-night stay) also has four simple but comfortable bedrooms.

## FOOD
### Cooking Classes

In summer, chef Terence Janericco (42 Fayette St., Boston, 617/426-7458, or after July 1 Box 226, Herrick Bay, Brooklin 04616, 207/359-2068, www.terencejanericcocookingclasses.com), author of a dozen cookbooks, moves his cooking school from Boston to Brooklin. The demonstration-only, three-hour classes are $65 pp, which includes dining on the foods prepared.

### Local Flavors

Competition is stiff for lunchtime seats at the **Morning Moon Café** (junction of Rte. 175 and Naskeag Point Rd., Brooklin, 207/359-2373, 7 A.M.–2 P.M. Tues.–Sun.), mostly because *WoodenBoat* staffers consider it an annex to their offices. "The Moon" is a friendly hangout for coffee, pizza, or great sandwiches and salads—or order it to go.

Across the street from the Morning Moon Café, the **Brooklin General Store** (1 Reach Rd., junction of Rte. 175 and Naskeag Point Rd., Brooklin, 207/359-8817, 5 A.M.–7 P.M. Mon.–Sat. and 7 A.M.–5 P.M. Sun.), vintage 1872, carries groceries, beer and wine, newspapers, take-out sandwiches, and local chatter.

In North Brooksville, where Route 175/176 crosses the Bagaduce River, stands the **Bagaduce Lunch,** a popular take-out stand (outdoor tables only) open 11 A.M.–7 or 8 P.M. daily early May–mid-September. Check the tide calendar and go when the tide is changing; order a clam roll or a hamburger, settle in at a picnic table, and watch the reversing falls. The food is so-so, but the setting is tops.

Lunch is the specialty at **Buck's Harbor Market** (Rte. 176, South Brooksville, 207/326-8683, 7 A.M.–7 P.M. Mon.–Fri., 8 A.M.–7:30 P.M. Sat., 8 A.M.–6 P.M. Sun. all year), a low-key, marginally yuppified general store popular with yachties in summer. There's a small deli/lunch counter in the back room open 11 A.M.–2 P.M.

Monday–Saturday, and for pizzas from 4:30 P.M. on Fridays and Saturdays. Behind the market is **Buck's Restaurant** (Rte. 176, South Brooksville, 207/326-8688, from 5 P.M. Mon.–Sat.), a quirky café with indoor and a few outdoor tables. The emphasis is on comfort food, with choices varying from sandwiches and pizza to nightly specials. With the café here at the market and summertime steel-band street concerts outside, this can be a busy corner.

## Ethnic Fare

Okay, I know it's hard to believe, but **El El Frijoles** (41 Caterpillar Rd./Rte. 15, Sargentville, 207/359-2486, 11 A.M.–8 P.M. Wed.–Sun.) gets good marks for its empanadas, burritos, and tacos. It's a small, somewhat funky, mostly take-out operation with a few seats inside and out. It's housed in a barn behind Coast to Coast Fine Arts.

## Country Inn Dining

An 1865 farmstead is the setting for the **Rusticator Restaurant** at the Oakland House Seaside Inn (435 Herrick Rd., Brooksville, 207/359-8521), open to the public by reservation mid-June–mid-September for its daily breakfast buffet, Sunday brunch, Thursday night shorefront lobster picnic, and superb dinners, with seating beginning at 6 P.M. Entrée range is $11–17, a steal. The dining rooms are in the property's original farmstead, which dates from 1865. At dinner, families dine in a separate room from couples, keeping everyone happy.

Almost everything on the menu is local or organic at **The Brooklin Inn** (Rte. 175, Brooklin, 207/359-2777, www.brooklininn.com, 5:30–9 P.M. Wed.–Mon.). The chef tries to know "who raised, grew, picked, or caught all the food," and all the fish are wild, free swimming, and locally caught. Entrées are $18–32; a children's menu is available. Downstairs an **Irish Pub** (5:30–10 P.M. daily) serves burgers, Guinness stew, pizza, and on Fridays all the fresh baked haddock you can eat for $10.

The chef seems to change annually at **The Lookout** (Flye Point Rd., off Rte. 175, North Brooklin, 207/359-2188, www.thelookoutinn.biz, 5:30–8 P.M. Mon.–Fri. and most Sat.). The inn and restaurant, at the tip of Flye Point, has a knockout view of Herrick Bay (as long as there's no fog). It's been owned and operated by Flye family descendants for more than 110 years (judging from the look of the place, little has changed in that period). It also has eight rustic rooms (with private and shared but all detached baths; $115–155, including breakfast) and seven rustic cottages with kitchens and woodstoves ($1,042–1,400/week, shorter stays sometimes available). Dogs are welcome in most cottages for $40 per pet per week or $10 per day.

## INFORMATION AND SERVICES

The best source of information about the region is the Blue Hill Peninsula Chamber of Commerce (28 Water St., Box 520, Blue Hill 04614, 207/374-2281, www.bluehillpeninsula.org). Another possibility, although somewhat outdated when I checked, is the website of the East Penobscot Bay Association (www.penobscotbay.com). Request a copy of its handy flyer/map. Once you've landed on Route 172 or 175, pop into one of the small roadside convenience stores and start asking questions. The clerks—often the owners—know it all cold, and these markets always have a fair share of local color. Of course, they won't object if you also buy something while you're there.

The public libraries in this area are small and welcoming, but hours are limited. Friend Memorial Library (Rte. 175, Brooklin, 207/359-2276) has a lovely Circle of Friends Garden, with benches and a brick patio. It's dedicated to the memory of longtime Brooklin residents E. B. and Katharine White. Also check out Free Public Library (1 Town House Rd., Rte. 176, Brooksville, 207/326-4560) and Sedgwick Village Library (Main St., Sedgwick, 207/359-2177).

# Castine

Castine (pop. 1,343) is a gem—a serene New England village with a tumultuous past. It's on the tip of a cape, surrounded by water on three sides, including the entrance to the Penobscot River, which made it a strategic defense point. Once beset by geopolitical squabbles, saluting the flags of three different nations (France, Britain, and Holland), its only crises now are local political skirmishes. This is an unusual community, a National Historic Register enclave that many people never find. The town celebrated its bicentennial in 1996. Today a major presence is Maine Maritime Academy, yet Castine remains the quietest imaginable college town. Students in search of a party school won't find it here; naval engineering is serious business.

What visitors discover is a year-round community with a busy waterfront, an easy-to-conquer layout, a handful of traditional inns and boutiques, wooded trails on the outskirts of town, an astonishing collection of splendid Georgian and Federalist architecture, and water views from nearly every which way you turn. If you're staying in Blue Hill or even Bar Harbor, spend a day here. Or book a room in one of the town's lovely inns, and use Castine as a base for exploring here and beyond. Either way, you won't regret it.

## HISTORY

Originally known as Fort Pentagoet, Castine received its current name courtesy of Jean-Vincent d'Abbadie, Baron de St.-Castin. A young French nobleman manqué who married a Wabanaki princess named Pidiwamiska, d'Abbadie ran the town in the second half of the 17th century and eventually returned to France.

A century later, in 1779, occupying British troops and their reinforcements scared off potential American seaborne attackers (including Colonel Paul Revere), who turned tail up the Penobscot River and ended up scuttling their more than 40-vessel fleet—a humiliation known as the Penobscot Expedition and still regarded as one of America's worst naval defeats.

When the boundaries for Maine were finally set in 1820, with the St. Croix River marking the east rather than the Penobscot River, the last British Loyalists departed, some floating their homes north to St. Andrews, in New Brunswick, Canada, where they can still be seen today. For a while, peace and prosperity became the bywords for Castine—with lively commerce in fish and salt—but it all collapsed during the California Gold Rush and the Civil War trade embargo, leaving the town down on its luck.

Of the many historical landmarks scattered around town, one of the most intriguing must be the sign on "Wind Mill Hill," at the junction of Route 166 and State Street:

> On Hatch's Hill there stands a mill. Old Higgins he doth tend it. And every time he grinds a grist, he has to stop and mend it.

In smaller print, just below the rhyme, comes the drama:

> Here two British soldiers were shot for desertion.

Castine indeed has quite a history.

## ◖ Castine Historic Tour

To appreciate Castine fully, you need to arm yourself with the Castine Merchants Association's visitors' brochure/map (all businesses and lodgings in town have copies) and follow the numbers on bike or on foot. With no stops, walking the route takes less than an hour, but you'll want to read dozens of historical plaques, peek into public buildings, shoot some photos, and perhaps even do some shopping.

Highlights of the tour include the late-18th-century **John Perkins House,** moved to Perkins Street from Court Street in 1969 and restored with period furnishings. It's open for

# MAINE MARITIME ACADEMY

The state's only merchant-marine college (and one of only seven in the nation) occupies 35 acres in the middle of Castine. Founded in 1941, the academy awards undergraduate and graduate degrees in such areas as marine engineering, ocean studies, and marina management, preparing a student body of about 825 men and women for careers as ship captains, naval architects, and marine engineers.

The academy owns a fleet of 60 vessels, including the historic research schooner *Bowdoin*, flagship of Arctic explorer Admiral Donald MacMillan, and the 499-foot training vessel TV *State of Maine*, berthed down the hill at the waterfront. In 1996-1997, the *State of Maine*, formerly the U.S. Navy hydrographic survey ship *Tanner*, underwent a $12 million conversion for use by the academy. It is still subject to deployment, and in 2005, the school had to quickly find alternative beds for students using the ship as a dormitory when it was called into service in support of rescue and rebuilding efforts after Hurricane Katrina in New Orleans. Midshipmen conduct free 30-minute tours of the vessel on weekdays in summer (about mid-July–late Aug.). The schedule is posted at the dock, or call 207/326-4311 to check; photo ID is required.

Weekday tours of the campus can be arranged through the Admissions Office (207/326-2206 or 800/227-8465 outside Maine, www.mainemaritime.edu). Campus highlights include three-story Nutting Memorial Library, in Platz Hall (open daily during the school year, weekdays in summer and during vacations); the Henry A. Scheel Room, a cozy oasis in Leavitt Hall containing memorabilia from late naval architect Henry Scheel and his wife, Jeanne; and the well-stocked bookstore (Curtis Hall, 207/326-9333, 8 A.M.-3 P.M. Mon.-Fri.).

---

guided tours 2–5 P.M. Sunday and Wednesday July and August; admission is $5.

Next door, **The Wilson Museum** (107 Perkins St., 207/326-8545, www.wilsonmuseum.org, 2–5 P.M. Tues.–Sun. late May–late Sept., free), founded in 1921, contains an intriguingly eclectic two-story collection of prehistoric artifacts, ship models, dioramas, baskets, tools, and minerals assembled over a lifetime by John Howard Wilson, a geologist/anthropologist who first visited Castine in 1891 (and died in 1936). Among the exhibits are Balinese masks, ancient oil lamps, cuneiform tablets, Zulu artifacts, pre-Inca pottery, and assorted local findings. Don't miss this, even though it's a bit musty, although that is changing thanks to a recent multimillion dollar bequest. (The only comparable Maine institutions are the Nylander Museum, in Caribou, and the L. C. Bates Museum, in Hinckley.) Open the same days and hours as the Perkins House are the **Blacksmith Shop,** where a smith does demonstrations, and the **Hearse House,** containing Castine's 19th-century winter and summer funeral vehicles. Both are free admission. The **Castine Scientific Society** (P.O. Box 196, Castine 04421), a private foundation, operates the five-building complex (the fifth being the Doudiet House, where the administrative offices are).

At the end of Battle Avenue stands the 19th-century **Dyce's Head Lighthouse,** no longer operating; the keeper's house is owned by the town. Alongside it is a public path (signposted) leading via a wooden staircase to a tiny patch of rocky shoreline and the beacon that has replaced the lighthouse.

Highest point in town is **Fort George State Park,** site of a 1779 British fortification. Nowadays, little remains except grassy earthworks, but there are interpretive displays and picnic tables.

**Main Street,** descending toward the water, is a feast for historic-architecture fans. Artist Fitz Hugh Lane and author Mary McCarthy once lived in elegant houses along the elm-lined street (neither building is open to the public). On Court Street between Main and Green stands turn-of-the-20th-century **Emerson Hall,** site of Castine's municipal offices. Since Castine has no official information booth, you may need to duck in here (it's open weekdays) for answers to questions.

Across Court Street, **Witherle Memorial Library,** a handsome early-19th-century building on the site of the 18th-century town jail, looks out on the Town Common. Also facing the Common are the Adams and Abbott Schools, the former still an elementary school. The **Abbott School** (10 A.M.–4 P.M. Tues.–Sat. and 1–4 P.M. Sun. July–Labor Day, reduced schedule spring and fall, free but donation welcome), built in 1859, has been carefully restored for use as a museum/headquarters for the **Castine Historical Society** (P.O. Box 238, Castine 04421, 207/326-4118, www.castinehistoricalsociety.org). A big draw at the volunteer-run museum is the 24-foot-long Bicentennial Quilt, assembled for Castine's 200th anniversary in 1996. The historical society, founded in 1966, organizes lectures, exhibits, and special events (some free) in various places around town.

On the outskirts of town, across the narrow neck between Wadsworth Cove and Hatch's Cove, stretches a rather overgrown canal (signposted British Canal) scooped out by the occupying British during the War of 1812. Effectively severing land access to the town of Castine, the Brits thus raised havoc, collected local revenues for eight months, and then departed for Halifax with enough funds to establish Dalhousie College (now Dalhousie University). Wear waterproof boots to walk the canal route; the best time to go is at low tide.

If a waterfront picnic sounds appealing, buy the fixings at Bah's Bakehouse and settle in on the grassy earthworks along the harborfront at **Fort Madison,** site of an 1808 garrison (then Fort Porter) near the corner of Perkins and Madockawando Streets. The views from here are fabulous, and it's accessible all year. A set of stairs leads down to the rocky waterfront.

## PARKS, PRESERVES, AND RECREATION
### Witherle Woods
This 96-acre preserve owned by Maine Coast Heritage Trust and managed by the Conservation Trust of Brooksville, Castine, and Penobscot is a popular walking area with a maze of trails and old woods roads leading to the water. The adjacent property is privately owned, so carry a trail map and stick to it. Many Revolutionary War–era relics have been found here; if you see any, do *not* remove them. Access to the preserve is via a shaded old woods road on Battle Avenue, between the water district property (at the end of the wire fence) and The Manor's exit driveway and diagonally across from La Tour Street. Several lodgings keep a supply of maps as does the nearby Adams Gallery, or contact (by phone or mail) the **Conservation Trust of Brooksville, Castine, and Penobscot** (P.O. Box 421, Castine 04421, 207/326-9711). The Trust has been protecting the natural resources of Castine, Penobscot, and Brooksville since the early 1980s. It also offers natural-history walks, canoe trips, and boat excursions. Also ask locally about the **Henderson Natural Area** and other preserves, some accessible only by boat.

### Bicycling
Bicycling is an easy way to see Castine. The terrain is gentle and traffic in town is light. Rental bikes are available hourly, daily, and weekly from **Dennett's Wharf** (207/326-9045).

### ◖ Sea Kayaking
Also based at Dennett's Wharf is **Castine Kayak Adventures** (15 Sea St., Castine, 207/326-9045, www.castinekayak.com), spearheaded by Maine Guide Karen Francoeur. Known locally as "Kayak Karen," she's particularly adept with beginners, delivering wise advice from beginning to end. All skill levels are accommodated. Three-hour half-day trips are $55; six-hour full-day tours are around $105 including lunch. Two-hour sunset tours are $40; the sunrise tour includes a

light breakfast for $55. Friday nights, there are special two-hour phosphorescence tours, under the stars (weather permitting), for $55 pp. Longer trips are available for $110 per day. If you have your own boat, call Karen for advice; she knows these waters.

## Swimming

**Backshore Beach,** a crescent of sand and gravel on Wadsworth Cove Road (turn off Battle Ave. at the Castine Golf Club) is a favorite saltwater swimming spot, with views across the bay to Stockton Springs. Be forewarned, though, that ocean swimming in this part of Maine is not for the timid. The best time to try it is on the incoming tide, after the sun has had time to heat up the mud. At mid- to high tide, it's also the best place to put in a sea kayak. Park along the road.

If a pool sounds more attractive, you can swim in the **Cary W. Bok indoor pool** at Maine Maritime Academy for $4. Call 207/326-4311, ext. 451, for open- and lap-swim times.

## Golf

The **Castine Golf Club** (200 Battle Ave., Castine, 207/326-8844, www.castinegolfclub.com) dates to 1897, when the first tee required a drive from a 30-step-high mound. Redesigned in 1921 by Willie Park Jr., the nine-hole course is open May 15–October 15. Starting times are seldom required, and greens fees are reasonable.

## Excursion Boat

On Fridays, Captain Melissa Terry's **Belfast Bay Cruises** (207/322-5530, www.belfastbaycruises.com, $28 adult, $15 ages 5–15) reverses its usual Belfast to Castine course and offers an afternoon trip to Belfast aboard the *Good Return.* Whereas Castine is all white clapboard, Belfast is red brick. Spend a few hours shopping the intriguing Main Street shops or exploring the town's three National Historical Districts on foot—pick up a walking map at the chamber of commerce (15 Main St.) or wander along the Museum in the Streets, a series of markers highlighting historic buildings and people. Another option with Belfast Bay

Cruises is a 45-minute **Castine Harbor Tour** ($10 adult, $8 child).

## SHOPPING
### Antiques and Galleries

Tucked into the back of the 1796 Parson Mason House, one of Castine's oldest residences, **Leila Day Antiques** (53 Main St., 207/326-8786, www.leiladayantiques.com) is a must for anyone in the market for folk art, period furniture, and quilts. Access is via a lovely, flower-lined walkway.

Traditional American craftwork is sold at **Castine Historical Handworks** (9 Main St., Castine, 207/326-4460, www.castinehistoricalhandworks.com). Among the selections are pottery, textiles, and folk art.

Oil paintings by local artists Joshua and Susan Adam are on view at **Adam Gallery** (140 Battle Ave., 207/326-8272, www.adamgalleryonline.com).

### Books

Driving toward Castine on Route 166, watch on your right for a small sign for **Dolphin Books and Prints** (314 Castine Rd., Castine, 207/326-0888, www.dolphin-book.com), where Pete and Liz Ballou have set up their antiquarian business with more than 10,000 books as well as framed prints and art.

In downtown Castine, a block up from the waterfront, **The Compass Rose Bookstore and Café** (3 Main St., 207/326-9366 or 800/698-9366, www.compassrosebooks.com) carries an ever-expanding selection of new books, cards, games, and prints chosen by owner Sharon Biggie. In the back of the shop is a café serving hot and cold drinks (espresso, too), soup, sandwiches, and tasty baked goods.

### Furniture

Bench-made Windsor chairs are the specialty at **M&E Gummel Chairworks** (600 Shore Rd., P.O. Box 767, Castine 04421, 207/326-8122, www.gummelchairworks.com). The father-and-son team use 18th-century methods when handcrafting the chairs, Colonial dining

© TOM NANGLE

The yellow Victorian Pentagöet Inn stands out in a town full of white houses.

tables, and bowls, one at a time in their late-19th-century barn workshop.

## ENTERTAINMENT

Best place for live music is **Dennett's Wharf** (15 Sea St., 207/326-9045). Some performances require a ticket. Also head to **The Reef** (facing the waterfront parking lot), for pizza and entertainment, and to **Stella's Jazz Nocturnal** for jazz.

The Trinitarian Church often brings in high-caliber musical entertainment. The Castine Town Band often performs on the common. Check www.castine.org/band.htm for its schedule.

## ACCOMMODATIONS
### Inns

Castine is blessed with three fine traditional inns. This is not the place to come if you require in-room phones, air-conditioning, or fancy bathrooms. Rather, the pace is relaxed and the accommodations reflect the easy elegance of a bygone era.

The three-story, Queen Anne–style **Pentagöet Inn** (26 Main St., P.O. Box 4, Castine 04421, 207/326-8616 or 800/845-1701, www.pentagoet.com, May–late Oct., $115–245 peak) is the perfect Maine summer inn, right down to the lace curtains billowing in the breeze, the soft floral wallpapers, and the intriguing curiosities that accent, but don't clutter, the rooms. Congenial innkeepers Jack Burke, previously with the foreign service, and Julie Van de Graaf, a pastry chef, took over the century-old inn in 2000 and have given it new life, upgrading rooms and furnishing them with Victorian antiques, adding handsome gardens, and carving out a niche as a dining destination. Their enthusiasm for the area is contagious. The inn's 16 rooms are spread out between the main house (with Wi-Fi service) and the adjoining house. A hot buffet breakfast and afternoon refreshments are provided. Jack holds court in Passports Pub (chock-full of vintage photos and prints and exotic antiques) every afternoon, advising guests on activities and opportunities. Borrow one of the inn's bikes and explore around town or simply walk—the Main Street location is convenient to everything Castine offers. Better yet, just sit on the wraparound porch and take it all in.

The three-story **Castine Inn** (33 Main St., P.O. Box 41, Castine 04421, 207/326-4365, www.castineinn.com, May–late Oct., $105–300) earns a stellar rating for its stunning semi-formal gardens and extremely helpful staff. The 16 rooms and three suites, updated from their 1890s origins, vary in style, from simple Maine to simple elegance (if you're looking for bathrooms with whirlpool tubs, this is the place). Lots of interesting artwork is everywhere and there's a very simpatico and unpretentious air, encouraged by enthusiastic innkeepers Amy and Tom Gutow. In the small, English-style pub, hikers, bicyclists, kayakers, and less energetic guests mingle with a loyal local clientele. A full breakfast is included.

Once the summer "cottage" of Arthur Fuller, a South Boston Yacht Club commodore, **The Manor Inn** (Battle Ave., P.O. Box 873, Castine 04421, 207/326-4861 or 877/626-6746, www.

manor-inn.com, $115–275) overlooks town and harbor from five mostly wooded acres elevated above Battle Avenue. Though the atmosphere is informal, there are lots of elegant architectural touches. Nancy Watson and Tom Ehrman took over in 1998, upgrading beds, linens, and furniture. They've expanded the dining room and continue to improve the inn each year. The 14 second- and third-floor rooms are an eclectic mix—some with canopied beds and fireplaces, all with private baths. A separate guest building has a TV and games as well as Nancy's yoga studio; guests are welcome to join her morning Iyengear classes (Mon., Wed., Fri., $12 drop-in fee). Wi-Fi is available. The trailhead for Witherle Woods is close by. The inn is often the site of weddings and receptions; ask before you book unless you don't mind being the odd man out. It's open mid-February–late December.

## Rental Cabins and Cottages

Perched in a field along the edge of Hatch's Cove, with terrific views, are the six two-bedroom, pine-paneled log cabins of **Castine Cottages** (33 Snapp's Way, Rte. 166, P.O. Box 224, Castine 04421, 207/326-8003, www.castinecottages.com), operated by Alan and Diana Snapp. Weekly rate is $625 late June–late September, $500 off-season; when available, cabins are rented nightly for $75–150. Well-behaved pets allowed. It's open May–October. You'll need to provide your own sheets and towels or pay an additional $10 per person.

## FOOD
## Local Flavors

Since 1920, locals have been buying lunch and ice cream at **Castine Variety** (1 Main St., Castine, 207/326-8625, 5 A.M.–10 P.M. daily in summer, to 7 P.M. the rest of the year). Go for the vintage feeling and the reasonably priced menu varying from sandwiches to pizza to lobster rolls, but don't expect anything approaching friendly service unless you're a local (although that attitude may be softening thanks to new owners).

Far more friendly are the folks at **The Breeze** (town dock, Castine, 207/326-9200), a waterfront take-out stand with reliably good basics—burgers, fried clams, ice cream. You can't beat the location or the view, but the lines can be very, very long.

At **Eaton's Boatyard** (Sea St., P.O. Box 123, Castine 04421, 207/326-8579), a full-service marina renting moorings by the day or week, you can buy live lobsters May–October and have them cooked or order them shipped anywhere year-round.

## Casual Dining

Here's a doubleheader: **Bah's Bakehouse** (26 Water St., Castine, 207/326-9510, 7 A.M.–6 P.M. Mon.–Sat., opens at 8 A.M. Sun.), and sharing the same location, **Stella's Jazz Nocturnal** (207/326-9710, opens at 4 P.M. Tues.–Sat., food service 5–9 P.M.). Upstairs is Bah's, a higgledy-piggledy eatery of three rooms and a deck at the end of an alleyway tucked between Main and Water Streets. Its slogan is "creative flour arrangements," and creative it is. Stop here for morning coffee, cold juices, interesting snacks and salads, homemade soups, wine or beer, and the best sandwiches in town. Be forewarned: If it's crowded, go elsewhere—the kitchen is quickly overwhelmed and service can be slow to frustrating. Underneath the deck is Stella's, an intimate lounge where live jazz is performed Thursday–Sunday. Listen while nibbling on a blue cheese burger, grilled lamb lollipops, pan-seared halibut, or other eclectic choices ($8.50–16).

On a warm summer day, it's hard to find a better place to while away a few hours than **Dennett's Wharf** (15 Sea St., 207/326-9045, www.dennettswharf.com, 11 A.M.–9 P.M. daily May–Columbus Day). Next to the town dock, it's a colorful barn of a place with outside deck and front-row windjammer-watching seats in summer. Kids are welcomed. The crayoned kids' menu includes all the usual favorites, such as mac-'n-cheese and gummy dinosaurs for dessert. Try attaching a dollar bill to the soaring ceiling; countless others have. Service is leisurely; don't dine here if you're in a hurry.

**The Pine Cone Pub** at The Manor Inn (76 Battle Ave., Castine, 207/326-4861) serves a light menu, with such choices as Caesar salad and fish-and-chips.

## Fine Dining

Jazz music plays softly and dinner is by candlelight at the **C Pentagöet** (26 Main St., Castine, 207/326-8616 or 800/845-1701, www.pentagoet.com, opens at 6 P.M. daily July and Aug., Mon.–Sat. May, June, Sept., Oct.). In fine weather, you can dine on the porch. Choices vary from roasted *loup de mer* to slow-cooked lamb shank, or simply make a meal of small plates, such as lamb lollipops and crab cakes and a salad. Don't miss the lobster bouillabaisse or the chocolate *budino*, a scrumptious warm Italian pudding that melts in your mouth (a must for chocoholics). Can't make up your mind? Order the Taste of the Pentagöet sampling platter ($45), with tasting portions of the most popular dishes. Most entrées are in the $18–29 range.

The bilevel dining room at **The Manor Inn** (76 Battle Ave., Castine, 207/326-4861, 6–8:30 P.M. Tues.–Sat. in summer, Thurs.–Sat. off-season) overlooks the gardens and lawn. Dinner is served from an extensive menu accented with Asian flavors and Indian curries and other world flavors, accompanied by home-baked breads, and always including vegetarian choices (most entrées $16–24). Reservations are essential on weekends and for the annual Fourth of July pig roast. It's open Valentine's Day–late December.

## INFORMATION AND SERVICES
### Information

Castine has no local information office, but all businesses and lodgings in town have copies of the Castine Merchants Association's visitors' brochure/map. For additional information, go to the Castine Town Office (Emerson Hall, 67 Court St., Castine, 207/326-4502, www.castine.me.us, 8 A.M.–3:30 P.M. Mon.–Fri.).

Check out Witherle Memorial Library (41 School St., 207/326-4375, ww.witherle.lib.me.us). Also accessible to the public is the Nutting Memorial Library, in Platz Hall on the Maine Maritime Academy campus.

### Public Restrooms

Castine has public restrooms on the town dock, at the foot of Main Street.

# Deer Isle

"Deer Isle is like Avalon," wrote John Steinbeck in *Travels with Charley*—"it must disappear when you are not there." Deer Isle (the name of both the island and its midpoint town) has been romancing authors and artisans for decades, but it's unmistakably real to the quarrymen and fishermen who've been here for centuries. These long-timers are a sturdy lot, as even Steinbeck recognized: "I would hate to try to force them to do anything they didn't want to do."

Early-18th-century maps show no name for the island, but by the late 1800s, nearly 100 families lived here, supporting themselves first by farming, then by fishing. In 1789, when Deer Isle was incorporated, 80 local sailing vessels were scouring the Gulf of Maine in pursuit of mackerel and cod, and Deer Isle men were circling the globe as yachting skippers and merchant seamen. At the same time, in the once-quiet village of Green's Landing (now called Stonington), the shipbuilding and granite industries boomed, spurring development, prosperity, and the kinds of rough hijinks typical of commercial ports the world over.

Green's Landing became the "big city" for an international crowd of quarrymen carving out the terrain on Deer Isle and nearby Crotch Island, source of high-quality granite for Boston's Museum of Fine Arts, the Smithsonian Institution, a humongous fountain for John D. Rockefeller's New York estate, and less showy projects all along the Eastern Seaboard. The heyday is long past, but the industry did extend into the 20th century (including a contract for the pink granite at President John F. Kennedy's Arlington National Cemetery gravesite). Today, Crotch Island is the site of Maine's only operating island granite quarry.

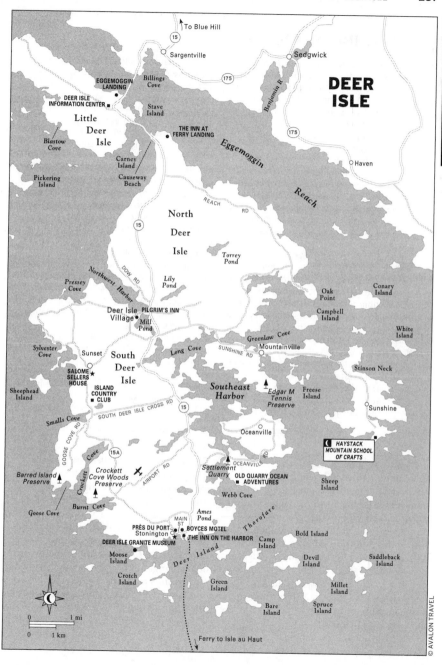

© AVALON TRAVEL

# THE MAINE ISLAND TRAIL

In the early 1980s, a "trail" of coastal Maine islands was only the germ of an idea. By the end of the millennium, the **Maine Island Trail Association (MITA)** counted about 4,000 members dedicated to conscientious (i.e., low- or no-impact) recreational use of more than 100 public and private islands along 325 miles of Maine coastline between Portland and Machias.

More than a dozen of these islands (each year, new ones are added and others are subtracted) are in the Acadia region – between Isle au Haut and Schoodic Point. In fact, one of the best island clusters along the entire trail is in the waters off Stonington on Deer Isle.

Access to the trail is only by private boat, and the best choice is a sea kayak, to navigate shallow or rock-strewn coves. Sea-kayak rentals are available in Bar Harbor, Southwest Harbor, Blue Hill, and Stonington, and several outfitters offer island tours (see specific sections for details). The best source of information is the Maine Association of Sea Kayaking Guides and Instructors (MASKGI), whose members agree to adhere to the Leave No Trace philosophy.

The trail's publicly owned islands – supervised by the state Bureau of Public Lands – are open to anyone; the private islands are restricted to MITA members, who pay $45 a year for the privilege (and, it's important to add, the responsibility). With the fee comes the **Maine Island Trail Guidebook,** providing directions and information for each of the islands. With membership comes the expectation of care and concern. "Low impact" means different things to different people, so MITA experienced acute growing pains when enthusiasm began leading to "tent sprawl."

To cope with and reverse the overuse, MITA has created an "adopt-an-island program," in which volunteers become stewards for specific islands and keep track of their use and condition. MITA members are urged to pick up trash, use tent platforms where they exist, and continue elsewhere if an island has reached its assigned capacity (stipulated on a shoreline sign and/or in the guidebook).

A superb complement to the *Maine Island Trail Guidebook* is a copy of *Hot Showers!* by Lee Bumsted, a former MITA staff member (see *Suggested Reading* in the *Resources* section). Recognizing the need for alternating island camping and warm beds (and hot showers), she has almost singlehandedly alleviated island stress and strain. Some of the B&Bs and inns listed in her guide give discounts to MITA members.

Membership information is available from Maine Island Trail Association (P.O. Box C, Rockland 04841, 207/596-6456, www.mita.org).

Measuring about nine miles north to south (plus another three miles for Little Deer Isle), the island of Deer Isle today has a handful of hamlets (including Sunshine, Sunset, Mountainville, and Oceanville) and two towns—Stonington and Deer Isle—with a population just under 3,000. Road access is via Route 15 on the Blue Hill Peninsula. A huge suspension bridge, built in 1939 over Eggemoggin Reach, links the Sargentville section of Sedgwick with Little Deer Isle; from there, a sinuous, 0.4-mile causeway connects to the northern tip of Deer Isle.

Deer Isle remains an artisans' enclave, anchored by the Haystack Mountain School of Crafts. Studios and galleries are plentiful, although many require noodling along back roads to find them. Stonington, a rough-and-tumble fishing port with an idyllic setting, is slowly being gentrified, as more and more galleries and upscale shops open for the summer each season. Locals are holding their collective breaths hoping that any improvements don't change the town too much (although most visitors could do without the car racing on Main Street at night). Already, real-estate prices and accompanying taxes have escalated way past the point where many a local fisherman can hope to buy, and in some cases, maintain a home.

# GETTING CRAFTY

Internationally famed artisans – sculptors and papermakers, weavers and jewelers, potters and printmakers – become the faculty each summer for the unique **Haystack Mountain School of Crafts.** Founded in 1950 by Mary Beasom Bishop (1885-1972) and a group of talented Maine artisans as a studio research and study program, Haystack has grown into one of the top craft schools in the country.

Under the direction of beloved former director Francis Merritt, the school opened its first campus near Haystack Mountain, in Montville, Maine, in 1951. Ten years later, when the state unveiled plans to build a new highway (Rte. 3) that would bisect that campus, the school moved to its present 40-acre oceanfront location at the end of the Sunshine Road in Deer Isle. Good move.

You would be hard-pressed to find a more artistically stimulating and architecturally stunning environment. Architect Edward Larrabee Barnes's award-winning campus perfectly complements its dramatic setting. The angular, cedar-shingled buildings are connected via walkways and teaching decks and a central staircase that cascades like a waterfall down the wooded hillside to the rocky coast below. The visual impression is one of spruce and ledge, glass and wood, islands and water.

One thing that makes Haystack work is its diverse student body. Students of all abilities, from beginners through advanced professionals, come from around the globe for the two- to three-week summer sessions, taking weekday classes and enjoying round-the-clock studio access to follow their creative muses. In a recent year, students ranged in age from 18 to 75, and in professions from a retired teacher to a physicist. What brings them all here, says current director Stuart Kestenbaum, is the "direct making experience." That experience draws not only those who make but those who collect. For a collector of fine craft, he says, taking a class is a "great way to get insight into the making process; it gives a different relationship with the craft being collected." Each session also includes a range of craft. These may include blacksmithing, drawing, metals, wood, beads, clay, fiber/design, printmaking, glass, weaving, mixed media, paper, and baskets.

## SIGHTS

Sightseeing on Deer Isle means exploring back roads, browsing the galleries, walking the trails, hanging out on the docks, and soaking in the ambience.

### ◖ Haystack Mountain School of Crafts

The renowned Haystack Mountain School of Crafts (Sunshine Rd., P.O. Box 518, Deer Isle 04627, 207/348-2306, www.haystack-mtn.org) in Sunshine (see the sidebar *Getting Crafty*) is open to the public on a limited basis, but if it fits in your schedule, go. Tours of the campus ($5) are given at 1 P.M. every Wednesday. These include a video, viewing works on display, and the opportunity to tour some studios. Free slide programs, lectures, demonstrations, and concerts, presented by faculty and visiting artists, start at 8 P.M. on varying weeknights

early June–late August. Perhaps the best opportunities are the End-of-Session auctions, held on Thursday nights every two or three weeks, when you can tour the studios free 4–6 P.M. and see the works the teachers and students have produced, then return for the auction preview at 7:30 P.M., followed by the auction at 8 P.M. It's a great opportunity to buy craftwork at often very reasonable prices.

### Historic Houses and Museums

The 1830 **Salome Sellers House** (416 Sunset Rd./Rte. 15A, Sunset Village, 207/367-2629, 1–4 P.M. Wed. and Fri. July–mid-Sept., free), a repository of local memorabilia, is the headquarters of the **Deer Isle-Stonington Historical Society.** Volunteer guides love to provide tidbits about various items; seafarers' logs and ship models are particularly intriguing. It's just north of the Island Country Club

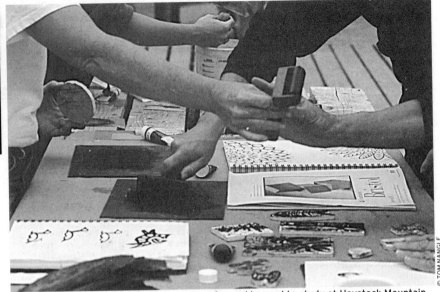

© TOM NANGLE

Students come from throughout North America and beyond to study at Haystack Mountain School of Crafts.

and across from Eaton's Plumbing. Donations are appreciated.

Close to the Stonington waterfront, the **Deer Isle Granite Museum** (51 Main St., Stonington, 207/367-6331) was established to commemorate the centennial of the quarrying business hereabouts. Best feature of the small museum is a 15-foot-long working model of Crotch Island, center of the industry, as it appeared at the turn of the 20th century. Flatcars roll, boats glide, and derricks move—it all looks very real. The museum is open late May–early September, but it's best to call for current days and hours of operation. Recommended donation is $5 per family.

Another downtown Stonington attraction is a Lilliputian complex known hereabouts as the **"Miniature Village."** Some years ago, the late Everett Knowlton created a dozen and a half replicas of local buildings and displayed them on granite blocks in his yard. Since his death, they've been restored and put on display each summer in town—along with a donation box to

support the upkeep. The village is set up on East Main Street (Rte. 15), below Hoy Gallery.

## Pumpkin Island Light

A fine view of Pumpkin Island Light can be had from the cul-de-sac at the end of the Eggemoggin Road on Little Deer Isle. If heading south on Route 15, bear right at the information booth after crossing the bridge and continue to the end.

## Penobscot East Resource Center

The purpose of the Penobscot East Resource Center, on the waterfront in Stonington (207/367-2708, www.penobscoteast.org), is "to energize and facilitate responsible community-based fishery management, collaborative marine science, and sustainable economic development to benefit the fishermen and the communities of Penobscot Bay and the Eastern Gulf of Maine." Bravo to that! It operates a **Lobster Hatchery** (Stonington Lobster Coop No. 1, 52 Indian Point Rd.), which was

# TED AMES, GENIUS

Ted Ames, the man behind the Penobscot East Resource Center and the Lobster Hatchery, in Stonington, was in 2005 awarded a $500,000 MacArthur Fellowship. These prestigious "genius grants" are awarded to "talented individuals who have shown extraordinary originality and dedication in their creative pursuits and a marked capacity for self-direction." The foundation credited Ames with fusing "the roles of fisherman and applied scientist in response to increasing threats to the fishery ecosystem resulting from decades of over-harvesting." Criteria for selection are: exceptional creativity, promise for important future advances based on a track record of significant accomplishment, and potential for the fellowship to facilitate subsequent creative work. No question, they found the right guy in Ted Ames.

A humble, soft-spoken man with dogged determination, Ames found little time to bask in the limelight from the award. While he certainly appreciated the money and the attention paid to his causes, the numerous interviews with TV, radio, and newspaper reporters took up valuable time, time he would rather use researching fisheries, collecting data, and devising ways to develop community-based fisheries management.

Ames is a fascinating guy, a combination of fisherman, lobsterman, and research scientist with deep Maine roots. "My family were some of the original settlers of Vinalhaven," he said. His ancestors on his father's side arrived in 1757, on the island off Rockland in Maine's Mid-Coast Region. "My mother's side came from Mount Desert." They were the original settlers on Bartlett's Island. When King George told the family to leave, they refused and stayed put, he recalled. Ames grew up in a fishing family on Vinalhaven and went on to gain a master's degree in biochemistry from the University of Maine. But fishing was in his blood, and he eventually returned to the sea as a lobsterman and ground fisherman.

His years on the water gave him first-hand experience watching the changes in Maine's fisheries. He watched Maine's coastal economy change as fishing ports became more gentrified, commercial piers gave way to oceanfront homes, and marine-related businesses gave way to fancy boutiques. His education combined with his experiences gave him tools and the insight needed to work toward developing new fisheries management practices and supporting fishing communities. He studied fishing patterns in the Gulf of Maine, noting spawning and habitat, and he complemented his research with listening to the stories and experiences of aging fishermen. By doing so, he was able to establish a fishing timeline beginning with historical patterns and following their evolution to current ones.

The Penobscot East Resource Center, which he founded with his wife, Robin, a former marine resources commissioner, and the Lobster Hatchery both are designed as research facilities as well as places for community members and others to learn more about fishing, to meet commercial fishermen and women, and to learn about their lifestyles in order to help support them and preserve the tradition and the economy. Ames, a master at gaining community support (due perhaps to his impeccable Maine credentials), managed to raise $25,000 from local fishing families and local businesses and individuals in an area not known for wealth.

Ames plans to use the unrestricted MacArthur Fellows Program money to continue his fisheries research and to develop ways for "community-based groundfishing management to make it sustainable, so coastal fishing communities can survive into the next century. That's a challenge, but we're in the midst of it." There's no better person to be on the forefront than Ted Ames.

constructed by volunteers from the lobster industry in donated space with $25,000 raised locally and a matching grant. Lobster production began in 2006. Guided tours are offered ($10 adults, $5 children); call 207/367-2708 for the schedule.

The man behind both ventures is Ted Ames, who won a $500,000 MacArthur Fellowship "Genius Grant" in 2005 (see sidebar *Ted Ames, Genius*).

## PARKS AND PRESERVES

Foresighted benefactors have managed to set aside precious acreage for respectful public use on Deer Isle. The Nature Conservancy owns two properties, **Crockett Cove Woods Preserve** and **Barred Island Preserve**. For information, contact The Conservancy (14 Maine St., Fort Andross, Brunswick 04011, 207/729-5181). The conscientious steward of other local properties is the **Island Heritage Trust** (3 Main St., at Rte. 15, P.O. Box 42, Deer Isle 04627, 207/348-2455, www.islandheritagetrust.org). When the office is open (usually 10:30 A.M.–3 P.M. weekdays July and Aug., 10 A.M.–2 P.M. Tues. and Thurs. off-season), you can pick up notecards, photos, T-shirts, and helpful maps and information on hiking trails and nature preserves. Proceeds benefit the IHT's efforts; donations are much appreciated.

### Settlement Quarry

Here's one of the easiest, shortest walks in the area, leading to an impressive vista. From the parking lot on Oceanville Road (just under a mile off Rte. 15), marked by a carved granite sign, it's about five minutes to the top of the old quarry, where the viewing platform (a.k.a. the "throne room") takes in the panorama—all the way to the Camden Hills on a good day. In early August, wild raspberries are an additional enticement. Three short loop trails lead into the surrounding woods from here. A map is available in the trailhead box.

### Edgar Tennis Preserve

The 145-acre Tennis Preserve, in particular, off the Sunshine Road, has very limited parking,

so don't try to squeeze in if there isn't room; schedule your visit for another hour or day. But do go, and bring at least a snack if not a full picnic to enjoy on one of the convenient rocky outcroppings (carry in, carry out, though). Allow at least 90 minutes to enjoy the walking trails, one of which skirts Pickering Cove, providing sigh-producing views. Another trail leads to an old cemetery. Parts of the trails can be wet, so wear appropriate footwear. And do bring binoculars for bird-watching. The preserve is open sunrise–sunset. To find it, take the Sunshine Road 2.5 miles to the Tennis Road, and follow it to the preserve.

### Shore Acres Preserve

The 38-acre preserve, a gift in 2000 from Judy Hill to the Island Heritage Trust, comprises old farmland, woodlands, clam flats, a salt marsh, and granite shorefront. Three walking trails connect in a 1.5-mile loop, with the Shore Trail section edging Greenlaw Cove. As you walk along the waterfront, look for the islands of Mount Desert rising in the distance and seals basking on offshore ledges. Do not walk across the salt marsh and try to avoid stepping on beach plants. To find the preserve, take the Sunshine Road 1.2 miles and then bear left at the fork onto the Greenlaw District Road. The preserve's parking area is just shy of one mile down the road. Park only in the parking area, not on paved road.

### Crockett Cove Woods Preserve

Donated to The Nature Conservancy by benevolent, eco-conscious local artist Emily Muir, 98-acre Crockett Cove Woods Preserve is Deer Isle's natural gem—a coastal fog forest laden with lichens and mosses. Four interlinked walking trails cover the whole preserve, starting with a short nature trail. Pick up the helpful map/brochure at the registration box. Wear rubberized shoes or boots and respect adjacent private property. The preserve is open sunrise–sunset daily all year. From Deer Isle Village, take Route 15A to Sunset Village. Go 2.5 miles to Whitman Road and then to Fire Lane 88. The local contact phone number is 207/367-2674.

## Barred Island Preserve

Owned by The Nature Conservancy, but managed by the Island Heritage Trust, Barred Island Preserve was donated by Carolyn Olmsted, grandniece of noted landscape architect Frederick Law Olmsted, who summered nearby. A former owner of Goose Cove Lodge donated an additional 48 acres of maritime boreal fog forest. A single walking trail, one mile long, leads from the parking lot to the point. At low tide, and when eagles aren't nesting, you can continue out to Barred Island. Another trail skirts the shoreline of Goose Cove, before retreating inland and rejoining with the main trail. From a high point on the main trail, you can see more than a dozen islands, many of which are protected from development, as well as Saddleback Ledge Light, 14 miles distant. To get to the preserve, follow Route 15A to Goose Cove Road and then continue to the parking area on the right. If it's full, return another day.

## Holt Mill Pond Preserve

The Stonington Conservation Commission administers this town-owned preserve, where more than 47 bird species have been identified (bring binoculars). It comprises four habitats: upland spruce forest, lowland spruce/mixed forest, freshwater marsh, and saltwater marsh. A self-guiding nature trail is accessible off the Airport Road (off Rte. 15 at the intersection with Lily's Café). Look for the Nature Trail sign just beyond the medical center. The detailed, self-guiding trail brochure, available at the trailhead registration kiosk, is accented with drawings by noted artist Siri Beckman.

## Ames Pond

Ames Pond is neither park nor preserve, but it might as well be. On a back road close to Stonington, it's a mandatory stop in July and August, when the pond wears a blanket of pink and white water lilies. From downtown Stonington, take Indian Point Road east, just under a mile, to the pond. There's no official parking, so if you're shooting photos, pull off the road as far as possible, respecting private property.

## Causeway Beach and Scott's Landing

If you're itching to dip your toes in the water, stop by Causeway Beach along the causeway linking Little Deer Isle to Deer Isle. It's popular for swimming and is also a significant habitat for birds and other wildlife. On the other side of Route 15 is Scott's Landing, with more than 20 acres of fields, trails, and shorefront.

# RECREATION
## Guided Walks

The Island Heritage Trust, along with the Stonington and Deer Isle Conservation Commissions, sponsors a Walks and Talks series. Guided walks cover topics such as Bird and Bird Calls for Beginners, Common Trees of Deer Isle, and Care and Culture of Your Small Woodlot. For information and reservations, call 207/348-2455.

## Sea Kayaking

With lots of islets and protected coves, sea kayaking in the waters around Deer Isle, especially off Stonington, is extremely popular.

If you sign up with the **Maine Island Trail Association** (Box C, Rockland, www.mita.org, $45 a year), you'll receive a handy manual that steers you to more than a dozen islands in the Deer Isle archipelago where you can camp, hike, and picnic—eco-sensitively, please. Boat traffic can be a bit heavy at the height of summer, so to best appreciate the tranquility of this area, try this in September, after the Labor Day holiday. Nights can be cool, but days are likely to be brilliant. Do remember this is a working harbor.

The six-mile paddle from Stonington to Isle au Haut is best left to experienced paddlers, especially since fishing folks refer to kayakers as "speed bumps."

For equipment rentals or guided trips, see *Sporting Outfitters and Guided Trips.* Old Quarry Ocean Adventures is especially helpful and provides many services for kayakers.

## Swimming

The island's only major freshwater swimming hole is the **Lily Pond,** northeast of Deer Isle

Village. Just north of the Shakespeare School, turn into the Deer Run Apartments complex. Park and take the path to the pond, which has a shallow area for small children.

## Golf

About two miles south of Deer Isle Village, watch for the large sign (on the left) for the **Island Country Club** (Rte. 15A, Sunset, 207/348-2379), a nine-hole public course that's been here since 1928. Starting times are first-come, first-served, and greens fees are low; no credit cards. It's open early June–late September. Also at the club are three beautifully maintained tennis courts. Or just commandeer a rocking chair and watch the action from one of the porches. The club's cheeseburgers and salads are among the island's best bargain lunches.

### Sporting Outfitters and Guided Trips

The biggest operation is **Old Quarry Ocean Adventures** (130 Settlement Rd., Stonington, 207/367-8977 or 877/479-8977, mobile 207/266-7778, www.oldquarry.com), with a broad range of outdoor-adventure choices. Bill Baker's ever-expanding enterprise rents canoes, kayaks, sailboats, bikes, moorings, platform tent sites, and cabins. Bicycle rentals are $20 a day or $100 a week. Canoes or rowboats are $42 half day, $52 full day, or $250 per week; sailboats are $80 or $100 half day, $100 or $150 full day. For all boat rentals, you must demonstrate competency in the vessel.

All-day guided tours in single kayaks are $105; tandems are $175. Half-day tours are $55 and $110, respectively. Plenty of other options are available, including sunset tours, family trips, and gourmet picnic paddles.

Sea-kayak rental rates are $57 per day for a single, $67 for a tandem. Half-day rates (based on a four-hour rental) are $42 and $52, respectively. Overnight rates (24-hour rental) are subject to a 10 percent surcharge. Weekly rentals are $300 single, $380 tandem.

A Registered Maine Guide leads overnight kayak-camping trips on nearby islands.

Rates, including meals, begin at $285 adult for one night.

If you're bringing your own kayak, you can park your car ($6 per night for up to two nights, $5 per night for three or more nights) and launch from here ($5 per boat for launching), and Old Quarry will take your trash and any trash you find. Old Quarry is off the Oceanville Road, less than a mile from Route 15, just before you reach the Settlement Quarry preserve. It's well signposted.

Next to the restaurant of the same name and owned by the same family is **Finest Kind** (Center District Crossroad, about halfway between Rtes. 15 and 15A, 207/348-7714). Bicycle rentals are $15 per day or $75 per week. Kayak or canoe rentals are $35 per day solo, $45 per day tandem, including paddles, life jackets, spray skirts, delivery, and pickup.

## EXCURSION BOATS
### Isle au Haut Boat Company

If you're not up for self-propulsion, the *Miss Lizzie* or the *Mink* departs twice daily, morning and afternoon mid-June–early September, from the Isle au Haut Boat Company dock in Stonington for a narrated 75-minute trip among the islands before landing at Duck Harbor; on morning tours, the crew hauls a string of lobster traps. Cost is $32 adults, $16 kids, $8 bike. A 45-minute trip to the Isle au Haut town dock operates five times daily ($32 adult, $16 kids under 12, family fare available); you can rent a bike on Isle au Haut for $20. Reservations are advisable, especially in July and August. Parking is available at the pier for $9. The *Miss Lizzie* and the *Mink* are owned by the Isle au Haut Boat Company (Seabreeze Ave., Stonington, 207/367-5193 or 207/367-6516, www.isleauhaut.com), the same company that operates the regular mail boat/passenger-ferry service to offshore Isle au Haut.

### Guided Island Tours

Captain Walter Reed's Guided Island Tours (207/348-6789, www.guidedislandtours.com) aboard the *Gael* are custom designed for a maximum of four passengers. Walt is a Registered Maine Guide and professional biologist who also is steward for Mark Island Lighthouse and several uninhabited islands in the area. He provides in-depth perspective and the local scoop. The cost is $37.50 pp for the first hour plus $15 pp for each additional hour. Reservations are required; box lunches are available for an additional fee.

## Old Quarry Ocean Adventures

Yet another aspect of the Old Quarry Ocean Adventures (Stonington, 207/367-8977 or 877/479-8977, mobile 207/266-7778, www. oldquarry.com) empire are sightseeing tours on the *Nigh Duck*. The three-hour trips, one in the morning (9 A.M.–noon) and one in the afternoon (1–4 P.M.) are $38 for adults and $22 for children under 12. Both highlight the natural history of the area, as Captain Bill navigates the boat through the archipelago. Lobster traps are hauled on both trips. The afternoon one features an island swimming break in a freshwater quarry. Also available is a 1.5-hour sunset cruise, departing one-half hour before sunset, for $30 adults and $20 kids under 12. And if that's not enough, Old Quarry also offers puffin, lighthouse, whale-watch, and island cruises, with rates beginning at $45 per adult, $305 for kids. Of course, if none of this floats your boat, you can also arrange for a custom charter for $175 per hour.

## ◖ ART AND CRAFT GALLERIES

Thanks to the presence and influence of Haystack Mountain School of Crafts, supertalented artists and artisans lurk in every corner of the island. Most are tucked away on back roads, so watch for roadside signs. Many have studios open to the public where you can watch the artists at work. First Friday open gallery nights are scheduled July–October (www.stoningtongalleries.com).

### Little Deer Isle

On Little Deer Isle, don't miss **Morrow Wilson**

**Studios** (455 Eggemoggin Rd., 207/348-6871, www.morrowwilsonstudios.com), Doug and Jennifer Morrow-Wilson's gallery. Doug has turned blacksmithing into an art form, while Jennifer makes paper by hand and then uses it in three-dimensional collages that often include internal lighting. Their collaborations are especially nice. Both often open their studios to visitors.

### North End of Deer Isle

Although the artist has died, his innovative and beautiful jewelry lives on in his eponymous **Ronald Hayes Pearson studio and gallery** (29 Old Ferry Rd., 207/348-2535), where artisans continue to create his designs under the watchful eye of his wife.

The nearby **Greene Ziner Gallery** (73 Reach Rd., 207/348-2601, www.melissagreene.com) is a double treat. Melissa Greene turns out incredible painted and incised pottery (she's represented in the Renwick) and Eric Ziner works magic in metal sculpture and furnishings. Your budget may not allow for one of Melissa's pots (in the four-digit range), but I guarantee you'll covet them. The gallery also displays the work of several other local artists.

### Deer Isle Village Area

One of the island's premier galleries is Elena Kubler's **The Turtle Gallery** (61 N. Deer Isle Rd., Rte. 15, 207/348-9977, www.turtlegallery. com), in a handsome space formerly known as the Old Centennial House Barn (owned by the late Haystack director Francis Merritt) and the adjacent farmhouse. Group and solo shows of contemporary paintings, prints, and crafts are hung upstairs and down in the barn; works by gallery artists are in the farmhouse; and there's usually sculpture in the gardens both in front and in back. It's just north of Deer Isle Village—across from the Shakespeare School, oldest on the island.

Although it's in a new location and craft queen Mary Nyburg is no longer at the helm, her **Blue Heron Gallery and Studio** (Main St., Deer Isle, www.blueherondeerisle.com) survives and continues to show the work of

© TOM NANGLE

A handful of shops can be found in Deer Isle Village.

Haystack's internationally renowned faculty—printmakers, blacksmiths, potters, weavers, papermakers, glassworkers, and more.

Just a bit south is **Dockside Quilt Gallery** (33 Church St., 207/348-2531), where Nancy Knowlton, her daughter Kelly Pratt, and daughter-in-law Rebekah Knowlton stitch heirloom-quality quilts. Also here are Re-Bears, one-of-a-kind teddy bears handcrafted from vintage furs and fabrics by ninth-generation islander Heather Cormier. Custom quilts and bears are available.

The **Deer Isle Artists Association** (13 Dow Rd., 207/348-2330) is headquartered less than a mile northwest of the village. The co-op gallery features two-week exhibits of paintings, prints, drawings, and photos by local pros. Horse fans won't want to miss Penelope Plumb's upstairs gallery **Equine Art** (207/348-6892, www.penelopeplumb.com). The entrance is in the back of the building.

Just down the street, the **dowstudio** (Dow Rd., 207/348-6498, www.dowstudiodeerisle.com) shows pottery, metalwork, jewelry, prints, and drawings by Ellen Wieske, Carole Ann Fer, and Susan Webster.

Carol Scott Wainright's hand-woven **River Horse Rugs** (Deer Isle Village, 207/348-2589, www.riverhorserugs.net) are unmistakable. Her tapestry-like designs feature organic or geometric shapes on linen warp and hand-dyed wool in deep, vivid colors. Call for an appointment.

## Sunshine Road

Now for a bit of whimsy. From Route 15 in Deer Isle Village, take the Sunshine Road east 2.9 miles to **Peter Beerits Sculpture** (600 Sunshine Rd., 800/777-6845, www.nervousnellies.com). The meadows and woods surrounding the studio teem with whimsical wood and metal sculptures, including dragons, Huns on horseback, moose, and more (all for sale). The property is also home to Beerits's other enterprise, **Nervous Nellie's Jams and Jellies,** known for outstandingly creative condiments; sample the hot pepper jelly or blackberry peach conserve or ginger syrup. The promotional brochures are hilarious. Best time to come is 9 A.M.–5 P.M. May–early October, when the shop operates the ultracasual **Mountainville Café,** serving tea, coffee, and delicious scones—with, of course, Nervous Nellie's products. They're delicious; stock up, because they're sold in only a few shops.

Nearby is the **Pitcher Masters Studio Gallery** (Good Dog Run, 45 French Camp Rd., off Sunshine Rd., 207/348-2322, www.pitchermasters.com). Buzz Masters and Frank Pitcher show their paintings and pottery along with selected works by other megatalented artists.

## Stonington

Cabinetmaker **Geoffrey Warner's Studio** (431 N. Main St., 207/367-6555, www.geoffwarnerstudio.com) features his work as well as that of other local woodworkers in rotating shows. Warner mixes classic techniques with contemporary styles accented by Eastern, nature-based, and arts-and-crafts accents to create some unusual and rather striking pieces.

Bright and airy **Isalos Fine Art** (Main St.,

The fishing village of Stonington, with its boat-filled harbor, tips Deer Isle.

Stonington, 207/367-2700, www.isalosart.com) shows the work of local artists in rotating shows.

Jack and Harriet Rawle Hemenway's **Green Head Forge** (Old Quarry Rd., 207/367-2632) is a delight. Downstairs is Jack's forge and a gallery filled with his sculpted and forged metalwork; upstairs, you can watch Harriet create fabulous jewelry and small objects in gold and silver.

Debi Mortenson shows her paintings, photography, and sculptures at **D Mortenson Galley** (10 W. Main St., 207/367-5875, www.debimortenson.com) year-round.

The **d.Watson Gallery** (68 Main St., 207/367-2900) is a fine art gallery representing a number of artists working in varied media.

More paintings, many in bold, bright colors, can be found at Jill Hoy's **Hoy Gallery** (E. Main St., 207/367-2368).

## OTHER SHOPPING
### Food
In the May 2005 issue of the *Rosengarten Report*, **Stonington Sea Products** (100 N. Main St., Stonington, 207/367-2400 or 888/402-2729, www.stoningtonseafood.com) had its hickory-smoked salmon, unsliced, named as one of the "25 Best Products" the noted food critic has ever recommended, describing it in terms including "Wow!" and "Bravo!" See for yourself, or try any of the company's other smoked products. If you don't visit in person, shop online.

### Antiques, Books, and Gifts
Three shops are in Deer Isle Village. **Old Fire House** (12 N. Deer Isle Rd./Rte. 15, Deer Isle, 207/348-9978), just north of Main Street, is chock-full of old furniture and collectibles. Don't miss the downstairs. In "downtown" Deer Isle Village, you'll find **The Periwinkle** (8 Main St., Deer Isle, 207/348-2256), where Neva Beck carries a fine inventory of Maine books, as well as crafts, notecards, and gifts. Look for Neva's hand-braided rugs and chair pads and baby quilts. Just south off Main Street you'll come to Janice Glenn's **Old Deer Isle Parish House Antiques** (7 Church St., Rte.

15, Deer Isle, 207/348-9964), a funky shop heavy into vintage textiles, kitchenware, and other collectibles, with an especially nice collection of quilts, rugs, and samplers. For browsers, this place is heaven. No credit cards.

At the bottom of the island, **The Clown** (6 Thurlow's Hill Rd., Stonington, 207/367-6348) awaits. The imaginative owners came up with this combination of art, antiques, and… food and wine. Look, it works. Part of the key is the owners' farm in Tuscany, source of extra-virgin olive oil, wines, Deruta pottery, unusual furnishings, and other "necessities." Art openings are also wine tastings—a fine idea.

In downtown Stonington, below the Opera House, **Dockside Books and Gifts** (W. Main St., P.O. Box 171, Stonington 04681, 207/367-2652) carries just what its name promises, with a specialty in marine and Maine books. The rustic two-room shop is open May–November. Don't miss the view from outside the shop.

## Eclectic Shops

If you're looking for Maine pottery, weaving, metalwork, pewterware, imported tiles, or walking sticks, go directly to the **Harbor Farm Store** (Rte. 15, P.O. Box 64, Little Deer Isle 04650, 207/348-7755 or 800/342-8003, www.harborfarm.com), one of the state's best gift shops. Based in a mid-19th-century schoolhouse a mile south of the Deer Isle suspension bridge, the shop carries thousands of very unusual, high-quality items, and it's also all available by mail. The selection of tile—from around the world—is beyond amazing.

After all this browsing, you just might need a double-dip cone from **Harbor Ice Cream,** across the street from The Periwinkle, or **Island Cow Ice Cream,** on the main drag in Stonington.

## Clothing

Women need to be cautious going into **The Dry Dock** (24 Main St., Stonington, 207/367-5528)—the merchandise instantly sells itself. Imported women's clothing from Nigerian, Tibetan, and Indian cottage industries, unique jewelry, and unusual notecards are just some of the options in one large room and a smaller back room.

# ENTERTAINMENT AND EVENTS

Stonington's National Historic Landmark, the 1912 **Opera House** (207/367-2788, www.operahousearts.org), is home to Opera House Arts, which hosts films, plays, lectures, concerts, family programs, and workshops year-round. A café operates during programs.

In mid-June, when lupine in various shades of pink and purple seems to be blooming everywhere, is the **Lupine Festival** (207/342676 or 207/367-2420). The weekend festival includes arts openings and shows, boat rides, a private-gardens tour, and entertainment, varying from a contra dance to movies.

**Seamark Community Arts** (207/348-2333, www.seamarkcommunityarts.com) hosts arts workshops for children and adults in areas such as book arts, nature crafts, pottery, drawing and painting, film and video, printmaking, basketry, textile arts, and more. The summer highlight is the themed annual auction, in which dozens of artists contribute their interpretations. For example, in 2007, it was "Time."

Mid-July brings the **Stonington Lobsterboat Races** (207/348-2804), very popular competitions held in the harbor, with lots of possible vantage points. Stonington is one of the major locales in the lobster-boat race circuit.

In early October is **Peninsula Potters Open Studios** (207/348-5681), during which more than two dozen potters welcome visitors.

Want to meet locals and learn more about the area? **Island Heritage Trust** (207/348-2455) sponsors a series of walks, talks, and tours mid-June–mid-September. Call for information and reservations.

# ACCOMMODATIONS
## Inns and Bed-and-Breakfasts

**Pilgrim's Inn** (20 Main St., P.O. Box 69, Deer Isle 04627, 207/348-6615, www.pilgrimsinn.com, $109–249 d) is a beautifully restored Colonial building and newer cottages overlooking the peaceful Mill Pond. The National Historic Register inn began life in 1793 as a boardinghouse named The Ark; be sure to check out the fascinating guestbook, with names dating to 1901. A bit of a disconnect from the peacefulness is the recently added TV room (request a room far away from it, as the noise carries) and the downstairs tavern (formerly a fine-dining restaurant). It's open early May–mid-October.

**C The Inn on the Harbor** (Main St., P.O. Box 69, Stonington 04681, 207/367-2420 or 800/942-2420, www.innontheharbor.com, $130–215 peak) is exactly as its name proclaims. Its expansive deck hangs right over the harbor. Although recently updated, the 1880s complex still has an air of unpretentiousness. Most of the 14 rooms and suites, each named after windjammers, have fantastic harbor views and private or shared decks where you can keep an eye on lobster boats, small ferries, windjammers, and pleasure craft. (Binoculars are provided.) Rooms on the street can be noisy at night. Rates include a continental buffet breakfast. An espresso bar is open 11 A.M.–4:30 P.M. Nearby are antique, gift, and craft shops; guest moorings are available. It's open all year, but call ahead off-season, when rates are lower.

In downtown Stonington, just up the hill from the Inn on the Harbor and convenient for walking to everything (even a small sandy beach a mile away) is **Près du Port** (W. Main St. and Highland Ave., P.O. Box 319, Stonington 04681, 207/367-5007, www.presduport.com, $125–150), a bright B&B run by amiable innkeeper Charlotte Casgrain. After many summers at a Deer Isle French summer camp, and a career as a Connecticut French teacher, she's settled here. Three rooms have detached baths, one has a private bath; there are vanity sinks in the rooms. Children are welcome; there's even a toy cupboard to entertain them. Adults can arrange for a Tuesday afternoon massage. No credit cards. It's open mid-June–mid-October. When Deer Isle beds are scarce at the height of summer, Charlotte is the best resource for dozens of last-minute overnight rooms in local homes. This location is ideal if you're en route to or returning from Isle au Haut.

Eggemoggin Reach is almost on the doorstep at **The Inn at Ferry Landing** (77 Old Ferry Rd., Deer Isle, 207/348-7760, www.ferrylanding.com, $120–175), overlooking the abandoned Sargentville–Deer Isle ferry wharf. The view is wide open from the inn's "great room," where guests gather to read, play games, talk, and watch passing windjammers. Professional musician Gerald Wheeler has installed two grand pianos in the room; it's a treat when he plays. His wife, Jean, is the hospitable innkeeper, managing three water-view guest rooms and a suite. A harpsichord and a great view are big pluses in the suite. The Mooring, an annex that sleeps five, is rented by the week ($1,500, without breakfast). The inn is open all year except Thanksgiving and Christmas; Wi-Fi throughout.

## Motels

Right in downtown Stonington, just across the street from the harbor, is **Boyces Motel** (44 Main St., P.O. Box 94, Stonington 04681, 207/367-2421 or 800/224-2421, www.boycesmotel.com, $65–125). Eleven units all have TV, phones, and refrigerators; some have kitchens and living rooms, and one has two bedrooms. Across the street, Boyce's has a private harborfront deck for its guests. Ask for rooms well back from Main Street to lessen the noise of locals cruising the street at night. It's open year-round.

## Seasonal Rentals

For house and cottage rentals by the week, month, or season, contact **Sargent's Rentals** (P.O. Box 115, Stonington 04681, 207/367-5156, www.sargentsrentalsinc.com). Plan well ahead, as the best properties get snapped up as much as a year in advance.

## Campgrounds

Plan well ahead if you want to camp at **Old Quarry Ocean Adventures Campground** (130 Settlement Rd., Stonington, 207/367-8977, www.oldquarry.com). It has both oceanfront and secluded sites for tents and just three

RV sites. Each site has a 12-by-12 platform, picnic table, deck chairs, and fire grill. Sites are $32–40 for two, plus $15–18 for each additional person. An overflow site, without platform, table, or fire ring, is $16 per night for two, plus $12 for each additional camper. Campground facilities include swimming pond, hiking trails, laundry, camp store (lobsters available), and kayak launch. Parking is designed so that vehicles are kept away from most campsites, but you can use a garden cart to transport your equipment between your car and your site. The campground is adjacent to Settlement Quarry Park.

# FOOD
## Local Flavors
Craving sweets? Head to **Susie Qu's Sweets and Curiosities** (40 School St., Stonington, 207/367-2415, 8 A.M.–4 P.M. Thurs.–Mon.). Susan Scott bakes a fine selection of cookies and pies, offers a limited selection of breakfast and lunch choices, and also carries gifty items. It's a Wi-Fi hotspot.

Best pizza on the island? Head for **Burnt Cove Market** (Rte. 15, Stonington, 207/367-2681, 6 A.M.–9 P.M., opens at 9 A.M. Sun.). Besides pizza, you can get fried chicken and sandwiches, plus beer and wine.

Creativity defines the menu at ◖ **Lily's Café** (450 Airport Rd. at Rte. 15, Stonington, 207/367-5936, 7 A.M.–5 P.M. Mon.–Fri.) in a cute house at the corner of the Airport Road just over two miles from downtown. It's all very casual; order at the counter and find a table. (Some of the tables have fun windowpane shadowboxes.) Eat here or assemble a *haut gourmet* picnic: veggie and meat sandwiches, Mediterranean salads, cheeses, and homemade soups and breads. Upstairs is the Chef's Attic, with a smattering of antiques as well as works by local artists. Out back is an organic produce stand. Alas, it's open only for lunch (although you can pick up the fixings for a fine takeout-and-eat-later dinner) and closed on weekends. Occasionally it hosts wine-tasting dinners.

The Island Community Center (School St., Stonington) is the locale for the lively **Island Farmers Market,** selling smoked and organic meats, fresh herbs and flowers, produce, Asian foods, maple syrup, jams and jellies, crafts, and more 10 A.M.–noon every Friday May–October.

## Family-Friendly Home Cooking
In July or August, don't show up at **Finest Kind Dining** (70 Center District Crossroad, Deer Isle, 207/348-7714, www.finestkinden-terprises.com, 5–8:30 P.M. Mon.–Sat. mid-May–mid-Oct.) without a dinner reservation. This log-cabin family restaurant is no longer a secret. Expect home-style all-American food served conscientiously in a come-as-you-are setting. Pizza, pasta, prime rib, and seafood are all available, and there's a salad bar, too ($8–20). And save room for dessert. Wheelchair access; liquor license. The restaurant, owned by the Perez family, is halfway between Route 15 and Sunset Road (Rte. 15A). The enterprising Perezes also own the adjacent **Round the Island Mini Golf** (same phone, open the same months) and rent canoes, kayaks, and bicycles.

**Harbor Café** (Main St., Stonington, 207/367-5099, 6 A.M.–8 P.M. Mon.–Sat., often later Fri.–Sat., and to 2 P.M. Sun.) is *the* place to go for breakfast (you can eavesdrop on the local fisherfolk if you're early enough), but it's also reliable for lunch and dinner (especially on Friday nights for the seafood fry, with free seconds). Try to snag the front window table.

The views are top-notch from **Fisherman's Friend Restaurant** (5 Atlantic Ave., Stonington, 207/367-2442, 11 A.M.–9 P.M. Sun.–Thurs., to 10 P.M. Fri.–Sat.), which moved in 2005 from its longtime uptown digs to a harborfront location, complete with outdoor deck seating. The restaurant gets high marks for respectable food, generous portions, fresh seafood, and outstanding desserts, but it seems to have lost its soul in the move. Still, where else can you get lobster prepared 30 different ways? Prices are reasonable—the Friday night fish fry, with free seconds, is $7.99. It's open mid-May–October.

## Casual Dining

Families are welcome at the **Whale's Rib Tavern** (20 Main St./Sunset Rd., Deer Isle Village, 207/348-5222, 5–9 P.M. daily), a comfy white-tablecloth tavern in the lower-level of the Pilgrim's Inn. Everyone can find something that appeals and is within budget on the menu, which varies from burgers to beef tenderloin, fish-and-chips to scampi.

You have a front seat—and a comfortable one at that—on all the harbor action at **Maritime Café** (27 Main St., Stonington, 207/367-2600, www.maritimecafe.com, 11:30 A.M.–3 P.M. and 5–8 P.M. daily). Big windows frame the harbor from the dining room, and there's also lunch seating on the harborside deck. The menu emphasizes seafood (no surprise), but there are other choices and always a vegetarian selection. Entrées run $16–28.

## Seafood in the Rough, or Not

When the weather's perfect, and you want seafood that's a bit different, in a fabulous setting, **Cockatu** (Carter's Seafood, 24 Carter La., off Oceanville Rd., Stonington, 207/367-0900, noon–8 P.M. daily late May–early Sept.) delivers. Fresh, fresh, fresh seafood, right out of the fish store, is cooked to order with some interesting, Portuguese-inspired preparations complementing the usual fried clams and lobster rolls. Most choices are $13–20, although lunch rolls (fish, crabmeat, scallop) begin at $8. It's takeout by definition: Order inside and then grab an outside table with serene views over idyllic Webb Cove and by the cockatoo, from which the operation gets its name. You won't find a finer place or better price for lobster, either. Do save room for the homemade but fancy European-style desserts. BYOB. While most folks arrive by car, you can also canoe or kayak here. A second location of the restaurant, **Cockatoo II** (Goose Cove Rd., Sunset, 207/348-2300, 11 A.M.–10 P.M. daily) opened in the lovely Goose Cove Lodge in 2007. The views are the best on the island, and there are both indoor and outdoor seating and a full bar; this menu is more extensive—and expensive, topping out at $40 for a 28-ounce porterhouse. Be forewarned: At either location, while the food earns raves, the service often is painfully sluggish—friends reported waiting more than two hours for their meal; if you're famished, go elsewhere.

# INFORMATION AND SERVICES
## Information

The Deer Isle–Stonington Chamber of Commerce (P.O. Box 459, Stonington 04681, 207/348-6124, www.deerislemaine.com) has a summer information booth, staffed by volunteers, on a grassy triangle on Route 15 in Little Deer Isle, a quarter of a mile after crossing the bridge from Sargentville (Sedgwick).

Across from the Pilgrim's Inn is the Chase Emerson Memorial Library (Main St., Deer Isle Village, 207/348-2899). At the tip of the island is the Stonington Public Library (Main St., Stonington, 207/367-5926).

## Public Restrooms

Public restrooms are at the Atlantic Avenue Hardware pier and at the Stonington Town Hall, Main Street; at the Chase Emerson Library in Deer Isle Village; and behind the information booth on Little Deer Isle.

# Isle au Haut

Eight miles off Stonington lies 4,700-acre Isle au Haut, roughly half of which belongs to Acadia National Park. Pronounced variously as "I'll-a-HO" or "I'LL-a-ho," the island has nearly 20 miles of hiking trails, excellent birding, and a tiny village.

About 60 souls call 5,800-acre Isle au Haut home year-round, most of them eking out a living from the sea. Each summer, the population temporarily swells with day-trippers, campers, and cottagers—then settles back in fall to the measured pace of life on an offshore island.

Samuel de Champlain, threading his way through this archipelago in 1605 and noting the island's prominent central ridge, came up with the name of Isle au Haut—High Island. Appropriately, the tallest peak (543 feet) is now named Mount Champlain.

More recent fame has come to the island thanks to island-based author Linda Greenlaw, of *Perfect Storm* fame, who wrote *The Lobster Chronicles*. Although that book piqued interest, Isle au Haut remains uncrowded and well off the beaten tourist track.

Most of the southern half of the six-mile-long island belongs to Acadia National Park, thanks to the wealthy summer visitors who began arriving in the 1880s. It was their heirs who, in the 1940s, donated valuable acreage to the federal government. Today, this offshore division of the national park has a well-managed 18-mile network of trails, a few lean-tos, several miles of unpaved road, and summertime passenger-ferry service to the park entrance.

In the island's northern half are the private residences of fisherfolk and summer folk, a minuscule village (including a market and post office), a five-mile paved road, and a lighthouse. The only vehicles on the island are owned by residents.

If spending the night on Isle au Haut sounds appealing (it is), you'll need to plan well ahead; it's no place for spur-of-the-moment sleepovers. (Even spontaneous day trips aren't always possible.) The best part about staying overnight on Isle au Haut is that you'll have so much more than seven hours to enjoy this idyllic island.

## ◖ ACADIA NATIONAL PARK

Mention Acadia National Park and most people think of Bar Harbor and Mount Desert Island, where more than three million visitors arrive each year. The Isle au Haut section of the park sees maybe 5,000 visitors a year—partly because only 48 people a day (not counting campers) are allowed to land here. But the remoteness of the island and the scarcity of beds and campsites also contribute to the low count.

Near the town landing, where the year-round mail boat and another boat dock, is the **Park Ranger Station** (207/335-5551), where you can pick up trail maps and park information—and use the island's only public facilities. (Do yourself a favor, though: Make your plans by downloading Isle au Haut maps and information from the Acadia National Park website, www.nps.gov/acad.)

### Hiking

Hiking on Acadia National Park trails is the major recreation on Isle au Haut, and even in the densest fog, you'll see valiant hikers going for it. A loop road circles the whole island; an unpaved section goes through the park, connecting with the mostly paved nonpark section. Walking on that is easy. Beyond the road, none of the park's 18 miles of trails could be labeled "easy"; the footing is rocky, rooty, and often squishy. But the park trails *are* well marked, and the views—of islets, distant hills, and ocean—make the effort worthwhile. Go prepared with proper footwear.

The most-used park trail is the four-mile, one-way **Duck Harbor Trail,** connecting the town landing with Duck Harbor. (You can either use this trail or follow the island road—mostly unpaved in this stretch—to get to the campground when the summer ferry ends its Duck Harbor runs.)

© TOM NANGLE

The Isle au Haut lighthouse is occasionally open to the public.

Even though the summit is only 314 feet, **Duck Harbor Mountain** is the island's toughest trail. Still, it's worth the 1.2-mile, one-way effort for the stunning, 360-degree views from the summit. Option: Rather than return via the trail's steep, bouldery sections, cut off at the Goat Trail and return to the trailhead that way.

For terrific shoreline scenery, take **Western Head** and **Cliff Trails** at the island's southwestern corner. They form a nice loop around Western Head. The route follows the coastline, ascending to ridges and cliffs and descending to rocky beaches, with some forested sections. Options: Close the loop by returning via the Western Head Road. If the tide is out (and *only* if it's out), you can walk across the tidal flats to the quaintly named Western Ear for views back toward the island. Western Ear is private, so don't linger. The **Goat Trail** adds another four miles (round-trip) of moderate coastline hiking east of the Cliff Trail; views are fabulous and birding is good, but if you're here only for a day, you'll need to decide whether there's time to catch the return mail boat. If you do have the time and the energy, you can connect from the Goat Trail to the **Duck Harbor Mountain Trail.**

## OTHER RECREATION
### Biking
Pedaling is limited to the 12 or so miles of mostly unpaved roads, and while it is a way to get around, frankly, the terrain is neither exciting, fun, nor view-worthy. Mountain bikes are not allowed on the park's hiking trails, and rangers try to discourage park visitors from bringing them to the island. If you're staying at the Inn at Isle au Haut, you can borrow a bike, which is handy around the "village" and for going swimming in Long Pond. You can also rent a bike ($18–20 per day) on the island from the Isle au Haut Ferry Service or Old Quarry Ocean Adventures. It costs $8 round-trip to bring your own bike aboard the Isle au Haut ferry. Both boats carry bikes *only* to the town landing, not to Duck Harbor.

### Swimming
For superb **freshwater swimming,** head for Long Pond, a skinny, 1.5-mile-long swimming hole running north-south on the east side of the island, abutting national park land. You can bike over there, clockwise along the road, almost five miles, from the town landing. Or bum a ride from an island resident. There's a minuscule beachlike area on the southern end with a picnic table and a float. If you're here only for the day, though, there's not enough time to do this *and* get in a long hike. Opt for the hiking—or do a short hike and then go for a swim (the shallowest part is at the southern tip).

## ACCOMMODATIONS AND FOOD
There are no restaurants serving breakfast or lunch on Isle au Haut, so if you're coming for a day trip, bring sufficient food and water.

On the east side of the island is **The Inn at Isle au Haut** (P.O. Box 78, Lighthouse Point, Isle au Haut 04645, off-island 207/335-5141, www.innatisleauhaut.com, $275–350 d), a mansard-roofed, waterfront Victorian home that Diana Santospago has turned into an inn. An accomplished cook, Diana whips up fabulous breakfasts, lunches, dinners for her guests; bring your own beer or wine. The downstairs room with private bath is most spacious. Three rather small rooms on the second floor share one bath; all but one have water views. Bikes are provided for guests, and it's an easy pedal to Long Pond for swimming or to connect with park trails. It's open June 1–Sept. 30.

## Camping

The only camping on Isle au Haut is in lean-tos at the Acadia National Park campground. So you'll need to get your bid in early to reserve one of the five six-person lean-tos at **Duck Harbor Campground,** open May 15–October 15. Before April 1, contact the park for a reservation request form: Acadia National Park (P.O. Box 177, Bar Harbor 04609, 207/288-3338, www.nps.gov/acad). Anytime from April 1 on *(not before, or the park people will send it back to you)*, return the completed form, along with a check for $25, covering camping for up to six people for a maximum of five nights May 15–June 14, three nights June 15–September 15, and five nights again September 16–October 15. Mark the envelope: "Attn: Isle au Haut Reservations." Competition is stiff in the height of summer, so list alternate dates. The park refunds the check if there's no space; otherwise, it's nonrefundable and you'll receive a "special-use permit" *(do not* forget to bring it along). There's no additional camping fee.

Unless you don't mind backpacking nearly five miles to reach the campground, try to plan your visit mid-June–Labor Day, when the mail boat makes a stop in Duck Harbor. It's wise to call the Isle au Haut Company for the current ferry schedule before choosing dates for a lean-to reservation.

Trash policy is carry-in/carry-out, so pack a trash bag or two with your gear. Also bring a container for carting water from the campground pump, since it's 0.3 mile from the lean-tos. It's a longish walk to the general store for

food—when you could be off hiking the island's trails—so bring enough to cover your stay.

The three-sided lean-tos are big enough (8 feet by 12 feet, 8 feet high) to hold a small (two-person) tent, so bring one along if you prefer being fully enclosed. A tarp will also do the trick. (Also bring mosquito repellent—some years, the critters show up here en masse.) No camping is permitted outside of the lean-tos, and nothing can be attached to trees.

## Food

Isle au Haut is pretty much a BYO place—and that means BYO food. There is no restaurant. Unless you're staying at the island's only inn, the only source of food is the **Isle au Haut General Store,** not far from the town landing. Thanks to the store, you won't starve. The inventory isn't extensive, but it can be intriguing, which is due to the store manager, who travels worldwide and stocks the shop with her finds. On the other hand, food probably won't be your prime interest here—Isle au Haut is as good as it gets.

## GETTING THERE

Until recently, unless you had your own vessel, the only access to Isle au Haut's town landing was the mail boat. That's still the only way to get there year-round, but two companies now offer transportation to and from the island. Use Isle au Haut Boat Company if your destination is the park, as it lands right at Duck Harbor twice daily during peak season.

### Isle au Haut Boat Company

The Isle au Haut Boat Company (Seabreeze Ave., P.O. Box 709, Stonington 04681, 207/367-5193, www.isleauhaut.com) generally operates five daily trips Monday–Saturday, plus two on Sunday mid-June–early September. Other months, there are 2–3 trips Monday–Saturday. The best advice is to request a copy of the current schedule, covering dates, variables, fares, and extras.

Round-trips April–mid-October are $32 adults, $16 kids under 12 (two bags per adult, one bag per child). Round-trip surcharges:

bikes ($16), kayaks/canoes ($30 minimum), pets ($8). If you're considering bringing a bike, be sure to inquire about on-island bike rentals ($20 per day). Weather seldom affects the schedule, but be aware that ultraheavy seas could cancel a trip.

There is twice-daily ferry service mid-June–Labor Day, from Stonington to Duck Harbor, at the edge of Isle au Haut's Acadia National Park campground. For a day trip, the schedule allows you 6.5 hours on the island Monday–Saturday and 4.5 hours on Sunday. No boats or bikes are allowed on this route, and no dogs are allowed in the campground. A ranger boards the boat at the town landing and goes along to Duck Harbor to answer questions and distribute maps. Before mid-June and after Labor Day, you'll be off-loaded at the Isle au Haut town landing, about five miles from Duck Harbor. The six-mile passage from Stonington to the Isle au Haut town landing takes 45 minutes; the trip to Duck Harbor is 1.25 hours.

Ferries depart from the Isle au Haut Boat Company dock (Seabreeze Ave., off E. Main St. in downtown Stonington). Parking ($9 outside, $11 indoors, per day) is available next to the ferry landing. Arrive at least an hour early to get all this settled so you don't miss the boat. Better yet, spend the night on Deer Isle before heading to Isle au Haut.

## Old Quarry Ocean Adventures

The new kid on the block offering seasonal service to Isle au Haut, Old Quarry Ocean Adventures (Stonington, 207/367-8977 or 877/479-8977, mobile 207/266-7778, www.oldquarry.com) transports passengers on the recently renovated *Nigh Duck*. The boat usually leaves Old Quarry at 9 A.M. and arrives at the island's town landing one hour later. It departs from the same point at 5 P.M., arriving back at Old Quarry around 6 P.M. The fee is $34 round-trip for adults, $17 for children under 12. You can add an island bike rental for an additional $20. Old Quarry also offers a taxi service to Isle au Haut for $140/hour for up to six people.

# ACADIA REGION

Summer folk have been visiting Mount Desert Island (MDI) for millennia. The earliest Native Americans discovered fabulous fishing and clamming, good hunting and camping, and invigorating salt air here. Today's arrivals find variations on the same theme: thousands of lodgings and campsites, hundreds of restaurant seats, dozens of shops, plus 40,000 acres of Acadia National Park.

It's no coincidence that artists were a large part of the 19th-century vanguard here: The dramatic landscape, with both bare and wooded mountains descending to the sea, still inspires everyone who sees it. Once the word got out, painterly images began confirming the reports, and the surge began. Even today, no saltwater locale on the entire Eastern Seaboard can compete with the variety of scenery on Mount Desert Island.

Those pioneering artists brilliantly portrayed this area, adding romantic touches to landscapes that really need no enhancement. From the 1,530-foot summit of Cadillac Mountain, preferably at an off hour, you'll sense the grandeur of it all—the slopes careening toward the bay and the handful of islands below looking like the last footholds between Bar Harbor and Bordeaux.

For nearly four centuries, controversy has raged about the pronunciation of the island's name, and we won't resolve it here. French explorer Samuel de Champlain apparently gets credit for naming it l'Ile des Monts Deserts, "island of bare mountains," when he sailed by in 1604. The accent in French would be on the second syllable, but today "Mount De-SERT" and "Mount DES-ert" both have their

© TOM NANGLE

# HIGHLIGHTS

◖ **Park Loop Road:** If you do nothing else on Mount Desert, drive this magnificent road that takes in many of Acadia National Park's highlights (page 316).

◖ **The Carriage Roads:** Whether you walk, bike, or ride in a horse-drawn carriage, do make it a point to see Mr. Rockefeller's roads and bridges (page 318).

◖ **Jordan Pond House:** For more than a century, afternoon tea and popovers on the lawn of the Jordan Pond House have been a tradition. Do make reservations for an afternoon pick-me-up, perhaps after walking or biking the many carriage roads that lead here (page 322).

◖ **Abbe Museum:** The downtown Abbe Museum and its seasonal museum at Sieur de Monts Springs are fascinating places to while away a few hours and learn about Maine's Native American heritage (page 324).

◖ **Oceanarium:** A fabulous introduction to the coastal ecology is provided at this low-tech, kid-friendly site (page 324).

◖ **Dive-In Theater Boat Cruise:** Got kids? Don't miss this tour, where Diver Ed brings the undersea world aboard (page 328).

◖ **Asticou Azalea Garden and Thuya Garden:** "Magical and enchanting" best describes these two peaceful gardens. While Zenlike Asticou is best seen in spring, Thuya delivers color through summer and also has hiking paths (page 339).

◖ **Wendell Gilley Museum:** Gilley's intricately carved birds, from miniature shorebirds to life-size birds of prey, are a marvel to behold (page 344).

LOOK FOR ◖ TO FIND RECOMMENDED SIGHTS, ACTIVITIES, DINING, AND LODGING.

◖ **Island Cruises:** Kim Strauss shares his deep knowledge of island ways and waters on the lunchtime cruise that allows time to explore Frenchboro (page 347).

◖ **Schoodic National Scenic Byway:** Loop through the Schoodic region on this route highlighted by artisans' studios, mesmerizing views, and the pink-granite shores of Acadia National Park's only mainland section (page 364).

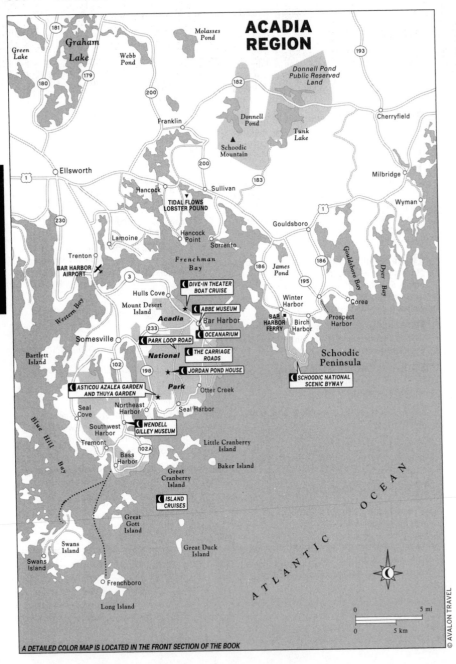

# ACADIA REGION

**181**

Graham Lake

Green Lake

Molasses Pond

Webb Pond

**193**

**179**

**180**

**200**

Donnell Pond Public Reserved Land

**182**

Donnell Pond

Cherryfield

Franklin

Schoodic Mountain

Tunk Lake

**1** Ellsworth

**200**

Hancock

**183**

Sullivan

Milbridge

Wyman

**230**

TIDAL FLOWS LOBSTER POUND

Lamoine

Hancock Point

Sorrento

Gouldsboro

**1**

Trenton

BAR HARBOR AIRPORT

Frenchman Bay

James Pond

**186**

**195**

Winter Harbor

Corea

Gouldsboro Bay

Dyer Bay

**3**

Hulls Cove

DIVE-IN THEATER BOAT CRUISE

Mount Desert Island

Acadia

ABBE MUSEUM

Bar Harbor

BAR HARBOR FERRY

Birch Harbor

Prospect Harbor

Western Bay

**233**

OCEANARIUM

Somesville

PARK LOOP ROAD

**102**

THE CARRIAGE ROADS

National

Schoodic Peninsula

Bartlett Island

**198**

JORDAN POND HOUSE

Park

Otter Creek

SCHOODIC NATIONAL SCENIC BYWAY

ASTICOU AZALEA GARDEN AND THUYA GARDEN

Seal Cove

Northeast Harbor

Seal Harbor

Blue Hill Bay

Southwest Harbor

WENDELL GILLEY MUSEUM

Tremont

**102A**

Little Cranberry Island

Bass Harbor

Great Cranberry Island

Baker Island

ISLAND CRUISES

Great Gott Island

Great Duck Island

ATLANTIC OCEAN

Swans Island

Swans Island

Frenchboro

Long Island

0          5 mi

0          5 km

© AVALON TRAVEL

**A DETAILED COLOR MAP IS LOCATED IN THE FRONT SECTION OF THE BOOK**

advocates, although the former gets the accuracy nod. In any case, the island is anything but deserted today. Even as you approach the island, via the shiretown of Ellsworth and especially in Trenton, you'll run the gauntlet of a minor-league Disneyland, with water slides, bumper cars, and enough high-cholesterol eateries to stun the surgeon general. Don't panic. Acadia National Park lies ahead. Even on the most crowded days, if you venture more than a few steps into the park, you'll find you have it nearly to yourself.

As you drive or bike around Mount Desert—vaguely shaped like a lobster claw and indented by Somes Sound (the only fjord on the United States' east coast)—you'll cross and recross the national-park boundaries, reminders that Acadia National Park, covering a third of the island, is indeed the major presence here. It affects traffic, indoor and outdoor pursuits, and, in a way, even the climate.

The other major presence is Bar Harbor, largest and best known of the island's communities. It's the source of just about anything you could want (if not need), from T-shirts to tacos, books to bike rentals. The contrast with Acadia is astonishing as the park struggles to maintain its image and character.

Bar Harbor shares the island with Southwest Harbor, Tremont, and a number of small villages: Bass Harbor, Bernard, Northeast Harbor, Seal Harbor, Otter Creek, Somesville, and Hall Quarry. From Bass, Northeast, and Southwest Harbors, private and state ferries shuttle bike and foot traffic to offshore Swans Island, Frenchboro (Long Island), and the Cranberry Isles (and cars to Swans Island).

Stay on Route 1, instead of taking Route 3 to the island, and the congestion disappears. The towns lining the eastern shore of Frenchman Bay have some of the best views of all: front-row seats facing the peaks of Mount Desert Island. It's no wonder many artists and artisans make their homes here—for the inspiring scenery, no doubt. And at the tip of the Schoodic Peninsula, a stunning pocket of Acadia National Park sees only a fraction of the visitors who descend on the main part of the park.

## PLANNING YOUR TIME

So much to do, so little time. That's the lament of most visitors. While you can circumnavigate Mount Desert Island in a day, hitting the highlights along the Park Loop with just enough time to oohhh and aahhh at each, to appreciate Acadia you need time to hike the trails, ride the carriage roads, get afloat on a whale-watching cruise or a sea kayak, visit museums, and explore an offshore island or two. A week or longer is best, but you can get a taste of Acadia in 3–4 days.

The region is very seasonal, with most restaurants, accommodations, and shops open mid-May–mid-October. May and June bring the new greens of spring and blooming rhododendrons and azaleas in Northeast Harbor's Asticou Garden, but mosquitoes and blackflies are at their worst, and weather is temperamental—perhaps sunny and hot one day, damp and cold the next, a packing nightmare. July and August bring summer at its best, along with the biggest crowds. September is a gem of a time to visit: no bugs, fewer people, less fog, and the golden light of fall. Foliage usually begins turning in early October, making it an especially beautiful time to visit (although the Columbus Day holiday weekend brings a spike in visitors). Winter is Acadia's silent season, best left for independent travelers who don't mind making do or perhaps making a meal of peanut-butter crackers if an open restaurant can't be found.

The only way onto Mount Desert Island is Route 3. Unless you're traveling in the wee hours of the morning or late at night, expect traffic. Avoid it during shift changes on island, 8–9 A.M. and 3–4 P.M. weekdays, when traffic slows to a crawl. On the island, use the Island Explorer bus system to avoid parking hassles.

# Ellsworth

The punchline to an old Maine joke is "Ya cahn't get they-ah from he-ah." The truth is, you can't get to Acadia without going through Ellsworth and Trenton. Indeed, when you're crawling along in bumper-to-bumper traffic, it might seem as if all roads lead to downtown Ellsworth. And the truth is, many do. Route 1, the main thoroughfare along the coast, and Route 1A, which connects to Bangor, meet in downtown Ellsworth. Route 172 leads to the Blue Hill Peninsula and on to Deer Isle, Stonington, and the mail boat to Isle au Haut. Route 1 continues north, providing access to the Schoodic Peninsula and a remote section of the park. And the Bar Harbor Road (Rte. 3) is something of an Achilles heel—often a summertime bottleneck as it funnels all traffic to Mount Desert Island.

While there are ways to skirt around a few of the worst bottlenecks, the region does have its calling cards. Ellsworth, Hancock County's shire town, has mushroomed with the popularity of Acadia National Park, but you can still find handsome architectural remnants of the city's 19th-century lumbering heyday (which began shortly after its incorporation in 1800). Brigs, barks, and full-rigged ships—built in Ellsworth and captained by local fellows—loaded lumber here and carried it round the globe. Despite a ruinous 1855 fire that swept through downtown, the lumber trade thrived until late in the 19th century, along with factories and mills turning out shoes, bricks, boxes, and butter.

These days, Ellsworth is the region's shopping mecca. Antique shops and small stores line Main Street, which doubles as Route 1 in the downtown section; supermarkets, strip malls, and big-box stores line Routes 1 and 3 between Ellsworth and Trenton.

One more plus for the area is the new Bar Harbor Chamber of Commerce Information Center, which opened in 2006 in the former Acadia Information Center location on Route 3 in Trenton. If you're day-tripping to Mount Desert Island, you can leave your car here and hop aboard the free Island Explorer bus, eliminating driving and parking hassles.

## SIGHTS
### Woodlawn

Very little has changed at the Woodlawn Museum, the Colonel **Black House** (Surry Rd./Rte. 172, Ellsworth, 207/667-8671, www.woodlawnmuseum.com, 10 A.M.–5 P.M. Tues.–Sat., 1–4 P.M. Sun. June–Sept., 1–4 P.M. Tues.–Sun. May and Oct., $7.50 adults, $3 children 5–12; grounds are free) since George Nixon Black donated it to the town in 1928. Completed in 1828, the Georgian house is a marvel of preservation, one of Maine's best, filled with Black family antiques and artifacts. Enthusiastic docents lead hour-long tours, beginning on the hour, to point out the circular staircase, rare books and artifacts, canopied beds, a barrel organ, and lots more. Even kids appreciate all the unusual stuff. Afterward, plan to picnic on the manicured grounds and then explore two sleigh-filled barns, the Memorial Garden, and the two miles of mostly level trails in the woods up beyond the house. Restrooms are next to the parking area. On several Wednesday afternoons in July and August, there are elegant teas in the garden (or in the carriage house if it's raining). China, silver, linens, special-blend tea, sandwiches, pastries, and live music—for $15 a person; reservations are required. The grounds are accessible all year. In winter, there's cross-country skiing on the trails. On Route 172, a quarter mile southwest of Route 1, watch for the small sign and turn into the winding uphill driveway.

### Birdsacre

En route to Bar Harbor, watch carefully on the right for the sign that marks Birdsacre (Rte. 3, Bar Harbor Rd., Ellsworth, 207/667-8460), a 185-acre urban sanctuary. Wander the trails in this peaceful preserve—spotting wildflowers, birds, and well-labeled shrubs and trees—and

© HILARY NANGLE

Take a break in downtown Ellsworth, where there are plenty of interesting shops and restaurants.

you'll have trouble believing you're surrounded by prime tourist territory. The sanctuary is open sunrise–sunset all year. At the sanctuary entrance is the 1850 **Stanwood Homestead Museum,** with period furnishings and wildlife exhibits. Once owned by noted ornithologist Cordelia Stanwood, the volunteer-operated museum is open for tours by chance or appointment, mid-May–mid-October. To be sure, call ahead for an appointment. Admission is free to the preserve and the homestead, but donations are needed and greatly appreciated. Birdsacre is also a wildlife rehabilitation center, so expect to see all kinds of winged creatures, especially hawks and owls, in various stages of rescue. Some will be returned to the wild, while others remain here for educational purposes. Stop by the Nature Center for even more exhibits.

## The New England Museum of Telephony

What was life like before cell phones or touch-tone dialing? Find out at The New England Museum of Telephony (166 Winkumpaugh Rd., Ellsworth, 207/667-9491, www.ellsworthme.org/ringring, 1–4 P.M. Thurs.–Sun. July–Sept., $5 adult, $2.50 kids), a hands-on museum with the largest collection of old-fashioned switching systems in the East, including many from Maine. Place a call to see how these old systems work. To find the museum, head 10 miles north on Route 1A (toward Bangor) and then go left on Winkumpaugh Road for one mile.

## Aerial Touring

Two businesses provide a variety of ways to get an eagle's-eye view of the area. Both are based on the Route 3 side of Hancock County/Bar Harbor Airport, just north of Mount Desert Island and 12 miles north of downtown Bar Harbor.

**Scenic Flights of Acadia** (Bar Harbor Rd., Rte. 3, Trenton, 207/667-6527, www.mainecoastalflight.com) offers low-level flightseeing services in the Mount Desert Island region. Flights range 22–60 minutes and

ACADIA REGION

ACADIA REGION

begin around $50 per person, with a two-passenger minimum.

**Scenic Biplane, Helicopter and Glider Rides** (968 Bar Harbor Rd./Rte. 3, Trenton, 207/667-7627, www.acadiaairtours.com) lets you soar in silence with daily glider flights. The one- or two-passenger gliders are towed to at least an altitude of 2,500 feet and then released. An FAA-certified pilot guides the glider. Rates begin at $179 for two, $129 for one, for a 20-minute flight. Or ride in a biplane: A 20-minute ride in an open-cockpit plane is $225 for two. Or go up in a chopper, with rates beginning at $230 for two; $345 for three. All flights are subject to an airport fee.

# ENTERTAINMENT

Ace lumberjack "Timber" Tina Scheer has been competing around the world since she was seven, and she shows her prowess at **The Great Maine Lumberjack Show** (Rte. 3, 207/667-0067, www.mainelumberjack.com, 7 P.M. daily mid-June–late Aug., $8.50 adult, $6.50 ages 4–11). During the 75-minute "Olympics of the Forest," you'll watch two teams compete in 14 events, including ax throwing, cross-cut sawing, log rolling, speed climbing, and more. Some are open to participation. (Kids can learn log rolling by appointment.) Performances are held rain or shine. Seating is under a roof, but dress for the weather if it's inclement. The ticket office opens at 6 P.M.

The carefully restored art deco **Grand Auditorium** of Hancock County (100 Main St., Ellsworth, 207/667-9500, www.grandonline.org) is the year-round site of films, concerts, plays, and art exhibits.

A summer highlight is the **Ellsworth Concert Band** concert series, held Wednesday evenings in July and August in the plaza outside Ellsworth City Hall (an imposing building just north of Main St.). If it rains, it's held inside City Hall. Practice begins at 6:30 P.M., concerts start at 8 P.M., and the 50-member community band even welcomes visitors with talent and instruments. Just show up at practice time. The repertoire is mostly marches and

show music; a prize goes to the person who correctly identifies a mystery tune.

# SHOPPING
## Specialty Shops

You're unlikely to meet a single soul who has left the **Big Chicken Barn Books and Antiques** (Rte. 1, 1768 Bucksport Rd., Ellsworth, 207/667-7308) without buying *something*. You'll find every kind of collectible on the vast first floor, courtesy of more than four dozen dealers. Climb the stairs for books, magazines, old music, and more. With 21,000 square feet, this place is addictive, with free coffee, restrooms, and hassle-free browsing. The Big Chicken is 11 miles east of Bucksport, 8.5 miles west of Ellsworth.

A fine collection of antiquarian and used books fills the shelves of **Apple Tree Books** (71 Main St., Ellsworth, 207/667-7999).

The 40-plus-dealer **Old Creamery Antique Mall** (13 Hancock St., Ellsworth, 207/667-0522) fills 6,000 square feet on two jam-packed floors.

Around the corner is **Atlantic Art Glass** (25 Pine St., Ellsworth, 207/664-0222), where you can watch Linda and Ken Perrin demonstrate glass blowing and buy their contemporary creations.

Don't miss **Rooster Brother** (29 Main St., Rte. 1, Ellsworth, 207/667-8675 or 800/866-0054, www.roosterbrother.com), for gourmet cookware, cards, and books on the main floor; coffee, tea, candy, cheeses, a huge array of exotic condiments, fresh breads, and other gourmet items on the lower level; and discounted merchandise on the second floor, open seasonally. You can easily pick up all the fixings for a fancy picnic here. The shop is in a handsome old riverside building on busy Route 1.

It's hard to categorize **J&B Atlantic Company** (142 Main St., Rte. 1, 207/667-2082). It takes up a good part of the block, with room after room filled with furniture, home accessories, gifts, books, and antiques.

**John Edwards Market** (158 Main St., Ellsworth, 207/667-9377) is a two-fold find. Upstairs is a natural-foods store. Downstairs is the

Wine Cellar Gallery, a terrific space showcasing Maine artists throughout the year.

## Discount Shopping

You can certainly find bargains at the **L. L. Bean Factory Store** (150 High St., Rte. 1, Ellsworth, 207/667-7753), but this is an outlet, so scrutinize the goods for flaws and blemishes before buying.

Across the road is **Reny's Department Store** (Ellsworth Shopping Center, High St., Rte. 1, Ellsworth, 207/667-5166), a Maine-based discount operation with a you-never-know-what-you'll-find philosophy. Trust me, you'll find something here.

And in an adjacent shopping plaza is **Marden's** (225 High St., Rte. 1A, Ellsworth, 207/669-6036, www.mardenssurplus.com), another Maine bit-of-this, bit-of-that enterprise with the catchy slogan: I shoulda bought it, when I saw it. Good advice.

## ACCOMMODATIONS
### Motels and Bed-and-Breakfasts

National chain (Comfort Inn, Holiday Inn, Travelodge) and independent motels line High Street (Rtes. 1 and 3), a densely commercial stretch in Ellsworth, and continue southward through Trenton toward Mount Desert Island. Most of the motels and cabin complexes along the Trenton stretch are smaller, family-owned operations—not fancy, but their rates are far lower than what you'd find on Mount Desert. (Bar Harbor is 20 miles from downtown Ellsworth.)

Family-owned, nicely landscaped, and meticulously maintained, the **Open Hearth Inn** (Rte. 3, Trenton, 207/667-2930 or 800/655-0234, www.openhearthinn.com, $70–120 d) is on the Island Explorer bus route, less than a quarter mile from the bridge connecting Trenton to Mount Desert, and within walking distance of four lobster restaurants. Choose an inn room with a three-course breakfast or opt for a cottage or motel room (both with continental buffet breakfast), or apartment with kitchen. All have TV, fridge, air-conditioning, and Wi-Fi. Also on the premises is an enclosed family

hot tub. The only drawback might be traffic noise. Kids under 12 are free; two pet-friendly rooms are an additional $25. Free pickup at Bar Harbor Airport. Open year-round.

**White Birches** (Rte. 1, P.O. Box 743, Ellsworth 04605, 207/667-3621 or 800/435-1287, www.whitebirchescountryclub.com) is a clean, generic, somewhat dated motel with 67 rooms ($70–105 d, in shoulder and peak seasons; kids 16 and younger free), nine-hole golf course ($11), and a restaurant. It's popular with tour groups. Rooms have phones and cable TV; some have air-conditioning. It's open all year. Small pets possible.

Simple accommodations are provided at **Mrs. Bancroft's Bed and Breakfast** (6 Wood St., Ellsworth, 207/667-4696, $55), a rambling 1876 home in a quiet, residential neighborhood within walking distance of downtown shops and restaurants.

## Campgrounds

Equally convenient (or not) to the Schoodic Region and Mount Desert Island is the 55-acre **Lamoine State Park** (23 State Park Rd., Rte. 184, Lamoine, 207/667-4778), which is just off the shortcut route from Mount Desert Island to Schoodic. Park facilities include a pebble beach and picnic area with a spectacular view, a boat-launch ramp, and a children's play area. Day-use admission is $3 adults, $1 children 5–11. Camping (62 sites) is $20 per site per night for nonresidents ($15 for Maine residents), plus a $2-per-night fee for reservations; no hookups; two-night minimum, 14-night maximum. (Camping season is mid-May–mid-September. From January 2, reserve online at www.state.me.us/doc/parks/reservations using a credit card, or call 207/287-3824 weekdays.) Leashed pets are allowed, but not on the beach, and cleanup is required.

## FOOD
### Local Flavors

Order breakfast anytime at **The Riverside Café** (151 Main St., Ellsworth, 207/667-7220, 6 A.M.–3 P.M. Mon.–Fri., opens at 7 A.M. Sat. and Sun., closes at 2 P.M. Sun.). The fresh-squeezed juices are fabulous, the buckwheat pancakes are outstanding, and there's even a vegetarian menu with vegan choices. Lunch menu includes homemade soups, salads, sandwiches, grilled sandwiches, and high-cal desserts. Sunday brunches are legendary. Breakfast is served all day; lunch service begins at 11 A.M. And the café's name? It used to be down the street, overlooking the Union River.

Less creative but no less delicious are the home-style breakfasts at **Martha's Diner** (Reny's Plaza, 151 High St., Ellsworth, 207/664-2495, 6 A.M.–2 P.M. Mon.–Sat., 7 A.M.–1 P.M. Sun.), where lunch is also served weekdays 11 A.M.–2 P.M. Almost everything on the menu is less than $5, booths are red leatherette and Formica, and the waitresses likely will call you "doll."

Ice cream doesn't get much finer than that sold at **Morton's Ice Cream** (9 School St., Ellsworth, 207/667-1146, closed Sun.), a tiny shop with a deservedly giant reputation for homemade Italian gelato, sorbet, and ice cream. It's half a block off Main Street.

The area's best pizza is served at **Finelli Pizzeria** (12 Rte. 1, Ellsworth, 207/664-0230, 11 A.M.–8 P.M. Mon.–Thurs., to 9 P.M. Fri. and Sat.), where the pizza dough and focaccia bread are made fresh daily. The specialty is New York-style, thin-crust pizza, but other options include calzones, pastas, subs, and salads.

Although the emphasis is on vegan and vegetarian at **Frankie's Café** (225 High St., 207/667-7701, 8 A.M.–8 P.M. Mon.–Fri., to 6 P.M. Sat., 9 A.M.–4 P.M. Sun.), inside Mr. Paperback in the Maine Coast Mall, other possibilities include roast beef, fresh roast turkey, and other not-so-green sandwiches.

## Casual Dining

**Cleonice Mediterranean Bistro** (112 Main St., Ellsworth, 207/664-7554, 11:30 A.M.–9 P.M. Mon.–Sat. and 5–9 P.M. Sun., but call ahead off-season) is named for chef/owner Richard Hanson's mother, Cleonice Renzetti. (It helps if you learn how to pronounce it: klee-oh-NEESE.) Gleaming woodwork and brass lighting fixtures combine for a golden glow in the long dining room, lined with wooden booths on one side, a 32-foot wooden bar, dating from 1938, on the other. The tapas and meze selection alone is worth the trip—covering the Mediterranean circuit (spanakopita, hummus, manchego cheese with pear sauce, and even *brandade de morue*); most are around $5. Dinner entrée range is $18–22.

A refurbished 1932 Windsor dining car now serves as the bar area at **Calypso** (156 Main St./Rte. 1, Ellsworth, 207/667-6554, www.calypsodining.com, 11 A.M.–9 P.M. Mon.–Sat., 5–9 P.M. Sun.), where the eclectic menu varies from burgers and mac and cheese to duck breast and tenderloin ($10–30). Good service, good food.

## Lobster

Route 3 (Bar Harbor Rd.) is lined with eateries, including several lobster "pounds" that deserve a stop. One of the best known and longest running (since 1956) is **Trenton Bridge Lobster Pound** (Rte. 3, Bar Harbor Rd., Trenton, 207/667-2977, www.trentonbridgelobster.com, 11 A.M.–7:30 P.M. Mon.–Sat. late May–mid-Oct.), on the right, next to the bridge leading to Mount Desert Island. Watch for the "smoke signals"—steam billowing from the huge vats; the lobster couldn't be much fresher.

Brian and Jane Langley's **Union River Lobster Pot** (8 South St., Ellsworth, 207/667-5077, www.lobsterpot.com, 11:30 A.M.–9 P.M. mid-June–early Sept., then 5 P.M.–close through mid-Sept.) is tucked behind Rooster Brother, right on the banks of the Union River. Lobster's the main attraction, but the menu delivers everything from burgers, steaks, and ribs to sandwiches, chowder, and fried food. And save room for the pie—especially the blueberry.

# INFORMATION AND SERVICES

The Ellsworth Area Chamber of Commerce (163 High St., P.O. Box 267, Ellsworth 04605, 207/667-5584, www.ellsworthchamber.org) has information and an area guidebook.

En route from Ellsworth on Route 3, and shortly before you reach Mount Desert, you'll see (on your right) the Bar Harbor Chamber of

Commerce (Rte. 3, Trenton, P.O. Box 158, Bar Harbor 04609, 207/288-5103 or 888/540-9990, www.barharbormaine.com). You'll find all sorts of info on the island as well as other locations, restrooms, phones, and a helpful staff.

Don't miss a chance to visit one of the state's loveliest libraries, the Ellsworth Public Library (46 State St., Ellsworth, 207/667-6363, www.ellsworth.lib.me.us). George Nixon Black, grandson of the builder of the Woodlawn Museum, donated the National Historic Register Federalist building to the city in 1897.

## GETTING AROUND

Route 1 of the **Island Explorer** bus system, which primarily serves Mount Desert Island with its fleet of propane-fueled, fare-free vehicles, connects the Hancock County/Bar Harbor Airport with downtown Bar Harbor. Operated by Downeast Transportation, the Island Explorer runs late June–Columbus Day.

# Acadia National Park on Mount Desert Island

Rather like an octopus, or perhaps an amoeba, Acadia National Park extends its reach here and there and everywhere on Mount Desert Island. America's first national park east of the Mississippi River, and the only national park in the northeastern United States, was created from donated parcels—a big chunk here, a tiny chunk there—and slowly but surely fused into its present-day size of more than 46,000 acres. Within the boundaries of this splendid space are mountains, lakes, ponds, trails, fabulous vistas, and several campgrounds. Each year, more than two million visitors bike, hike, and drive into and through the park. Yet even at the height of summer, when the whole world seems to have arrived here, it's possible to find peaceful niches and less-trodden paths.

Acadia's history is unique among national parks and indeed fascinating. Several books have been written about some of the high-minded (in the positive sense) and high-profile personalities who provided the impetus (and wherewithal) for the park's inception and never flagged in their interest and support. Just to spotlight a few, we can thank the likes of George B. Dorr, Charles W. Eliot, and John D. Rockefeller Jr. for what we have today.

The most comprehensive guide to the park and surrounding area is *Moon Acadia National Park.*

## NATIONAL PARK INFORMATION

Anyone entering the park by any means should buy a pass. Entrance fees, covering pedestrians, bicyclists, and motorized vehicles, are $20 late June–early October; $10 May 1–late June and most of October. That covers one vehicle for seven days. If you're traveling alone, an individual seven-day pass is $5. An annual pass to Acadia is $40, the America the Beautiful pass covering all federal recreation sites is $80, a lifetime senior pass is $10, and an access pass for disabled citizens is free. Passes are available at the visitors centers.

### Hulls Cove Visitor Center

The modern Hulls Cove Visitor Center (Rte. 3, Hulls Cove, 207/288-3338, 8 A.M.–4:30 P.M. daily mid-April–late Oct. and to 6 P.M. July and Aug.) is eight miles southeast of the head of Mount Desert Island and well signposted. Here you can buy your park pass, make reservations for ranger-guided natural- and cultural-history programs, watch a 15-minute film about Acadia, study a relief map of the park, buy books, park souvenirs, and cassette guides, and use the restrooms. Pick up a copy of the *Beaver Log,* the tabloid-format park newspaper that lists the schedule of park activities, plus tide calendars and the entire schedule for the excellent **Island Explorer** shuttle-bus system, which

© TOM NANGLE

Big views await those who hike Great Head Trail.

operates late June–Columbus Day. The Island Explorer is supported by entrance fees (park pass required), as well as by Friends of Acadia and L. L. Bean. If you have children, enroll them for $2.25 in the park's **Junior Ranger Program.** They'll receive a booklet. To earn a Junior Ranger Patch, they must complete the activities and join one or two ranger-led programs or walks.

### Thompson Island Visitor Center

As you cross the bridge from Trenton toward Mount Desert Island, you might not even notice that you arrive first on tiny Thompson Island, site of a visitors center (8 A.M.–6 P.M. daily mid-May–mid-Oct.), established jointly by the chambers of commerce of Mount Desert Island's towns and Acadia National Park. In season, a park ranger usually is posted here to answer questions and provide basic advice on hiking trails and other park activities, but consider this a stopgap—be sure also to continue to the park's main visitors center.

### Acadia National Park Headquarters

From November to April, information is available at Acadia National Park Headquarters (Eagle Lake Rd./Rte. 233, 8 A.M.–4:30 P.M. daily), about 3.5 miles west of downtown Bar Harbor. During the summer, it's open weekdays only.

## SIGHTS
### ◖ Park Loop Road

The 27-mile Park Loop Road takes in most of the park's big-ticket sites. It begins at the visitors center, winds past several of the park's scenic highlights (with parking areas), ascends to the summit of **Cadillac Mountain,** and provides overlooks to magnificent vistas. Along the route are trailheads and overlooks, as well as **Sieur de Monts Spring** (Acadia Nature Center, Wild Gardens of Acadia, Abbe Museum summer site, and the convergence of several spectacular trails), **Sand Beach, Thunder Hole, Otter Cliffs, Fabbri picnic area** (there's one wheelchair-accessible picnic table), **Jordan**

# WITH A LITTLE HELP FROM OUR FRIENDS...

As federal funding for national parks shrinks year after year, every park in America needs a safety net like **Friends of Acadia (FOA),** a dynamic organization headquartered in Bar Harbor. Historic stone bridges need repairs? FOA raises the funds. Propane-powered shuttle-bus service needs expanding? FOA finds a million-dollar donor. Well-used trails need maintenance? FOA organizes volunteer work parties. New connector trails needed? FOA gets them done. No vacuum seems to go unfilled.

FOA — one of Acadia National Park's greatest assets — is both reactive and proactive. It's an amazingly symbiotic relationship. When informed of a need, the Friends stand ready to help; when they themselves perceive a need, they propose solutions to park management and jointly figure out ways to make them happen. It's hard to avoid sounding like a media flack when describing this organization.

Founded in 1986 to preserve and protect the park for resource-sensitive tourism and myriad recreational uses, since 1995 FOA has contributed more than $6.5 million to the park and surrounding communities for trail upkeep, carriage-road maintenance, park research, and other conservation projects. Plus it cofounded the Island Explorer bus system and instigated the Acadia Trails Forever program, a joint park–FOA partnership for trail rehabilitation. It's now working on establishing an off-island transportation hub, among other projects.

Friends of Schoodic (www.friendsofschoodic.org), an FOA committee, does much of the same type of work to preserve and protect the Schoodic section of the park. It also assists in staffing the park's information center, maintaining the Schoodic Education and Research Center buildings, inventorying natural resources, and counting visitors.

You can join FOA and support this worthy cause for $35 a year, or $100 for a family (43 Cottage St., P.O. Box 45, Bar Harbor 04609, 207/288-3340 or 800/625-0321, www.friendsofacadia.org). You can also lend a hand (or two) while you're here. FOA and the park organize volunteer work parties for Acadia trail, carriage-road, and other outdoor maintenance (8:30 A.M.-12:30 P.M. Tues., Thurs., Sat. June-Oct.). Call the recorded information line (207/288-3934) for the work locations, or 207/288-3340 or 800/625-0321 for answers to questions. The meeting point is Park Headquarters (Eagle Lake Rd., Rte. 233, Bar Harbor), about three miles west of town. This is a terrific way to give something back to the park, and the camaraderie is contagious. Be sure to take your own water, lunch, and bug repellent. Dress in layers and wear closed-toe shoes.

Each summer, Friends of Acadia also sponsors a handful of **Ridge Runners,** who work under park supervision and spend their days out and about on the trails repairing cairns, watching for lost hikers, and handing out Leave No Trace information.

If you happen to be in the region on the first Saturday in November, call the FOA office to register for the annual carriage-road cleanup, which usually draws 250 or so volunteers. Bring water and gloves; there's a free hot lunch at midday for everyone who participates. It's dubbed Take Pride in Acadia Day — indeed an apt label.

**Pond House, Bubble Pond, Eagle Lake,** and the summit of **Cadillac Mountain.** Just before you get to Sand Beach, you'll see the Park Entrance Station, where you'll need to buy a pass if you haven't already done so. (If you're here during nesting/fledgling season—April–mid-August—be sure to stop in the Precipice Trailhead parking area.)

Start at the parking lot below the Hulls Cove Visitor Center and follow the signs; part of the loop is one-way, so you'll be doing the loop clockwise. Traffic gets heavy at midday in midsummer, so aim for an early-morning start if you can. Maximum speed is 35 mph, but be alert for gawkers and photographers stopping without warning, and pedestrians dashing across the road from stopped cars or tour buses. If you're out here at midday in midsummer, don't be surprised to see cars and RVs parked in the right lane in the one-way sections; it's permitted.

Allow a couple of hours so you can stop along the way. You can rent an audio tour on cassette or CD for $12.95 (including directions, instruction sheet, and map) at the Hull's Cove Visitor Center. Another option is to pick up the drive-it-yourself tour booklet, *Motorist Guide: Park Loop Road* ($1.50), available at the Thompson Island and Hulls Cove Visitor Centers.

## ◖ The Carriage Roads

In 1913, John D. Rockefeller Jr. began laying out what eventually became a 57-mile carriage-road system, overseeing the project through the 1940s. Motorized vehicles have never been allowed on these lovely graded byways, making them real escapes from the auto world. Devoted now to multiple uses, the "Rockefeller roads" see hikers, bikers, baby strollers, horse-drawn carriages, even wheelchairs. Busiest times are 10 A.M.–2 P.M.

Pick up a free copy of the carriage-road map at any of the centers selling park passes. Fortunately, a $6 million restoration campaign, undertaken during the 1990s, has done a remarkable job of upgrading surfaces, opening overgrown panoramas, and returning the roads to their original 16-foot width.

The most crowded carriage roads are those closest to the visitors center—the Witch Hole Pond Loop, Duck Brook, and Eagle Lake. Avoid these, opting instead for roads west of Jordan Pond. Or go early in the morning or late in the day. Better still, go off-season, when you can enjoy the fall foliage (late September–mid-October) or winter's cross-country skiing.

If you need a bicycle to explore the carriage roads, you can rent one in Bar Harbor or Southwest Harbor. Be forewarned that hikers are allowed on the carriage roads that spill over onto private property south of the Jordan Pond House, but they are off-limits to bicyclists. The no-biking areas are signaled with Green Rock Company markers. The carriage-road map clearly indicates the biking/no-biking

areas. *Bicyclists must be especially speed-sensitive on the carriage roads, keeping an eye out for hikers, horseback riders, small children, and the hearing impaired.*

To recapture the early carriage-roads era, take one of the horse-drawn open-carriage tours run by **Carriages in the Park,** based at Wildwood Stables (Park Loop Rd., P.O. Box 241, Seal Harbor 04675, 207/276-3622, www.acadia.net/wildwood), a mile south of the Jordan Pond House. Six one- and two-hour trips start at 9:30 A.M. daily mid-June–Columbus Day. Reservations are not required, but they're encouraged, especially in midsummer. Best outing is the two-hour **Sunset at the Summit** ($22 adults, $9 ages 6–12, $6 ages 2–5) to the top of Day Mountain. Other routes are $16–18 per adult, $8–9 children, $4.50–6 little kids. If you take the two-hour carriage ride to Jordan Pond House, departing at 1:15 P.M. daily ($18 adults, not counting food and beverage), you're guaranteed a reserved lawn chair for tea and popovers.

## Bass Harbor Light

At the southern end of Mount Desert's western "claw," follow Route 102A to the turn-off toward Bass Harbor Head. Drive or bike to the end of Lighthouse Road, walk down a steep wooden stairway, and look up and to the right. Voilà! Bass Harbor Head Light—its red glow automated since 1974—stands sentinel at the eastern entrance to Blue Hill Bay. Built in 1858, the 26-foot tower and lightkeeper's house are privately owned, but the dramatic setting is a photographer's dream.

## Baker Island

The best way to get to—and to appreciate—wildlife-rich Baker Island is on the ranger-narrated Acadia National Park Baker Island Tour aboard the *Miss Samantha,* booked through **Bar Harbor Whale Watch Co.** (1 West St., Bar Harbor, 207/288-2386 or 888/942-5374, $32 adult, $18 ages 6–15, $8 5 and younger). The 4.5-hour tours depart Monday–Saturday late June–mid-September and include access via skiff to the 130-acre island with farm-

© TOM NANGLE

No two bridges are alike in the Carriage Road system.

stead, lighthouse, and intriguing rock formations. The return trip provides a view of Otter Cliffs, Thunder Hole, Sand Beach, and Great Head from the water.

## RECREATION
### Hikes

If you're spending more than a day on Mount Desert Island, plan to buy a copy of *A Walk in the Park: Acadia's Hiking Guide,* by Tom St. Germain (see the *Suggested Reading* in the *Resources* section), which details more than 60 hikes, including some outside the park. Remember that pets are allowed on park trails, but only on leashes no longer than six feet. Four of the Island Explorer bus routes are particularly useful for hikers, alleviating the problems of backtracking and car-jammed parking lots. Here's a handful of favorite Acadia hikes, from easy to rugged.

These three easy trails are ideal for young families. **Jordan Pond Nature Trail:** Start at the Jordan Pond parking area. This is an easy, one-mile, handicapped-accessible, wooded loop

trail; pick up a brochure. Include Jordan Pond House (for tea and popovers) in your schedule. **Ship Harbor Nature Trail:** Start at the Ship Harbor parking area, on Route 102A between Bass Harbor and Seawall Campground, in the southwestern corner of the island. The easy, 1.3-mile loop trail leads to the shore; pick up a brochure at the trailhead. Ship Harbor is particularly popular among birders seeking warblers, and you just might spot an eagle while you picnic on the rocks. **Wonderland:** An even easier trail, with its parking area just east of the Ship Harbor parking area, Wonderland is 1.4 miles round-trip.

**Great Head Trail:** This moderately easy, 1.4-mile loop trail starts at the eastern end of Sand Beach, off the Park Loop Road. Park in the Sand Beach parking area and cross the beach to the trailhead. Or take Schooner Head Road from downtown Bar Harbor and park in the small area where the road dead-ends. There are actually two trail loops here, both of which have enough elevation to provide terrific views.

**Gorham Mountain:** Another moderate hike

with great views is this 1.8-mile round-trip. It's a great family hike, as kids especially love the Cadillac Cliffs section. Access is off the Park Loop Road, just beyond Thunder Hole.

**Beech Mountain:** A moderate hike, Beech Mountain's summit has an abandoned fire tower, from which you can look out toward Long Pond and the Blue Hill Peninsula. A knob near the top is a prime viewing site for the migration of hawks (and other raptors) in September. Round-trip on the wooded route is about 1.2 miles, although a couple of side trails can extend it. You'll have less competition here, in a quieter part of the park. Take Route 102 south from Somesville, heading toward Pretty Marsh. Turn left onto Beech Hill Road and follow it to the parking area at the end.

**Beehive Trail** and **Precipice Trail:** These two are the park's toughest routes, with sheer faces and iron ladders; Precipice often is closed (usually mid-Apr.–late July) to protect nesting peregrine falcons. If challenges are your thing and these trails are open (check beforehand at the visitors center), go ahead. But a fine alternative in the difficult category is the **Beachcroft Trail** on Huguenot Head. Also called the Beachcroft Path, the trail is best known for its 1,500 beautifully engineered granite steps. Round-trip is about 2.2 miles, or you can continue a loop at the top, taking in the **Bear Brook Trail** on Champlain Mountain, for about 4.4 miles. The parking area is just north of Route 3, near Sieur de Monts Spring, and just west of the Park Loop Road, near the Jackson Laboratory.

## Rock Climbing

Acadia has a number of splendid sites prized by climbers: the sea cliffs at Otter Cliffs and Great Head; South Bubble Mountain; Canada Cliff (on the island's western side); and the South Wall and the Central Slabs on Champlain Mountain. If you haven't tried climbing, *never* do it yourself, without instruction. **Acadia Mountain Guides Climbing School** (198 Main St., Bar Harbor, 207/288-8186 or 888/232-9559, www.acadiamountainguides.com) and **Atlantic Climbing School (ACS)** (24 Cottage St., 2nd floor, P.O. Box 514, Bar Harbor 04609, 207/288-2521) both provide instruction and guided climbs. Costs depend upon the site, experience, session length, and number of climbers; call for details.

## Swimming

Slightly below the Park Loop Road (take Island Explorer Rte. 3/Sand Beach), **Sand Beach** is the park's (and the island's) biggest sandy beach. Lifeguards are on duty during the summer, and even then, the biggest threat can be hypothermia. The salt water is terminally glacial—in mid-July, it still might not reach 60°F. The best solution is to walk to the far end of the beach, where a warmer, shallow stream meets the ocean. On a hot August day, arrive early; the parking lot fills up.

The park's most popular freshwater swimming site, staffed with a lifeguard and inevitably crowded on hot days, is **Echo Lake,** south of Somesville on Route 102 and well signposted (take Island Explorer Rte. 7/Southwest Harbor).

If you have a canoe, kayak, or rowboat, you can reach swimming holes in **Seal Cove Pond** and **Round Pond,** both on the western side of Mount Desert. The eastern shore of **Hodgdon Pond** (also on the western side of the island) is accessible by car (via Hodgdon Rd. and Long Pond Fire Rd.). **Lake Wood,** at the northern end of Mount Desert, has a small beach and auto access. To get to Lake Wood from Route 3, head west on Crooked Road to unpaved Park Road. Turn left and continue to the parking area, which will be crowded on a hot day, so arrive early.

## PARK RANGER PROGRAMS

When you stop at the Hulls Cove Visitor Center and pick up the current issue of the park's *Beaver Log* newspaper (or download it ahead of time at www.nps.gov/acad), you'll find a whole raft of possibilities for learning more about the park's natural and cultural history.

The park ranger programs, lasting 1–3 hours, are great—and most are free. During July and August, there are about 100 programs

# JORDAN POND HOUSE

In the late 19th century, when Bar Harbor was in the throes of becoming "the great new place" to escape the heat of Washington, New York, Philadelphia, and the Midwest, gentle ladies and men patronized an unassuming farmhouse/teahouse on the shores of Jordan Pond. By 1895 or 1896, under the stewardship of Thomas McIntire, it became Jordan Pond House – a determinedly rustic establishment, with massive fieldstone fireplaces, serving afternoon tea and leisurely luncheons during the summer and fall.

And rustic it remained, well into the late 20th century – until leveled by a disastrous fire in the summer of 1979. At that point, it was owned by Acadia National Park. John D. Rockefeller Jr. had bought it in the 1930s and donated it to the park in the early 1940s. Since then, it's been managed on behalf of the park by concessionaires – at present the Acadia Corporation (which also operates gift shops in several locations).

Today, Jordan Pond House, the only restaurant within Acadia National Park, must rely on its framed antique photos to conjure a bit of nostalgia for the bygone era. The building is modern and open, the pace in summer is frenetic, and the food is average. But the view from the lawn over Jordan Pond and the astounding Bubbles is incredible. Surely *it* hasn't changed.

So...at least once, brave the crowds and have afternoon tea on the lawn at Jordan Pond House. Order tea or Oregon chai or even cappuccino and fresh popovers (two) with extraordinary strawberry jam.

If you need a popover fix when you return home, you can always buy a package of the mix along with the jam in the gift shop, but if you don't, here's the Jordan Pond House recipe:

### JORDAN POND HOUSE POPOVERS
2 large eggs
1 cup whole milk
1 cup all-purpose flour (presifted)
$1/2$ teaspoon salt
$1/8$ teaspoon baking soda

Preheat oven to 425°F. Beat eggs with electric mixer at high speed three minutes. Reduce mixer speed to lowest setting and very gradually pour in half the milk. In separate bowl, combine sifted flour, salt, and baking soda and sift again.

With mixer still running at slowest speed, add dry ingredients to egg-and-milk mixture. Turn off mixer and use rubber spatula to blend mixture thoroughly.

Set mixer to medium speed and very gradually pour in remaining milk, blending one minute. Raise mixer speed to highest setting and beat 10 minutes.

Strain batter through fine-mesh strainer to remove lumps and then pour into well-buttered popover or custard cups. Bake 15 minutes. Without opening the oven, reduce heat to 350° and bake 15 more minutes (20 minutes if oven door has a window).

Serve immediately with fresh jam and room-temperature butter.

Hint: Popovers turn out significantly better if baked in ovenproof cups rather than in metal or glass.

The recipe makes two popovers. Increase as desired, but be sure to measure carefully.

ACADIA REGION

each week, all listed in the *Log*. Included are early-morning (7 A.M.) birding walks; mountain hikes (moderate level); tours of the historic Carroll Homestead, a 19th-century farm; Cadillac summit natural-history tours; children's expeditions to learn about tide pools and geology (an adult must accompany kids); trips for those in wheelchair; and even a couple of tours a week in French. Some tours require reservations, some do not; a few, including boat tours, have fees.

Park rangers also give the evening lectures during the summer in the amphitheaters at Blackwoods and Seawall Campgrounds.

## CAMPING

Mount Desert Island has at least a dozen private (commercial) campgrounds, but there are only two—Blackwoods and Seawall—within park boundaries on the island; neither has hookups. Both have seasonal restrooms (no showers) and dumping stations. Both also have seasonal amphitheatres, where rangers present evening programs.

## Blackwoods Campground

With more than 300 campsites, Blackwoods, just off Route 3, five miles south of Bar Harbor, is open all year. Because of its location on the east side of the island, it's also the more popular of the two campgrounds. Reservations are suggested May 1–October 31, when the fee is $20 per site per night. Call 877/444-6777; have your credit card handy. Or register online at www.recreation.gov. Reservations can be made up to six months prior. In April and November, camping is $10; December–March it's free.

## Seawall Campground

Reservations are not accepted at Seawall Campground, on Route 102A in the Seawall district, four miles south of Southwest Harbor—it's first-come, first-served. But in midsummer, you'll need to arrive as early as 8:30 A.M. (when the ranger station opens) to secure one of the 200 or so sites. Seawall is open Memorial Day weekend–September. Cost is $20 per night for drive-up sites and $14 per night for walk-in sites.

RV length at Seawall is limited to 35 feet, with the width limited to an awning extended no more than 12 feet. Generators are not allowed in the campground.

## ◖ JORDAN POND HOUSE

The only restaurant within the park is the Jordan Pond House (Park Loop Rd., 207/276-3316, 11:30 A.M.–8 P.M. daily mid-May–late Oct., to 9 P.M. late June–early Sept.), a modern facility in a spectacular waterside setting. Jordan Pond House began life as a rustic 19th-century teahouse; wonderful old photos still line the walls of the current incarnation, which went up after a disastrous fire in 1979. Afternoon tea is still a tradition, with tea, popovers, and extraordinary strawberry jam, served on the lawn until 5:30 P.M. daily in summer, weather permitting. Not exactly a bargain at $8.75, but it's worth it. However, Jordan Pond is far from a secret, so expect to wait for seats at the height of summer. Jordan Pond House is on the Island Explorer's Route 5. *A health note:* Perhaps because of all the sweet drinks and jam served outdoors, patrons at the lawn tables sometimes find themselves pestered by bees. They don't usually sting unless you pester them back, but if you're hyperallergic to bee stings, or are with anyone who is, be alert.

# Bar Harbor and Vicinity

In 1996, Bar Harbor celebrated the bicentennial of its founding (as the town of Eden). In the late 19th century and well into the 20th, the town grew to become one of the East Coast's fanciest summer watering holes.

In those days, ferries and steam yachts arrived from points south, large and small resort hotels sprang up, and exclusive mansions (quaintly dubbed "cottages") were the venues of parties thrown by summer-resident Drexels, DuPonts, Vanderbilts, and prominent academics, journalists, and lawyers. The "rusticators" came for the season, with huge entourages of

servants, children, pets, and horses. The area's renown was such that by the 1890s, even the staffs of the British, Austrian, and Ottoman embassies retreated here from summers in Washington, D.C.

The establishment of the national park in 1919 and the arrival of the automobile changed the character of Bar Harbor and Mount Desert Island; two World Wars and the Great Depression took an additional toll in myriad ways; but the coup de grâce for Bar Harbor's era of elegance came with the Great Fire of 1947.

Nothing in the history of Bar Harbor and

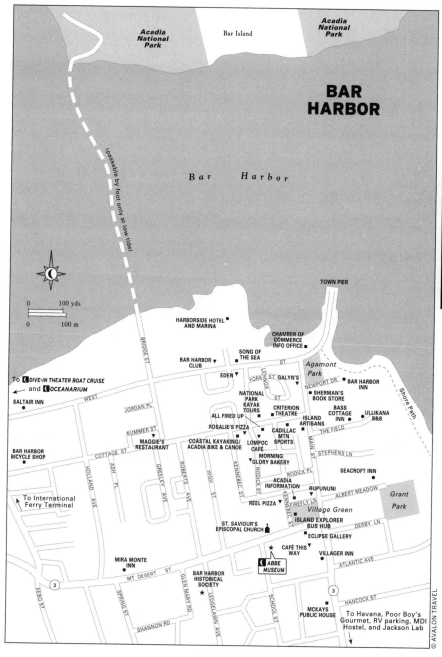

Acadia National Park

Bar Island

Acadia National Park

# BAR HARBOR

B a r    H a r b o r

(passable by foot only at low tide)

0    100 yds
0    100 m

TOWN PIER

HARBORSIDE HOTEL AND MARINA

CHAMBER OF COMMERCE INFO OFFICE

Agamont Park

SONG OF THE SEA

BAR HARBOR CLUB

EDEN

GALYN'S

LENNOX ST

YORK ST

NEWPORT DR

SHERMAN'S BOOK STORE

BAR HARBOR INN

To **◖**DIVE-IN THEATER BOAT CRUISE
and **◖**OCEANARIUM

WEST

SALTAIR INN

JORDAN PL

NATIONAL PARK KAYAK TOURS

CRITERION THEATRE

BASS COTTAGE INN

ULLIKANA B&B

ALL FIRED UP

ISLAND ARTISANS

ROSALIE'S PIZZA

CADILLAC MTN SPORTS

THE FIELD

SUMMER ST

BAR HARBOR BICYCLE SHOP

MAGGIE'S RESTAURANT

COASTAL KAYAKING/ ACADIA BIKE & CANOE

LOMPOC CAFÉ

COTTAGE ST

MORNING GLORY BAKERY

RODICK PL

STEPHENS LN

SEACROFT INN

To International Ferry Terminal

HOLLAND AVE

ASH PL

GREELEY AVE

ROBERTS AVE

HIGH ST

KENNEBEC ST

RODICK ST

ACADIA INFORMATION

RUPUNUNI

ALBERT MEADOW

Grant Park

REEL PIZZA

FIREFLY LN

Village Green

ISLAND EXPLORER BUS HUB

DERBY LN

ST. SAVIOUR'S EPISCOPAL CHURCH

ECLIPSE GALLERY

MIRA MONTE INN

MT DESERT ST

BAR HARBOR HISTORICAL SOCIETY

CAFÉ THIS WAY

★ ◖ABBE MUSEUM

VILLAGER INN

ATLANTIC AVE

KEBO ST

SPRING ST

GLEN MARY RD

LEDGELAWN AVE

SCHOOL ST

3

MCKAYS PUBLIC HOUSE

HANCOCK ST

To Havana, Poor Boy's Gourmet, RV parking, MDI Hostel, and Jackson Lab

SHANNON RD

MAIN ST

KENNEBEC ST

Shore Path

© AVALON TRAVEL

Mount Desert Island stands out like the Great Fire of 1947, a wind-whipped conflagration that devastated more than 17,000 acres on the eastern half of the island and leveled gorgeous mansions, humble homes, and more trees than anyone could ever count. Only three people died, but property damage was estimated at $2 million. Whole books have been written about the October inferno; fascinating scrapbooks in Bar Harbor's Jesup Memorial Library dramatically relate the gripping details of the story. Even though some of the elegant cottages have survived, the fire altered life here forever.

# SIGHTS
## ◖ Abbe Museum

The fabulous Abbe Museum is a superb place to introduce children (and adults) to prehistoric and historic Native American tools, crafts, and other cultural artifacts, with an emphasis on Maine's Micmac, Maliseet, Passamaquoddy, and Penobscot tribes. Everything about this privately funded museum, established in 1927, is tasteful. It has two campuses. The new main campus (26 Mt. Desert St., Bar Harbor, 207/288-3519, www.abbemuseum.org, 10 A.M.–6 P.M. daily Apr.–Dec.—reduced days and hours before mid-May and after early Nov., $6 adults, $2 ages 6–15), built in 2001 and incorporating the former YMCA, is home to a collection spanning nearly 12,000 years. Museum-sponsored events include craft workshops, hands-on children's programs, archaeological field schools, and the **Native American Festival** (held at the College of the Atlantic usually the first Saturday after the Fourth of July). The museum's gift shop has an especially nice selection of Native American–made baskets.

Admission to the in-town Abbe also includes admission to the museum's original site in the park, about 2.5 miles south of Bar Harbor, at Sieur de Monts Spring, where Route 3 meets the Park Loop Road (9 A.M.–4 P.M. daily late May–early Oct., $2 adults, $1 children 6–15). Everything about this small, privately funded museum is tasteful, including the park setting, a handsome National Historic

Register building, and displays from a 50,000-item collection.

While you're at the summertime Abbe Museum, take the time to wander the paths in the adjacent **Wild Gardens of Acadia,** a three-quarter-acre microcosm of more than 400 plant species native to Mount Desert Island. Twelve separate display areas, carefully maintained and labeled by the Bar Harbor Garden Club, represent native plant habitats; pick up the map/brochure that explains each.

## St. Saviour's Episcopal Church

St. Saviour's (41 Mt. Desert St., Bar Harbor, 207/288-4215, 7 A.M.–dusk daily), close to downtown Bar Harbor, boasts Maine's largest collection of Tiffany stained-glass windows. Ten originals are here; an 11th was stolen in 1988 and replaced by a locally made window. Of the 32 non-Tiffany windows, the most intriguing is a memorial to Clarence Little, founder of the Jackson Laboratory and a descendant of Paul Revere. Images in the window include the laboratory, DNA, and mice. In July and August, volunteers regularly conduct free tours of the Victorian-era church (completed in 1878); call for the schedule or make an appointment for an off-season tour. The church is open for self-guided tours (8 A.M.–8 P.M.)—pick up a brochure in the back. If old cemeteries intrigue you, spend time wandering the 18th-century town graveyard next to the church.

## ◖ Oceanarium

At the northern edge of Mount Desert Island, 8.5 miles northwest of downtown Bar Harbor, is this understated but fascinating spot, also called the Maine Lobster Museum and Hatchery (1351 Rte. 3, Bar Harbor, 207/288-5005, 9 A.M.–5 P.M. Mon.–Sat. mid-May–mid-Oct.), one of the island's two related oceanariums. This low-tech, high-interest operation awes the kids, and it's pretty darn interesting for adults, too. David and Audrey Mills have been at it since 1972 and are determined to educate visitors while showing them a good time. At this facility (there's also a sister site in Southwest Harbor), visitors on tour view thousands of tiny lobster hatchlings, enjoy a museum, and meander along a salt-marsh walk, where you can check out tidal creatures and vegetation. All tours begin on the hour and half hour. Allow 1–2 hours to see everything. Tickets are $10 adults, $6 children 4–12 for a program with two talks; an expanded program includes a 45-minute Marsh Walk for $12 adults, $7 children; an all-access pass to both sites is $16 adults and $10.50 children.

## College of the Atlantic

A museum, a gallery, and a pleasant campus for walking are reasons to visit the college (105 Eden St., Rte. 3, Bar Harbor, 207/288-5395, www.coamuseum.org), which specializes in human ecology, or man's interrelationship with the environment. In a handsome renovated building, the **George B. Dorr Natural History Museum** (207/288-5015) showcases regional birds and mammals in realistic dioramas made by COA students. The biggest attraction for children is the please-touch philosophy, allowing kids to feel fur, skulls, and even whale baleen. Tickets are $3.50 adults, $1.50 teenagers, and $1 children (3–12). The museum is open 10 A.M.–5 P.M. Monday–Saturday mid-June–Labor Day and by appointment at other times.

Across the way is the **Ethel H. Blum Gallery** (10 A.M.–4 P.M. Tues.–Sat. in summer, 9 A.M.–5 P.M. weekdays during the academic year), a small space that hosts some intriguing exhibits.

Also on campus is a **Beatrix Farrand Garden** that was undergoing restoration. The garden, designed in 1928, contained more than 50 varieties of roses and was the prototype for the rose garden at Dumbarton Oaks in Washington, D.C. Both are known for Farrand's use of garden rooms, such as the terraces in this garden.

## Bar Harbor Whale Museum

Inside the Bar Harbor Whale Museum (52 West St., Bar Harbor, 207/288-0288, www.barharborwhalemuseum.org, 9 A.M.–9 P.M. daily July and Aug., noon–8 P.M. daily June, 10 A.M.–8 P.M. daily Sept. and Oct.), also affiliated with the college, are a life-size model of a prehistoric walking whale, a pilot whale skeleton, seals, marine birds, a 22-foot-long minke porpoise, and exhibits on whales. There's also a mesmerizing video of whales in their habitat. Admission is free, but donations support marine mammal research and conservation. Ask about the Friday evening lecture series.

## Bar Harbor Historical Society

The Bar Harbor Historical Society (33 Ledgelawn Ave., Bar Harbor, 207/288-0000, 1–4 P.M. Mon.–Sat. mid-June–mid-Oct., free), in its own National Register building, has fascinating displays, stereopticon images, and a scrapbook about the 1947 fire that devastated the island. The photographs alone are worth the visit. Also here are antique maps, Victorian-era hotel registers, and much other local memorabilia. In winter, it's open by appointment. For a sample of Bar Harbor before the great fire, wander over to upper West Street, which is on the National Historic Register thanks to the remaining grand cottages that line it.

## Mount Desert Island Biological Laboratory

Some of the world's top scientists work year-round or come to Bar Harbor in summer to work at Mount Desert Island Biological Laboratory (Old Bar Harbor Rd., Salisbury Cove, 207/288-3147, www.mdibl.org), one of the few scientific research institutions in the world dedicated to studying marine animals to learn more about human health and environmental health and the only comprehensive effort in the country to sequence genomes. Public tours are offered on Wednesdays (call for time) late June–late August, beginning at Maren Auditorium. The program begins with a presentation by a laboratory scientist about the lab's history and research, and a short video. Then a naturalist talks about animal life in Frenchman Bay and how it pertains to the lab's research. It includes a hands-on presentation at the touch tank, filled with marine animals from Frenchman Bay, a visit to a 15-foot glass tank with other marine creatures, and a stroll through the visitors center, where there are smaller tanks. The tour takes about 1.5 hours. To avoid crowds, go on a nice day. The lab also presents an evening lecture series. Most are serious scientific talks, but there's also usually a children's program.

## Bar Harbor and Park Tours

The veteran of the Bar Harbor–based bus tours is **Acadia National Park Tours** (tickets at Testa's Restaurant, Bayside Landing, 53 Main St., P.O. Box 52, Bar Harbor 04609, 207/288-3327, www.acadiatours.com), operating May–October. A 2.5-hour, naturalist-led tour of Bar Harbor and Acadia departs at 10 A.M. and 2 P.M. daily from downtown Bar Harbor (Testa's is across from Agamont Park, near the Bar Harbor Inn). Reservations are wise in midsummer and during fall-foliage season (late September and early October); pick up reserved tickets 30 minutes before departure. Cost is $20 adults, $10 children under 12.

If there's a time crunch, take the one-hour trolley-bus tour operated by **Oli's Trolley** (P.O. Box 794, Bar Harbor 04609, 207/288-9899, www.acadiaislandtours.com), which departs downtown Bar Harbor five times daily (between 10 A.M. and 6 P.M.) in July and August, including Bar Harbor mansion drive-bys and the Cadillac summit. Starting point is the Oli's Trolley Ice Cream Shop (58 Cottage St.), across from the post office. (Tickets are also available at Harbor Place, the waterfront marketplace near the Bar Harbor Inn.) Dress warmly if the air is at all cool; it's an open-air trolley. Cost is $15 adults, $10 children under 12. Reservations are advisable. The trolley also does 2.5-hour park tours at 10 A.M. and 2 P.M. May–October. Tickets are $20 adults, $10 children under 12. The bus and trolley routes both include potty stops.

Note: While the Island Explorer buses do reach a number of key park sights, they are not tour buses. There is no narration, the bus cuts off the Park Loop at Otter Cliffs, and it excludes the summit of Cadillac Mountain.

## Birding and Nature Tours

For private tours of the park and other parts of the island, contact Michael Good at **Down East Nature Tours** (P.O. Box 521, Bar Harbor 04609, 207/288-8128, www.downeastnaturetours.com). A biologist and Maine Guide, Michael Good is simply batty about birds. He's spent more than 25 years studying the birds of North America, and he's even turned his home property on Mount Desert Island into a bird sanctuary. Good specializes in avian ecology in the Gulf of Maine, giving special attention to native and migrating birds. Whether you're a first-timer wanting to spot eagles, peregrine falcons, shorebirds, and warblers or a serious birder seeking to add to your life list, perhaps with a Nelson's sharptailed sparrow, Good's your man. Prices begin at $50 pp for two hours and include transportation from your lodging; family rates are available. Bring your own binoculars, but Michael supplies a spotting scope.

# RECREATION
## Walks

A real treat is a stroll along downtown Bar Harbor's **Shore Path,** a well-trodden, granite-edged byway built around 1880. Along the craggy shoreline are granite-and-wood benches, town-owned **Grant Park** (great for picnics), birch trees, and several handsome mansions that escaped the 1947 fire. Offshore are the four Porcupine Islands. The path is open 6:30 A.M.–dusk, and leashed pets are okay. Allow about 30 minutes for the mile loop, beginning next to the town pier and the Bar Harbor Inn and returning via Wayman Lane.

Check local newspapers or the Bar Harbor Chamber of Commerce visitor booklet for the times of low tide and then walk across the gravel bar (wear hiking boots or rubberized shoes) to wooded **Bar Island** (formerly Rodick's Island) from the foot of Bridge Street in downtown Bar Harbor. Shell heaps recorded on the eastern end of the island indicate that Native Americans enjoyed this turf in the distant past. You'll have the most time to explore the island during new-moon or full-moon low tides, but no more than four hours—about two hours before and two hours after low tide. Be sure to wear a watch so you don't get trapped (for up to 10 hours). The foot of Bridge Street is also an excellent kayak-launching site.

About a mile from downtown, along Main Street, Route 3, is **Compass Harbor,** a section of the park where you can stroll through woods to the water's edge and explore the overgrown ruins of park cofounder George Dorr's home.

Bear right at the fork just after the Thompson Island information center on Route 102/198 to reach **Indian Point/Blagden Preserve,** a lovely preserve owned by The Nature Conservancy. Five trails wind through forested, 110-acre Indian Point/Blagden Preserve, a rectangular parcel with island, hill, and bay vistas. Seal-watching and birding are popular—harbor seals on offshore rocks and woodpeckers (plus 130 other species) in blowdown areas. To spot the seals, plan your hike around low tide, when they'll be sprawled on the rocks close to shore. Wear rubberized shoes. Bring binoculars or use the telescope installed here for the purpose. To keep from disturbing the seals, watch quietly and avoid jerky movements. Park near the preserve entrance and follow the Big Woods Trail, which runs the length of the preserve. A second parking area is farther in, but then you'll miss much of the preserve. When you reach the second parking area, just past an old field, bear left along the Shore Trail to see the seals. Register at the caretaker's house (just beyond the first parking lot, where you can pick up bird and flora checklists), and respect private property on either side of the preserve. It's open dawn–6 P.M. daily all year. From the junction of Routes 3 and 102/198, continue 1.8 miles to Indian Point Road and turn right. Go 1.7 miles to a fork and turn right. Watch for the preserve entrance on the right, marked by a Nature Conservancy oak leaf.

## Bicycle Rentals and Rides

With all the great biking options, including 45 miles of carriage roads (12 miles of which are off-limits to bicycles) and some of the best roadside bike routes in Maine, you'll want to bring a bike or rent one here. Expect to pay about $20 per day for a rental bike, including helmet, lock, and map. It's wise to make reservations.

The Minutolo family's **Bar Harbor Bicycle Shop** (141 Cottage St., Bar Harbor, 207/288-3886, www.barharborbike.com), on the corner with Route 3, has been in business since 1977 and has earned an excellent reputation (it's also known as Island Adventures). If you have your own bike, stop here for advice on routes—the Minutolos have cycled everywhere on the island and can suggest the perfect mountain-bike or road-bike loop based on your ability and schedule. The shop organizes free Sunday morning group road rides, usually 9 A.M.–noon, with a longer option for more experienced cyclists. Evening rides for various abilities, including a Ladies Ride, are also organized. The shop has rentals varying from standard mountain bikes to full-suspension models and even tandems as well as all the accessories and gear you might need. Hours in summer are 8 A.M.–8 P.M. daily, 9 A.M.–5:30 P.M. Tuesday–Saturday other months.

## Sea Kayaking

**National Park Kayak Tours** (39 Cottage St., Bar Harbor, 207/288-0342 or 800/347-0940, www.acadiakayak.com) limits its Registered Maine Guide–led tours to a maximum of six tandem kayaks per trip. Four-hour morning, midday, afternoon, or sunset paddles are offered, including shuttle service, a paddle/safety lesson, and a brief stop, for $46 per person in July and August, $42 off-season. Most trips cover about six miles. Multiday camping trips also are offered. Try to make reservations at least one day in advance.

## Golf

Duffers first teed off in 1888 at **Kebo Valley Golf Club** (100 Eagle Lake Rd., Rte. 233, Bar Harbor, 207/288-5000, www.kebovalleyclub.com, May–Oct.), Maine's oldest club and the eighth-oldest in the nation. The 17th hole became legendary when it took President William Howard Taft 27 tries to sink the ball in 1911. Kebo is very popular, with a gorgeous setting, an attractive clubhouse, and decent food service, so tee times are essential; you can reserve up to six days in advance. Greens fees are the highest on the island, but afternoon and twilight rates are available.

## EXCURSION BOATS
### ◖ Dive-In Theater Boat Cruise

You don't have to go diving in these frigid waters; others will do it for you. When the kids are clamoring to touch slimy sea cucumbers and starfish at various touch tanks in the area, they're likely to be primed for Diver Ed's Dive-In Theater Boat Cruise (P.O. Box 870, Bar Harbor 04609, 207/288-3483, www.div-ered.com), operating from the College of the Atlantic pier (105 Eden St.). Former Bar Harbor harbormaster Ed Monat heads the crew aboard the 46-passenger *Seal,* which goes a mile or two offshore and sends down two professional divers (including Ed) with video cameras. You and the kids stay on deck, all warm and dry, and watch the action on a TV screen. There's communication back and forth, so the kids can ask questions as the divers pick up urchins, starfish, crabs, lobsters, and other sea life. When the diver surfaces, he or she brings a bag of touchable specimens—another chance to pet some slimy creatures (which go back into the water after show-and-tell). Great concept. Watch the kids' expressions—this is a big hit. The two-hour trips depart three times daily Monday–Friday, twice daily Saturday, and once on Sunday in July and August, with fewer trips in spring and fall. Cost is $30 adults, $25 seniors, $20 children ages 5–11, $5 younger than 5; usually twice weekly there's a park ranger or naturalist on board and the tour lasts for three hours—check the park's *Beaver Log* newspaper or Diver Ed's website for the schedule and reservation information—these trips cost an additional $5.

## Whale-Watching and Puffin-Viewing Excursions and Nature Cruises

Whale-watching boats go as much as 20 miles offshore, so no matter what the weather in Bar Harbor, dress warmly and bring more cloth-ing than you think you'll need—even gloves, if you're especially sensitive to cold. Motion-sensitive children and adults should plan for appropriate medication, such as pills or patches.

Whale-watching, puffin-watching, and combo excursions are offered by **Bar Harbor Whale Watch Company** (1 West St., Bar Harbor, 207/288-2386 or 800/942-5374, www.BarHarborWhales.com), sailing from the town pier (1 West St.) in downtown Bar Harbor. The company operates under various names, including Acadian Whale Watcher, and has a number of boats. Most trips are accompanied by a naturalist (often from Allied Whale at the College of the Atlantic), who regales passengers with all sorts of interesting trivia about the whales, porpoises, seabirds, and other marine life spotted along the way. In season, some trips go out as far as the puffin colony on Petit Manan light. Trips depart daily late May–late October, but with so many options, it's impossible to list the schedule, so call. Tickets are $49 adults, $26 children 6–14, $8 children under 6. Part of the ticket price benefits Allied Whale, which researches and protects marine animals in the Gulf of Maine. Note: Trips often go longer than the 2.5–3 hours advertised. Don't plan anything else too tightly around the trip. Either before or afterward, be sure to visit the Whale Museum.

Scenic nature cruises (1.5–2 hours), lighthouse viewing, and kid-friendly lobster and seal-watch cruises (1.5 hours) also are offered. Rates for these are $22–32 for adults, $15–20 ages 6–14, $5–8 age 5 and younger.

## Sailing

Captain Steve Pagels's **Downeast Windjammer Cruises** (207/288-4585 or 207/288-2373, www.downeastwindjammer.com, $32 adult, $22 kids under 12) offers 1.5–two-hour day sails on the 151-foot steel-hulled *Margaret Todd,* a gorgeous four-masted schooner with tanbark sails that he designed and launched in 1998. Trips depart three times daily mid-May–mid-October (weather permitting) from the Bar Harbor Inn pier, just east of the town pier in downtown Bar Harbor. You'll get the best

Whale-watching and puffin-watching tours go as much as 20 miles offshore.

© TOM NANGLE

ACADIA REGION

wildlife sightings on the morning trip; better sailing on the afternoon trip; and live music on the sunset one. Some morning sails are narrated by a park ranger.

### Sea/Venture Cruise

Captain Winston Shaw's custom boat tour by Sea/Venture (207/288-3355, www.svboattours.com) lets you design the perfect trip aboard *Reflection,* a 20-foot motor launch. Captain Shaw, a Registered Maine Guide and committed environmentalist, specializes in nature-oriented tours. He was involved in the inaugural Earth Day celebration in 1970. The founder and director of the Coastal Maine Bald Eagle Project, he's been studying Maine's coastal bald eagles since the late 1970s. You can pick from 10 recommended cruises lasting 1–8 hours or design your own. In any case, the boat is yours. Boat charter rate is $85 per hour for 1–2 passengers, $95 for 3–4, or $105 for 5–6. Captain Shaw can also arrange for picnic lunches. On longer trips, restroom stops are available.

### Lobster Cruise

When you're ready to learn The Truth about lobsters, sign up for a cruise aboard Captain John Nicolai's *Lulu,* a traditional Maine lobster boat. *Lulu* departs 4–5 times daily May–September from the Harborside Hotel and Marina in Bar Harbor (55 West St., 207/963-2341 or 866/235-2341, www.lululobsterboat.com, $27 adult, $24 senior, $15 kids under 12). Captain Nicolai provides an entertaining commentary on anything and everything, but especially about lobsters and lobstering. He hauls a lobster trap and explains intimate details of the hapless critter. (Lobstering is banned on Sunday June–August; the cruises operate, but there's no hauling that day.) Reservations are required; six passengers maximum. No credit cards. There's free parking in the hotel's lot.

## SHOPPING

Bar Harbor's boutiques—running the gamut from attractive to kitschy—are indisputably visitor oriented; many shut down for the winter.

Downtown Bar Harbor's best craft gallery

is **Island Artisans** (99 Main St., Bar Harbor, 207/288-4214, www.islandartisans.com). More than 100 Maine artists are represented here, and the quality is outstanding. Don't miss it. You'll find basketwork, handmade paper, wood carvings, blown glass, jewelry, weaving, metalwork, ceramics, and more. **Eclipse Gallery** (12 Mount Desert St., Bar Harbor, 207/288-9048) specializes in handblown glass and complementary works and represents more than 100 contemporary American artists.

Toys, cards, and newspapers blend in with the new-book inventory at **Sherman's Book Store** (56 Main St., Bar Harbor, 207/288-3161). It's just the place to pick up maps and trail guides for fine days and puzzles for foggy days.

Souvenir shops are *everywhere* on Mount Desert Island, so why single out the Acadia Shops? If you need Maine-made mementos for Uncle Harry and Aunt Mary, if the kids need trinkets for friends back home, the Acadia Corporation has several shops in downtown Bar Harbor that can cover it all. Price range is broad, quality is fairly high, and clerks are especially friendly at **The Acadia Shop** (85 Main St., Bar Harbor, 207/288-5600, www.acadiashops.com). Another branch, **Acadia Outdoors** (45 Main St., Bar Harbor, 207/288-2422), features sportswear and outdoor accessories.

Most vacationers don't expect to shop for musical instruments, but everyone with an affinity for folkloric music gravitates toward **Song of the Sea** (47 West St., Bar Harbor 207/288-5653, www.songsea.com), a unique, jam-packed harborfront shop where you can find guitars, banjos, harmonicas, and tin whistles—but also such esoterica as hammered dulcimers, doumbeks, didgeridoos, psalteries, and Chilean rainsticks. Ed and Anne Damm are extremely knowledgeable and helpful, even to the point of playing instruments over the phone for call-in orders.

# ENTERTAINMENT

At the height of the summer season, plenty of live entertainment varies from pub music to films to classical concerts.

The **Bar Harbor Town Band** performs free at 8 P.M. Monday and Thursday July–mid-August on the Village Green (Main St. and Mount Desert St., Bar Harbor).

Above Rupununi's restaurant, **Carmen Verandah** (119 Main St., Bar Harbor, 207/288-2766) is the weekend place to be and be seen. Everything gets rolling about 9:30 P.M.—blues, rock, salsa, funk, zydeco, ska, reggae, you name it—and there's lots of space for dancing. Other nights, there's a DJ. Darts and billiards round out the picture. It's open all year.

You never know quite what's going to happen at **Improv Acadia** (15 Cottage St., Bar Harbor, 207/288-2503, www.improvacadia.com, $15 adults, $10 kids 12 and younger). Every show is different, as actors use audience suggestions to create spots; the 8 P.M. show is family friendly.

The **Bar Harbor Music Festival** (207/288-5744 in July and Aug., 212/222-1026 off-season, www.barnharbormusicfestival.org), a summer tradition since 1967, emphasizes up-and-coming musical talent in a series of classical, jazz, and pops concerts, usually Fridays and Sundays, at various island locations, including local inns and an annual outdoor concert in Acadia National Park, early July–early August. A relatively new addition to the schedule is an opera, which received rave reviews in its debut season. Tickets begin at $25 adult, $15 student, available at the festival office building (59 Cottage). Preconcert dinners are also sometimes available at $30. Reservations are wise.

## Cinemas

In 2001, new owners assumed the reins of the beautifully refurbished National Historic Landmark **Criterion Theatre** (35 Cottage St., Bar Harbor, 207/288-3441 for films or 207/288-5829 for concerts, www.criterionthe-atre.com), built in 1932. Now, in addition to screening films, the Criterion puts on concerts, plays, and other special events. You'll soak up the nostalgia in this art deco classic with nearly 900 seats (including an elegant floating balcony). Beer, wine, and light fare are available.

Combine pizza with your picture show at **Reel Pizza Cinerama** (33 Kennebec Pl., Bar

Harbor, film 207/288-3811, food 207/288-3828, www.reelpizza.com). There are two showings nightly on each of two screens. All tickets are $6; pizzas are $13–20. Doors open at 4:30 P.M.; go early for the best seats.

## EVENTS

Bar Harbor is home to numerous special events. Here's just a sampling. For more, call 207/288-5103 or visit www.barharbor-maine.com.

In late May, the annual **Warblers and Wildflowers Festival** attracts birders and nature lovers. Events include morning birdsong walks, garden tours, art, lectures, and other events.

In late June **Legacy of the Arts** is a week-long celebration of music, art, theater, dance, and history, with tours, exhibits, workshops, concerts, lectures, demonstrations, and more.

The Abbe Museum, the College of the Atlantic, and the Maine Indian Basketmakers Alliance sponsor the annual **Native American Festival,** 10 A.M.–4 P.M. the first Saturday after the Fourth of July, featuring baskets, beadwork, and other handicrafts for sale, and Indian drumming and dancing. Free admission; it's held at College of the Atlantic, Bar Harbor.

In even-numbered years, the **Mount Desert Garden Club Tour** presents a rare chance to visit some of Maine's most spectacular private gardens the second or third Saturday in July (confirm the date with the Bar Harbor Chamber of Commerce).

The **Directions Craft Show** fills a weekend in late July or early August with extraordinary displays and sales of crafts by members of Directions. You'll find it at Mount Desert Island High School (Rte. 233, Eagle Lake Rd.). Hours are 5–9 P.M. Friday, 10 A.M.–5 P.M. Saturday and Sunday.

## ACCOMMODATIONS

Most properties are seasonal. Rates reflect high season.

### Hotels and Motels

One of the town's best-known, most-visible,

and best-situated hotels is the **Bar Harbor Inn** (Newport Dr., P.O. Box 7, Bar Harbor 04609, 207/288-3351 or 800/248-3351, www.bar-harborinn.com, $199–379), a sprawling complex on eight acres overlooking the harbor and Bar Island. Facilities include an outdoor pool, a spa, and two restaurants. The 153 rooms and suites, in three different buildings, vary considerably in style, from traditional inn to motel. Continental breakfast is included, and special packages, with meals and activities, are available—an advantage if you have children. Rooms in the Oceanfront Lodge are good choices, with reasonable rates and terrific views. The Main Inn rooms have seen the most recent upgrades. Service is attentive. It's open late March–late November.

The newest and fanciest hotel in town is **Harborside Hotel and Marina** (55 West St., Bar Harbor, 207/288-5033 or 800/238-5033, www.theharborsidehotel.com, $299–499), fronting on the water in downtown Bar Harbor. Almost all of the 185 rooms and suites have a water view and semiprivate balconies; some have whirlpool tubs; deluxe rooms have marble baths, and some have large outdoor hot tubs. Some of the one- to three-bedroom suites have whirlpools or fireplaces; penthouse suites have full kitchens. Rates include a continental breakfast buffet. Facilities include two restaurants, outdoor-heated pool and whirlpool, full-service spa, and fitness room.

In town, the family-owned **Villager** (207 Main St., Bar Harbor, 207/288-3211 or 888/383-3211 or winter 207/288-2270), www.barharborvillager.com, $90–140) delivers clean standard motel rooms (air-conditioning, phone, TV, Wi-Fi) with an outdoor pool and friendly service and advice. The location puts all of downtown sights within walking distance, and the Bangor bus stop is here.

Also on the lower end of the budgetary scale are two neighboring motels: **Edenbrook Motel** (96 Eden St., Rte. 3, Bar Harbor, 207/288-4975 or 800/323-7819, www.acadia.net/eden-brook, $70–130), with panoramic views of Frenchman Bay from some rooms, and the wee bit fancier **Highbrook Motel** (94 Eden St.,

Rte. 3, Bar Harbor, 207/288-3591 or 800/338-9688, www.highbrookmotel.com, $79–128). Both are about 1.5 miles from Acadia's main entrance, one mile from downtown, and 500 yards from the ferry servicing Canada.

Downright cheap is **Robbins Motel** (396 Rte. 3, Bar Harbor, 207/288-4659 or 800/858-0769, $58 d), an older motel with 30 small, but clean, queen-bedded rooms (air-conditioning, TV, Wi-Fi) and an outdoor pool.

## Inns and Bed-and-Breakfasts

Few innkeepers have mastered the art of hospitality as well as Roy Kasindorf and Helene Harton, owners of the 【 **Ullikana Bed and Breakfast** (16 The Field, Bar Harbor, 207/288-9552, www.ullikana.com, $180–330), a 10-room, Victorian Tudor inn, built by Alpheus Hardy, Bar Harbor's first "cottager" in 1885. They genuinely enjoy their guests. Helene's a whiz in the kitchen; after one of her multicourse breakfasts, usually served on the water-view patio, you won't be needing lunch. She's also a decorating genius, blending antiques and modern art, vibrant color with soothing hues, folk art and fine art, with a result like a finely tuned orchestra. Roy excels at helping guests select just the right hike, bike route, or other activity. Afternoon refreshments provide a time for guests to gather and share experiences. Ten comfortable rooms all have private baths; many have working fireplaces, and some have private terraces with water views. Helene and Roy also own The Yellow House, next door, with six lovely rooms decorated in old Bar Harbor style and a huge living room filled with antique wicker. They're in a quiet downtown location close to Bar Harbor's Shore Path. French spoken.

Right next door is the fabulously renovated and rejuvenated 【 **Bass Cottage** (14 The Field, P.O. Box 242, Bar Harbor 04609, 207/288-1234 or 866/782-9224, www.basscottage.com, $195–350). Corporate refugees Teri and Jeff Anderholm bought the 26-room 1885 cottage in 2003 and spent a year gutting it, salvaging the best of the old, and blending in new to turn it into a luxurious and stylish 10-room inn. It retains its Victorian bones, yet is most un-Victorian in style. Guest rooms are soothingly decorated with cream and pastel-colored walls and have phones and TV with DVD (a DVD library is available; a godsend on a yucky day); many rooms have fireplaces and whirlpool tubs. The spacious and elegant public rooms—expansive living rooms, cozy library, porches—flow from one to another. Teri puts her culinary degree to use preparing baked goods, fruits, and savory and sweet entrées for breakfast and evening refreshments. A guest pantry is stocked with tea, coffee, and snacks.

Much less pricey and a find for families is the **Seacroft Inn** (18 Albert Meadow, Bar Harbor, 207/288-4669 or 800/824-9694, www.seacroftinn.com, $99–139), well situated just off Main Street and near the Shore Path. All rooms in Bunny and Dave Brown's white, multigabled cottage have air-conditioning, phone, TV, refrigerator, and microwave, and in season, continental breakfast (subtract $5 from the rate if you don't want it). Housekeeping is $10 per day. Some rooms can be joined as family suites. There's also an apartment, available by the week for $1,550.

Energetic Marian Burns, a former math/science teacher, is the reason everything runs smoothly at **Mira Monte Inn** (69 Mount Desert St., Bar Harbor, 207/288-4263 or 800/553-5109, www.miramonte.com, $170–235), close (but not too close) to downtown. Born and raised here, and an avid gardener, Marian's a terrific resource for island exploring. Try to capture her during afternoon wine and cheese, and ask about her experience during the 1947 Bar Harbor fire. And don't miss her collection of antique Bar Harbor hotel photos. The 13 Victorian-style rooms have air-conditioning, cable TV, and either a balcony or fireplace, and some have whirlpool tubs; two efficiency suites and one fully equipped apartment-style unit in a separate building are ideal for families. Early and late in the season, Marian organizes special-rate theme weekends. Rates include an extensive hot-and-cold breakfast buffet.

Matt and Kristi Losquadro, and their three young children, welcome guests to **The Saltair**

**Inn** (1221 West St., Bar Harbor, 207/288-2882, www.saltairinn.com, $225–345), an elegant, yet casual, waterfront bed-and-breakfast in the historical district. Three of the four rooms have water views, one has a two-person whirlpool tub, two have balconies, and all have at least one gas fireplace, TV, and Wi-Fi. A full breakfast is served either in the dining room or on the water-view deck. It's steps from downtown, but really, with a location like this, why leave?

Outside of town in a serene location with fabulous views of Frenchman Bay is Jack and Jeani Ochtera's ❰ **Inn at Bay Ledge** (150 Sand Point Rd., Bar Harbor, summer 207/288-4204 or winter 207/875-3262, www.innatbayledge.com, $150–475), an oasis of calm tucked under towering pines and atop an 80-foot cliff. A long veranda lined with wicker chairs and settees descends to decks, a pool, and on to the lawn, which stretches to the cliff's edge. Stairs descend to a private stone beach below. Almost all guest rooms have water views, some rooms have whirlpool tubs, some private decks. Breakfast is served on the water-view porch.

On a budget? Consider the pleasant but few-frills **Llangolan Inn and Cottages** (865 Rte. 3, Bar Harbor, 207/288-3016, www.llangolan.com), seven miles from downtown. The well-cared-for property includes a B&B and cottages. Five rooms, one with private bath and four sharing two baths, are comfortable and welcoming and go for a bargain $70–80, including a continental breakfast. Also available are basic housekeeping cottages sleeping 2–5, each with kitchenette, TV, and heat ($85–120 d). This property is right on Route 3, so expect traffic noise. Ask for rooms facing the back or for a cottage well away from the road. Even then, you'll probably hear the passing *vroom.*

Another budget choice is the **Otter Creek Inn** (Rte. 3, Otter Creek, 207/288-5151 or 800/845-5852, www.ottercreekme.com, $85–125), a well-maintained complex with a small motel-like inn, an apartment, and cottages. Rooms have minifridge, TV, and include continental breakfast. A two-bedroom apartment rents for $125–175; two housekeeping cabins are $95–125. There are laundry facili-

ties, and all accommodations are adjacent to the Otter Creek Market, which has everything from camping supplies to lobster and wine.

## Hostels

The **Bar Harbor/Mount Desert Island Hostel** (321 Main St., P.O. Box 32, Bar Harbor 04609, 207/288-5587, www.barharborhostel.com), in a beautifully renovated building on the edge of town, has dorms for men and women ($25 pp), a family room ($80), and a well-equipped kitchen; outside are an organic garden (planted by College of the Atlantic students), where you can help yourself to the produce, and tent platforms ($10 pp). No smoking, no liquor, no credit cards, midnight curfew. Reservations (best by mail) are essential, as this is a popular location. It's open in winter by chance or reservation.

## Seasonal Rentals

Contact **Lynam Real Estate** (227 Main St., P.O. Box C, Bar Harbor 04609, 207/288-3334, www.lynams.com) or **Maine Island Properties** (P.O. Box 1025, Mount Desert 04660, 207/244-4308, fax 207/244-0588, www.maineislandproperties.com) for listings of houses/cottages available by the week or month.

## FOOD

You won't go hungry in Bar Harbor, and you won't find chain fast-food places. The island's best collection of good, inexpensive restaurants, most open year-round, are along Rodick Street, from Reel Pizza down to Rosalie's, which actually fronts on Cottage Street. You'll find a good ethnic mix here, from Mexican to Thai to Italian. For sit-down restaurants, make reservations as far in advance as possible.

## Local Flavors

Only a masochist could bypass **Ben and Bill's Chocolate Emporium** (66 Main St., Bar Harbor, 207/288-3281 or 800/806-3281), a long-running taste-treat-cum-experience in downtown Bar Harbor. The homemade candies and more than 50 ice-cream flavors (including a dubious lobster flavor) are nothing short of outrageous; the whole place smells like the inside of a chocolate truffle. It opens daily at 10 A.M., with closing dependent upon season and crowds, but usually late into the evening.

If ice cream is your passion, another must-stop is **Mt. Desert Ice Cream** (325 Main St. and 7 Firefly La., Bar Harbor, 207/460-5515) for outrageous flavors.

Probably the least-expensive lunch or ice-cream option in town is **West End Drug Co.** (105 Main St., Bar Harbor, 207/288-3318), where you can get grilled cheese sandwiches ($1.40), PBJ, and other old-fashioned white-bread basics as well as frappes (a Maineism—frappes are made with ice cream, milk shakes aren't) and sundaes at the fountain.

Bar Harbor has a super natural-foods store, the **Alternative Community Market** (16 Mount Desert St., Bar Harbor, 207/288-8225), where you can buy pastries, sandwiches, panini, get an espresso, or even fruit smoothies from the organic juice bar. There's limited seating indoors and on the deck. It's open 7 A.M.–10:30 P.M. daily.

The **Eden Farmer's Market** operates out of the YMCA parking lot off Lower Main Street in Bar Harbor 9 A.M.–noon each Sunday Mother's Day–late October. You'll find fresh meats and produce, local cheeses and maple syrup, bread, honey, preserves, even prepared Asian foods.

**J. H. Butterfield Co.** (152 Main St., Bar Harbor, 207/288-3386) is a fine place to pick up fixings for a fancy picnic.

Efficient, friendly, cafeteria-style service makes **EPI Sub and Pizza Shop** (8 Cottage St., Bar Harbor, 207/288-5853, 10 A.M.–8 P.M. daily, to 8:30 P.M. July and Aug.) an excellent choice for picnics or a quick break from sightseeing. The dozen-plus sub-sandwich choices at EPI's (short for epicurean) are bargains (try the Cadillac); it also serves salads, pizza, and Italian dinners. If the weather closes in, there are always the pinball machines in the back room. No credit cards.

For a light, inexpensive breakfast or lunch, you can't go wrong at ◖ **Morning Glory Bakery** (39 Rodick St., Bar Harbor, 207/288-

3041, 7 A.M.–4 P.M. Mon.–Fri., 8 A.M.–1 P.M. Sat.). Espresso and other fancy coffees, fresh-squeezed juices, smoothies, and fresh-baked goodies are all made from scratch. Planning a day in the park? Call ahead for a boxed lunch.

When it comes to pub-grub favorites, such as burgers and fish sandwiches, **The Thirsty Whale Tavern** (40 Cottage St., Bar Harbor, 207/288-9335) does it right; it's open for lunch and dinner daily.

## Picnic Fare

Adeena and Chris Fisher concentrate their culinary efforts on **Not Quite the Corner Cafe** (65 Main St., Bar Harbor, 207/288-1006, 10:30 A.M.–4 P.M. daily). The tiny shop that's—you guessed it—one store up from the intersection with Cottage Street is an excellent source for take-out hot or cold sandwiches, wraps, soups, side salads, and treats, all a tad above the ordinary in creative flair.

Also earning high marks is **Michelle's Brown Bag Cafe** (164 Main St., Bar Harbor, 207/288-5858) for its paninis, salads, and sandwiches. Eat in or take it to go.

Far less fancy is **Adelmann's Deli** (224 Main St., Bar Harbor, 207/288-0455, 6 A.M.–3 P.M. daily). Build-your-own egg sandwiches are $3.49; build-your-own lunch sandwiches are $6.75. Choose from a variety of breads, Boar's Head brand meats and cheeses, veggies, condiments, and more.

If you happen to be on Route 102 in the Town Hill area around lunchtime, plan to pick up picnic fare at **Mother's Kitchen** (Rte. 102, Town Hill, Bar Harbor, 207/288-4403). The plain, miniscule building next to Salsbury's Organic Garden Center (look for the Real Good Food sign) is deceiving—it's been operating since 1995 and turns out 20 different sandwiches, as well as deli salads, scones, breakfast sandwiches, great cookies, and pies. It'll even pack up box lunches. Calling ahead would save time, but the whimsically named sandwich combos are tough to describe over the phone. (How about Charlie Noble—homemade chicken salad with walnuts and tarragon, cranberry sauce, and lettuce on onion walnut dill bread.) If you're desperately hungry, there are a few picnic tables outside, but you can find better picnic settings elsewhere. Mother's Kitchen is open 8 A.M.–2 P.M. Monday–Saturday mid-April–October.

## Brewpubs and Microbreweries

Bar Harbor's longest-lived brewpub is the **Lompoc Café** (36 Rodick St., Bar Harbor, 207/288-9392, www.lompoccafe.com, 11:30 A.M.–9 P.M. daily late Apr.–mid-Dec.), serving creative lunches and dinners ($8–19). How about a lobster and avocado quesadilla? After 9 P.M., there's just beer and thin-crust pizza until about 1 A.M. The congenial café has a beer garden, a bocce court, and open mic night Thursdays and live entertainment (blues, bluegrass, and jazz) Fridays and Saturdays May–October.

Lompoc's signature Bar Harbor Real Ale and five or six others are brewed by the **Atlantic Brewing Company** (15 Knox Rd., Town Hill, in the upper section of the island, 207/288-2337 or 800/475-5417, www.atlanticbrewing.com). Free brewery tours, including tastings, are given at 2, 3, and 4 P.M. daily Memorial Day–Columbus Day. Also based here is **Mainely Meat Bar-B-Q** (207/288-9200), offering daily specials and an all-you-can-eat barbecue on Saturdays.

**Bar Harbor Brewing Company and Soda Works** (135 Otter Creek Rd., Rte. 3, Bar Harbor, 207/288-4592), begun in 1990 by Tod and Suzi Foster as a mom-and-pop operation, remains a small, friendly, hands-on enterprise producing five kinds of beer and ale in a basement microbrewery. Start off at the log-cabin tasting room/gift shop, where kids can sample Old Fashioned Bar Harbor Root Beer. Free tours begin every 20 minutes 3:30–5 P.M. Tuesday–Friday late June–August. The brewery is 4.5 miles south of downtown Bar Harbor.

## Casual Family-Friendly Dining

Once a Victorian boarding house and later a 1920s speakeasy, **Galyn's Galley** (17 Main St., Bar Harbor, 207/288-9706, www.galynsbarharbor.com, 11:30 A.M.–10 P.M. daily March–Nov.)

has been a popular eatery since 1986. Lots of plants, modern decor, reliable service, a great downtown location, and several indoor and outdoor dining areas contribute to the loyal clientele. The cuisine is consistently good (dinner entrées $15–25). Reservations advisable.

Set back from the road behind a garden is the very popular **McKays Public House** (231 Main St., Bar Harbor, 207/288-2002, www.mckayspublichouse.com, 11:30 A.M.–3 P.M. and 5–10 P.M. daily), a comfortable pub with seating indoors in small dining rooms or at the bar or outdoors in the garden. Classic pub fare includes Reubens, shepherd's pie with lamb, burgers, and fish-and-chips ($8–10). At dinner, fancier entrées, such as coq au vin and seafood risotto, are also available, most in the $14–23 range.

Good food at a fair price reels them into **Poor Boy's Gourmet** (300 Main St., Bar Harbor, 207/288-4148, www.poorboysgourmet.com, opens at 4:30 P.M. daily). Until 6 P.M. it serves an Early Bird menu with about a half-dozen entrées as well as another 10 all-you-can-eat pasta choices for $8.95. The price jumps just a bit after that, with most entrées running $11–15. There's even a lobster feast for $21.

Fifties memorabilia and old toys fill **Route 66 Restaurant** (21 Cottage St., Bar Harbor, 207/288-3708, www.bhroute66.com, 7 A.M.–8 P.M. or so daily), a fun restaurant that's a real hit with kids (check out the train running around just below the ceiling). There's nothing fancy here, but it has a wide-ranging menu that includes sandwiches, burgers, pizza, steak, chicken, seafood, and kids' choices. Dinner choices run around $8–18, breakfast $3–7, lunch $7–12. The Reece family, various members of which run other restaurants on the island, operates it.

An unscientific but reliable local survey gives the best-pizza ribbon to **Rosalie's Pizza and Italian Restaurant** (46 Cottage St., Bar Harbor, 207/288-5666, opens 11:30 A.M. daily), where the Wurlitzer jukebox churns out tunes from the 1950s. This family-owned standard gets high marks for consistency with its homemade pizza (in four sizes or by the slice), calzones, and subs—lots of vegetarian options. If you need something a bit heartier, try the Italian dinners—spaghetti, eggplant parmigiana, and others—all around $7, including a garlic roll. Beer and wine are available.

## Eclectic Fare

Escape the humdrum at ◖ **Café This Way** (14 Mt. Desert St., Bar Harbor, 207/288-4483, www.cafethisway.com), where creativity reigns but isn't overdone—consider crab cakes with tequila-lime sauce or Thai-grilled salmon. The breakfast menu is a genuine wake-up call; try Green Eggs and Sam. Dinner entrées are in the $14–24 range; the wine list is very selective and the desserts are outstanding. It's open for breakfast (7–11 A.M. Mon.–Sat., 8 A.M.–1 P.M. Sun.) and for dinner (5:30–9 P.M. daily).

Another breakfast or lunch treat is **2 Cats** (130 Cottage St., Bar Harbor, 207/288-2808 or 800/355-2828, www.2catsbarharbor.com, 7 A.M.–1 P.M. daily), where you can dine inside or on the patio. Three upstairs rooms are $165–195, with breakfast, of course.

**Town Hall Bistro** (Rte. 102 and Crooked Rd., Bar Harbor, 207/288-1011, 5:30–9:30 P.M. Tues.–Sat.) promises interesting, creative cuisine served with a sense of humor, and it delivers. Possibilities include small and large plates, making it easy to please mixed appetites, and menu items fluctuate with what's fresh and available. The small dining area is simply adorned.

## Ethnic and Vegetarian Fare

For Thai food, **Siam Orchard** (30 Rodick St., Bar Harbor, 207/288-9669, 5–9 P.M. daily, to 9:30 P.M. July and Aug.) gets the locals' nod. House specials run $14–17, curries and noodle dishes, such as pad thai, run $8–14 at dinner. There are plenty of choices for vegetarians. Beer and wine only. It's open all year.

Sharing the same building is **Gringo's** (30 Rodick St., Bar Harbor, 207/288-2326, 11 A.M.– 9 P.M. Mon.–Sat., noon–8 P.M. Sun.), a Mexican hole-in-the-wall specializing in take-out burritos, wraps, handmade salsas, and smoothies, with almost everything less than $7.50. For a real kick, don't miss the jalapeño brownies.

There's a good chance **Eden** (28 West St.,

Bar Harbor, 207/288-4422, www.barharbor-vegetarian.com, 5–9:30-ish P.M. daily) could make a vegetarian out of even the most diehard meat lover. This small restaurant is dedicated to using organic ingredients from area farms and preparing vegan entrées ($11–18).

For "American fine dining with Latin flair," head to ◖ **Havana** (318 Main St., Bar Harbor, 207/288-2822, www.havanamaine.com, 5–10 P.M. daily May–late Oct., Wed.–Sat. the rest of the year), where the innovative, Cubanesque menu (entrées $16–35) changes almost daily to take advantage of what's locally available. Inside, bright orange walls and white tablecloths set a tone that's equally festive and accomplished. It's easy to make a meal of appetizers here.

It's back! Longtime favorite **Miguel's** (51 Rodick St., Bar Harbor, 207/288-5117, 4:30–9 P.M. daily) disappeared for a few years, but it's back serving the usual Mexican dishes along with a few surprises.

Italian with pizzazz is served in both half and full portions (yay!) at **Guinness and Porcelli's** (191 Main St., Bar Harbor, 207/288-0300, 4:30 P.M.–close daily). Unusual pizzas, such as lobster or wild boar, creative soups and salads, and entrées are a winning combo. The risotto *al arragosta,* made with lobster, sweet peas, and leeks, is a keeper, as is the butternut squash ravioli.

## Fancy to Fine Dining

The view's the thing at the Bar Harbor Inn's **Reading Room Restaurant** (Newport Dr., Bar Harbor, 207/288-3351, www.barharborinn.com); request a window seat. Once the stuffy Bar Harbor Reading Room, a gentlemen's club, the dining room still has a sweeping curve of windows overlooking Bar Island and Frenchman Bay. Dinner is available, but opt for the Sunday brunch buffet (11:30 A.M.–2:30 P.M., $26 adults, $13 kids).

The stylish **Bar Harbor Club** (111 West St., 207/288-5033, 7–11 A.M. and 5–10 P.M. daily) was the playground of the Rockefellers, Pulitzers, Astors, Cornings, and other wealthy and famous residents during Bar Harbor's heyday. It survived the fire and hung on until

1989 and then sat abandoned and deteriorating for years. In 2005, after a multimillion dollar renovation, it reopened under the same ownership as the adjacent Harborside Hotel. Once again, it's providing elegant, harbor-view dining (as long as there isn't an events tent set up on the lawn; ask before you book if the view is important to you). Entrées, such as pan-roasted wild halibut and roast spring lamb, range $22–32. Ask for a table away from the large TV in the Vanderbilt Lounge.

Fresh, fresh, fresh seafood—that's what you'll find at **Maggie's Restaurant** (6 Summer St., Bar Harbor, 207/288-9007, www.maggies-barharbor.com, 5–9:30 P.M. Mon.–Sat. June–Oct.). The restaurant grew out of owner Maggie O'Neil's experiences as a fishmonger, and much of the equally fresh produce comes from Maggie's own farm. Entrées, such as Maine seafood Provençal or bronzed cod with Latin lime tartar sauce, run $16–25. Hint: The lobster crepes are renowned. Soft music and good service complement the dining experience.

Five miles south of Bar Harbor in the village of Otter Creek (which itself is in the town of Mount Desert) is the inauspicious-looking ( **Burning Tree** (Rte. 3, Otter Creek, 207/288-9331, 5–10 P.M. Wed.–Mon. late June–early Oct., also closed Mon. after Labor Day), which is anything but nondescript inside. Chef/owners Allison Martin and Elmer Beal Jr. have created one of Mount Desert Island's best restaurants. Bright and airy, with about 16 tables crowded in three areas, it serves a casually chic crowd. Reservations are essential in summer. Specialties are imaginative seafood entrées—such as curry pecan flounder, cioppino—and vegetarian dishes made from organic produce. Scallop kebabs have *lots* of scallops, the specialty crab cakes are 90 percent crabmeat, and edible flowers garnish the entrées ($18–25). The homemade breads and desserts are delicious. At the height of summer, service can be a bit rushed and the kitchen runs out of popular entrées. Solution: Plan to eat early; it's worth it.

## Lobster

Lobster, lobster, and more lobster—that's what

ACADIA REGION

© HILARY NANGLE

Eden Farmer's Market in Bar Harbor

you'll find at **The Lobster Claw** (54 West St., Bar Harbor, 207/288-4489, 11 A.M.–8:30 P.M.), a take-out shack with a few tables. Sure there are other choices on the menu, including organic and vegetarian specials and a kiddie menu, but the lobster served here is fresh picked and never frozen. Lobster rolls come in four varieties, and there's always the lobsta-ka-bobsta, a grilled lobster meat kebab with accompaniments. Ask about local delivery.

## INFORMATION AND SERVICES
### Information
The Bar Harbor Chamber of Commerce (1201 Bar Harbor Rd./Rte. 3, Trenton, P.O. Box 158, Bar Harbor 04609, 207/288-5103 or 888/540-9990, www.barharbormaine.com) is open daily in summer, weekdays off-season. Late May–mid-October, you'll find a "branch" chamber office at Harbor Place, 1 West Street, next to the town pier. (Some Bar Harbor information is also available at the Thompson Island Information Center, just after you cross the bridge from Trenton toward Mount Desert Island.) Bar Harbor's annual visitors information booklet usually is off the presses in January—a big help in making early plans for a summer vacation.

Check out Jesup Memorial Library (34 Mount Desert St., Bar Harbor, 207/288-4245, www.jesup.lib.me.us).

### Public Restrooms
Downtown Bar Harbor has public restrooms in the Harbor Place complex at the town pier, in the municipal building (fire/police station) across from the village green, and on the School Street side of the athletic field, where there is RV parking. Restrooms are also at the Mount Desert Island Hospital and the International Ferry Terminal.

### Parking
Make it easy on yourself and help improve the air quality and reduce stress levels by leaving your car at your lodging, or if day-tripping at the chamber's visitors center on Route 3 in Trenton, and taking the Island Explorer.

RVs are not allowed to park near the town pier; designated RV parking is alongside the athletic field, Lower Main and Park Streets, about eight blocks from the center of town.

# Northeast and Seal Harbors

Ever since the late 19th century, the upper crust from the City of Brotherly Love has been summering in and around Northeast Harbor. Sure, they also show up in other parts of Maine, but it's hard not to notice the preponderance of Pennsylvania license plates surrounding Northeast Harbor's elegant "cottages" mid-July–mid-August. (In the last decade or so, the Pennsylvania plates have been joined by growing numbers from Washington, D.C., New York, and Texas.)

Actually, even though Northeast Harbor is a well-known name with special cachet, it isn't even an official township; it's a zip-coded village within the town of Mount Desert, which collects the breathtaking property taxes and doles out the municipal services.

The attractive boutiques and eateries in Northeast Harbor's small downtown area cater to a casually posh clientele, while the well-protected harbor attracts a tony crowd of yachties. For their convenience, a palm-size annual directory, *The Redbook,* discreetly lists owners' summer residences and winter addresses—but no phone numbers.

## SIGHTS
### Somes Sound
As you head toward Northeast Harbor on Route 198 from the northern end of Mount Desert Island, you'll begin seeing cliff-lined Somes Sound on your right. This glacier-sculpted fjord juts five miles into the interior of Mount Desert Island from its mouth, between Northeast and

## THE MAINE SEA COAST MISSION

Remote islands and other isolated communities along Maine's rugged coastline may still have a church, but few have a full-time minister; fewer yet have a health-care provider. Yet these communities aren't entirely shut off from either preaching or medical assistance.

Since 1905, the Maine Sea Coast Mission, nondenominational, nonprofit organization rooted in a Christian ministry, has offered a lifeline to these communities. The mission, based in Bar Harbor (127 West St., 207/288-5097 or 888/824-7258), serves nearly 2,800 people on eight different islands, including Frenchboro, the Cranberries, Swans, and Isle au Haut, as well as others living in remote coastal locations on the mainland. Its numerous much-needed services include a Christmas program; in-school, after-school, and summer-school programs; emergency financial assistance; food assistance; a thrift shop, ministers to island and coastal communities; scholarships; and health services.

Many of these services are delivered via the mission's *Sunbeam V*, a 75-foot diesel boat that has no limitation on when it can travel and few on where it can travel. In winter, it even serves as an icebreaker, clearing harbors and protecting boats from ice damage.

A nurse and a minister usually travel on the *Sunbeam*. The minister may conduct services on the island, or on the boat, which also functions as a gathering place for fellowship, meals, and meetings. The minister also reaches out to those in need, marginalized, or ill, and often helps with island funerals. Onboard telemedicine equipment enables the nurse to provide much-needed health care, including screening clinics for diabetes, cholesterol, and prostate and skin cancer; flu and pneumonia vaccines; and tetanus shots.

During your travels in the Acadia region, you might see the *Sunbeam* homeported in Northeast Harbor or on its rounds. If you want to learn more about or support this worthwhile organization, visit www.seacoast-mission.org.

Southwest Harbors. Watch for the right-hand turn for Sargent Drive (no RVs allowed) and follow the lovely, granite-lined route along the east side of the sound. Halfway along, a marker explains the geology of this natural fjord, the only one on the Eastern Seaboard. There aren't many pullouts en route, and traffic can be fairly thick in midsummer, but don't miss it. An ideal way to appreciate Somes Sound is from the water—sign up for an excursion out of Northeast or Southwest Harbor.

### ◀ Asticou Azalea Garden and Thuya Garden

If you have the slightest interest in gardens (even if you don't, for that matter), allow time for Northeast Harbor's two marvelous public gardens. Information about both is available from the local chamber of commerce. If gardens are extra-high on your priority list, inquire locally about visiting the private Rockefeller garden, accessible on a very limited basis.

One of Maine's best spring showcases is the Asticou Azalea Garden, a 2.3-acre pocket where about 70 varieties of azaleas, rhododendrons, and laurels—many from the classic Reef Point garden of famed landscape designer Beatrix Farrand—burst into bloom. When Charles K. Savage, beloved former innkeeper of the Asticou Inn, learned the Reef Point garden was being undone in 1956, he went into high gear to find funding and managed to rescue the azaleas and provide them with the gorgeous setting they have today, across the road and around the corner from the inn. Oriental serenity is the key—with a Japanese sand garden, stone lanterns, granite outcrops, pink-gravel paths, and a tranquil pond. Try to visit early in the season, early in the morning, to savor the effect. The garden is on Route 198, at the northern edge of Northeast Harbor, immediately north of the junction with Peabody Drive (Rte. 3). Watch for a tiny sign on the left (if you're coming from the north) marking access to the parking area. Asticou is open sunrise–sunset daily May–November, and blossoming occurs here May–August, but prime time for azaleas is roughly mid-May–mid-June. A small pillar box suggests a $1 donation, and another box contains an attractively designed garden guide ($2). Pets are not allowed in the garden. Take Island Explorer Route 5/Jordan Pond or Route 6/Brown Mountain and request a stop.

Behind a carved wooden gate on a forested hillside not far from Asticou lies an enchanted garden also designed by Charles K. Savage and inspired by Beatrix Farrand. Special features of Thuya Garden are perennial borders, sculpted shrubbery, and Oriental touches. On a misty summer day, when few visitors appear, the colors are brilliant. Adjacent to the garden is **Thuya Lodge** (207/276-5130), former summer cottage of Joseph Curtis, donor of this awesome municipal park. The lodge, with an extensive botanical library and quiet

Bear Island, at the mouth of Somes Sound, is within Acadia National Park and is best viewed from the water.

© HILARY NANGLE

rooms for reading, is open 10 A.M.–4:30 P.M. Monday–Saturday and noon–4:30 P.M. Sunday late June–Labor Day. The garden is open 7 A.M.–7 P.M. daily May 1–October 31. A collection box next to the front gate requests a $5 per adult donation. To reach Thuya, continue on Route 3 beyond Asticou Azalea Garden and watch for the Asticou Terraces parking area (no RVs, two-hour limit) on the right. Cross the road and climb the Asticou Terraces Trail (0.4 mile) to the garden. Or drive 0.2 mile beyond the Route 3 parking area, watching for a minuscule Thuya Garden sign on the left. Go half a mile up the steep, narrow and curving driveway to the parking area. Take Island Explorer Route 5/Jordan Pond and request a stop.

After you've visited Thuya Garden, open the back gate, where you'll see a sign for the **Eliot Mountain Trail,** a 1.4-mile moderately difficult round-trip (lots of exposed roots). Near the summit, Northeast Harbor spreads out before you. If you're here in August, sample the wild blueberries. Much of the Eliot Mountain Trail is on private land, so stay on the path and be respectful of private property.

## Petite Plaisance

On Northeast Harbor's quiet South Shore Road, Petite Plaisance is a special-interest museum commemorating noted Belgian-born author and college professor Marguerite Yourcenar (pen name of Marguerite de Crayencour), the first woman elected to the prestigious Académie Française. From the early 1950s to 1987, Petite Plaisance was her home, and it's hard to believe she's no longer here; her intriguing possessions and presence fill the two-story house—of particular interest to Yourcenar devotees. Free, hour-long tours of the first floor are given in French or English, depending on visitors' preferences. (French-speaking visitors often make pilgrimages here.) The house is open for tours daily June 15–August 31. No children under 12 are allowed. Call 207/276-3940 9 A.M.–4 P.M. at least a day ahead for an appointment and directions, or write: Petite Plaisance Trust, P.O. Box 403, Northeast Harbor 04662. Yourcenar admirers should request

Asticou Azalea Garden may be small, but it's a masterpiece.

cial floats at the end of the concrete municipal pier on Sea Street.

### Sea Princess

The 75-foot *Sea Princess* (207/276-5352, www.acadiainfo.com/seaprincess.htm) carries visitors as well as an Acadia National Park naturalist on a 2.5-hour morning trip around the mouth of Somes Sound and out to Little Cranberry Island (Islesford) for a 50-minute stopover. The boat leaves Northeast Harbor at 10 A.M. daily mid-May to mid-October ($25). A narrated afternoon trip departs at 1 P.M. on the same route. A scenic 1.5-hour Somes Sound cruise departs at 3:45 P.M. daily late June–early September. The same months, two sunset cruises are offered. The three-hour sunset/dinner cruise departs for the Islesford Dock Restaurant on Little Cranberry (Islesford) at 5:15 P.M. Dinner is on your own at the restaurant. A 1.5-hour sunset cruise of Somes Sounds departs at 7 P.M. Cost for all tours is $20–25 adult, $15 children 5–12, $5 for children under 5. Reservations are advisable for all trips, although even that provides no guarantee, since the cruises require a rather hefty 15-passenger minimum. Arrive at least one half hour before departure to buy tickets at the booth next to the harbormaster's office, at the head of the municipal pier.

directions to Brookside Cemetery in Somesville, seven miles away, where she is buried.

### Great Harbor Maritime Museum

Annual exhibits focusing on the maritime heritage of the Mount Desert Island area are held in the small, eclectic Great Harbor Maritime Museum (125 Main St., Northeast Harbor, 207/276-5262, 10 A.M.–5 P.M. Tues.–Sat. late June–Labor Day, plus weekends in Sept. and Oct., $3), housed in the old village fire station and municipal building. ("Great Harbor" refers to the Somes Sound area—Northeast, Southwest, and Seal Harbors, as well as the Cranberry Isles.) Yachting, coastal trade, and fishing receive special emphasis. Special programs and exhibits are held during the summer.

## RECREATION

Northeast Harbor is the starting point for a couple of boat services headed for the Cranberry Isles. (Other boats depart from Southwest Harbor.) The vessels leave from the commer-

## SHOPPING

Upscale shops, galleries, and boutiques, with clothing, artworks, housewares, antiques, and antiquarian books, line both sides of Main Street, making for intriguing browsing and expensive buying (but be sure to check the sale rooms of the clothing shops for bona fide bargains). The season is short, though, with some shops open only in July and August.

One must-visit is **Shaw Contemporary Jewelry** (100 Main St., 207/276-5000 or 877/276-5001, www.shawjewelry.com). Besides the spectacular silver and gold beachstone jewelry created by Rhode Island School of Design alumnus Sam Shaw, the work of more than 100 other jewelers is displayed exquisitely. Plus there are sculptures, Asian art, and rotating art exhibits. It all leads back toward a lovely, light-filled garden. Prices are in the stratosphere, but appropriately so. As one well-dressed customer was overhead sighing to her companion: "If I had only one jewelry store to go to in my entire life, this would be it." The gallery is open all year, with a varying schedule depending on the season.

# ENTERTAINMENT
## Mount Desert Festival of Chamber Music

Since 1964, the Mount Desert Festival of Chamber Music (207/276-3988, www.mtdesertfestival.org) has presented concerts. Concerts are staged in the century-old Neighborhood House on Main Street at 8:15 P.M. Tuesdays mid-July–mid-August. Past musicians have included the Borromeo String Quartet and the Miami String Quartet. Tickets ($20 general admission; $10 student section) are available at the Neighborhood House box office on Mondays and Tuesdays during the concert season or by phone reservation.

# ACCOMMODATIONS
## Inns

If money's no object and you're yearning for a classic, old-timey experience, spring for the **Asticou Inn** (Rte. 3, P.O. Box 337, Northeast Harbor 04662, 207/276-3344 or 800/258-3373, www.asticou.com). Do splurge; less-pricey rooms just don't make the grade. Built in 1883 and refurbished periodically, the classic harbor-view inn has 31 second-, third-, and fourth-floor rooms and suites in the main building, plus 16 rooms and suites in several more modern cottages. Facilities include an excellent restaurant, clay tennis courts, outdoor pool, and access to the Northeast Harbor Golf Club. The inn is open mid-May–late October. July and August rates are $225–240 d, including continental breakfast. Try to plan a late-May or early-June visit; you're practically on top of the Asticou Azalea Garden, Thuya Garden is a short walk away, and the rates are lowest ($130–215 d). The Asticou is a popular wedding venue, so if you're looking for a quiet weekend, check the inn's wedding schedule before you book a room.

# Bed-and-Breakfasts

Less pricey and far less formal, **The Maison Suisse Inn** (144 Main St., Northeast Harbor, 207/276-5223 or 800/624-7668, www.maisonsuisse.com, $185–375) is a lovely Shingle-style inn set off the street behind a rustic garden. Ten rooms are in the main inn, another five in the guest cottage behind it. All have private baths, TV, phone, and Wi-Fi; some have a fireplace. Breakfast is provided at a restaurant across the street.

The casual elegance of a bygone era still exists at **Grey Rock Inn** (Rte. 3/198, Northeast Harbor, summer 207/276-9360, winter 207/244-4437, www.greyrockinn.com, $185–375, mid-May–late Oct.), an antiques-filled 1910 mansion with to-die-for views over Northeast Harbor to the outer islands. Guest rooms are comfortable and large; many have fireplaces. Common rooms, most with fireplaces, flow from one to another. Trails lace the property's seven acres, which are bordered by Acadia National Park on two sides. Head out for a hike, perhaps to the summit of Noumbega Mountain, or stroll down the street to downtown Northeast Harbor. Rates include a full breakfast. Note: The owners can be eccentric.

In 1888, architect Fred Savage designed the two Shingle-style buildings that make up the three-story **Harbourside Inn** (Main St., P.O. Box 178, Northeast Harbor, 207/276-3272, www.harboursideinn.com, $125–295, mid-June–mid-Sept.). The Sweet family has preserved the old-fashioned feel by decorating the 17 spacious rooms and three suites with antiques, yet modern amenities include some kitchenettes and phones. Most rooms have working fireplaces. A continental breakfast is served. Trails to Norumbega Mountain and Upper Hadlock Pond leave from the back of the property. Do note that through the years, the waterfront property has been sold so despite the inn's name, only glimpses of the harbor can be seen.

## Motel

Although it's a bit dated—every room has two double beds—and the decor is uninspired, you can't beat the location of the **Kimball Terrace Inn** (10 Huntington Rd., P.O. Box 1030, Northeast Harbor 04662, 207/276-3383 or 800/454-6225, www.kimballterrace-inn.com, $167–187, open Apr.–late Oct.). The three-story motel overlooks the harbor, and every room has a patio or private balcony (ask for a harbor-facing room), TV, phone, and air-conditioning. Do bring binoculars for yacht-spotting. The motel has a pool, a restaurant serving three meals daily, lounge, and is a short walk to Northeast Harbor's downtown. It is a popular wedding venue, so ask if there are any groups in-house before you book if that's a concern. Early and late season, rates plummet, and there are especially wallet-friendly packages.

## FOOD
### Local Flavors

In the **Pine Tree Market** (121 Main St., Northeast Harbor, 207/276-3335, 7 A.M.–7 P.M. Mon.–Sat., 8 A.M.–6 P.M. Sun.), you'll find gourmet goodies, a huge wine selection, resident butcher, fresh fish, deli, homemade breads, pastries, sandwiches, and salads.

Pop into **Full Belli Deli** (Sea St., Northeast Harbor, 207/276-4299, 8 A.M.–4 P.M. Mon.–Sat., to 2 P.M. Sun.) for soups, fat sandwiches, and breakfast fare.

The **Northeast Harbor Farmers Market** is set up 9 A.M.–noon each Thursday from June well into October across from the Kimball Terrace Inn on Huntington Road. Look for the usuals, as well as cheeses, cider, maple syrup, breads and cookies, yarns and related fiber products, and prepared Asian foods.

### Casual Dining

Real local color and crab cakes and crab sandwiches are *the best* at the **Docksider** (14 Sea St., Northeast Harbor, 207/276-3965, 11 A.M.–9 P.M. daily, summer only), a low-key, family-friendly, unassuming, hole-in-the-wall place inevitably jammed with devoted locals

and summer folk. Just up the hill from the chamber office, the Docksider has an outside deck, plus a couple of veteran (since forever) waitresses, no view, and a reputation far and wide. Prices reflect market rates, with choices beginning around $8, and more popular ones in the $14–20 range. If you're smitten, buy one of the T-shirts, featuring an upright lobster announcing, "Frankly, I don't give a clam." Note: Early-bird specials and a 10 percent discount apply 4:30–6 P.M.

Tucked in a shady corner of a parking lot behind Shaw's Jewelry is a taste of the Mediterranean. **Bassa Cocina de Tapeo** (5 Old Firehouse La., Northeast Harbor, 207/276-0555, www.bassacocina.com), a perfect choice for a hot, sultry night, lets you pick and choose from a tapas menu ($3–12) or splurge on entrées ($15–35), all representing the flavors of the Mediterranean: Spain, France, Italy, and Morocco (hint: The paella is divine). A martini and wine bar serves grappas, sherries, and Mediterranean wines. Dine inside or on the patio. It's open for lunch and dinner daily in summer, dinner only in spring and fall.

Casual, yet sophisticated, **Redbird Provisions** (11 Sea St., Northeast Harbor, 207/276-3006, 11:30 A.M.–2:30 P.M. and 6–9 P.M. Wed.–Sat., www.redbirdprovisions.com) is the perfect neighborhood restaurant—if your neighbors are the yachting type. Lunch and dinner ($10–26) are served in a renovated home that also houses Bella Spa.

### Fine Dining

The elegant, mural-lined dining room at the **Asticou Inn** (Rte. 3, 207/276-3344 or 800/258-3373, 7–9 A.M., 11:30 A.M.–2 P.M., and 6–9 P.M. daily) is open to the public for breakfast, lunch, Sunday brunch, and dinner ($27–35). Lunch is served on the harborside deck, with serene views over Northeast Harbor. Jackets and ties are advised for dinner.

## INFORMATION AND SERVICES
### Information

The Chamber Information Bureau (also called the Yachtsmen's Building) of the Mount

Desert Chamber of Commerce (18 Harbor Rd., P.O. Box 675, Northeast Harbor 04662, 207/276-5040, 8 A.M.–5 P.M. daily mid-June–mid-Oct.) covers the villages of Somesville, Northeast Harbor, Seal Harbor, Otter Creek, Pretty Marsh, Hall Quarry, and Beech Hill. Request a free copy of the annual *Mount Desert Chamber of Commerce Village/Island Guide and Northeast Harbor Port Directory.*

## Public Restrooms

Restrooms are at the end of the building housing the Great Harbor Maritime Museum, in the town office on Sea Street, and at the harbor.

## GETTING AROUND

Northeast Harbor is serviced by Route 5/Jordan Pond and Route 6/Brown Mountain of the Island Explorer bus system.

# The Quiet Side

Southwest Harbor considers itself the hub of Mount Desert Island's "quiet side." In summer, its tiny downtown district is probably the busiest spot on the whole western side of the island (west of Somes Sound), but that's not saying a great deal. "Southwest" has the feel of a settled community, a year-round flavor that Bar Harbor sometimes lacks. And it competes with the best in the scenery department. The Southwest Harbor area serves as a very convenient base for exploring Acadia National Park, as well as the island's less-crowded villages and offshore Swans Island, Frenchboro, and the Cranberry Isles.

The quirky nature of the island's four town boundaries creates complications in trying to categorize various island segments. Officially, the town of Southwest Harbor includes only the villages of Manset and Seawall, but nearby is the precious (really!) hamlet of Somesville. The Somesville National Historic District, with its distinctive arched white footbridge, is especially appealing, but traffic gets congested here along Route 102, so rather than just rubbernecking, plan to stop and walk around.

The "quiet side" of the island becomes even more quiet as you round the southwestern edge into Tremont, which includes the villages of Bernard, Bass Harbor, home of **Bass Harbor Head Light** and ferry services to offshore islands, and Seal Cove. Tremont occupies the southwesternmost corner of Mount Desert Island. It's about as far as you can get from

Bar Harbor, but the free Island Explorer bus service, Route 7/Southwest Harbor, comes through here regularly.

Be sure to drive or bike these small villages. Views are fabulous, the pace is slow, and you'll feel as if you've stumbled upon "the real Maine."

## SIGHTS
### Wendell Gilley Museum

In the center of Southwest Harbor, the Gilley Museum (Herrick Rd., corner of Rte. 102, Southwest Harbor, 207/244-7555, www.wendellgilleymuseum.org, 10 A.M.–4 P.M. Tues.–Sun. June–Oct., to 5 P.M. in July and Aug., Fri.–Sun. in May, Nov., and Dec., $5 adults, $2 kids 5–12) was established in 1981 to display the lifework of local woodcarver Wendell Gilley (1904–1983), a one-time plumber who had gained a national reputation for his carvings by the time of his death. The modern, energy-efficient museum houses more than 200 of his astonishingly realistic bird specimens carved over more than 50 years. Most days, a local artist gives woodcarving demonstrations. The gift shop carries an ornithological potpourri—books to binoculars to carving tools. Kids over eight appreciate this more than younger ones. If the carving bug catches you, workshops are available varying from 90-minute introductory lessons for adults and children ($25) offered most weekdays during the summer to multiday classes on specific birds.

## Southwest Harbor Oceanarium

Touching a sea cucumber or a starfish may not be every adult's idea of fun, but kids sure enjoy the hands-on experience at the Oceanarium (Clark Point Rd., Southwest Harbor, 207/244-7330, www.theoceanarium.com, 9 A.M.–5 P.M. Mon.–Sat. mid-May–late Oct., $10 adult, $7 ages 4–12), sister site to the Bar Harbor Oceanarium (combo tickets at 25 percent discount). A knowledgeable naturalist introduces creatures from a watery touch tank during a tour of the oceanarium. Twenty tanks hold a range of sea creatures. In addition, exhibits line the walls of the intriguing, low-tech museum. It's next to the Coast Guard station.

## Mount Desert Island Historical Society Museum and Gardens

This tiny museum (Rte. 102, Somesville, 207/276-9323, 1–4 P.M. Tues.–Sat., seasonal) is adjacent to the gently curving white bridge in Somesville, so there's a good chance you're going to stop, if just for a photo. In season, the heirloom garden, filled with flowering plants and herbs of the 19th and early 20th centuries, is worth a photo or two in and of itself. The tiny one-room museum has local artifacts and memorabilia displayed in a themed exhibit that changes annually. You can buy a walking-tour guide to Somesville in the museum. If you're especially interested in history, ask about the museum's programs, which include speakers, demonstrations, and workshops.

## Butterfly Garden

It's easy to miss the **Charlotte Rhoades Park and Butterfly Garden** (Rte. 102, Southwest Harbor), but that would be a mistake. This tiny, seaside, town-owned park was donated to the town in 1973 and is maintained entirely by volunteers. It's seldom busy, and it's a delightful place for a picnic. A kiosk is stocked with butterfly observation sheets. It's on the water side of Route 102 between the Causeway Golf Club and the Seal Cove Road.

## The Seal Cove Auto Museum

On the westernmost side of the island, but eas-ily accessible from Southwest Harbor, a nondescript blue building camouflages The Seal Cove Auto Museum (Pretty Marsh Rd., Rte. 102, Seal Cove, 207/244-9242, www.sealcoveautomuseum.org, 10 A.M.–5 P.M. daily June–late Sept., $5 adults, $2 kids under 12), one of the largest collections of Brass Era (1905–1917) autos in the country comprising more than 100 antique autos and 35 antique motorcycles. All are in as-found condition; this varies from fresh-from-the-barn to meticulously restored. It's easy for kids of any age to spend an hour here, reminiscing and/or fantasizing. Among the highlights are a 1907 Chadwick Touring Car and a 1910 Chadwick Racer, two of only three Chadwicks still in existence; a 1915 F.R.P., the fifth of only nine built and the only one still in existence; an original 1903 Ford Model A, the first car commercially produced by the Ford Motor Co., and a 1909 Ford Model T "Tin Lizzie," from the first year of production. The oldest car in the collection is an 1899 DeDion-Bouton, one of the earliest cars produced in the world. The museum is about six miles southwest of Somesville. Or, if you're coming from Southwest Harbor, take Route 102 North to Seal Cove Road (partly unpaved) west to the other side of Route 102 (it makes a giant loop) and go north about 1.5 miles. This is not on the Island Explorer route.

## Country Store Museum

Stepping inside the former general store that's now headquarters for the Tremont Historical Society (Bass Harbor, 207/244-9753, www.tremontmainehistory.us) is like stepping into the 1800s. Displays highlight the local heritage. If you're lucky, the society's president, seventh-generation islander Muriel Davidson might be on duty and regale you with stories about her aunt, author Ruth Moore. You can buy copies of Moore's books here—good reads all. The museum, across from the Seafood Ketch, is open Wednesday and Saturday afternoons July–mid-October; donation appreciated.

# RECREATION

Acadia National Park, of course, is the recreational focus throughout Mount Desert Island;

on the island's western side, the main nonpark recreational activities are bike, boat, and picnic related.

At the Southwest Harbor/Tremont Chamber of Commerce office, or at any of the area's stores, lodgings, and restaurants, pick up a free copy of the *Trail Map/Hiking Guide,* a very handy foldout map showing more than 20 hikes on the west side of Mount Desert Island. Trail descriptions include distance, time required, and skill levels (easy to strenuous).

## Bicycle Rentals

A veteran business with a first-rate reputation, **Southwest Cycle** (Main St., Southwest Harbor, 207/244-5856 or 800/649-5856) rents bikes by the day and week and is open all year (hours are 8:30 A.M.–5:30 P.M. Mon.–Sat. and 10 A.M.–4 P.M. Sun. June–Sept.; shorter hours in winter). The staff at Southwest Cycle will fix you up with maps and lots of good advice for three loops (10–30 miles) on the western side of Mount Desert. (See *Islands near Mount Desert* for planning biking day trips to Swans Island or the Cranberry Isles.) Rentals are around $20. The shop also rents every imaginable accessory, from baby seats to jogging strollers.

## Sea Kayaking

On the outskirts of Southwest Harbor's downtown, close to the chamber of commerce, is **Maine State Sea Kayak** (254 Maine St., Southwest Harbor, 207/244-9500 or 877/481-9500, www.mainestatekayak.com). Staffed with experienced, environmentally sensitive kayakers (several are Registered Maine Guides), the company offers four-hour trips (8:30 A.M.–12:30 P.M., 10 A.M.–2 P.M., 2–6 P.M. and a sunset tour) with a choice of half a dozen routes (depending on tide, visibility, and wind conditions). The trip is for $46 pp ($42 late May–June and September) and it includes shuttle transportation, paddling equipment, and a guide. Most trips also include island or beach breaks. Maximum group is six tandems; minimum age is 12. Neophytes are welcome.

If you have your own boat, consider putting in at either the park's Pretty Marsh picnic area, off Route 102, in Pretty Marsh, or at the public boat launch at the end of Bartlett's Landing Road, off the Indian Point Road near the Route 102 end. From either put-in, you can paddle around privately owned Bartlett Island. For a longer trip, head north along the shoreline past Black and Green Islands, both privately owned, to Alley Island, which is open for day access.

## Calm-Water Paddling

Just west of Somesville (take the Pretty Marsh Rd.), and across the road from Long Pond, the largest lake on Mount Desert Island, **National Park Canoe and Kayak Rental** (145 Pretty Marsh Rd., Rte. 102, Mount Desert, 207/244-5854 or 877/378-6907, www.acadia.net/canoe) makes canoeing and kayaking a snap. Just rent the boat, carry it across the road to Pond's End, and launch it. Be sure to pack a picnic. Half-day rate (8:30 A.M.–12:30 P.M. or 1–5 P.M.) for a canoe is $25, full-day rate is $45; solo kayak is $24 half day, $40 full day, $140 per week; tandem kayak is $27 half day, $52 full day, $185 per week. A do-it-yourself sunset canoe or kayak tour (from 5 P.M.–sunset) is $16 pp. Reservations are advisable and essential in July and August. It's open mid-May–mid-October.

If you've brought your own canoe (or kayak), launch it here at Pond's End and head off. It's four miles to the southern end of the lake. If the wind kicks up, skirt the shore; if it *really* kicks up from the north, don't paddle too far down the lake, as you'll have a devil of a time getting back.

Another option is to launch your canoe on the quieter, cliff-lined southern end of the lake, much of which is in the park. To find the put-in, take the Seal Cove Road (on the east end of downtown Southwest Harbor). Go right on Long Cove Road to the small parking area at the end near the pumping station. You can also put in from the Long Pond Fire Road, off Route 102, in Pretty Marsh.

Almost the entire west side of Long Pond is Acadia National Park property, so plan to picnic and swim along there; tuck into the sheltered area west of Southern Neck, a crooked finger of land that points northward from the western shore. Stay clear of private property on the east side of the lake.

### Deep-Sea Fishing
Go fishing with the **Masako Queen Fishing Company** (Beal's Wharf, Clark Point Rd., Southwest Harbor, 207/244-5385, www.masakoqueen.com) aboard *The Vagabond,* and you might return with a lobster. The boat goes 8–20 miles offshore for mackerel, bluefish, codfish, and more, but on each trip every passenger is assigned a lobster trap. When that trap is hauled, any legal-size lobster in your trap is yours. Trips last 5–7 hours, and all equipment is included. Dress warmly.

### Boat Rentals and Lessons
**Mansell Boat Rental Co.** (135 Shore Rd., Manset, next to Hinckley, 207/244-5625, www.mansellboatrentals.com) rents sail- and powerboats, with rates varying by type of boat and duration, but expect to pay close to $200 for a day rental. Sailing lessons also are available.

### Golf
Play a quick nine at the **Causeway Club** (Fernald Point Rd., 207/244-3780), which edges the ocean. Be forewarned: It's more challenging than it looks.

## EXCURSION BOATS
Southwest Harbor is the starting point for a couple of boat services headed for the Cranberry Isles. (Other boats depart from Northeast Harbor; see the *Northeast and Seal Harbors* section; see the *Cranberry Isles* section for information on the regular ferry/mail-boat service between Northeast Harbor and the Cranberries—the ferries are slightly less expensive, but there's no narration.)

### ◖ Island Cruises
High praise goes to Captain Kim Strauss's Island Cruises (Little Island Marine, Shore Rd., Bass Harbor, 207/244-5785, www.bassharborcruises.com) for its daily, narrated 3.5-hour lunch cruise to Frenchboro. The 49-passenger *R. L. Gott,* which Strauss built, departs

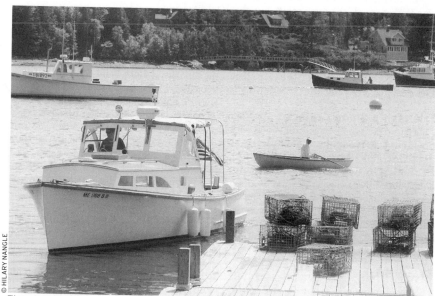

There's more than one way to get around Southwest Harbor.

at 11 A.M. daily during the summer. Kim has been navigating these waters for more than 55 years, and his experience shows not only in his boat handling but also in his narration. Expect to pick up lots of local heritage and lore about once-thriving and now-abandoned granite-quarrying and fishing communities, the sardine industry, and lobstering, and to see seals, cormorants, guillemots, and often eagles, too. The trip allows enough time on Frenchboro for a picnic (or lunch at the summertime deli on the dock) and a short village stroll, and then a return through the sprinkling of islands along the 8.3-mile route. Kim also hauls a few traps and explains lobstering. He also earns major points for maneuvering the boat around so that passengers on both sides get an up-close view of key sights. It's an excellent, enthralling tour for all ages. Round-trip cost is $27 adults, $17 children 11 and younger. Be sure to reserve, and if the weather looks iffy, call ahead to confirm. Most of the trip is in sheltered water, but rough seas can put the kibosh on it. Island Cruises also does a two-hour afternoon nature cruise among the islands that covers the same topics but that spends a bit more time at seal ledges and other spots. On either trip, don't forget to bring binoculars. You'll find the Island Cruises dock by following signs to the Swans Island Ferry and turning right at the sign shortly before the state ferry dock.

### Friendship Sloop Cruises

Charter a traditional Friendship sloop with **Downeast Friendship Sloop Charters** (P.O. Box 1533, Southwest Harbor 04679, 207/266-5210, www.downeastfriendship-sloop.com). Private charters start at $125 per hour, including appetizer; shared trips are $50 for two hours, $75 for three hours. A sunset sail is a lovely way to end a day. One of the boats used is the oldest known Friendship sloop still sailing.

## SHOPPING

The best shopping locale on this side of the island is Southwest Harbor. You'll also find a few (okay, very few) shops in Somesville. Mind you, there aren't *lots* of shops, but the small selection is interesting.

### Art, Antiques, and Gifts

In the middle of Southwest Harbor's small shopping area is **Sand Castle Ocean and Nature Store** (360 Main St., Southwest Harbor, 207/244-4118), a delightful shop with a huge range of handcrafted items, most with a marine theme. Representing the work of several dozen artisans, the shop has wind chimes, jewelry, ceramics, ship models, and lots of other surprises.

Stop in at **E. L. Higgins** (Bernard Rd., Bernard, 207/244-3983, www.antiquewicker .com). In two onetime classrooms in an 1890s schoolhouse, Edward Higgins has the state's best collection of antique wicker furniture, about 400 pieces at any given time.

Right next door is **Linda Fernandez Handknits** (Bernard Rd., Bernard, 207/244-7224), with beautiful hand-knit sweaters, mittens, hats, socks, Christmas stockings, and embroidered pillowcases all handcrafted by the talented and extended Fernandez family. The kids' lobster sweaters are especially cute. It's a great place to stock up on mittens for holiday gift giving.

Fine art of the 19th and early 20th century is the specialty at **Clark Point Gallery** (46 Clark Point Rd., Southwest Harbor, 207/244-0920, www.clarkpointgallery.com). Most works depict Maine and Mount Desert Island.

Jewelry approaches fine art at **Aylen and Son Jewelers** (Main St., Rte. 102, Southwest Harbor, 207/244-7369, www.peteraylen.com). Since opening in 1979, Peter and Judy Aylen have been crafting and selling jewelry in 18-karat gold and sterling silver and augmenting it with fine gemstones or intriguing beads.

Potters Lisbeth Faulkner and Edwin Davis can often be seen working in their studio at **Seal Cove Pottery and Gallery** (Kelleytown Rd., Seal Cove, 207/244-3602). In addition to their functional hand-thrown or hand-built pottery, they exhibit Davis's paintings as well as crafts from other island artisans.

## Books, Charts, and Music

The two-story **Port in a Storm Bookstore** (Main St., Rte. 102, Somesville, Mount Desert, 207/244-4114 or 800/694-4114, www.portinastormbookstore.com) is one of Maine's best independent bookstores. It's totally seductive, guaranteed to lighten your wallet. High ceilings, comfortable chairs, whimsical floor sculptures, open space, and Somes Cove views all contribute to the ambience. Inventory is not huge, but it's well selected—especially nature and children's books—and the staff is very knowledgeable. Especially in summer, noted authors often appear to lecture or sign their books. In the summer, the shop operates the **Port Side** outpost in the much-photographed, buoy-adorned, weathered faux lighthouse on Steamboat Wharf, in Bernard.

Don Gooding's **Mainely A Cappella** (11 Seal Cove Rd., Southwest Harbor, 800/827-2936, www.acappella.com) is the largest source of a cappella music in the world, with more than 3,000 a capella–related items. Available are CDs, sheet music, videos, songbooks, instructional materials, and more from all over the globe.

## ENTERTAINMENT
### Life Is a Cabaret

It's not too far to drive from Southwest Harbor to Bar Harbor for evening dinner and entertainment, but Southwest has a cabaret theater that even draws customers in the reverse direction for great entertainment and so-so food: **The Deck House Restaurant and Cabaret Theater** (Great Harbor Marina, 11 Apple La., off Rte. 102, Southwest Harbor, 207/244-5044). Try to arrive for dinner by 6:30 P.M. to enjoy the spectacular harbor view and order your meal (entrées are $18–28). The cathedral-ceilinged dining room holds 140, and the table is yours for the evening for an additional $10 pp cover charge (reservations are essential in midsummer). About 8:15 P.M., the young waitstaff, chameleonlike, unveils its other talents—singing, dancing, even storytelling and puppetry. After hearing the dozen or so numbers, you won't be surprised to learn that many

Deck House staff have moved on to Broadway and beyond. The performers aren't compensated, so be prepared to leave a tip.

## Repertory Theater

Somesville is home to the **Acadia Repertory Theatre** (Rte. 102, Somesville, P.O. Box 106, Mount Desert 04660, 207/244-7260 or 888/362-7480, www.acadiarep.com, $22 adults, $16 seniors, students, and military, $10 kids under 16), which has been providing first-rate professional thespian summer stock on the stage of Somesville's antique Masonic Hall since the 1970s. Classic plays by Wilde, Goldsmith, even Molière, have been staples, as has the annual Agatha Christie mystery. Performances in the 144-seat hall run at 8:15 P.M. Tuesday–Sunday late June–late August, with 2 P.M. matinees on the last Sunday of each play. Special children's plays occur at 10:30 A.M. Wednesday and Saturday in July and August. Tickets for children's theater programs are $8 adults, $5 kids. (No credit cards; pay at the box office before the performance.)

## EVENTS

In early October, Smuggler's Den Campground on Route 102 in Southwest Harbor is home to the annual **Oktoberfest International Food Festival and Craft Fair** (207/244-9264 or 800/423-9264, www.acadiachamber.com), a one-day celebration with crafts, food, games, music, and about two dozen Maine microbrewers presenting about 80 different brews.

## ACCOMMODATIONS

As the Asticou Inn is to Northeast Harbor, the Claremont is to Southwest Harbor. On the other end of the lodging scale, there are several commercial campgrounds in this part of the island, plus an Acadia National Park campground.

### Inn

When you're ready to splurge, **The Claremont** (22 Claremont Rd., Southwest Harbor, 207/244-5036 or 800/244-5036, www.the-claremonthotel.com) may well be your choice, but you'll have to plan a year ahead to land a room in July or August. The most popular time is the first week in August, during the annual Claremont Croquet Classic. An elegant grande dame, dressed in yellow clapboard, the Claremont dominates a six-acre hilltop overlooking Somes Sound and caters to honeymooners, yuppies, and gentrified folk. The views are stupendous. Guests have access to croquet courts, a clay tennis court, bikes, rowboats, and a library. Dating from 1884, the main building has 26 rooms (with bath and phones), most of them recently refurbished yet pleasantly old-fashioned and nonfancy. Other accommodations are in the six-room Phillips House, one-suite Clark House, and Cole Cottage, with two rooms and one efficiency. Rooms in these buildings are $185–245 including breakfast, early July–early September, plus a hefty 15 percent service charge and Maine sales tax. Also on the premises are 14 cottages ($205–300, early July–early Sept.); they can go as high as $3,500 a week in midsummer. No pets, no smoking, and, surprisingly, no credit cards. Children are welcome. The hotel and dining room are open early June–mid-October; cottages are open late May–mid-October.

## Bed-and-Breakfasts

Many of Southwest Harbor's B&Bs are clustered downtown, along Main Street and the Clark Point Road.

Set on a corner, well back from the Clark Point Road, is ◖ **Harbour Cottage Inn** (9 Dirigo Rd., P.O. Box 258, Southwest Harbor 04679, 207/244-5738 or 888/843-3022, www.harbourcottageinn.com), appealingly revamped in 2002, when Javier Montesinos and Don Jalbert took over the reins. Built in 1870, it was the "annex" for one of the island's original hotels and housed the increasing numbers of rusticators who patronized this part of the island. It has evolved into a lovely B&B with eight rooms ($159–175) and three suites ($205–259), decorated in a colorful and fun cottage style. Most rooms have whirlpool baths or steam-sauna showers, some have fireplaces, and all have telephones, TV, and Wi-Fi. Rates include a multicourse breakfast and use of

beach bicycles. The inn stocks a nice selection of wine and beer. Also part of Harbour Cottage is **Pier One,** which offers five weekly waterfront suites ($1,260–1,575), including a studio cottage, all with kitchens, TV, and phone. Guests have private use of a 150-foot pier, and they can dock or launch canoes or kayaks or other small boats from right outside their doors; dockage is available for larger boats. It's all within walking distance of downtown.

The linden-blossom fragrance can be intoxicating in summer at the **Lindenwood Inn** (118 Clark Point Rd., P.O. Box 1328, Southwest Harbor 04679, 207/244-5335 or 800/307-5335, www.lindenwoodinn.com, $125–325). Jim King, the Australian owner, has imaginatively decorated the inn's nine rooms and poolside bungalow with artifacts from everywhere in a style that's sophisticated, yet comfortable. After you hike Acadia's trails, the heated pool and hot tub are especially welcome, and after that, perhaps the inn's full bar. Some rooms have harbor views. It's open all year.

At the Victorian **Inn at Southwest** (371 Main St., Rte. 102, P.O. Box 593, Southwest Harbor 04679, 207/244-3835, www.innatsouthwest.com, $135–185), guests gather for games, reading, conversation, and afternoon tea in a huge living room with fireplace and comfortable couches. Built in 1884 as the Freeman Cottage, the elegant building has 13 dormers and a wraparound veranda. Seven second- and third-floor guest rooms—named for Maine lighthouses and full of character—are fitted out with wicker furniture, ceiling fans, down comforters, and lots more. Some have gas stoves or limited water views. The inn is Wi-Fi wired. It's open May–October. Breakfast is a feast, with such treats as cheesecake crepes and eggs Florentine.

Across the lane **The Kingsleigh Inn 1904** (373 Main St., P.O. Box 1426, Southwest Harbor 04679, 207/244-5302, www.kingsleighinn.com, $140–190) is a very attractive Queen Anne manse with eight well-thought-out rooms (private baths) on three floors. If you're sensitive to street noise, request a back-facing (harbor-view) room, although air-conditioners and in-room sound machines muffle the sound in summer. The huge turret suite, with fireplace, TV, telescope, large bathroom, and lots of comfortable wicker furniture, is $295. Breakfast is an elegant, three-course affair, served on the water-view porch, weather permitting. Afternoon refreshments are served, and chocolates and port wine are replenished daily in guest rooms.

From the front, the **Cranberry Hill Inn** (60 Clark Point Rd., P.O. Box 222, Southwest Harbor 04679, 207/244-5007, www.cranberryhillinn.com, 495–135) appears as a simple white extended farmhouse behind a white picket fence. From the rear, it opens up with big windows and big decks taking in the harbor views. It has five guest rooms, some with private baths, and a big living room that invites settling in with a good read by the fire. A full breakfast and afternoon tea are provided. Innkeeers Patti and Jerry Sellig operate the B&B seasonally.

In 2004, Ann and Charlie Bradford sold the family home that had housed their long-time B&B and reopened a petite version of the **Island House** (36 Freeman Ridge, P.O. Box 1006, Southwest Harbor 04679, 207/244-5180, www.islandhousebb.com, $115 d) in their new custom home, built atop a ridge in a quiet neighborhood about a mile from downtown. They've downsized the guest space to just two comfy rooms, plus a guest living/dining room, all on one level (a great place for anyone with mobility problems, although it's not wheelchair-accessible). Anne's warm hospitality and delicious full breakfasts remain the same. Also available is a separate, two-bedroom apartment, with a tiny deck offering glimpses of distant islands, above the garage ($150 d). It's open all year.

In Manset, adjacent to the Hinckley Yacht complex and with jaw-dropping views down Somes Sound, is **The Moorings** (Shore Rd., P.O. Box 744, Southwest Harbor 04679, 207/244-5523, 207/244-3210, or 800/596-5523, www.mooringsinn.com, $70–125), owned and operated by the King family since 1960. The oceanfront complex is part motel, part cottage rental, and part old-fashioned B&B, and the rates are terrific. Ten rooms in the Main House are named after locally built sailing vessels. Rates include juice, coffee, and doughnuts. The Lighthouse View Wing has motel-style rooms with refrigerator, microwave, waterfront decks, and incredible views (spend the afternoon counting the Hinckley yachts). Also on the property are cottage units, a combination of rooms and efficiencies ($115–175). Bikes, canoes, and kayaks are available for guests, so you can paddle around the harbor.

## Motels and Cottages

Smack on the harbor and just a two-minute walk from downtown is the appropriately named **Harbor View Motel and Cottages** (11 Ocean Way, P.O. Box 701, Southwest Harbor 04679, 207/244-5031 or 800/538-6463, www.maine-sunshine.com/harbview). The family-owned complex comprises motel rooms ($55–125) spread out in two older one-story buildings and a newish three-story one that fronts on the harbor. A continental breakfast is served to motel room guests July 1–Labor Day. Also on the premises are seven housekeeping cottages with kitchenettes varying from studios to two-bedrooms (weekly rentals only; $480–1,170).

Right across from the famed seawall and adjacent to the park is the **Seawall Motel** (566 Seawall Rd./Rte. 102A, Southwest Harbor, 207/244-9250 or 800/248-9250, www.seawall-motel.com, $75–110). The no-surprises, two-story motel (upstairs rooms have the best views) has free Wi-Fi, in-room phones, and cable TV. A continental breakfast is included mid-May–October. Kids 12 and under stay free. The location's excellent for bird-watchers—there are a freshwater pond, pine forest, and the ocean. The motel is also home to the Acadia Workshop Center (207/244-3020 or 800/248-9250, www.acadiaworkshopcenter.com), which offers five-day art classes May–October. Packages are available that include lodging, meals, airport transportation, workshop, and park tour.

## Campgrounds

On the eastern edge of Somesville, just off Route 198 at the head of Somes Sound, the

**Mount Desert Campground** (516 Somes Sound Dr., Rte. 198, Somesville, Mount Desert, 207/244-3710, www.mountdesertcampground.com) is especially centrally located for visiting Bar Harbor, Acadia, and the whole western side of Mount Desert Island. The campground has 152 wooded tent sites, about 45 on the water, spread out on 58 acres. Reservations are essential in midsummer—one-week minimum for waterfront sites, three days for off-water sites in July and August. (Campers book a year ahead for waterfront sites here.) This deservedly popular and low-key campground gets high marks for maintenance, noise control, and convenient tent platforms. Another plus is The Gathering Place, where campers can relax, play games, and buy coffee and fresh-baked treats or ice cream. Summer rates are $30–45 a night for two adults and two children younger than 18. Electrical hookups are available for $2 per night. No pets July–early September. No trailers longer than 20 feet. Kayak and canoe rentals are available. It's open mid-June–mid-September.

If staying at a quiet, no-frills campground in an outstanding setting appeals, head for Hall Quarry, a few miles south of Somesville. **Somes Sound View Campground** (86 Hall Quarry Rd., Mount Desert, 207/244-3890, www.ssvc.info), among the smallest campgrounds on the island, has 60 tight tent and RV (maximum 28 feet) sites on a hillside, with some on the ocean's edge. Facilities include hot showers (if you're camping on the lowest levels, it's a good hike up to the bathhouse), a pool, dock, and pond with paddleboats; nearest store is two miles. Canoe rentals are available, and you can swim in the sound (from a rocky beach). Leashed pets are allowed. Sites are $29–49 in July and August, less early and late in the season. No credit cards. It's open late May–mid-October. The campground is two miles south and east of Somesville and a mile east of Route 102.

**Smuggler's Den Campground** (Rte. 102, P.O. Box 787, Southwest Harbor, 207/244-3944, www.smugglersdencampground.com) is a midsize campground between Echo Lake and downtown Southwest Harbor. It's also the site of the annual Oktoberfest. Trails lead to back roads to both Echo Lake (1.25 miles) and Long Pond (one mile). Big-rig sites are grouped in the top third; pop-ups and small campers are in the middle third; tenting sites are in the lower third and in the woods rimming the large recreation field. Summer rates covering four adults vary from $28 (tent) to $49 (full hookups with concrete pads) for the 96 sites, 54 of which are designated for tents. Also available are four camping cabins that rent for $500 per week. Facilities include a heated pool and kiddy pool, laundry, free hot showers, lobsters and ice cream for sale, and entertainment. Well-behaved pets are a possibility.

## Cottage Rentals

**LSRobinson Co.** (337 Main St., P.O. Box 1480, Southwest Harbor 04679, 207/244-5563, www.lsrobinson.com) has an extensive list of area rentals. The Southwest Harbor/Tremont Chamber of Commerce also keeps a helpful listing of privately owned homes/cottages available for rent. The chamber's annual summer guide usually contains a couple of pages of ads with photos.

# FOOD
## Local Flavors

Lots of goodies for picnics can be found at **Sawyer's Market** (Main St., Southwest Harbor, 207/244-7061, 5:30 A.M.–7:30 P.M. Mon.–Sat.); for wine and cheese head across the street to **Sawyer's Specialties** (Main St., Southwest Harbor, 207/244-3317), open daily.

Hot diggity dog! **Maddy's** (7 Clark Point Rd., Southwest Harbor, 207/244-0011, 7 A.M.–3 P.M., to 1 P.M. Sun.) welcomes kids with paper-topped, crayon- and game-stocked tables, and kid-pleasing basics and hot dog connoisseurs with gourmet tube steaks, all at reasonable prices. Soups, salads, sausages, chili, burgers, and even Mexican standards are on the menu, and breakfast is served all day.

The students at College of the Atlantic run **Beech Hill Farm** (Beech Hill Rd., Mount Desert, 207/244-5204, 8 A.M.–5 P.M. Tues., Wed.,

Fri., and Sat.), a five-acre MOFGA-certified organic farm that also has acres of heirloom apple trees and 65 acres of forestland. Visit the farmstand for fresh produce.

## Ethnic Fare

**C XYZ Restaurant** (80 Seawall Rd., Rte. 102A, Manset, 207/244-5221, 5:30–9 P.M. daily) isn't easy to find, but it's well worth the effort. It's at the end of a dirt driveway rising slowly to a crest—look for the faux cacti marking the parking lot. There's dining inside and on the porch. No gloppy Mexican fare here; rather this popular spot (do make reservations) delivers the flavors of interior Mexico: Xalapa, Yucatán, and Zacatecas (hence XYZ). Most popular dish? *Cochinitas*—citrus-marinated pork rubbed with achiote paste (it's worthy of its reputation). Entrées are $21. The margaritas are classic—requiring, allegedly, 1,100 pounds of fresh limes each year. For dessert, try the exquisite XYZ pie.

From the outside, it doesn't look like much, but locals know you can count on **C DeMuro's Top of the Hill** (Rte. 102, Southwest Harbor, 207/244-0033, 4:30 P.M.–close daily) for a really good meal at a very fair price. Dine in the country-style, pine dining room or on the weatherized patio. The Italian-influenced menu (try the excellent veal Italiano) has something in all price ranges ($9–18), but the real steal is the Lobster Paloozah special, including a cup of clam chowder, steamed mussels, a boiled lobster, pasta or potato, and vegetable, all for about $19. Early-bird specials are served 4:30–6:30 P.M.

## Casual Dining

Some of the island's most creative sandwiches and pizza toppings emerge from Arthur and Kate Jacobs's **Little Notch Café** (340 Main St., Southwest Harbor, 207/244-3357, 11 A.M.–8 P.M. Mon.–Sat. May–Oct., 11 A.M.–7 P.M. weekdays Nov.–Apr.), next to the library in Southwest Harbor's downtown. How about a broccoli, sausage, and black olive pizza? Or a prosciutto sandwich with asiago and roasted peppers? All this plus Little Notch Bakery's famed breads, sinful desserts, a couple of pasta choices, and homemade soups, stews, and chowders make the café a winner.

By day, **Eat-a-Pita** (326 Main St., Southwest Harbor, 207/244-4344, www.eatapita-chefmarc.com, 8 A.M.–9 P.M. daily) is a casual, order-at-the-counter restaurant, serving breakfast and lunch. At night, it morphs into **Café 2,** a tad more formal with full service. The dining room is furnished with old oak tables and chairs and an eclectic collection of stuff. Start the day with a Greek or Acapulco omelet. Lunch emphasizes pita sandwiches and salads (delicious! Call in advance for takeout); dinner choices ($8–22) include a half dozen pastas and entrées such as poached Atlantic salmon and boneless lamb loin. Desserts are homemade.

Good food, good coffee, and good wine mix with a Mediterranean-influenced menu at **Sips** (4 Clark Point Rd., Southwest Harbor, 207/244-4550, 6:30 A.M.–10 P.M. Mon.–Sat., 9 A.M.–2 P.M. Sun.). Small- and large-plate and tapas-style choices range $8–21.

Earning high praise for its internationally accented fare, good service, fabulous views over the harbor, and incredible martinis is **Fiddlers' Green** (411 Main St., Southwest Harbor, 207/244-9416, www.fiddlersgreenrestaurant.com, 11 A.M.–2:30 P.M. and 5:30 P.M.–close daily). House specialties, such as Asian vegetarian hot pot, pork *cubano,* and lobster pot pie, range $16–27.

## Fine Dining

The dreamy views from **Claremont Dining Room** (22 Claremont Rd., 207/244-5036 or 800/244-5036, 6–9 P.M. daily) descend over the lawns and croquet courts, to the boathouse and dock, and beyond to the water backed by mountains. It's truly a special place for an elegant meal complemented by an old-fashioned grace. Unfortunately chefs seem to change annually, so it's hard to predict the quality; it's best to ask locally (jackets and ties requested for dinner, entrées $19–28). Dining-room reservations are wise in midsummer. In July and August, informal lunches and cocktails are served in the shorefront Boat House, also open to the public.

ACADIA REGION

Red sky at night, diners delight. Gold walls, artwork, wood floors, and a giant hearth set a chic tone for splurge-worthy **Red Sky** (14 Clark Point Rd., 207/244-0476, www.redskyrestaurant.com, 5:30–9:30 P.M. daily), one of the island's premier restaurants. The creative fare (entrées $19–30) emphasizes fresh seafood, hand-cut meats, and local organic produce, and there's always a vegetarian choice. Bread is baked daily and the desserts are homemade. The restaurant is open Valentine's Day–New Year's Eve.

### Seafood and Lobster in the Rough

If you have a penchant for puns—or can tune them out—head for the family-run **Seafood Ketch Restaurant** (McMullin Ave., Bass Harbor, 207/244-7463, 11 A.M.–9 P.M. daily late May–mid-Oct.). The corny humor begins with "Please no fishing from dining room windows or the deck," and "What foods these morsels be," and goes up or down from there (depending on your perspective). But there's nothing corny about the seafood roll, an interesting change from the usual lobster or crab roll. There are a few "landlubber delights," but mostly the menu has fresh seafood dishes—including the baked lobster-seafood casserole (a recipe requested by *Gourmet*). Most entrées run $18–20, but sandwiches and lighter fare are available. This is a prime family spot (with a kids' menu), where the best tables are on the flagstone patio overlooking Bass Harbor. Follow signs for the Swans Island ferry terminal.

**( Thurston's Lobster Pound** (Steamboat Wharf Rd., Bernard, 207/244-7600, 11 A.M.–8 P.M. daily early and late in the season, to 8:30 P.M. in July and Aug., open Memorial Day–Columbus Day) wins the award for the island's best lobster pound, with a screened dining room that practically sits in the water. Family-oriented Thurston's also has chowders, sandwiches, and terrific desserts. Beer and wine are available. Be sure to read the directions at the entry and order before you find a table on one of two levels.

Much more rustic, although less so after its 2007 renovations, is **The Captain's Galley at Beal's Lobster Pier** (182 Clark Point Rd., 207/244-7178 or 207/244-3202, 9 A.M.–8 P.M. daily, closes at 5 P.M. after Labor Day), where you dine on covered picnic tables on the working dock. In addition to lobster, steamers, and fresh fish, you'll find chowders, sandwiches, ice cream, and baked desserts. It's at the end of the road, adjacent to the Coast Guard Base.

# INFORMATION AND SERVICES
## Information

Near the public parking lots and fire station (behind Sawyer's Market) is the Southwest Harbor/Tremont Chamber of Commerce (P.O. Box 1143, Southwest Harbor 04679, 207/244-9264 or 800/423-9264, www.acadiachamber.com).

Check out Southwest Harbor Public Library (338 Main St., Southwest Harbor, 207/244-7065, www.swhplibrary.org).

## Public Restrooms

In downtown Southwest Harbor, public restrooms are at the southern end of the parking lot behind the Main Street park and near the fire station. Across Main Street, Harbor House also has a restroom, and there are port-o-lets at the town docks. There's also a public restroom at the Swan's Island ferry terminal.

# GETTING AROUND

Southwest Harbor, Tremont, and Bass Harbor are serviced by Route 7/Southwest Harbor of the Island Explorer bus system.

# Islands near Mount Desert

Sure, Mount Desert is an island, but for a sampling of real island life, you'll want to make a day trip to one of the offshore islands. Most popular are the Cranberry Isles and Swans Island, but Frenchboro (see sidebar *Frenchboro, Long Island*) has begun seeing a steadier stream of visitors.

## CRANBERRY ISLES

The Cranberry Isles, south of Northeast and Seal Harbors, comprise Great Cranberry, Little Cranberry (called Islesford), Sutton, Baker, and Bear Islands. Islesford and Baker include property belonging to Acadia National Park. Bring a bike and explore the narrow, mostly level roads on the two largest islands (Great Cranberry and Islesford), but *remember to respect private property.* Unless you've asked permission, *do not* cut across private land to reach the shore.

The Cranberry name has been attributed to 18th-century loyalist governor Francis Bernard, who received these islands (along with all of Mount Desert) as a king's grant in 1762. Cranberry bogs (now long gone) on the two largest islands evidently caught his attention. Permanent European settlers were here in the 1760s, and there was even steamboat service by the 1820s.

Lobstering and other fishing industries are the commercial mainstay, boosted in summer by the various visitor-related pursuits. Artists and writers come for a week, a month, or longer; day-trippers spend time on Great Cranberry and Islesford.

Largest of the islands is **Great Cranberry,** with a general store, a small historical museum, and a gift shop, but not much else except pretty views.

The second-largest island is **Little Cranberry,** locally known as Islesford. It's easy to spend the better part of a day here exploring. Begin at **The Islesford Historical Museum** operated by the National Park Service (207/288-3338, 10 A.M.–noon and 12:30–4:30 P.M. Mon.–Sat. and 10:45 A.M.–noon and 12:30–4:30 P.M. Sun. mid-June–Labor Day, free). The exhibits focus on local history, much of it maritime, so displays include ship models, household goods, fishing gear, and other memorabilia. Also on Islesford are public restrooms (across from the museum), a handful of galleries, and a general store. For lunch, bring a picnic or head to **The Islesford Dock** (207/244-7494, 11 A.M.–3 P.M. and 5–9 P.M. Tues.–Sat., 10 A.M.–2 P.M. Sun. late June–Labor Day), where prices are moderate, the food is home-cooked, and the views across to Acadia's mountains are incredible. If you want to spend the night, reserve at the **Braided Rugs Inn** (Box 15, Islesford 04646, 207/244-5943, $100), with three shared-bath rooms. For **cottage rentals,** see www.islesford.com.

**ACADIA REGION**

The Islesford Dock is the place to have lunch or dinner on Little Cranberry Island.

## Getting There

Decades-old, family-run **Beal and Bunker**

ACADIA REGION

# FRENCHBORO, LONG ISLAND

Since Maine has more Long Islands than anyone cares to count, most of them have other labels for easy distinction. Here's a case in point – a Long Island known universally just as Frenchboro, the name of the village that wraps around Lunts Harbor. With a year-round population hovering at 50, Frenchboro has had ferry service only since 1960. Since then, the island has acquired phone service, electricity, and satellite TV, but don't expect to notice much of that when you get there. It's a very quiet place where islanders live as islanders always have – making a living from the sea and proud of it. In 1999, when more than half the island (914 acres, including 5.5 miles of shorefront) went up for sale by a private owner, an incredible fund-raising effort collected nearly $3 million, allowing purchase of the land in January 2000 by the Maine Coast Heritage Trust. Some of the funding has been put toward restoration of the village's church and one-room schoolhouse; islanders and visitors will still have full access to all the acreage, and interested developers will have to look elsewhere.

Frenchboro is a delightful day trip. A good way to get a sense of the place is to take the 3.5-hour lunch cruise run by Captain Kim Strauss of **Island Cruises** (Little Island Marine, Shore Rd., Bass Harbor, 207/244-5785, www.bassharborcruises.com; see Island Cruises under Recreation in The Quiet Side section). For an even longer day trip to Frenchboro, plan to take the passenger ferry R. L. Gott during her weekly run for the Maine State Ferry Service. The Gott departs Bass Harbor at 8 A.M. each Friday early April–late October, arriving in Frenchboro at 9 A.M. The return trip to Bass Harbor is at 6 P.M., allowing nine hours on the island. Round-trip cost is $9 adults, $4.25 children (children under 5 are free).

Extra ferries operate for the island's annual **lobster festival,** usually the second Saturday in August, when islanders and hundreds of visitors gather in the village for lobster galore, games, and more. For info, call the Lunt and Lunt Lobster Company (207/334-2922).

When you go, take a picnic with you, or stop at **Lunt's Dockside Deli** (207/334-2922), open only in July and August. It's a very casual establishment – order at the window, grab a picnic table, and wait for your name to be called; lobster rolls and fish chowder are the specialties, but there are plenty of other choices, including sandwiches, hot dogs, and even vegetable wraps; of course, you can get lobster, too. It's inexpensive; the view is wonderful; and you might even get to watch lobsters being unloaded from a boat.

The **Frenchboro Historical Society Museum,** just up from the dock, has interesting old tools, other local artifacts, and a small gift shop. It's usually open afternoons late May–early September. The island has a network of maintained trails through the woods and along the shore, easy and not-so-easy; some can be squishy and some are along bouldery beachfront. The trails are rustic and most are unmarked, so proceed carefully. In the center of the island is a beaver pond. (You'll get a sketchy map on the boat, but you can also get one at the Historical Society.)

Frenchboro is the subject of Hauling by Hand: The Life and Times of a Maine Island, a fascinating, well-researched "biography" published in 1999 by eighth-generation islander Dean Lunt, now a journalist in Portland. (See Suggested Reading.) His website (www.islandportpress.com) has helpful info for visiting the island.

(P.O. Box 33, Cranberry Isles 04625, 207/244-3575) provides year-round mail-boat/passenger service to the Cranberries from Northeast Harbor. The ferries don't carry cars, but you can take a bike. Or just plan to explore on foot. The schedule makes it possible to do both islands in one day. The summer season, with more frequent trips, runs late June–Labor Day. The first boat departs Northeast Harbor's municipal pier at 7:30 A.M. Monday–Saturday; first Sunday boat is 10 A.M. The last boat for Northeast Harbor leaves Islesford at 6:30 P.M. and leaves (Great) Cranberry at 6:45 P.M. The boats do a bit of to-ing and fro-ing on the three-island route (including Sutton in summer), so be patient as they make the circuit. It's a people-watching treat. If you just did a round-trip and stayed aboard, the loop would take about 1.5 hours. Round-trip tickets (covering the whole loop, including intraisland if you want to visit both Great Cranberry and Islesford) are $16 adults, $10 kids under 12 (free for kids under 3). Bicycles are $5 round-trip. The off-season schedule runs early May–mid-June and early September–mid-October; the winter schedule runs mid-October–April. In winter, the boat company advises phoning ahead on what Mainers quaintly call "weather days."

The **Cranberry Cove Ferry** (upper town dock, Clark Point Rd., Southwest Harbor, 207/244-5882 or cell 207/460-1981, www .downeastwindjammer.com) operates a summertime service to the Cranberries, mid-May–mid-October, aboard the 47-passenger *Island Queen*. The ferry route begins at the upper town dock (Clark Point Rd.) in Southwest Harbor, with stops in Manset and Great Cranberry before reaching Islesford an hour later. (Stops at Sutton can be arranged.) In summer (mid-June–mid-September), there are six daily round-trips, with two additional evening trips Tuesdays, Thursdays, and Saturdays. The first departure from Southwest Harbor is 7 A.M.; last departure from Islesford is 6 P.M. Round-trip fares are $22 adults, $14 children, $6 bicycle.

The **MDI Water Taxi** (207/244-7312), a con-

verted lobster boat, makes frequent on-demand trips to the Cranberries.

Captain John Dwelley (207/244-5724) also operates a water-taxi service to the Cranberries. His six-passenger *Delight* makes the run from Northeast, Southwest, or Seal Harbor for $55–70 per trip, depending upon time of day, early June–late September. Reservations are required for trips 6–11 P.M. and 6–8 A.M. Custom cruises are available, including excursions to Baker's Island.

## SWANS ISLAND

Six miles off Mount Desert Island lies scenic, 6,000-acre Swans Island (pop. 327), named after Colonel James Swan, who bought it and two dozen other islands as an investment in 1786. As with the Cranberries, fishing—especially lobstering—is the year-round way of life here; summer sees the arrival of artists, writers, and other seasonal visitors. The island has no campsites, few public restrooms (ferry dock and a port-o-let outside the museum), a tiny motel, and two small, traditional-style B&Bs. Visitors who want to spend more than a day tend to rent cottages by the week.

You'll need either a bicycle or a car to get around on the island, as the ferry comes in on one side, and the village center is on the other. Should you choose to bring a car, it's wise to make reservations for the ferry, especially for the return trip. Bicycling is a good way to get around, but be forewarned that the roads are narrow, lacking shoulders, and hilly in spots.

If you can be flexible, wait for a clear day, pack a picnic, and catch the first ferry (7:30 A.M.) from Bass Harbor. At the ferry office in Bass Harbor, request a Swans Island map (and take advantage of the restroom). Keep an eye on your watch so you don't miss the last ferry (4:30 P.M.) back to Bass Harbor.

The ferry arrives in the northeast corner of the island. Head off down the main road toward Burnt Coat Harbor. (The island has three villages—Atlantic, Minturn, and Swans Island.) First stop is the tiny **Seaside Hall Museum,** which describes itself as "The Island's Attic." It's usually open noon–3 P.M.,

© TOM NANGLE

**Take the state ferry to Swans Island.**

but it's run by volunteers, so that's not a sure thing. Admission is a $1 donation.

Pedal around to the west side of the harbor and down the peninsula to **Hockamock Head Light** (officially, Burnt Coat Harbor Light). From the ferry landing, Hockamock Head is 4.5 miles. The distinctive square lighthouse, built in 1872 and now automated, sits on a rocky promontory overlooking Burnt Coat Harbor, Harbor Island, lobster-boat traffic, and crashing surf. The keeper's house is unoccupied; the grounds are great for picnics.

If it's hot, ask for directions to one of two prime island swimming spots: **Fine Sand Beach** (salt water) or **Quarry Pond** (fresh water). Fine Sand Beach is on the west side of Toothacher Cove; you'll have to navigate about a mile of unpaved road to get there, but it's worth the trouble. Be prepared for chilly water, however. Quarry Pond is in Minturn, on the opposite side of Burnt Coat Harbor from the lighthouse. Follow the one-way loop around, and you'll see it on your right as you're rounding the far side of the loop.

Shopping options are few on Swans, but there

are two worth noting. If you head left at the end of Ferry Terminal Road, you'll come to **Saturn Press** (463 Atlantic Rd., 207/526-4000), where designer Jane Goodrich and printer James Van Pernis create notecards and papers using antique letterpresses. The shop is usually open 9 A.M.–5 P.M. Monday–Friday, and the informal tours explain the letterpress process (you can usually see them in action) and visit the studios where the designs, based on the company's library of tens of thousands of graphic image ephemera, are created. Afterward, pick up some notecards in the small shop or at least a catalog. Saturn has few retail outlets as most of its products are carried by museums and fine-paper stores.

Although Swan's Island Blankets are no longer produced on Swans Island (the company was sold and moved to Lincolnville in 2005), you can still buy the blankets here. The shop at 135 North Road (on the way to Fine Sand Beach) is usually open 2–5 P.M. daily in July, August, and September; call 207/526-4120 for details or directions.

A Swans Island summer highlight is the

**Sweet Chariot Music Festival,** a three-night midweek extravaganza in early August. Windjammers arrive from Camden and Rockland, enthusiasts show up on their private boats, and the island's Oddfellows Hall is standing room only for three evenings of folk singing, storytelling, and impromptu hijinks. In midafternoon of the first two days (about 3:30 P.M.), musicians go from boat to boat in Burnt Coat Harbor, entertaining with sea chanteys. Along the route from harbor to concert, enterprising local kids peddle lemonade, homemade brownies, and kitschy craft items. It's all very festive, but definitely a "boat thing," not very convenient for anyone without waterborne transport.

Overnight accommodations are available at **The Harbor Watch Motel** (111 Minturn Rd., Swans Island, 207/526-4563 or 800/532-7928, www.swansisland.com, $95–120). Dining choices are limited and include the **Swan's Island Store** (Minturn Rd.), the **Island Bake Shop** (73 Ferry Terminal Rd., 207/526-4123, 7 A.M.–2 P.M. Mon.–Sat.), and **The Boat House** (207/526-4201), a take-out restaurant and gift shop clinging to a cliffside overlooking the harbor on the way to the lighthouse.

## Getting There and Around

Swans Island is a six-mile, 40-minute trip on the state-operated car ferry *Captain Henry Lee.* The ferry makes 5–6 round-trips a day mid-April–late October, the first from Bass Harbor at 7:30 A.M. (9 A.M. Sun.) and the last from Swans Island at 4:30 P.M. Other months, the first and last runs are the same, but there are only 4–5 trips. For more information, contact **Maine State Ferry Service** (P.O. Box 114, Bass Harbor 04653, 207/244-3254; 303 Atlantic Rd., Swans Island, 207/526-4273; daily recorded info 800/491-4883, www.state.me.us/mdot/opt/ferry/ferry). Round-trip fares are $14.50 adults, $6.25 children 5–11. Bikes are $13.75 round-trip per adult, $7 per child. Round-trip ticket for vehicle and driver is $42 May–October. Reservations are accepted only for vehicles (be in line at least 15 minutes before departure or you'll risk forfeiting your space, reservation fee is $7 each way).

To reach the Bass Harbor ferry terminal on Mount Desert Island, follow the distinctive blue signs, marked Swans Island Ferry, along Routes 102 and 102A. Parking, when available, is $7 per day.

# Schoodic Peninsula

Slightly more than 2,366 of Acadia National Park's acres are on the mainland Schoodic Peninsula—the rest are all on islands (including Mount Desert). World-class scenery and the relative lack of congestion, even at the height of summer, are just two reasons to sneak around to the eastern side of Frenchman Bay. Others are abundant opportunities for outdoor recreation, two scenic byways, and, believe it or not, shopping. You can easily do your gift shopping for the year at the dozens of artists' and artisans' studios tucked throughout this region.

Still, the biggest attractions in this area are the spectacular vignettes and vistas—of offshore lighthouses, distant mountains, and close-in islands—and the unchanged villages. Winter

Harbor (pop. 988), known best as the gateway to Schoodic, shares the area with an old-money, low-profile, Philadelphia-linked summer colony on exclusive Grindstone Neck.

Gouldsboro (pop. 1,941)—including the not-to-be-missed villages of Birch Harbor, Corea, and Prospect Harbor—earned its own minor fame from Louise Dickinson Rich's 1958 book *The Peninsula,* a tribute to her summers on Corea's Cranberry Point, "a place that has stood still in time." Since 1958, change has crept into Corea, but not so's you'd notice. It's still the same quintessential lobster-fishing community, perfect for photo ops. A new section of the Maine Coastal Islands National Wildlife Reserve, the 431-acre **Corea Heath Unit,** has taken over former Navy lands along Route 195

# GALLERY HOPPING

Art and artisan studios and galleries are numerous, and it's easy to while away a foggy day browsing and buying. Begin by picking up copies of the *Artist Studio Tour Map*, which details and provides directions to about a dozen galleries in Franklin, Sullivan, and Hancock, and the *Schoodic Peninsula* brochure, which notes galleries and shops on the peninsula. Both are widely available and free. Hours and days of operation vary; it's best to call first if you really want to visit a gallery. Here's a sampling to get you started.

## HANCOCK AND SULLIVAN

Take the Point Road 2.5 miles to find Russell and Akemi Wray's **Raven Tree Gallery** (536 Point Rd., Hancock, 207/422-8273). Russell specializes in wood sculpture, bronzes, prints, and jewelry; Akemi crafts pottery. Out front is a small sculpture gallery. Continue another two miles to the **Ragna Bruno Torkanowsky Studio and Gallery** (983 Point Rd., Hancock, 207/422-6252). Torkanowsky's home gallery is filled with her sculpture and paintings and selections from other artists.

Return to Route 1 and take Eastside Road, just before the Hancock-Sullivan Bridge, and drive 1.5 miles south to **Gull Rock Pottery** (325 Eastside Rd., Hancock, 207/422-3990), where Torj and Kurt Wray (Russell's parents) have a magical waterfront setting and sculpture gallery. Inside is wheel-thrown, hand-painted, dishwasher-safe pottery decorated with blue-and-white motifs representing local landscapes.

Cross the Hancock–Sullivan Bridge and then take your first left off Route 1 onto Taunton

Drive to find the next three galleries. Drawing from her experiences as an oil painter and from her life in Japan, Peg McAloon creates masterful one-of-a-kind quilts at **Wildfire Run Quilt Boutique** (148 Taunton Dr., Sullivan, 207/422-3935, www.maineus.com/wildfirerun).

Nearby **Lunaform** (Cedar La., West Sullivan, 207/422-0923, www.lunaform.com) is in a class by itself. First there's the setting – the beautifully landscaped grounds surrounding an abandoned granite quarry. Then there's the realization that many of the wonderfully aesthetic garden ornaments created here look like hand-turned *pottery*, when in fact they're hand turned, but made of steel-reinforced concrete. It takes a bit of zigging and zagging to get here. Go right onto Track Road; after a half mile, go left onto Cedar Lane.

Bet you can't keep from smiling at the whimsical animal sculptures and fun furniture of talented sculptor/painter Philip Barter. His work is the cornerstone of the eclectic **Barter Family Gallery** (Shore Rd., Sullivan, 207/422-3190, www.barterfamilygallery.com). But there's more: Barter's wife and seven children have put their considerable skills to work producing hooked and braided rugs, jewelry, and other craft items. Follow Taunton Road 2.5 miles from Route 1.

Continue north on Taunton Road, and it will loop around Hog Bay and onto Route 200, for the next three stops. Charles and Susanne Grosjean's **Hog Bay Pottery** (245 Hog Bay Rd., Rte. 200, Franklin, 207/565-2282) is another double treat. Inside the casual, laid-back showroom are Charles's functional, nature-themed pottery and Susanne's stunning handwoven rugs.

---

in Corea. Plans call for developing trails, including one along the shorefront (call 207/546-2124 for updated information). In another initiative, the Frenchman Bay Conservancy is seeking to acquire the 600-acre Northern Corea Heath, across the highway, home to Grand Marsh and Grand Marsh Bay.

Between Ellsworth and Gouldsboro are Hancock, Sullivan, and Sorrento. Venture down the ocean-side back roads, and you'll discover an old-timey summer colony at Hancock Point, complete with library, post office, yacht club, and tennis courts.

Meander inland to find the lakes for boating and fishing and peaks for hiking.

## SCHOODIC SECTION OF ACADIA NATIONAL PARK

The Schoodic section of Acadia has an entirely different feel from the main part on Mount

Handwoven textiles are the specialty at **Moosetrack Studio** (388 Bert Gray Rd./Rte. 200, Sullivan, 207/422-9017), where the selections vary from handwoven area rugs to shawls woven from merino wool and silk. Camilla Stege has been weaving since 1969 and her work reflects her experience and expertise.

Paul Breeden, best known for the remarkable illustrations, calligraphy, and maps he's done for *National Geographic*, Time-Life Books, and other national and international publications, displays and sells his paintings at the **Spring Woods Gallery and Willowbrook Garden** (40A Willowbrook La., Sullivan, 207/422-3007, www. springwoodsgallery.com, www.willowbrookgarden.com). Also filling the handsome modern gallery space are paintings by Ann Breeden and metal sculptures and silk scarves by the talented Breeden offspring. Be sure to allow time to meander through the sculpture garden, where there's even a playhouse for kids.

## SCHOODIC PENINSULA

From Route 1, loop down to Winter Harbor and back up on Route 186 through Prospect Harbor to find these galleries.

Architectural stoneware, with a specialty in sinks, is the drawing card at **Maine Kiln Works** (115 S. Gouldsboro Rd./Hwy. 186, Gouldsboro, 207/963-5819, www.waterstonesink.com), but you'll also find functional pottery in the shop. You might also see Dan Weaver at work on the wheel in the back room.

If you're lucky, you might catch Susan Dickson-Smith throwing a pot at **Stave Island Gallery/Proper Clay Stoneware** (Rte. 186, South Gouldsboro, 207/963-2040, www. properclay.com).

An old post office houses **Lee Art Glass** (679 S. Gouldsboro Rd./Rte. 196, Gouldsboro, 207/963-7280). Although Rod Lee has died, his works live on, thanks to Wayne Tucker and Sheldon R. Bickford, who bought the business after training with Lee. The fused-glass tableware is created by taking two pieces of window glass and firing them on terra-cotta or bisque molds at 1,500°F. What makes the end result so appealing are the colors and the patterns – crocheted doilies or stencils – impressed into the glass. The almost-magical results are beautiful, delicate-looking, yet functional.

Every piece handcrafted at **Gypsy Moose Glass Studio** (Main St., Winter Harbor, 207/963-2674, www.gypsymooseglass.com) is made from a single glass rod, which means no two are alike. You'll find glass beads, fused-glass earrings, swan weather predictors, and much more.

Visiting the **U.S. Bells Foundry and Watering Cove Pottery** (56 W. Bay Rd., Rte. 186, Prospect Harbor 04669, 207/963-7184, www. usbells.com) is a treat for the ears, as browsers try out the many varieties of cast-bronze bells made in the adjacent foundry by Richard Fisher. If you're lucky, he may have time to explain the process – particularly intriguing for children and a distraction from their instinctive urge to test every bell in the shop. The store also carries quilts by Dick's wife, Cindy, and wood-fired stoneware and porcelain by their daughter-in-law Liza Fisher. U.S. Bells is 0.25 mile up the hill from Prospect Harbor's post office.

ACADIA REGION

Desert. It's much smaller, less busy, and provides fewer recreational opportunities, but it's still magnificent and well worth visiting. There's no official visitors center in this area, so you'll want to stop at the main Acadia Visitor Center on Mount Desert Island, or download Schoodic information before you come.

As with so much of Acadia's acreage on Mount Desert Island, the Schoodic section became part of the park largely because of the deft diplomacy and perseverance of George B. Dorr. No obstacle ever seemed too daunting to Dorr. In 1928, when the owners objected to donating their land to a national park tagged with the Lafayette name (geopolitics being involved at the time), Dorr even managed to obtain congressional approval for the 1929 name change to Acadia National Park—and Schoodic was part of the deal.

There's no camping in this section of the

© TOM NANGLE

**Pink granite ledges surround Schoodic Point.**

park, but private camping and other lodging options are available in the area. There are no restaurants or other food sources in the park, but you won't need to go far.

To reach the park boundary from Route 1 in Gouldsboro, take Route 186 south to Winter Harbor. Continue through town, heading east, and then turn right and continue to the park-entrance sign, just before the bridge over Mosquito Harbor.

You can also tour the park using the free Island Explorer bus, which circulates through Winter Harbor, around the Schoodic Loop, and on to Prospect Harbor, with stops along the way. It's an efficient and environmentally friendly way to go.

Perhaps one of the best ways to get to know the park is to become involved with the **Friends of Schoodic** (P.O. Box 194, Prospect Harbor 04669, www.friendsofschoodic.org), which supports the park with clean-up projects, trail and building maintenance, and staffing the visitors information booth at the Gatehouse.

## Schoodic Loop

The major sights of Acadia's Schoodic section lie along the six-mile one-way road that meanders counterclockwise around the tip of the Schoodic Peninsula. You'll discover official and unofficial picnic areas, the hiking trailheads, offshore lighthouses, and turnouts with scenic vistas. Also named the Park Loop Road, it's best referred to as the Schoodic Loop to distinguish it from the one on Mount Desert. From this side of Frenchman Bay, the vistas of Mount Desert's summits are gorgeous, behind islands sprinkled here and there.

The first landmark is **Frazer Point Picnic Area,** with lovely vistas, picnic tables, and wheelchair-accessible restrooms. Other spots are fine for picnics, but this is the only official one. If you've brought bikes, leave your car here and do a counterclockwise 12.2-mile loop through the park and back to your car via Birch Harbor and Route 186. It's a fine day trip.

From the picnic area, the road becomes one-way. Unlike the Park Loop Road on Mount Desert, no parking is allowed in the right lane. There are periodic pullouts, but not many cars can squeeze in. Despite the fact that this is far from the busiest section of Acadia, it can still be frustrating in the summer to be unable to find a space. Best advice, therefore: Stay in the area and do this loop early in the morning or later in the afternoon, perhaps in May or June. (The late-September and early-October foliage is gorgeous, but traffic *does* increase then.) While you're driving, if you see a viewpoint you like (with room to pull off), stop; it's a long way around to return.

At 2.2 miles from the picnic area, watch for a narrow, unpaved road on the left, across from an "open" beach vista. It winds for a mile (keep left at the fork) up to a tiny parking circle, from which you can follow the trail (signposted "Schoodic trails") to the open ledges on 440-foot Schoodic Head. From the circle, there's already a glimpse of the view, but it gets much better. If you bear right at the fork, you'll come to a grassy parking area with access to the Alder Trail and the Schoodic Head Trail.

Continue on the Park Loop Road and hang a right onto a short, two-way spur to **Schoodic Point,** the highlight of this section of the park. Although crowds gather at the height of summer, especially when the surf is raging, the two-tiered parking lot, amazingly, seldom fills up. (There are restrooms here, too.) Check local newspapers for the time of high tide and try to arrive here then; the word *awesome* is overused, but it sure describes Schoodic Point's surf performance on the rugged pink granite. The setting sun makes it even more brilliant. This area is open 6 A.M.–10 P.M. only.

*Caution:* If you've brought children, keep them well back from the water; a rogue wave can sweep them off the rocks all too easily. It *has* happened. Picnics are great here (make sure you bring a litter bag), and so are the tide pools at mid- to low tide. Birding is spectacular during spring and fall migrations.

Just before the point is a small info center, staffed by volunteers and park rangers, on the site of a former top-secret U.S. Navy base that became part of the park in 2002. The campus is now the Schoodic Education and Re-

search Center (locally called by its acronym, SERC); occasional lectures and programs are held here and it's the site of the biennial sculpture symposium.

From Schoodic Point, return to the Loop Road. Look to your right, and you'll see Little Moose Island, which is accessible at low tide. Be careful, though, and don't get stranded here. Continue to the **Blueberry Hill** parking area (about one mile from the Schoodic Point/Loop Rd. intersection), a moorlike setting where the low growth allows almost 180-degree views of the bay and islands. There are a few trails in this area—all eventually converging on **Schoodic Head,** the highest point on the peninsula. (Don't confuse this with Schoodic Mountain, which is well north of here.) Across the road and up the road a bit is the trailhead for the 180-foot-high **Anvil** headland. The Schoodic Head Loop hike comprises three connecting trails, and it can be hiked in either direction, or if time is tight, choose just one trail to hike (allow 2–3 hours for the full loop). Clockwise begins with the easiest terrain and ends with a downhill scramble over a steep and rocky hillside. As one ranger noted, it's tough on the knees and you have to be very careful with your footing in this direction. If you hike it counterclockwise, beginning with the Anvil Trail, you'll get the toughest terrain out of the way first.

As you continue along this stretch of road, keep your eyes peeled for eagles, which frequently soar here. There's a nest on the northern end of Rolling Island; you can see it with binoculars from some of the roadside pullouts.

From Blueberry Hill, continue 1.2 miles to a pullout for the East Trail, the shortest and most direct route to Schoodic Head. From here, it's about another mile to the park exit, in Wonsqueak Harbor. It's another two miles to the intersection with Route 186 in Birch Harbor. (If you didn't bring a picnic, Bunker's Wharf Restaurant is an excellent stop.)

## SCENIC BYWAYS

Just how gorgeous is this region? Well, it has not one, but two scenic byways: one coastal and one inland. You can link the two together via Route 1 between Gouldsboro and Cherryfield.

## ◖ Schoodic National Scenic Byway

Beginning at the bridge on Route 1 in Sullivan, 27-mile Schoodic Byway (www.schoodicbyway.org) passes a reversing falls and takes in vistas of Frenchman Bay and Acadia's peaks before looping down and around the Schoodic Peninsula via Route 186 and the Park Road, before ending in Prospect Harbor, with views of the boat-filled harbor and Prospect Harbor Lighthouse. Recent improvements have provided pullouts just where you want to stop and admire the views. Hint: Do yourself a favor and from Prospect Harbor, take Route 195 to Corea Harbor.

## Maine Scenic Byway

A few miles east of Ellsworth, Route 182 veers northeast off Route 1 to Franklin and on to Cherryfield, a 25-mile stretch of sparkling ponds, brilliant colors, and no civilization. Schoodic Mountain, Donnell Pond, and Tunk Lake are just three of the natural treasures along the way. As you enter Washington County and land in Cherryfield, you're brought gently back to civilization by a whole town full of architectural treasures. This route is simply gorgeous in autumn.

## RECREATION
### Donnell Pond Public Reserved Land

More than 15,000 acres have been preserved for public access in Donnell Pond Public Reserved Land (Maine Bureau of Parks and Lands, 207/827-1818, www.state.me.us/doc/parks), a huge mountain-and-lake area north and east of Sullivan. Developers had their eyes on this gorgeous real estate in the 1980s, but preservationists fortunately rallied to the cause. Outright purchase of 7,316 of the acres, in the Spring River Lake area, came through the foresighted Land for Maine's Future program. Hikers can climb Schoodic, Black, and Caribou Mountains; paddlers and anglers have

Donnell Pond, Tunk Lake, Spring River Lake, Long Pond, Round Pond, and Little Pond, among others. Route 182, an official Scenic Highway, cuts right through the Donnell Pond preserve. The preserve encompasses lakes for boating and fishing, mountains for hiking, and primitive campsites. Do note: Hunting is permitted, so take special care during hunting season.

### Schoodic Mountain, Donnell Pond Public Reserved Land

The hiking isn't easy here, but it isn't technical. And the options are many. The interconnecting trail system takes in Schoodic Mountain, Black Mountain, and Caribou Mountain. Follow the Schoodic Mountain Loop clockwise, heading westward first. To make a day of it, pack a picnic and take a swimsuit (and don't forget a camera and binoculars for the summit views). On a brilliantly clear day, you'll see Baxter State Park's Katahdin, the peaks of Acadia National Park, and the ocean beyond. And in late July/early August, blueberries are abundant on the summit. For such rewards, this is a popular hike, so don't expect to be alone, especially on fall weekends, when the foliage colors are spectacular.

The Black Mountain ascent begins easily enough and then climbs steadily through the woods, easing off a bit before reaching bald ledges. Continue to the true summit by taking the trail past Wizard Pond. Views take in the forested lands, nearby lakes and peaks, and out to Acadia's peaks. You can piggyback it with Schoodic Mountain, using that trailhead base for both climbs. Another possibility is to add Caribou Mountain. That loop exceeds seven miles, making a full day of hiking.

Trailheads are accessible by either boat or vehicle. To reach the vehicle-access trailhead for Schoodic Mountain from Route 1 in East Sullivan, drive just over four miles northeast on Route 183 (Tunk Lake Rd.). Cross the Maine Central Railroad tracks and turn left at the Donnell Pond sign onto an unpaved road (marked as a jeep track on the USGS map). Go about 0.25 mile and then turn left for the parking area and trailhead for Schoodic Mountain, Black Mountain, Caribou Mountain, and a trail to Schoodic Beach. If you continue straight, you'll come to another trailhead for Black and Caribou Mountains. Water-access trailheads are at Schoodic Beach and Redman's Beach.

## Shore Path

A pleasant and short shore path begins and ends at the **Dixon Memorial Rock** and follows the water's edge, rising through the woods and passing by cottages on eastern Grindstone Neck. The views are fabulous. To find it, take Beach Street to Club House Lane, proceed across the four-way intersection, and then go right on Steamboat Lane, following it to the oval at the end.

## Bicycling

The best choices for cycling are the **Schoodic Loop** and the quiet roads of **Grindstone Neck** and **Corea.** Bike rentals ($15 per 24 hours) are available from **SeaScape Kayaking** (18 East Schoodic Dr., Birch Harbor, 207/963-7223, www.seascapekayaking.com), an ideal location for the Schoodic Loop.

## Canoeing and Kayaking

Experienced sea kayakers can explore the coastline throughout this region. Canoeists can paddle the placid waters of Jones Pond, on the Schoodic Peninsula. In Donnell Pond Public Reserved Land, the major water bodies are **Donnell Pond** (big enough by most gauges to be called a lake) and **Tunk** and **Spring River Lakes;** all are accessible for boats (even, alas, powerboats).

To reach the boat-launching area for Donnell Pond from Route 1 in Sullivan, take Route 200 North to Route 182. Turn right and go about 1.5 miles to a right turn just before Swan Brook. Turn and go not quite two miles to the put-in; the road is poor in spots but adequate for a regular vehicle. The Narrows, where you'll put in, is lined with summer cottages ("camps" in the Maine vernacular); keep paddling eastward to the more open part of the lake. Continue on Route 182 to find the boat launches

for Tunk Lake and Spring River Lake (hand-carry only). Canoeists and kayakers have access to Tunk Stream from Spring River Lake.

Still within the preserve boundaries, but farther east, you can put in a canoe at the northern end of Long Pond and paddle southward into adjoining Round Pond. In early August, Round Mountain, rising a few hundred feet from Long Pond's eastern shore, is a great spot for gathering blueberries and huckleberries. The put-in for Long Pond is on the south side of Route 182 (park well off the road), about two miles east of Tunk Lake.

## Outfitters and Trips

Paddle around the waters of Schoodic or Flanders Bay with Ed and Cheryl Brackett's **SeaScape Kayaking** (18 E. Schoodic Dr., Birch Harbor, 207/963-7223, www.seascapekayaking.com). Guided three- to four-hour tours are $45 pp, including fortification: homemade blueberry scones for morning trips and blueberry-white chocolate chip cookies in the afternoon. Canoe rental for lake usage is $40 per day; kayaks are $40 double, $30 single.

Master Maine Guides Darrin Kelly and Megan Gahl are committed to sustainability and education—they not only talk the talk, they walk the walk, living off the grid in a yurt surrounded by protected lands. Their enthusiasm and knowledge come through on their trips. **Ardea Expeditions** (242 S. Gouldsboro Rd., Gouldsboro, 207/460-9731, www.ardea-ecoexpeditions.com) offers a wide range of sea kayaking options, from half- and full-day trips to camping or inn-to-inn overnights to research expeditions. Half-day coastal eco-adventures begin at $59 adult, $49 child; a full day of island hopping is $105, including lunch. Family trips are available as are instructional trips, a first-light sunrise tour geared to birders, and a sunset tour that can be combined with a lobster bake. Custom overnights begin at $145 pp/day. Ask about voluntourism research expeditions, including island inventory and monitoring and seabird surveys. Ardea donates 1 percent of sales to local nonprofits—all the more reason to choose this outfitter.

ACADIA REGION

Antonio Blasi, a Registered Maine Sea Kayak and Recreational Guide, leads guided tours of Frenchman or Taunton Bay and hiking and camping expeditions through **Hancock Point Kayak Tours** (58 Point Rd., Hancock, 207/422-6854, www.hancockpointkayak.com). A three-hour paddle, including all equipment, safety and paddling demonstrations, and usually an island break, is $45. You have a choice of single or double kayak. Minimum age is 9 for a double, 12 for a single. Overnight kayak camping trips are $150 per person. Antonio also leads overnight backpacking trips for $125 pp, and cross-country skiing and snowshoe tours are available in winter.

## Swimming

The best freshwater swimming in the area is at **Jones Beach,** a community-owned recreation area on Jones Pond in West Gouldsboro. Here you'll find restrooms, a nice playground, picnic facilities, boat launch, swim area with a float, and a small beach. It's at the end of Recreation Road, off Route 195, which is 0.3 mile south of Route 1.

Two beach areas on Donnell Pond are also popular for swimming—**Schoodic Beach** and **Redman's Beach**—and both have picnic tables, fire rings, and pit toilets. It's a half-mile hike to Schoodic Beach from the parking lot. Redman's Beach is accessible only by boat. Other pocket beaches are also accessible by boat, and there's a rope swing (use at your own risk) by a roadside pullout for Fox Pond.

## Golf

Play a nine-hole round at the **Grindstone Neck Golf Course** (Grindstone Ave., Winter Harbor, 207/963-7760, www.grindstonegolf.com, May–Oct.), just for the dynamite scenery and for a glimpse of this exclusive, late-19th-century summer enclave. Established in 1891, the public course attracts a tony crowd; 150-yard markers are cute little birdhouses.

## SHOPPING
## Art and Antiques

Browsers, dreamers, and collectors are welcome at **Art and Old Things** (70 Taunton Dr., Sullivan, 207/422-3551), a one-stop antiques and collectibles shop, art gallery, and sculpture garden that's just plain fun to visit. The eclectic gallery features the work of Joe Martell and other regional artists; the shop is filled with antiques, junktiques, and shabby chic furniture, decorative items, home accents, and architectural pieces; the garden is accented with granite and marble sculptures and unique functional artwork. The shop is just 500 yards off Route 1, just beyond Gazebo Park.

**Winter Harbor Antiques and Works of Hand** (424–426 Main St., Winter Harbor, 207/963-2547) is a double treat. Antiques fill one building and works by local craftspeople and artists fill the other. It's across from Hammond Hall and set behind colorful, well-tended gardens.

Barbara Noel makes most of the sea glass jewelry, mobiles, and other creations at **Harbor Treasures** (358 and 368 Main St., Winter Harbor, 207/963-7086).

Here's a nifty place: **Chapter Two** (611 Corea Rd., Corea, 207/963-7269) is home to the Corea Rug Hooking company and Accumulated Books Gallery. Spread out in three buildings are a nice selection of used and antiquarian books, locally made crafts, and Rosemary's hand-hooked rugs. Sip on tea or coffee while browsing. Yarn, rug-hooking supplies, and lessons are available.

Ever seen a palmara, durian jack, pangium edule, or dompaum? Even know what they are? **Coastal Antiques** (Rte. 186, Prospect Harbor, 207/963-5546) has the original nut collection from Perry's Nut House, which pulled in tourists from around the globe in Belfast until its demise. Some specimens are amazing to see. The shop, which also sells antiques, shares a building with DeMarco Realty at the intersection with the Corea Road/Route 195.

## Food and Wine

German and Italian presses, Portuguese corks, and Maine fruit all go into the creation of Bob and Kathe Bartlett's award-winning dinner and dessert wines: apple, pear, blueberry,

Just about everyone shops Winter Harbor's five-and-dime.

raspberry, blackberry, strawberry, and loganberry. Founded in 1982, **Bartlett Maine Estate Winery** (175 Chicken Mill Pond Rd., Gouldsboro, 207/546-2408, www.bartlettwinery.com, 10 A.M.–5 P.M. Mon.–Sat. late May–mid-Oct., or by appointment off-season) produces more than 20,000 gallons annually in a handsome wood-and-stone building designed by the Bartletts. No tours, but you're welcome to sample the wines, and you can buy single bottles and gift packages. Bartlett's is a half mile south of Route 1 in Gouldsboro.

Organic fruit and honey wines are produced at family-operated **Shalom Orchard Organic Winery and Bed and Breakfast** (158 Eastbrook Rd., P.O. Box 4, Franklin 04634, 207/565-2312, www.shalomorchard.com). The certified-organic farm is well off the beaten path but worth a visit not only for the wines, but also for yarns, pelts, fleece, and especially the views of Frenchman Bay from the hilltop orchard. The farm also has two simple rooms, sharing one bath and kitchenette. A full farm breakfast is included in the $55–65 rate. Pets and kids are

welcome. To find it, take Route 182 to Route 200/Eastbrook Road, and go 1.6 miles.

This area has two excellent smokehouses. Defying its name, **Sullivan Harbor Smokehouse** (Rte. 1, Hancock, 207/422-3735 or 800/422-4014, www.sullivanharborfarm.com) has moved to spacious, modern new digs in Hancock. Big interior windows allow visitors to see into the production facility and watch the action. Among the offerings are Scottish-style smoked salmon, gravlax, smoked scallops, smoked trout, smoked Arctic char, smoked salmon pâté, and more.

The newer **Grindstone Neck of Maine** (311 Newman St., Rte. 186, just north of downtown Winter Harbor, 207/963-7347, or 866/831-8734, www.grindstoneneck.com) also earns high marks for its smoked salmon, shellfish, spreads, and pâtés, all made without preservatives or artificial ingredients. Also available are fresh fish, wine, and frozen foods for campers. Best seller: a can of Road Kill Stew; go figure.

## This and That

You can find just about anything at the

**Winter Harbor 5 and 10** (Main St., Winter Harbor, 207/963-7927, www.winterharbor-5and10.com). It's the genuine article, an old fashioned five-and-dime that's somehow still surviving in the age of Wal-Mart.

# ENTERTAINMENT AND EVENTS

Winter Harbor's biggest wingding is the annual **Lobster Festival** (www.acadia-schoodic.org) the second Saturday in August. The gala daylong event includes a parade, live entertainment, lobster-boat races (a serious competition in these parts), crafts fair, games, and more crustaceans than you could ever consume.

## Arts and Science

The **Pierre Monteux School for Conductors and Orchestra Musicians** (Rte. 1, Hancock, 207/422-3280, www.monteuxschool.org), a prestigious summer program founded in 1943, has achieved international renown for training dozens of national and international classical musicians. It presents two well-attended concert series starting in late June and running through July. The Wednesday series (7:30 P.M., $10 adults, $5 kids) features chamber music; the Sunday concerts (5 P.M., $15 adults, $5 students) feature symphonies. An annual children's concert usually is held on a Monday (1 P.M.) in early to mid-July. Recently, it's been scheduling concerts in August, too. All concerts are held in the school's Forest Studio.

Concerts, art classes, coffeehouses, workshops, and related activities are presented year-round by the energetic **Schoodic Arts for All** (207/963-2569, www.schoodicarts.org), a volunteer organization. Many are held at historic Hammond Hall in downtown Winter Harbor. A summer series presents monthly concerts on Friday evenings May–October. In early August, the two-week **Schoodic Arts Festival** is jam-packed with daily workshops and nightly performances for all ages. Register early for any program that you don't want to miss.

Seeking to add more vibrancy and diversity to the peninsula's entertainment offerings and to indulge their own interests in music and

the sciences, the owners of Oceanside Meadows Inn created the **Innstitute for Arts and Sciences** (207/963-5557, www.ocean-inn.com), which presents a series of Thursday night events late June–late September, with a break during the Schoodic Arts Festival. The wide-ranging calendar includes lectures and concerts as well as art shows. Some are free, others are $10 in advance or $12 at the door.

Acadia Partners (P.O. Box 277, Winter Harbor 04693, 207/288-1326, www.acadiapartners.orgt) is working with Acadia National Park to create a scientific research center at **Schoodic Education and Research Center,** on the old Navy base on Schoodic Point, locally called SERC. In 2007, it launched a biennial international sculpture symposium, with the aim of creating granite sculptures to place within coastal communities throughout the region.

# ACCOMMODATIONS

There are no lodgings in the Schoodic section of the park, but within less than a half hour of the Schoodic parkland, you'll have your choice of an impressive range of places to sleep—from an elegant French-style country inn with a fantastic restaurant to a rustic campground with lovely wilderness sites.

## Country Inns

Buffered from the highway by a tall hedge, **Le Domaine** (Rte. 1, HC 77, Box 496, Hancock 04640, 207/422-3395 or 800/554-8498, www.ledomaine.com) has gained a five-star reputation for its restaurant, founded in 1946—long before fine dining had cachet here. But that's only part of the story. Above the restaurant is a charming, five-room, country-French inn. The 80-acre inn property, nine miles east of Ellsworth, is virtual Provence, an oasis transplanted magically to Maine. On the garden-view balconies, or on the lawn out back, you're oblivious to the traffic whizzing by. Better yet, follow the lovely wooded trail to a quiet pond. Three guest rooms ($285 d, including breakfast and dinner; $200 B&B) and two suites ($370 d, MAP, $285 B&B) all are named after locales in Provence. Continental breakfast, usually including freshly made croissants and jams, can be served in your room or in the dining room. Alert the inn if you'll be arriving after 5:30 P.M., when the staff has to focus on dinner. The ultra-French restaurant is open to the public 6–9 P.M. Tuesday–Sunday. Reservations are essential, especially in July and August. Le Domaine's season is mid-June–early November.

Follow Hancock Point Road 4.8 miles south of Route 1 to the three-story, gray-blue **Crocker House Country Inn** (967 Point Rd., HC 77, Box 171, Hancock 04640, 207/422-6806, www.crockerhouse.com, $110–165), Rich and Liz Malaby's antidote to Bar Harbor's summer traffic. Built as a summer hotel in 1884, the inn underwent rehabbing a century later, but it retains a decidedly old-fashioned air, although Wi-Fi is now available. Breakfast is included. Guests can relax in the common room or reserve spa time in the carriage house. One kayak and a few bicycles are available. Nearby are clay tennis courts, quiet walking routes past Hancock Point's elegant seaside "cottages," and a unique octagonal public library. The Malabys will pack picnic lunches (extra charge) for day trips to Campobello Island, Acadia, or Lamoine State Park. If you're arriving by boat, request a mooring. The inn's dining room is a draw in itself.

## Bed-and-Breakfasts

Overlooking the Gouldsboro Peninsula's only sandy saltwater beach, **Oceanside Meadows Innstitute** (Rte. 195, Corea Rd., P.O. Box 90, Prospect Harbor 04669, 207/963-5557, www.oceaninn.com, $128–198, May–late Oct.) is a jewel of a place on 200 acres with fabulous gardens, wildlife habitat, and walking trails. The elegant 1860s Captain's House has seven attractive rooms, and the 1820 Shaw farmhouse next door has another seven. Each room has a copy of Louise Dickinson Rich's *The Peninsula*—a thoughtful touch. Breakfast is an impressive four-course event, usually featuring herbs and flowers from the inn's gardens. Energetic husband-and-wife team of Sonja Sundaram and Ben Walter seem to have thought

of everything—hot drinks available all day, a guest fridge, beach toys, even detailed guides to the property's trails and habitats (great for entertaining kids). As if all that weren't enough, Sonja and Ben have totally restored the 1820 timber-frame barn out back—creating the **Oceanside Meadows Innstitute for the Arts and Sciences.** Local art hangs on the walls, and June–September, the 125-seat barn has a full schedule of classical concerts and lectures on natural history, Native American traditions, and more, usually on Thursday nights. Some are free, some require tickets; all require reservations. The inn's website is also a phenomenal resource on area activities. Oceanside Meadows is six miles off Route 1.

Watch lobster boats unload their catch at the dock opposite **Elsa's Inn on the Harbor** (179 Main St., Prospect Harbor, 207/963-7571, www.elsasinn.com, $105–155). Jeffrey and Cynthia Alley, their daughter, Megan, and her husband, Glenn Moshier, and grandsons Andrew and Emmett have turned Jeff's mother Elsa's home into a warm and welcoming inn. The Alley family roots in the area go back more than 10 generations, so you're guaranteed to receive solid information on where to go and what to do. Every room has an ocean view, and Megan, an experienced innkeeper whose career included positions at Ritz-Carlton and luxury boutique hotels, pampers guests with luxurious linens, down duvets, terry robes, and a hearty hot breakfast. After a day exploring, settle into a rocker on the veranda and gaze over the boat-filled harbor out to Prospect Harbor Light. And afterward? Well perhaps a lobster bake. Upon request, Megan's dad will bring over some fresh lobster and Megan will prepare a complete lobster dinner—corn on the cob, cole slaw, homemade rolls, and a seasonal dessert, all for about $22 pp, depending upon market rates.

Set well back from Route 1, **Acadia View Bed and Breakfast** (175 Rte. 1, Gouldsboro, 207/963-7457 or 866/963-7457, www.acadiaview.com, $135–165) is built on a bluff with views across Frenchman Bay to the peaks of Mount Desert and a path down to the shorefront. Pat and Jim Close built the oceanfront house as a B&B, opening it in 2005. The building may be new, but it's filled with antique treasures from the Closes's former life in Connecticut. Each of the four guest rooms has a private deck. The Route 1 location, while next to nothing, is convenient for everything.

Off the beaten path is Bob Travers and Barry Canner's **Black Duck Inn on Corea Harbor** (Crowley Island Rd., P.O. Box 39, Corea 04624, 207/963-2689, www.blackduck.com, $140–170, May–mid-Oct.), literally the end of the line on the Gouldsboro Peninsula. Set on 12 acres in this timeless fishing village, the B&B has four handsomely decorated rooms and plenty of common space. Across the way, perched on the harbor's edge, are two little seasonal cottages, one rented by the day (three-night minimum) and one by the week ($825–900). The inn and Corea are geared to wanderers, readers, and anyone seeking serenity (who isn't?). Rocky outcrops dot the property and a nature trail meanders to a millpond; in early August, the blueberries are ready. If the fog socks in, the large parlor has comfortable chairs and loads of books.

Something of a categorical anomaly, **The Bluff House Inn** (Rte. 186, P.O. Box 249, Gouldsboro 04607, 207/963-7805, www.bluffinn.com, $65–100) is part motel, part hotel, part B&B—a seemingly successful mix in a contemporary building overlooking Frenchman Bay on the west side of the Gouldsboro Peninsula. Verandas wrap around the first and second floors, so bring binoculars for osprey and bald eagle sightings. Pine walls and flooring give a lodge feeling to the open first floor. Settle by the stone fireplace or grab a seat by the window. Breakfast, a generous continental with excellent baked goodies, is served here. The eight second-floor rooms are decorated "country" fashion, with quilts on the very comfortable beds. (In hot weather, request a corner room.) Also available is a two-bedroom housekeeping apartment ($120/day or $670/week) built above a garage. It's open all year.

About 12 miles east of Ellsworth is the **Island View Inn** (12 Miramar Ave., Sullivan, 207/422-3031, www.maineus.com/islandview,

$145–165, late May–mid-Oct.); its name is the height of understatement. Out front are the peaks of Mount Desert, a remarkable panorama. Four of the seven rooms (all with decks) capture the view from this updated 1889 summer home run by Evelyn Joost and her daughter Sarah. The inn evokes the easy elegance of days gone by. The Island View has a private beach, but the water is terminally chilly. Sailing excursions are available by reservation on the inn's Rhodes 18 sloop. Guests have free use of a canoe and a dinghy. Pets and kids over six are welcome.

**The White Elephant Inn** (25 Main St./Rte. 182, Franklin, 207/565-2020, $90) is anything but. Owner Dana Geel, a history teacher and lover of all things old and odd, has filled his circa 1830 Colonial farmhouse overlooking Hog Bay with antique treasures highlighted by his collection of 5,000 (!) elephants. Dana's owned a number of houses on Mount Desert and has amassed a collection of notable antiques in the process, including some furnishings from the estate of Evalyn Walsh McLean, one-time owner of the Hope diamond, and even a camel table—this you simply must see. Public rooms ramble from one to another, varying from formal ones to a cozy den. A full breakfast is served. Dana knows the region well and has even opened an info center in the barn.

Sustainable living is the focus of Karen and Ed Curtis's peaceful **◖ Three Pines Bed and Breakfast** (HC 77, Box 349AA, Hancock 04640, 207/460-7595, www.threepinesbandb.com, $85–115, year-round), fronting on Sullivan Harbor, just below the Reversing Falls. Their quiet, off-the-grid, oceanfront farm faces Sullivan Harbor and is home to llamas, pigs, chickens, and ducks, as well as a large organic garden, berry bushes, a developing orchard, and greenhouses. Photovoltaics provide electricity; appliances are primarily propane powered; satellite technology operates the phone, TV, and Internet systems. Two inviting guest rooms have private entrances and waterviews. A full vegetarian breakfast (with fresh eggs from the farm available) is served. Bring kayaks or bikes. You can walk or pedal along an abandoned railway line down to the point or up to the lobster pound, and you can launch your kayak from the back—or is it the front—yard. Children welcome; pets are a possibility.

Innkeeper Carolyn Bucklin is determined to create the perfect B&B experience at **Cottage by the Sea** (38 Kilkenny Cove, Hancock, 207/422-6783, www.cottagebytheseamaine.com, $140–160, June 1–mid-Oct.). Top-quality linens, fully equipped rooms (satellite TV, irons and ironing boards, hair dryers, telephones), evening turndown service, and air-conditioning make it hard to tear yourself away from the oceanfront inn. Three rooms are available, one with a view of Kilkenny Cove. Breakfast is a multicourse affair; afternoon refreshments are served. No pets, as there is a resident dog.

Sorrento is such a low-key place that lots of people don't realize it has a B&B, an ultra-casual homestay-style one at that. **Bass Cove Farm Bed and Breakfast** (312 Eastside Rd., Rte. 185, Sorrento, 207/422-3564, www.basscovefarm.com, $65–100) was opened in 1992 by spinner/weaver/gardener/editor Mary Ann Solet and her husband, Michael Tansey, a group-home supervisor whose résumé also includes the Harry S. Truman Manure Pitchoff Championship at the annual Common Ground Country Fair. The 1840s-era farmhouse uses solar-heated water; the cleaning is done with nontoxic products. Mary Ann can rattle off dozens of ideas for exploring the area, particularly in the craft department, and she raids her extensive vegetable garden daily to produce a hearty, healthful breakfast. Guest rooms have quilt-covered beds and other homey touches—some share baths. A one-bedroom apartment on the second floor rents for $375–395 a week.

## Cottages

Roger and Pearl Barto, whose family roots in this region go back five generations, have four rental accommodations on their Henry's Cove oceanfront property, **Main Stay**

**Cottages** (66 Sargent St., P.O. Box 459, Winter Harbor 04693, 207/963-2601, www.awaweb.com/stayinn, $80–115). Most unusual is the small, one-bedroom Boat House, which has stood since the 1880s. It hangs over the harbor, with views to Mark Island Light, and you can hear the water gurgling below you at high tide. Other options include a very comfortable efficiency cottage, a one-bedroom cottage, and a second-floor suite, with private entrance, in the main house. All have big decks and fabulous views over the lobster boat–filled harbor; watch for the eagles that frequently soar overhead. Main Stay is on the Island Explorer route and just a short walk from where the Bar Harbor Ferry docks.

Rustic, but charming in a sweet, old-fashioned way, are **Albee's Cottages** (Rte. 186, Prospect Harbor, 207/963-2336 or 800/963-2336, www.theshorehouse.com, $73–114/night, May–late Sept.), a cluster of 10 somewhat ramshackle cottages, decorated with braided rugs, fresh flowers, and other homey touches. Two things make this place special: the waterfront location—and it's truly waterfront; many of the cottages are just a couple of feet from the high-tide mark—and the management. Owner Richard Rieth goes out of his way to make guests feel welcome. Pick up lobsters and say what time you want dinner, and they'll be cooked and delivered to your cottage. Richard sometimes brings home-baked sweets and other treats to cottages when he has the time and inclination. He's slowly fixing up the simple cottages, first tackling much-needed new roofs and exterior painting. Now he's updating the interiors. In peak season, cottages rent on a Saturday-to-Saturday basis, but shorter rentals are often available. Dogs allowed.

## Campgrounds

On a wooded finger of land projecting eastward from the Schoodic Peninsula, **☾ Ocean Wood Campground** (P.O. Box 111, Birch Harbor 04613, 207/963-7194, early May–late Oct.) gets kudos for eco-sensitivity, noise control, and 17 fantastic wilderness sites, most on the ocean. Don't expect frills; nature provides the entertainment. The 70 campsites (20 with hookups) are $20–39, depending on location and services. Pets (leashed) and guests are allowed at regular sites, but not at the wilderness ones. No credit cards; free hot showers. The campground is a terrific base for exploring the Schoodic section of Acadia National Park. (Note, however, that the campground is at the *end* of the one-way Schoodic Loop Road. It's no problem hiking back into the park area the wrong way, but if you're driving or biking, you'll need to go around, about five miles, via Route 186, to do the loop.)

## Donnell Pond Public Reserved Land

A handful of authorized, primitive campsites can be found on Tunk Lake (southwestern corner) and Donnell Pond (at Schoodic Beach and Redman's Beach), all accessible by foot or boat. Each has a table, fire ring, and nearby pit toilet. Many of the sites are lakefront. All are first-come, first-served (no fees or permits required), and are snapped up quickly on midsummer weekends. You can camp elsewhere within the unit, excepting day-use areas, but fires are not permitted on unauthorized sites.

## FOOD
### Local Flavors

Make a point to attend one of the many **public suppers** held throughout the summer in this area and so many other rural corners of Maine. Typically benefiting a worthy cause, these usually feature beans, chowder, or spaghetti and the serendipity of plain potluck. Everyone saves room for the homemade pies. Notices of such suppers are usually posted on public bulletin boards in country stores and in libraries, on signs in front of churches, and at other places people gather.

Delicious soups and sandwiches, baked goods, and a nice selection of prepared foods are available at **Mano's Market** (1517 Rte. 1, Hancock, 207/422-6500, 7 A.M.– 6 P.M. Tues.–Sat.), a gourmet and prepared foods and wine market.

Pick up veggies, meats, eggs, cheeses, and handcrafted fiber products as well as jams, preserves, and baked goods at the **Winter Harbor Farmers Market** (parking lot, corner Newman St. and Rte. 186, Winter Harbor, 9 A.M.– noon Tues. late June–early Sept.).

Once a true, old-fashioned country store with a classic traditional soda fountain and penny candy, **J. M. Gerrish Provisions** (352 Main St., Winter Harbor, 207/963-2727, 8 A.M.–8 P.M. daily), known as Gerrish's Store, has undergone many changes in recent years. It's now an upscale specialty-foods store, coffee bar with Wi-Fi, ice-cream parlor, and café, but that might change under new ownership.

Craving curry? Call in your order before 3 P.M., and **Tandoor Downeast** (Eastbrook Rd., Franklin, 207/565-3598, www.tandoor-downeast.com) will prepare authentic Indian cuisine for you to take away. The menu is extensive, and prices are reasonable, with most choices $6–8. A selection is usually also available at the Winter Harbor Farmers Market.

### Family Fare

The best place for grub and gossip in Winter Harbor is **Chase's Restaurant** (193 Main St., Winter Harbor, 207/963-7171, 7 A.M.–8 P.M., to 2 P.M. Sun.), a seasoned, no-frills booth-and-counter operation that turns out first-rate fish chowder, fries, and onion rings, wraps, home-style dinners, and downright cheap breakfasts.

In "downtown" Prospect Harbor, the **Downeast Deli** (corner Rtes. 186 and 195, Prospect Harbor, 207/963-2700, 11 A.M.– 7 P.M. Sun.–Thurs., to 8 P.M. Fri.–Sat.) will fix you right up with dozens of sandwich choices: hot or cold hoagies, hot dogs and burgers, Reubens, deli-style sandwiches, and good pizza with a wide array of mix-and-match choices.

Don't be put off by the lobster "sculpture" outside **Ruth and Wimpy's Kitchen** (792 Rte. 1, Hancock, 207/422-3723, 11 A.M.– 9 P.M. daily Apr.–Dec.); you'll probably see a crowd as well. This family-fare standby serves hefty sandwiches, lobster prepared in 30 ways, pizza, pasta, and steak. Prices begin at less than $3 for a cheeseburger and climb to about $25 for a twin-tail lobster dinner. Locals praise the lobster roll as the cheapest and best around. Antique license plates and collections of miniature cars and trucks accent the interior. It's five miles east of Ellsworth, close to the Hancock Point turnoff.

Good food served by friendly folks is what pulls the locals into **🄒 Chester Pike's Galley** (2236 Rte. 1, Sullivan, 207/422-8200, 6 A.M.–2 P.M. Mon.–Sat., opens at 7 A.M. Sun., and 4:30–8:30 P.M. Fri. and Sat.). The prices are low, the portions big. If you're on a diet, don't even *look* at the glass case filled with fresh-baked pies, cakes, and cookies. Go early if you want to snag one of the homemade doughnuts (and order dessert first). It's also open Friday nights for a fish fry with free seconds, and Saturday nights for roast beef.

Here's a surprise: You can't get much farther from Mexico than Coastal Maine and still be in the States, but **The Mexican Restaurant** (1166 Rte. 1, Hancock, 207/422-3723, 11 A.M.–8 P.M. daily) has earned a reputation for being a hot spot for authentic Mex. Originally in Harrington, where it catered to the region's migrant blueberry pickers, it's moved to Hancock, where it shares a huge log building with a motorcycle shop. It's bright and cheerful inside, with tables also on the porch and a few picnic tables on the lawn. Almost everything on the menu is $3–8, and there are plenty of choices.

## Casual Dining

Make it a point to find **Bunkers Wharf** (260 E. Schoodic Dr., Birch Harbor, 207/963-2244, www.bunkerswharfrestaurant.com, 11:30 A.M.–10 P.M. daily), just one mile from the end of the Schoodic loop. The dining room overlooks a working wharf, and there's a big stone fireplace to ward off the chill on inclement days. Crisp white linens and fresh flowers add a formal touch in the dining room, yet the feeling is unpretentious. You can also dine in the pub or on a patio that's practically in the harbor. Only drawback: Dinners are pricey: entrées are $18 and up. Open seasonally.

**The Fisherman's Inn** (7 Newman St., Rte. 186, Winter Harbor, 207/963-5585, 5–9 P.M. daily late May–mid-Oct.), estab-

lished in 1947, has had a roller-coaster history, with good phases and bad ones. It's now under the ownership of Kathy Johnson and her award-winning chef/husband, Carl. The only remaining tradition seems to be the "gourmet cheese spread" served to every table—but you'll also have a sample of salmon pâté from Carl's latest venture, Grindstone Neck of Maine. Seafood is the specialty here, and there's a good chance that the guy at the neighboring booth caught your lobster or fish. Asian influences are evident, too. Entrée range is $14–25, although some dishes can top that given seasonal market rates.

It's easy to miss **Chipper's** (Rte. 1, Hancock, 207/422-8238, 5–9 P.M., closed Sun.–Mon.), a simple Cape-style building hard by Route 1, but that would be a mistake. Chip definitely knows his way around the kitchen. The wide-ranging menu includes rack of lamb and even chateaubriand, but the emphasis is on seafood; the crab cakes earn their rave reviews. Meals include a sampling of tasty haddock chowder and a salad, but save room for the homemade ice cream for dessert. Entrées are in the $16–30 range, but some appetizer/salad combo options provide budget options.

## Fine Dining

The ultra-French restaurant **🄒 Le Domaine** (1515 Rte. 1, P.O. Box 519, Hancock 04640, 207/422-3395 or 800/544-8498, www.ledomaine.com, Tues.–Sat. mid-June–early Nov.) has gained a five-star reputation. Although ownership changed in 2005, the same crew is in the kitchen and the menu remains très French. The restaurant is equally renowned for its 5,000-bottle wine cellar and lovely Provençal decor. Reservations are essential, especially in July and August. Opt for the five-course fixed-price menu for $35; otherwise the tab may dent your budget (entrées $22–31), but stack that up against plane fare to France.

The unpretentious dining rooms at the **Crocker House Country Inn** (967 Point Rd., Hancock Point, 207/422-6806, www.crockerhouse.com, 5:30–9 P.M.) provide a setting for well-prepared, continental fare with flair, crafted from fresh and local ingredients (entrées $22–32) and Sunday brunch (11 A.M.–2 P.M.); reservations are essential as this is one of the area's most consistent and popular dining spots. The dining room is open daily May 1–October 31 and Thursday–Sunday in April, November, and December.

## Lobster in the Rough

Thank the Ellsworth-based Frenchman Bay Conservancy for buying the four-acre **Tidal Falls Preserve** (off Eastside Rd., Hancock), overlooking Frenchman Bay's only reversing falls (roiling water when the tide turns), and opening it to public access. When a half-century-old lobster pound went on the market a few years ago, the conservancy hastened into action, raised more than half a million dollars, and bought the property. Today, a dozen picnic tables on the lawn overlook the falls, and seals often haul out on nearby ledges. There's also a screened-in dining pavilion and free Wi-Fi. It's an idyllic spot. **Tidal Falls Lobster Pound** (207/422-6457, 11 A.M.–8:30 P.M. daily late May–early Sept.) leases the site. Come for the lobster (pricey for a lobster shack, but the view makes up for it); landlubbers will find a wood-fired barbecue smoker disguised as a train (really!). Order at the window and then grab a seat. BYOB. Eastside Road is off Route 1 (on your right, if you're heading north) just south of the Hancock–Sullivan bridge; follow it one mile and look for a sign on your left. Follow the gravel road to the end.

## INFORMATION AND SERVICES

For advance information about the region, contact the Schoodic Peninsula Chamber of Commerce (P.O. Box 381, Winter Harbor 04693, 207/963-7658, www.acadia-schoodic.org) and request its handy map and brochure, revised annually. For information on the National and Maine Scenic Byways in this region, visit www.byways.org or www.exploremaine.org/byways.

Check out Dorcas Library (Rte. 186, Prospect Harbor, 207/963-4027, www.dorcas.lib.me.us) or Winter Harbor Public Library (18 Chapel La., Winter Harbor, 207/963-7556, www.winterharbor.lib.me.us). The octagonal Hancock Point Library (207/422-6400), formed in 1899, is a center for village activities. Check the bulletin boards by the entrance to find out what's happening when.

## GETTING AROUND

The **Bar Harbor Ferry** (207/288-2984, www.barharborferry.com, round-trip $29.50 adult, $19.50 child, $6 bike), owned by Captain Steve Pagels (who also operates the four-masted schooner *Margaret Todd* and ferry service to the Cranberry Isles), runs his Bar Harbor–to–Winter Harbor, passenger-only ferry late June–late September. You can board the ferry with a bike in Bar Harbor (at the Bar Harbor Inn pier), disembark in Winter Harbor (at Winter Harbor Marine, on Sargent St.), pedal the short distance to Schoodic, then bike the Schoodic Loop Road, and return later to Bar Harbor on the ferry (last boat is 5 P.M.). The ferry departs Bar Harbor on even hours 8 A.M.–6 P.M., returning on odd hours from Winter Harbor 9 A.M.–5 P.M. (no ferry after 4 P.M. in Sept.).

Since the ferry's summer schedule is coordinated with the free **Island Explorer** (www.exploreacadia.com) bus's summertime Schoodic route, you can board the ferry in Bar Harbor, pick up the bus at the dock in Winter Harbor, and be shuttled along the Schoodic Loop. Stop where you like for a picnic and then board a later bus. Take the last bus back to the ferry and return to Bar Harbor. It's super car-free excursion!

# THE DOWN EAST COAST

"Down East," people say, is the direction the wind blows—the prevailing southwest wind that powered 19th-century sailing vessels along this rugged coastline. But to be truly Down East, in the minds of most Mainers, you have to be physically here, in Washington County—a stunning landscape of waterways, forests, blueberry barrens, rocky shoreline dotted with islands and lighthouses, and independent, pocket-size communities, many still dependent upon fishing or lobstering for their economies.

At one time, *most* of the Maine coast used to be as underdeveloped as this part of it. You can set your clock back a generation or two while you're here; you'll find no giant malls and only a couple of fast-food joints. While there are a handful of restaurants offering fine dining, for the most part, your choices are lim-ited to family-style restaurants specializing in home cooking with an emphasis on fresh (usually fried) seafood and lobster rolls. Nor will you find grand resorts or even not-so-grand hotels. Motels, tourist cabins, and small inns and B&Bs dot the region. The upside is that prices, too, are a generation removed. If you're searching for Maine of your memories or your imagination, this is it.

When eastern Hancock County flows into western Washington County, you're on the Down East Coast (also called the Sunrise Coast). From Steuben eastward to Jonesport, Machias, and Lubec—then "around the corner" to Eastport, and Calais—Washington County is twice the size of Rhode Island, covers 2,528 square miles, has about 35,000 residents, and stakes a claim as the first U.S. real

# HIGHLIGHTS

◖ **Maine Coastal Islands National Wildlife Refuge:** More than 300 birds have been sighted at Petit Manan Point, but even if you're not a birder, come for the hiking and, in August, the blueberries (page 379).

◖ **Great Wass Island Preserve:** The finest natural treasure in this part of Maine is the Great Wass Archipelago, partly owned by The Nature Conservancy, with opportunities for hiking and birding (page 383).

◖ **Machias Seal Island Puffin Tour:** Excursion boats depart from Jonesport and Cutler for Machias Seal Island, home to Atlantic puffins (the clowns of the sea), as well as razorbill auks, Arctic terns, and common murres (pages 386 and 392).

◖ **West Quoddy Head State Park:** The candy-striped lighthouse is a Maine Coast icon and even a short hike along the paths edging the cliffs reaps big rewards (page 396).

◖ **Roosevelt Campobello International Park:** Make it an international vacation by venturing over to this New Brunswick park, home to the Roosevelt Cottage and miles of hiking trails, jointly managed by the United States and Canada (page 402).

◖ **Shackford Head State Park:** The reward for this easy hike are panoramic views over Cobscook Bay, from Eastport to Campobello (page 408).

LOOK FOR ◖ TO FIND RECOMMENDED SIGHTS, ACTIVITIES, DINING, AND LODGING.

◖ **Whale-Watching and Scenic Cruises:** Cruise into Passamaquoddy Bay, pass the Old Sow Whirlpool, and ogle seabirds and whales (page 409).

estate to see the morning sun. The region also includes handfuls of offshore islands—some accessible by ferry, charter boat, or private vessels. (Some, with sensitive bird-nesting sites, are off-limits during the summer.) At the uppermost point of the coast, and conveniently linked to Lubec by a bridge, New Brunswick's Campobello Island is a popular day-trip destination—the locale of Franklin D. Roosevelt's summer retreat. Other attractions in this area include festivals, concert series, art and antique galleries, lighthouses, two Native American

reservations, and the great outdoors for hiking, biking, birding, sea kayaking, whale-watching, camping, swimming, and fishing. Hook inland to Grand Lake Stream to find a remote, wild land of lakes famed for fishing and old-fashioned family-style summer vacations.

One of the Down East Coast's millennial buzzwords has been eco-tourism, and local conservation organizations and chambers of commerce have targeted and welcomed visitors willing to be careful of the fragile ecosystems here—visitors who will contribute to the

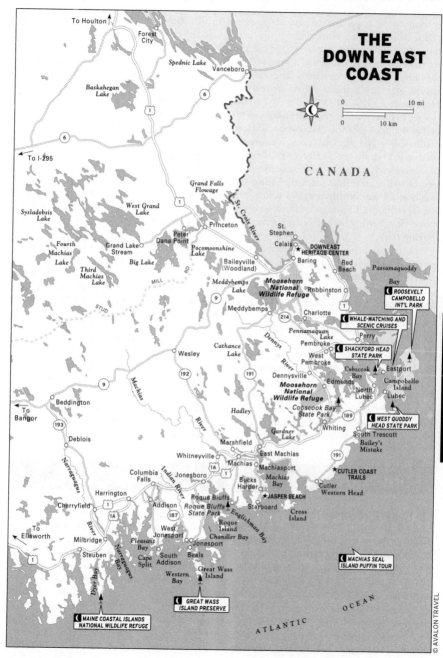

# THE DOWN EAST COAST

To Houlton

Forest City

Spednic Lake

Vanceboro

Baskahegan Lake

6

6

To I-295

CANADA

Grand Falls Flowage

West Grand Lake

Sysladobsis Lake

Fourth Machias Lake

Grand Lake Stream

Big Lake

Third Machias Lake

Princeton

Peter Dana Point

Pocomoonshine Lake

St. Croix River

St. Stephen

Calais

DOWNEAST HERITAGE CENTER

Baring

Red Beach

Passamaquoddy Bay

Baileyville (Woodland)

Meddybemps Lake

Moosehorn National Wildlife Refuge

Robbinston

ROOSEVELT CAMPOBELLO INT'L PARK

MILL RD

Meddybemps

Charlotte

214

WHALE-WATCHING AND SCENIC CRUISES

STUD

Wesley

Cathance Lake

Pennamaquan Lake

Dennys River

Perry

Pembroke

SHACKFORD HEAD STATE PARK

West Pembroke

Eastport

Cobscook Bay

Campobello Island

192

191

Dennysville

Edmunds

North Lubec

Lubec

Moosehorn National Wildlife Refuge

Cobscook Bay State Park

189

WEST QUODDY HEAD STATE PARK

To Bangor

Beddington

Hadley

Gardner Lake

Whiting

South Trescott

193

Deblois

Machias River

Marshfield

East Machias

Bailey's Mistake

191

9

Whitneyville

Machias

Machiasport

CUTLER COAST TRAILS

1A

1

Machias Bay

Columbia Falls

Jonesboro

Bucks Harbor

JASPER BEACH

Cutler

Western Head

Harrington

Indian River

Addison

Roque Bluffs

Starboard

Cross Island

Cherryfield

1

Roque Bluffs State Park

Englishman Bay

187

1A

Roque Island

Chandler Bay

To Ellsworth

Milbridge

West Jonesport

Jonesport

Beals

MACHIAS SEAL ISLAND PUFFIN TOUR

Steuben

Pleasant Bay

South Addison

Great Wass Island

Narraguagus River

Cape Split

Western Bay

Narraguagus Bay

Dyer Bay

MAINE COASTAL ISLANDS NATIONAL WILDLIFE REFUGE

GREAT WASS ISLAND PRESERVE

ATLANTIC OCEAN

0    10 mi
0    10 km

© AVALON TRAVEL

economy while respecting the natural resources and leaving them untrammeled, visitors who don't cross the fine line between light use and overuse. Low-impact tourism is essential for this area. However, outfitters and canoe-, kayak-, and bicycle-rental outlets are few and far between.

One natural phenomenon no visitor can affect is the tide—the inexorable ebb and flow, predictably in and predictably out. If you're not used to it, even the six- to 10-foot tidal ranges of southern Maine may surprise you. But along this coastline, the tides are astonishing—as much as 28 feet of difference in water level within six hours. Old-timers tell stories of big money lost betting on horses racing the fast-moving tides.

Another surprise to visitors may be how early the sun rises—and sets—on the Sunrise Coast. Keep in mind that if you cross into Canada in either Lubec or Calais, you enter Atlantic time, and you'll need to set your clock ahead one hour.

Yet another distinctive natural feature of Washington County is its blueberry barrens (fields). Depending on the time of year, the fields will be black (torched by growers to jump-start the crop), blue (ready for harvest), or maroon (fall foliage, fabulous for photography). In early summer, a million rented bees set to work pollinating the blossoms. By August, when a blue haze forms over the knee-high shrubs, bent-over bodies use old-fashioned wooden rakes to harvest the ripe berries. It's backbreaking work, but the employment lines usually form quickly when newspaper ads announce the advent of the annual harvest.

One bit of advice you might not receive from the tourism people is that warm clothing is essential in this corner of Maine. It may be nicknamed the Sunrise Coast, but it also gets plenty of fog, rain, and cool temperatures. Temperatures tend to be warmer, and the fog diminishes, as you head toward the inland parts of the county, but you can *never* count on that. Mother Nature is an accomplished curveball pitcher, and el Niño and la Niña periodically provide an assist.

## PLANNING YOUR TIME

Downeast Maine is not for those in a hurry. Traffic ambles along. Towns are few and far between. Nature is the biggest calling card here, and to appreciate it, you'll need time to hike, bike, canoe, sea kayak, or take an excursion boat. Although Route 1 follows the coast in general, it's often miles from the water. You'll want to ramble down the peninsulas to explore the seaside villages, see lighthouses, or hike in parks and preserves, and perhaps wander inland to the unspoiled lakes. You'll need at least three days to begin to cover the territory, ideally five days or longer if you want to really explore it.

# Milbridge

The pace begins to slow a bit by the time you've left Hancock County and entered western Washington County, the beginning of the Down East Coast. In this little pocket are the towns of Steuben, Milbridge, Cherryfield, and Harrington.

Life can be tough here nowadays, where once great wooden ships slid down the ways and brought prosperity and trade to shippers, builders, and barons of the timber industry. Cherryfield's stunning houses are evidence enough. The barons now control the blueberry fields, covering much of the inland area of western Washington County and annually shipping millions of pounds of blueberries out of headquarters in Milbridge (pop. 1,330) and Cherryfield (pop. 1,200). The big names here are Jasper Wyman and Sons and Cherryfield Foods.

Milbridge straddles Route 1 and the Narraguagus River (Nar-ra-GWAY-gus, a Native American name meaning "above the boggy place"), once the state's premier source of Atlantic salmon. Cherryfield is at the tidal limit of the Narraguagus. Even though Route 1A trims maybe three miles off the trip from Milbridge to Harrington (pop. 900), resist the urge to take it. Take Route 1 from Milbridge to Cherryfield—the Narraguagus Highway— and then continue to Harrington. You just shouldn't miss Cherryfield.

Steuben's claim to fame is the Petit Manan section of the Maine Coastal Islands National Wildlife Refuge.

## SIGHTS
### ◖ Maine Coastal Islands National Wildlife Refuge

Occupying a 2,166-acre peninsula in Steuben with 10 miles of rocky shoreline (and three offshore islands) is the refuge's outstandingly scenic Petit Manan Point Division (Pigeon Hill Rd., Steuben, mailing address P.O. Box 279, Milbridge 04658, 207/546-2124, www.fws.gov/northeast/mainecoastal). The remote location means it sees only about 15,000 visitors a year, most of those likely birders, as more than 250 different birds have been sighted here. The refuge's primary focus is restoring colonies of nesting seabirds. Among the other natural highlights here are stands of jack pine, coastal raised peatlands, blueberry barrens, fresh- and saltwater marshes, granite shores, and cobble beaches. When asking directions locally, you'll hear it called 'tit Manan.

The moderately easy, four-mile round-trip Birch Point Trail and easy, 1.5-mile round-trip Hollingsworth or Shore Trail provide splendid views and opportunities to spot wildlife along the shore and in the fields, forests, and marshland. The Hollingsworth Trail, leading you to the shoreline, is the best. This is foggy territory, but on clear days, you can see the 123-foot lighthouse on Petit Manan Island, 2.5 miles offshore. The Birch Point Trail heads through blueberry fields to Dyer Bay and loops by the waterfront, with much of the trail passing through woods.

From Route 1, on the east side of Steuben, take Pigeon Hill Road. Six miles down is the first parking lot, for the Birch Point Trail; another half mile takes you to the parking

Petit Manan Light is part of the Maine Coastal Islands National Wildlife Refuge.

**THE DOWN EAST COAST**

area for the Hollingsworth Trail; space is limited. If you arrive in August, help yourself to blueberries. The refuge is open sunrise–sunset daily all year; cross-country skiing is permitted in winter.

## Milbridge Historical Society Museum

A group of energetic residents worked tirelessly to establish the Milbridge Historical Society Museum (S. Main St., Milbridge, 207/546-4471, www.milbridgehistoricalsociety.org, 1–4 P.M. Sat. and Sun. June and Sept., and Tues. July and Aug., donations accepted). Displays in the large exhibit room focus on Milbridge's essential role in the shipbuilding trade, but kids will enjoy such oddities as an amputation knife used by a local doctor and a re-created country kitchen.

## Scenic Fall-Foliage Routes

In fall—roughly early September–early October in this part of Maine—the postharvest blueberry fields take on brilliant scarlet hues, then maroon. They're gorgeous. The best barren-viewing road is Route 193 between Cherryfield and Beddington, via Deblois, the link between Routes 1 and 9—a 21-mile stretch of granite outcrops, pine windscreens, and fiery-red fields.

## Cherryfield Historic District

Imagine a little town this far Down East having a 75-acre National Register Historic District with 52 architecturally significant buildings. If architecture appeals, don't miss Cherryfield. The **Cherryfield-Narraguagus Historical Society** (P.O. Box 96, Cherryfield 04622) has produced a free brochure/map, *Guide to the Cherryfield Historic District,* which you can obtain in advance or pick up once you get here. Architectural styles included on the route are Greek Revival, Italianate, Queen Anne, Colonial Revival, Second Empire, Federal, and Gothic Revival—dating from 1803 to 1940, with most being late 19th century. Especially impressive for such a small town are the Second Empire–style homes.

## BOATING EXCURSIONS

Captain Jaime Robertson's **Robertson Sea Tours and Adventures** (Milbridge Marina, Fickett's Point Rd., 207/546-3883 or 207/461-7439, www.robertsonseatours.com, May 15–Oct. 1) offers a puffin and seabird cruise to Petit Manan Island, a scenic island cruise, a lobstering cruise, and others from Milbridge aboard the *Mairi Leigh,* a classic Maine lobster boat. The puffins and seabirds cruise lasts three hours and is $60 for adults, $45 for kids 12 and younger, with a $150 boat minimum. The island cruise ($50 for adults, $35 for kids, $125 boat minimum) lasts 2–2.5 hours, passes seven islands, and highlights the region's aquaculture industry. The lobstering cruise lasts 1.5–2 hours and costs $30 per adult, $20 per child, with an $80 boat minimum. An option includes a lobster lunch ($75 adult, $50 kids, boat minimum $200), complete with a steamed lobster served aboard. All cruises depart from the Milbridge Marina and require reservations.

Captains Harry "Buzzy" and Esther Shinn's **Downeast Coastal Cruises** (207/546-7720 or cell 207/598-7740, www.downeastcoastalcruises.com) depart from the Milbridge Landing aboard the comfortable *Alyce K.* for island cruises, lobster cruises (complete with meal), sunset cruises, and charters. Cruises last 2–4 hours and cost $45–75 per adult, $35–65 per child; boat minimums apply. Both Shinns have seawater flowing through their veins.

## SHOPPING

**Arthur Smith** (Rogers Point Rd., Steuben, 207/546-3462) is the real thing when it comes to chainsaw carvings. He's an extremely talented folk artist who looks at a piece of wood and sees an animal in it. His carvings of great blue herons, eagles, wolves, porcupines, flamingoes, and other creatures are incredibly detailed, and his wife, Marie, paints them in lifelike colors. Don't expect a fancy studio; much of the work can be viewed roadside.

Also in Steuben, but on the other end of the

Cherryfield's National Historic District has 52 architecturally significant buildings.

spectrum, is **Ray Carbone** (460 Pigeon Hill Rd., Steuben, 207/546-2170), whose masterful wood, stone, and bronze sculptures and fine furniture are definitely worth stopping to see, if not buy. Don't miss the granite sculptures and bird baths in the garden.

## ENTERTAINMENT AND EVENTS

The biggest event in this end of Washington County, and even beyond, is the **Milbridge Anniversary Celebration,** the last weekend in July, drawing hundreds of visitors. The Saturday-afternoon highlight is the codfish relay race—hilarious enough to have been featured in *Sports Illustrated* and on national television. The four-member teams, clad in slickers and hip boots, *really do* hand off a greased cod instead of the usual baton. Race rules specify that runners must be "reasonably sober" and not carry the codfish between their teeth or legs. Also on the schedule are blueberry pancake breakfasts, a fun parade, kids' games, auction, dance, beano and cribbage tournaments, craft booths, and a lobster bake. You have to be there. The relay race has been going since the mid-1980s; the festival has been going for a century and a half.

Check locally for the concert schedule of the **Cherryfield Band,** an impressive community group with about three dozen enthusiastic members. They're in demand May–December, but best of all are their concerts, usually Tuesday evenings, in the lovely downtown bandstand overlooking the Narraguagus River.

**The Humboldt Field Research Institute** (59 Eagle Hill Rd., Steuben, 207/546-2821, www.eaglehill.us, 7:30 P.M. Thurs. early July–late Aug., free) offers lectures, sometimes preceded by optional dinners (fee), by guest lecturers, authors, and scholars on wide-ranging, usually scientific topics. Call for the current schedule. The institute is four miles off Route 1. Take Dyer Bay Road off Route 1, bearing left at the fork onto Mogador Road for a total of 3.6 miles, then left on Schooner Point Road, then right on Eagle Hill Road. Programs take place in the dining hall lecture room. Most are free.

## ACCOMMODATIONS
### Bed-and-Breakfasts and Motels

One of Cherryfield's 52 Historic Register buildings, the 1793 Archibald-Adams House is now the **Englishman's Bed and Breakfast** (122 Main St., Cherryfield, 207/546-2337, www.englishmansbandb.com, $95–155). The magnificently restored Federal-style home borders the Narraguagus River and makes a superb base for exploring inland and Down East Maine. The lovely grounds have gardens and a screened-in gazebo. Owners Peter (the Englishman) and Kathy Winham are archaeologists and serious tea drinkers—they also sell fine teas online (www.teasofcherryfield.com) and in area specialty stores; afternoon tea is a treat (reservation required). Two guest rooms in the main house have river views. One has a private half bath but shares a full bath. A riverside guesthouse, built in the 1990s, melds beautifully with the inn's architecture and is self-catering; pets are allowed here for $7 per night.

Another B&B in a historic Federal-style house bordering the Narraguagus River is the 1803 **Ricker House** (49 Park St., Cherryfield, 207/546-9737, $75 d, $65 s), in one of the town's five oldest buildings. Jean and Bill Conway are enthusiastic hosts who welcome visitors into their comfy home and serve a full breakfast. Two guest rooms share one bath. Pore over the *Adventures* book in the living room or relax on the screened-in porch. It's a fine base for taking a stroll around the neighborhood of historical homes. No credit cards.

Billy and Jackie Majors' strikingly modern **Guagus River Inn** (295B Kansas Rd., Milbridge, 207/546-2780, www.guagusriverinn.com, $70–150) is passive solar design. There's plenty of space to spread out here in a huge recreation room with exercise equipment, an indoor lap pool, living room, deck, and rolling lawns down to the river. Rates include a full breakfast.

Many of the 28 rooms at **The Red Barn Motel** (5 N. Main St., Milbridge, 207/546-7721, hleighton@mainline.net, $70) overlook the Narraguagus River. All have air-conditioning and TV. Pets are welcome. Meals are available at the adjacent restaurant.

## Campgrounds

Since 1958, the Ayers family has opened its quiet, well-off-the-beaten-path property on Joy Cove to campers. **Mainayr Campground** (321 Village Rd., Steuben, 207/542-2690, www.mainayr.com) has 35 tenting and RV sites, which go for $25–30, depending on type and hookups. Also on the premises are a playground, laundry, beach for tidal swimming, camp store, berries for picking, and fresh lobsters. If that's not enough, David Ayr enjoys regaling campers with stories.

Covering seven acres on the tidal Harrington River, Kurt and Patsy Petzold's small, low-key **Sunset Point Campground** (102 Marshville Rd., Harrington, 207/483-4412, www.sunsetpointcampground.com, May 15–Oct. 15) has 30 open sites ($16 tent sites, $22–26 RV sites), a playground, free Wi-Fi, laundry facility, and saltwater swimming. Lobster, clams, and clams usually are available, either live or cooked. Leashed pets are allowed. From Route 1, east of Harrington, take the road toward Marshville for 2.8 miles; the campground is on the right.

## FOOD
### Local Flavors

You can easily pick up enough goodies for a picnic lunch or to stock a cottage kitchen at the **Milbridge Farmers Market** (Milbridge Market parking lot, Main St., Milbridge, 9 A.M.–noon Sat. early June–early Oct.). Choose from fresh baked goods, goat cheese, organic veggies and meats, and eggs as well as wool products, soaps, and skin lotions. Go early for the best selection.

"Where rich espresso meets fattening pastries" is the motto at the artsy-themed and curiously named **Chicamoose Café** (1 N. Main St., Milbridge, 207/546-7495). Local artwork is featured, and open mic nights are occasion-

ally held. A small selection of sandwiches is offered daily in this casual place—settle into a sofa or at a table. Free Wi-Fi.

Cinnamon doughnut muffins are just one reason to dip off Route 1 to **Wildflour Bakery** (314 Village Rd., Steuben, 207/546-0978, 8 A.M.–noon Wed., Thurs., and Sat.), a tiny bakery with some seating offering good breads, English muffins, and other goodies.

If you're heading out to Petit Manan Wildlife Refuge, trust me on this. Ignore the exterior and venture into **Country Charm** (336 Village Rd., Steuben, 207/546-3763, 5:30 A.M.–8 P.M., until 7 P.M. Sun.). The fried fish is fabulously fresh, crispy, light, and cheap, even by local standards. You easily can get out of here for less than $10 pp, far less if you're on a tight budget. The original dining room has, well, country charm (sit here if you want to listen in on the local gossip); the newer ones (added when a real kitchen replaced the original blue trailer) are purely functional. Hungry? Order the Charm Special: two eggs, bacon, sausages, pancakes, toast, and coffee all for a whopping $5; omelettes begin at $2.50.

### Casual Dining

Best choice is **44 Degrees North** (17 Main St., Milbridge, 207/546-4440, www.44-degrees-north.com, 11 A.M.–8 P.M., Fri.–Sat. to 9 P.M.). The front room is family oriented, with booths, tables, and cheerful decor. The back room doubles as a bar and has a big-screen TV. Expect good home cooking, with a few surprises and, as is usually the case in this part of Maine, mouthwatering desserts. Prices top out at $15 for the house specialty, seafood lasagna. The pub side opens daily at 11 A.M. and stays open through "last call."

## INFORMATION

The best source for area info is the Machias Bay Area Chamber of Commerce (207/255-4402, www.machiaschamber.org).

# Jonesport/Beals Area

Between western Washington County and the Machias Bay area is the molar-shaped Jonesport Peninsula, reached from the west via the attractive little town of Columbia Falls, bordering Route 1. Rounding the peninsula are the picturesque towns of Addison, Jonesport, and Beals Island, and less scenic Jonesboro. First settled around 1762, Columbia Falls (pop. about 550) still has a handful of houses dating from the late 18th century, but its best-known structure is the early-19th-century Ruggles House.

On the banks of the Pleasant River, just south of Columbia Falls, Addison (pop. 1,150) once had four huge shipyards cranking out wooden cargo vessels that circled the world. Since that 19th-century heyday, little seems to have changed, and the town today may be best known as the haunt of painter John Marin, who first came to Maine in 1914.

Jonesport and Beals Island, with a combined population of about 2,185, are traditional hard-working fishing communities—old-fashioned, friendly, and photogenic. Beals, connected to Jonesport via an arched bridge over Moosabec Reach, is named for Manwarren Beal Jr. and his wife, Lydia, who arrived around 1773 and quickly threw themselves into the Revolutionary War effort. But that's not all they did—the current phone book covering Jonesport and Beals Island lists dozens of Beal descendants (as well as dozens of Alleys and Carvers, other early names).

Even more memorable than Manwarren Beal was his six-foot, seven-inch descendent Barnabas, dubbed "Tall Barney" for obvious reasons. The larger-than-life fellow became the stuff of legend all along the Maine coast—and a popular Jonesport restaurant preserves his name.

Also legendary here is the lobster-boat design known as the Jonesport hull. People from away won't recognize its distinctive shape, but count on the fishing pros to know it. The harbor here is jam-packed with Jonesport lobster boats, and souped-up versions are consistent winners in the summertime lobster-boat-race series.

## SIGHTS
### ◀ Great Wass Island Preserve

Allow a whole day to explore 1,579-acre Great Wass Island, an extraordinary preserve, even when it's drenched in fog—a not-infrequent event. Owned by The Nature Conservancy (Fort Andross, 14 Maine St., Brunswick, 207/729-5181), the preserve is at the tip of Jonesport's peninsula. Easiest hiking routes are the wooded, two-mile Little Cape Point and 1.5-mile Mud Hole Trails, retracing your path for each. (Making a loop by connecting the two along the rocky shoreline adds considerably to the time and difficulty, but do it if you have time; allow about six hours and wear waterproof footwear.) Expect to see beach-head iris (like a blue flag) and orchids, jack pine, a peat bog, seals, pink granite, pitcher plants, lots of warblers, and maybe some grouse. Carry water and a picnic; wear bug repellent. No camping, fires, or pets; no toilet facilities. Daytime access only. To reach the preserve from Route 1, take Route 187 to Jonesport (12 miles) and then cross the arched bridge to Beals Island. Continue across Beals to the Great Wass causeway (locally called "the Flying Place") and then go three miles on Black Duck Cove Road to the parking area (on the left). Watch for The Nature Conservancy oak-leaf symbol. At the parking area, pick up a trail map and a bird checklist.

Also owned by The Nature Conservancy is 21-acre **Mistake Island,** accessible only by boat. Low and shrubby, Mistake has a Coast Guard–built boardwalk from the landing at the northwest corner to **Moose Peak Light,** standing 72 feet above the water at the eastern end of the island. The only negative on this lovely island is rubble left behind when the government leveled the keeper's house.

## Ruggles House

Behind a picket fence on a quiet street in Columbia Falls stands the remarkable Ruggles House (Main St., P.O. Box 99, Columbia Falls

# PUFFINS

The chickadee is the Maine state bird, and the bald eagle is our national emblem, but probably the best-loved bird along the Maine coast is the Atlantic puffin (Fratercula arctica), a member of the auk (Alcidae) family. Photographs show an imposing-looking creature with a quizzical mien; amazingly, this larger-than-life seabird is only about 12 inches long. Black-backed and white-chested, the puffin has bright orange legs, "clown-makeup" eyes, and a distinctive, rather outlandish red-and-yellow beak. Its diet is fish and shellfish.

Almost nonexistent in this part of the world as recently as the 1970s, the puffin (or "sea parrot") has recovered dramatically thanks to the unstinting efforts of Cornell University ornithologist Stephen Kress and his Project Puffin. Starting with an orphan colony (of two) on remote Matinicus Rock, Kress painstakingly transferred nearly a thousand puffin chicks (also known fondly as "pufflings") from Newfoundland and used artificial nests and decoys to entice the birds to adapt to and reproduce on Eastern Egg Rock in Muscongus Bay.

In 1981, thanks to the assistance and persistence of hundreds of interns and volunteers, and despite the predations of great black-backed gulls, puffins finally were fledged on Eastern Egg, and the rest, as they say, is history. Within 20 years, more than three dozen puffin couples were nesting on Eastern Egg Rock, and still more had established nests on other islands in the area. Kress's methods have received international attention, and his proven techniques have been used to reintroduce bird populations in remote parts of the globe. In 2001, Down East magazine singled out Kress to receive its prestigious annual Environmental Award.

## HOW AND WHERE TO SEE PUFFINS

Puffin-watching, like whale-watching, involves heading offshore, so be prepared with warm clothing, rubber-soled shoes, a hat, sunscreen, binoculars, and, if you're motion sensitive, appropriate medication.

Although the Maine Audubon Society undertakes evening excursions from New Harbor to Eastern Egg Rock 2-3 times a summer, and Hardy Boat Cruises has puffin-watching trips from New Harbor daily early June-mid-August, there are daily up-close-and-personal opportunities for puffin-watching along the Down East Coast – specifically, on Machias Seal Island, aboard boats departing from Cutler and Jonesport. Weather permitting, you'll be allowed to disembark on the 20-acre island.

Naturalist and skilled skipper Andy Patterson begins his puffin tours from Cutler in mid-May, departing each morning (about 7 A.M.) aboard the 40-footer Barbara Frost. The season wraps up in late August. Cost is $80 a person. Contact **Bold Coast Charters** (207/259-4484).

Captain John Norton – son of Barna Norton, the veteran of puffin-watching trips – departs from the waterfront in Jonesport at about 7 A.M. daily, late May-August. Cost is $100. Contact **Norton of Jonesport** (207/497-5933 or 888/551-4895).

## ADOPT-A-PUFFIN PROGRAM

Stephen Kress's Project Puffin has devised a clever way to enlist supporters via the Adopt-a-Puffin program. For a $100 donation, you'll receive a certificate of adoption, vital statistics on your adoptee, annual updates, and a T-shirt. Email adoption requests to orders@projectpuffin.org.

© TOM NANGLE

The Ruggles House is an architectural masterpiece.

04623, 207/483-4637, www.ruggleshouse. org, 9:30 A.M.–4:30 P.M. Mon.–Sat., 11 A.M.– 4:30 P.M. Sun. June 1–Oct. 15, $5 adults, $2 children). Built in 1818 for Judge Thomas Ruggles—lumber baron, militia captain, even postmaster—the tiny house on a grand scale boasts a famous flying (unsupported) staircase, intricately carved moldings, Palladian window, and unusual period furnishings. Rescued in the mid-20th century and maintained by the Ruggles House Society, this gem has become a magnet for savvy preservationists. A quarter mile east of Route 1, it's open for hour-long guided tours.

At the house, pick up a copy of the Columbia Falls walking-tour brochure, which details the intriguing history of other houses in this hamlet.

## Maine Central Model Railroad

Here's nirvana for model-train enthusiasts. Harold ("Buz") Beal and his wife, Helen, have created a fantastic model railroad layout—the Maine Central Model Railroad— covering about 900 square feet in a building next to their house. It features 4,000 trees, 396 train cars, 3,000 feet of track, 11 bridges and trestles, 200 switches…. The trains wind through towns modeled on real Maine places. Look for Stephen King's house in Bangor. Buz Beal, a 26-year Coast Guard veteran, figures railroading is in his blood; his grandfather was a Canadian Pacific engineer. Visitors are welcome any day of the year, but it's best to call ahead (207/497-2255) to be sure someone's home. On Route 187, about four miles northeast of downtown Jonesport, watch for the Church Enterprises sign on the right and then take the next left to the Beals' house. A railroad crossing sign marks the driveway. (Route 187 makes a loop through the peninsula; the Beals are on the easternmost side of the loop—7.7 miles south of Route 1.) There's no charge, but donations are welcomed. Buzz will usually run at least one train for visitors, but it takes three people to operate the full model. That usually occurs on Sunday evenings.

## Downeast Institute for Applied Marine Research and Education

University of Maine at Machias professor Brian Beals founded the Beals Island Regional Shellfish Hatchery, now the Downeast Institute (Black Duck Cove, Great Wass Island, 207/497-5769, www.downeastinstitute. org), a marine field station for the University of Maine at Machias. Learn everything there is to know about shellfish, especially soft-shell clams, on this eight-acre property, with two natural coves. Tours are by appointment.

## Wild Salmon Research Center

Established in 1922, the center (Columbia Falls, 207/483-4336, www.mainesalmonrivers.org, 8 A.M.–4 P.M. Mon.–Fri., free) has a few educational displays and a library. In the basement is a volunteer-run fish hatchery that raises 50,000 Atlantic salmon fry annually. Staff welcome visitors and explain the efforts to save Maine's endangered salmon. You might also ask about the status of the East Machias Aquatic Research Center, a new facility under development by the Downeast Salmon Federation. Planned are a fish hatchery, laboratories, resources center, and small museum.

## EXCURSION BOATS
### ◖ Machias Seal Island Puffin Tour

A great-grandson of legendary local "Tall Barney" Beal, Captain Barna Norton began offering puffin-watching trips to Machias Seal Island (MSI) in 1940 in a 33-foot boat incautiously named *If.* Now his son, Captain John, has taken over the helm of **Norton of Jonesport** (118 Main St., Box 330, Jonesport 04649, 207/497-5933 or 207/497-5933, www.machiassealisland.com, $100). He captains *Chief,* heading 20 miles offshore to an island claimed by both the United States and Canada—a colorful saga. To preserve the fragile nesting sites of Atlantic puffins and arctic terns, access to the 15-acre island is restricted. Passengers are off-loaded into small boats, but sea swells sometimes prevent landing. (The captain supplies wristbands to queasy passengers.) The trip is *not* appropriate for small children or unsteady adults. The boat departs Jonesport around 7 A.M. and returns around noon. Wear waterproof hiking boots, take a hat, and pack some munchies.

## Other Cruises

Operating as **Coastal Cruises** (Kelley Point Rd., R.R. 1, Box 1360, Jonesport, 207/497-3064 or 207/497-2699), Captain Laura Fish and her brother Harry Fish, a certified dive master, offer three-hour Moosabec Reach cruises in the 23-foot powerboat *Aaron Thomas.* Among the sights are Great Wass Island and Mistake Island. Cost is $45 pp, six-person maximum. Dive trips are a possibility. Reservations are required. Trips depart from Jonesport and operate May–mid-October.

## ENTERTAINMENT AND EVENTS

For a taste of real Maine, don't miss the early April **Fried Smelt Dinner.**

The biggest annual event hereabouts is the wingding Jonesport **Fourth of July** celebration, with several days of special activities, including barbecues, beauty pageant, kids' games, fireworks, and the famed **Jonesport Lobsterboat Races** in Moosabec Reach.

The mid-August **Maine Wild Blueberry Festival,** in neighboring Machias, is an easy jaunt from the Jonesport/Beals area.

**Peabody Memorial Library** presents bimonthly art shows and sponsors a summer music series.

## SHOPPING

Flower-design majolica pottery and whimsical terra-cotta items are specialties at **Columbia Falls Pottery** (150 Main St., Columbia Falls, 207/483-4075 or 800/235-2512), an appealing shop in a rehabbed country store next to the Ruggles House. Veteran potter April Adams keeps the inventory fresh, and the company does a hefty mail-order business. A newly renovated, two-bedroom apartment is available for rent upstairs either as one unit by the week for $700 or, when available, by the room, for $120–150 per night.

Two adjacent antiques shops brighten Jonesport's waterfront: **Harbor House on Sawyer Cove** (32 Sawyer Sq., 207/497-5417) and **Moospecke Antiques** (Sawyer Sq., 207/497-2457).

In downtown Jonesport, **Church's True Value** (Main St., Rte. 187, Jonesport, 207/497-2778) carries all the usual hardware items, plus gifts, souvenirs, and sportswear. Helpful owners John and Sharon Church can also answer any question about the area and solve most any problem.

Bob and Charlene Nelson's combined talents are on view at **Nelson Decoys Downeast Gallery** (Cranberry La., Jonesport, 207/497-3488). Bob's a talented woodcarver, and Charlene paints his creations. They also display works by other area artists in their gallery. It's just off Main Street downtown.

## ACCOMMODATIONS
### Bed-and-Breakfasts

How about staying in a beautiful, modern farmhouse overlooking the water—with llamas llolling outside? At **C** **Pleasant Bay Bed and Breakfast and Llama Keep** (338 West Side Rd., P.O. Box 222, Addison 04606, 207/483-4490, www.pleasantbay.com, $50–135), Joan and Lee Yeaton manage to pamper more than 40 llamas and a herd of red deer as well as their two-legged guests. Three miles of trails wind through the 110 acres, and a canoe is available for guests. Three lovely rooms (private and shared baths) and one suite, with microwave and refrigerator, all have water views. Rates include a delicious breakfast. Arrange in advance for a llama walk ($15 per llama). It's open all year. The farm borders Pleasant Bay, 3.9 miles southwest of Route 1.

The fanciest digs in Jonesport are at **C** **Harbor House on Sawyer Cove** (P.O. Box 468, Sawyer Sq., Jonesport 04649, 207/497-5417, www.harborhs.com, $125), hospitably run by Maureen and Gene Hart—she an ex-nurse, he an ex-engineer. Relatively new to Jonesport, they've adopted it with a passion, enjoying sharing it with Harbor House guests. Two very comfortable and spacious second-floor rooms—

named Beach Rose and Lupine and decorated accordingly—have incredible views of Moosabec Reach. Binoculars are provided so you can watch the action, including passengers embarking on the Norton puffin trip. The rooms also have TV and Wi-Fi, and a guest phone, fridge, and microwave are provided. The Harts operate an antiques shop, selling what they call "curiosities," on the first floor of this fascinating old building, once Jonesport's telegraph office. Maureen serves a great breakfast—early enough for birders—on the harbor-view porch. Harbor House is open all year.

### Cottages and Apartments

Close to the best sandy beach on the peninsula, the **Church's Ocean Front Cottages** (49 Sandy River Beach Rd., Jonesport, 207/497-2886, www.oceancottagesmaine.com), managed by Linda Church, are three rustic, well-maintained cottages, all with Wi-Fi and direct TV/VCR, available by the week. Best view is from Sandpiper, which sleeps six and rents for $1,000 a week; the others (Linnet and Lemon Drop) are $700 a week. Bring your own sheets and towels. It's open May–October. The cottages are seven miles south of Route 1 and four miles northeast of downtown Jonesport. A fourth cottage, Harborview ($500/week or $100/day), an eccentric little place with a spectacular panoramic view, is on Main Street in downtown Jonesport.

Proprietor Dorothy Higgins's **Cranberry Cove Cottages** (56 Kelley Point Rd., Jonesport, 207/497-2139, ddhiggi@hotmail.com, $125) comprise two second-story cottage-style apartments, each distinctively furnished in cottage style and with TV, phone, and harbor view. Both have kitchenettes provisioned with all sorts of goodies, from fresh eggs to wine and cheese. Pets are welcome. Rates decrease with length of stay.

Abigail Oates-Alley has two two-bedroom units in an oceanfront duplex called **Moose-a-bec** (34 Old House Point, P.O. Box 557, Jonesport 04649, 207/497-2121, $125). Both have big views, full baths with laundries, TV, and phones with answer machines. It's adjacent to a working wharf, so expect to see and hear the boats going out and returning each day. The downstairs unit is handicapped-friendly. The upstairs unit has a tiny second bedroom.

### Campgrounds

The town of Jonesport operates the low-key, no-frills **Jonesport Campground** (Henry Point, Kelley Point Rd., Jonesport) on two acres with fabulous views over Sawyer Cove and Moosabec Reach. Basic facilities include outhouses, picnic tables, and fire rings; three power poles provide hookups. Showers and washing machines are available across the cove at Jonesport Shipyard (207/497-2701). The campground is exposed to wind off the water, so expect nights to be cool. Sites are allocated on a first-come, first-served basis. It's open early May–Labor Day. Avoid the campground during Fourth of July festivities; it's jam-packed. From Route 187 at the northeastern edge of Jonesport, turn right onto Kelley Point Road and then right again to Henry Point.

### FOOD

Craving carbs? Head for Lois Hubbard's home bakery, called **The Farm** (1561 Mason's Bay Rd., Rte. 187, R.R. 1, Box 3115, Jonesport, 207/497-5949). In addition to specialty breads, Lois produces 15 flavors of whoopie pies, including blueberry. The bakery, 3.3 miles south of the Jonesboro end of Route 1, is open all year.

Good road food is available at **Dallas Lobstah Take Out** (Rte. 1, Harrington, 207/483-2227, 4–8 P.M. Mon.–Fri., noon–8 P.M. Sat. and Sun.), right on Route 1 with picnic tables.

For local color, start at **Tall Barney's** (52 Main St., Rte. 187, Jonesport, 207/497-2403, www.tallbarneys.com), where you'll find homemade baked beans and chowders, pizza, and more—and you won't break the bank. Sit back and watch the servers chat up the lobstermen regulars camped out at the big center table, known locally as the Liars' Table. Join them, if you dare. No credit cards. The restaurant is just before the bridge to Beals Island; watch for the statue of Barney. Days and hours of operation change frequently, so call.

### INFORMATION AND SERVICES

The Machias Bay Area Chamber of Commerce (12 E. Main St., Machias, 207/255-4402, www.machiaschamber.org) handles inquires for the Machias area as well as Jonesport.

In downtown Jonesport, the best source of local information is Church's True Value (Main St., Rte. 187, Jonesport, 207/497-2778), open every day but Sunday. Another reliable source is Maureen Hart at Antiques on the Harbor (on Sawyer Cove, 207/497-5417).

## Machias Bay Area

The only negative thing about Machias (Muh-CHY-us, pop. about 2,500) is its Micmac Indian name, meaning "bad little falls" (even though that's accurate—the midtown waterfall here *is* treacherous). A contagious local esprit pervades this shire town of Washington County, thanks to antique homes, a splendid river-valley setting, Revolutionary War monuments, and a small but busy university campus.

If you regard crowds as fun, an ideal time to land here is during the renowned annual Machias Wild Blueberry Festival, third weekend in August, when harvesting is under way in Washington County's blueberry fields and you can stuff your face with blueberry-everything—muffins, jam, pancakes, ice cream, pies. You can also collect blueberry-logo napkins, T-shirts, magnets, pottery, and jewelry. The menu at the local McDonald's even lists blueberry pancakes and sundaes that weekend.

Among the other summer draws are a chamber-music series, art shows, and semiprofessional theater performances. Within a few miles are

# TWO SCENIC ROUTES

The drives described below can also be bike routes (easy to moderately difficult), but be forewarned that the roads are narrow and shoulderless, so caution is essential. Heed biking etiquette.

## ROUTE 191, THE CUTLER ROAD

Never mind that Route 191, between East Machias and West Lubec, is one of Maine's most stunning coastal drives – you can still follow the entire 27-mile stretch and meet only a handful of cars. **East Machias** even has its own historic district, with architectural gems dating from the late 18th century along High and Water Streets. Farther along Route 191, you'll find fishing wharves, low moorlands, a hamlet or two, and islands popping over the horizon. The only peculiarly jarring note is the 26-tower forest of North Cutler's Naval Computer and Telecommunications Station, nearly 1,000 feet high – monitoring global communications – but you'll see this only briefly. (At night, the skyscraping red lights are really eerie, especially if you're offshore aboard a boat.) Off Route 191 are minor roads and hiking trails worth exploring, especially the coastal trails of the Cutler Coast Public Preserve. About three miles south of the Route 191 terminus, you can also check out **Bailey's Mistake,** a hamlet with a black-sand (volcanic) beach. And the name? Allegedly it stems from one Captain Bailey who, misplotting his course and thinking he was in Lubec, drove his vessel ashore here one night in the late 19th century.

Unwilling to face the consequences of his lapse, he and his crew off-loaded their cargo of lumber and built themselves dwellings. Whether true or not, it makes a great saga. Even though it's in the town of **Trescott,** and the hamlet is really South Trescott, everyone knows this section as Bailey's Mistake.

## ROUTE 92, STARBOARD PENINSULA

Pack a picnic and set out on Route 92 (beginning at Elm Street in downtown Machias) down the 10-mile length of the Starboard Peninsula to a stunning spot known as the Point of Maine. Along the way are the villages of Larrabee, Bucks Harbor, and Starboard, all part of the town of Machiasport. In Bucks Harbor is the turnoff (a short detour to the right) to **Yoho Head,** a controversial upscale development overlooking Little Kennebec Bay.

South of the Yoho Head turnoff is the sign for **Jasper Beach.** From the Jasper Beach sign, continue 1.4 miles to two red buildings (the old Starboard School House and the volunteer fire department). Turn left onto a dirt road and continue to a sign reading Driveway. Go around the right side of a shed and park on the beach. (Keep track of the tide level, though.) You're at **Point of Maine,** a quintessential Down East panorama of sea and islands. On a clear day, you can see offshore **Libby Island Light,** the focus of Philmore Wass's entertaining narrative *Lighthouse in My Life: The Story of a Maine Lightkeeper's Family* (see *Suggested Reading* in the *Resources* section).

day trips galore—options for hiking, biking, golfing, swimming, and sea kayaking.

Also included within the Machias sphere are the towns of Roque Bluffs, Jonesboro, Whitneyville, Marshfield, East Machias, and Machiasport. Just to the east, between Machias and Lubec, are the towns of Whiting and Cutler.

## HISTORICAL SIGHTS

History is a big deal in this area, and since Machias was the first settled Maine town east of the Penobscot River, lots of enthusiastic amateur historians have helped rescue homes and sites dating from as far back as the Revolutionary War.

English settlers, uprooted from communities farther west on the Maine coast, put down permanent roots here in 1763, harvesting timber to ensure their survival. Stirrings of revolutionary discontent surfaced even at this remote outpost, and when British loyalists in Boston began usurping some of the valuable harvest, Machias patriots plotted revenge. By 1775, when the armed British schooner *Margaretta* arrived as a cargo escort, local residents aboard the sloop *Unity,* in a real David-and-Goliath episode, chased and captured the *Margaretta.* On June 12, 1775, two months after the famed Battles of Lexington and Concord (and five days before the Battle of Bunker Hill), Machias Bay was the site of what author James Fenimore Cooper called "The Lexington of the Sea"—the first naval battle of the American Revolution. The name of patriot leader Jeremiah O'Brien today appears throughout Machias—on a school, a street, a cemetery, and a state park. In 1784, Machias was incorporated; it became the shire town in 1790.

## Museums

One-hour guided tours vividly convey the atmosphere of the 1770 **Burnham Tavern** (Main St., Rte. 192, Machias, 207/255-4432, www.burnhamtavern.com, 9 A.M.–5 P.M. Mon.–Fri. mid-June–Sept., or by appointment, $5 adults, $0.25 for kids under 12), where upstart local patriots met in 1775 to plot revolution against the British. Job and Mary Burnham's tavern/home next served as an infirmary for casualties from the Revolution's first naval battle, just offshore. Lots of fascinating history lies in this National Historic Site maintained by the Daughters of the American Revolution. Hanging outside is a sign reading, "Drink for the thirsty, food for the hungry, lodging for the weary, and good keeping for horses, by Job Burnham." If you're here in early August, you can join in the museum's annual **lawn party,** including lunch, tours, and handicraft sales.

Headquarters for the Machiasport Historical Society and one of the area's three oldest residences, the 1810 **Gates House** (344 Port Rd., Machiasport, 207/255-8461, 12:30–4:30 P.M. Tues.–Sat. July and Aug., donation appreciated) was snatched from ruin and restored in 1966. The National Historic Register building overlooking Machias Bay contains fascinating period furnishings and artifacts, many related to the lumbering and shipbuilding era. The museum, four miles southeast of Route 1, has limited parking on a hazardous curve.

## Centre Street Congregational Church

Machias's most distinctive landmark is the steeple of the 1836 Gothic Revival Centre Street Congregational Church (7 Center St., Machias, 207/255-6665, www.centrestreetchurch.org), paradoxically situated on *Center* Street. The community-oriented parishioners spearhead the annual Maine Wild Blueberry Festival, and the church is the site of the July and August Machias Bay Chamber Concerts.

## O'Brien Cemetery

Old-cemetery buffs will want to stop at O'Brien Cemetery, resting place of the town's earliest settlers. It's next to Bad Little Falls Park, close to downtown, off Route 92 toward Machiasport. A big plus here is the view, especially in autumn, of blueberry barrens, the waterfall, and the bay.

## Fort O'Brien State Memorial

The American Revolution's first naval battle was fought just offshore from Fort O'Brien in June 1775. Now a State Historic Site, the fort was built and rebuilt several times—originally to guard Machias during the Revolutionary War. Only Civil War–era earthworks now remain, plus well-maintained lawns overlooking the Machias River. Steep banks lead down to the water; keep small children well back from the edge. No restrooms or other facilities, but there's a playground at the Fort O'Brien School, next door. Officially, the park is open Memorial Day weekend–Labor Day, but it's easily accessible all year. Admission is free. Take Route 92 from Machias about five miles toward Machiasport; the parking area is on the left.

## UNIVERSITY OF MAINE AT MACHIAS

Founded in 1909 as Washington State Normal School, University of Maine at Machias (9 O'Brien Ave., Machias, 207/255-1200, www.umm.maine.edu) is now part of the state university system. The **UMM Art Galleries,** in Powers Hall, feature works from the university's expanding permanent collection of Maine painters—including John Marin, William Zorach, Lyonel Feininger, and Reuben Tam. Rotating exhibits occur throughout the school year. Hours are 1–4 P.M. Monday–Friday when school is in session, or by appointment.

UMM's **Center for Lifelong Learning** has a state-of-the-art fitness center, six-lane heated pool, and the George Simpson Murdock Bookstore, which stocks more than textbooks. The pool and fitness room are open to the public daily; call for schedule.

Also open to the public is **Merrill Library** (207/255-1284).

# RECREATION
## Parks and Preserves
Just as dedicated as the historical preservationists are the hikers, birders, and other eco-sensitive outdoors enthusiasts who've helped preserve thousands of acres in this part of Maine for public access and appreciation.

At **Bad Little Falls Park,** alongside the Machias River, stop to catch the view from the footbridge overlooking the roiling falls (especially in spring). Bring a picnic and enjoy this midtown oasis tucked between Routes 1 and 92.

Thanks to a handful of foresighted year-round and summer residents, spectacular, crescent-shaped **Jasper Beach**—piled high with ocean-polished jasper and other rocks—has been preserved by the town of Machiasport. No sand here, just stones, in intriguing shapes and colors. Resist the urge to fill your pockets with souvenirs, maybe settling for just a single special rock. Parking is limited; no facilities. From Route 1 in downtown Machias, take Route 92 (Machias Rd.) 9.5 miles southeast, past the village of Bucks Harbor. Watch for a large sign on your left. The beach is on Howard's Cove, 0.2 mile off the road, and accessible all year.

Southwest of Machias, six miles south of Route 1, is **Roque Bluffs State Park** (Roque Bluffs Rd., Roque Bluffs, 207/255-3475). Saltwater swimming this far north is for the young and brave, but this park also has a 60-acre freshwater pond warm and shallow enough for toddlers and the old and timid. Facilities include primitive changing rooms, outhouses, a play area, and picnic tables (no food or lifeguards). Views go on forever from the wide-open, mile-long sweep of sand beach. Admission is $3 adults, $1 children 5–11. The fee box relies on the honor system. The park is open daily May 15–September 15, but the beach is accessible all year.

On Route 191, about 4.5 miles northeast of the center of Cutler, watch for the parking area (on the right) for the **Cutler Coast Public Preserve,** a 12,000-acre preserve with nearly a dozen miles of beautifully engineered hiking trails on the seaward side of Route 191. Allow 5–6 hours to do the shorter, 5.8-mile Black Point Brook Loop, providing an easy start for about 1.5 miles before getting to the Coastal Trail, a stretch of moderately rugged hiking southward along dramatic, tree-fringed shoreline cliffs. Then head back via the Black Point Brook cutoff and connect with the Inland Trail to return to your car (or bicycle). Bring binoculars and a camera; the views from this wild coastline are fabulous. Also bring insect repellent—inland boggy stretches are buggy. Carry a picnic and commandeer a granite ledge overlooking the surf. Precipitous cliffs and narrow stretches can make the shoreline section of this trail perilous for small children or insecure adults, so use extreme caution and common sense. There are no facilities in the preserve. If you're here in August, you can stock up on blueberries and even some wild raspberries. Another option, the 9.8-mile Fairy Head Loop, starts the same way as the Black Point Brook Loop but continues southward along the coast, leading to three primitive campsites (stoves only, no fires), available on a first-come, first-served basis. There's no way to reserve these, so you take your chances. Unless you have gazelle genes, the longer loop almost demands an overnight. Information on the preserve, including a helpful map, is available from the **Maine Bureau of Parks and Lands** (22 State House Station, Augusta 04333, 207/287-3821, www.state.me.us/doc/parks). Originally about 2,100 acres, this preserve was quintupled in

1997, when several donors, primarily the Richard King Mellon Foundation, deeded to the state 10,055 acres of fields and forests across Route 191 from the trail area, creating a phenomenal tract that now runs from the ocean all the way back to Route 1. Mostly in Cutler but also in Whiting, it was Maine's second-largest public-land gift—after Baxter State Park.

Next to the post office, on Route 1, in East Machias is the riverside **Eagle Watch picnic area,** which isn't much of a picnic area at all, but it is a great place to watch eagles soar in the spring and early summer.

## Golf

With lovely water views, and tidal inlets serving as obstacles, the nine-hole **Great Cove Golf Course** (387 Great Cove Rd., off Roque Bluffs Rd., Jonesboro, 207/434-7200) is a good challenge. It has reasonable greens fees, carts, and a snack bar; you can also rent clubs. From Jonesboro (Rte. 1), go 3.5 miles east and south on Roque Bluffs Road. It's open May–October. You can play a quick nine at **Barren View Golf Course** (Rte. 1, Jonesboro, 207/434-6531, www.barrenview.com). A pro shop, snack bar, carts, and club rentals are available.

## Canoeing, Sea Kayaking, and Bicycling

If you've brought your own sea kayak, there are public launching ramps in Bucks Harbor (east of the main Machias Rd.) and at Roque Bluffs State Park. You can also put in at Sanborn Cove, beyond the O'Brien School on Route 92, about five miles south of Machias, where there's a small parking area. Before setting out, be sure to check the tide calendar and plan your strategy so you don't have to slog through acres of muck when you return.

**Sunrise Canoe and Kayak** (0.02 mile off Rte. 1 on an unsigned road, behind Margaretta Motel, Machias, 207/255-3375 or 877/980-2300, www.sunrisecanoeandkayak.com) rents canoes and kayaks for $20 per day, sit-on-top kayaks for $15 per day, and offers half-day sea-kayak excursions on Machias Bay, including one to a petroglyph site ($48 pp). It also rents 24-speed mountain bikes for $15 per day. Pickup and delivery service is $25. It also offers fully outfitted, multiday canoeing and kayaking excursions on the Machias and St. Croix Rivers and along the Bold Coast.

The spectacular **Machias River,** one of Maine's most technically demanding canoeing rivers, is a dynamite trip mid-May–mid-June, but no beginner should attempt it. The best advice is to sign on with an outfitter/guide. The run lasts 4–6 days, the latter if you start from Fifth Machias Lake. Expect to see such wildlife as osprey, eagles, ducks, loons, moose, deer, beaver, and snapping turtles. Be aware, though, that the Machias is probably the buggiest river in the state, and blackflies will form a welcoming party. Bring khaki duds; the bugs are attracted to colors. The major portage is at Upper Holmes Falls; trying to run the half-mile-long rips would buy you a ticket to the morgue. In addition to Sunrise Canoe and Kayak, **Sunrise Expeditions** (4 Union Plaza, Ste. 2, Bangor, 207/942-9300 or 800/748-3730, www.sunrise-exp.com) also offers fully outfitted trips.

## ◖ Machias Seal Island Puffin Tour

Andy Patterson, the skipper of the 40-footer *Barbara Frost,* operates the **Bold Coast Charter Company** (P.O. Box 364, Cutler 04626, 207/259-4484, www.boldcoast.com), homeported in Cutler Harbor. Andy provides knowledgeable narration, answers questions in depth, and shares his considerable enthusiasm for this pristine corner of Maine. He's best known for his five-hour puffin-sighting trips to Machias Seal Island (departing between 7 and 8 A.M. mid-May–Aug.). All trips are dependent on weather and tide conditions, and reservations are required. Cost is $80 (but don't bring small children or unsteady adults). No credit cards. Daily access to the island is restricted, and swells can roll in, so passengers occasionally cannot disembark, but the curious puffins often surround the boat, providing plenty of photo opportunities. A seabird tour, without an island visit, is available for $80 adult, $45 kids 14 and younger. No matter what the air temperature on the mainland, be sure to dress warmly, and wear sturdy shoes. The *Barbara Frost*'s wharf is on Cutler Harbor, just off Route 191. Look for the Little River Lobster Company sign; you'll depart from the boat-launching ramp.

## ENTERTAINMENT, FESTIVALS, AND EVENTS

The University of Maine at Machias is the cultural focus in this area, particularly during the school year. **Stage Front: The Arts Downeast** puts on an annual series of concerts, plays, recitals, and other events in the Performing Arts Center at the university. The summer series, once a month, usually features classical and pops concerts, including at least one performance by the energetic Steuben-based Opera Maine organization. Contact UMM (207/255-1384) for schedule information.

**Machias Bay Chamber Concerts** (207/255-3849) occur at 7:30 P.M. Tuesday evenings early July–mid-August at the Centre Street Congregational Church. Art exhibits accompany concerts. Tickets are $12 for adults, $6 for students, and free for kids age 12 and younger. Call for a current schedule.

The **Machias Wild Blueberry Festival** (www.machiasblueberry.com) is the summer highlight, running Friday–Sunday the third weekend in August, featuring a pancake breakfast, road races, concerts, a craft show, a baked-bean supper, a homegrown musical, and more. The blueberry motif is everywhere. It's organized by Centre Street Congregational Church in downtown Machias.

## SHOPPING

Influenced by traditional Japanese designs, Connie Harter-Bagley markets her dramatic ceramics at **Connie's Clay of Fundy** (Rte. 1, Box 345, East Machias, 207/255-4574, www.clay-offundy.com), on the East Machias River, four miles east of Machias. If she's at the wheel, you can also watch her work.

A number of regional artists and artisans show and sell their wares at **Unique Possibilities** (300 E. Main St./Rte. 1, Ma-

chias, 207/255-3337), in the Causeway Common building (same complex as Dunkin' Donuts). Also here is **The Country Tea Room** (207/255-3337), a relaxing place to sip tea and snack on sweets.

Need a read? **Jim's Books, etc.** (8 Elm St., Machias, 207/255-9058), at the third house on the left on Route 32, just beyond the university campus, is open by chance or appointment.

## ACCOMMODATIONS
### Bed-and-Breakfasts and Inns

The first three B&Bs feature dining rooms open to the public (see *Food* for details).

The beautifully restored **C Chandler River Lodge** (654 Rte. 1, Jonesboro, 207/434-2540, $100–175) sits well off the highway and overlooks treed lawns that roll down to the Chandler River. It's an idyllic spot, with Adirondack-style chairs positioned just where you want to sit and take in the views. Or you might just want to sit on the porch. Upstairs are four guest rooms, three with private bath, one with detached bath. Downstairs is a fine-dining restaurant. Rates include a continental breakfast.

Victoriana rules at the **Riverside Inn** (Rte. 1, P.O. Box 373, East Machias 04630, 207/255-4134, www.riversideinn-maine.com, $95–130), a meticulously restored early-19th-century sea captain's home with two rooms and two suites (one with kitchenette). Relax on the deck overlooking the East Machias River and you'll forget you're a few steps from a busy highway. Sit in the lovely terraced perennial gardens and you'll feel the same way. There's also a popular dining room, where reservations are essential.

Fronting on the tidal Machias River, the barn-red **Inn at Schoppee Farm** (Rte. 1, Machias, 207/255-4648, www.schoppeefarm.com, $110) is earning fame as a dining and lodging destination. The 19th-century farm operated as a dairy for three generations before Machias natives David and Julie Barker returned home to operate it as a B&B. They welcome guests with two rooms, each furnished with antiques and such niceties as air-conditioning, Wi-Fi, whirlpool baths, and soft down comforters in addition to river views and a full breakfast. Also available is a two-bedroom suite with kitchen ($250 per night or $900 per week). The dining room is open for five-course dinners Thursday–Saturday, by reservation. Just east of the causeway, it's a healthy walk to downtown diversions.

The second generation now operates **Micmac Farm Guesthouses** (Rte. 92, Machiasport, 207/255-3008, www.micmacfarm.com, $80–95/night, $495–595/week, May–late Oct.). Stay in one of Anthony and Bonnie Dunn's three comfortable, well-equipped cottages, and you'll find yourself relaxing on the deck overlooking the tidal Machias River and watching for seabirds, seals, and eagles. No breakfast is provided, but each wood-paneled cottage has a kitchenette and dining area. Pets and children are welcome. There's also a river-view room in the restored 18th-century Gardner House, with a private bath with whirlpool tub. Guests have use of the farmhouse, including a library. A light breakfast is provided for Gardner House guests. Micmac Farm, 2.5 miles south of Machias, is a lovely oasis.

## Motels

The best feature of the two-story **Machias Motor Inn** (26 E. Main St., Rte. 1, Machias, 207/255-4861, www.machiasmotorinn.com, $70–110) is its location overlooking the tidal Machias River; sliding doors open onto decks with a view. Twenty-eight guest rooms and six efficiencies have extra-long beds, plus cable TV, air-conditioning, Wi-Fi, and phone. Next door is Helen's Restaurant—famed for seasonal fruit pies and an all-you-can-eat weekend breakfast buffet. Pets ($5 fee) are welcome at the motel. The motel is within easy walking distance to downtown; perfect if you're here for the Blueberry Festival. It's open all year.

For inexpensive digs, you can't beat the ◖ **Blueberry Patch** (550 Rte. 1, Jonesboro, 207/434-5411, $48–68), a clean and bright motel and tourist cabins, with three efficiency units. Nothing fancy here, but all rooms have satellite TV, air-conditioning, Wi-Fi, and phones, and there's even a pool and small playground. If you're taller than six feet, choose a motel room rather than a cabin (cabin bathrooms are tiny). Rates include coffee and pastry in the morning, but the Whitehouse Restaurant, next door, is open for breakfast, lunch, and dinner.

The second generation now runs **The Bluebird Motel** (Rte. 1, Machias, 207/255-3332, $65–70), a clean, upgraded 1950s-style motel. Forty pine-paneled rooms have cable TV, phones, air-conditioning, and large baths. The motel is set back from Route 1 enough to keep down noise, but request a room in the rear section if you're a light sleeper. The motel, a mile south of downtown, has wheelchair-accessible rooms. Pets are allowed in some units. It's open all year.

## FOOD

Watch the local papers for listings of **public suppers, spaghetti suppers,** or **baked bean suppers,** a terrific way to sample the culinary talents of local cooks. Most begin at 5 P.M., and it's wise to arrive early to get near the head of the line. The suppers often benefit needy individuals or struggling nonprofits—always worth supporting—and where else can you eat nonstop for under $10?

### Local Flavors

**Fat Cat Deli** (50 Main St., Machias, 207/255-6777, 11 A.M.–8:15 P.M. Mon.–Sat., 4–8:15 P.M. Sun.) makes the area's best pizzas and sandwiches and often has live music.

Craving something healthful? You can pick up breads and muffins as well as sandwiches and soups at **Whole Life Organic Market** (80 Main St., Machias, 207/255-8855, 9 A.M.–6 P.M. Mon.–Sat., 10 A.M.–2 P.M. Sun.). There's a small but pleasant seating area, too. It's open year-round.

Another source for fresh, healthful foods is the **Machias Valley Farmers Market** (8 A.M.–noon Sat. and often Wed. and Fri. May–Oct.). It's held on "The dike," a low causeway next to the Machias River. It's usually a good source for blueberries in late July and August.

### Family-Friendly Home Cooking

Family-owned, and very popular all day long,

is **The Blue Bird Ranch Family Restaurant** (3 E. Main St./Rte. 1, Machias, 207/255-3351, www.norumbegablue.com, 6 A.M.–8 P.M. daily), named for the Prout family's other enterprise, Blue Bird Ranch Trucking Company. Service is efficient, food is hearty, and portions are ample in the three dining rooms. The breakfast buffet, served 8–11 A.M., is $6.

Although pie aficionados say it's not what it used to be, **Helen's** (28 E. Main St./Rte. 1, Machias, 207/255-8423, 6 A.M.–8:30 P.M. daily) is renowned for its blueberry pie. It's also a source of inexpensive, family-style fare. The Sunday breakfast buffet, served 8–10:30 A.M., is $6, and the soup-and-salad bar is $6 anytime.

## Casual Dining

Machias lucked out when Susan Ferro, owner, artist, and chef—she claims she got her start garnishing mud pies as a kid—opened the **❮ Artist's Café** (3 Hill St., Machias, 207/255-8900, 11 A.M.–2 P.M. Mon.–Fri. and 5–8 P.M. Mon.–Sat.) in a small house across from the university. The dining rooms are decorated with paintings by Ferro and other local artists. Luncheon sandwiches—named The Impressionist, Garden of Eden, The Rococo, and so on, are always a reasonably priced adventure ($5–7). Dinner entrées, which change frequently and usually include a vegetarian option, are $22–28. Beer and wine are available. Be sure to reserve for dinner, especially on weekends.

## Fine Dining

Reservations are essential at the popular dining room at the **Riverside Inn** (Rte. 1, East Machias, 207/255-4134, www.riversideinn-maine.com, open for dinner 5–8 P.M. Tues.–Sun. in peak season). The pricey menu might include entrées such as lobster and scallops in champagne sauce or Riverside Wellington as well as more budget-friendly main-course salads.

Machias's newest fine-dining restaurant, **Chandler River Lodge** (654 Rte. 1, Jonesboro, 207/434-2540, 5–8 P.M. Tues.–Sat.) has views over the Chandler River, and the grounds are perfect for a stroll either before or afterward. At dinner, entrées ($28–35) might include guava mango chicken, blueberry pork, or five-pepper steak. All include fresh baked breads and salad. If you don't want to splurge on dinner, lunch is served seasonally. Call for days and hours.

Far more intimate is the **❮ Inn at Schoppee Farm** (Rte. 1, Machias, 207/255-4648, www.schoppeefarm.com, 5–8 P.M. Mon.–Sat.), which serves five-course dinners ($36–44) in the Hannah Weston dining room by reservation. Seating is limited to 15, so call early. Usually the menu offers a choice of four entrées, varying from seafood, beef, chicken, duck, or lamb. The river-view dining room complements the farmhouse's Federal-style architecture—bright and airy, with pine floors, hand-hewn beams, and antiques. BYOB.

## INFORMATION AND SERVICES

The Machias Bay Area Chamber of Commerce (12 E. Main St, Machias, 207/255-4402, www.machiaschamber.org) stocks brochures, maps, and information on area hiking trails. The office is generally open 10 A.M.–3 P.M. Monday–Friday.

THE DOWN EAST COAST

# Lubec and Vicinity

Literally the beginning of America—at the nation's easternmost point—Lubec (pop. 1,730) can serve as a base for exploring New Brunswick's Campobello Island, the Cutler coastline, and territory to the west. With a couple of appealing B&Bs and more than 90 miles of meandering waterfront, Lubec conveys the aura of realness: a hardscrabble fishing community that extends a welcome to visitors. Lubec residents love to point out that the closest traffic light is 50 miles away.

Settled in 1780 and originally part of Eastport, Lubec was split off in 1811 and named for the German port of Lübeck (for convoluted reasons still not totally clear). The town's most famous resident was Hopley Yeaton, first captain in the U.S. Revenue-Marine (now the U.S. Coast Guard), who retired here in 1809.

Along the main drag (Water St.), a number of shuttered buildings reflect the town's roller-coaster history. Once the world's sardine capital, Lubec no longer has a packing plant, but aquaculture has come to the forefront, and new businesses are slowly arriving.

## ◖ WEST QUODDY HEAD STATE PARK

Beachcombing, hiking, picnicking, and an up-close look at Maine's only red-and-white-striped lighthouse are the big draws at 480-acre Quoddy Head State Park (West Quoddy Head Rd., Lubec, 207/733-0911, 9 A.M.–sunset May 15–Oct. 15, $2 adults, $1 kids), the easternmost point of U.S. land. Begin with a visit to the **Visitor Center** (Keeper's House, 207/733-2180, www.westquoddy.com, 10:10 A.M.–4 P.M. daily late May–mid-Oct., free), operated by the enthusiastic West Quoddy Head Light Keepers Association, a volunteer group. Inside are exhibits on lighthouse memorabilia, local flora and fauna, and area heritage; a gallery displaying local works; and a staffed information desk.

**West Quoddy Head Light,** towering 83 feet above mean high water, was built in 1808. (Its counterpart, East Quoddy Head Light, is on

New Brunswick's Campobello Island.) Views from the lighthouse grounds are fabulous, and whale sightings are common in summer. The lighthouse tower is open annually for one day in June or early July, during Lighthouse Week, and other times when the Coast Guard is on-site.

The cliffs of Canada's Grand Manan Island are visible from the park's grounds. A 1.75-mile, moderately difficult trail follows the 90-foot cliffs to Carrying Place Cove, and an easy, mile-long boardwalk winds through a unique moss and heath bog designated as a National Natural Landmark. Be forewarned that the park gate is locked at sunset. In winter, the park is accessible for snowshoeing. From Route 189 on the outskirts of Lubec, take South Lubec Road (well signposted) to West Quoddy Head Road. Turn left and continue to the parking area.

Candy-striped West Quoddy Head Light is sometimes open for tours.

© TOM NANGLE

# TIDES

Nowhere in Maine is the adage "Time and tide wait for no man" more true than along the Washington County coastline. The nation's most extreme tidal ranges occur in this area, so the hundreds of miles of tidal shore frontage between Steuben and Calais provide countless opportunities for observing tidal phenomena. Every six hours or so, the tide begins either ebbing or flowing. The farther Down East you go, the higher (and lower) the tides. Although tides in Canada's Bay of Fundy are far higher, the highest tides in New England occur along the St. Croix River, at Calais.

Tides govern coastal life – particularly Down East, where average tidal ranges may be 10-20 feet and extremes approach 28 feet. Everyone is a slave to the tide calendar, which coastal-community newspapers diligently publish. Boats tie up with extra-long lines; clammers and wormdiggers schedule their days by the tides; hikers have to plan for shoreline exploring; and kayakers need to plan their routes to avoid getting stuck in the muck.

Tides, as we all learned in elementary school, are lunar phenomena, created by the gravitational pull of the moon; the tidal range depends on the lunar phase. Tides are most extreme at new and full moons – when the sun, moon, and Earth are all aligned. These are spring tides, supposedly because the water springs upward (the term has nothing to do with the season). And tides are smallest during the moon's first and third quarters – when the sun, Earth, and moon have a right-angle configuration. These are neap tides ("neap" comes from an Old English word meaning "scanty"). Other lunar/solar phenomena, such as the equinoxes and solstices, can also affect tidal ranges.

The best time for shoreline exploration is on a new-moon or full-moon day, when low tide exposes mussels, sea urchins, sea cucumbers, starfish, periwinkles, hermit crabs, rockweed, and assorted nonbiodegradable trash. Rubber boots or waterproof, treaded shoes are essential on the wet, slippery terrain.

Caution is also essential in tidal areas. Unless you've carefully plotted tide times and heights, don't park a car or bike or boat trailer on a beach; make sure your sea kayak is lashed securely to a tree or bollard; don't take a long nap on shoreline granite; and don't cross a low-tide land spit without an eye on your watch.

A perhaps apocryphal but almost believable story goes that one flatlander stormed up to a ranger at Cobscook Bay State Park one bright summer morning and demanded indignantly to know why they had had the nerve to drain the water from her shorefront campsite during the night. When it comes to tides...you have to go with the flow.

## SIGHTS
### Mulholland Market and McCurdy Smokehouse

**Lubec Landmarks** (207/733-2068) is working to preserve these two local landmarks. The smokehouse complex, the last operating herring-smoking operation in the country, can be seen on the water side of Water Street. In 2007, after years of effort, it finally reopened to the public for tours. Mulholland Market is the organization's headquarters. Inside are displays about the smokehouses and exhibits of local art. It's volunteer operated, so hours change frequently.

### Lubec Historical Society

The society's small museum in the **Old Columbian Store** (Main St., 207/733-4696, 9 A.M.–3 P.M. Mon., Wed., and Fri., free) doubles as a visitors information center. Among the historical and genealogical displays is a working model of the machine used in the infamous Gold from Seawater swindle of 1898. Volunteers will glad fill you in on that or you can pick up a brochure. While here, also pick up the *Lubec Historic Walking Tour* brochure, which highlights about a dozen historical sites in downtown Lubec. The museum is on the left as you're entering town, just beyond Uncle Kippy's restaurant.

Lubec Landmarks' Mulholland Market building is one of the bright spots in downtown Lubec.

## Lubec Breakwater

Even the humongous tides and dramatic sunsets over Johnson Bay can get your attention if you hang out at the breakwater. Across the channel, on Campobello Island, is red-capped **Mulholland Point Lighthouse,** an abandoned beacon built in 1885. As the tide goes out—18 or so feet of it—you'll also see hungry harbor seals dunking for dinner. And if you're lucky, you might spot the eagle pair that nests on an island in the channel (bring binoculars).

## RECREATION
### Tours

Native Lubec residents, often with roots going back generations and with specialties as diverse as wildlife, birding, photography, and diving, deliver insights and share their knowledge on **Tours of Lubec and Cobscook** (24 Water St., P.O. Box 535, Lubec 04652, 207/733-2997 or 888/347-9302, www.toursoflubecandcobscook.com). Credit enthusiastic Lubec resident Ruta Jordans for creating the nonprofit Association to Promote and Protect the Lubec

Environment (APPLE) to learn more about Lubec. APPLE sponsors personalized interpretive tours in areas covering area art, culture, the environment, history, and heritage. Rates range $20–40 pp. Call or visit the website to create an itinerary that works for you.

### Hiking and Walking

Tag along with Lubec's **Pathfinders Walking Group** (207/733-4984 or 207/733-0988)—enthusiastic area residents who go exploring every Sunday year-round, usually meeting at 2 P.M. for a two-hour ramble. Nonmembers are welcome, there's no fee, and you'll see a Lubec (and more) that most visitors never encounter.

A fine place for a walk is the Maine Coast Heritage Trust's 376-acre **Hamilton Cove Preserve.** To find it, take Route 189 to the South Lubec Road toward Quoddy Head, but bear right at the fork and continue 2.4 miles to a small parking lot on the left. There's a kiosk with maps about 100 feet or so down the trail. The 1.5 miles of ocean frontage are highlighted by cobble beaches, rocky cliffs, and jaw-dropping views (on a clear day) of Grand Manan. It's about one mile to an observation platform and another half mile to the bench at the trail's end.

For information on other hikes in the area, pick up a copy of *Cobscook Trails,* a guidebook with maps and trail details. It's available at local stores for $6.50 or from the **Quoddy Regional Land Trust** (Rte. 1, Whiting 04691). Another resource available locally is *Self-Guided Birding Explorations, Washington County, Maine,* published in conjunction with the Down East Spring Birding Festival (see *Entertainment and Events.* It lists and maps walks and hikes and notes habitats and bird species.

## ENTERTAINMENT AND EVENTS

Classical music is the focus (for the most part) at **SummerKeys** (207/733-2316 or off-season 973/316-6220, www.summerkeys.com), a music camp for adults, no prior experience required, with weeklong programs in piano, voice, oboe, flute, clarinet, guitar, violin, and cello. Free concerts by visiting artists, faculty, and students are held at 7:30 P.M. Wednesday evenings late June–early September in the Congregational Christian Church, on Church Street.

**Live music** is usually on tap weekends at Cohill's Inn and Annabell's Pub, both on Water Street.

During summer, concerts are often held at the town bandstand on Main Street.

An ambitious, grassroots group has launched **Cobscook Community Learning Center** (207/733-2233, Timber Cove Rd., Trescott, www.thecclc.org). Two timber-frame buildings house CCLC's year-round programs, an open pottery studio, fiber-arts studio, and multiuse classrooms. Under construction are an outdoor amphitheater with dance floor, hiking and walking trails, and more on the center's 60-acre campus. The center's mission is "to enrich the lives of local community members through grassroots collaboration, using the arts, the rich social fabric, and the natural surroundings as the medium." Festivals, adult education, indigenous education, sustainable and value-added eco-ventures, youth programs, and more are

planned. Open-jam music nights, held on the second, fourth, and fifth Mondays each month (7–10 P.M., donation appreciated), bring in as many as 20 musicians and a good crowd of listeners. Do call to see what's on the schedule.

Birding is big here, and spring brings **The Down East Spring Birding Festival** (P.O. Box 42, Whiting 04691, 207/733-2201, www.downeastbirdfest.org) to the Cobscook Bay Area, held annually in late May. Guided and self-guided explorations, presentations, and tours fill schedule, and participation is limited, so register early.

## SHOPPING

Within strolling distance of each other downtown are **Dianne's Glass Gallery** (72 Water St., Lubec, 207/733-2458, www.diannesglass.com), where Dianne Larkin sells her handcrafted glass jewelry, plates, and other creations; **Northern Tides** (24 Water St., Lubec, 207/733-2500), with a nice selection of mostly local artwork; and **Downeast Artisans** (60 Washington St., Lubec, 207/733-8811), a collaborative gallery with works in varied media.

On the way to West Quoddy Head, detour off the main road just after the fork, taking a right on Carrying Place Cove to find **Le Cadeau Originals** (53 Carrying Place Cove, Lubec, 207/733-2940), where Judith Ashley weaves and sells her creations and photography.

Lighthouse buffs must stop at **West Quoddy Gifts** (Quoddy Head Rd., one mile before the lighthouse, 207/733-2457). It's stocked with souvenirs and gifty items, most with a lighthouse theme.

## ACCOMMODATIONS

Many visitors use Lubec as a base for day trips to Campobello Island, so it's essential to make reservations at the height of summer. Several lodgings are also available on Campobello.

### Bed-and-Breakfasts

Built in 1860 by a British sea captain, **Peacock House Bed and Breakfast** (27 Summer St., Lubec, 207/733-2403 or 888/305-0036, www.peacockhouse.com, $90–130) has long been one of Lubec's most prestigious residences. Among the notables who have stayed here are Donald MacMillan, the famous Arctic explorer, and U.S. Senators Margaret Chase Smith and Edmund Muskie. It has three rooms and four suites; suites have TV and sitting area; one has a gas fireplace and a refrigerator. One room is wheelchair-accessible.

Unusual antiques fill the guest and sitting rooms of the 19th-century **Home Port Inn** (45 Main St., Lubec, 207/733-2077 or 800/457-2077 outside Maine, www.homeportinn.com, mid-May–mid-Oct., $90–105), ensconced on a Lubec hilltop. Each of the seven rooms has a private bath, although some are detached; some have water views. Rates include a generous continental breakfast. The inn also serves dinner by reservation.

Piano students at SummerKeys often practice on the living room piano at **BayViews** (6 Monument St., Lubec, 207/733-2181, $50–80, May 1–Oct. 31), providing impromptu concerts for other guests. The 1824 Victorian house sits on two acres edging Johnson Bay. It's a relaxed B&B, filled with eclectic antiques, art, and books. (Owner Kathryn Rubeor has a master's in English literature.) It's an easy walk to town if you can tear yourself away from the back deck or lawn chairs or hammock. Breakfast is a bountiful continental, with fresh fruit and juice, home-baked bread, and homemade granola and toppings. One huge suite perfect for a family and one twin room, with a piano, have private baths; two doubles and one single share a bath. A five-bedroom, three-bath waterfront house also is available for $1,100 per week.

## Motel

If you're traveling with small children, the lackluster **Eastland Motel** (County Rd., Rte. 189, R.R. 1, Box 6915, Lubec, 207/733-5501, www.eastlandmotel.com, $65–76) is Lubec's best bet. Four miles southwest of town, near the Lubec Municipal Airport (used infrequently), the motel has 20 rooms with cable TV and air-conditioning. Request one of the 12 rooms in the newer section. Free continental breakfast. Small pets possible ($10).

## Rental Properties

The farmhouse on the Bell family's 200-year-old saltwater farm, **Tide Mill Farms** (40 Tide Mill Rd., Edmunds, two miles north of Rte. 189, 207/733-2110, www.tidemillfarm.com), is available for weekly rental. Ocean views are available from throughout the century-old farmhouse, which has five bedrooms and 1.5 baths. Amenities include a TV/VCR, washer/dryer, and gas grill. Linens are provided. Original settler Robert Bell built a tidal gristmill here, and one of the stones still lies on the point. Explore the farm's 1,600 acres, including six miles of shorefront as well as forest and mountain trails. Watch for eagles, seals, and loons. The property is home to the organic farm of the same name, and you'll see farm animals and operations.

Bill Clark has rescued the former Coast Guard Station at West Quoddy Head and restored, renovated, and reopened it as ◖ **West Quoddy Station** (S. Lubec Rd., Lubec, Maine, 207/733-4452 or 877/535-4714, www.quoddyvacation.com), with five one-bedroom units (four in the lodge and one separate cabin), or opt for the five-bedroom, 2.5-bath Station House. All have kitchens, Wi-Fi, and DirecTV. Views are stupendous and extend to East Quoddy Head on Campobello; West Quoddy Head is about a half-mile walk. Rates begin at $75 per night, when available, but weekly rentals ($550–1,500) get first preference.

## Campgrounds

A 3.5-mile network of nature trails, picnic spots, great birding and berry picking, hot showers, a boat launch, and wooded shorefront campsites make 888-acre **Cobscook Bay State Park** (Rte. 1, Edmunds Township, 207/726-4412) one of Maine's most spectacular state parks. It's even entertaining just to watch the 24-foot tides surging in and out of this area at five or so feet an hour; there's no swimming because of the undertow. Reserve well ahead to get a place on the shore. To guarantee a site in July and August, using MasterCard or Visa, call 207/287-3824 or visit www.campwithme.com; reservation fee is $2 per site per night, two-night minimum. The park is open daily mid-May–mid-October; trails are groomed in winter for cross-country skiing, and one section goes right along the shore. Summer day-use fees are $3 adults, $1 children 5–11; under 5 or over 65 are free. The nonresident camping fee is $19 per site per night; the fee for Maine residents is $14.

The 80-acre **South Bay Campground** (591 County Rd./Rte. 189, R.R. 1, Box 6565, Lubec, 207/733-1037 or 877/733-1037, southbay@midmaine.com, mid-May–mid-Oct.) has 74 RV and tent sites, a third on the shore of beautiful South Bay. Eight private island sites (accessible on foot at low tide) are also available. Noise regulations are strictly enforced. Facilities include a game room and a pool. Leashed pets are allowed. The campground is about seven miles from Route 1.

## FOOD
### Local Flavors
You can't go wrong with a stop at **Bold Coast Smokehouse** (224 County Rd./Rte. 189, 207/733-8912 or 888/733-0807, www.boldcoastsmokehouse.com). Vinny Gartmayer is a master of the smoking process, creating delectable hot and cold smoked salmon, smoked fish spreads, smoked salmon sticks (great for picnics; try the garlic-pepper), and other goodies.

Oh my! ◼ **Monica's** (56 Pleasant St., 866/952-4500, www.monicaschocolates.com) gives meaning to the term sinfully delicious. Monica Elliott creates sumptuous handmade gourmet chocolates using family recipes from her native Peru. Visitors can sample chocolates before buying (Smart move: You're guaranteed to buy after you taste.) Among the chocolates are scrumptious bonbons, blueberry wine and raspberry wine truffles, peanut butter cups made with homemade peanut butter, and other mouthwatering treats. Yum!

Stave off a midday hunger attack with home-baked goodies with an organic twist from **Sun Porch Industries** (99 Johnson St., 207/733-7587, 11 A.M.–5 P.M. Wed.–Sun.), a tiny natural and organic foods store.

The **Atlantic House Coffee Shop** (52 Water St., Lubec, 207/733-0906, www.atlantichouse.net, 7 A.M.–7 P.M. daily May–Oct.) is one of the brightest spots on a rather forlorn street. Breakfast pastries, tasty sandwiches, pizzas, great desserts, and decent coffee—load up before you head out for a hike. Give yourself time, though, as service can be slow.

### Dining
Dining in Lubec is a bit of a crapshoot. It's wise to ask locally about current reputations, although often you'll find even mixed reviews then.

Depending on your source, **Uncle Kippy's** (County Rd., Rte. 189, Lubec, 207/733-2400, 11 A.M.–8 P.M. Sun.–Thurs., to 9 P.M. Fri. and Sat.) gets high and higher marks in Lubec for wholesome cooking. A sign out front announces, "Stop in or we'll both starve." Steak and seafood are specialties—at unfancy prices—and the pizza is the area's best ($7–29).

The nicest dining room in the area is at the **Home Port Inn** (45 Main St., Lubec, 207/733-2077 or 800/457-2077 outside Maine, www.homeportinn.com, 5–8 P.M. daily). Reservations are advisable for this very popular restaurant—a sunken dining room with tables for 30. The specialty is seafood (entrées run $12–24), but the food often doesn't match the setting. Open in summer only.

## INFORMATION AND SERVICES
The Cobscook Bay Area Chamber of Commerce (P.O. Box 42, Whiting 04691, www.cobscookbay.com) covers the Cobscook Bay region, including Lubec. Local sources of information include: The Puffin Pines (240 Rte. 1, Whiting); the Old Columbian Store (Main St., Lubec, 207/733-4696, limited hours Mon., Wed., and Fri.), home of the Lubec Historical Society; and the Visitor Center (West Quoddy Head Lighthouse, 207/733-2180, www.westquoddy.com, 10:10 A.M.–4 P.M. daily late May–mid-Oct.).

Lubec Memorial Library (corner of Water and School Sts., Lubec, 207/733-2491) has a public restroom.

THE DOWN EAST COAST

# Campobello Island

## ◀ ROOSEVELT CAMPOBELLO INTERNATIONAL PARK

Just over the Franklin D. Roosevelt Memorial Bridge from Lubec lies nine-mile-long Campobello Island, in Canada's New Brunswick province. Since 1964, 2,800 acres of the island have been under joint U.S. and Canadian jurisdiction as Roosevelt Campobello International Park, commemorating U.S. President Franklin D. Roosevelt. FDR summered here as a youth, and it was here that he contracted infantile paralysis (polio) in 1921. The park, covering most of the island's southern end, has well-maintained trails, picnic sites, and dramatic vistas, but its centerpiece is the imposing Roosevelt Cottage, a mile northeast of the bridge. Interesting to note that before becoming a summer retreat for wealthy Americans, Campobello was the feudal fiefdom of a Welsh family. King George III awarded the grant to Captain William Owen in 1767, and he arrived in 1770.

### Roosevelt Cottage/Visitor Centre

Little seems to have changed in the 34-room red-shingled Roosevelt "Cottage" overlooking Passamaquoddy Bay since President Roosevelt last visited in 1939. The grounds are beautifully landscaped, and the many family mementos—especially those in the late president's den—bring history alive. It all feels very personal, far less stuffy than most presidential memorials.

Stop first at the park's Visitor Centre, where you can pick up brochures (including a trail map, birding guide, and bog guide), use the restrooms, and see a short video setting the stage for the cottage visit. Then walk across to the house/museum (10 A.M.–6 P.M. Atlantic daylight time, 9 A.M.–5 P.M. eastern daylight time, last tour at 5:45 P.M., mid-May–mid-Oct., free). Guides are stationed in various rooms to explain and answer questions. Be sure to also visit the neighboring **Hubbard Cottage,** reopened to the public in 2006, and

open July 1–early September whenever it isn't in use by conferences. Free outside walking tours of the estate and on-site presentations on local ecology are given, weather and staff permitting. For more information, contact Executive Secretary, Roosevelt Campobello International Park (P.O. Box 129, Lubec 04652, or 459 Rte. 774, Welshpool, Campobello, NB, Canada E5E 1A4, 506/752-2922 seasonal, www.fdr.net).

### The Park by Car

If time is short, or you're unable to hike, at least take some of the park's driving routes—**Cranberry Point Drive,** 5.4 miles round-trip from the Visitor Centre; **Liberty Point Drive,** 12.4 miles round-trip, via Glensevern Road, from the Visitor Centre; and **Fox Hill Drive,** a 2.2-mile link between the other two main routes. Even with the car, you'll have access to beaches, picnic sites, spruce and fir forests, and great views of lighthouses, islands, and the Bay of Fundy.

Just west of the main access road from the bridge is the **Mulholland Point picnic area,** where you can spread out your lunch next to the distinctive red-capped lighthouse overlooking Lubec Narrows.

### Hiking/Picnicking

Within the international park are 8.5 miles of walking/hiking trails, varying from dead easy to moderately difficult. Easiest is the 1.2-mile (round-trip) walk from the Visitor Centre to **Friar's Head picnic area,** named for its distinctive promontory jutting into the bay. For the best angle, climb up to the observation deck on the "head." Grills and tables are here for picnickers. Pick up a brochure at the Visitor Centre detailing natural sights along the route.

The most difficult—and most dramatic—trail is a 2.4-mile stretch from **Liberty Point to Raccoon Beach,** along the southeastern shore of the island. Precipitous cliffs can make parts of this trail chancy for small children or

© TOM NANGLE

Be sure to have required identification and any necessary paperwork before crossing the bridge between Lubec, Maine, and Campobello Island, Canada.

insecure adults, so use caution. Liberty Point is incredibly rugged, but observation platforms make it easy to see the tortured rocks and wide-open Bay of Fundy. Along the way is the SunSweep Sculpture, an international art project by David Barr. At broad Raccoon Beach, you can walk the sands, have a picnic, or watch for whales, porpoises, and osprey. To avoid returning via the same route, park at Liberty Point and walk back along Liberty Point Drive from Raccoon Beach. If you're traveling with nonhikers, arrange for them to meet you with a vehicle at Con Robinson's Point.

A fascinating boardwalk, perfect for those in wheelchairs, is **Eagle Hill Bog,** 2.9 km down the Glensevern Road. Interpretive signs explain the lichens, scrub pines, pitcher plants, and other flora and fauna within the bogs. A spur trail leads to a trail that climbs quickly to an observation deck.

You can also walk the park's perimeter, including just more than six miles of shoreline, but only if you're in good shape, have water-

proof hiking boots, and can spend an entire day on the trails. Before attempting this, however, inquire at the Visitor Centre about trail conditions and tide levels.

## CAMPOBELLO BEYOND THE INTERNATIONAL PARK

Take a day or two and explore Campobello beyond the park; overnighters have several lodging and food options. You can also continue by ferry from here to New Brunswick's Deer Island and on to Eastport.

### Herring Cove Provincial Park

New Brunswick's provincial government does a conscientious job of running Herring Cove Provincial Park (506/752-2396 or 800/561-0123), with picnic areas, 91 campsites (506/752-7010), a four-mile trail system, a mile-long sandy beach, freshwater Glensevern Lake, and the nine-hole championship-level **Herring Cove Golf Course** (506/752-2467). The park is open early June–September.

## East Quoddy Head Light

Consult the tide calendar before planning your assault on East Quoddy Head Light (also known as Head Harbour Light), at Campobello's northernmost tip. It's on an islet accessible only at low tide. The distinctive white light tower bears a huge red cross. (You're likely to pass near it on whale-watching trips out of Eastport.) From the Roosevelt cottage, follow Route 774 through the village of Wilson's Beach and continue to the parking area. A stern Canadian Coast Guard warning sign tells the story:

> Extreme Hazard. Beach exposed only at low tide. Incoming tide rises 5 feet per hour and may leave you stranded for 8 hours. Wading or swimming are extremely dangerous due to swift currents and cold water. Proceed at your own risk.

So there. It's definitely worth the effort for the bay and island views from the lighthouse grounds, often including whales and eagles. Allow about an hour before and after dead low tide (be sure your watch coincides with the Atlantic-time tide calendar).

In 2005, **The Friends of the Head Harbour Lightstation** (916 Rte. 774, Welshpool, NB E5E 1B1 Canada, www.campobellow.com/lighthouse), a local group, took over maintenance of the station to preserve it. They hope to eventually open it to the public with an interpretive center highlighting the lighthouse's history, maritime ecosystems in the Bay of Fundy, and whale-rescue efforts. In the meantime, work parties provide an opportunity to peek inside. You can support the efforts with a membership, available for US$15 individual or US$25 family.

## Whale-Watching and Boat Tours

**Island Cruises** (506/752-1107 or 888/249-4400) departs three times daily from Head Harbor Wharf for scenic whale-watching cruises aboard the *Mister Matthew*, a 37-foot traditional Bay of Fundy fishing boat that carries 20 passengers. Owner Mac is a member of the Fundy Whale Rescue Team, so he has great insights and stories to share.

## ACCOMMODATIONS AND FOOD

In midsummer, if you'd like to overnight on the island, be sure to reserve lodgings well in advance; Campobello is a popular destination. The nearest backup beds are in Lubec, and those fill up, too.

**The Owen House** (11 Welshpool St., Welshpool, Campobello Island, NB, Canada, 506/752-2977, www.owenhouse.ca, late May–mid-Oct., $107–210 Canadian), is the island's best address, a comfortably elegant early-19th-century inn on 10 acres on Deer Point overlooking Passamaquoddy Bay and Eastport in the distance. Nine guest rooms (two with shared baths) on three floors are decorated with antiques and family treasures along with owner Joyce Morrel's paintings (Joyce grew up in this house) and assorted handmade quilts. There's a first-floor room that's ideal for those with mobility problems. Joyce and innkeeper Jan Meiners are very active in the lighthouse preservation efforts. Just north of the inn is the Deer Island ferry landing.

**The Lupine Lodge** (610 Rte. 774, Welshpool, Campobello Island, NB, Canada, 506/752-2555, www.lupinelodge.com, early June–mid-Oct., $85–140 Canadian), a log lodge complex, is only a quarter mile from the Roosevelt cottage. Bay views from the 11-acre grounds and a few of the 11 rooms are terrific, but rooms are pretty basic. The adjacent restaurant serves breakfast, lunch, and dinner. Out the back door are the Adams Estate trails of the provincial park.

Campsites are available at **Herring Cove Provincial Park** (506/752-7010). Tent cabins also are available.

Don't expect culinary creativity on Campobello, but you won't starve—at least during the summer season. Best choice is **Family Fisheries** (1977 Rte. 774, Wilson's Beach, 506/752-2470, 10 A.M.–8 or 9 P.M. daily), a seafood restaurant and fish market toward the northern end of the island. Portions are huge,

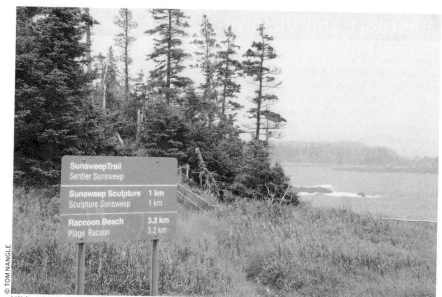

© TOM NANGLE

Hiking trails in the international park hug the rugged coastline of Campobello Island.

service is friendly, the fish is superfresh, and the homemade desserts are heavenly. BYOB. The only restaurant open year-round is **Sweet Time Bakery** (Rte. 774, 7 A.M.–8 or 9 P.M. daily), serving good home cooking and fresh-baked breads. The only island restaurant with a liquor license is Lupine Lodge.

## INFORMATION AND SERVICES

To visit Campobello, you'll have to pass Customs checkpoints on the U.S. and Canada ends of the Franklin D. Roosevelt Memorial Bridge (Lubec, U.S., Customs 207/733-4331; Campobello, Canada, Customs 506/752-2091, fax 506/752-1080). Be sure to have required identification.

Be aware that crossing this short little bridge takes an hour, because there's a one-hour time difference between Lubec and Campobello. Lubec (like the rest of Maine) is on east-

ern standard time; Campobello, like the rest of Canada's Maritime Provinces, is on Atlantic time, an hour later. As soon as you reach the island, set your clock ahead an hour.

There is no need to convert U.S. currency to Canadian for use on Campobello; U.S. dollars are accepted everywhere on the island, but prices tend to be quoted in Canadian dollars.

Just after Canadian Customs waves you through from Lubec, stop at the Tourist Information Centre (44 Rte. 774, Welshpool, NB, 506/752-7043, May–Oct.), on your right. The staff can fix you up with an island map, trail maps of the international park, tide info for lighthouse visits, and New Brunswick propaganda, and then steer you toward the Roosevelt property.

For information on Campobello Island, contact Campobello Island Tourism Association (506/752-7010, www.campobello.com).

# Eastport and Vicinity

When you leave Whiting, and continue north on Route 1 around Cobscook Bay, it's hard to believe that life could slow down any more than it already has, but it does. The landscape's raw beauty is occasionally punctuated by farmhouses or a convenience store, but little else.

Edmunds Township's claims to fame are its splendid public lands—Cobscook Bay State Park and a unit of Moosehorn National Wildlife Refuge. Just past the state park, loop along the scenic shoreline before returning to Route 1.

Pembroke, once part of adjoining Dennysville, claims Reversing Falls Park, where you can watch (and hear) ebbing and flowing tides draining and filling Cobscook Bay.

If time allows a short scenic detour, especially in fall, turn left (northwest) on Route 214 and drive 10 miles to quaintly named Meddybemps, allegedly a Passamaquoddy word meaning "plenty of alewives (herring)." Views over Meddybemps Lake, on the north side of the road, are spectacular, and you can launch a canoe or kayak into the lake here, less than a mile beyond the junction with Route 191 (take the dead-end unpaved road toward the water).

Backtracking to Route 1, heading east from Pembroke, you'll come to Perry, best known for the Sipayik (Pleasant Point) Indian Reservation, a Passamaquoddy settlement, two miles east of Route 1, that's been here since 1822. Drop down Route 191 that cuts through the reservation's heart. If there's time, stop at the small Waponahki Museum. Or plan a visit around the reservation's August Indian Days celebration.

The city (yes, it's officially a city) of Eastport (pop. 1,900) is on Moose Island, connected by causeway to the mainland at Sipayik (Pleasant Point). Views are terrific on both sides, especially at sunset, as you hopscotch from one blob of land to another and finally reach this minicity, where the sardine industry was introduced as long ago as 1875. Five sardine canneries once operated here, employing hundreds of local residents who snipped the heads off herring and stuffed them into cans—one of those esoteric skills not easily translatable to other tasks. In the 1990s, the focus was on fish farming. In the new century, entrepreneurs and artisans seem to be leading the way.

Settled in 1772, Eastport has had its ups and downs, mostly mirroring the fishing industry. It's now on an upswing, as people "from away" have arrived to soak up the vibe of a small town with a heavy Down East accent. Artists, artisans, and antiques shops are leading the town's rejuvenation as a tourist destination, with The Tides Institute at the forefront. A big push came in 2001, when the Fox Network reality-TV series *Murder in Small Town X* was filmed here; the city morphed into the village of Sunrise, Maine, and local residents eagerly filled in as extras. The huge waterfront statue of a fisherman is a remnant of the filming.

The biggest controversy in these parts now is the possibility of a liquefied natural gas terminal on the coastline, something many locals on both sides of the border are fighting.

Until 1811, the town also included Lubec, which is about 2.5 miles across the water in a boat, but 40-something in a car. A ferry now shuttles passengers back and forth for Lubec's SummerKeys concerts, and locals hold out hope that a regular schedule will be established.

## SIGHTS
### Historic Walking Tour

The best way to appreciate Eastport's history is to pick up and follow the route in *A Walking Guide to Eastport,* available locally for $2. The handy map/brochure spotlights the city's 18th-, 19th-, and early-20th-century homes, businesses, and monuments, many now on the National Register of Historic Places. Among the highlights are historic homes converted to B&Bs, two museums, and a large chunk of downtown Water Street, with many handsome brick buildings erected after a disastrous fire swept through in 1886. A free walking map, with far fewer details, also is available.

## THE QUODDY LOOP

It's easy to make it a two-nation vacation and avoid backtracking along Route 1 by looping through Canada. In July and August, **East Coast Ferries** (Deer Island, New Brunswick, Canada, 506/747-2159 or 877/747-2159, www.eastcoastferries.nb.ca) operates funky, bargelike car ferries between Eastport and Deer Island, and then on to Campobello Island – and vice versa. The ferry schedule is in Atlantic time, so adjust for the one-hour time distance when planning, since Eastport is on eastern time and the two Canadian islands are on Atlantic time. Campobello departures are on the hour, beginning at 9 A.M. Atlantic time (8 A.M. eastern time). Eastport departures are on the half hour, beginning at 9:30 A.M. Atlantic time (8:30 A.M. eastern time). Check the schedule carefully to avoid missing the last boat back to Eastport. (If you take a car, you can drive back to Eastport from Campobello via Lubec. It's 1.5 miles by water and almost 50 miles by road.) The ferry landing in Eastport is just off Water Street, 0.3 mile north of Washington Street, next to the Eastport Chowder House Restaurant. Fees, in Canadian funds, for car and driver, are $15 for Deer Island/Campobello, $12 for Deer Island/Eastport, no charge for kids 12 and younger, and passengers without cars are $3 on each (no credit cards, fare collected on board). It all seems very informal, and the trip is an adventure, but remember that you're crossing the Canadian border. United States citizens need required identification; non-U.S. citizens need a passport; most non-Europeans also need a Canadian visa.

## Raye's Mustard Mill Museum

How often do you have a chance to watch mustard being made in a turn-of-the-20th-century mustard mill? Drive by J. W. Raye and Co. (83 Washington St., Rte. 190, Eastport, 207/853-4451 or 800/853-1903, www.rayesmustard.com, 9 A.M.–5 P.M. daily), at the edge of Eastport, and stop in for a free 15-minute tour (call for schedule). You'll get to see the granite millstones, the mustard seeds being winnowed, and enormous vats of future mustard. Raye's sells mustard under its own label and produces it for major customers under their labels. The shop stocks all of Raye's mustard varieties (samples available), other Maine-made food, and gift items, and it also has a small café, where you can buy sandwiches, soups, and salads. Even Martha Stewart has discovered Ray's, which took home both gold and bronze medals from the 2007 World Wide Mustard Competition.

## The Tides Institute and Museum of Art

One of the most promising additions to Eastport's downtown is The Tides (43 Water St., 207/853-4047, www.tidesinstitute.org, 10 A.M. to 4 P.M. Tues.–Sat., free), in a former bank that owner/director Hugh French, an Eastport native, is restoring. The institute's impressive goals are to build significant cultural collections and to produce new culturally important works employing printmaking, letterpress, photography, bookmaking, oral history, and other media. For its collection, the institute is focusing on works by artists and photographers associated with Maine and Maritime Canada. Already, it has significant works by artists such as John Marin and photographers such as Lewis Hine, a nice selection of baskets by Native Americans, and two organs made by the local Pembroke Organ Co. in the 1880s. These and others are displayed in rotating shows that also highlight contemporary area artists. The research and reference library has more than 4,000 volumes. The institute also offers workshops by visiting artists in printmaking and other topics. These are open to the public by reservation. Definitely stop in for a visit.

## Passamaquoddy Indian Reservation

Baskets, tools, beadwork, a birch-bark canoe, and photo-lined walls are all part of the

THE DOWN EAST COAST

Watch stoneground mustard being made at Raye's Mustard Mill.

**Waponahki Museum** (Rte. 190, Perry, 207/853-4001, call for hours) on Sipayik (Pleasant Point Reservation). The small collection is dedicated to preserving the history and culture of Maine's Passamaquoddy Indians. The museum has spurred revival of the Passamaquoddy language, now being taught and written. The museum—two miles east of Route 1 and seven miles north of Eastport—is open all year. Admission is free, but donations are welcomed.

Ask at the museum or locally about basket makers who might sell from their homes. The fancy and work baskets are treasures, constantly escalating in price. It's a real treat to be able to buy one from the maker.

## PARKS AND PRESERVES
### ◖ Shackford Head State Park
Ninety-acre Shackford Head (off Deep Cove Rd., Eastport, trailhead and parking area just east of the Washington County Community College Marine Technology Center at the southern end of town, free) is on a peninsula that juts into Cobscook Bay. It has five miles of wooded

trails, with the easiest being the one-mile round-trip to Shackford Head and its continuation onto the steeper Ship Point Trail, which adds another half mile, rising gently to a 175-foot-high headland with wide-open views of Eastport and, depending on weather, Campobello Island, Lubec, Pembroke, and even Grand Manan. This state preserve is a particularly good family hike. Use bug repellent and carry binoculars and a camera. There's a toilet near the parking area, but no other facilities. Also here is a memorial with plaques detailing the history of five Civil War ships that were decommissioned and burned on Cony Beach between 1901 and 1920 by the U.S. government. Eastport's huge tides allowed the ships to be brought in and beached and then taken apart as the tide receded. Of note is that 14 Eastport men served on four of the ships.

### Reversing Falls Park
There's plenty of room for adults to relax and kids to play at the 140-acre Reversing Falls Park in West Pembroke—plus shorefront ledges and a front-row seat overlooking a fas-

cinating tidal phenomenon. Pack a picnic and then check newspapers or information offices for the tide times, so you can watch the salt water surging through a 300-yard-wide passage at about 25 knots, creating a whirlpool and churning "falls." The park is at Mahar Point in West Pembroke, 7.2 miles south of Route 1. Coming from the south (Dennysville), leave Route 1 in West Pembroke when you see the Triangle Grocery Store. Turn right and go 0.3 mile to Leighton Point Road, where you'll see a sign saying, "Shore Access 5.5 miles." Turn right and go 3.8 miles, past gorgeous meadows, low shrubs, and views of Cobscook Bay. Turn right on Clarkside Road, at a very tiny Reversing Falls sign, posted high on a telephone pole. Go about 1.5 miles to the end and then turn left onto a gravel road and continue two miles to the park.

## Gleason Cove

This quiet park and boat launch is a delightful place to walk along the shorefront or to grab a table and spread out a picnic while drinking in the dreamy views over fishing weirs and islands in Passamaquoddy Bay. It's now threatened with a liquified natural-gas port, so it may not be around in this form much longer. To get here, take Shore Road (opposite the New Friendly Restaurant) and then take a right on Gleason Cove Road. No facilities.

## RECREATION
### Golf

**Downeast Adventure Golf** (Rte. 1, Perry, 207/731-9595, $6 adults, $5 kids 5–11) is an 18-hole championship miniature golf course on 2.5 acres, with night lights. Also on-site is a practice green.

## ◖ Whale-Watching
## and Scenic Cruises

Eastporter Butch Harris gave the waterfront a shot in the arm when he bought the sleek *Sylvina Beal,* a historic, 84-foot schooner built in 1911. His company, **Eastport Windjammers** (104 Water St. at the head of the breakwater, 207/853-2500, 207/853-4303 before

© TOM NANGLE

Book a day trip or longer on one of Eastport's windjammers for an upclose view of Passamaquoddy Bay.

10 A.M. and 6–8 P.M., www.eastportwind-jammers.com) offers a number of options to sail. The three-hour whale-watching cruise departs at 1:30 P.M. daily and heads out into the prime whale-feeding grounds of Passamaquoddy Bay—passing the Old Sow whirlpool (largest tidal whirlpool in the Northern Hemisphere), salmon aquaculture pens, and Campobello Island. En route, you'll see bald eagles, porpoises, possibly puffins and osprey, and more. Best months are July and August, when sightings are frequent, but Butch is a skilled spotter, so if they're there, he'll find them. The cost is $35 for adults, $18 for children 12 and younger. A two-hour sunset cruise departs the Eastport Pier at 7 P.M. and costs $25 for adults, $15 for children.

The newest addition to Captain Harris's fleet is the *Halie and Matthew,* a 92-foot schooner he built with John Bishop at Eastport's boat school. Each of the eight staterooms has double berths and private head

© TOM NANGLE

Downtown Eastport fronts on the harbor.

THE DOWN EAST COAST

with shower. Two- to five-day cruises range from $500 to more than $1,000 pp.

## Deep-Sea Fishing

**Eastport Windjammers** also offers a four-hour fishing trip on the *Quoddy Dam,* with all equipment provided. No license is required for recreational saltwater fishing. Bring a cooler or fish container if you want to keep your catch. The trip costs $25 for adults and $15 for children. It leaves from the Eastport Breakwater at 8 A.M.

## Sea Kayaking, Canoeing, and Hiking

Explore the region by sea kayak with **Cobscook Hikes and Paddles** (13 Woodcock Way, Robinston, 207/726-4776 summer, 207/454-2130 winter, www.cobscookhikesandpaddles.com), which services the area between Whiting and Calais. Registered Maine Guides Stephen and Tessa Ftorek lead three-hour ocean or lake paddles, designed to meet your interests and ability, for $50 pp. Two-hour sunrise or sunset

paddles are $40. On Friday nights, you can watch luminescent organisms sparkle in the water on a two-hour Phosphorescent Paddle, for $45. The Ftoreks also offer guided full-day ($80) and half-day ($40) hikes and snowshoeing adventures in winter. They opened an outpost in Eastport at Eastport Framing.

**Quoss Boats** (Rte. 1, Perry, 207/731-9595) rents lake kayaks for $40 per day, including paddle, life jacket, and portage. Renters must be swimmers, older than 21, and provide a major credit card for deposit. A half-day rental, when available, is $27. Kayaks are only for lake and estuary paddling, and introductory lessons are available. You can take them to one of the many pretty lakes on the inland side of Route 1.

## Star-Gazing

The Downeast Amateur Astronomers' **Downeast Observatory** (356 Old County Rd., Pembroke, 207/726-4621, www.downeastaa.com), with eight-inch DE8 reflector and three- and five-inch refractors, is open to the public for free by appointment. Contact Charlie Sawyer at the number above for details.

## ENTERTAINMENT

The **Eastport Arts Center** (36 Washington St., Eastport, 207/853-2358, www.eastportartscenter.com) is an umbrella organization for local arts groups, with headquarters and performing space in a former church. You can pick up a brochure with a complete schedule, which usually includes concerts, films, puppet shows, productions by local theater group **Stage East,** an Elderhostel program, and other cultural events. Also based here is **SummerArts** (207/853-6179, www.summerarts.com), a five-week series of classes and workshops.

The center works with Butch Harrison to provide a ferry to the free **SummerKeys** concerts, held Wednesday nights late June–early September in Lubec. Transportation is aboard the *Quoddy Dam,* departing Eastport at 6:30 P.M. and returning around 9:30 P.M. Ferry tickets are $14 in advance, $17 for walk-ins, space available, buy at the *Sylvina Beal* ticket office on Water Street or call 207/853-2500.

For **live music** in Eastport on weekends, try The Rose Garden (9 Dana St.).

## FESTIVALS AND EVENTS

For a small community, Eastport manages to pull together and put on plenty of successful events during the year.

Eastport's annual four-day **Fourth of July–Old Home Week** extravaganza includes a parade, pancake breakfasts, barbecues, a flea market, an auction, races, live entertainment, and fireworks. This is one of Maine's best Fourth of July celebrations and attracts a crowd of more than 10,000. Lodgings are booked months in advance, so plan ahead.

**Indian Ceremonial Days,** a three-day Native American celebration, includes children's games, canoe races, craft demos, talking circles, fireworks, and traditional food and dancing at Sipayik, the Pleasant Point Reservation, in Perry, the second weekend in August.

The **Eastport Salmon Festival** celebrates the area's aquaculture industry. If you like salmon, you'll *love* this event, which combines a salmon barbecue, craft booths, live entertainment, and boat trips at the Eastport breakwater 11 A.M.–4 P.M. the Sunday after Labor Day.

## SHOPPING
### Art, Crafts, and Antiques

Eastport has long been a magnet for artists and craftspeople yearning to work in a supportive environment, but the influx has increased in recent years. Proof of this is **The Eastport Gallery** (74 Water St., Eastport, 207/853-4166, www.eastportgallery.com, mid-June–Sept.), a cooperative whose works in varied media line the walls of a downtown building. The gallery also sponsors the annual **Paint Eastport Day,** usually held the second Saturday in September, when anyone is invited to paint a local scene; a reception and "wet paint" auction follow.

Relatively new on Eastport's art scene is **The Commons** (51 Water St., 207/853-4123), a waterfront building that's been beautifully renovated by a gaggle of energetic women with local ties into a fabulous gallery displaying works by 60 area artists and artisans. The group has plans to renovate a nearby waterfront warehouse into more shops and perhaps a hotel.

**Earth Forms** (5 Dana St., Eastport, 207/853-2430, www.earthforms.biz) features potter Donald Sutherland's intriguing (and sometimes whimsical) wheel-thrown work—self-described as "functional, nonfunctional, and dysfunctional" pottery. You can often see him at work on his wheel. It's tough to walk out without buying one of these special pieces.

Next door to Earth Forms is **Rose Garden Antiques and Design** (9 Dana St., 207/853-9598), an eclectic collection of antiques, collectibles, and art. Owners Linda and Al Salleroli are renovating the building and have included an indoor garden, café, and space for independent vendors as well as public restrooms.

Woodworker Roland LaVallee's gallery **Crow Tracks** (11 Water St., 207/853-2336, www.crowtracks.com) is filled with his intricate carvings of birds and local fauna. The tiny garden entryway just doubles the pleasure of a visit.

It's a delight to wander through the sculpted mermaids, angels, goddesses, flora, and fauna in the garden at **Ostrander** (83 Clark St., corner of Brewster St., Eastport, 207/853-4342). Inside are more sculptures, paintings, and garden art by Elizabeth Ostrander.

A number of very talented artists and artisans are tucked along the back roads of the area. You might get lucky and find them open, but it's wise to call before making a special trip. These include the **Salt Meadow Gallery and Studio** (Hersey Rd., Pembroke, 207/726-5153), in a log cabin chock-full of hand-painted floorcloths and woodcuts by Beverly Runyan; **Done Roving Farm and Carding Mill** (20 Charlotte Rd., Charlotte, 207/454-8148), a working farm where fiber artist Paula Farra creates and sells handspun yarns and felts in a variety of fibers and displays the works of other area artisans; **Wrenovations** (84 Mill Stream Rd., Robbinston, 207/454-2382), stained art creations by Mark Wren; and **Susan Designs** (behind Loring's Body Shop on Gin Cove Rd., Perry, 207/853-4315), where gifted quilt artist Susan Plachy sells her creations.

### Hand-Sewn Shoes

Shoemaking was once a major industry in Maine, although today only a couple of places still sew shoes by hand. One of them is **Quoddy Trail Moccasin Co.** (1041 Rte. 1, Perry, 207/853-2488, www.quoddytrail.com). The company was started by Harry Smith Shorey and is now run by his descendent Kevin Shorey and his wife, Kirsten. Overruns and seconds are sold at discounted prices at the Shoreys' store, the **Quoddy Wigwam** (Rte. 1 and Shore Rd., 207/853-4812), where you can also see a huge stuffed moose and buy Native American baskets and souvenirs. Call or ask at the store to arrange a tour of the low-key factory to see where the leather is cut and how it's sewn into moccasins, boat shoes, slippers, and other models, or to arrange for a custom pair ($70 and up; the bestselling model retails for $140) to be made.

### Gifts and a Whole Lot More

Describing **45th Parallel: The Store** (Rte. 1, Perry, 207/853-9500) is a tough assignment. You really have to *go there* and see for yourself. The aesthetic displays are worth the trip to this eclectic emporium. Housed in a one-story log building two miles (in the Calais direction) from the junction of Routes 190 and 1, the 45th Parallel is part antiques shop, part gift shop, part global marketplace—and entirely seductive. Tiny white lights glimmer here and there, antique architectural remnants hang from the ceiling, and every little niche holds yet another fascinating treasure.

Do stop in, if only for a few minutes, at **S. W. Wadsworth and Son** (42 Water St., 207/853-4343), the oldest ship chandlery in the country and the oldest retail business in Maine. In addition to hardware and marine gear, you'll find nautical gifts and souvenirs.

## ACCOMMODATIONS

Lodgings in Eastport can fill up in summer, and since it's literally the end of the road, it's wise to reserve ahead.

### Bed-and-Breakfasts

In 1833, renowned artist John James Audubon stayed at the elegant **Weston House** (26 Boynton St., Eastport, 207/853-2907 or 800/853-2907, www.westonhouse-maine.com, $70–85), so one of the three second-floor guest rooms bears his name—and walls lined with Audubon bird prints. All rooms share 2.5 baths, but don't let that dissuade you from staying at this lovely home. Jett and John Peterson's family antiques and interesting art and crafts fill the beautifully decorated house on a quiet side street two blocks above the waterfront. Breakfast is outstanding (Jett is Eastport's favorite caterer), complete with candelabra and classical music. Outside are croquet and badminton facilities, plus lovely gardens with a gazebo, chairs, and table. Tea and sherry are available in the afternoon. With notice, Jett will prepare a private dinner and serve it in the formal dining room, a smart and delicious choice given Eastport's limited restaurants.

Pretty gardens surround the **(** **Chadbourne House** (19 Shackford St., Eastport, 207/853-2727 or 888/853-2728, www.chadbourne-house.com, $110–140), Eastport's most elegant B&B. Jill and David Westphal's antiques-filled, Federal-style home has four guestrooms, two with fireplaces and one that fills most of the third floor. The double living room has two fireplaces. Guests gather each morning at the dining room table for David's breakfasts, and they can arrange in advance for a seafood dinner feast to be served in the garden. It's walking distance to downtown. One caveat: You'll have to remove your shoes in the entryway. Wi-Fi throughout.

The comfortably furnished **Milliken House Bed and Breakfast** (29 Washington St., Eastport, 207/853-2955 or 888/507-9370, www.eastport-inn.com, $75–85) is a good choice for families, but be forewarned that you'll have to carry your luggage up at least one, and perhaps two, tall flights of stairs. Hosts Bill and Mary Williams welcome children and pets to their in-town home that's an easy walk to shops and restaurants. Breakfasts are huge and served family-style in the very-Victorian dining room. There's a big TV in the double parlor downstairs, Wi-Fi throughout, and a phone is available. Call ahead in winter.

## Motel

Here's a motel with the spirit of a B&B. Enthusiastic about their adopted community, host Owen Lawlor and manager Deb Moore at **The Motel East** (23A Water St., Eastport, 207/853-4747, www.eastportme.info, $105–120) provide all kinds of advice and guarantee you'll enjoy the area. Got a problem or question? Owen or Deb can solve it or answer it. Guests have front-row seats on Passamaquoddy Bay, overlooking Campobello Island, and you can walk to everything downtown. Six good-size rooms and eight efficiency suites have Wi-Fi, phones, and cable TV, although the rooms could use freshening. Request a balcony room; avoid those on the basement level. Free coffee in the lobby. It's open all year. The separate Friar Roads Cottage is available for $150 d a day.

## Apartments

On the second floor of **The Commons** (51 Water St., 207/853-4123, www.thecommonseastport.com), a newly renovated downtown building on the waterfront, are two nicely appointed, two-bedroom apartments, with decks and spectacular harbor views. Tide Watcher has two baths and rents for $950 per week; Water's Edge has one bath and rents for $900; either is $150 per night/three-night minimum, when available. Both are nicely decorated, have well-equipped kitchens and comfy living rooms, laundries, and big decks over the harbor, complete with gas grills.

## Campground

On the outskirts of town is the quiet, well-maintained, waterfront **Seaview Campground** (16 Norwood Rd., Eastport, 207/853-4471, www.eastportmaine.com), just off Route 190, with 70 tent and RV open and semiwooded sites, nine cabins, and a four-unit motel. Shorefront sites on Harrington Cove have great views, but they're snapped up quickly. Cabins have excellent vistas. The camp store, open 7 A.M.–10 P.M., sells lobster live or cooked by the pound. There are also a recreation hall, dock, laundry, and a restaurant (open 7 A.M.–8 P.M.) serving breakfast, lunch, and dinner. Leashed pets are allowed only at RV and tent sites. Campsites are based on a family of four. Tent sites are $14–20, RV sites are $25–40, depending upon location and season. One-to three-bedroom cabins are $70–145 per day or $425–800 a week; motel rooms are $55–80 a day. It's open mid-May–mid-October. Pets are $10 per day, with a two-pet limit.

## FOOD

While you won't go hungry in Eastport, you won't be wowed by the food, either. As always in this region, ask locally about the current reputations.

## Local Flavors

The best pizza in Eastport comes from **Bank Square and Deli** (34 Water St., Eastport, 207/853-2709, www.banksquarepizza.com, 11 A.M.–8 P.M. Mon.–Sat.), where you can also get subs, wraps, burgers, salads, chicken, and even pasta. It has only a few seats, so grab your stuff and eat it elsewhere. No credit cards.

When you're wandering around the Eastport breakwater, you'll notice the line at **Rosie's Hot Dog** (municipal pier, Eastport, no phone, opens at 11 A.M. Mon.–Sat., at noon Sun.), a veteran takeout stand open only in summer. Rosie's tube steaks are the best around.

The **Sunrise County Farmers Market** sets up its tables next to Raye's Mustard Mill (Washington St., Eastport) 11 A.M.–2 P.M. every Thursday late June–October.

**Moose Island General Store** (corner of Water and Washington Sts., 207/853-2622, 5 A.M.–10 P.M. daily) serves breakfast baked goods, pizza, and other foods and must-haves. Bonus points for the harborfront deck.

Casual, friendly, and inexpensive is **The Happy Crab** (35 Water St., 207/853-9400, 11 A.M.–8 P.M. Mon.–Sat., 2–8 P.M. Sun.), a grill and sports bar. Pizza and finger food are usually available after 8 P.M. until the bar closes. Play pool while you wait. If the weather's fine, grab a seat on the deck. It's sometimes open for breakfast, too.

You might find ceviche or curry on the limited menu served at the **Rose Garden** (9 Dana St., 207/853-9598), a combination antiques, art, and curiosities shop that doubles as a café. It's open 10 A.M.–7 P.M. Monday–Wednesday, with a later closing and live entertainment Friday and Saturday in July and August. Dinner is served on Friday night only. It schedules poetry readings about once a month.

Here's something a bit different. **Blueberry Point Chefs** (Rte. 1, P.O. Box 58, Perry 04667, 207/853-4629, www.blueberrypointchefs.com) is a cooking school held on a 150-acre blueberry farm with panoramic views over Passamaquoddy Bay. Chef Audrey Patterson teaches two-day classes 5–8:30 P.M. Mondays and Tuesdays late May–late September for $80 pp or $50 for one night. Each evening concludes with a meal, and classes include opportunities for local culinary tours. Check the website for the specifics of each class. Also on the premises is the **Ice House Wine and Cheese Shop** (10 A.M.–5 P.M. Tues.–Sat.), a gourmet food and wine shop.

## Casual Dining

One of Eastport's dining secrets is Hilda and Sidney Lewis's **The Blue Iris** (31 Water St., Eastport, 207/853-2440, 6:30 A.M.–2 P.M. Tues.–Sat.), which shares space with a floral shop. Well-spaced indoor tables and outdoor ones on a bilevel deck all have water views. Breakfast is served all day; lunch is available beginning at 11 A.M., dinner is served on special occasions. With the exception of lobster and crabmeat rolls or clubs, a chicken Caesar, and perhaps daily specials, nothing on the menu is more than $5. It's all good, and the service is cheerful but, uhm, leisurely.

A popular roadside eatery with a well-deserved reputation, the aptly named **New Friendly Restaurant** (1014 Rte. 1, Perry, 207/853-6610, 11 A.M.–8 P.M. Mon.–Fri.) lays on home-cooked offerings for "dinnah" (a Maine-ism meaning lunch), specializing in steak and seafood, including what many label the area's best lobster roll. Don't be surprised to find it crowded.

A downtown Eastport institution since 1924, the **Wa-Co Diner and Dining Room** (47 Water St., 207/853-4046, 6 A.M.–9 P.M. daily), pronounced WHACK-o, short for Washington County *or,* the story goes, for Nelson Watts and Ralph Colwell, is a must-do local-color stop. Choose from the front diner, with counter and booths, the more refined dining room, or the waterfront deck. Expect diner fare with a dose of attitude; a few fancier items top out around $25, but most are inexpensive. New ownership took over in 2007, so ask locally as reviews have been mixed. No credit cards.

Time your meal right, and you can watch the Deer Isle ferry arrive and depart or view the windjammer *Sylvina Beal* sail by from the bilevel **Eastport Chowder House** (167 Water St., 207/853-4700, 11 A.M.–9 P.M. daily). Seafood, natch, is the specialty, with entrées in the $12–15 range. One drawback is the bar underneath—the jukebox is so loud that the tables in the dining room shake.

For more than a decade, the easternmost Mexican restaurant in the United States anchored downtown Eastport; expected to replace it is **The Pickled Herring** (32 Water St., 207/853-2323, www.thepickledherring.com), which is billing itself as a martini bar with fine dining. Locals are hopeful but bemused by the concept.

## INFORMATION AND SERVICES
### Information
Brochures are available at the Quoddy Maritime Museum and Visitor Center (70 Water St., 10 A.M.–6 P.M. daily June–Sept.). In the museum section of the center is a huge model of the failed 1936 Passamaquoddy Tidal Power Project (an idea whose time hadn't come when it was proposed).

Information also is available from the Eastport Chamber of Commerce (207/853-3633, www.eastport.net) and online at www.cobscookbay.com/eastport.htm.

The handsome stone Peavey Memorial Library (26 Water St., Eastport, 207/853-4021), built in 1893, is named after the inventor of the Peavey grain elevator.

### Public Restrooms
Restrooms are available at the library, and in summer, there are portable toilets on Eastport's breakwater.

# Calais and Vicinity

Calais (CAL-us) is as far as you'll get on the coast of Maine; from here on, you're headed inland.

Europeans showed up in this area as early as 1604, when French adventurers established an ill-fated colony on St. Croix Island in the St. Croix River—16 whole years before the Pilgrims even thought about Massachusetts. After a winter-long debacle, all became relatively quiet until 1779, when the first permanent settler arrived.

The most interesting time to show up in Calais (pop. 3,890) is during the nine-day International Festival, the first or second week in August, when the city and neighboring St. Stephen, New Brunswick, go all out with dances, concerts, races, barbecues, and fireworks—reinforcing the transborder cooperation that has long benefited both communities. In late 2008, a third international bridge should open, connecting Route 1 north of downtown Calais to St. Stephen. It joins a downtown bridge, also connecting to St. Stephen, and a quieter, smaller crossing a few miles north, connecting with Mill Town.

Southeast of Calais is tiny Robbinston, a booming shipbuilding community in the 19th century but today little more than a 500-person blip on the map. Highlights nowadays are a wonderful chocolate shop and the Calais-Robbinston "milestones."

## SIGHTS
### Downeast Heritage Center
The $6.5 million Downeast Heritage Center (39 Union St., Calais, 207/454-7878 or 877/454-2500, www.downeastheritage.org, 10 A.M.–5 P.M. daily mid-May–mid-Oct., free) opened in the renovated Calais Train Station in May 2004 and now has three permanent, interactive, low-tech exhibits highlighting more than 12,000 years of regional cultural and natural history. These explain the region's shipbuilding, forestry, blueberrying, and fishing heritage; Passamaquoddy culture; and the St. Croix settlement. Among the highlights are a handmade Passamaquoddy canoe crafted using traditional tribal tools, a touch tank with marine creatures, and a riverfront walk, from which, if you're lucky, you might spot soaring eagles.

### Walking Tour
Pick up a copy of the *Walking Tour Guide to Calais Residential Historic District* at the Maine Tourism Information Center, on the waterfront. The guide, produced by the St. Croix Historical Society, briefly covers the town's history and maps and describes the architecture and early owners of 23 historic houses, four of which are listed on the National Register of Historic Places.

# GRAND LAKE STREAM

For a tiny community of about 200 year-rounders, Grand Lake Stream has a well-deserved, larger-than-life reputation. It's the center of a vast area of rivers and lakes, ponds and streams – a recreational paradise, and more than 27,000 acres, including 62 miles of shore frontage, has been preserved by the **Downeast Lakes Land Trust** (www.downeastlakes.org). It's the literal town at the end of the world, remote in every sense of the word, yet just a half hour or so inland from Calais.

The famous stream is a narrow, three-mile neck of prime scenic and sportfishing water connecting West Grand Lake and Big Lake. A dam spans the bottom of West Grand, and just downstream is a state-run salmon hatchery. Since the mid-19th century, the stream and its lakes have been drawing fishing fans to trout and landlocked-salmon spawning grounds, and fourth and fifth generations now return here each year.

Fly-fishing enthusiasts arrive in May and June for landlocked salmon and smallmouth bass (the stream itself is fly-fishing only); families show up in July and August for canoeing, birding, swimming, fishing, and hiking; hunters arrive in late October for game birds and deer; and snowmobilers, snowshoers, and cross-country skiers descend as the snow piles up.

Canoe building has contributed to the area's mystique. The distinctive Grand Lake canoe (or "Grand Laker"), a lightweight, square-sterned, motorized 20-footer, was developed in the 1920s specifically for sportfishing in these waters. In the off-season, several villagers still hunker down in their workshops and turn out these stable cedar beauties. (Interested? Call Bill Shamel, 207/796-8199.)

## ACTIVITIES

If you're in Grand Lake Stream only for the day, head for the **public landing** and bear right after the intersection with the Pine Tree Store, where you'll find a parking area, a dock, a portable toilet, and a boat launch. You can also walk the path on the western shore of the stream. Or, armed with a map from the Pine Tree Store, hike the 2.6-mile **Little Mayberry Cove Trail** edging the western shoreline of West Grand Lake.

Better yet, plan a day with a guide. The region has the greatest concentration of Registered Maine Guides in the state, which gives you an indication of the fishing, hunting, and

## St. Croix Island

Unless you have your own boat, you can't get over to 6.5-acre St. Croix Island, an International Historic Site under joint U.S. and Canadian jurisdiction (Rte. 1, Red Beach Cove, eight miles south of Calais, www.nps.gov/maac, free).

The island is the site of the pioneering colony established by French explorers Samuel de Champlain and Pierre du Gua (Sieur de Monts) in 1604. Doomed by disease, mosquitoes, lack of food, and a grueling winter, 35 settlers died; in spring, the emaciated survivors abandoned their effort and moved on to Nova Scotia. In 1969, archaeologists found graves of 23 victims, but the only monument on the island is a commemorative plaque dating from 1904.

The current in the St. Croix River is strong, and tidal ranges can be as high as 28 feet, so neophyte boaters shouldn't even attempt a crossing, but local residents often picnic and swim off the island's sandy beach on the southern end. For a better understanding of the historic colony, visit the Downeast Heritage Center. The attractive 16-acre roadside rest area on Route 1 at **Red Beach Cove** was greatly improved for the 400th anniversary of the settlement in 2004. A short heritage trail, with bronze statues depicting various key persona or cultures in the development of the colony, ends on the point with views of the island. Also here are picnic tables, restrooms, a gravel beach, and a boat launch. It's a great place to stop for a picnic.

## Whitlock Mill Lighthouse

From the lovely Pikewoods Rest Area, beside

canoeing opportunities here. Truly the best way to experience Grand Lake Stream is with a member of the **Grand Lake Stream Guides Association** (www.grandlakestreamguides.com). The website lists members and specialties. You can arrange for one of these skilled guides to lead you on a fishing expedition, wildlife or photographic safari, or canoeing trip for a half day or longer.

### FOLK ART FESTIVAL

A great time to visit the village is the last full weekend in July for the annual **Grand Lake Stream Folk Art Festival** (207/796-8199, 10 A.M.-5 P.M. Sat. and Sun., $5 one day, $8 both days), held on the town's grassy ballfield. Tents shelter approximately 50 top-notch juried artisans. Nonstop bluegrass and folk music is another attraction. An exhibit highlights the region's canoe-building tradition and another displays antique and contemporary quilts. Breakfast, lunch, and snacks are available. Complementing the festival are lakeside barbecues by the guides, usually lobster on Friday evening, chicken on Saturday evening, with tickets available at the Pine Tree Store, across from the festival grounds. A contra dance takes place Saturday night, and a music jam, open to anyone, takes place Sunday morning. Leashed pets are welcome on festival grounds.

### INFORMATION AND SERVICES

The volunteer-run Grand Lake Stream Chamber of Commerce (P.O. Box 124, Grand Lake Stream 04637, www.grandlakestream.com) produces a brochure listing accommodations, shops, and services.

The heart of Grand Lake Stream is Kurt and Kathy Cressey's Pine Tree Store (3 Water St., P.O. Box 129, Grand Lake Stream 04637, 207/796-5027, www.pinetreestore.com). People have been getting their gas and groceries here for more than 60 years. It's also a good source of local information (and gossip), and it sells pizza, sandwiches, and general-store merchandise. Be sure to check out their handmade pack baskets (sold at L. L. Bean).

To get to Grand Lake Stream, head north on Route 1 from Calais through Princeton. About two miles north of Princeton, turn left (west) onto Grand Lake Stream Road (also called Princeton Rd). Continue about 10 miles to the village.

Route 1, about four miles southeast of Calais, there's a prime view of 32-foot-high Whitlock Mill Lighthouse, on the southern shore of the St. Croix River. Built in 1892, the green flashing light is accessible only over private land, so check it out from this vantage point. Besides, you can also have a picnic break here.

## Calais-Robbinston Milestones

A quirky little local feature, the Calais-Robbinston milestones are a dozen red-granite chunks marking each of the 12 miles between Robbinston and Calais. Presaging today's highway mileage markers, late-19th-century entrepreneur and journalist James S. Pike had the stones installed on the north side of Route 1 to keep track of the distance while training his pacing horses.

## RECREATION
### Parks and Preserves

More than 50 miles of trails and gravel roads wind through the 17,257-acre Baring Unit of the **Moosehorn National Wildlife Refuge** (Charlotte Rd., Baring, 207/454-7161, http://moosehorn.fws.gov, sunrise–sunset daily, free), on the outskirts of Calais. Start with the 1.2-mile nature trail near the refuge headquarters, and get ready for major-league wildlife-watching: 35 mammal and 220 bird species have been spotted in the refuge's fields, forests, ponds, and marshes. Wear waterproof shoes and insect repellent. In August, help yourself to wild blueberries. During November deer-hunting season, either avoid the refuge Monday–Saturday or wear a hunter-orange hat and vest. Trails are accessible by

THE DOWN EAST COAST

snowshoes, snowmobile, or cross-country skis in winter. To reach refuge headquarters, take Route 1 north from downtown Calais about three miles. Turn left onto the Charlotte Road, and go 2.4 miles to the headquarters sign. The office is open 8 A.M.–4 P.M. Monday–Friday all year (except major national holidays); you can pick up free trail maps, bird checklists, and other informative brochures. If you want to help support the conservation of wildlife in eastern Maine and educational programs, you can join Friends of Moosehorn National Wildlife Refuge (R.R. 1, Box 202, Ste. 12, Baring, ME 04694). A check for a mere $10 will do the trick.

By the way, if you don't have time to walk the trails, watch for the elevated man-made nesting platforms—avian high-rises for bald eagles—outside of Calais alongside Route 1 North (near the junction with the Charlotte Road). Depending on the season, you may spot a nesting pair or even a fledgling. The chicks (usually twins but occasionally triplets) hatch around mid-May and try their wings by early August. A 400-square-foot observation deck across Route 1 is the best place for eagle-watching.

Continuing on the Charlotte Road past the Moosehorn Refuge headquarters, you'll come to **Round Lake** (locally called Round Pond), a lovely spot where you can picnic, swim, or put in a kayak or canoe. Across the road, with a great lake view, is the interesting old Round Pond Cemetery, dating from the early 19th century. (Why do graveyards always have the best views?) Just after the cemetery, a left turn puts you on Pennamaquam Lake Road (or Charlotte Rd.) toward Perry; a right turn takes you to Route 214, near Pembroke.

About six miles south of Calais, watch for signs pointing to **Devil's Head** and take the dirt road on the river side. The 315-acre site has a mile of frontage on the St. Croix River estuary and views to St. Croix Island. A road, with two parking areas, descends to the shoreline, and there are pit toilets and a marked hiking trail, approximately 1.5 miles looping from the road, leading to the highest point of coastal land north of Cadillac Mountain. According to locals, the headland was originally called d'Orville Head but it morphed into Devil's Head.

Calais has a lovely riverfront park at the foot of North Street. **Pike's Park** is the perfect place for a picnic. From here you have access to the **Calais Waterfront Walk,** which edges the river, running for 0.9 mile upriver and 0.6 downriver.

## Golf

At the nine-hole **St. Croix Country Club** (River Rd., Rte. 1, Calais, 207/454-8875, late April–late Oct.), the toughest and most scenic hole is the seventh, one of five holes on the river side of Route 1.

## River Tours

Captain Louis Bernardini shares his knowledge of the St. Croix River's tides, history, flora, and fauna on **Up Close Tours** (207/454-2844 day, 207/454-2285 night, www.up-closetours.com). Boat tours depart from the Robbinston boat landing 2–3 times daily Monday–Friday, and once on Saturday, and last for about two hours. The boat visits St. Croix Island, and lobstering is demonstrated. Adults are $25, children 12 and younger are $15. The boat carries a maximum of six passengers, and the minimum fee is $50. No credit cards.

# ENTERTAINMENT AND FESTIVALS

First-run films show at the three-screen **State Cinemas** (79 Main St., Calais, 207/454-8830, $6). Sunday matinees are usually at 1:30 P.M.

**Music on the Green** is a series of free concerts presented at 6:30 P.M. Wednesdays at Triangle Park in downtown Calais. When the weather doesn't cooperate, concerts are moved to the Downeast Heritage Museum.

The **Brewer House** (Rte. 1, Robbinston, 12 miles south of Calais, 207/454-0333) sometimes hosts chamber music concerts featuring resident violinist Trond Saeverud.

Calais, Maine, and St. Stephen, New Brunswick, collaborate the first or second week of August for the nine-day **International Festival** of dinners, concerts, dances, a craft fair, ball games, and cross-border parade and road race. Newspapers carry schedules (just be sure to note which events are on eastern time and which are on Atlantic time).

## SHOPPING

Downtown Calais has a few shops worthy of a look-see. **St. Croix Valley Antiques and Collectibles** (4 Monroe St., 866/420-1167) is a big shop with a wide range of furniture, quilts, baskets, and tableware. The **Urban Moose** (80 Main St., 207/454-8277) has an eclectic inventory that invites browsing. Perhaps most intriguing is Captain Craig Little's **Little Ships of the Maritimes** (32 North St./Rte. 1), which specializes in custom scale models. Nearly two dozen regional artists and artisans sell their works at **Cat's Eye Gallery** (272 North St., Calais, 207/454-2020). Books new, old, and rare are sold at the **Calais Book Shop** (405 Main St., 207/454-1110), which also sponsors a reading group.

If you stop in at **Katie's on the Cove** (Rte. 1, Mill Cove, Robbinston, 207/454-3297 or 800/494-5283, 10 A.M.–5 P.M. Tues.–Sat. late May–mid-Oct.), do it at your own risk. Chocoholics may need a restraining order. Joseph and Lea Sullivan's family operation, begun in 1982, has become a great success story. They now produce about four dozen varieties of homemade fudge, truffles, caramels, peanut brittle, even marzipan. The candies are available in Washington County gift shops and elsewhere in Maine (including Maine Black Bear Paws at L. L. Bean), and the Sullivans do mail orders, but the aroma alone is worth a trip to the source (call first, though, as days and hours are limited). The shop, 12 miles southeast of Calais and about 15 miles west of Eastport, is no place for unruly or demanding kids—space is limited and the candy is pricey.

## ACCOMMODATIONS
### Bed-and-Breakfasts

The classic, Greek Revival–style [ **Brewer House** (Rte. 1, P.O. Box 88, Robbinston 04671, 207/454-0333, www.thebrewerhousebnb.com, $95–155 d) commands a knoll opposite the boat launch in Robbinston. Built by Captain John N. Marks in 1828, the house is distinguished by columns both in front and back, French nine-over-nine windows with carved Grecian moldings, Ionic pilasters, marble fireplaces, silver doorknobs, and an elliptical staircase—obviously the good captain was successful. The house also served as a stop on the Underground Railroad. The four guest rooms are furnished with antiques; some have ocean views, and some have shared baths. There's also a two-bedroom apartment ($125 d), where pets are welcome ($15 fee). A full breakfast is served. The B&B has an artsy feel, as the J. B. Siem Gallery is on the property, and chamber concerts featuring violinist Trond Saeverud are presented here. The innkeepers speak English, German, Danish, Norwegian, Swedish, and a little Japanese.

Within easy walking distance of downtown is **Greystone Bed and Breakfast** (13 Calais Ave., Calais, 207/454-2848, www.greystonecalaisme.com, $80), Alan and Candace Dwelley's masterfully restored, 1840 Greek Revival home. The property, listed on the National Historic Register, is an architectural gem within, with Corinthian columns and black marble fireplace mantels, and two guest rooms (one of which can be paired with a third, smaller room). The Dwelleys serve a more-than-full breakfast and are eager to share their recommendations for local sights and shopping.

### Motels/Cottages

Local motel accommodations are all quite dated, but rooms are clean and serviceable and better yet, rates are very low.

The Gothic-styled, gingerbread-trimmed **Redclyffe Shore Motel and Dining Room** (Rte. 1, Robbinston, 207/454-3270, www.redclyffeshoremotorinn.com, $75) sits on a bluff jutting into the St. Croix River as it widens into Passamaquoddy Bay. The 16 motel units have cable TVs, phones, and sunset-facing river views. Redclyffe is locally popular for its greenhouse-style dining room, with ocean views, serving moderately priced entrées ($12–22) 5–9 P.M. daily. Dinner reservations are a good idea in July and August, especially during the

International Festival. It's 12 miles south of Calais. The motel is open mid-May–October; the restaurant is open mid-May–December.

About 5.5 miles southeast of Calais, family-run **Heslin's Motel and Cottages** (Rte. 1, Calais, 207/454-3762, www.mainerec.com/heslins.html, May 1–late Oct.) has motel rooms ($62–70), cabins ($49–80), and rustic housekeeping cottages ($70–100 night, $420–600 week) on 60 acres alongside the St. Croix River. Some cottages are oceanfront. All units are heated and have TV; motel rooms have air-conditioning and phones; the more expensive cottages have kitchens. A big plus is a heated swimming pool. In the motel's informal river-view restaurant, steaks and fresh seafood ($12–20) are the specialties, served 5–9 P.M. daily. Small portions are available for kids and seniors. The cocktail lounge draws a loyal local clientele.

### Campgrounds

High enough for a great view of the St. Croix River, **Hilltop Campground** (317 Ridge Rd., R.R. 1, Box 298, Robbinston, 207/454-3985 or 866/454-3985, www.hilltopcampground-maine.com, mid-May–mid-Oct.) has 84 tent and RV sites on 100 wooded and open acres, plus a pool, basketball court, a trout pond, a small store, Wi-Fi service, and laundry facilities. Sites are $22–32 a night.

## FOOD
### Local Flavors

If you're near downtown Calais, order picnic sandwiches to go at **Border Town Subz** (311 Main St., Calais, 207/454-8562, 10 A.M.–7 P.M. Mon.–Fri., 11 A.M.–3 P.M. Sat.), a reliable local favorite. It offers lots of choices, including vegetarian, and three sandwich lengths.

Another choice for picnic fixings, cottage staples, and other goodies is the **Sunrise County Farmers Market** (11 A.M.–3 P.M. Tues. late June–Oct.). Look for it in the downtown park.

### Casual Dining

White Christmas lights brighten the ceiling of **⟨ Bernardini's** (257 Main St., Calais, 207/454-2237, 11 A.M.–8 P.M. Mon.–Sat.), a very popular downtown restaurant that has earned its repute with always-reliable Tuscany-inspired Italian cuisine, augmented by a few surprises, such as a crabmeat-stuffed avocado special that's a real winner; entrées are $10–15. The pleasant dining room is accented by woodwork salvaged from a local church. Save room for the tiramisu.

Calais's other restaurant is on a side street, off Route 1, just north of the center of town (and behind McDonald's). **The Chandler House** (20 Chandler St., Calais, 207/454-7922, 4–11 P.M. Tues.–Sun.) serves the usuals and is known for its prime rib.

## INFORMATION AND SERVICES
### Information

Sharing space with the Downeast Heritage Museum, near the Ferry Point Bridge just off Route 1 (Main St.) in downtown Calais, is a Maine Visitor Information Center (39 Union St., Calais, 207/454-2211), with clean restrooms and scads of brochures, including those produced by the St. Croix Valley Chamber of Commerce (207/454-2308 or 888/422-3112, www.visitcalais.com). The information center is open 8 A.M.–6 P.M. daily mid-May–mid-October, 9 A.M.–5:30 P.M. daily the rest of the year.

Check out Calais Free Library (Union St., Calais, 207/454-2758, www.calais.lib.me.us).

### Public Restrooms

Restrooms are available at the Maine Visitor Information Center (39 Union St., Calais) and the St. Croix International Heritage Site, in Red Beach.

### Crossing into Canada

If you plan to cross into Canada, you'll have to pass Customs checkpoints on both the Calais (U.S., 207/454-3621) and St. Stephen (Canada, 506/466-2363) ends of the bridges. Be sure to have the required identification and paperwork.

Pay attention to your watch, too—Calais is on eastern time, while St. Stephen (and the rest of Canada's Maritime Provinces) is on Atlantic time, one hour later.

# BACKGROUND

## The Land

### IN THE BEGINNING...

Maine is an outdoor classroom for Geology 101, a living lesson in what the glaciers did and how they did it. Geologically, Maine is something of a youngster; the oldest rocks, found in the Chain of Ponds area in the western part of the state, are only 1.6 billion years old—more than two billion years younger than the world's oldest rocks.

But most significant is the great ice sheet that began to spread over Maine about 25,000 years ago, during the late Wisconsin Ice Age. As it moved southward from Canada, this continental glacier scraped, gouged, pulverized, and depressed the bedrock in its path. On it continued, charging up the north faces of mountains, clipping off their tops and moving southward, leaving behind jagged cliffs on the mountains' southern faces and odd deposits of stone and clay. By about 21,000 years ago, glacial ice extended well over the Gulf of Maine, perhaps as far as the Georges Bank fishing grounds.

But all that began to change with meltdown, beginning about 18,000 years ago. As the glacier melted and receded, ocean water moved in, covering much of the coastal plain and working its way inland up the rivers. By 11,000 years ago,

© HILARY NANGLE

# ESTUARIES AND MUDFLATS

Maine's estuaries, where fresh- and salt water meet, are ecosystems of outstanding biological importance. South of Cape Elizabeth, where the Maine coast is low and sandy, estuaries harbor large salt marshes of spartina grasses that can tolerate the frequent variations in salinity as runoff and tides fluctuate. Producing an estimated four times more plant material than an equivalent area of wheat, these spartina marshes provide abundant nutrients and shelter for a host of marine organisms that ultimately account for as much as 60 percent of the value of the state's commercial fisheries.

The tidal range along the Maine coast varies 9-26 vertical feet, southwest to northeast. Where the tide inundates sheltered estuaries for more than a few hours at a time, spartina grasses cannot take hold, and mudflats dominate. Although it may look like a barren wasteland at low tide, a mudflat is also a highly productive environment and home to abundant marine life. Several species of tiny primitive worms called nematodes can inhabit the mud in densities of 2,000 or more per square inch. Larger worm species are also very common. One, the bloodworm, grows up to a foot long and is harvested in quantity for use as sportfishing bait.

More highly savored among the mudflat residents is the soft-shell clam, famous for its outstanding flavor and an essential ingredient of an authentic Maine lobster bake. But because clams are suspension feeders – filtering phytoplankton through their long siphon, or "neck" – they can accumulate pollutants that cause illness, including hepatitis. Many Maine mudflats are closed to clam harvesting because of leaking septic systems, so it's best to check with the state's Department of Marine Resources or the local municipal office before digging a mess of clams yourself.

For birds – and birders – salt marshes and mudflats are an unparalleled attraction. Long-legged wading birds such as glossy ibis, snowy egret, little blue heron, great blue heron, tricolored heron, green heron, and black-crowned night heron frequent the marshes in great numbers throughout the summer, hunting the shallow waters for mummichogs and other small salt-marsh fish, crustaceans, and invertebrates. Mid-May-early June, and then again mid-July-mid-September, migrating shorebirds pass through Maine to and from their subarctic breeding grounds. On a good day, a discerning birder can find 17 or more species of shorebirds probing the mudflats and marshes with pointed bills in search of their preferred foods. In turn, the large flocks of shorebirds don't escape the notice of their own predators – merlins and peregrine falcons dash in to catch a meal.

*(Contributed by William P. Hancock, Maine Audubon)*

---

glaciation had pulled back from all but a few minor corners at the top of Maine, revealing the south coast's beaches and the unusual geologic traits—eskers and erratics, kettleholes and moraines, even a fjord—that make the rest of the state such a fascinating natural laboratory.

## Today's Landscape

Three distinct looks make up the contemporary Maine coastal landscape. (Inland are even more distinct biomes: serious woodlands and mountains as well as lakes and ponds and rolling fields.)

Along the **Southern Coast,** from Kittery to Portland, are fine-sand beaches, marshlands, and only the occasional rocky headland. The **Mid-Coast** and **Penobscot Bay,** from Portland to the Penobscot River, feature one finger of rocky land after another, all jutting into the Gulf of Maine and all incredibly scenic. **Acadia** and the **Down East Coast,** from the Penobscot River to Eastport and including fantastic Acadia National Park, has many similarities to the Mid-Coast (gorgeous rocky peninsulas, offshore islands, granite everywhere), but, except on Mount Desert Island, takes on

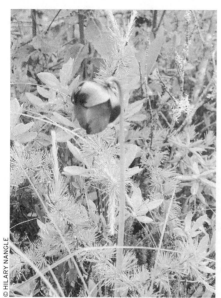
© HILARY NANGLE

Pitcher plants can often be sighted in the peat bogs along the Maine Coast.

a different look and feel by virtue of its slower pace, higher tides, and quieter villages.

## GEOGRAPHY

Bounded by the Gulf of Maine (Atlantic Ocean), the St. Croix River, New Brunswick Province, the St. John River, Québec Province, and the state of New Hampshire (and the only state in the Union bordered by only one other state), Maine is the largest of the six New England states, roughly equivalent in size to the five others combined—offering plenty of space to hike, bike, camp, sail, swim, or just hang out. The state—and the coastline—extends from 43° 05' to 47° 28' north latitude, and 66° 56' to 80° 50' west longitude. (Technically, Maine dips even farther southeast to take in five islands in the offshore Isles of Shoals archipelago.) It's all stitched together by 22,574 miles of highways and 3,561 bridges.

Maine's more than 5,000 rivers and streams provide nearly half of the watershed for the Gulf of Maine. The major rivers are the Pe-nobscot (350 miles), the St. John (211 miles), the Androscoggin (175 miles), the Kennebec (150 miles), the Saco (104 miles), and the St. Croix (75 miles). The St. John and its tributaries flow northeast; all the others flow more or less south or southeast.

## CLIMATE

Whoever invented the state's oldest cliché—"If you don't like the weather, wait a minute"—must have spent at least several minutes in Maine. The good news, though, is that if the weather is lousy, it's bound to change before too long. And when it does, it's intoxicating. Brilliant, cloud-free Maine weather has lured many a visitor to put down roots, buy a retirement home, or at least invest in a summer retreat.

The serendipity of it all necessitates two caveats: *Always pack warmer clothing than you think you'll need.* And *never arrive without a sweater or jacket—even at the height of summer.*

The National Weather Service assigns Maine's coastline a climatological category distinct from climatic types found in the interior.

The **coastal** category, which includes Portland, runs from Kittery northeast to Eastport and about 20 miles inland. Here, the ocean moderates the climate, making coastal winters warmer and summers cooler than in the interior (relatively speaking, of course). From early June through August, the Portland area—fairly typical of coastal weather—may have three to eight days of temperatures over 90°F, 25–40 days over 80°, 14–24 days of fog, and 5–10 inches of rain. Normal annual precipitation for the Portland area is 44 inches of rain and 71 inches of snow (the snow total is misleading, though, since intermittent thaws clear away much of the base).

### The Seasons

Maine has four distinct seasons: summer, fall, winter, and mud. Lovers of spring need to look elsewhere in March, the lowest month on the popularity scale with its mud-caked vehicles, soggy everything, irritable temperaments, tank-trap roads, and often the worst snowstorm of the year.

Look atop telephone poles and on rocky ledges for osprey nests.

Summer can be idyllic—with moderate temperatures, clear air, and wispy breezes—but it can also close in with fog, rain, and chills. Prevailing winds are from the southwest. Officially, summer runs June 20 or 21–September 20 or 21, but June, July, and August is more like it, with temperatures in the Portland area averaging 70°F during the day and in the 50s at night. The normal growing season is 148 days.

A poll of Mainers might well show autumn as the favorite season—days are still warmish, nights are cool, winds are optimum for sailors, and the foliage is brilliant. Fall colors usually begin appearing far to the north about mid-September, reaching their peak in that region by the end of the month. The last of the color begins in late September in the southernmost part of the state and fades by mid-October. Early autumn, however, is also the height of hurricane season, the only potential flaw this time of year.

Winter, officially December 20 or 21–March 20 or 21, means deep snow and cold inland and an unpredictable potpourri along the coastline. When the cold and snow hit the coast, it's time for cross-country skiing, ice fishing, snowshoeing, ice-skating, ice climbing, and winter trekking and camping.

Spring, officially March 20 or 21–June 20 or 21, is the frequent butt of jokes. It's an ill-defined season that arrives much too late and departs all too quickly. Ice floes dot inland lakes and ponds until "ice-out" (see *Glossary*), in early–mid-May; spring planting can't occur until well into May; lilacs explode in late May and disappear by mid-June. And just when you finally can enjoy being outside, blackflies stretch their wings and satisfy their hunger pangs. Along the coast, onshore breezes often keep the pesky creatures to a minimum.

## Northeasters and Hurricanes

A northeaster is a counterclockwise, swirling storm that brings wild winds out of—you guessed it—the northeast. These storms can occur any time of year, whenever the conditions brew them up. Depending on the season, the winds are accompanied by rain, sleet, snow, or all of them together.

# THE ROCKY SHORELINE AND THE MARINE ENVIRONMENT

On Maine's more exposed rocky shores – the dominant shoreline from Cape Elizabeth all the way Down East to Lubec – where currents and waves keep mud and sand from accumulating, the plant and animal communities are entirely different from those in the inland aquatic areas. The most important requirement for life in this impenetrable, rockbound environment is probably the ability to hang on tight. Barnacles, the calcium-armored crustaceans that attach themselves to the rocks immediately below the high-tide line, have developed a fascinating battery of adaptations to survive not only pounding waves but also prolonged exposure to air, solar heat, and extreme winter cold. Glued in place, however, they cannot escape being eaten by dog whelks, the predatory snails that also inhabit this intertidal zone. Whelks are larger and more elongate than the more numerous and ubiquitous periwinkle, accidentally transplanted from Europe in the mid-19th century.

Also hanging onto these rocks, but at a lower level, are the brown algae – seaweeds. Like a marine forest, the four species of rockweed provide shelter for a wide variety of life beneath their fronds. A world of discovery awaits those who make the effort to go out onto the rocks at low tide and look under the clumps of seaweed and into the tide pools they shelter. Venture into these chilly waters with mask, fins, and wet suit and still another world opens for natural-history exploration. Beds of blue mussels, sea urchins, sea stars, and sea cucumbers dot the bottom close to shore. In crevices between and beneath the rocks lurk rock crabs and lobsters. Now a symbol of the Maine coast and the delicious seafood it provides, the lobster was once considered "poor man's food" – so plentiful that it was spread on fields as fertilizer. Although lobsters are far less common than they once were, they are one of Maine's most closely monitored species, and their population continues to support a large and thriving commercial fishing industry.

The same cannot be said for most of Maine's other commercially harvested marine fish. When Europeans first came to these shores four centuries ago, cod, haddock, halibut, hake, flounder, herring, and tuna were abundant. No longer. Overharvested, their seabed habitat torn up by relentless dragging, these groundfish have all but disappeared. It will be decades before these species can recover – and then only if effective regulations can be put in place soon.

The familiar doglike face of the harbor seal, often seen peering alertly from the surface just offshore, provides a reminder that wildlife populations are resilient – if given a chance. A century ago, there was a bounty on harbor seals because it was thought they ate too many lobsters and fish. Needless to say, neither fish nor lobsters increased when the seals all but disappeared. With the bounty's repeal and the advent of legal protection, Maine's harbor seal population has bounced back to an estimated 15,000-20,000. Scores of them can regularly be seen basking on offshore ledges, drying their tan, brown, black, silver, or reddish coats in the sun. Though it's tempting to approach for a closer look, avoid bringing a boat too near these haul-out ledges, as it causes the seals to flush into the water and imposes an unnecessary stress on the pups, which already face a first-year mortality rate of 30 percent.

Positive changes in our relationships with wildlife are even more apparent with the return of birds to the Maine coast. Watching the numerous herring gulls and great black-backed gulls soaring on a fresh ocean breeze today, it's hard to imagine that a century ago, egg collecting had so reduced their numbers that they were a rare sight. In 1903, there were just three pairs of common eiders left in Maine; today, 25,000 pairs nest along the coast. With creative help from dedicated researchers using sound recordings, decoys, and prepared burrows, Atlantic puffins are recolonizing historic offshore nesting islands. Osprey and bald eagles, almost free of the lingering vestiges of DDT and other pesticides, now range the length of the coast and up Maine's major rivers.

*(Contributed by William P. Hancock, Maine Audubon)*

Hurricane season officially runs June–November but is most prevalent late August–September. Some years, the Maine coast remains out of harm's way; other years, head-on hurricanes and even glancing blows have eroded beaches, flooded roads, splintered boats, downed trees, knocked out power, and inflicted major residential and commercial damage. Winds—the greatest culprit—average 74–90 mph. A **hurricane watch** is announced on radio and TV about 36 hours beforehand, followed by a **hurricane warning,** indicating that the storm is imminent. Find shelter, away from plate-glass windows, and wait it out. If especially high winds are predicted, make every effort to secure yourself, your vehicle, and your possessions. Resist the urge to head for the shore to watch the show; rogue waves, combined with ultrahigh tides, have been known to sweep away unwary onlookers.

## Sea Smoke and Fog

Sea smoke and fog, two atmospheric phenomena resulting from opposing conditions, are only distantly related. But both can radically affect visibility and therefore be hazardous. In winter, when the ocean is at least 40°F warmer than the air, billowy sea smoke rises from the water, creating great photo ops for camera buffs but especially dangerous conditions for mariners.

In any season, when the ocean (or lake or land) is colder than the air, fog sets in, creating perilous conditions for drivers, mariners, and pilots. Romantics, however, see it otherwise, reveling in the womblike ambience and the muffled moans of foghorns. Between April and October, Portland averages about 31 days with heavy fog, when visibility may be a quarter mile or less.

## Storm Warnings

The National Weather Service's official daytime signal system for wind velocity consists of a series of flags representing specific wind speeds and sea conditions. Beachgoers and anyone planning to venture out in a kayak, canoe, sailboat, or powerboat should heed these signals. The flags are posted on all public beaches, and warnings are announced on TV and radio weather broadcasts, as well as on cable TV's Weather Channel and the NOAA broadcast network.

# History

## Prehistoric Mainers: The Paleoindians

As the great continental glacier receded northwestward out of Maine about 11,000 years ago, some prehistoric grapevine must have alerted small bands of hunter-gatherers—fur-clad Paleoindians—to the scrub sprouting in the tundra, burgeoning mammal populations, and the ocean's bountiful food supply. Because come they did—at first seasonally and then year-round. Anyone who thinks tourism is a recent Maine phenomenon needs only to explore the shoreline in Damariscotta, Boothbay Harbor, and Bar Harbor, where heaps of cast-off oyster shells and clamshells document the migration of early Native Americans from woodlands to waterfront. "The shore" has been a summertime magnet for millennia.

Archaeological evidence from the Archaic period in Maine—roughly 8000–1000 B.C.—is fairly scant, but paleontologists have unearthed stone tools and weapons and small campsites attesting to a nomadic lifestyle supported by fishing and hunting (with fishing becoming more extensive as time went on). Toward the end of the tradition, during the late Archaic period, emerged a rather anomalous Indian culture known officially as the Moorehead phase but informally called the Red Paint People; the name is due to their curious trait of using a distinctive red ocher (pulverized hematite) in burials. Dark red puddles and stone artifacts have led excavators to burial pits as far north as the St. John River. Just as mysteriously as they had arrived, the Red Paint People disappeared abruptly and inexplicably around 1800 B.C.

Following them almost immediately—and almost as suddenly—hunter-gatherers of the Susquehanna Tradition arrived from well to the south, moved across Maine's interior as far as the St. John River, and remained until about 1600 B.C., when they, too, enigmatically vanished. Excavations have turned up relatively sophisticated stone tools and evidence that they cremated their dead. It was nearly 1,000 years before a major new cultural phase appeared.

The next great leap forward was marked by the advent of pottery making, introduced about 700 B.C. The Ceramic period stretched to the 16th century, and cone-shaped pots (initially stamped, later incised with coiled-rope motifs) survived until the introduction of metals from Europe. Houses of sorts—seasonal wigwam-style dwellings for fishermen and their families—appeared along the coast and on offshore islands.

## The Europeans Arrive

The identity of the first Europeans to set foot in Maine is a matter of debate. Historians dispute the romantically popular notion that Norse explorers checked out this part of the New World as early as A.D. 1000. Even an 11th-century Norse coin found in 1961 in Brooklin (on the Blue Hill Peninsula) probably was carried there from farther north.

Not until the late 15th century, the onset of the great Age of Discovery, did credible reports of the New World (including what's now Maine) filter back to Europe's courts and universities. Thanks to innovations in naval architecture, shipbuilding, and navigation, astonishingly courageous fellows crossed the Atlantic in search of rumored treasure and new routes for reaching it.

John Cabot, sailing from England aboard the ship *Mathew,* may have been the first European to reach Maine, in 1498, but historians have never confirmed a landing site. No question remains, however, about the account of Giovanni da Verrazzano, an Italian explorer

commanding *La Dauphine* under the French flag, who reached the Maine coast in May 1524, probably at the tip of the Phippsburg Peninsula. Encountering less-than-friendly Indians, Verrazzano did a minimum of business and sailed onward. His brother's map of the site labels it "The Land of Bad People." Esteban Gomez and John Rut followed in Verrazzano's wake, but nothing came of their exploits.

Nearly half a century passed before the Maine coast turned up again on European explorers' itineraries. This time, interest was fueled by reports of a Brigadoon-like area called Norumbega (or Oranbega, as one map had it), a myth that arose, gathered steam, and took on a life of its own in the decades after Verrazzano's voyage.

By the early 17th century, when Europeans began arriving in more than twos and threes and getting serious about colonization, Native American agriculture was already under way at the mouths of the Saco and Kennebec Rivers, the cod fishery was thriving on offshore islands, Indians far to the north were hot to trade furs for European goodies, and the birchbark canoe was the transport of choice on inland waterways.

In mid-May 1602, Bartholomew Gosnold, en route to a settlement off Cape Cod aboard the *Concord,* landed along Maine's southern coast. The following year, merchant trader Martin Pring and his boats *Speedwell* and *Discoverer* explored farther Down East, backtracked to Cape Cod, and returned to England with tales that inflamed curiosity and enough sassafras to satisfy royal appetites. Pring produced a detailed survey of the Maine coast from Kittery to Bucksport, including offshore islands.

On May 18, 1605, George Waymouth, skippering the *Archangel,* reached Monhegan Island, 11 miles off the Maine coast, and moored for the night in Monhegan Harbor (still treacherous even today, exposed to the weather from the southwest and northeast and subject to meteorological beatings and heaving swells; yachting guides urge sailors not to expect to anchor, moor, or tie up there). The next day, Waymouth crossed the bay and scouted the mainland. He took five Indians hostage and sailed up the St. George River, near present-day Thomaston. As maritime historian Roger Duncan has put it:

> The Plimoth Pilgrims were little boys in short pants when George Waymouth was exploring this coastline.

Waymouth returned to England and awarded his hostages to officials Sir John Popham and Sir Ferdinando Gorges, who, their curiosity piqued, quickly agreed to subsidize the colonization effort. In 1607, the *Gift of God* and the *Mary and John* sailed for the New World carrying two of Waymouth's captives. After returning them to their native Pemaquid area, Captains George Popham and Raleigh Gilbert continued westward, establishing a colony (St. George or Fort George) at the tip of the Phippsburg Peninsula in mid-August 1607 and exploring the shoreline between Portland and Pemaquid. Frigid weather, untimely deaths (including Popham's), and a storehouse fire doomed what's called the Popham Colony, but not before the 100 or so settlers built the 30-ton pinnace *Virginia,* the New World's first such vessel. When Gilbert received word of an inheritance waiting in England, he and the remaining colonists returned to the Old World.

In 1614, swashbuckling Captain John Smith, exploring from the Penobscot River westward to Cape Cod, reached Monhegan Island nine years after Waymouth's visit. Smith's meticulous map of the region was the first to use the "New England" appellation, and the 1616 publication of his *Description of New-England* became the catalyst for permanent settlements.

## The French and the English Square Off

English dominance of exploration west of the Penobscot River in the early 17th century coincided roughly with French activity east of the river.

In 1604, French nobleman Pierre du Gua, Sieur de Monts, set out with cartographer Samuel de Champlain to map the coastline, first reaching Nova Scotia's Bay of Fundy and then sailing up the St. Croix River. In midriver, just west of present-day Calais, a crew planted gardens and erected buildings on today's St. Croix Island while de Monts and Champlain went off exploring. The two men reached the island Champlain named l'Isle des Monts Deserts and present-day Bangor before returning to face the winter with their ill-fated compatriots. Scurvy, lack of fuel and water, and a ferocious winter wiped out nearly half of the 79 men. In spring 1605, de Monts, Champlain, and other survivors headed southwest, exploring the coastline all the way to Cape Cod before heading northeast again and settling permanently at Nova Scotia's Port Royal (now Annapolis Royal).

Eight years later, French Jesuit missionaries en route to the Kennebec River ended up on Mount Desert Island and, with a band of French laymen, set about establishing the St. Sauveur settlement. But leadership squabbles led to building delays, and English marauder Samuel Argall—assigned to reclaim English territory—arrived to find them easy prey. The colony was leveled, the settlers were set adrift in small boats, the priests were carted off to Virginia, and Argall moved on to destroy Port Royal.

By the 1620s, more than four dozen English fishing vessels were combing New England waters in search of cod, and year-round fishing depots had sprung up along the coast between Pemaquid and Portland. At the same time, English trappers and dealers began usurping the Indians' fur trade—a valuable income source.

The Massachusetts Bay Colony was established in 1630 and England's Council of New England, headed by Sir Ferdinando Gorges, began making vast land grants throughout Maine, giving rise to permanent coastal settlements, many dependent on agriculture. Among the earliest communities were Kittery, York, Wells, Saco, Scarborough, Falmouth, and Pemaquid—places where they tilled the acidic soil, fished the waters, eked out a barely-above-subsistence living, coped with predators and endless winters, bartered goods and services, and set up local governments and courts.

By the late 17th century, as these communities expanded, so did their requirements and responsibilities. Roads and bridges were built, preachers and teachers were hired, and militias were organized to deal with internecine and Indian skirmishes.

Even though England yearned to control the entire Maine coastline, her turf, realistically, was primarily south and west of the Penobscot River. The French had expanded from their Canadian colony of Acadia, for the most part north and east of the Penobscot. Unlike the absentee bosses who controlled the English territory, French merchants actually showed up, forming good relationships with the Indians and cornering the market in fishing, lumbering, and fur trading. And French Jesuit priests converted many a Native American to Catholicism. Intermittently, overlapping Anglo-French land claims sparked locally messy conflicts.

In the mid-17th century, the strategic heart of French administration and activity in Maine was Fort Pentagoet, a sturdy stone outpost built in 1635 in what is now Castine. From here, the French controlled coastal trade between the St. George River and Mount Desert Island and well up the Penobscot River. In 1654, England captured and occupied the fort and much of French Acadia, but, thanks to the 1667 Treaty of Breda, title returned to the French in 1670, and Pentagoet briefly became Acadia's capital.

A short but nasty Dutch foray against Acadia in 1674 resulted in Pentagoet's destruction ("levell'd with ye ground," by one account) and the raising of a third national flag over Castine.

## The Indian Wars (1675-1760)
Caught in the middle of 17th- and 18th-century Anglo-French disputes throughout Maine were the Wabanaki (People of the Dawn), the collective name for the state's major Native American tribal groups, all of whom spoke Algonquian languages. Modern ethnographers label these groups the Micmacs, Maliseets, Passamaquoddies, and Penobscots.

In the early 17th century, exposure to European diseases took its toll, wiping out three-quarters of the Wabanaki in the years 1616–1619. Opportunistic English and French traders quickly moved into the breach, and the Indians struggled to survive and regroup.

But regroup they did. Less than three generations later, a series of six Indian wars began, lasting nearly a century and pitting the Wabanaki most often against the English but occasionally against other Wabanaki. The conflicts, largely provoked by Anglo-French tensions in Europe, were King Philip's War (1675–1678), King William's War (1688–1699), Queen Anne's War (1703–1713), Dummer's War (1721–1726), King George's War (1744–1748), and the French and Indian War (1754–1760). Not until a get-together in 1762 at Fort Pownall (now Stockton Springs) did peace effectively return to the region—just in time for the heating up of the revolutionary movement.

## Comes the Revolution
Near the end of the last Indian War, just beyond Maine's eastern border, a watershed event led to more than a century of cultural and political fallout. During the so-called Acadian Dispersal, in 1755, the English expelled from Nova Scotia 10,000 French-speaking Acadians who refused to pledge allegiance to the British Crown. Scattered as far south as Louisiana and west toward New Brunswick and Québec, the Acadians lost farms, homes, and possessions in this *grand dérangement*. Not until 1785 was land allocated for resettlement of Acadians along both sides of the Upper St. John River, where thousands of their descendants remain today. Henry Wadsworth Longfellow's epic poem *Evangeline* dramatically relates the sorry Acadian saga.

In the District of Maine, on the other hand, with relative peace following a century of intermittent warfare, settlement again exploded, particularly in the southernmost counties. The 1764 census tallied Maine's population at just under 25,000; a decade later, the number had doubled. New towns emerged almost overnight, often heavily subsidized by wealthy investors from the parent Massachusetts Bay

Colony. With almost 4,000 residents, the largest town in the district was Falmouth (later renamed Portland).

In 1770, 27 Maine towns became eligible, based on population, to send representatives to the Massachusetts General Court, the colony's legislative body. But only six coastal towns could actually afford to send anyone, sowing seeds of resentment among settlers who were thus saddled with taxes without representation. Sporadic mob action accompanied unrest in southern Maine, but the flashpoint occurred in the Boston area.

On April 18, 1775, Paul Revere set out on America's most famous horseback ride—from Lexington to Concord, Massachusetts—to announce the onset of what became the American Revolution. Most of the Revolution's action occurred south of Maine, but not all of it.

In June, the Down East outpost of Machias was the site of the war's first naval engagement. The well-armed but unsuspecting British vessel HMS *Margaretta* sailed into the bay and was besieged by local residents angry about a Machias merchant's sweetheart deal with the British. Before celebrating their David-and-Goliath victory, the rebels captured the *Margaretta,* killed her captain, and then captured two more British ships sent to the rescue.

In the fall of 1775, Colonel Benedict Arnold—better known to history as a notorious turncoat—assembled 1,100 sturdy men for a flawed and futile "March on Québec" to dislodge the English. From Newburyport, Massachusetts, they sailed to the mouth of the Kennebec River, near Bath, and then headed inland with the tide. In Pittston, six miles south of Augusta and close to the head of navigation, they transferred to a fleet of 220 locally made bateaux and laid over three nights at Fort Western in Augusta. Then they set off, poling, paddling, and portaging their way upriver. Skowhegan, Norridgewock, and Chain of Ponds were among the landmarks along the grueling route. The men endured cold, hunger, swamps, disease, dense underbrush, and the loss of nearly 600 of their comrades before reaching Québec in late 1775. In the Kennebec River Valley, Arnold Trail historical signposts today mark highlights (or, more aptly, lowlights) of the expedition.

Four years later, another futile attempt to dislodge the British, this time in the District of Maine, resulted in America's worst naval defeat until World War II—a little-publicized debacle called the Penobscot Expedition. On August 14, 1779, as more than 40 American warships and transports carrying more than 2,000 Massachusetts men blockaded Castine to flush out a relatively small enclave of leftover Brits, a seven-vessel Royal Navy fleet appeared. Despite their own greater numbers, about 30 of the American ships turned tail up the Penobscot River. The captains torched their vessels, exploding the ammunition and leaving the survivors to walk in disgrace to Augusta or even Boston. Each side took close to 100 casualties, three commanders—including Paul Revere—were court-martialed, and Massachusetts was about $7 million poorer.

The American Revolution officially came to a close on September 3, 1783, with the signing of the Treaty of Paris between the United States and Great Britain. The U.S.-Canada border was set at the St. Croix River, but, in a massive oversight, boundary lines were left unresolved for thousands of square miles in the northern District of Maine.

## Trade Troubles and the War of 1812

In 1807, President Thomas Jefferson imposed the Embargo Act, banning trade with foreign entities—specifically, France and Britain. With thousands of miles of coastline and harbor villages dependent on trade for revenue and basic necessities, Maine reeled. By the time the act was repealed, under President James Madison in 1809, France and Britain were almost unscathed, but the bottom had dropped out of New England's economy.

An active smuggling operation based in Eastport kept Mainers from utter despair, but the economy still had continued its downslide. In 1812, the fledgling United States declared war on Great Britain, again disrupting coastal trade. In the fall of 1814, the situation reached its nadir when the British invaded the Maine coast and occupied all the shoreline between the St. Croix and Penobscot Rivers. Later that same year, the Treaty of Ghent finally halted the squabble, forced the British to withdraw from Maine, and allowed the locals to get on with economic recovery.

## Statehood

In October 1819, Mainers held a constitutional convention at the First Parish Church on Congress Street in Portland. (Known affectionately as "Old Jerusalem," the church was later replaced by the present-day structure.) The convention crafted a constitution modeled on that of Massachusetts, with two notable differences: Maine would have no official church (Massachusetts had the Puritans' Congregational Church), and Maine would place no religious requirements or restrictions on its gubernatorial candidates. When votes came in from 241 Maine towns, only nine voted against ratification.

For Maine, March 15, 1820, was one of those good news/bad news days: After 35 years of separatist agitation, the District of Maine broke from Massachusetts (signing the separation allegedly, and disputedly, at the Jameson Tavern in Freeport) and became the 23rd state in the Union. However, the Missouri Compromise, enacted by Congress only 12 days earlier to balance admission of slave and free states, mandated that the slave state of Missouri be admitted on the same day. Maine had abolished slavery in 1788, and there was deep resentment over the linkage.

Portland became the new state's capital (albeit only briefly; it switched to Augusta in 1832), and William King, one of statehood's most outspoken advocates, became the first governor.

## Trouble in the North Country

Without an official boundary established on Maine's far northern frontier, turf battles were always simmering just under the surface. Timber was the sticking point—everyone wanted the vast wooded acreage. Finally, in early 1839, militia reinforcements descended on the dis-

puted area, heating up what has come to be known as the Aroostook War, a border confrontation with no battles and no casualties (except a farmer who was shot by friendly militia). It's a blip in the historical timeline, but remnants of fortifications in Houlton, Fort Fairfield, and Fort Kent keep the story alive today. By March 1839, a truce was negotiated, and the 1842 Webster-Ashburton Treaty established the border once and for all.

## Maine in the Civil War

In the 1860s, with the state's population slightly more than 600,000, more than 70,000 Mainers suited up and went off to fight in the Civil War—the greatest per-capita show of force of any northern state. About 18,000 of them died in the conflict. Thirty-one Mainers were Union Army generals, the best known being Joshua L. Chamberlain, a Bowdoin College professor, who commanded the Twentieth Maine regiment and later became president of the college and governor of Maine.

During the war, young battlefield artist Winslow Homer, who later settled in Prouts Neck, south of Portland, created wartime sketches regularly for such publications as *Harper's Weekly*. In Washington, Maine Senator Hannibal Hamlin was elected vice president under Abraham Lincoln in 1860 (he was removed from the ticket in favor of Andrew Johnson when Lincoln came up for reelection in 1864).

## Maine Comes into Its Own

After the Civil War, Maine's influence in Republican-dominated Washington far outweighed the size of its population. In the late 1880s, Mainers held the federal offices of acting vice president, Speaker of the House, secretary of state, Senate majority leader, Supreme Court justice, and several important committee chairmanships. Best known of the notables were James G. Blaine (journalist, presidential aspirant, and secretary of state) and Portland native Thomas Brackett Reed, presidential aspirant and Speaker of the House.

In Maine itself, traditional industries fell into

decline after the Civil War, dealing the economy a body blow. Steel ships began replacing Maine's wooden clippers, refrigeration techniques made the block-ice industry obsolete, concrete threatened the granite-quarrying trade, and the output from Southern textile mills began to supplant that from Maine's mills.

Despite Maine's economic difficulties, however, wealthy urbanites began turning their sights toward the state, accumulating land (including islands) and building enormous summer "cottages" for their families, servants, and hangers-on. Bar Harbor was a prime example of the elegant summer colonies that sprang up, but others include Grindstone Neck (Winter Harbor), Prouts Neck (Scarborough), and Dark Harbor (on Islesboro in Penobscot Bay). Vacationers who preferred fancy hotel-type digs reserved rooms for the summer at such sprawling complexes as Kineo House (on Moosehead Lake), Poland Spring House (west of Portland), or the Samoset Hotel (in Rockland). Built of wood and catering to long-term visitors, these and many others all eventually succumbed to altered vacation patterns and the ravages of fire.

As the 19th century spilled into the 20th, the state broadened its appeal beyond the well-to-do who had snared prime turf in the Victorian era. It launched an active promotion of Maine as "The Nation's Playground," successfully spurring an influx of visitors from all economic levels. By steamboat, train, and soon by car, people came to enjoy the ocean beaches, the woods, the mountains, the lakes, and the quaintness of it all. (Not that these features didn't really exist, but the state's aggressive public relations campaign at the turn of the 20th century stacks up against anything Madison Avenue puts out today.) The only major hiatus in the tourism explosion in the century's first two decades was 1914–1918, when 35,062 Mainers joined many thousands of other Americans in going off to the European front to fight in World War I. Two years after the war ended, in 1920 (the centennial of its statehood), Maine women were the first in the nation to troop to the polls after ratification of the 19th Amendment granted universal suffrage.

Maine was slow to feel the repercussions of the Great Depression, but eventually they came, with bank failures all over the state. Federally subsidized programs, such as the Civilian Conservation Corps (CCC) and the Works Progress Administration (WPA), left lasting legacies in Maine.

Politically, the state has contributed notables on both sides of the aisle. In 1954, Maine elected as its governor Edmund S. Muskie, only the fifth Democrat in the job since 1854. In 1958, Muskie ran for and won a seat in the Senate, and in 1980 he became secretary of state under President Jimmy Carter. Muskie died in 1996.

Elected in 1980, Waterville's George J. Mitchell made a respected name for himself as a Democratic senator and Senate majority leader before retiring in 1996, when Maine became only the second state in the union to have two women senators (Olympia Snowe and Susan Collins, both Republicans). After his 1996 reelection, President Bill Clinton appointed Mitchell's distinguished congressional colleague and three-term senator, Republican William Cohen of Bangor, as secretary of defense, a position he held through the rest of the Clinton administration. Mitchell spent considerable time during the Clinton years as the U.S. mediator for Northern Ireland's "troubles" and subsequently headed an international fact-finding team in the Middle East. Both Mitchell and Cohen have retired to the private sector, but no one will be surprised to see them on the national stage again.

# Government and Economy

## STATE GOVERNMENT

Politics in Maine isn't quite as variable and unpredictable as the weather, but pundits are almost as wary as weather forecasters about making predictions. Despite a long tradition of Republicanism dating from the late 19th century, Maine's voters and politicians have a national reputation for being independent-minded—electing Democrats, Republicans, or independents more for their character than their political persuasions.

Four of the most notable recent examples are Margaret Chase Smith, Edmund S. Muskie, George J. Mitchell, and William Cohen—two Republicans and two Democrats, all Maine natives. Republican Senator Margaret Chase Smith proved her flintiness when she spoke out against McCarthyism in the 1950s. Ed Muskie, the first prominent Democrat to come out of Maine, won every race he entered except an aborted bid for the presidency in 1972. George Mitchell, as mentioned, has gained a stellar reputation, as has William Cohen. In a manifestation of Maine's strong tradition of bipartisanship, Mitchell and Cohen worked together closely on many issues to benefit the state and the nation (they even wrote a book together).

In the 1970s, Maine elected an independent governor, James Longley, whose memory is still respected (Longley's son was later elected to Congress as a Republican, and his daughter to the state senate as a Democrat). In 1994, Maine voted in another independent, Angus King, a relatively young veteran of careers in business, broadcasting, and law. The governor serves a term of four years, limited to two terms.

The state's Supreme Judicial Court has a chief justice and six associate justices.

Maine is ruled by a bicameral, biennial citizen legislature comprising 151 members in the House of Representatives and 35 members in the state senate, including a relatively high percentage of women and a fairly high proportion of retirees. Members of both houses serve two-year terms. Along with the governor, they meet at the State House in Augusta to pass legislation and administer an annual state budget of around $2 billion. In 1993, voters passed a statewide term-limits referendum restricting legislators to four terms.

Whereas nearly two dozen Maine cities are ruled by city councils, about 450 smaller towns and plantations retain the traditional form of rule: annual town meetings. Town meetings generally are held in March, when newspaper pages bulge with reports containing classic quotes from citizens exercising their rights to vote and vent. A few examples: "I believe in the pursuit of happiness until that pursuit infringes on the happiness of others"; "I don't know of anyone's dog running loose except my own, and I've arrested her several times"; and "Don't listen to him; he's from New Jersey."

Nonresidents are welcome to attend town meetings. Although, of course, you can't vote, a town meeting is a great way to experience true local government. Refreshments are usually available—typically, proceeds benefit some local cause—and sometimes there's even a potluck lunch or supper. The meeting provides the live entertainment.

## ECONOMY

When the subject of the economy comes up, you'll often hear reference to the "two Maines," as if a line bisected the state in half, east to west. There's much truth to the image. Southern Maine is prosperous with good jobs (although never enough), lots of small businesses, and a highly competitive real-estate market. Northern Maine struggles along, suffering from its immensity and lack of infrastructure as much as from its low population density.

The coast follows that same pattern. The Southern Coast reaps the benefit of its proximity to Boston. Not only is it a favorite weekend getaway for Boston-area residents, it's increasingly becoming part of Boston's suburbs as more and more people move there and commute to the city. Tourism thrives here seasonally. Retail is strong, thanks to Kittery. And traditional maritime-related businesses continue, although real-estate pressures have contributed to their weakening, as fishermen struggle to hold on to wharves and to live near where they work.

Portland is the state's largest city and has a strong economy, supported by tourism and maritime-related businesses. Years ago, Portland made the wise decision to preserve its waterfront for maritime use, so it's still very much a working waterfront. Not surprisingly, Freeport's economy is retail based. Brunswick, Bath, and the surrounding towns are supported by the three Bs: Bowdoin College, Brunswick Naval Air Station, and Bath Iron Works.

Mid-Coast and Penobscot Bay and increasingly the Blue Hill Peninsula have strong maritime-related businesses, including lobstering, fishing, clamming, worm digging, and their support services. Also driving this region is a vital creative economy of artists and artisans, boatbuilders and cabinetmakers, and entrepreneurial professionals, such as architects and designers. Small businesses, technology-based companies, and telemarketing provide employment, as does tourism. These three regions are also extremely popular with retirees, who often take up second careers or are active in the local community as mentors and volunteers.

The farther Down East you travel, the harder it is to eke out a living. In Washington County, many folks cobble together some semblance of year-round employment in wreath making, fishing, clamming, guiding, logging, blueberry raking, and whatever else is available. Tribal officials in this region are hoping to bring a liquefied natural-gas port to Perry, increasing prospects for tribal members, but strong opposition exists. As one local official told me: "Everyone complains that there are no jobs, but whenever an opportunity comes along, no one wants to risk changing the lifestyle." And that's a conundrum that's bound to continue for at least the foreseeable future.

# The People

Maine's population didn't top the one-million mark until 1970. Thirty years later, according to the 2000 census, the state had 1,274,923 residents. Along the coast, Cumberland County, comprising the Greater Portland area, has the highest head count.

Despite the longstanding presence of several substantial ethnic groups, plus four Native American tribes (about 1 percent of the population), diversity is a relatively recent phenomenon in Maine, and the population is about 95 percent Caucasian. A steady influx of refugees, beginning after the Vietnam War, forced the state to address diversity issues, and it continues to do so today.

## Natives and "People from Away"

People who weren't born in Maine aren't natives. Even people who *were* may experience close scrutiny of their credentials. In Maine, there are natives and *natives*. Every day, the obituary pages describe Mainers who have barely left the houses in which they were born—even in which their grandparents were born. We're talking roots!

Along with this kind of heritage comes a whole vocabulary all its own—lingo distinctive to Maine or at least New England. (For help in translation, see the *Glossary*.)

Part of the "native" picture is the matter of "native" produce. Hand-lettered signs sprout everywhere during the summer advertising native corn, native peas, even—believe it or not—native ice. In Maine, homegrown is well grown.

"People from away," on the other hand, are those whose families haven't lived here year-round for a generation or more. But people from away (also called flatlanders) exist all over Maine, and they have come to stay, putting down roots of their own and altering the way the state is run, looks, and *will* look. Senators Snowe and Collins are natives, but Governor

King came from away, as did most of his cabinet members. You'll find other flatlanders as teachers, corporate executives, artists, retirees, writers, town selectmen, and even lobstermen.

In the 19th century, arriving flatlanders were mostly "rusticators" or "summer complaints"—summer residents who lived well, often in enclaves, and never set foot in the state off-season. They did, however, pay property taxes, contribute to causes, and provide employment for local residents. Another 19th-century wave of people from away came from the bottom of the economic ladder: Irish escaping the potato famine and French Canadians fleeing poverty in Québec. Both groups experienced subtle and overt anti-Catholicism but rather quickly assimilated into the mainstream, taking jobs in mills and factories and becoming staunch American patriots.

The late 1960s and early 1970s brought bunches of "back-to-the-landers," who scorned plumbing and electricity and adopted retro ways of life. Although a few pockets of diehards still exist, most have changed with the times and adopted contemporary mores (and conveniences).

Today, technocrats arrive from away with computers, faxes, cell phones, and other high-tech gear and "commute" via the Internet and modern electronics. Maine has played a national leadership role in telecommunications reform—thanks to the university system's early push for installation of state-of-the-art fiber optics.

## Native Americans

In Maine, the *real* natives are the Wabanaki (People of the Dawn)—the Micmac, Maliseet, Penobscot, and Passamaquoddy tribes of the eastern woodlands. Many live in or near three reservations, near the headquarters for their tribal governors. The Passamaquoddies are at Pleasant Point, in Perry, near Eastport, and at Indian Township, in Princeton, near Calais. The Penobscots are based on Indian Island, in Old Town, near Bangor. Other Native American population clusters—known as "off-reservation Indians"—are the Aroostook Band of Micmacs, based in Presque Isle, and

the Houlton Band of Maliseets, in Littleton, near Houlton.

In 1965, Maine became the first state to establish a Department of Indian Affairs, but just five years later the Passamaquoddy and Penobscot tribes initiated a 10-year-long land-claims case involving 12.5 million Maine acres (about two-thirds of the state) weaseled from the Indians by Massachusetts in 1794. In late 1980, a landmark agreement, signed by President Jimmy Carter, awarded the tribes $80.6 million in reparations. Despite this, the tribes still struggle to provide jobs on the reservations and to increase the overall standard of living. A 2003 referendum to allow the tribes to build a casino was defeated. The latest attempt to increase jobs and money is a controversial plan to bring a liquified natural gas port to tribal lands in Perry.

One of the true success stories of the tribes is the revival of traditional arts as businesses. The Maine Indian Basketmakers Association has an active apprenticeship program, and two renowned basket makers—Mary Gabriel and Clara Keezer—have achieved National Heritage Fellowships. Several well-attended annual summer festivals—in Bar Harbor, Grand Lake Stream, and Perry—highlight Indian traditions and heighten awareness of Native American culture. Basket making, canoe building, and traditional dancing are all parts of the scene. The splendid Abbe Museum in Bar Harbor features Indian artifacts, interactive displays, historic photographs, and special programs. Gift shops have begun adding Native American jewelry and baskets to their inventories.

## Acadians and Franco Americans

Within about three decades of their 1755 expulsion from Nova Scotia in *le grand dérangement*, Acadians had established new communities and new lives in northern Maine's St. John Valley. Gradually, they explored farther into central and southern coastal Maine and west into New Hampshire. The Acadian diaspora has profoundly influenced Maine and its culture, and it continues to do so today. Along the coast, French is spoken on the streets of

Biddeford, where there's an annual Franco American festival and an extensive Franco American research collection.

## African Americans

Although Maine's African American population is small, the state has had an African American community since the 17th century; by the 1764 census, there were 322 slaves and free blacks in the District of Maine. Segregation remained the rule, however, so in the 19th century, blacks established their own parish, the Abyssinian Church, in Portland. Efforts are under way to restore the long-closed church as an African American cultural center and gathering place for Greater Portland's black community. For researchers delving into "Maine's black experience," the University of Southern Maine, in Portland, houses the African-American Archive of Maine, a significant collection of historic books, letters, and artifacts donated by Gerald Talbot, the first African American to serve in the Maine legislature.

## Finns

Finns came to Maine in several 19th-century waves, primarily to work the granite quarries on the coast and on offshore islands and the slate quarries in Monson, near Greenville. Finnish families clustered near the quarries in St. George and on Vinalhaven and Hurricane Islands—all with landscapes similar to those of their homeland. Today, names such as Laukka, Lehtinen, Hamalainen, and Harjula are interspersed among the Yankee names in the Mid-Coast region.

## Russians, Ukrainians, and Byelorussians

Arriving after World War II, Slavic immigrants established a unique community in Richmond, just inland from Bath. Only a tiny nucleus remains today, along with an onion-domed church, but a stroll through the local cemetery hints at the extent of the original colony.

## The Newest Arrivals: Refugees from War

War has been the impetus for the more recent arrival of Asians, Africans, Central Americans, and Eastern Europeans. Most have settled in the Portland area, making that city the state's center of diversity. Vietnamese and Cambodians began settling in Maine in the mid-1970s. A handful of Afghanis who fled the Soviet-Afghan conflict also ended up in Portland. Somalis, Ethiopians, and Sudanese fled their war-torn countries in the early to mid-1990s, and Bosnians and Kosovars arrived in the last half of the 1990s. With every new conflict comes a new stream of immigrants—world citizens are becoming Mainers, and Mainers are becoming world citizens.

# Culture

Mainers are an independent lot, many exhibiting the classic Yankee characteristics of dry humor, thrift, and ingenuity. Those who can trace their roots back at least a generation or two in the state and have lived here through the duration can call themselves natives; everyone else, no matter how long they've lived here, is "from away."

Mainers react to outsiders depending upon how those outsiders treat them. Treat a Mainer with a condescending attitude, and you'll receive a cold shoulder at best. Treat a Mainer with respect, and you'll be welcome, perhaps even invited in to share a mug of coffee. Mainers are wary of outsiders and often with good reason. Many outsiders move to Maine because they fall in love with its independence and rural simplicity, and then they demand that the farmer stop spreading that stinky manure on his farmlands, or they insist that the town initiate garbage pickup, or they build a glass-and-timber McMansion in the midst of white clapboard historical homes.

In most of Maine, money doesn't impress folks. The truth is, that lobsterman in the old truck and the well-worn work clothes might be sitting on a small fortune. Or living on it. Perhaps nothing has caused more troubles between natives and newcomers than the rapidly increasing value of land and the taxes that go with that. For many visitors, Maine real estate is a bargain they can't resist.

If you want real insight into Maine character, listen to a CD or watch a video by one Maine master humorist, Tim Sample. As he often says, "Wait a minute; it'll sneak up on you."

## FINE ART

In 1850, in a watershed moment for Maine landscape painting, Hudson River School artist par excellence Frederic Edwin Church (1826–1900) vacationed on Mount Desert Island. Influenced by the luminist tradition of such contemporaries as Fitz Hugh Lane (1804–1865), who summered in nearby Castine, Church accurately but romantically depicted the dramatic tableaux of Maine's coast and woodlands that even today attract slews of admirers.

By the 1880s, however, impressionism had become the style du jour and was being practiced by a coterie of artists who collected around Charles Herbert Woodbury (1864–1940) in Ogunquit. His program made Ogunquit the best-known summer art school in New England. After Hamilton Easter Field established another art school in town, modernism soon asserted itself. Among the artists who took up summertime Ogunquit residence was Walt Kuhn (1877–1949), a key organizer of New York's 1913 landmark Armory Show of modern art.

Meanwhile, a bit farther south, impressionist Childe Hassam (1859–1935), part of writer Celia Thaxter's circle, produced several hundred works on Maine's remote Appledore Island, in the Isles of Shoals off Kittery, and illustrated Thaxter's *An Island Garden*.

Another artistic summer colony found its niche in 1903, when Robert Henri (born Robert Henry Cozad, 1865–1929), charis-

matic leader of the Ashcan School of realist/modernists, visited Monhegan Island, about 11 miles offshore. Artists who followed him there included Rockwell Kent (1882–1971), Edward Hopper (1882–1967), George Bellows (1882–1925), and Randall Davey (1887–1964). Among the many other artists associated with Monhegan images are William Kienbusch (1914–1980), Reuben Tam (1916–1991), and printmakers Leo Meissner (1895–1977) and Stow Wengenroth (1906–1978).

But colonies were of scant interest to other notables, who chose to derive their inspiration from Maine's stark natural beauty and work mostly in their own orbits. Among these are genre painter Eastman Johnson (1824–1906); romantic realist Winslow Homer (1836–1910), who lived in Maine for 27 years and whose studio in Prouts Neck (Scarborough) still overlooks the surf-tossed scenery he so often depicted; pointillist watercolorist Maurice Prendergast (1858–1924); John Marin (1870–1953), a cubist who painted Down East subjects, mostly around Deer Isle and Addison (Cape Split); Lewiston native Marsden Hartley (1877–1943), who first showed his abstractionist work in New York in 1909 and later worked in Berlin; Fairfield Porter (1907–1975), whose family summered on Great Spruce Head Island, in East Penobscot Bay; Andrew Wyeth (b. 1917), whose reputation as a romantic realist in the late 20th century surpassed that of his illustrator father, N. C. Wyeth (1882–1945).

On a parallel track was sculptor Louise Nevelson (1899–1988), raised in a poor Russian-immigrant family in Rockland and far better known outside her home state for her monumental wood sculptures slathered in black or gold. Two other noted sculptors with Maine connections were William Zorach (1887–1966) and Gaston Lachaise (1882–1935), both of whom lived in Georgetown, near Bath.

Today, Maine has no major community known exclusively for its summer art colony. Sure, there are artistic clusters here and there, united by the urge for creative networking and moral support—especially when threatened with reduced government subsidy. Among these artistic pockets, all close to the ocean, are the Kennebunks, Portland, Monhegan Island, Rockland, Blue Hill, Deer Isle, Gouldsboro, and Eastport.

Year-round or seasonal Maine residents with national (and international) reputations include Lincolnville's Neil Welliver and Alex Katz, North Haven's Eric Hopkins, Deer Isle's Karl Schrag, Tenants Harbor's Jamie Wyeth (third generation of the famous family), Kennebunk's Edward Betts, and Cushing's Lois Dodd and Alan Magee.

The two best collections of Maine art are at the **Portland Museum of Art** (7 Congress Sq., Portland, 207/775-6148) and the **Farnsworth Art Museum** (16 Museum St., Rockland, 207/596-6457). The Farnsworth, in fact, focuses only on Maine art, primarily from the 20th century. In 1996, both museums saw their already-impressive holdings greatly enhanced when philanthropic collector Elizabeth Noyce bequeathed her comprehensive Maine collection to them. The Farnsworth is the home of the Wyeth Center, featuring the works of three generations of Wyeths.

The **Ogunquit Museum of American Art,** appropriately, also has a very respectable Maine collection (in a spectacular setting). Other Maine paintings, not always on exhibit, are at the Bowdoin College Museum of Art, in Brunswick.

## CRAFTS

Any survey of Maine art, however brief, must include the significant role of crafts in the state's artistic tradition. As with painters, sculptors, and writers, craftspeople have gravitated to Maine—most notably since the establishment in 1950 of the **Haystack Mountain School of Crafts.** Started in the Belfast area, the school put down roots on Deer Isle in 1960. Each summer, internationally famed artisans—sculptors, glassmakers, weavers, jewelers, potters, papermakers, and printmakers—become the faculty for the unique school, which has weekday classes and 24-hour studio access for adult students on its handsome 40-acre campus. For information: Haystack Mountain School of

Crafts, Sunshine Road, P.O. Box 518, Deer Isle 04627, 207/348-2306, fax 207/348-2307, www.haystack-mtn.org. Portland is the headquarters for the **Maine Crafts Association** (15 Walton St., Portland, 207/780-1807, www.mainecrafts.org), which has nearly 150 members and produces a very useful annual directory of artisans and exhibits.

## DOWN EAST LITERATURE

Maine's first big-name writer was probably the early 17th-century French explorer Samuel de Champlain (1570–1635), who scouted the Maine coast, established a colony in 1604 near present-day Calais, and lived to describe in detail his experiences. Several decades after Champlain's forays, English naturalist John Josselyn visited Scarborough and in the 1670s published the first two books accurately describing Maine's flora and fauna (aptly describing, for example, blackflies as "not only a pesterment but a plague to the country").

Today, Maine's best-known author lives not on the coast but just inland in Bangor—Stephen King (b. 1947), wizard of the weird. Many of his dozens of horror novels and stories are set in Maine, and several have been filmed for the big screen here. King and his wife, Tabitha, also an author, are avid fans of both education and team sports and have generously distributed their largesse among schools and teams in their hometown as well as other parts of the state.

### Chroniclers of the Great Outdoors

John Josselyn was perhaps the first practitioner of Maine's strong naturalist tradition in American letters, but the Pine Tree State's rugged scenic beauty and largely unspoiled environment have given rise to many ecologically and environmentally concerned writers.

The 20th century saw the arrival in Maine of crusader Rachel Carson (1907–1964), whose 1962 wake-up call, *Silent Spring,* was based partly on Maine observations and research. The Rachel Carson National Wildlife Refuge, headquartered in Wells and comprising 10 chunks of environmentally sensitive coastal real estate, covers nearly 3,500 acres between Kittery Point and the Mid-Coast region.

The tiny town of Nobleboro, near Damariscotta, drew nature writer Henry Beston (1888–1968), author of, among other things, *The Outermost House* (about Cape Cod); his *Northern Farm* lyrically chronicles a year in Maine. Beston's wife, Elizabeth Coatsworth (1893–1986), wrote more than 90 books—including *Chimney Farm*, about their life in Nobleboro.

Fannie Hardy Eckstorm (1865–1946), born in Brewer to Maine's most prosperous fur trader, graduated from Smith College and became a noted expert on Maine (and specifically Native American) folklore. Among her extensive writings, *Indian Place-Names of the Penobscot Valley and the Maine Coast,* published in 1941, remains a sine qua non for researchers.

The out-of-doors and inner spirits shaped Cape Rosier adoptees Helen and Scott Nearing, whose 1954 *Living the Good Life* became the bible of Maine's back-to-the-landers.

## Classic Writings on the State

Historical novels, such as *Arundel,* were the specialty of Kennebunk native Kenneth Roberts (1885–1957), but Roberts also wrote *Trending into Maine,* a potpourri of Maine observations and experiences (the original edition was illustrated by N. C. Wyeth). Kennebunkport's Booth Tarkington (1869–1946), author of the *Penrod* novels and *The Magnificent Ambersons,* described 1920s Kennebunkport in *Mary's Neck,* published in 1932.

A little subgenre of sociological literary classics comprises astute observations (mostly by women) of daily life in various parts of the state. Some are fiction, some nonfiction, some barely disguised romans à clef. Probably the best-known chronicler of such observations is Sarah Orne Jewett (1849–1909), author of *The Country of the Pointed Firs,* a fictional 1896 account of "Dunnet's Landing" (actually Tenants Harbor); her ties, however, were in the South Berwick area, where she spent most of her life. Also in South Berwick, Gladys Hasty Carroll (1904–1999) scrutinized everyday life in her hamlet, Dunnybrook, in *As the Earth Turns* (a

title later "borrowed" and tweaked by a soap-opera producer). Lura Beam (1887–1978) focused on her childhood in the Washington County village of Marshfield in *A Maine Hamlet,* published in 1957, while Louise Dickinson Rich (1903–1972) entertainingly described her coastal Corea experiences in *The Peninsula,* after first having chronicled her rugged wilderness existence in *We Took to the Woods.* Ruth Moore (1903–1989), born on Gott's Island, near Acadia National Park, published her first book at the age of 40. Her tales, recently brought back into print, have earned her a whole new, appreciative audience. Elisabeth Ogilvie (b. 1917) came to Maine in 1944 and lived for many years on remote Ragged Island, transformed into "Bennett's Island" in her fascinating "tide trilogy": *High Tide at Noon, Storm Tide,* and *The Ebbing Tide.* Ben Ames Williams (1887–1953), the token male in this roundup of perceptive observers, in 1940 produced *Come Spring,* an epic tale of hardy pioneers founding the town of Union, just inland from Rockland.

Seldom recognized for her Maine connection, antislavery crusader Harriet Beecher Stowe (1811–1896) lived in Brunswick in the mid-19th century, where she wrote *The Pearl of Orr's Island,* a folkloric novel about a tiny nearby fishing community.

Mary Ellen Chase was a Maine native, born in Blue Hill in 1887. She became an English professor at Smith College in 1926 and wrote about 30 books, including some about the Bible as literature. She died in 1973.

Two books do a creditable job of excerpting literature from throughout Maine—something of a daunting task. The most comprehensive is *Maine Speaks: An Anthology of Maine Literature,* published in 1989 by the Maine Writers and Publishers Alliance. *The Quotable Moose: A Contemporary Maine Reader,* edited by Wesley McNair and published in 1994 by the University Press of New England, focuses on 20th-century authors.

## A World of Her Own

For Marguerite Yourcenar (1903–1987), Maine provided solitude and inspiration for

# THE LOBSTER EXPERIENCE

No Maine visit can be considered complete without the "real Maine" experience of a "lobsta dinnah" at a lobster wharf/pound/shack. Keep an eye on the weather, pick a sunny day, and head out.

If you spot a lobster place with Restaurant in its name and no outside dining, keep going. What you're looking for is the genuine article. You want to eat outdoors, at a wooden picnic table, with a knockout view of boats and the sea. Whatever place you choose, the drill is much the same, and the "dinners" are served anytime from noonish on (some places close as early as 7 P.M.).

First of all, dress very casually so you can manhandle the lobster without messing up your good clothes. If you want beer or wine, call ahead and ask if the place serves it; you may need to bring your own, since many such operations don't have beer/wine licenses, much less liquor licenses. In the evening, carry some insect repellent, in case mosquitoes crash the party.

A basic one-pound lobster and go-withs (cole slaw or potato salad, potato chips, perhaps corn on the cob, and butter or fake butter for dipping) should run $15 or less, but of course that depends on the current market. Depending on your hunger, though, you may want to indulge in a shore dinner (lobster, steamed clams, potato chips, and maybe chowder, cole slaw, or corn), for which you may have to part with $18-24. Don't skip dessert; many lobster pounds are known for their homemade pies.

It's not unusual, either, to see lobster-wharf devotees carting picnic baskets with hors d'oeuvres, salads, and baguettes. I've even seen candles and champagne. Creativity abounds, but don't stray too far from the main attraction – the crustaceans.

Typically, you'll need to survey a chalkboard or whiteboard menu and step up to a window to order. You'll either give the person your name or get a number. A few places have staff to take your order or deliver your meal, but usually you head back for the window when your name or number is called. Don your plastic lobster bib and begin the attack. If you're a neophyte, watch a pro at a nearby table. Some pounds have "how-to" info on printed paper placemats. If you're really worried (you needn't be), contact the Maine Lobster Promotion Council (382 Harlow St., Bangor, www.mainelobsterpromotion.com). It publishes a brochure with detailed instructions. Don't worry about doing it "wrong"; you'll eventually get what you came for, and it'll be an experience to remember.

For the ultimate lobster feeding frenzy, plan to be in Rockland the first weekend in August, when volunteers at the annual Maine Lobster Festival stoke up the world's largest lobster cooker and serve thousands of pounds of lobsters nonstop to more than 50,000 enthusiastic diners.

Here (by region, in alphabetical order) are

---

subjects ranging far beyond the state's borders. Yourcenar was a longtime Northeast Harbor resident and the first woman elected to the prestigious Académie Française. Her house, now a shrine to her work, is open to the public by appointment in summer.

## Essayists, Critics, and Humorists Native and Transplanted

Maine's best-known essayist is and was E. B. White (1899–1985), who bought a farm in tiny Brooklin in 1933 and continued writing for *The New Yorker*. *One Man's Meat*, pub-lished in 1944, is one of the best collections of his wry, perceptive writings. His legions of admirers also include two generations raised on his classic children's stories *Stuart Little*, *Charlotte's Web*, and *The Trumpet of the Swan*.

Writer and critic Doris Grumbach (b. 1918), who settled in Sargentville, not far from Brooklin but far from her New York ties, wrote two particularly wise works from the perspective of a Maine transplant: *Fifty Days of Solitude* and *Coming into the End Zone*.

Maine's best contemporary exemplar of hugreat places to experience lobster. All are described in more detail in the regional chapters.

## SOUTHERN COAST
**Kittery Point:** Chauncey Creek Lobster Pier, 207/439-1030
**Ogunquit:** Barnacle Billy's Lobster Pound, 207/646-5575

## GREATER PORTLAND
**Cape Elizabeth (near Portland):** The Lobster Shack, 207/799-1677
**Portland:** Portland Lobster Company, 207/775-2112
**South Freeport:** Harraseeket Lunch and Lobster Company, 207/865-3535

## MID-COAST
**Boothbay Harbor:** The Lobster Dock, 207/635-7120
**Cundy's Harbor:** Holbrook's Wharf, 207/729-0848
**Damariscotta/Pemaquid Peninsula:** Broad Cove Marine Services, Medomak, 207/529-5186; Shaw's Fish and Lobster Wharf, New Harbor, 207/677-2200; Pemaquid Fishermen's Co-op, Pemaquid Harbor, 207/677-2801; Muscongus Bay Lobster, Round Pond, 207/529-5528; Round Pond Lobster Co-Op, Round Pond, 207/529-5725; South Bristol Fishermen's Co-op, South Bristol, 207/644-8224
**Georgetown:** Five Islands Lobster Company, 207/371-2990

**Small Point:** The Lobster House, 207/389-1596
**Southport:** Robinson's Wharf, 207/633-3830

## PENOBSCOT BAY
**East Belfast:** Young's Lobster Pound Restaurant, 207/338-1160
**Lincolnville Beach:** The Lobster Pound, 207/789-5550
**South Thomaston (near Rockland):** Waterman's Beach Lobster, 207/596-7819
**Spruce Head (near Rockland):** Miller's Lobster Company, 207/594-7406
**Tenants Harbor:** Dip Net, 207/372-6307

## BLUE HILL AND DEER ISLE
**Castine:** Dennett's Wharf, 207/326-9045
**Stonington:** Cockatu, 207/367-0900

## ACADIA
**Bernard (Mount Desert Island):** Thurston's Lobster Pound, 207/244-7600
**Hancock:** Tidal Falls Lobster Pond, 207/422-6457
**Southwest Harbor:** Beal's Lobster Pier, 207/244-3202
**Trenton:** Trenton Bridge Lobster Pound, 207/667-2977

## DOWN EAST
**Eastport:** Eastport Chowder House, 207/853-4700

---

morous writing is the late John Gould (1908–2003), whose life in rural Friendship has provided grist for many a tale. Gould's hilarious columns in the *Christian Science Monitor* and his steady book output have made him the icon of Maine humor.

## Pine Tree Poets
Born in Portland, Henry Wadsworth Longfellow (1807–1882) is Maine's most famous poet; his marine themes clearly stem from his seashore childhood (in "My Lost Youth," he wistfully rhapsodized, "Often I

think of the beautiful town/That is seated by the sea…").

Widely recognized in her own era, poet Celia Thaxter (1835–1894) held court on Appledore Island in the Isles of Shoals, welcoming artists, authors, and musicians to her summer salon. Today, she's best known for *An Island Garden*, published in 1894 and detailing her attempts at horticultural TLC in a hostile environment.

Edna St. Vincent Millay (1892–1950) had connections to Camden, Rockland, and Union and described a stunning Camden panorama in "Renascence."

# MAINE FOOD SPECIALTIES

Everyone knows Maine is *the* place for lobster, but there are quite a few other foods that you should sample before you leave.

For a few weeks in May, right around Mother's Day (the second Sunday in May), a wonderful delicacy starts sprouting along Maine woodland streams: **fiddleheads,** the still-furled tops of the ostrich fern *(Matteuccia struthiopteris)*. Tasting vaguely like asparagus, fiddleheads have been on May menus ever since Native Americans taught the colonists to forage for the tasty vegetable. Don't go fiddleheading unless you're with a pro, though; the lookalikes are best left to the woods critters. If you find them on a restaurant menu, indulge.

As with fiddleheads, we owe thanks to Native Americans for introducing us to **maple syrup,** one of Maine's major agricultural exports. The annual crop averages 110,000 gallons. The syrup comes in four different colors/flavors (from light amber to extra dark amber), and inspectors strictly monitor syrup quality. The best syrup comes from the sugar or rock maple, *Acer saccharum.* On Maine Maple Sunday (usually the fourth Sunday in March), several dozen syrup producers open their rustic sugarhouses to the public for "sugaring-off" parties – to celebrate the sap harvest and share the final phase in the production process. Wood smoke billows from the sugarhouse chimney while everyone inside gathers around huge kettles used to boil down the watery sap. (A single gallon of syrup starts with 30-40 gallons of sap.) Finally, it's time to sample the syrup every which way – on pancakes and waffles, in tea, on ice cream, in puddings, in muffins, even just drizzled over snow. Most producers also have containers of syrup for sale. For a list of participating sugarhouses, contact the Maine Department of Agriculture (207/287-3491, www.getrealmaine.com).

The best place for Maine maple syrup is atop pancakes made with Maine **wild blueberries.** Packed with antioxidants and all kinds of good-for-you stuff, these flavorful berries are prized by bakers because they retain their form and flavor when cooked. Much smaller than the cultivated versions, wild blueberries are also raked, not picked. Although most of the Down East barren barons harvest their crops for the lucrative wholesale market, a few growers let you pick your own blueberries in mid-August. Contact the Wild Blueberry Commission (207/581-1475) or the state Department of Agriculture (207/287-3491) for locations, recipes, and other wild-blueberry information, or log on to the website of the Wild Blueberry Association of North America, headquartered in Bar Harbor: www.wildblueberries.com.

The best place to simply *appreciate* blueberries is Machias, site of the renowned annual Wild Blueberry Festival, held the third weekend in August. While harvesting is under way in the surrounding fields, you can stuff your face with blueberry-everything – muffins, jam, pancakes, ice cream, pies. Plus you can collect blueberry-logo napkins, T-shirts, fridge magnets, pottery, and jewelry.

Another don't miss while in Maine is Maine-made **ice cream.** Skip the overpriced Ben and Jerry's outlets. Locally made ice cream and gelato are fresher and better and often come in an astounding range of flavors. The big name in the state is Gifford's, with regional companies being Shain's and Round Top. All beat the out-of-state competition by a long shot. Even better are some of the one-of-a-kind dairy bars and farm stands. Good bets are Brown's, in York; Morton's, in Ellsworth; and Mt. Desert Ice Cream and Ben and Bill's, both in Bar Harbor.

Finally, whenever you get a chance, shop at a **farmers market.** Their biggest asset is serendipity – you never know what you'll find. Everything is locally grown and often organic. Herbs, unusual vegetables, seedlings, baked goods, meat, free-range chicken, goat cheese, herb vinegars, berries, exotic condiments, smoked salmon, maple syrup, honey, and jams are just a few of the possibilities. For a list of all the markets (including those in inland areas), contact the Maine Department of Agriculture.

Whitehead Island, near Rockland, was the birthplace of Wilbert Snow (1883–1977), who went on to become president of Connecticut's Wesleyan University. His 1968 memoir, *Codline's Child,* makes fascinating reading.

A longtime resident of York, May Sarton (1912–1995) approached cult status as a guru of feminist poetry and prose—and as an articulate analyst of death and dying during her terminal illness.

Among respected Maine poets today are Philip Booth (b. 1925), a resident of Castine; William Carpenter (b. 1940), of Stockton Springs; and Appleton's Kate Barnes (b. 1932), named Maine's Poet Laureate from 1996 to 1999. Although she comes by her acclaim legitimately, Barnes is also genetically disposed, being the daughter of writers Henry Beston and Elizabeth Coatsworth.

## Maine Lit for Little Ones

Besides E. B. White's children's classics, *Stuart Little, Charlotte's Web,* and *The Trumpet of the Swan,* America's kids were also weaned on books written and illustrated by Maine island summer resident Robert McCloskey (b. 1914), notably *Time of Wonder, One Morning in Maine,* and *Blueberries for Sal.* Neck-and-neck in popularity is prolific Walpole illustrator-writer Barbara Cooney (1917–1999), whose award-winning titles included *Miss Rumphius, Island Boy,* and *Hattie and the Wild Waves.* Cooney produced more than 100 books, and it seems as if everyone has a different favorite.

Maine can also lay partial claim to Kate Douglas Wiggin (1856–1923), author of the eternally popular *Rebecca of Sunnybrook Farm;* she spent summers at Quillcote, in Hollis, just west of Portland.

# ESSENTIALS

## Getting There

Coastal Maine has two major airports, two major bus networks, a toll highway, limited Amtrak service, and some ad hoc local transportation systems that fill in the gaps.

### BY AIR

Coastal Maine's major airline gateway is **Portland International Jetport** (PWM; 207/774-7301, www.portlandjetport.org), although visitors headed farther northeast sometimes prefer **Bangor International Airport** (BGR; 207/947-0384, www.flybangor.com). The "international" in their names is a bit misleading. Charter flights from Europe often stop at Bangor for refueling and customs clearance,

and sometimes bad weather also diverts flights there. Boston's Logan Airport is the nearest airport with direct flights from Europe and other worldwide destinations.

You'll undoubtedly want to fly into Bangor if you're going to Bar Harbor and Acadia National Park or the Down East coastal counties of Washington and Hancock. But Portland is the more logical airport choice if you're visiting southern Maine—the beaches, Portland, or the coastal towns up to Damariscotta. If your destination is the Camden/Rockport area, which is equidistant between the two airports, your choice is a toss-up. Being on the coast, the Portland airport is more subject to fog shut-

© TOM NANGLE

downs than Bangor, but many Bangor flights originate (or stop) in Boston, where fog delays can afflict Logan Airport even more.

Increasingly popular choices for bargain hunters are **Southwest Airlines** (800/435-9792), which operates economical flights into Manchester, New Hampshire, and **Jet Blue** (800/538-2583), which services Portland. Ground transportation is available between Manchester and the Portland Jetport.

All the airlines increase their flight frequency during the summer to accommodate stepped-up demand.

Airlines serving Portland and/or Bangor are **AirTran** (800/433-7300), **Continental** (800/523-3273), **Delta** (800/221-1212), **Jet Blue** (800/538-2583), **Northwest** (800/225-2525), **United Express** (800/864-8331), and **US Airways** (800/428-4322).

## Portland Jetport Facilities

Portland's amenities include a newsstand/gift shop, coffee shop, restaurant/lounge, restrooms, large waiting area, ATM, and plenty of coin- and card-operated telephones. Avis, Budget, Hertz, and National car-rental agencies have offices in the terminal; nearby Alamo runs a shuttle. A business center in the gate area has Internet access. Visitor information is dispensed from a desk (not always staffed, unfortunately) between the gates and the baggage-claim area. There's no need to rush out to grab your luggage, though—Portland has one of the slowest baggage-claim operations in the country. Plan to stop at the restrooms, browse through the gift shop, and pick up tourism information after you arrive—and even then you may still have to wait for your luggage. Complaints to management elicit the response that Portland is the terminus of many airline routes, and the airline companies (which provide the baggage handlers and unloading equipment) give low priority to locations that don't require fast turnaround. As a result, carry-on luggage is a plus here. Baggage-handling offices surround the luggage carousels. Airlines are responsible for luggage, so if you have a problem, contact a representative from your airline. If

you have an emergency, contact the airport manager (207/773-8462).

**Ground Transportation:** The **Explorer** (207/774-9891 or 800/377-4457, www.portland-explorer.org) buses link all Portland transportation hubs—the airport, Portland Transportation Center, Vermont Transit terminal, Scotia Prince Ferry, and Casco Bay Lines—with hotels on the route. Portland's **Metro** bus line (207/774-0351) provides scheduled service throughout the city. **Taxis** are available outside baggage claim.

If you're planning to arrive in Portland and head directly up the coast anywhere between the airport and Camden, call ahead to **Mid-Coast Limousine** (207/236-2424 or 800/937-2424) and schedule a pickup. You might be lucky and find one of its limos at the airport, but it operates by reservation, so don't take the chance.

## Bangor Airport Facilities

Bangor's airport has scaled-down versions of Portland's facilities but all the necessary amenities: Avis, Budget, Hertz, National and Alamo rental cars (with Enterprise and Thrifty nearby); newsstand/gift shop; and waiting area with restrooms and phones. If you need help, contact the airport manager (207/947-0384).

**Ground Transportation: Bangor Area Transportation** (BAT; 207/882-4670, www.bgrme.org) buses connect the airport to downtown Bangor. Buses run Monday–Saturday. **West's Coastal Connection** (207/546-2823 or 800/596-2823, www.westbusservice.com) has scheduled service along Route 1 to Calais, with stops in Ellsworth, Gouldsboro, Machias, and Perry. It makes flag stops on request in Hancock, Sullivan, Milbridge, Columbia Falls, Jonesboro, Whiting, Dennysville, and Pembroke. **Taxis** are available outside baggage claim.

## Regional Airports

Airports accessible via US Airways/Business Express from Boston are **Hancock County Airport** (BHB; 207/667-7329, www.bhbairport.com) near Bar Harbor and **Knox County Regional Airport** (RKD; 207/594-4131, http://knoxcounty.midcoast.com) at Owls Head, near Rockland and Camden. Colgan

Air is the local affiliate of US Airways Express at these two airports. Hancock County Airport has rental-car offices for Budget and Hertz and is also serviced by the Island Explorer bus late June–Columbus Day. Knox County has a Budget car-rental desk.

## Boston Logan Airport

If you fly into Boston (BOS), you easily can get to Maine via rental car (all majors at the airport, but it's not pleasant to navigate Logan in a rental car) and Concord Trailways bus (easiest and least-expensive option). You'll need to connect to North Station to take Amtrak's Downeaster train. Another option is **Mermaid Transportation** (800/696-2463, www.gomermaid.com), which operates the best van service between Boston and Portland. Pickup and dropoff, by reservation only, are at Portland Jetport and Logan airport. Mermaid also provides daily van service between Manchester, New Hampshire, and the Portland Jetport.

## BY CAR

The major highway access to Maine from the south is **I-95,** which roughly parallels the coast until Bangor, before shooting up to Houlton. Other busy access points are **Route 1,** also from New Hampshire, exiting the state in Calais at the New Brunswick province border; **Route 302,** from North Conway, New Hampshire, entering Maine at Fryeburg; **Route 2,** from Gorham, New Hampshire, to Bethel, **Route 201,** entering from Québec province, just north of Jackman, and a couple of crossing points from New Brunswick into Aroostook and Washington Counties in northeastern Maine.

## BY BUS

**Concord Trailways** (800/639-3317, www.concordtrailways.com) departs downtown Boston (South Station Transportation Center) and Logan Airport for Portland almost hourly from the wee hours of the morning until late at night, making pickups at all Logan airline terminals (lower level). Most of the buses continue directly to Bangor. The Portland bus terminal is the Portland Transportation Center, Thompson Point Road, just west of I-295. If you're headed for downtown Portland from the bus terminal, board the Metro city bus at the terminal and show your Concord Trailways bus ticket to receive a free trip.

Three daily nonexpress buses continue from Portland along the coast as far as Searsport and then head inland to the Trailways terminal in Bangor.

## BY RAIL

**Amtrak's Downeaster** (800/872-7245, www.thedowneaster.com) makes five daily round-trip runs between Boston's North Station and Portland's Transportation Center, with stops in Wells, Saco, and seasonally in Old Orchard Beach (May 1 to October 31). The Wells Regional Transportation Center is staffed for information, has restrooms, ATM, and a climate-controlled waiting area. There's seasonal trolley service to the beach. Taxis are on-site. The Saco station is near downtown and on the Tri-Town Shuttlebus route; taxis are available on-site. The Old Orchard Beach station is adjacent to the chamber of commerce and steps from the beach. From the Portland station, Portland's Metro municipal bus service will take you gratis to downtown Portland; just show your Amtrak ticket stub.

## BY FERRY

An oceangoing car-and-passenger ferry *The Cat* (877/359-3760, www.catferry.com) links Portland and Bar Harbor with Yarmouth, in western Nova Scotia, Canada, with up to two daily trips from one port or the other between early June and mid-October. When making plans, remember that Yarmouth is on Atlantic time—an hour later than Maine's eastern time. Check for the current operating schedule and fees, but expect a 5.5-hour journey when departing from Portland, three hours from Bar Harbor. The ferry carries up to 900 passengers and 240 cars. Because of maritime law, the ferry can't operate between Portland and Bar Harbor without a stop in Canada.

# Getting Around

## By Bus

Ground transportation exists in Maine, but it's far from adequate. For instance, only two long-distance bus companies cover the state, and only one covers coastal Maine. There's no smoking on the buses.

**Concord Trailways** (800/639-3317, www.concordtrailways.com) has the most extensive bus network, with routes designed to assist students, island ferry passengers, and day-trippers. Buses from Boston's Logan Airport stop in downtown Portland and follow a mostly coastal route through Brunswick, Bath, Wiscasset, Damariscotta, Waldoboro, Rockland, Camden, Belfast, and Searsport, ending in Bangor, and then follow the same route in reverse. (During the school year, the route also includes Bowdoin College in Brunswick and the University of Maine campus in Orono.)

Once-a-day buses to and from Calais coordinate with the Bangor bus schedules. The Calais line, stopping in Ellsworth, Gouldsboro, Machias, and Perry (near Eastport), is operated by **West's Coastal Connection** (207/546-2823 or 800/596-2823, www.westbusservice.com). Flag stops along the route are permitted (see the regional chapters for information).

Portland and South Portland have **city bus service,** with some wheelchair-accessible vehicles. A number of smaller communities have established **local shuttle vans** or **trolley-buses,** but most of the latter are seasonal. Trolley-buses operate (for a fee) in Ogunquit, Wells, the Kennebunks, Portland, Bath, and Boothbay. Mount Desert Island and the Schoodic Peninsula have the **Island Explorer,** an excellent free summer (from late June) bus service.

## By Car

No matter how much time and resourcefulness you summon, you'll never really be able to appreciate Coastal Maine without a car. Down every little peninsula jutting into the Atlantic lies a picturesque village or park or ocean view. Even I-95, the state's major artery, boasts scenic vistas that bring photographers to a screeching halt. (Of course, a radar-equipped cop can deliver the same result for any driver.)

Note that the interstate can be a bit confusing to motorists; it's important to consult a map and pay close attention to the green directional signs to avoid heading off in the wrong direction. Between York and Augusta, I-95 is the same as the Maine Turnpike, regulated by The Maine Turnpike Authority (877/682-9433 or 800/675-7453 travel conditions, www.maineturnpike.com). I-295 splits from I-95 in Portland and heads up the coast to Brunswick before veering inland and rejoining I-95 in Gardiner. Service areas are infrequent on the turnpike and interstate and are not on both sides of the highway, so stop when you see one; don't wait for the next one. All exit numbers along I-95 reflect distance in miles from the border. Exits on I-295 reflect distance from where it splits from I-95 just south of Portland at Exit 44.

The Maine Department of Transportation (800/877-9171, www.state.me.us/mdot) has general road information on its website and also operates the Explore Maine site (www.exploremaine.org), which has information on all forms of transportation in Maine. For real-time information on road conditions, weather, construction, and major delays, dial 511 in Maine, 866/282-7578 from out of state, or visit www.511maine.gov. Information is available in both English and French.

If your destination is the Mid-Coast, take I-295 to Brunswick and then pick up Route 1 North. If it's Penobscot Bay, consider taking I-95 (you'll save time by splitting off and looping around on I-295) to Augusta and then taking Route 17 to Rockland or Route 3 to Belfast. If your destination is the Blue Hill Peninsula or above, stay on I-95 to Bangor and then take Route 1A to the coast. If it's Calais, stay on I-95 to Bangor and then take Route 9 to Route 1 South to Calais.

Maximum speed on I-95 and the Maine Turnpike is 65 mph—55 mph on some stretches.

## CAN YOU GET THERE FROM HERE?

Countless names for Maine cities, towns, villages, rivers, lakes, and streams have Native American origins; some are variations on French; and a few have German derivations. Below are some pronunciations to give you a leg up when requesting directions along the Maine coast.

**Arundel** – Uh-RUN-d'l
**Bangor** – BANG-gore
**Bremen** – BREE-m'n
**Calais** – CAL-us
**Castine** – Kass-TEEN
**Damariscotta** – dam-uh-riss-COTT-uh
**Harraseeket** – Hare-uh-SEEK-it
**Isle au Haut** – i'll-a-HO, I'LL-a-ho (subject to plenty of dispute, depending on whether or not you live in the vicinity)
**Katahdin** – Kuh-TA-din
**Lubec** – Loo-BECK

**Machias** – Muh-CHIGH-us
**Matinicus** – Muh-TIN-i-cuss
**Medomak** – Muh-DOM-ick
**Megunticook** – Muh-GUN-tuh-cook
**Monhegan** – Mun-HE-gun
**Mount Desert** – Mount Duh-ZERT
**Narraguagus** – Nare-uh-GWAY-gus
**Naskeag** – NASS-keg
**Passagassawakeag** – Puh-sag-gus-uh-WAH-keg
**Passamaquoddy** – Pass-uh-muh-QUAD-dee
**Pemaquid** – PEM-a-kwid
**Saco** – SOCK-oh
**Schoodic** – SKOO-dick
**Steuben** – Stew-BEN
**Topsham** – TOPS-'m
**Wiscasset** – Wiss-CASS-it
**Woolwich** – WOOL-itch

In snow, sleet, or dense fog, the limit drops to 45 mph; only rarely does the highway close. On other highways, the speed limit is usually 55 mph in rural areas and posted in built-up areas. Note that the Maine Turnpike is a toll highway.

Two lanes wide from Kittery in the south to Fort Kent at the top, U.S. Route 1 is the state's most congested road, particularly in July and August. Mileage distances can be extremely deceptive, since it will take you much longer than anticipated to get from point A to point B. If you ask anyone about distances, chances are good that you'll receive an answer in hours rather than miles. Plan accordingly. If you're trying to make time, it's best to take the Maine Turnpike or I-95; if you want to see Maine, take U.S. 1 and lots of little offshoots.

That said, bear in mind that the Maine Turnpike itself becomes megacongested on summer weekends, and especially summer *holiday* weekends. More than 300,000 vehicles use the turnpike on Memorial Day, Fourth of July, and Labor Day weekends. Worst times on the turnpike are 4–8 P.M. Friday (north-bound), 11 A.M.–2 P.M. Saturday (southbound; most weekly cottage rentals run from Saturday noon to Saturday noon), and 3–7 P.M. Sunday (southbound). On three-day holiday weekends, avoid heading southbound between 3 and 7 P.M. on Monday.

**Rental cars** are available at the Portland, Bangor, and most smaller airports. All the major chains are represented—Alamo, Avis, Budget, Hertz, National, Thrifty, even Rent-a-Wreck. If you're planning to arrive on a July or August weekend, or a summer holiday weekend, call well ahead for a reservation or you may be out of luck.

Almost all **gas stations** in Maine are self-serve (pumps are marked Self; at those marked Full, an attendant will pump the gas for you), and many now allow you to pay at the pump with a credit card. (Many also have ATMs, but you'll usually have to pay a bank surcharge.)

**Important Driving Regulations:** Seat belts are mandatory in Maine. You cannot be stopped for not wearing one, but if you're stopped for any other reason, you can be fined if you're not buckled in. Maine allows right turns at red lights after you stop and check for oncoming traffic. In rare cases, you'll see a No Turn on Red sign—in which case, heed it. *Never* pass a stopped school bus in either direction. Wait until the bus's red lights have stopped flashing and all children are well off the road. Maine law also requires drivers to turn on their car's headlights any time the windshield wipers are operating.

**Roadside Assistance:** Since Maine is enslaved to the automobile, it's not a bad idea for vacationers to carry membership in AAA in case of breakdowns, flat tires, and other car crises. Contact your nearest AAA office or AAA Northern New England (425 Marginal Way, Portland 04101, 207/780-6800 or 800/482-7497, www.aaanne.com). The emergency road service number is 800/222-4357.

## Hitchhiking

Even though Maine's public transportation network is woefully inadequate, and the crime rate is one of the lowest in the nation, it's still risky to hitchhike or pick up hitchhikers.

# Tips for Travelers

## VISAS AND OFFICIALDOM

Since 9/11, security has been excruciatingly tight for foreign visitors, with customs procedures in flux. For current rules, visit www.usa.gov/visitors/arriving.shtml and www.dhs.gov/xtrvlsec. It's crucial to plan well ahead, pack diligently, and have all necessary paperwork. It's also wise to make two sets of copies of all paperwork, one to carry separately on your trip and another left with a trusted friend or relative at home.

## SMOKING

Maine now has laws banning smoking in restaurants, bars, and lounges as well as enclosed areas of public places, such as shopping malls. Only a handful of B&Bs and country inns permit smoking, and more and more motels, hotels, and resorts are limiting the number of rooms where smoking is permitted. Many accommodations have instituted high fines for anyone who smokes in a nonsmoking room. If you're a smoker, motels with direct outdoor access make it easy to satisfy a craving.

## ACCOMMODATIONS, FOOD, AND ALCOHOL
### Accommodations

For all accommodation listings, rates are quoted for peak season, which is usually July and August but may extend through foliage (mid-October). Rates drop, often dramatically, in the shoulder and off-season at accommodations that remain open. Especially during peak season, many accommodations require a two- or three-night minimum.

For the best rates, be sure to check Internet specials and to ask about packages. Many accommodations also provide discounts for members of travel clubs such as AAA, to seniors and the military, and other such groups.

Unless otherwise noted, accommodations have private baths.

### Food

Days and hours of operation listed for places serving food are for peak season. These do change often, sometimes even within a season, and it's not uncommon for a restaurant to close early on a quiet night. To avoid disappointment, call before making a special trip.

### Alcohol

As in the rest of the country, Maine's minimum drinking age is 21 years—and bar owners, bartenders, and serving staff can be held legally accountable for serving underage imbibers. Owners and employees also may be held liable for accidents caused by *legal* drinkers.

# ADVENTURES IN LEARNING

A surprising number of educational programs operate along the Maine coast. Whether you want to improve your foreign-language skills, learn to take photographs, want to craft furniture, learn to sail or even build a boat, or have a family-oriented nature-based vacation, there's a course for you. Here's a sampling.

## HOME, SWEET HOME

In 1974, enterprising entrepreneurs Pat and Patsy Hennin jumped on the do-it-yourself bandwagon and established the **Shelter Institute** (873 Rte. 1, Woolwich, 207/442-7938, www.shelterinstitute.com) to train neophytes in energy-efficient home design and construction techniques. Since then, thousands of students have taken courses here, and enthusiastic alumni (and their building projects) span the globe. Students range in age from late teens to early 80s. A one-week post-and-beam course, for instance, is $975 pp, $1,500 per couple. Courses take place on the school's 68-acre campus in Woolwich, five miles north of Bath. Visitors are welcome any time, and anyone who appreciates fine woodworking tools *has* to visit the institute's **Woodbutcher Tools** retail shop and bookstore, open 9 A.M.-4:30 P.M. Monday-Friday, 9 A.M.-3 P.M. Saturday.

## CONTEMPLATIVE SKIFF BUILDING

Word of mouth seems to be the best marketing tool for **The Carpenter's Boatshop** (440 Old County Rd., Pemaquid, 207/677-3768). Founded in 1979 by Bobby Ives, an engaging Congregational minister, and his late wife, Ruth, the boatshop accepts interested applicants of any denomination to join a community dedicated to both spirituality and boatbuilding. This is no laid-back, contemplative religious retreat; serious boatbuilding supports the community. Sessions run mid-September-mid-June, and there's no tuition. Room and board are provided. The diverse group of 6-8 students all become part of the boatbuilding crew, working at least 40 hours a week in the huge shingled barn/boatshop. Each student builds a 9.5-foot Monhegan skiff, contributes to the construction of three types of stock

wooden boats, helps with all the daily chores, and spends Saturday morning doing valuable community service on the Pemaquid Peninsula. During daily prayer gatherings, students can participate or use the time for reading or other reflective pursuits. Marine author Peter Spectre, an admitted skeptic, admiringly describes this unique program: "Just consider what all these people have done for themselves and the community."

## CREATING A SMALLER WORLD

Begun in 1986 to provide language classes for adults, **Penobscot School** (28 Gay St., Rockland, 207/594-1084, www.languagelearning.org) has become a multicultural clearinghouse with ties around the globe. In fall, winter, and spring, the school offers day and evening courses in nearly a dozen languages, sponsors ethnic dinners and festivals, organizes language-immersion weekends, and puts on international study programs in local schools. July-September, international students (ages 18-65) arrive at the school for intensive three-week English-language courses. On summer weekdays, visitors are often invited for lunch at the school to interact with students practicing their English. Call for information.

## SAILING, SAILING

The best way to explore Maine's coast is aboard a boat. **Bay Island Sailing School** (117 Tillson Ave., Rockland, 207/596-7550 or 800/421-2492, www.sailme.com) is an American Sailing Association-approved summer program that has weekday, weekend, and live-aboard learn-to-sail classes – and special courses for teenagers and women. Contact the school for details.

## YOU OUGHTA BE IN PICTURES

Students come from all over the world to the prestigious **Maine Media Workshops** (P.O. Box 200, Rockport 04856, 207/236-8581 or 877/577-7700, www.meworkshops.com), where international photo and film luminaries teach one- and two-week courses, summer and fall, to neophytes and professionals. A degree-grant-ing program, called **Rockport College,** continues during the winter. Courses are fairly pricey; evening slide lectures are open to the public.

## FURNISH YOUR FUTURE

Alumni of the one-, two-, and 12-week workshops at the **Center for Furniture Craftsmanship** (25 Mill St., Rockport, 207/594-5611, www.woodschool.org), established in 1993, can't say enough about their experiences. One-week to nine-month courses are for various skill levels, from beginner to pro. The center can help arrange for lodging and meals. It's open all year.

## DRAMA FOR THE DEAF

Based at Belfast's former Crosby Middle School, the **National Theatre Workshop of the Handicapped** (96 Church St., P.O. Box 1138, Belfast 04915, 207/338-6894, www.ntwh.org) is a phenomenal organization founded in 1977 and introduced to Belfast in 1998. Jesuit Brother Rick Curry, disabled since birth, established NTWH in New York City's Soho district to provide jobs in the performing and fine arts for people with disabilities. Author of *The Secrets of Jesuit Breadmaking*, as well as countless articles on drama and disabilities, Brother Curry oversees art and drama workshops and productions in Belfast for 50 residential students May–October.

## MUSICAL INTERLUDE

You're never too old to learn how to play a musical instrument or to sing. **Summerkeys** (207/733-2316 June 15–Oct. 15, 973/316-6220 Oct. 15–June 15, www.summerkeys.com) is a music school without admission requirements. Its premise is the inviting: "Come as you are to enjoy the study, the work and the beauty of the Maine Coast." The Lubec school offers instruction in a number of musical instruments, including piano, violin, flute, guitar, cello, and clarinet as well as in voice. Beginners are welcome. Cost is about $500 per week.

## WOODWISE BOAT WAYS

Build a boat, a canoe, a classic sea chest, or a remote-control pond yacht. Those are just a sampling from the dozens of boatbuilding and related craft courses offered each summer at the 60-acre waterfront campus of **The WoodenBoat School** (41 WoodenBoat La., P.O. Box 79, Brooklin 04616, 207/359-4651, www.thewoodenboatschool.com). There's even a popular family week program. Prices begin around $650; lodging and meals packages are available.

## B.A. IN FAMILY FUN

Explore tide pools, learn about animal tracks, discover the diversity of bats, go whale-watching, and take a hike and learn about the natural world in the process at College of the Atlantic's **Family Nature Camp** (105 Eden St., Bar Harbor, 800/597-9500, www.coa.edu/summer). This hands-on, participatory, naturalist-led program provides plenty of fodder for those "What I Did on My Summer Vacation" essays. The minimum age is five; extended family is welcome. Camp includes campus lodging, meals, field trips, and some boat tours.

## ISLAND IMMERSION

Spend a few days or up to a week at one of the themed sessions offered on Hog Island by **Hog Island Audubon Camp** (Keene Neck Rd., off Rte. 32, Bristol, mailing address 20 Gilsland Farm Rd., Falmouth 04105, 207/781-2332 or 888/325-5261, www.maineaudubon.org), an Audubon-owned, 330-acre island that's part of Todd Audubon Sanctuary. Sessions for adults, youth, and families range about $500-1,200 and include accommodations and meals, as well as guided activities. Possibilities might include birding, natural history, and yoga led by specialists.

## TO EVERYTHING, TURN, TURN, TURN

Founded in 2004 by Ken Keoughan, the **Woodturning School** (10 Cappelletti Dr., off Rte. 129/130, Damariscotta, mailing address P.O. Box 190, Friendship 04547, 207/380-8076, www.woodturningschool.org) introduces students to woodturning, a woodworking skill that produces hollow vessels. All tools are provided.

Stiff anti-drunken-driving efforts in Maine (including random roadblocks, license revocation or suspension, hefty fines, and jail terms) have reduced but by no means halted the fatalities. If your blood alcohol level is 0.08 percent or higher, you are legally considered to be operating under the influence.

## TIME ZONE

All of Maine is in the eastern time zone—the same as New York, Washington, D.C., Philadelphia, and Orlando, Florida. Eastern standard time (EST) runs from the last Sunday in October to the first Sunday in April; eastern daylight time (EDT), one hour later, prevails otherwise. Surprising to many first-time visitors is how early the sun rises in the morning and how early it sets at night in midsummer.

If your itinerary also includes Canada, remember that the provinces of New Brunswick and Nova Scotia are on Atlantic time—one hour later than eastern—so if it's noon in Maine, it's 1 p.m. in these provinces.

# Health and Safety

There's too much to do in Maine, and too much to see, to spend even a few hours laid low by illness or mishap. Be sensible—be sure to get enough sleep, wear sunscreen and appropriate clothing, know your limits and don't take foolhardy risks, heed weather and warning signs, carry water and snacks while hiking, don't overindulge in food or alcohol, always tell someone where you're going, and watch your step. If you're traveling with children, you should quadruple your caution.

## MEDICAL CARE

In the event of any emergency, dial 911.

### Southern Coast

**York Hospital** (15 Hospital Dr., York, emergency room 207/351-2157); **Wells Urgent Care** (109 Sanford Rd., Wells, 207/646-5211, 8 a.m.–7 p.m.); **Kennebunk Walk-In Clinic** (24 Portland Rd., Rte. 1, Kennebunk, 207/985-6027); **Southern Maine Medical Center** (Rte. 111, Biddeford, 207/283-7000, emergency 207/283-7100).

### Greater Portland

**Maine Medical Center** (22 Bramhall St., Portland, emergency 207/871-2381); **Mercy Hospital** (144 State St., Portland, emergency 207/879-3265).

### Mid-Coast

**Mid-Coast Hospital** (Bath Rd., Cooks Corner, Brunswick, 207/729-0181); **Parkview Hospital** (329 Maine St., a mile south of Bowdoin College, Brunswick, 207/373-2000); **St. Andrews Hospital and Healthcare Center** (3 St. Andrews La., Boothbay Harbor, 207/633-2121); **Miles Memorial Hospital** (Bristol Rd., Rte. 130, Damariscotta, 207/563-1234).

### Penobscot Bay

**Penobscot Bay Medical Center** (Rte. 1, Rockport, 207/596-8000); **Waldo County General Hospital** (118 Northport Ave., Belfast, 207/338-2500 or 800/649-2536).

### Blue Hill and Deer Isle

**Blue Hill Memorial Hospital** (57 Water St., Blue Hill, 207/374-3400, emergency 207/374-2836, www.bhmh.org).

### Acadia Region

**Maine Coast Memorial Hospital** (50 Union St., Ellsworth 04605, 207/664-5311 or 888/645-8829, emergency room 207/664-5340, www.mainehospital.org); **Mount Desert Island Hospital** (10 Wayman La., Bar Harbor, 207/288-5081, www.mdihospital.org).

### Down East

**Down East Community Hospital** (Upper

Court St., Rte. 1A, Machias, 207/255-3356); **Regional Medical Center at Lubec** (43 S. Lubec Rd., Lubec, 207/733-5541); **Eastport Health Care** (Boynton St., 207/853-6001); **Calais Regional Hospital** (50 Franklin St., Calais, 207/454-7521).

# AFFLICTIONS
## Lyme Disease

A bacterial infection that causes severe arthritis-like symptoms, Lyme disease (named after the Connecticut town where it was first identified in 1975) has been documented in Maine since 1986. Health officials monitor the situation carefully and issue cautionary warnings during prime tick season—mid-May into August. Atlanta's Centers for Disease Control and Prevention (www.cdc.gov) has cited the wooded, marshy areas of Maine's southernmost counties, York and Cumberland, as the highest-risk areas. From there northward along the coast to Mount Desert Island, the risk is considered low to moderate.

Lyme disease is spread by bites from tiny deer ticks (not the larger dog ticks; they don't carry it), which feed on the blood of deer, mice, songbirds, and humans. Symptoms include joint pain, extreme fatigue, chills, a stiff neck, headache, and a distinctive ringlike rash. Except for the rash, which occurs in about 80 percent of victims, the symptoms mimic those of other ailments, such as the flu, so the disease is hard to diagnose. The rash, which expands gradually and usually is not painful, may appear from three days to a month after a bite. If left untreated, Lyme disease eventually can cause heart and neurological problems and debilitating arthritis. Preventive measures are essential. If you suspect you've been exposed, seek medical assistance.

The best advice is to take precautions: Wear a long-sleeved shirt and long pants, and tuck the pant legs into your socks. Light-colored clothing makes the ticks easier to spot. Buy tick repellent at a supermarket or convenience store and use it liberally on your legs. Spray it around your cuffs and beltline. While you're hiking, try to keep to the center of trails, away from long grasses. After any hike, check for ticks—especially behind the knees, and in the armpits, navel, and groin. Monitor children carefully. If you find a tick or suspect you have been bitten, head for the nearest hospital emergency room. If you spot a tick on you (or anyone else), remove it with tweezers and save it for analysis. Not all deer ticks are infected.

## Rabies

Incidents of rabies—a life-threatening, nerve-attacking disease for which there is no cure unless treated immediately—have increased dramatically in Maine since 1994. No human has ever survived a case of rabies, and the disease is horrible, so *do not* approach, or let any child approach, any of the animals known to transmit it: raccoons, skunks, squirrels, bats, and foxes. Domestic dogs are required to have biennial rabies inoculations, thus providing a front line of defense for humans. If you're bitten by any animal, especially one acting suspiciously, head for the nearest hospital emergency room. For statewide information about rabies, contact the Maine Disease Control Administration in Augusta (207/287-3591).

## Allergies (in the Land of Bees and Lobster)

If your medical history includes extreme allergies to shellfish or bee sting, you know the risks of eating a lobster or wandering around a wildflower meadow. However, if you come from a landlocked area and are new to crustaceans, you might not be aware of the potential hazard. Statistics indicate that less than 2 percent of adults have a severe shellfish allergy, but for those victims, the reaction can set in quickly. Immediate treatment is needed to keep the airways open. If you have a history of severe allergic reactions to *anything,* be prepared when you come to the Maine coast dreaming of lobster feasts. Ask your doctor for a prescription for EpiPen (epinephrine), a preloaded, single-use syringe containing 0.3 mg of the drug—enough to tide you over until you can get to a hospital.

## Seasickness

Samuel Butler, the 19th-century author of *Erewhon*, wrote, "How holy people look when they are sea-sick." And he wasn't kidding. Seasickness conjures visions of the pearly gates and an overwhelming urge for instant salvation. Fortunately, even though the ailment seems to last forever, it's only temporary—depending on where you are, what remedies you have, and how your system responds. If you're planning to do any boating in Maine—particularly sailing—you'll want to be prepared. (Being prepared in fact may keep you from succumbing, since fear of seasickness just about guarantees you'll get it.)

Seasickness allegedly stems from an inner-ear imbalance caused by boat motion, but researchers have had difficulty explaining why some people on a vessel become violently ill and others have no problem at all.

To prevent seasickness, try to stay in good shape. Get enough sleep and food, and keep your clothing warm and dry (not easy, of course, on a heeling sailboat). Some veteran sailors swear by salted crackers, sips of water, and bites of fresh ginger. If you start feeling queasy, keep your eyes on the horizon and stay as far away as possible from odors from the engine, the galley, the head, and other seasick passengers. If you become seasick, keep sipping water to prevent dehydration.

Dramamine, Marezine, and Bonine, taken several hours before a boat trip, have long been the preventives of choice. They do cause drowsiness, but anyone who's been seasick will tell you he'd rather be drowsy. Another popular preventive is the scopolamine patch (available by prescription under the trademark Transderm Scop; not advised for pregnant women, the elderly, or children), which gradually releases medication into the bloodstream for up to three days. Discuss the minor side effects with the physician who gives you the prescription, and read directions and cautions carefully before using.

And some people swear by the pressure bracelet, which operates somewhat on the principle of acupressure, telling your brain to ignore the fact that you're not on terra firma. Great success has been reported with these prophylactics in the last decade. Before embarking, especially if the weather is at all iffy, go ahead and put on a patch or a bracelet. Any such preventive measure also improves your mental attitude, relieving anxiety.

## Sunstroke

Since Maine lies between 43° and 48° north latitude, sunstroke is not a major problem, but don't push your luck by spending an entire day frying on the beach in southern coastal Maine. Not only do you risk sunstroke and dehydration, but you're also asking for skin cancer down the road. Early in the season, slather yourself, and especially children, with plenty of PABA-free sunblock. (PABA can cause skin rashes and eruptions, even on people not abnormally sensitive.) Depending on your skin tone, use sun protection factor (SPF) 15 or higher. If you're in the water a long time, slather on some more. Start with 15–30 minutes of solar exposure and increase gradually each day. If you don't get it right, watch for symptoms of sunstroke: fever, profuse sweating, headache, nausea or vomiting, extreme thirst, and sometimes hallucinations. To treat someone with sunstroke, find a breezy spot and place a cold, wet cloth on the victim's forehead. Change the cloth frequently so it stays cold. Offer lots of liquids—strong tea or coffee, fruit juice, water, and soft drinks (no alcohol).

## Hypothermia and Frostbite

Wind and weather can shift dramatically in Maine, especially at higher elevations, creating prime conditions for contracting hypothermia and frostbite. At risk are hikers, swimmers, canoeists, kayakers, sailors, skiers, even cyclists.

When body temperature plummets below the normal 97° to 98.6°F, hypothermia is likely to set in. Symptoms include disorientation, a flagging pulse rate, prolonged shivering, swelling of the face, and cool skin. Quick action is essential to prevent shock and keep body temperature from dropping into the 80s, where cardiac arrest can occur. Emergency treatment begins with removal of as much wet clothing as possible without causing further exposure. Wrap the victim in anything dry—blankets, sleeping bag, clothing, towels, even large plastic trash bags—to keep body heat from escaping. Be sure the neck and head are covered. Or practice the buddy system—climb into a sleeping bag with the victim and provide skin contact. Do not rub the skin, apply hot water, or elevate the legs. If he or she is conscious, offer high-sugar snacks and nonalcoholic hot drinks (but, again, no alcohol; it dilates blood vessels and disrupts the warming process). As quickly as possible, transport the victim to a hospital emergency room.

When extremities begin turning blue or gray, with red blotches, frostbite may be setting in. As with hypothermia, add warmth slowly but do not rub frostbitten skin. Offer snacks and warm, nonalcoholic liquids.

Even during the height of summer, be on the alert for mild hypothermia when children stay in the ocean too long. Bouncing in and out of the water, kids become preoccupied, refuse to admit they are cold, and fall prey to wind chill.

To prevent hypothermia and frostbite, dress in layers and remove or add them as needed. Wool, waterproof nylon (such as Gore-Tex), and synthetic fleece (such as Polartec) are the best fabrics for repelling dampness. Polyester fleece lining wicks excess moisture away from your body. If you plan to buy a down jacket, be sure it has a waterproof shell; down will just suck up the moisture from snow and rain. Especially in winter, always cover your head, since body heat escapes quickly through the head; a ski mask will protect ears and nose. Wear wool- or fleece-lined gloves and wool socks.

## Special Considerations During Hunting Season

During Maine's fall hunting season (October–Thanksgiving weekend)—and especially during the November deer season—walk or hike only in wooded areas marked No Hunting, No Trespassing, or Posted. And even if an area *is* closed to hunters, don't decide to explore the woods during deer or moose season without wearing a "hunter orange" (read: eye-popping fluorescent) jacket or vest. If you take your dog along, be sure it, too, wears an orange vest. Deer hunters are required to wear two items of orange clothing—a hat and usually a vest. Orange gear is available in sporting-goods stores, hardware stores, and some supermarkets and convenience stores. Hunting is illegal on Sundays.

During hunting season, moose and deer are on the move and made understandably skittish by the hunters invading their turf. Moose are primarily found inland, but deer are everywhere, and even the occasional moose strays into Coastal Maine. At night, particularly in wooded areas, these huge creatures often end up alongside or in the roads, so ratchet up your defensive-driving skills. Reduce your normal speed, use high beams when there's no oncoming traffic, and remain extra-alert. In a moose-vs.-car encounter, no one wins, and human fatalities are common. An encounter between a deer and a car may be less dangerous to humans (although the deer usually dies), but some damage is inevitable.

# Information and Services

## MONEY
### Currency
Since Maine's Down East Coast borders Canada, don't be surprised to see a few Canadian coins mixed in with American ones when you receive change from a purchase. In such cases, Canadian and U.S. quarters are equivalent, although the exchange rate is in fact drastically different. Most services (including banks) will accept a handful of Canadian coins at par, but you'll occasionally spot No Canadian Currency signs.

If you need to exchange foreign currency—other than Canadian dollars—do it at or near border crossings or in Portland. In small communities, such transactions are more complicated; you may end up spending more time and money than necessary.

### Banks and Automated Teller Machines
Typical banking hours are 9 A.M.–3 P.M. weekdays, occasionally with later hours on Friday. Drive-up windows at many banks tend to open as much as an hour earlier and stay open an hour or so after lobbies close. Some banks also maintain Saturday morning hours. But as long as you have an automated teller machine (ATM) or debit card or a credit card, you can go anywhere in coastal Maine at any time and withdraw money from your personal checking, savings, or credit-card account.

### Credit Cards/Travelers Checks
Bank credit cards have become so preferred and so prevalent that it's nearly impossible to rent a car or check into a hotel without one (the alternative is payment in advance or a hefty cash deposit). MasterCard and Visa are most widely accepted in Maine, and Discover and American Express are next most popular; Carte Blanche, Diners Club, and EnRoute (Canadian) lag far behind. Be aware, however, that small restaurants (including lobster pounds), shops, and B&Bs off the beaten track might not accept credit cards or nonlocal personal checks; you may need to settle your account with cash or travelers check.

### Taxes
Maine charges a 5 percent sales tax on items such as gifts, snacks, books, clothing, and video rentals, and a 7 percent tax on all bar, restaurant, and lodging bills. Bear in mind, especially when making reservations by phone, that restaurants and lodgings usually do *not* include the 7 percent tax when quoting their prices. A whopping 10 percent tax is added to car-rental rates.

### Tipping
The longtime restaurant tipping standard—15 percent of the total bill—still prevails in most of Maine. One exception is Portland, where a big-city 20 percent rate isn't unusual in the upscale restaurants. Of course, the restaurant tip always should depend on the quality of the service. If you've ever worked in a restaurant, you know how much tips are appreciated—but they need to be earned. Don't penalize a waitperson for the kitchen's mistakes or incompetence, but do reduce the tip if the service is sloppy. If for any reason you don't tip, do let a host or hostess know the reason, so you're not just considered chintzy.

Taxi drivers expect a 15 percent tip; airport porters expect at least $1 per bag, depending on the difficulty of the job. If a porter simply unloads a suitcase from a car, $0.50 is plenty; if he has to escort you to a ticket counter—and especially if he arranges for speedier service—a dollar per bag is appropriate.

The usual tip for housekeeping services in accommodations is $1–2 per person, per night, depending upon the level of service. It's not necessary to tip at B&Bs if the owners do the housekeeping.

Some accommodations add a 10- to 15-percent service fee to rates.

# TIPS FOR TIGHTWADS AND THE BUDGET CONSCIOUS

At first glance, Maine might seem pricey, but take another look. It is possible to keep a vacation within a reasonable budget, and here are a few tips for doing so.

For starters, avoid the big-name towns and seek out accommodations in smaller, nearby ones instead. For example, instead of Damariscotta, consider Waldoboro; instead of Camden, try Belfast or Searsport; in place of Bar Harbor, check Trenton or Southwest Harbor. Or simply explore the Down East Coast, where rates are generally far lower than in other coastal regions.

Small, family-owned motels tend to have the lowest rates. Better yet, book a cabin or cottage for a week, rather than a room by the night. Not only can you find reasonable weekly rentals – especially if you plan well in advance – but also you'll have cooking facilities, which allow you to avoid eating all meals out.

Speaking of food, buy or bring a small cooler so you can stock up at supermarkets and farmers markets for picnic meals. Most Hannaford and Shaw's supermarkets have large selections of prepared foods and big salad bars and bakeries, and many local groceries have pizza and sandwich counters.

Do check local papers and bulletin boards for Public Supper notices. Most are very inexpensive, raise money for a good cause, and provide an opportunity not only for a good meal, but also to meet locals and gain a few insider tips.

Of course, sometimes you want to have a nice meal in a nice place. Consider going out for lunch, which is usually far less expensive than dinner, or take advantage of early-bird specials or of the Friday night, all-you-can-eat fish fries offered at quite a few home-cooking restaurants.

Take advantage of Maine's vast outdoor-recreation opportunities; many are free. Even Acadia, with its miles and miles of trails and carriage roads, and its Explore bus service, is a bargain; buy a park pass and it's all yours to use and explore.

Instead of taking the family on a sailing excursion, hop aboard a ferry. State ferries to Vinalhaven and North Haven, from Rockland, and to Swan's Island, from Bass Harbor, and Casco Bay Lines, servicing the islands off Portland, are reasonably priced ways to get afloat.

Take advantage of free events: concerts, lectures, farmers markets, art shows and openings, and family events. Most are usually listed in local papers.

Avoid parking hassles and fees and save gas by using local transportation services when available, such as the trolley network on the Southern Coast and the Explorer bus system on Mount Desert Island.

Finally, before making reservations for anything, check to see if there's a special Internet rate or ask about any discounts that might apply to you: AAA, senior, military, government, family rate, and so forth. If you don't ask, you won't get.

## TOURISM INFORMATION AND MAPS
### Maine Tourism Association

The Maine Tourism Association (325 Water St., Hallowell, Maine 04347, 207/623-0363, www.mainetourism.com) publishes the free, annual magazine-style guidebook *Maine Invites You*, which details sights throughout the state and provides listings of chambers of commerce and other info helpful for travelers. Call, write, or visit the website to request a copy and a state map.

## State Visitors Information Centers

The Maine Tourism Association operates state visitors information centers in Calais, Fryeburg (May–October), Hampden, Houlton, Kittery, and Yarmouth. These are excellent places to visit to stock up on brochures, pick up a map, ask advice, and use restrooms.

## Maine Online

The Maine Office of Tourism has established an award-winning website: www.visitmaine.com.

You'll find chamber of commerce addresses, articles, photos, information on lodgings, and access to a variety of Maine tourism businesses. But hundreds of other Maine pages are also up and running, so surf away. You can use the website to request a free state map and copy of *Maine Invites You*. The state's toll-free information hotline is 888/MAINE-45 (888/624-6345).

## Local Chambers of Commerce and Tourism Offices

Tourism is Maine's second-largest source of revenue, so almost every community of any size has some kind of information office, varying from York's mansionlike quarters to tiny log cabins. Information on these is listed in the destination chapters.

## Maps

Peek in any Mainer's car, and you're likely to see a copy of *The Maine Atlas and Gazetteer*, published by DeLorme Mapping Company, in Yarmouth. Despite an oversize format inconvenient for hiking and kayaking, this 96-page paperbound book just about guarantees that you won't get lost (and if you're good at map reading, it can get you out of a lot of traffic jams). Scaled at one-half inch to the mile, it's meticulously compiled from aerial photographs, satellite images, U.S. Geological Survey maps, GPS readings, and timber-company maps, and it is revised annually. It details back roads and dirt roads and shows elevation, boat ramps, public lands, campgrounds and picnic areas, and trail heads. DeLorme products are available nationwide in book and map stores, but you can also order direct (800/452-5931, www.delorme.com). The atlas is $19.95 and shipping is $4 (Maine residents need to add 5 percent sales tax).

The Maine Tourism Association also publishes a less detailed but free state map.

## COMMUNICATIONS AND MEDIA
## Postal and Shipping Services

Post offices in Maine cities and towns are open six days a week, usually 8 A.M.–5 P.M. Monday–Saturday, although Saturday service in small communities typically is 8 A.M.–noon.

Cities and large towns have strategically placed Express Mail, UPS, and Federal Express boxes. To contact Federal Express, call 800/463-3339; to contact UPS, call 800/742-5877. Other national/international delivery services available in Maine are Airborne Express (800/247-2676) and DHL (800/225-5345). Ask locally about businesses that provide packing and shipping services.

If you expect to receive mail while visiting Maine, have your correspondents address it to you c/o General Delivery in the town or city where you expect to be and mark it "Hold for arrival on [your estimated arrival date]." Be sure to give them that post office's correct zip code (every post office has a national zip code directory; overseas residents can check with the nearest U.S. embassy or consulate, or log on to www.usps.com).

## Area Code

Maine still has only one telephone area code, 207. To call long distance in state and out of state, dial 1 plus the area code before the number. For directory assistance, dial 411.

## Toll-Free Calling

Any number with an area code of 800, 888, 877, 866, 855, 844, 833, or 822 is toll free.

## Cell Phones

When you're on vacation, a ringing telephone should be the absolute last thing you want to think about, but needs do arise, and cellular phones have become a fact of life. Transmission towers are now sprinkled everywhere in Maine; only a few pockets—mostly down peninsulas and in remote valleys and hollows—are out of cellular-phone range. That said, getting reception often requires doing the dance—moving left, right, up, and down to find the strongest signal.

## Internet Access

Internet access is widely available at libraries and coffeehouses. Most hotels and many inns and B&Bs also offer Internet access; many provide dataports or Wi-Fi.

# RESOURCES

## Glossary

To help you translate some of the lingo off the beaten track (e.g., country stores and county fairs, farmstands and flea markets), here's a sampling of local terms and expressions.

**alewives** herring

**ayuh** yes

**barrens** as in "blueberry barrens"; fields where wild blueberries grow

**beamy** wide (as in a boat or a person)

**beans** shorthand for the traditional Saturday-night meal, which always includes baked beans

**blowdown** a forest area leveled by wind

**blowing a gale** very windy

**camp** a vacation house (small or large), usually on freshwater and/or in the woods

**chance** serendipity or luck (as in "open by appointment or by chance")

**chicken dressing** chicken manure

**chowder (pronounced "chowdah")** soup made with lobster, clams, or fish, or a combination thereof; lobster version sometimes called lobster stew

**chowderhead** mischief or troublemakers, usually interchangeable with idiot

**coneheads** tourists (because of their presumed penchant for ice cream)

**cottage** a vacation house (anything from a bungalow to a mansion), usually on salt water

**culch (also cultch)** "stuff"; the contents of attics, basements, and some flea markets

**cull** a discount lobster, usually minus a claw

**cunnin'** cute (usually describing a baby or small child)

**dinner (pronounced "dinnah")** the noon meal

**dinner pail** lunch box

**dite** a very small amount

**dooryard** the yard near a house's main entrance

**Down East** with the prevailing wind; the old coastal sailing route from Boston to Nova Scotia

**downcellar** in the basement

**dry-ki** driftwood, usually remnants from the logging industry

**ell** a residential structural section that links a house and a barn; formerly a popular location for the "summer kitchen," to spare the house from woodstove heat

**exercised** upset; angry

**fiddleheads** unopened ostrich-fern fronds, a spring delicacy

**finest kind** top quality; good news; an expression of general approval; also, a term of appreciation

**flatlander** a person not from Maine, often but not exclusively someone from the Midwest

**floatplane** a small plane equipped with pontoons for landing on water; the same aircraft often becomes a skiplane in winter

**flowage** a water body created by damming, usually beaver handiwork (also called "beaver flowage")

**frappe** a thick drink containing milk, ice cream, and flavored syrup, as opposed to a milk shake, which does not include ice cream (but beware: a frappe offered in other parts of the United

States is an ice-cream sundae topped with whipped cream!)

**from away** not native to Maine

**galamander** a wheeled contraption formerly used to transport quarry granite to building sites or to boats for onward shipment

**gore** a sliver of land left over from inaccurate boundary surveys. Maine has several gores; Hibberts Gore, for instance, has a population of one.

**got done** quit a job; was let go

**harbormaster** local official who monitors water traffic and assigns moorings; often a very political job

**hardshell** lobster that hasn't molted yet (more scarce, thus more pricey in summer)

**hod** wooden "basket" used for carrying clams

**ice-out** the departure of winter ice from ponds, lakes, rivers, and streams; many communities have ice-out contests, awarding prizes for guessing the exact time of ice-out, in April or May

**Italian** long soft bread roll sliced on top and filled with peppers, onions, tomatoes, sliced meat, black olives, and sprinkled with olive oil, salt, and pepper; veggie versions available

**jimmies** chocolate sprinkles, like those on an ice-cream cone

**lobster car** a large floating crate for storing lobsters

**Maine Guide** a member of the Maine Professional Guides Association, trained and tested for outdoor and survival skills; also called Registered Maine Guide

**market price** restaurant menu term for "the going rate," usually referring to the price of lobster or clams

**molt** what a lobster does when it sheds its shell for a larger one; the act of molting is called ecdysis (as a stripper is an ecdysiast)

**money tree** a collection device for a monetary gift

**mud season** mid-March to mid-April, when back roads and unpaved driveways become virtual tank traps

**nasty neat** extremely meticulous

**near** stingy

**notional** stubborn, determined

**off island** the mainland, to an islander

**place** another word for a house (as in "Herb Pendleton's place")

**pot** trap, as in "lobster pot"

**public landing** see "town landing"

**rake** hand tool used for harvesting blueberries

**rusticator** a summer visitor, particularly in bygone days

**scooch (or scootch)** to squat; to move sideways

**sea smoke** heavy mist rising off the water when the air temperature suddenly becomes much colder than the ocean temperature

**select** a lobster with claws intact

**Selectmen** the elected men and women who handle local affairs in small communities; the First Selectman chairs meetings. In some towns, "people from away" have tried to propose substituting a gender-neutral term, but in most cases the effort has failed.

**shedder** a lobster with a new (soft) shell; generally occurs in July and August (more common then, thus less expensive than hardshells)

**shire town** county seat

**shore dinner** the works: chowder, clams, lobster, and sometimes corn on the cob, too; usually the most expensive item on a menu

**short** a small, illegal-size lobster

**slumgullion** tasteless food; a mess

**slut** a poor housekeeper

**slut's wool** dust balls found under beds, couches, and so on

**snapper** an undersize, illegal lobster

**softshell** see "shedder"

**soda** cola, root beer, and so on (often referred to as "pop" in other parts of the country

**some** very (as in "some hot")

**spleeny** overly sensitive

**steamers** clams (before or after they are steamed)

**sternman** a lobsterman's helper (male or female)

**summer complaint** a tourist

**supper (pronounced "suppah")** evening meal, eaten by Mainers around 5 or 6 P.M. (as opposed to flatlanders and summer people, who eat dinner between 7 and 9 P.M.)

**tad** slightly; a little bit

**thick-o'-fog** zero-visibility fog
**to home** at home
**tomalley** a lobster's green insides; considered a delicacy by some
**town landing** shore access; often a park or a parking lot, next to a wharf or boat-launch ramp

**upattic** in the attic
**Whoopie! Pie** the trademarked name for a high-fat, calorie-laden, cakelike snack that only kids and dentists could love
**wicked cold!** frigid
**wicked good!** excellent
**williwaws** uncomfortable feeling

# Suggested Reading

## DESCRIPTION AND TRAVEL

Batignani, K. W., *Maine's Coastal Cemeteries: A Historic Tour.* Camden, ME: Down East Books, 2004. A guide to 35 cemeteries with intriguing histories, unusual epitaphs, and notable carvings.

Bumsted, L. *Hot Showers! Maine Coast Lodgings for Kayakers and Sailors.* 2d ed. Brunswick, ME: Audenreed Press, 2000. Excellent, well-researched resource for anyone cruising the shoreline and yearning for alternatives to a sleeping bag. It offers some information on kayak access (but also see the *Recreation* section).

Calhoun, C. C., and T. M. Szelog. *Maine.* 4th ed. New York: Fodor's Travel Publications, Compass American Guides, 2000. Entertaining, literate prose; outstanding photography.

Curtis, W., and T. Seymour. *Maine: Off the Beaten Path.* 8th ed. Old Saybrook, CT: Globe Pequot Press, 2008. Introduction to offbeat and unexpected locales; a good supplementary guide for would-be explorers.

Dwelley, M. J. *Spring Wildflowers of New England.* 2d ed. Camden, ME: Down East Books, 2000. Back in print after several years, this beautifully illustrated gem is an essential guide for exploring spring woodlands.

Dwelley, M. J. *Summer and Fall Wildflowers of New England.* 2d ed. Camden, ME: Down East Books, 2004. Flowers are grouped by color; more than 700 lovely colored-pencil drawings simplify identification.

Hancock, T. *The Gardens of Maine.* Farmington, ME: Heritage Publishing, 1997. Parks, public gardens, and significant landscaping throughout the state. The biggest emphasis is on southern Maine.

Karlin, L., and R. Sawyer-Fay. *Gardens Maine Style.* Camden, ME: Down East Books, 2001. A beautiful book depicting and describing private and some public gardens.

*The Maine Atlas and Gazetteer.* Yarmouth, ME: DeLorme, updated annually. You'll be hard put to get lost if you're carrying this essential volume; 70 full-page (oversize format) topographical maps with GPS grids.

Morrison, P. M. *The Guide to Maine Golf Courses.* Camden, ME: Down East Books, 2000. Useful, descriptive information about Maine golf courses built before publication.

Nangle, H. *Moon Maine.* 4th ed. Berkeley, CA: Avalon Travel, 2008. Explore the far reaches of Maine with a Maine resident and veteran travel writer.

Pierson, E. C., J. E. Pierson, and P. D. Vickery. *A Birder's Guide to Maine.* Camden, ME: Down East Books, 1981. An expanded version of *A Birder's Guide to the Coast of Maine.* No ornithologist, novice or expert, should explore Maine without this valuable guide.

Taft, H., J. Taft, and C. Rindlaub. *A Cruising

*Guide to the Maine Coast.* 5th ed. Peaks Island, ME: Diamond Pass Publishing, 2007. Don't even consider cruising the coast without this volume.

Vietze, A. *Insiders' Guide to the Maine Coast.* 2d ed. Guilford, CT: Globe Pequot Press, 2004. Longtime *Down East* magazine editor Andy Vietze, who really *is* an insider, shares the results of his zillions of explorations.

## LITERATURE, ART, AND PHOTOGRAPHY

Curtis, J., W. Curtis, and F. Lieberman. *Monhegan: The Artists' Island.* Camden, ME: Down East Books, 1995. Fascinating island history interspersed with landscape and seascape paintings and drawings by more than 150 artists, including Bellows, Henri, Hopper, Kent, Porter, Tam, and Wyeth.

*Maine Speaks: An Anthology of Maine Literature.* Brunswick, ME: Maine Writers and Publishers Alliance, 1989.

McNair, W., ed. *The Maine Poets: An Anthology of Verse.* Camden, ME: Down East Books, 2003. McNair's selection of best works by Maine's finest poets.

Middleton, D., and B. Morrison. *The Photographers Guide to the Maine Coast.* Woodstock, VT: Countryman Press, 2004. Find out where to go, how to get there, when to go, and how to take perfect photos.

Spectre, P. H. *Passage in Time.* New York: W. W. Norton, 1991. A noted marine writer cruises the coast aboard traditional windjammers; gorgeous photos complement the colorful text.

Van Riper, F. *Down East Maine: A World Apart.* Camden, ME: Down East Books, 1998. Maine's Washington County, captured with incredible insight and compassion by a master photographer and insightful wordsmith.

## LOBSTER AND LIGHTHOUSES

Caldwell, W. *Lighthouses of Maine.* Camden, ME: Down East Books, 1986. A historical tour of Maine's lighthouses, with the emphasis on history, legends, and lore.

Corson, T. *The Secret Life of Lobsters.* New York: HarperCollins, 2004. Everything you wanted—or perhaps didn't want—to know about lobster.

Hartnett, R., and P. D. Bachelder. *Maine Lighthouse Map and Guide.* Howes Cave, NY: Hartnett House Map Publishers, 2000. An illustrated map and guide providing directions on how to find all Maine beacons as well as brief histories.

Thompson, C. *Maine Lighthouses: A Pictorial Guide.* 3d ed. Mount Desert, ME: CatNap Publications, 2001. What they look like, how to find them, and a bit of background detail.

## HISTORY

Duncan, R. F., E. G. Barlow, K. Bray, K., and C. Hanks. *Coastal Maine: A Maritime History.* Woodstock, VT: Countrymen Press, 2002. Updated version of the classic work.

Isaacson, D., ed. *Maine: A Guide "Down East."* 2d ed. n.p.: Maine League of Historical Societies and Museums, 1970. Revised version of the Depression-era WPA guidebook. Still interesting for background reading.

Judd, R. W., E. A. Churchill, and J. W. Eastman, eds. *Maine: The Pine Tree State from Prehistory to the Present.* Orono: University of Maine Press, 1995. The best available Maine history, with excellent historical maps.

Paine, L. P. *Down East: A Maritime History of Maine.* Gardiner, ME: Tilbury House, 2000. A noted maritime historian provides an enlightening introduction to the state's seafaring tradition.

## MEMOIRS

Dawson, L. B. *Saltwater Farm*. Westford, ME: Impatiens Press, 1993. Witty, charming stories of growing up on the Cushing peninsula.

Greenlaw, L. *The Lobster Chronicles: Life on a Very Small Island*. New York: Hyperion, 2002. Swordfishing boat Captain Linda Greenlaw's account of returning to life on Isle au Haut after weathering the *The Perfect Storm*.

Lunt, D. L. *Hauling by Hand: The Life and Times of a Maine Island*. Frenchboro, ME: Islandport Press, 1999. A sensitive history of Frenchboro (a.k.a. Long Island), eight miles offshore, written by an eighth-generation islander, now a journalist.

Peavey, E. *Maine and Me: 10 Years of Down East Adventures*. Camden, ME: 2004. A collection of essays and articles by a writer for *Down East* magazine.

Wass, P. B. *Lighthouse in My Life: The Story of a Maine Lightkeeper's Family*. Camden, ME: Down East Books, 1987. Offshore adventures, growing up on Libby Island, near Machias.

## NATURAL HISTORY

Bennett, D. *Maine's Natural Heritage: Rare Species and Unique Natural Features*. Camden, ME: Down East Books, 1988. A dated book that examines both the special ecology of the state and how it's threatened.

Conkling, P. W. *Islands in Time: A Natural and Cultural History of the Islands of the Gulf of Maine*. 2d ed. Camden, ME: Down East Books, and Rockland, ME: Island Institute, 1999. A thoughtful overview by the president of Maine's Island Institute.

Kendall, D. L. *Glaciers and Granite: A Guide to Maine's Landscape and Geology*. Unity, ME: North Country Press, 1993. Explains why Maine looks the way it does.

*Maine's Ice Age Trail Down East Map and Guide*.

Orono: University of Maine Press, 2007. Also available online at http://iceagetrail.umaine.ecu. Information on 46 glacial sites.

## RECREATION
### Hiking and Walking

*AMC Maine Mountain Guide*. 9th ed. Boston: Appalachian Mountain Club Books, 2005. The definitive statewide resource for going vertical. In a handy small format. (AMC has eliminated Acadia National Park and expanded its separate guide on Acadia's peaks.)

*Cobscook Trails: A Guide to Walking Opportunities around Cobscook Bay and the Bold Coast*. 2d ed. Whiting, ME: Quoddy Regional Land Trust, 2000. Essential handbook for exploring this part of the Down East Coast. Excellent maps.

Collins, J., and J. E. McCarthy. *Nature Walks in Southern Maine*. Boston: Appalachian Mountain Club Books, 1996. Easy walks, mostly horizontal, and good natural-history commentary. Maps are primitive but do the job.

Gibson, J. *50 Hikes in Coastal and Southern Maine*. 3d ed. Woodstock, VT: Countryman Press/Backcountry Guides, 2001. Well-researched, detailed resource by a veteran hiker.

Roberts, P. *On the Trail in Lincoln County*. Newcastle/Damariscotta, ME: Lincoln County Publishing, 2003. A great guide to more than 60 walks in preserves from Wiscasset through Waldoboro, with detailed directions to trailheads.

Seymour, T. *Hiking Maine*. 2d ed. Helena, MT: Falcon Press, 2002. Helpful—especially for less-well-known hikes in the Mid-Coast Region. Not as comprehensive, statewide, as the Gibson hiking guide or the *AMC Maine Mountain Guide*.

### Paddling

*AMC River Guide: Maine*. 3d ed. Boston: Appalachian Mountain Club Books, 2002. Detailed guide to canoeing or kayaking Maine's large and small rivers.

*The Maine Island Trail: Stewardship Handbook and Guidebook.* Rockland, ME: Maine Island Trail Association, updated annually. Available only with MITA membership (annual dues $45), providing access to dozens of islands along the watery trail.

Miller, D. *Kayaking the Maine Coast: A Paddler's Guide to Day Trips from Kittery to Cobscook.* 2nd ed. Woodstock, VT: Countryman Press/Backcountry Guides, 2006. A well-researched volume by a veteran kayaker. With her book and a copy of *Hot Showers!* (see *Description and Travel*), you're all set.

Wilson, A., and J. Hayes. *Quiet Water Canoe Guide, Maine: Best Paddling Lakes and Ponds for All Ages.* 2d ed. Boston: Appalachian Mountain Club Books, 2005. Comprehensive handbook, with helpful maps, for inland paddling.

## Bicycling

Stone, H. *25 Bicycle Tours in Maine: Coastal and Inland Rides from Kittery to Caribou.* 3d ed. Woodstock, VT: Countryman Press/Backcountry Guides, 1998.

# ACADIA NATIONAL PARK/ MOUNT DESERT ISLAND

Abrell, D. *A Pocket Guide to the Carriage Roads of Acadia National Park.* 2nd ed. Camden, ME: Down East Books, 1995.

Brechlin, E. D. *A Pocket Guide to Paddling the Waters of Mount Desert Island.* Camden, ME: Down East Books, 1996.

Gillmore, R. *Great Walks of Acadia National Park and Mount Desert Island.* Rev. ed. Goffstown, NH: Great Walks, 1994.

Helfrich, G. W., and G. O'Neil. *Lost Bar Harbor.* Camden, ME: Down East Books, 1982. Fascinating collection of historic photographs of classic, turn-of-the-century "cottages," many obliterated by Bar Harbor's Great Fire of 1947.

Minutolo, A. *A Pocket Guide to Biking on Mount Desert Island.* Camden, ME: Down East Books, 1996.

Monkman, J., and M. Monkman. *Discover Acadia National Park: A Guide to the Best Hiking, Biking, and Paddling.* Boston: Appalachian Mountain Club Books, 2000. A comprehensive guide to well-chosen hikes, bike trips, and paddling routes, accompanied by an excellent pullout map.

Nangle, H. *Moon Acadia National Park.* 2nd ed. Emeryville, CA: Avalon Travel Publishing, 2006. A Mainer since childhood and veteran travel writer is the ideal escort for exploring this region in depth.

Perrin, S. *Acadia: The Soul of a National Park.* North Atlantic Books, 2003. A wonderful guide to 60 hikes, with details and descriptions combined with the author's experiences.

Roberts, A. R. *Mr. Rockefeller's Roads.* Camden, ME: Down East Books, 1990. The story behind Acadia's scenic carriage roads, written by the granddaughter of John D. Rockefeller (who created them).

St. Germain, T. A., Jr. *A Walk in the Park: Acadia's Hiking Guide.* 10th ed. Bar Harbor, ME: Parkman Publications, 2004. The best Acadia National Park hiking guide, in a handy Michelin-type vertical format. Part of the proceeds go to Friends of Acadia's Acadia Trails Forever campaign.

# Internet Resources

## GENERAL INFORMATION

### State of Maine
www.maine.gov

Everything you wanted to know about Maine and then some, with links to all government departments and Maine-related sites. Among other information on this site is info on accessible arts and recreation.

### Maine Office of Tourism
www.visitmaine.com

The biggest and most useful of all Maine-related tourism sites, with sections for where to visit, where to stay, things to do, trip planning, packages, calendar of events, and a search capabilities. Also lodging specials and a comprehensive calendar of events.

### Maine Tourism Association
www.mainetourism.com

Find lodging, camping, restaurants, attractions, services, and more as well as links for weather, foliage, transportation planning, and chambers of commerce.

### Maine Information
www.maine.info

A privately operated site with a mother lode of links handy for vacation planners.

### Portland Papers
www.mainetoday.com

Home site for Maine's largest newspaper has current news as well as extensive information on travel, outdoor activities, entertainment, and sports.

### Maine Emergency Management Association
www.state.me.us/mema/weather/weather.htm

Five-day weather forecasts broken down by 32 zones.

### Island Institute
www.islandinstitute.org

The institute serves as a clearinghouse/advocate for Maine's islands; the website provides links to the major year-round islands.

## TRANSPORTATION

### Maine Department of Transportation
www.exploremaine.org

An invaluable site for trip planning, with information on and links to airports, rail service, bus service, automobile travel, and ferries, as well as links to other key travel-planning sites.

### Maine Department of Transportation
www.511maine.gov

Provides real-time information about major delays, accidents, road construction, and weather conditions. You can get the same info and more by dialing 511 in-state.

### Portland Maine Transportation Page
www.transportme.com

Provides information on all modes of transit to, from, and within Portland. You can connect to bus, train, and airport information, including schedules.

## PARKS AND RECREATION

### Department of Conservation, Maine Bureau of Parks and Lands
www.maine.gov/doc/parks

Information on state parks, public reserved lands, and state historic sites, details on facilities such as campsites, picnic areas, and boat launches. Make state campground reservations online.

### Acadia National Park
www.nps.gov/acad

Information on all sections of Acadia National Park. Make ANP campground reservations online.

### Maine Audubon
**www.maineaudubon.org**

Information about Maine Audubon's eco-sensitive headquarters in Falmouth and all of the organization's environmental centers statewide. Activity and program schedules are included.

### The Nature Conservancy
**www.nature.org/wherewework/northamerica/states/maine**

Information about Maine preserves, field trips, and events.

### Maine Land Trust Network
**www.mltn.org**

Maine has dozens of land trusts statewide managing lands that provide opportunities for hiking, walking, canoeing, kayaking, and other such activities.

### Healthy Maine Walks
**www.healthymainewalks.com**

Lists places for walking statewide.

### Maine Island Trail Association
**www.mita.org**

Information about the association and its activities along with membership details.

### Maine Professional Guides Association
**www.maineguides.org**

Find licensed and Registered Maine Guides for sporting adventures, including sea kayaking, hunting, fishing, and recreation (such as canoeing trips and wildlife safaris).

### Maine Association of Sea Kayaking Guides and Instructors
**www.maineseakayakguides.com**

Information and links to about two dozen members who meet state requirements to lead commercial trips.

### Bicycle Coalition of Maine
**www.bikemaine.org**

Tons of information for bicyclists, including routes, shops, events, organized rides, and much more.

### Golf Maine
**www.golfme.com**

Lists member courses, stay-and-play packages, and golf links statewide.

### Maine Birding
**www.mainebirding.net**

A must-visit site for anyone interested in learning more about birding in Maine, including news, checklists, events, forums, trips, and more.

### Maine Windjammer Association
**www.sailmainecoast.com**

Windjammer schooners homeported in Rockland, Camden, and Rockport belong to this umbrella organization; links to the websites of all the vessels for online and phone information and reservations.

### L. L. Bean
**www.llbean.com**

The mega-outdoor retailer not only sells equipment but also offers courses.

## ARTS AND ENTERTAINMENT

### Music
**www.mainemusic.org**

Comprehensive site covering almost everything having to do with music in the state, from performances and festivals to musicians, composers, and instrument makers.

### Maine Fiber Arts
**www.mainefiberarts.org**

Everything you wanted to know about fiber artists, farms producing fiber, fiber-related events and festivals, fiber-arts teachers, fiber-arts exhibitions, and more.

### Maine Archives and Museums
**www.mainemuseums.org**

Information on and links to museums, archives, historical societies, and historic sites in Maine.

### Maine Art Museum Trail
**www.maineartmuseums.org**

Information on art museums with significant

collections statewide, including Ogunquit Museum of Art (Ogunquit); Portland Museum of Art (Portland); Bowdoin College Museum of Art (Brunswick); and Farnsworth Art Museum (Rockland).

### Maine Maritime Heritage Trail
### www.maritimemaine.org

Information about and links to maritime museums, boatbuilding schools, lighthouses, historic homes, fishing, naval history, forts, historic sites, and much more.

## SHOPPING

### Maine Antiques Dealers Association
### www.maineantiques.org

Lists member dealers statewide by location and specialty and provides information on upcoming antiques events.

### Maine Antiquarian Booksellers Association
### www.mainebooksellers.org

Lists independent shops that specialize in used, antiquarian, and rare books.

## ACCOMMODATIONS

### Maine Innkeepers Association
### www.maineinns.com

Lodging search for member motels, hotels, inns, and B&Bs statewide and lodging specials.

### Maine Campground Owners Association
### www.campmaine.com

Find private campgrounds statewide.

## FOOD AND DRINK

### Maine Restaurant Association
### www.mainerestaurant.com

Statewide trade organization site provides searchable listings of member restaurants by name or location.

### Maine Department of Agriculture
### www.getrealmaine.com

Information on all things agricultural, including fairs, farmers markets, farm vacations, places to buy Maine foods, berry- and apple-picking sites, and more.

### Maine Lobster Promotion Council
### www.mainelobsterpromo.com

All lobster, all the time, with links for ordering Maine lobster and organizing your own lobster bake, plus recipes for preparing lobster in more ways than you ever thought possible.

### Wild Blueberry Association of North America
### www.wildblueberries.com

Information on blueberries as well as numerous recipes.

# Index

## A

Abbe Museum: 23, 307, 324
Abbott School: 282
Acadia National Park: general discussion 16; Isle au Haut 258, 302-303; itinerary tips 20, 23; maps 4-5; Mount Desert Island 315-322; park ranger programs 320-321; reading suggestions 464; Schoodic Peninsula section 20, 23, 360-363; tours 326; transportation services 304-305
Acadians: 429, 435-436
Acadia Region: general discussion 306, 309; Bar Harbor 322-338; Ellsworth 310-315; food/restaurants 25; itinerary tips 25; maps 308; Northeast Harbor 338-344; planning tips 309; Schoodic Peninsula 359-374; Southwest Harbor 344-354; see also Acadia National Park
accommodations: general discussion 449; see also vacation rentals; specific place
African Americans: 436
afternoon tea: 16, 321, 322
air travel: 444-446
Alamo Theatre: 260-261
alcoholic beverages: 449, 452
Aldermere Farm: 228
alewives: 174
algae: 425
allergies: 453
Alna: 154
Amato's: 24, 113
American Revolution: 429-430
Ames, Ted: 291
Ames Pond: 293
amusement parks: 14, 78
Androscoggin River Bicycle Path: 131
Anglers Restaurant: 25, 255
animals: Baker Island 318-319; boat excursions 200, 328; Boothbay Peninsula 162-163, 165; Brunswick 131; Calais 417-418; Campobello Island 402-403, 404; Deer Isle 292-293; educational programs 451; estuaries and mudflats 422; Freeport 117; itinerary tips 23; Machias Bay 392-393; Pemaquid Peninsula 180; Portland 99-100; shoreline and marine environment 425; tours 181
antiquarian bookstores: Camden-Rockport area 234; Castine 283; Damariscotta 182; Portland 105; Wells 26, 53
antiques: general discussion 14-15; Bath 147;

Blue Hill 267; Boothbay Peninsula 167; Brooklin area 275; Brunswick 134; Calais 419; Castine 283; Damariscotta 182; Deer Isle 297-298; Eastport 411; Ellsworth 312; itinerary tips 26-27; The Kennebunks 68; Schoodic Peninsula 360-361, 366; Searsport 253-254; Southwest Harbor 348; Thomaston 195; Wells 53; Wiscasset 156
Antiques on Nine: 26, 68
Anvil headland: 363
Aquaboggan Water Park: 78
archery: 120
architectural walking tours: 14, 62-63, 140, 153, 194-195, 245
architecture trail: 27
area codes: 458
Arey's Neck Woods: 221
Armbrust Hill Town Park: 222
Arnold, Benedict: 430
Arnold Trail, The: 430
Aroostook War: 431
Arrows: 24, 58
art galleries: general discussion 14-15; Belfast 247; Blue Hill 265; Boothbay Peninsula 166-167; Brooklin area 275-276; Brunswick 134; Calais 419; Castine 283; Damariscotta 182; Deer Isle 258, 295-297; Eastport 411-412; itinerary tips 19, 23; The Kennebunks 68; Machias Bay 390-391; North Haven 225; Ogunquit 50-51, 53; Pemaquid Peninsula 174-175; Portland 105; Rockland 214-215; Schoodic Peninsula 366; St. George Peninsula 200; Vinalhaven 223; Wiscasset 156
artist colonies/studios: 16, 206
art museums: general discussion 14-15, 438; Brunswick 128-129; Eastport 407; itinerary tips 27-28; Machias Bay 390-391; Maine Art Museum Trail 27; Ogunquit 30, 48, 438; Portland 19, 83, 92-93, 438; Rockland 192, 209, 211, 438; Waldoboro 178
arts and crafts: general discussion 438; Bar Harbor 329-330; Blue Hill 265; Boothbay Peninsula 166-167; Brooklin area 275-276; Brunswick 134; Damariscotta 182; Deer Isle 258, 289, 295-297; Portland 105; Schoodic Peninsula 360-361, 366; Searsport 254; Southwest Harbor 348; Wiscasset 156
Arts District (Portland): 111-112
Arundel Beach: 65
A. S. Fales and Son Store: 196-197

Asticou Azalea Garden: 16, 23, 307, 339-340
astronomical observatories: 410-411
Atlantic puffins: 425
Atlantic Seal Cruises: 83, 120
Audubon Ecology Camp: 180
automated teller machines (ATMs): 456
automobile museums: 51, 211, 345
Avalon Antiques Market: 26, 156

# B

Back Cove: 98
Back Cove Trail: 90
Backshore Beach: 283
Backwoods Mountain: 274
Bad Little Falls Park: 391
Bagaduce Ferry Landing: 274
Bagaduce Music Lending Library: 264, 266
Bailey Island: 97
Bailey's Mistake: 389
Baker Island: 318-319
bald eagles: 425
Bald Mountain: 231
Bald Rock Trail: 241
Bangor International Airport: 444, 445
banks: 456
Bar Harbor: general discussion 16, 322;
    accommodations 331-333; entertainment
    and events 330-331; food/restaurants 25,
    333-338; maps 323; outdoor recreation
    326-329; shopping 329-330; sightseeing
    tips 324-326; tours 326
Bar Harbor Historical Society: 325
Bar Harbor Whale Museum: 325
Bar Island: 326-327
barnacles: 425
Barnes, Kate: 443
Barred Island Preserve: 293
Barrett's Cove: 232
bars: 103-104
baseball: 102
Basin, the: 142-143
Bass Harbor Head Light: 344
Bass Harbor Light: 318
Bates-Morse Mountain Preserve: 142, 143-144
Bath: general discussion 15; accommodations
    147-150; entertainment and events 146-147;
    food/restaurants 150-152; itinerary tips 21,
    26; maps 140-141; outdoor recreation 138-
    143; shopping 147; sightseeing tips 139-140,
    142-143
Bath Iron Works: 139-140
Bay Island Sailing School: 450
Bayside: 92, 112-113, 245

Beachcroft Trail: 320
beaches: general discussion 14; Bath
    143-144; Brunswick 132; Castine 283; The
    Kennebunks 65; Lincolnville 241; Mount
    Desert Island 320; Ogunquit 51; Pemaquid
    Peninsula 180-181; Portland 98-99;
    Rockland 213; Schoodic Peninsula 366; St.
    George Peninsula 199; Swans Island 358;
    Vinalhaven 222; Wells 51; The Yorks 41-42;
    see also swimming
Beals Island: 383
Beam, Lura: 439
beanhole beans: 197
Bear Brook Trail: 320
Beatrix Farrand Garden: 325
bed-and-breakfasts: see accommodations;
    specific place
Beech Mountain Trail: 320
Beehive Trail: 320
bees: 453
Belfast: 243-250
Belfast City Park: 245-246
Bellows, George: 437
Ben and Bill's Chocolate Emporium: 25,
    333-334
Benedict Arnold Trail: 430
Berwick Academy: 35
Berwicks, The: 35-37
Beston, Henry: 439
bicycling: see biking
Biddeford: 76-77, 81
Biddeford City Theater: 79
Big Garden Island: 221
Big White Island: 221
biking: general discussion 14; Acadia National
    Park 303; Bar Harbor 327; Bath 145;
    Boothbay Peninsula 164; Brooklin area 274;
    Brunswick 131-132; Camden-Rockport area
    230-231; Casco Bay Islands 89; Castine
    282; itinerary tips 20, 23; The Kennebunks
    65-66; Machias Bay 392; North Haven 225;
    Pemaquid Peninsula 180; Portland 100;
    reading suggestions 464; rentals 327, 346;
    Rockland 214; Schoodic Peninsula 365;
    Searsport 252-253; Southwest Harbor 346;
    Vinalhaven 222; see also mountain biking
Birch Point Beach State Park: 213
Birch Point Trail: 379
Birdsacre: 23, 310-311
birds/birding: general discussion 14, 16; Bath
    143-144; Brunswick 131; Bucksport 261;
    Deer Isle 292-293; educational programs
    451; estuaries and mudflats 422; Freeport

117; Grand Lake Stream 416; itinerary tips 23; Machias Bay 392-393; Milbridge 379; Monhegan Island 206; Old Orchard Beach 77; Portland 99; tours 326; The Yorks 41
Biscay Pond: 181, 182
black-crowned night herons: 422
blackflies: 17
Black House: 310
Black Mountain: 364-365
Black Point Brook Loop: 391
Blacksmith Shop: 281
Blackwoods Campground: 322
bloodworm: 422
Blowing Cave: 62
blueberries: 442
Blueberry Hill (Schoodic Peninsula): 363
Blue Hill: 23, 263-271
Blue Hill Falls: 266
Blue Hill Heritage Trust: 266
Blue Hill Mountain: 258, 266
Blue Hill Peninsula: general discussion 15-16, 257-258; Blue Hill 263-271; Brooklin area 271-279; Bucksport 260-263; Castine 280-286; Isle au Haut 302-305; itinerary tips 23; maps 259; planning tips 258, 260
Blue Hill Town Park: 266
BlueJacket Shipcrafters: 15, 192, 251-252
blue mussels: 425
Blue Sky on York Beach: 24, 47
boating/boat excursions: general discussion 15, 16; Bar Harbor 328-329; Bath 145-146; Belfast 246; Blue Hill 266-267; Boothbay Peninsula 164; Brunswick 132-133; Camden-Rockport area 232-233; Castine 283; Deer Isle 294-295; educational programs 451; itinerary tips 20, 21; Jonesport area 386; The Kennebunks 66; lighthouses 181; lobster fishing 66, 101, 120, 329; Milbridge 380; Northeast Harbor 341; Ogunquit 52; Pemaquid Peninsula 181; Portland 101; rentals 347; Rockland 213-214; Southwest Harbor 347-348; St. George Peninsula 200
Boggs Schoolhouse: 177
Bok Amphitheatre: 229
bookstores: Belfast 247; Blue Hill 267; Boothbay Peninsula 167; Brunswick 134; Camden-Rockport area 234; Castine 283; Damariscotta 182; Deer Isle 298; Ellsworth 312; The Kennebunks 68; Portland 105; Rockland 215; Southwest Harbor 349; St. George Peninsula 200; Thomaston 195; Wells 53; see also antiquarian bookstores
Boon Island Light: 40

Booth, Philip: 443
Boothbay Peninsula: 15, 160-172
Boothbay Railway Village: 160
Boothbay Region Land Trust: 162-163
Booth Quarry: 222
border crossings: 405, 420
Boston Logan Airport: 446
botanical gardens: general discussion 16; Bar Harbor 324; Boothbay Peninsula 163; itinerary tips 23, 27-28; Northeast Harbor 307, 339-340; Southwest Harbor 345
Bowdoin College: 15, 126, 128-129
Bowdoin College Museum of Art: 128-129
Bradbury Mountain State Park: 118
Bradley Pond Farm Preserve: 131
Brave Boat Harbor: 33
Bresca: 24, 110
brewpubs: Bar Harbor 335; Portland 103-104
Brick Store Museum, The: 62
Bristol Mills: 181
Broad Cove Church: 197
Brooklin: 271-279
Brooksville: 271-279
Brown's Head Light: 220-221
Brunswick: general discussion 15; accommodations 135-136; entertainment and events 133-134; food/restaurants 136-138; itinerary tips 26; outdoor recreation 130-133; shopping 134; sightseeing tips 128-130
Brunswick Hydro generating station: 130
Brunswick Literary Art Walk: 130
Brunswick-Topsham Land Trust: 131
Brunswick Women's History Trail: 130
Bubble Pond: 317
Bucksport: 260-263
Bucksport Waterfront Walkway: 261
budget tips: 457
bug repellent: 18
Burnham Tavern: 390
Burning Tree: 25, 337
Burnthead Trail: 206
Burnt Island Tour: 15, 21, 126, 160-161
Bush Estate: 62
bus service: 446, 447
Butler Preserve: 65
butterflies: 162, 345
Byelorussians: 436

# C

Cabot Mill Antiques: 26, 134
Cadillac Mountain: 20, 316-317
Calais: 20, 22, 415-420

Calais-Robbinston milestones: 417
Calais Waterfront Walk: 418
calm-water paddling: see canoeing
Camden Amphitheatre: 229
Camden Area History Center: 228
Camden Harbor Park: 229
Camden Hills State Park: 15, 20, 192, 229, 231, 237
Camden-Rockport area: 22, 226-240
Camp Ellis: 76, 80
camping/campgrounds: Acadia National Park 304; Bath 149-150; Belfast 249; Boothbay Peninsula 169; Bucksport 262; Calais 420; Camden-Rockport area 237; Deer Isle 299-300; Eastport 413; Ellsworth 313; Freeport 118, 122; Jonesport area 388; Lubec 400-401; Milbridge 382; Mount Desert Island 321-322; Pemaquid Peninsula 187; Schoodic Peninsula 371-372; Searsport 255; Southwest Harbor 351-352; St. George Peninsula 201-202; Thomaston 195; The Yorks 44-45
Campobello Island: 402-405
canoeing: general discussion 14, 16; Bath 146; Blue Hill 267; Brooklin area 274-275; Bucksport 261; Camden-Rockport area 230-231; Eastport 410; educational programs 451; Freeport 118, 120; Grand Lake Stream 416; The Kennebunks 66; Lincolnville 241; Machias Bay 392; Ogunquit 52; Pemaquid Peninsula 181-182; Portland 99; reading suggestions 463-464; rentals 52, 66, 120; Schoodic Peninsula 365; Southwest Harbor 346-347; Wiscasset 155
Cape Elizabeth: 14, 19, 97
Cape Elizabeth Light: 21
Cape Neddick: 24, 44
Cape Porpoise: 62
Cape Rosier: 274
Captain Alfred Skolfield Nature Preserve: 131
Captain and Patty's Piscataqua River Tours: 33
Caribou Mountain: 364-365
Carpenter, William: 443
Carpenter's Boatshop: 450
Carriage-Road System: 16, 307, 318
Carroll, Gladys Hasty: 439
Carson, Rachel: 438-439
car travel: general discussion 14, 446, 447-449; driving regulations 448-449; rentals 448
Casco Bay Islands: 88-89, 97
Casco Bay Tour: 14, 19, 83, 97
Castine: 16, 23, 280-286
Castine Historic Tour: 258, 280-282

Castle Tucker: 26, 153
Caterpillar Hill: 274
Cathedral Woods Trail: 206
Causeway Beach: 293
cell phones: 458
cemeteries: Bath 142; Blue Hill 264; Machias Bay 390; Portland 92, 99
Center for Furniture Craftsmanship: 451
Center for Maine Contemporary Art: 228
Center Pond Preserve: 144
Centre Street Congregational Church: 390
Chamberlain, Joshua L.: 129
Chamberlain Museum: 15, 130
chambers of commerce: 458
Champlain, Samuel de: 428, 438
Chapman-Hall House: 174
Charles Pond: 144
Charlotte Rhoades Park and Butterfly Garden: 345
charters: 146, 348
Chase, Mary Ellen: 439
Cherryfield Historic District: 380
Chester Pike's Galley: 25, 373
Chickawaukee Lake: 213
children's literature: 443
Children's Museum of Maine: 95
chocolate shops: 419
Christmas Cove: 181
Church, Frederic Edwin: 437
churches, historic: 175-176
cinemas: Bar Harbor 330-331; Bucksport 260-261; Calais 418
Civil War: 28, 88, 130, 431
clambakes: 170
clams: 422
Cliff Island: 97
Cliff Path: 40-41
Cliff Trail (Acadia National Park): 303
Cliff Trail (Monhegan Island): 206
climate: 17-18, 423-424, 426
clothing tips: 18
Coastal Maine Botanical Gardens: 126, 163
Coastal Mountains Land Trust: 228
Coastal Trail: 391
Coatsworth, Elizabeth: 439
Cobscook: 23, 398
cod: 425
Coffin Pond: 132
Coleman Pond: 241
Colombia Falls: 23
Colonial Pemaquid State Historic Site: 126, 175
Colony Beach: 65
comedy clubs: 104

common eiders: 425

Compass Harbor: 327

concerts: Bar Harbor 330; Bath 146; Berwick 36; Blue Hill 267-268; Boothbay Peninsula 166; Brunswick 133-134; Calais 418; Camden-Rockland area 233; Eastport 411; Freeport 120; The Kennebunks 67; Kittery 33; Lubec 399; Machias Bay 393; Milbridge 381; Ogunquit 52-53; Old Orchard Beach 79; Portland 102-103; Schoodic Peninsula 368; The Yorks 42; see also music

Congress Street: 91

cooking classes: 278

Cooney, Barbara: 443

Corea: 365

Corea Heath Unit: 359-360

cottages: see specific place

Counting House: 36-37

Country Store Museum: 345

Cox Pinnacle: 131

Craig Brook National Fish Hatchery: 261

Cramer Museum: 227-228

Cramer Park: 229

Cranberry Isles: 355, 357

Cranberry Point Drive: 402

credit cards: 456

Crescent Beach State Park: 51, 90

Crockett Cove Woods Preserve: 292

cross-country skiing: Freeport 117, 120; Grand Lake Stream 416; Rockland 211; Searsport 252

cruises: general discussion 14; Bar Harbor 328-329; Bath 145-146; Belfast 246; Boothbay Peninsula 164; Brooklin area 275; Bucksport 262; Camden-Rockport area 232-233; Castine 283; Eastport 409-410; island cruises 307, 347-348; itinerary tips 20, 21; Jonesport area 386; Milbridge 380; Pemaquid Peninsula 181; Portland 83, 101-102; Southwest Harbor 347-348; St. George Peninsula 200; see also windjammer cruises

cultural-heritage trails: 27-28, 130

Cumberland and Oxford Canal: 92

curling: 246

currency/currency exchange: 456

Curtis Island: 229-230

Cushing Peninsula: 196-198

Cutler Coast Public Reserve: 391-392

Cutler Road: 389

cycling: see biking

## D

Damariscotta: 172, 173, 187-189

Damariscove Island: 163-164

Darling Marine Research Center: 176

Davey, Randall: 437

Davistown Museum: 244

Day's Antiques: 26, 134

deep-sea fishing: general discussion 14; Eastport 410; Ogunquit 52; Southwest Harbor 347

Deering Oaks: 98

Deer Isle: 15-16, 23, 286-301

Deer Isle Granite Museum: 290

Deer Isle Village: 295-296

demographics: 434-436

Desert of Maine: 119

Devil's Head: 418

Diamond Cove: 88

discount shopping: 156-157, 234, 313

Discovery Trail: 179

Dive-In Theater Boat Cruise: 307, 328

Dixon Memorial Rock: 365

Dock Square: 19, 30, 63, 67

Dodge Point Preserve: 179

dog whelks: 425

Donnell Pond Public Reserved Land: 364, 372

Dorr Museum of Natural History: 325

Douglas N. Harding Rare Books: 26, 53

Down East Coast: general discussion 16, 375-376, 378; Calais 415-420; Campobello Island 402-405; Eastport 406-415; Grand Lake Stream 416-417; Jonesport area 383-388; Lubec 396-401; Machias Bay 388-395; maps 377; Milbridge 378-382

Downeast Heritage Center: 415

Downeast Institute for Applied Marine Research and Education: 386

Downeast Observatory: 410-411

Downtown Arts District: 91

Drakes Island Beach: 51

Dresden: 154

Dromore Burying Ground: 142

Duck Harbor Mountain: 303

Duck Harbor Mountain Trail: 303

Duck Harbor Trail: 302

dunes: 143, 144

Dyce's Head Lighthouse: 281

## E

Eagle Hill Bog: 403

Eagle Island: 89, 102, 120, 132-133

Eagle Lake: 317

eagles: 425

earth-friendly products: 68

East End: 91-92, 113-114

East End Beach: 98

East End Point: 89
Eastern Cemetery: 92
Eastern Promenade Trail: 90
East Machias: 389
East Point Sanctuary: 30, 77
Eastport: 20, 22, 406-415
East Quoddy Head Light: 404
Echo Lake: 320
Eckstorm, Fannie Hardy: 439
economy: 433-434
Edgar Tennis Preserve: 292
educational programs: 450-451
Eggemoggin Reach Regatta: 276
Eighth Maine Regimental Memorial: 88
Eliot Mountain Trail: 340
Ellsworth: 310-315
Emerson Hall: 282
Emmons Preserve: 65
endangered species: 425
entertainment: *see specific place*
estuaries: 422
Ethel H. Blum Gallery: 325
European exploration and settlement: 427-429
Evergreen Cemetery: 99

# F

Fabbri picnic area: 316
factory outlets: 14, 116-117
Fairy Head Loop: 391
falcons: 422
Fales's Store: 196-197
fall foliage: general discussion 424; Blue Hill
    266; Milbridge 379-380; planning tips 17
Falmouth: 99-100
Family Nature Camp: 451
farmers markets: general discussion 442;
    Bar Harbor 334; Bath 147; Blue Hill 270;
    Boothbay Peninsula 170; Brunswick 137;
    Calais 420; Camden-Rockport area 238;
    Damariscotta 187; Deer Isle 300; Eastport
    414; The Kennebunks 73; Machias Bay
    394; Milbridge 382; Northeast Harbor
    343; Portland 109; Rockland 217; Schoodic
    Peninsula 372; Wells 58; The Yorks 46
Farnsworth Art Museum and the Wyeth Center:
    15, 192, 209, 211, 438
Farnsworth Homestead: 209, 211
fauna: *see* wildlife
Fernald's Neck Preserve: 230
Ferry Beach State Park: 77
ferry service: general discussion 446;
    Brunswick 132; Campobello Island 407;
    Cranberry Isles 357; Eastport 407;
    Lincolnville 241; North Haven 226; Portland
    115; Rockland 214; Schoodic Peninsula 374;
    Swans Island 359
festivals and events: Bar Harbor 331; Bath 146-
    147; Belfast 247; Blue Hill 268; Boothbay
    Peninsula 166; Brooklin area 276; Brunswick
    134; Calais 418-419; Camden-Rockport
    area 233-234; Deer Isle 298; Eastport 411;
    Grand Lake Stream 417; Jonesport 386;
    The Kennebunks 67; Lubec 399; Machias
    Bay 393; Milbridge 381; Ogunquit 53; Old
    Orchard Beach 79-80; Pemaquid Peninsula
    182; Portland 104-105; Schoodic Peninsula
    368; Southwest Harbor 349; Thomaston
    195; Wiscasset 155-156; The Yorks 42
fiddleheads: 442
Fifth Maine Regiment Center: 88
fine arts: 437-438; *see also* art galleries; arts
    and crafts
Fine Sand Beach: 358
Finns: 436
fireworks: 79
First Church: 245
First Parish Church: 130
Fisherman's Museum: 21, 174
Fisherman's Walk: 41
fish/fishing: general discussion 14, 16, 425; Bath
    146; Brunswick 130; charters 146; commercial
    fishing 434; deep-sea fishing 52, 347;
    educational facilities 198-199; fish hatcheries
    261; fly fishing 120, 416; Grand Lake Stream
    416-417; The Kennebunks 66; Searsport 252;
    sportfishing 66; The Yorks 42
Five Fifty-Five: 24, 112
Flash in the Pans Community Steel Band: 15,
    23, 258, 276
flatlanders: 434-435
flea markets: 26-27, 147
flightseeing tours: Ellsworth 311-312; Rockland
    212
Flo's Steamed Dogs: 24, 45
flounder: 425
Flye Point Music and Arts Festival: 276
fly fishing: 120, 416
fog: 426
food/restaurants: general discussion 449;
    itinerary tips 24-25; Maine specialties 442;
    *see also* lobsters/lobster dinners; *specific
    place*
Footbridge Beach: 51
Fore River Sanctuary: 98-99
Fore Street: 24, 111
Fort Allen Park: 98

Fort Baldwin: 142
Fort Edgecomb: 155
Fort Foster: 32-33
Fort George State Park: 281
Fort Knox State Historic Site: 23, 192, 252-253
Fort Madison: 282
Fort McClary Historic Site: 32
Fort McKinley: 88
Fort O'Brien State Memorial: 390
Fort Point Light: 252
Fort Point State Park: 252
Fort Popham Historic Site: 142, 143
Fort Pownall: 252
Fort William Henry: 126, 175
Fort Williams Park: 19
Four Seasons Farm: 273
Fox Hill Drive: 402
Francine Bistro: 25, 239
Franco Americans: 435-436
Frazer Point Picnic Area: 362
Freeport: general discussion 14;
    accommodations 120-122; entertainment
    and events 120; food/restaurants 122-124;
    itinerary tips 20, 21; outdoor recreation
    117-120; shopping 116-117
Frenchboro: 356
Frenchboro Historical Society Museum: 356
Friar's Head picnic area: 402
Friends of Acadia (FOA): 317
frostbite: 454-455
Funtown/Splashtown USA: 78
furniture stores: 283-284

## G

galamanders: 219-220
gardens and landscapes: general discussion 16;
    Bar Harbor 324, 325; Boothbay Peninsula
    163; Camden-Rockport area 230; itinerary
    tips 23, 27-28; Northeast Harbor 307, 339-
    340; Southwest Harbor 345; tours 331
Gates House: 390
Geary's Beach: 222
geography: 423
geology: 421-423
George B. Dorr Museum of Natural History: 325
Georges Highland Path, The: 231-232
Georges River Land Trust, The: 228
Georges River Scenic Byway: 244
Georgetown Peninsula: 149
Ghostly Tours: 40
Giant Stairs: 131
Gilsland Farm: 99-100
glaciation: 421-422

Gleason Cove: 409
Glidden Midden: 179
glider flights: 212, 312
glossary: 459-461
glossy ibis: 422
Goat Island Light: 40, 62
Goat Trail: 303
Goldenrod, The: 24
golf courses: Bar Harbor 327-328; Bath 145;
    Belfast 246; Brunswick 132; Bucksport 262;
    Calais 418; Camden-Rockport area 232;
    Campobello Island 403; Castine 283; Deer
    Isle 294; Eastport 409; The Kennebunks
    66; Machias Bay 392; Ogunquit 52; Old
    Orchard Beach 77, 79; Pemaquid Peninsula
    180; Portland 100; Rockland 213; Schoodic
    Peninsula 366; Southwest Harbor 347; The
    Yorks 41
Gooch's Beach: 65
Good Life Center, The: 258, 272-273
Googins Island: 118
Goose Rocks Beach: 65
Gorham Mountain Trail: 319-320
Gould, John: 441
Gouldsboro: 361
government: 433
Grand Lake Stream: 16, 416-417
granite quarries: 286, 290
Grant Park: 326
great black-backed gulls: 425
great blue herons: 422
Great Chebeague Island: 88-89, 97
Great Cranberry Island: 355
Great Diamond Island: 88, 97
Great Harbor Maritime Museum: 341
Great Head Trail: 319
Great Pond Mountain: 261
Great Wass Island Preserve: 16, 23, 376, 383
green herons: 422
Grindle Point Light: 241
Grindstone Neck: 365
Grumbach, Doris: 440
Guided Island Tours: 294-295
guided trips: Castine 23; Deer Isle 294-295;
    sea kayaking 23
gulls: 425
Gut, The: 177
G. W. Hodson Park: 230

## H

haddock: 425
hake: 425
halibut: 425

Hamilton Beach: 89
Hamilton Cove Preserve: 398
Hamilton House: 36
Hamilton Sanctuary: 143
Hancock: 360
handicrafts: see arts and crafts
hand-sewn shoes: 412
Harbor Park: 213
harbor seals: 425
Harbor Walk: 41
Harrington House: 119-120
Harrington Meeting House: 175
Hartley, Marsden: 437
Hassam, Childe: 437
Haystack Mountain School of Crafts: 16, 258, 289, 438
Head Beach: 144
Head Tide Church: 154
Head Tide Village: 154
health care: 452-455
Hearse House: 281
helicopter tours: 212, 312
Henderson Natural Area: 282
Hendricks Hill Museum: 162
Henri, Robert: 437
Heritage Park: 246
herons: 422
herring: 425
Herring Cove Provincial Park: 403
herring gulls: 425
Herring Gut Learning Center: 198-199
hiking: general discussion 14, 16; Acadia National Park 302-303; Bar Harbor 326-327; Bath 143-145; Boothbay Peninsula 162-163; Brooklin area 274; Brunswick 131; Bucksport 261-262; Calais 417-418; Camden-Rockport area 229-230, 231-232; Campobello Island 402-403; Castine 282; Deer Isle 292-293; Freeport 117-118; Grand Lake Stream 416; itinerary tips 20, 23; Jonesport 383; The Kennebunks 64-65; Lincolnville 241; Lubec 396, 398-399; Machias Bay 391-392; Milbridge 379; Monhegan Island 206; Mount Desert Island 316-317, 319-320; Old Orchard Beach 77; packing tips 18; Pemaquid Peninsula 178-180; Phippsburg 143-145; Portland 90-91, 100; reading suggestions 463; Schoodic Peninsula 363; self-guided trails 144; Wells 49-50; The Yorks 41
historical background: 426-432
historic churches: 175-176
historic homes: general discussion 14; Belfast 245; Blue Hill 264; Castine 280-281; Damariscotta 174; Deer Isle 289-290; Freeport 119-120; Jonesport 383, 385; The Kennebunks 62-63; Portland 94, 96; Sedgwick 272; Thomaston 194; tours 39; Wiscasset 153, 155
Historic Meetinghouse Museum: 51
hitchhiking: 449
Hockamock Head Light: 358
Hockomock Nature Trail: 180
Hodgdon Pond: 320
Hodson Park: 230
Hog Island: 180
Hog Island Audubon Camp: 451
Holbrook Island Sanctuary State Park: 258, 274
Hollingsworth Trail: 379
Holt House: 264
Holt Mill Pond Preserve: 293
H.O.M.E. (Homeworkers Organized for More Employment): 261
Homer, Winslow: 91, 437
Hopper, Edward: 437
horseback riding: 118-119
Horseshoe Trail: 144
hospitals: see medical services; specific place
hostels: 333; see also accommodations; specific place
hotels: see accommodations; specific place
Hubbard Cottage: 402
Huber Preserve: 221
Hugo's: 24, 114
Hulls Cove Visitor Center: 315-316
Humboldt Field Research Institute: 381
hunting: 416
hunting season safety: 455
hurricanes: 424, 426
hypothermia: 454-455

**I**

ice cream: 442
ice harvest: 177
ice hockey: 102
ice-skating: 99
Indian Point/Blagden Preserve: 327
Indians: see Native Americans
Indian Wars, The: 429
indigenous peoples: 426-427, 435
indoor pools: 283
Inland Trail: 391
inns: see accommodations; specific place
insects: 18
Internet access: 458
Internet resources: 465-467
island cruises: 307, 347-348

Isle au Haut: 16, 23, 258, 302-305
Isle au Haut Boat Company: 294, 304-305
Isle au Haut Mountain: 221
Islesboro: 240-241
Islesford: 355
Islesford Historical Museum: 355
itinerary tips: 19-28

## J

James P. White House: 245
Jasper Beach: 389, 391
Jewell Falls: 98
Jewett, Sarah Orne: 35-36, 198, 439
John Perkins House: 280-281
Johnson, Eastman: 437
Johnson Memorial Park: 213
Jones Beach: 366
Jonesport: 20, 23, 383-388
Jordan Pond House: 16, 23, 307, 316-317, 321, 322
Jordan Pond House Popovers: 321
Jordan Pond Nature Trail: 319
Josephine Newman Sanctuary: 144
Joshua L. Chamberlain Museum: 15, 130
Josselyn, John: 438
Just Barb's: 25, 255-256

## K

kayaking: 155; see also sea kayaking
Kennebunk Beach: 65
Kennebunkport: 14, 19, 65
Kennebunks, The: accommodations 68-72;
    entertainment and events 67; food/
    restaurants 72-75; maps 61; outdoor
    recreation 65-66; shopping 67-68;
    sightseeing tips 60, 62-65
Kent, Rockwell: 437
Kienbusch, William: 437
King, Stephen: 438
Kittery: 32-35
Kittery Historical and Naval Museum: 32
Knight's Pond: 241
Kuhn, Walt: 437

## L

Lachaise, Gaston: 437
Lady Pepperrell House: 32
Laite Beach Park: 232
Lake Pemaquid: 182
Lake St. George State Park: 244
Lake Wood: 320
Lamoine State Park: 313
Lane, Fitz Hugh: 437

Lane's Island Preserve: 221-222
Langlais, Bernard: 196
Laudholm Farm: 30, 49-50
La Verna Preserve: 180
Lawson's Quarry: 222
Le Domaine: 25, 373
Libby Island Light: 389
Liberty: 244
Liberty Graphics Outlet Store: 244
Liberty Point Drive: 402
Liberty Post Office: 244
Liberty Tool Company: 27, 244
Library Park: 143
Lighthouse Depot: 21, 40, 53-54
lighthouses: general discussion 14-16;
    Biddeford 40; boat excursions 181;
    Calais 416-417; Campobello Island 404; Castine
    281; Deer Isle 290; itinerary tips 19, 21-22;
    Jonesport area 383; The Kennebunks 40,
    62; Lincolnville 241; Lubec 396, 398; Machias
    Bay 389; Monhegan Island 205; Mount
    Desert Island 318; museums 22, 23, 198, 211;
    Pemaquid Peninsula 174-175; Portland 40;
    Rockland 211, 212; Searsport 252; Southwest
    Harbor 344; St. George Peninsula 198;
    Swans Island 358; tours 40; Vinalhaven 220-
    221; Wells 40, 53-54; The Yorks 39, 40
Lily Pond: 293-294
Lincoln County Jail and Museum: 155
Lincolnville: 26, 240-243
Lincolnville Beach: 241
Linekin Preserve: 163
Literary Art Walk: 130
literature: 438-441, 443
little blue herons: 422
Little Cape Point Trail: 383
Little Chebeague Island: 89, 97
Little Cranberry Island: 355
Little Deer Isle: 295
Little Diamond Island: 97
Little Mayberry Cove Trail: 416
live music: see concerts; music
L. L. Bean: 14, 20, 21, 83, 116-117
L. L. Bean Outdoor Discovery Schools: 83, 120
lobsters/lobster dinners: general discussion
    14-16, 425, 440-441; Bar Harbor 337-338;
    Bath 151; Belfast 250; Blue Hill 270; boat
    excursions 83, 329; Boothbay Peninsula
    170; Brunswick 138; Deer Isle 290, 301;
    Ellsworth 314; Freeport 123-124; Frenchboro
    356; itinerary tips 21, 25; The Kennebunks
    75; Kittery 35; lobsterboats 66, 101; lobster
    hatchery 290, 292; Monhegan Island 208;

Ogunquit 57; Pemaquid Peninsula 126, 189; Portland 101, 110, 114-115; Schoodic Peninsula 374; Southwest Harbor 354; St. George Peninsula 202; tours 21; Wells 58-59; Wiscasset 157-158; The Yorks 47; *see also* food/restaurants
Longfellow, Henry Wadsworth: 94, 441
Long Island: 97, 356
Loop Trail: 117
Lubec: 20, 23, 396-401
Lubec breakwater: 398
Lubec Historical Society Museum: 397
Lucky Catch Lobster Tours: 21
Lyme disease: 50, 453

# M

Machias Bay: 388-395
Machias River: 392
Machias Seal Island Puffin Tour: 16, 23, 376, 386, 392-393
Mackworth Island: 100
Maiden's Cliff Trail: 229
mail boats: 21, 97
Main Beach: 51
Maine Antique Toy and Art Museum: 178
Maine Architecture Trail: 27
Maine Archives and Museum Directory: 28
Maine Art Museum Trail: 27
Maine Central Model Railroad: 385
Maine Coastal Islands National Wildlife Refuge: 16, 376, 379
Maine Discovery Center: 211
Maine Garden and Landscape Trail: 27-28
Maine History Gallery: 94
Maine Institute for the Healing Arts Herb Garden: 230
Maine Island Trail: 288, 293
Maine Lighthouse Museum: 22, 211
Maine Maritime Academy: 281
Maine Maritime Heritage Trail: 28
Maine Maritime Museum: general discussion 15, 126, 140; boat excursions 145-146; entertainment and events 147; itinerary tips 20, 21, 26
Maine Media Workshops: 450-451
Maine Narrow Gauge Railroad Company and Museum: 94
Maine Online: 457-458
Maine Outdoor Sculpture Guide: 28
Maine Scenic Byway: 364
Maine Sea Coast Mission: 339
Maine State Ferry Service: 214, 226, 359
Maine State Prison Showroom Outlet: 195

Maine Tourism Association: 457
Maine Turnpike: 59
Maine Wildlife Park: 117
Main Street (Castine): 281-282
Main Street Historic District (Rockland): 212
Manana Island: 204
maple syrup: 442
maps: map libraries 96; retail sources 458
Marginal Way: 30, 48-49
Marie Reed Memorial Park: 212
Marin, John: 437
marine environment: 425
Marine Park: 229
Marine Resources Aquarium: 161-162
Maritime Heritage Trail: 28
Marshall Point Lighthouse Museum: 22, 198
marshes: 99, 144
Mary-Lea Park: 229
Massacre Pond: 99
Mast Landing Sanctuary: 117
McCloskey, Robert: 443
McCurdy Smokehouse: 397
medical services: 452-453
Meissner, Leo: 437
Menigawum (Stratton Island) Preserve: 182
MERI Center for Marine Studies: 266
merlins: 422
Merrill Auditorium: 102
Merrill House: 272
Merryspring Park: 229
microbreweries: 95-96, 335
Mid-Coast region: general discussion 15, 125-126; Bath 139-152; Boothbay Peninsula 160-172; Brunswick 128-138; maps 127; Pemaquid Peninsula 172-190; planning tips 126-127; Wiscasset 153-159
Middle Beach: 65
Middle Mountain Park: 221
Milbridge: 378-382
Milbridge Historical Society Museum: 379
Millay, Edna St. Vincent: 441
Miniature Village: 290
Mistake Island: 383
mobile phones: 458
model railroads: 385
money: 456
Monhegan Historical and Cultural Museum: 205-206
Monhegan Island: general discussion 15, 203-208; accommodations 206-207; boat excursions 181, 200; food/restaurants 207-208; itinerary tips 20, 22; sightseeing tips 205-206; visitor rules 204

Monhegan Lighthouse: 205
Monhegan Museum: 192, 205-206
Montpelier: 194
Montsweag Flea Market: 26, 147
Montsweag Preserve: 144-145
Moody: 48
Moody Beach: 51
Moore, Ruth: 439
Moosehorn National Wildlife Refuge: 417-418
Moose Peak Light: 383
Moose Point State Park: 252
motels: see accommodations; specific place
Mother's Beach: 65
mountain biking: Freeport 118; rentals 52; see also biking
Mountain Trail: 118
Mount Desert Festival of Chamber Music: 342
Mount Desert Island: general discussion 16, 315-316; accommodations 321-322; food/restaurants: 25, 322; itinerary tips 20, 23; maps 4-5; outdoor recreation 319-321; reading suggestions 464; sightseeing tips 316-319
Mount Desert Island Biological Laboratory: 325-326
Mount Desert Island Historical Society Museum and Gardens: 345
Mt. Agamenticus: 41
Mt. Battie: 20, 229
Mt. Battie Trail: 229
mudflats: 422
Mud Hole Trail: 383
Mulholland Market: 397
Mulholland Point Lighthouse: 398
Mulholland Point picnic area: 402
mummichogs: 422
Munjoy Hill: 91-92
Museum at Portland Head Light: 97
museum directory: 28
Museum in the Streets: 194-195, 245
Museum of African Culture: 94-95
music: Bar Harbor 330; Blue Hill 267-268; Brooklin area 276; Brunswick 133-134; Calais 418; Castine 284; Eastport 411; educational programs 451; The Kennebunks 67; Northeast Harbor 342; Ogunquit 52-53; Schoodic Peninsula 368; Southwest Harbor 349; see also concerts
Musical Wonder House: 26, 155
mustard: 407

**N**

Narrows Park: 222
Naskeag Point: 274

National Theatre Workshop of the Handicapped: 451
Native Americans: 28, 426-427, 435
Nature Trail: 229
Nearing, Helen and Scott: 439
nematodes: 422
Nequasset Lake: 146
Nevelson, Louise: 437
Newbury Neck: 266
Newcastle: 172, 173
New England Museum of Telephony: 311
Newman, Josephine Oliver: 144
Newman Sanctuary: 144
Nickels-Sortwell House: 26, 153, 155
nightlife: 102-104
Nobleboro: 26, 182
Nobleboro Antique Exchange: 26
northeasters: 424, 426
Northeast Harbor: 23, 338-344
Northeast Historic Film (NHF): 260
North Haven: 224-226
North Haven Village: 225
Norton Pond: 241
Nott House, The: 62-63
Nubble Light: 21, 30, 39, 40

**O**

O'Brien Cemetery: 390
Oceanarium: 307, 324-325
Ocean Park: 76
Odd Fellows Hall: 219
Ogilvie, Elisabeth: 439
Ogunquit: 48-60
Ogunquit Arts Collaborative Gallery: 50-51
Ogunquit Beach: 19, 51
Ogunquit Heritage Museum: 51
Ogunquit Museum of American Art (OMAA): 14, 30, 48, 438
Old Berwick Historical Society: 36-37
Old Cemetery, The: 264
Old Columbian Store: 397
Old Conway Homestead and Cramer Museum: 227-228
Old German Church: 175-176
Old Orchard Beach: 76-81
Old Orchard Pier: 78
Old Port: 14, 83, 91, 109-111
Old Quarry Ocean Adventures: 295, 305
Old Walpole Meeting House, The: 175
Old York: 14
Old York Historical Society: 30, 39
Olson House: 197-198, 211
Osher Map Library: 96

osprey: 425
Otter Cliffs: 316
outdoor recreation: general discussion 14;
    itinerary tips 20; reading suggestions 463-
    464; rentals 66, 230-231; *see also specific
    place; activity*
Outdoor Sculpture Guide: 28
outfitters: Blue Hill 267; Deer Isle 294;
    Schoodic Peninsula 365-366
Ovens Mouth Preserve: 162-163
Owls Head Light: 15, 22
Owls Head Light State Park: 192, 212-213
Owls Head Transportation Museum: 15, 192, 211

## P

Palace Playland: 78
Paleoindians: 426-427
Parker Point Road: 266
parking: 338
Park Loop Road: 16, 20, 23, 307, 316-318
parks and preserves: general discussion 14,
    16; Bath 143-145; Belfast 245-246; Blue Hill
    266; Boothbay Peninsula 162-164; Brooklin
    area 274; Bucksport 261-262; Calais 417-418;
    Camden-Rockport area 228-230; Castine
    282; Deer Isle 292-293; Eastport 408-409;
    Freeport 117-120; itinerary tips 23; The
    Kennebunks 63-65; Machias Bay 391-392;
    Old Orchard Beach 77; Pemaquid Peninsula
    178-180; Portland 98-100; Searsport 252-
    253; Vinalhaven 221-222;
    *see also specific park*
Parkside: 92
Parson Fisher House: 23, 258, 264
Passamaquoddy Indian Reservation: 407-408
Payson Park: 98
Peaks Island: 88
Peary, Robert: 89, 102
Peary-MacMillan Arctic Museum: 128
Pejepscot Museum: 129
Pemaquid Beach Park: 181
Pemaquid Peninsula: general discussion
    15, 172-173; accommodations 184-187;
    entertainment and events 182; itinerary tips
    21, 26; outdoor recreation 180-182; parks
    and preserves 178-180; shopping 182-184;
    sightseeing tips 174-180
Pemaquid Point Lighthouse: 15, 21, 126, 174-175
Penobscot Bay: general discussion 15;
    Belfast 243-250; Camden-Rockport area
    226-240; Cushing Peninsula 196-198; food/
    restaurants 25; itinerary tips 25; Lincolnville
    240-243; maps 193; Monhegan Island 203-

208; planning tips 191, 193-194; Rockland
    209-219; Searsport 250-256; St. George
    Peninsula 198-202; Thomaston 194-195;
    Vinalhaven 219-224
Penobscot East Resource Center: 290, 292
Penobscot Marine Museum: 15, 192, 251
Penobscot Maritime Museum: 27
Penobscot Narrows Bridge and Observatory:
    23, 192, 253
Penobscot School: 450
peregrine falcons: 422
periwinkles: 425
Perkins Cove: 49
Perkins House: 280-281
Perry Creek Preserve: 221
Petite Plaisance: 340-341
Petit Manan Island: 379
Petit Manan National Wildlife Refuge: 23
Pettengill Farm: 120
Phippsburg: 142
Phippsburg Congregational Church: 142
Phippsburg Peninsula: 142-143, 148-149
picnic areas: Campobello Island 402-403;
    Freeport 118; Lubec 396
Picnic Rock: 65
Pike's Park: 418
Pineland Farms: 118-119
Pine Point: 76
Pitcher Pond: 241
Pitch Pine Barren Loop: 131
planetariums: 96
planning tips: 17-18
poetry: 441
Point of Maine: 389
Polly Cove Preserve: 221
Pooduck Beach: 274
Popham Beach State Park: 15, 126, 142, 143
popover recipe: 321
population: 434-436
Port Clyde: 22
Porter, Fairfield: 437
Porter Preserve: 162
Porthole, The: 24, 109
Portland: general discussion 14, 82, 86;
    accommodations 106-108; entertainment
    and events 102-105; food/restaurants
    24, 108-115; historical background
    85-86; itinerary tips 24; maps 84, 87;
    neighborhoods 86, 90-92; outdoor
    recreation 100-102; planning tips 85;
    shopping 105-106; sightseeing tips 92-100
Portland Freedom Trail: 95
Portland Harbor Museum: 21, 96-97

Portland Head Light: 14, 19, 21, 83, 90, 97
Portland International Jetport: 444, 445
Portland Museum of Art (PMA): 14, 19, 83, 92-93, 438
Portland Observatory: 14, 83, 93
Portland Women's History Trail: 90
post offices: 458
Pownalborough Court House: 154
Precipice Trail: 320
precipitation: 423-424
prehistoric cultures: 426-427
Prendergast, Maurice: 437
Primo: 25, 218
Project Puffin Visitor Center: 211-212
pronunciation guide: 448
Prospect Harbor: 361
Provence: 24, 57
public meals: 109
public restrooms: Bar Harbor 338; Bath 152; Belfast 250; Blue Hill 271; Boothbay Peninsula 171; Bucksport 263; Calais 420; Camden-Rockport area 240; Castine 286; Deer Isle 301; The Kennebunks 75; Northeast Harbor 344; Portland 115; Rockland 219; Southwest Harbor 354; Wiscasset 159
public suppers: 372
puffins/puffin-watching tours: general discussion 16, 384, 425; Bar Harbor 328; Boothbay Peninsula 165; itinerary tips 20, 23; Jonesport 386; Machias Bay 392-393; Milbridge 380; Pemaquid Peninsula 181; Rockland 211-212; St. George Peninsula 200
Pumpkin Island Light: 290
Pumpkin Patch: 27

## QR

quarries: 286, 292
Quarry Pond: 358
rabies: 453
Raccoon Beach: 402-403
Rachel Carson National Wildlife Refuge: 33, 50
Rachel Carson Salt Pond: 180
rail service: general discussion 446; Brunswick 130-131; model railroads 385; museums 94, 154; Portland 115; Rockland 212; vintage trains 130-131; Wiscasset 154
rainfall: 17, 423-424
rare books: see antiquarian bookstores
Raye's Mustard Mill Museum: 407
Red Beach Cove: 416
Redman's Beach: 366
regional airports: 445-446
Reid State Park: 144

rentals: biking 327, 346; boats 347; car travel 448; outdoor recreation 52, 66, 120, 230-231, 294
Reny's: 184, 313
restaurants: see food/restaurants
restrooms: see public restrooms
Reverend Daniel Merrill House: 272
Reversing Falls Park: 408-409
Rhoades Park and Butterfly Garden: 345
Rich, Louise Dickinson: 439
Richmond Island: 90
Ridgewell Preserve: 144
river tours: 418
River Tree Arts (RTA): 67
R. Jorgensen Antiques: 26, 53
Robert P. Tristram Coffin Wildflower Sanctuary: 145
Roberts, Kenneth: 439
Robinson, Edwin Arlington: 154
rock climbing: 320
rock crabs: 425
Rockland: accommodations 215-216; entertainment and events 214; food/restaurants 216-218; itinerary tips 22; outdoor recreation 212-214; shopping 214-215; sightseeing tips 209, 211-212
Rockland Breakwater: 192, 212
Rockland Breakwater Light: 15, 22, 212
Rockport: see Camden-Rockport area
Rockport College: 451
Rocks Beach: 65
rockweed: 425
Rocky End Trail: 144
roller coasters: 78
Roosevelt Campobello International Park: 376, 402-403
Roosevelt Cottage: 402
Roque Bluffs State Park: 391
Round Lake: 418
Round Pond (Calais): 418
Round Pond (Mount Desert Island): 320
Route 92: 389
Route 191: 389
Ruggles House: 23, 383, 385
Russian immigrants: 436

## S

Saco: 76, 80-81
Saco Heath Preserve: 77
Saco Museum: 77
safety tips: hunting season 455; illnesses 453-455
Sagadahoc Preservation: 140

sailing: Bar Harbor 328-329; Boothbay Peninsula 165; Brooklin area 275; Camden-Rockport area 232-233; Portland 101-102
Sailors' Memorial Museum: 241
salmon: 416
Salome Sellers House: 289
Salt Bay Farm Heritage Center: 178
Salt Bay Preserve Heritage Trail: 178
salt marshes: 99, 422
Sand Beach: 316, 320
sand dunes: 143, 144
Sarah Orne Jewett House: 35-36
Sarton, May: 443
Sayward-Wheeler House: 39
Scarborough Beach Park: 99
Scarborough Marsh: 99
Scarborough River Wildlife Sanctuary: 99
scenic routes: Acadia Region 307; Belfast area 244; Blue Hill 266; Brooklin area 274; Campobello Island 402; Machias Bay 389; Milbridge 379-380; Schoodic Peninsula 307, 363-364
Schoodic Beach: 366
Schoodic Head: 363
Schoodic Loop: 362-363, 365
Schoodic Mountain: 364-365
Schoodic National Scenic Byway: 307, 364
Schoodic Peninsula: general discussion 16; Acadia National Park 20, 23, 360-363; accommodations 368-372; entertainment and events 368; food/restaurants 372-374; outdoor recreation 364-366; shopping 360-361, 366-368; sightseeing tips 360-364
Schoodic Point: 363
Scott's Landing: 293
scuba diving: 42
Sculpture Garden Tour: 28
Seacoast Fine Dining Club: 45
sea cucumbers: 425
seagulls: 425
sea kayaking: general discussion 14, 15-16; Bar Harbor 327; Bath 146; Boothbay Peninsula 165; Brooklin area 274; Brunswick 133; Camden-Rockport area 230-231; Castine 258, 282-283; Deer Isle 288, 293; Eastport 410; Freeport 118, 120; guided trips 23; itinerary tips 20, 23; The Kennebunks 66; Lincolnville 241; Machias Bay 392; Ogunquit 52; Old Orchard Beach 79; Pemaquid Peninsula 181-182; Portland 100-101; rentals 52, 66, 120, 294; Rockland 22, 213; Schoodic Peninsula 365; Southwest Harbor 346; St. George

Peninsula 199-200; Vinalhaven 222; The Yorks 42; see also kayaking
Seal Cove Auto Museum, The: 345
Seal Cove Pond: 320
Seal Harbor: see Northeast Harbor
seals: 425
Seapoint Beach: 33
Sea Princess: 341
Sears Island: 252
Searsport: 27, 250-256
Searsport Antique Mall: 27
Seashore Trolley Museum: 14, 30, 60, 62
seasickness: 454
Seaside Hall Museum: 357-358
sea smoke: 426
seasons: 17-18, 423-427
sea stars: 425
sea urchins: 425
Sea/Venture cruise: 329
Seawall Campground: 322
seaweeds: 425
Sedgwick Historic District: 272
Seguin Island: 120
Seguin Museum: 146
self-guided tours: 23, 140, 144, 226-227
Settlement Quarry: 292
Shackford Head State Park: 16, 376, 408
Sheepscot: 154
shellfish allergies: 453
Shelter Institute: 450
shipbuilding industry: 14-15, 142, 250-251
Ship Harbor Nature Trail: 319
ship models: 15, 192, 251-252
shipping services: 458
Shirttail Point: 232
shopping: general discussion 14-15; itinerary tips 19-20; offbeat shopping 105-106, 182-183, 267, 298; see also specific place
Shore Acres Preserve: 292
shoreline environments: 425
Shoreline Walk: 118
Shore Path (Bar Harbor): 326
Shore Path (Schoodic Peninsula): 365
Shore Path (The Yorks): 41
Shore Trail (Damariscotta): 179
shuttle services: The Kennebunks 75; Old Orchard Beach 81; Wells 60; The Yorks 48
Sieur de Monts Spring: 316
Silver Lake: 261
skiing: 230
Ski Shelter Trail: 241
Skolfield-Whittier House: 129
Skoog Memorial Park: 221

slave trade: 90, 95
Slavic immigrants: 436
sloop cruises: 348
Small Point: 142
smoking: 449
snowfall: 17, 423-424
snowmobiling: 416
snowshoeing: Freeport 120; Grand Lake Stream 416; Lubec 396
Snow, Wilbert: 443
snowy egrets: 422
soaring tours: 212
soft-shelled clams: 422
Sohier Park: 30, 39
Somes Sound: 16, 23, 338-339
South Bristol: 177
Southern Coast: general discussion 14, 29-30; The Berwicks 35-37; The Kennebunks 60-75; Kittery 32-35; maps 31; Ogunquit-Wells area 48-60; Old Orchard Beach 76-81; planning tips 30-31; The Yorks 37-48
Southern Maine Community College (SMCC): 90
Southport Island: 162
Southport Memorial Library: 162
Southwest Harbor: 23, 344-354
Southwest Harbor Oceanarium: 345
Southworth Planetarium: 96
spartina grasses: 422
spectator sports: 102
Spirit Pond Preserve: 144
sportfishing: 66
Spouting Rock: 62
Spring Point Ledge Light: 21, 90
Spring Point Shoreline Walkway: 90
Spring River Lake: 365
Squirrel Island: 162
St. Andrew's Episcopal Church: 176
St. Ann's Church: 62
St. Anthony's Monastery: 30, 64
Stanwood Homestead Museum: 311
Starboard Peninsula: 389
star-gazing: 410-411
State Beach: 222
state government: 433
statehood: 431
St. Croix Island International Historic Site: 416
Steedman Woods: 41
St. George Peninsula: 198-202
St. Lawrence Arts and Community Center: 103
Stonington: 23, 296-297
storm warnings: 426
Stowe, Harriet Beecher: 130, 439
St. Patrick's Catholic Church: 176

Stratton Island: 182
Stroudwater: 92
St. Saviour's Episcopal Church: 324
Sullivan: 25, 360-361
Summerkeys: 451
Sunset Rock Park: 221
Sunshine Road: 296
sunstroke: 454
surfing: The Kennebunks 66; Ogunquit 52; Old Orchard Beach 79; Portland 99; rentals 52; The Yorks 42
Swans Island: 357-359
swimming: general discussion 16; Acadia National Park 303; Brunswick 132; Camden-Rockport area 232; Castine 283; Deer Isle 293-294; Freeport 118; Lincolnville 241; Mount Desert Island 320; Pemaquid Peninsula 180-181; Portland 99; Rockland 213; Schoodic Peninsula 366; St. George Peninsula 199; Swans Island 358; Vinalhaven 222; The Yorks 41-42; see also beaches
symphonies: 102

**T**
Tam, Reuben: 437
Tarkington, Booth: 439
Tate House: 96
taxes: 456
taxis: 456
tea: 16, 321, 322
temperatures: 17-18, 423-424
Temple Heights Spiritualist Camp: 245
Tennis Preserve: 292
Thaxter, Celia: 441
theater: Belfast 247; Berwick 37; Biddeford 79; Damariscotta 182; Ogunquit 52; Portland 102-103; Southwest Harbor 349
Thomas Point Beach: 132
Thomaston: 26, 194-195
Thompson Ice House, The: 177
Thompson Island Visitor Center: 316
Thorn Head Preserve: 143
Thunder Hole: 316
Thuya Garden: 16, 23, 307, 339-340
ticks: 50, 453
tide pools: 144, 180, 425
tides: 22, 397
Tides Institute and Museum of Art: 407
time zones: 452
tipping: 456
Tip-Toe Mountain: 221
Todd Wildlife Sanctuary: 180
toll-free calling: 458

Tote Road Trail: 118
tourism industry: 433-434
tourist information and services: general discussion 457-458; *see also specific place*
tours: general discussion 14; Acadia National Park 326; architectural tours 140, 245; Bar Harbor 326; Bath 140; Calais 418; Casco Bay Islands 88-89, 97; Cobscook 398; Eagle Island 89, 102, 120, 132-133; ghost tours 40; lighthouses 40; lobsters 21; Lubec 23, 398; microbreweries 95-96; Portland 90, 97-98, 102; river tours 33; Sculpture Garden Tour 28; self-guided tours 140, 226-227; wildlife 181; *see also* flightseeing tours; walks/walking tours
Town Commons (Brunswick): 131
Town Pound: 177
Tracy Shore Preserve: 179-180
train service: general discussion 446; Brunswick 130-131; model railroads 385; museums 94, 154; Portland 115; Rockland 212; vintage trains 130-131; Wiscasset 154
transportation services: general discussion 444-449; Acadia National Park 304-305; Cranberry Isles 355, 357; The Kennebunks 75; Portland 115; Schoodic Peninsula 374; Swans Island 359; The Yorks 47-48; *see also specific place*
travelers checks: 456
Trescott: 389
tricolored herons: 422
trolley service: Bar Harbor 326; The Kennebunks 75; Ogunquit 59-60; Old Orchard Beach 81; The Yorks 47-48
tuna: 425
Tunk Lake: 365
Two Lights State Park: 90

## UV

Ukrainians: 436
Umbrella Cover Museum: 88
Underground Railway: 95
University of Maine at Machias: 390-391
vacation rentals: Bar Harbor 333; Belfast 249; Blue Hill 269-270; Boothbay Peninsula 169-170; Brunswick 136; Camden-Rockport area 237; Castine 285; Deer Isle 299; Eastport 413; Lubec 400; Southwest Harbor 352; The Yorks 44; *see also* accommodations; *specific place*
Vaughn's Island Preserve: 64-65
Vaughn Woods State Park: 36
Vesper Hill Children's Chapel: 228

Victoria Mansion: 14, 83, 93
Vinalhaven: 219-224
Vinalhaven Historical Society: 220
vintage cars: 51, 211, 345
vintage trains: 130-131
visas: 405, 449
visitor information centers: 457

## WXYZ

*Wabanaki Guide to Maine: A Visitor's Guide to Native American Culture in Maine:* 28
Wabanaki Trail: 28
Wadsworth-Longfellow House: 94
Waldoboro: 172-173, 187
Waldoborough Historical Society Museum: 177-178
Walker Park: 229, 232
Walker's Point: 62
Walk-On Adventures: 120
walks/walking tours: general discussion 14; architectural tours 62-63, 140, 194-195, 245; Bar Harbor 326-327; Belfast 245; Brunswick 130; Bucksport 261; Calais 415; Castine 23; Deer Isle 293; Eastport 406; ghost tours 40; Lubec 398-399; Monhegan Island 206; Old Port 91; packing tips 18; Portland 86, 90, 95, 97-98, 100; reading suggestions 463; Schoodic Peninsula 364-365; Searsport 252-253; The Yorks 40-41
Waponahki Museum: 407-408
War of 1812: 430-431
war refugees: 436
Warren Island State Park: 240-241
waterfalls: 98
Waterfront Park: 143
Waterman's Beach Lobster: 22, 25
water parks: 78
weather: 17-18, 423-424, 426
Wedding Cake House: 62
Wells: 26, 48-60
Wells Auto Museum: 51
Wells Beach: 51
Wells Reserve at Laudholm Farm: 30, 49-50
Wendell Gilley Museum: 23, 307, 344
Wengenroth, Stow: 437
West End: 91, 112
Western Head Trail: 303
West Quoddy Head Light: 396
West Quoddy Head State Park: 16, 20, 23, 376, 396
Whaleback Lighthouse: 40
Whaleback Park: 179
whale watching: Bar Harbor 328; Boothbay

Peninsula 165; Campobello Island 402–403, 404; Down East Coast 376; Eastport 22, 409–410; itinerary tips 20, 23; The Kennebunks 66; Portland 100
White, E. B.: 273, 440
White Barn Inn: 24, 74–75
Whitehead Trail: 206
White House: 245
White's Beach: 132
white-water rafting: 266
Whitlock Mill Lighthouse: 416–417
Wiggin, Kate Douglas: 443
wild blueberries: 442
wildflowers: 145
Wild Gardens of Acadia: 324
wildlife: Baker Island 318–319; boat excursions 200, 328; Boothbay Peninsula 162–163, 165; Brunswick 131; Calais 417–418; Campobello Island 402–403, 404; Deer Isle 292–293; educational programs 451; estuaries and mudflats 422; Freeport 117; itinerary tips 23; Machias Bay 392–393; Pemaquid Peninsula 180; Portland 99–100; shoreline and marine environment 425; tours 181
Wild Salmon Research Center: 386
Willard Beach: 90
Williams, Ben Ames: 439
Wilson Museum: 281
windjammer cruises: Bar Harbor 328–329; Brooklin area 275; Camden-Rockport area 232–233; Eastport 409–410; Portland 102; Rockland 210
wines/wineries: Blue Hill 267; Brooklin area 276; Rockland 216–217; Schoodic Peninsula 366–367

Winnegance: 142
Winslow Memorial Park: 118
winter sports: Belfast: 246; Freeport: 120
Wiscasset: 15, 26, 153–159
Wiscasset, Waterville, and Farmington Railway: 154
Witch Island Preserve: 182
Witherle Memorial Library: 282
Witherle Woods: 282
Wolfe's Neck Farm: 118
Wolfe's Neck Woods State Park: 118
Women's History Trail: 130
Wonderland Trail: 319
Woodbury, Charles Herbert: 437
*WoodenBoat* Publications: 271–272
WoodenBoat School: 451
Wood Island Lighthouse: 21, 40
Woodlawn Museum: 310
Woodturning School: 451
Woolwich: 26, 143
Woolwich Historical Society Museum: 143
Wyeth, Andrew: 196–198, 211, 437
Wyeth, Jamie: 211
Wyeth, N. C.: 211, 437
Wyeth Center: *see* Farnsworth Art Museum and the Wyeth Center
Yoho Head: 389
York Beach: 24, 44
Yorks, The: 37–48
York's Wild Kingdom: 39–40
Yourcenar, Marguerite: 439–440
zoos: 39–40
Zorach, William: 437

# Acknowledgments

*For Tom*

Although I've lived in Maine since childhood (yes, I will always be a "from away"), and have traveled extensively for both work and pleasure, every time I revisit a place, I find something new or changed, sometimes subtly, other times dramatically. Restaurants open and close. Outfitters change their offerings. B&Bs are sold. New trails are cut. Museums expand. Hotels renovate. And on it goes. Which all goes to say, I couldn't have done this without the help of many people, who served as additional eyes and ears.

I'll start with Kathleen Brandes, who wrote the original editions of this book and whose friendship I valued and whose work and dedication I respected long before I took over with the last edition of this book. My appreciation for her meticulous research, her ability to capture a place or a person with a quick turn of phrase, and her dead-on accuracy has no bounds.

More thank-yous are due the folks at Avalon Travel who shepherded me through the process, Bill Newlin, Rebecca Browning, Kevin McLain, and most especially my editor, Kathryn Ettinger. Also thank you to Nicole Schultz, Kevin Anglin, Erin Van Rheenen, Dylan Wooters, and the many other behind-the-scenes Avalon staffers who worked on this book.

Special thank-yous, too, to those who sat down with me and shared local info, sheltered me along the way, fed me, helped with arrangements, verified information, called me with updates, or simply encouraged me: Bill and Cathy Shamel, Maureen Hart, Valerie Kidney, Jan Meiners and Joyce Morrel, Kathryn Rubeor, Alan Furth, Ben and Sonja Walter-Sundaram, Roy Kasindorf and Helene Harton, Darrin Kelly, Bill Haefele, Don Jalbert and Javier Montesinos, Risteen Masters, Mary and Don Hartley, Jack Burke and Julie Van de Graaf, Traci Klepper, Marti Mayne, Cathy Keating and Deb Bush, Bob Smith, Ellen Chandler, Abbe Levin, Rob Blood, Bruce Jackson, Jean Ginn Marvin, Patricia and Ken Mason, Gary Dominguez, Greg and Heather Burke, Kathryn Weare, Chip Gray, Barbara Whitten, Barbara and Tim Rogers, Sarah Wills and Steve Viega, Elaine Abel, and most especially Nancy Marshall, Charlene Williams, and Rose Whitehorse, of Nancy Marshall Communications. I couldn't have done this without all of your help and support.

I save my biggest thanks for my husband, Tom, who drove me everywhere and didn't complain (too much) when I made him backtrack two or three times along the same stretch of road, while seeking an elusive address; who waited patiently while I visited practically every restaurant, inn, and B&B from Kittery to Calais; who let me order for him in restaurants; who tackled research projects; and who supported me in every way possible throughout the entire process, all while shooting photographs for the book. I couldn't have done it without him.

And to you, dear reader, thank you for using this book to plan your visit to Maine. Do me a favor, will you? Give me feedback to help make the next edition will be even better. Contact me at Hilary@HilaryNangle.com, and link to my blog for updates on this book.

# www.moon.com

For helpful advice on planning a trip, visit www.moon.com for the **TRAVEL PLANNER** and get access to useful travel strategies and valuable information about great places to visit. When you travel with Moon, expect an experience that is uncommon and truly unique.

HANDBOOKS | METRO | OUTDOORS | LIVING ABROAD

# MAP SYMBOLS

| | | | |
|---|---|---|---|
| ▦ Expressway | 【 Highlight | ✗ Airfield | ⚐ Golf Course |
| ▦ Primary Road | ○ City/Town | ✈ Airport | P Parking Area |
| ▦ Secondary Road | ◉ State Capital | ▲ Mountain | ▰ Archaeological Site |
| ▦ Unpaved Road | ⊛ National Capital | + Unique Natural Feature | ▮ Church |
| - - - - Trail | ★ Point of Interest | | |
| ⋯⋯ Ferry | • Accommodation | ⧖ Waterfall | ▯ Gas Station |
| ┼─┼─┼ Railroad | ▼ Restaurant/Bar | ▲ Park | ⬭ Glacier |
| ▦ Pedestrian Walkway | ▪ Other Location | ▯ Trailhead | ▱ Mangrove |
| ▯▯▯ Stairs | Λ Campground | ⚑ Skiing Area | ▱ Reef |
| | | | ▱ Swamp |

# CONVERSION TABLES

°C = (°F – 32) / 1.8
°F = (°C x 1.8) + 32
1 inch = 2.54 centimeters (cm)
1 foot = 0.304 meters (m)
1 yard = 0.914 meters
1 mile = 1.6093 kilometers (km)
1 km = 0.6214 miles
1 fathom = 1.8288 m
1 chain = 20.1168 m
1 furlong = 201.168 m
1 acre = 0.4047 hectares
1 sq km = 100 hectares
1 sq mile = 2.59 square km
1 ounce = 28.35 grams
1 pound = 0.4536 kilograms
1 short ton = 0.90718 metric ton
1 short ton = 2,000 pounds
1 long ton = 1.016 metric tons
1 long ton = 2,240 pounds
1 metric ton = 1,000 kilograms
1 quart = 0.94635 liters
1 US gallon = 3.7854 liters
1 Imperial gallon = 4.5459 liters
1 nautical mile = 1.852 km

**MOON COASTAL MAINE**

Avalon Travel
a member of the Perseus Books Group
1700 Fourth Street
Berkeley, CA 94710, USA
www.moon.com

Editor and Series Manager: Kathryn Ettinger
Copy Editor: Karen Gaynor Bleske
Graphics Coordinator: Stefano Boni
Production Coordinators: Amber Pirker,
  Tabitha Lahr
Cover Designer: Nicole Schultz
Map Editor: Kevin Anglin
Cartographers: Kat Bennett, Chris Markiewicz
Proofreader: Jamie Andrade
Indexer: Judy Hunt

ISBN-10: 1-56691-753-0
ISBN-13: 978-1-56691-753-7
ISSN: 1538-5051

Printing History
1st Edition – 2002
3rd Edition – May 2008
5 4 3 2 1

## KEEPING CURRENT

If you have a favorite gem you'd like to see included in the next edition, or see anything
that needs updating, clarification, or correction, please drop us a line. Send your
comments via email to feedback@moon.com, or use the address above.